CW00829000

The Famine of 1896–1897 in Bengal

The Famine of 1896–1897 in Bengal

Availability or Entitlement Crisis?

MALABIKA CHAKRABARTI

ORIENT LONGMAN PRIVATE LIMITED

Registered Office
3-6-752 Himayatnagar, Hyderabad 500 029 (A.P.), India
e-mail : hyd2_orlongco@sancharnet.in

Other Offices
Bangalore, Bhopal, Bhubaneshwar, Chennai,
Ernakulam, Guwahati, Hyderabad, Jaipur, Kolkata,
Lucknow, Mumbai, New Delhi, Patna

ISBN 81 250 2389 5

Maps by Cartography Department
Sangam Books (India) Private Limited, Hyderbad

Typeset by
Johann Integrated Services
Chennai

Printed in India at
Chaman Enterprises
New Delhi

Published by
Orient Longman Private Limited
1/24 Asaf Ali Road
New Delhi 110002
e-mail : olldel@del6.vsnl.net.in

The external boundaries and coastline of India as depicted in the maps in this book are neither correct nor authentic.

Contents

Tables

Charts

Preface

This micro-study of a famine brings out the agony of a peasant society thrown out of gear in an abnormal situation, and the crisis of identities that ensued. The famine of 1896–97 in Bengal was the most devastating of its kind in eastern India since the Orissa famine of 1866–67. The present work is a focused treatment of the famine both as a "process" and an "event". It analyses the socio-economic and cultural determinants of the famine in order to evolve a coherent framework for its study. This is followed by an exposition of the actual event in its totality, with a distinct emphasis on the problems and responses of the different famine tracts, most notably the tribal belts.

This close-up of a peasant economy in the throes of a crisis raises many issues in the areas of demography, ecology, gender inequalities, etc. in the context of famine, which are likely to evoke an interdisciplinary interest. It also affords a close parallel with the Potato Famine in Ireland.

A central theme of this work has been to review the famine of 1896–97 in the light of Professor Amartya Sen's theory of the Failure of Exchange Entitlements (FEE), as distinct from that of Food Availability Decline (FAD). Sen, in his book *Poverty and Famines* has formulated this theory through several case studies of Afro-Asian famines in the twentieth century. The present publication projects this theory on to a nineteenth-century famine situation in Bengal and finds that a market-based entitlement failure precipitating severe famine conditions "even without receiving any impulse from food production", has little relevance here.

The analysis shows:

The decline in food availability due to *crop failure* was real and determinate during the Bengal famine of 1896–97. The study graphically brings out how a combination of untoward natural circumstances in the winter of 1896 brought into play the extreme fragility of the rice economy in Bengal.

The availability crisis was due not only to crop deficiency, but also to a widespread *supply failure* in the grain market, which made food inaccessible to a large section of the population. The inability of the market to respond and cater to the needs of the moment is explained as much by trade, logistics and policy problems, as by the lack of adequate "pull" or purchasing capacity.

In fact, this potent question of *pull failure* or *exchange failure* in connection with the famine of 1896–97 focuses on certain inherent or long-term exchange problems in the rural economy, which were persistently reducing the food entitlement of various sections of the peasant society throughout the 1890s. As far as short-term or immediate exchange failures are concerned, the crisis of 1896–97 was primarily the effect of crop-related failures. An exchange crisis resulting exclusively from coincidental shifts in market-based entitlements independent of food production was by no means typical of the nineteenth-century peasant economy in Bengal.

In conclusion, it may be said that though FAD alone did not lead to famine. It reacted on the entitlement problems within the peasant economy in such a way that the crisis deepened into famine. In the socio-economic context of Bengal in 1896-97, therefore, FAD does not appear to be an antithesis of FEE: rather, both these factors acted in unison to create a famine situation.

I take this opportunity to express my gratitude to Professor Binay Bhushan Chaudhuri for his help and advice during various stages of this work. I am also indebted to Professor Peter Marshall of King's College and Professor K. N. Chaudhuri of the School of African and Oriental Studies, London, for their valuable and insightful comments. I have greatly benefited from Professor Tapan Raychaudhuri's observations on the pattern of grain trade in several famine-hit districts, where availability tended to become a function of exchange failure. I owe much to my teacher, Dr Niharkana Majumdar, who has acted as a friend, mentor and guide since my college days. Finally, I would like to acknowledge my intellectual debt to Professor Amartya Sen, whose writings have been a source of inspiration and around whose theory of exchange entitlement the present work has grown.

I have drawn on the resources of many libraries and archives, especially the National Library and the State Archives, Calcutta, the Town Library at Runcorn, Cheshire, and the India Office Library, London. Special mention is due to Ms Antonia Moon of the India Office Records, London. I wish to thank Dr Nandini Rao of Orient Longman for the publication and Ms Priti Anand and Mr Nikhil Bhoopal for taking such meticulous care during the copy-editing process. Thanks are also due to Dr Shibani Maitra and Ms Patricia Sharpe, for helping with the maps and typing.

Abbreviations

an.	anna
app.	appendix
Br.	branch
ch.	chitak
CHJ	*Calcutta Historical Journal*
Comm.	Commissioner
cwt.	hundredweight
DCAR	*Divisional Commissioner's Annual Report*
DG	*District Gazetteer*
Dist.	District
Div.	Division
Dy.	Deputy
FRFRO	Final Report on Famine Relief Operations.
ICS	Indian Civil Service
LRP	Land Revenue Department Proceedings, Bengal.
md.	maund
NWP	North-West Provinces
Prgs.	Parganas
SDO	Sub-Divisional Officer
Secy.	Secretary
Settl.	Settlement
SR	*Report on Survey and Settlement Operations*
sr.	seer
Sup.	Superintendent

Introduction

[1] *Scope of the Study*

Famine was a recurrent feature in British Indian history. It grew in frequency and dimension since the 1860s until, by the turn of the century, it became the most critical problem threatening the entire peasant economy.

Of several famines in eastern India between 1896 and 1911, that of 1896–97 was the most devastating. The crop failure was particularly extensive, affecting not only Bengal but the United Provinces, Central Provinces, Bombay and Madras. The area in acute distress measured about 125,000 sq. miles, with a population of 35 million. This reacted sharply on the local situation, for the fear psychology took a stronger grip, and the terms of trade moved against the famine-hit zones of Bengal.

Most studies of famine in British India have analysed the general background of famines, rather than the actual phenomenon and its aftermath. Even the analysis of the general background has not always emphasised the vital question of the differences in regional problems and economies, especially of the tribal areas. In fact, the famine problem in this period has generally been given a political slant by both the nationalists and the British, who dealt with it summarily, as a sub-topic in general studies of India's economic condition under British rule.

This study will focus not only on the background and causes of the famine of 1896–97 in Bengal but also on its development and intensification, with special reference to the distinctive problems and responses of the different economic regions.

[2] *Famine Historiography*

British officials of the ICS, on the one hand, and anti-government and nationalist writers like William Digby,

R. C. Dutt and Dadabhai Naoroji, on the other, were mainly concerned with the political controversy as to whether and how far British colonial policies contributed to the local famine situation.

The works of G. W. Forrest and C. W. McMinn are typical examples of the official version of famines in British India. Forrest's emphasis is on government policy and relief measures during the famines of 1866, 1873–74, and 1896–97 in Bengal. Though supporting the government policy of non-interference with private grain trade during famines, Forrest admitted the danger of applying such general principles without regard to local circumstances, as was apparent during the Orissa famine of 1866.[1] The study by C. W. McMinn represents a deeper shade of political bias. By his own definition, it is "not a monogram on famines" but an attempt to "expose" the alleged famine falsehoods "employed by several Bengali writers and Congress orators to blacken the character of English officers and administration".[2]

Contrarily, critics of the government dealt with famines mainly as an effect of the economic policy and principles of the British administration. R. C. Dutt emphasised the overassessment of agricultural land in British India as the main cause of famines; Naoroji focussed on the bullion drain from India to England; while later writers like K. C. Ghosh and P. C. Ray elaborated on particular aspects of the British policy, such as the export of foodgrains and non-interference of the government with the private grain trade during famines. As noted, all these famine histories have distinct political overtones.

B. M. Bhatia and H. S. Srivastava have concentrated on a more detailed and secular study of the problems in rural society which were, however, aggravated by the policies of the British government. Dietmar Rothermund, Asok Sen, and others have focussed on the intricacies of tenancy legislation in the context

1 G. W. Forrest, *The Famine in India* (London: Horace Cox, 1897), p. 16.

2 C. W. McMinn, *Famines: Truths, Half-Truths, Untruths* (Calcutta: Thacker, Spink and Co., 1902), p. 39.

of peasant agriculture in the nineteenth century.

Michelle Burge McAlpin, in explaining the frequency of famines in western India between 1870 and 1920, challenges such views and underscores the role of climate in causing crop failures. This approach, based on rainfall statistics and climatology, emphasises the natural or ecological, rather than the institutional or policy background of famines. According to McAlpin, the rainfall was unusually short in the Bombay Presidency during 1898–1906, which accounted for the frequency of famines in this region at the turn of the century. For example, the rainfall index showed a decline of 20 per cent between the periods 1886–1897 and 1898–1906, and 6 per cent during 1907 to 1916.[3]

The population theory or traditional analysis of famines, however, emphasises any reduction in the total output, current supply and per capita availability of foodgrains as the focal point of famine. It is based on the Malthusian theory of a fast-increasing population bearing down with unrelenting force on the available resources of the land. Developing the argument further, the neo-Malthusians held that this mounting demographic pressure disturbed the ecological balance, leading to exhaustion of the soil, erosion, deforestation, and a host of related problems. Hence, "whenever the limits set by nature are ignored, and there is unwise and violent interference with man's agricultural-economic environment, nature reasserts herself with destructive energy".[4] This view directly links crop failure, and the consequent decline in aggregate production, with food shortage and starvation.

Amartya Sen in his theory of the Failure of Exchange Entitlements (FEE) questions this approach of Food Availability Decline or FAD, as he calls it. He criticises it as being too gross

[3] Michelle B. McAlpin, "Dearth, Famine and Risk: The Changing Impact of Crop Failures in Western India, 1870–1920", *Journal of Economic History* 39, no. 1, March 1979, p. 145. A shade of environmental determinism is also evident in the Structuralist approach of the 'Annales School', as represented by scholars like Goubert, Braudel and Ladurie.

[4] B. N. Ganguli, *Trends of Agriculture and Population in the Ganges Valley* (London: Methuen, 1938), p. 45.

and simplistic, which fails to make note of the finer distinctions of income distribution and the changing entitlement values in a market economy.

There may be various types of entitlement to foodgrains in a rural economy: direct or production-based entitlement, as of the landed proprietor, big farmer, small peasant and tenant-cultivator producing food staples, who command varying proportions of the crop grown;[5] trade-based entitlement, as of cash-crop cultivators, fishermen, craftsmen, weavers, retailers, etc., who meet their food requirements by selling their respective commodities; and own-labour entitlement, by which production-based and trade-based entitlements relate to one's labour power.[6]

According to Sen, most famines are caused less by a decline in food supply than by a coincidental shift in the existing pattern of exchange relations. Several case studies of twentieth-century famines, as in Bengal in 1943, Ethiopia in 1973–74, Bangladesh in 1974, and the Sahel countries in Africa during 1968–73, show that as food prices rise due to partial crop failure or other exogenous factors, the values of different commodities, including labour, not only remain static but begin to fall due to a variety

5 Strictly speaking, owners of lands under food crops, whether receiving rentals in kind or cash, have ownership entitlements to a share of the produce. But in a wider sense they may be said to have a production-based entitlement to food, as they own the main ingredient of production, that is, land.

6 Own-labour entitlement overlaps to some extent with production- and trade-based entitlement. Thus, a small peasant or a tenant who personally cultivates his land is entitled to the produce of his labour by production-based as well as own-labour entitlement. The hired labour on another's land, however, has only a labour-based entitlement to a share of the produce or its equivalent in cash, paid either in instalments or on a daily basis. Similarly, a craftsman or cash-crop cultivator who is directly engaged in producing the commodity sold by him to the retailers or middlemen may be said to have a trade-based and labour-based entitlement to food, while one who hires out his labour to the cash-crop producer, artisan or fisherman has only the exchange value of his own labour power in relation to that particular trade. Hence, a purely labour-based entitlement to foodgrains in a rural economy may be said to exist in case of those who live primarily on their labour, i.e., the hired labourer either in foodgrain production or trade.

of other reasons. This results in a sharp contrast between relative rates, as of foodgrains on the one hand, and of labour and different commodities on the other, thus further limiting the purchasing power or "foodgrain entitlement" of the wage earner, and of the dealers in those particular commodities. Famine is viewed not only as a food crisis, but as a total economic disaster: food shortage is no more than one possible factor in a cluster of variables, some of which might interact to cause strains and shifts within the framework of entitlement relations, and precipitate severe famine conditions "even without receiving any impulse from food production".[7]

The peasant's attitudes and responses to such falling entitlement levels during a crisis have been underlined by the 'subaltern' approach to famines. Morris D. Morris breaks new ground in analysing the Indian peasant's flexibility and "rational adaptations" in the context of crop failures.[8] R. C. Cobb, at one point, admits that the peasants' fear of dearth is not irrational, famine and scarcity being "the greatest single threat to their existence".[9] David Arnold's study of peasant attitudes and responses in the context of the Madras famine of 1876–78 tries "to use the crisis of famine as a window onto subaltern consciousness and action".[10]

James C. Scott views the pattern of interactions between the labourer, the peasant-proprietor and the landlord, or between the debtor and the creditor, as part of a "moral economy" in rural society.[11] Viewed in terms of "reciprocity", this patron-client relationship, as Paul Greenough calls it, emphasised the

7 Amartya Sen, *Poverty and Famine: An Essay on Entitlement and Deprivation* (Oxford: Clarendon Press, 1981), p. 158.

8 Morris D. Morris, "What is a Famine?" *Economic and Political Weekly* 9, 2 Nov. 1974, pp. 1855–64.

9 R. C. Cobb, *The Police and the People: French Popular Protest, 1789–1820* (London: Oxford University Press, 1970), pp. xvii–xviii, 215.

10 David Arnold, "Famine in Peasant Consciousness and Peasant Action: Madras 1876–8", in *Subaltern Studies*, vol. 3, ed. R. Guha (Delhi: Oxford University Press, 1984), p. 64.

11 James C. Scott, *The Moral Economy of the Peasant: Rebellion and Subsistence in Southeast Asia* (New Haven: Yale University Press, 1976).

patron's moral obligation to protect the client in return for his services, acknowledging in the process his "right to subsist".[12] According to David Hardiman, however, this seemingly permanent relationship was based not on a static system of reciprocal morality, but on a dynamic and unequal class conflict. In analysing the interaction of the Bhils with the Shahukars of eastern Gujarat, he shows how, especially in the case of tribal societies, such relationships represented the meeting of two alien cultures at specific points in time, to fulfil the historical needs of the moment.[13] The *kamia-malik* (servant-master) relationship in south Bihar is defined by Gyan Prakash as being juridical or contractual (debt-based) in form, economic in content (labour-control), yet expressed in terms of reciprocity.[14] As Arnold points out, an unequal relationship based on such conflicting interests could not stand the stress of a crisis like a famine, war or revolution, for "crises heighten social realities: they rarely negate them".[15] In the shake-up which followed, the existing ties and obligations in rural society were dissolved, giving way to a new exchange pattern in which the entitlement of the subordinate groups suffered in every instance.

A sense of betrayal and "moral outrage" during such crises provoked the peasants into various forms of grain-related crimes, as discussed by David Arnold in his monograph on famines and described most vividly by David Hardiman in his study of the Bhil uprising at Jhalod in September 1899. The peasants' protest against exploitation, however, did not always assume a violent form; a surer and more effective means, as pointed out by J. C. Scott, involved the prosaic or 'everyday' forms of resistance, such as

[12] Paul R. Greenough, "Indian Famines and Peasant Victims: The Case of Bengal in 1943–44", *Modern Asian Studies* 14, no. 2, April 1980, pp. 205–35.

[13] David Hardiman, "The Bhils and Shahukars of Eastern Gujarat", *Subaltern Studies,* vol. 5, ed. R. Guha (Delhi: Oxford University Press, 1987), p. 50.

[14] Gyan Prakash, *Bonded Histories: Genealogies of Labor Servitude in Colonial India* (Cambridge: Cambridge University Press, 1990).

[15] Arnold, "Famine in Peasant Consciousness", p. 64.

[16] James C. Scott, *Weapons of the Weak: Everyday Forms of Peasant Resistance* (Delhi: Oxford University Press, 1990).

poaching, pilfering, slander, arson, sabotage, evasion or desertion.[16] Aditee Nag Chowdhury-Zilly elaborates on vagrancy and peasant desertions as a form of protest after the famine of 1770 in Bengal.[17] According to Gyan Prakash, such flights marked "an enduring pattern of resistance" by the *kamia*s (bonded labourers) against exploitation by their *malik*s (landlords) in south Bihar.

[3] *Logic of the Study*

The present work, though analysing the apprehensions and responses of the subalterns in the face of a looming subsistence crisis, does not deal with it from the viewpoint of any particular group or community. Nor is it area specific, as is the recent trend in famine historiography. The focus is, rather, on the event in its totality, i.e., on the development and intensification of the famine in itself, and the crisis of identities that ensued. In course of the analysis, several current issues are raised (ecology, market mechanisms, demographic implications, nutrition, gender bias) which may evoke an interdisciplinary interest.

To see the famine in its proper perspective, it is essential to shift the emphasis of study from government policies to the inherent problems of an agrarian society, with its delicate balance between agriculture and ecology; the complex inter-relationships as between *zamindar*s (landlords), tenure holders, occupancy and non-occupancy *raiyat*s (peasants), agricultural labourers (whether free or bonded), artisans, *mahajan*s (creditors) and traders; the working of the rural market system, and the mechanism of surplus control. Hence, an in-depth study or a close-up of the peasant

[17] Aditee Nag Chowdhury-Zilly, *The Vagrant Peasant: Agrarian Distress and Desertion in Bengal, 1770–1830* (Wiesbaden: Steiner, 1982).

[18] Most recent works on famine belong to disciplines other than history, which focusses more on essays and monographs on the subject. As the present work is a micro study of a famine from a historical perspective, the following categories are not comparable: i) theoretical analyses of famine as a general phenomenon (e.g. D. Arnold); ii) compilations of papers on famine-related topics (as ed. by Dreze and Sen, T. Dyson, G. A. Harrison, and others); iii) works concentrating exclusively on specialised areas like demography (T. Dyson, A. Maharatna), market responses (M.

economy in the context of famines, is historically relevant.[18]

In the process, "climate" appears as a major variable, but not the focal point of famine. The local rainfall pattern in Bengal does not suggest any marked change or deterioration at the end of the nineteenth century. It is true that the proximate cause of crop failure has always been the lack of adequate and timely rainfall, as in the scarcity years of 1884, 1891–92, 1895–96 and 1896–97. But crop failure alone did not lead to famine; it merely intensified the chronic problems in the rural economic structure, which eventually led to the crisis.[19]

The population theory, too, underplays this vital aspect. Population growth as a factor contributing to the famine situation in any region cannot be studied in isolation, but only in the context of its socio-economic environment. For instance, though about one-third of the population perished from the ravages of the Black Death in Europe and of the great famine of 1770 in Bengal, the former revived due to the favourable trends of urbanisation and capitalist farming, while Bengal suffered more intensively from the negative effects of a colonial economy. Again, the loss of population from malaria in the "moribund delta" of Bengal during 1850–1900 coincided with a decline in agricultural productivity, due to the simultaneous presence of other depressing factors like the decaying river system and recurring cattle murrains.[20] Besides, by directly linking famine with a decline in the total volume of foodgrains available, the population theory ignores the disparities in its distribution, for a famine seldom, if ever, affects all classes in a given society.

In the final analysis, therefore, the emphasis falls mainly on the social framework of agriculture, which rendered the peasant economy peculiarly liable to famines. The very fact that a crop

---

Ravallion), nutritional and gender studies (S. R. Osmani, A. Whitehead, B. Harriss and others).

19 Famine is thus represented both as an event and a process, the complexities of which could not be captured either by climatological explanations, or by the "overly reductionist" approach of the Structuralists.

20 B. B. Chaudhuri, "Agricultural Production in Bengal, 1850–1900: Co-existence of Decline and Growth", *Bengal Past and Present* 88, 1969, pp. 157–70.

failure could so deeply affect the exchange structure as to create a crisis of such dimensions, is a reflection on the anachronisms present in the peasant society, which were slowly but surely undermining the production-, labour- and trade-based entitlements of various sections of the rural population.

The present work attempts to review the famine of 1896–97 in Bengal in terms of the theory of exchange entitlement. The three background chapters focus respectively on: the distinctive features in agriculture and ecology, especially the crop pattern and irrigation, in explaining the high incidence of crop failures in the region; the inequalities and entitlement problems in the rural economy, which transformed the crop failure into famine; and the interplay of these two variables, that is, crop failure and exchange failure, in causing and prolonging the famine situation during the thirty years preceding the crisis of 1896–97. In the process, a distinct emphasis is laid on the study of the Orissa famine of 1866, as a stark manifestation of FAD, or Food Availability Decline. The analysis tends to show that an exchange crisis resulting exclusively from coincidental shifts in market-based entitlements, independent of foodcrop production, was by no means typical of the nineteenth-century peasant economy in Bengal. Applied to the famine of 1896–97, FAD and FEE thus seem to lose their force as counter-arguments and appear, rather, as supplementary factors leading to the crisis.

A critical assessment of the nature and extent of crop failure during the year of famine confirms this hypothesis. The magnitude of the problem, as seen in chapter 4, indicates that the decline in food availability was both real and determinate. An attempt is made in chapter 5 to show how this shortfall reacted on the peasant economy to create an exchange crisis of grave dimensions, as reflected in the abnormal rise in foodgrain prices, the growth of a psychology of scarcity, and the varied responses of the peasantry in the face of imminent disaster. Chapter 6 traces the increasing intensity of the famine as indicated by the behavioural pattern of socially dominant groups like the rent receivers, mahajans and traders, who exploited this fluid situation to further reduce the entitlements of their subordinates and to perfect their mechanism of surplus control. Chapters 7 and 8 analyse the reactions of the government and of the grain-trade sector in creating entitlements to, and increasing the availability of, foodgrains in this context.

1

The Agricultural-Ecological Environment

As crop failure was the proximate cause of famines, a study of the distinctive regional problems in agriculture relating to the pattern of cultivation, rainfall, irrigation, floods, drainage, relief and soil will help to demarcate the traditional famine zones in Bengal in the late nineteenth century.

[1] *The Crop Pattern in Bengal*

The crop pattern in Bengal was such that almost all depended on the outcome of a single crop, namely, rice. By the end of the century, rice covered 39 million acres, i.e., 74.9 per cent of the total area under food crops, or an area three times that under all other food crops put together.[1] The rice crop featured prominently in all the three harvests of the year. The *rabi* (spring harvest), consisting of *boro* rice in Bengal proper and Orissa, and of wheat, barley and pulses in Bihar, was reaped chiefly in March, April and May; the *bhadoi* (autumn harvest), consisting principally of *aus* rice in Bengal proper and Orissa, and *makai* (maize) and millets in Bihar and Chotanagpur, was reaped in August–September; the *aghani* (winter harvest), corresponding to the *kharif* in the North-West Provinces and consisting of the *aman* or the great winter rice crop, was reaped during November–January. The winter rice or aman was the most important and often the sole crop grown in the districts of Bengal, Bihar and Orissa. It covered 32,101,000 acres out of a total of 67,243,100

1 *Selection of Papers Relating to the Famine of 1896–97 in Bengal* (Calcutta: Bengal Secretariat Press, 1897–98), vol. I: p. 1.

acres of net cropped area in the Province, thus amounting to 47.74 per cent of the total cultivation.[2]

[1.1] Extension of rice cultivation

[a] Suitability of rice to the local conditions

This emphasis on rice cultivation was not unreasoned. The soil, climate and topography in Bengal-Bihar-Orissa were ideal for rice production. Except in parts of South Bihar and the Chotanagpur Plateau, conditions were seldom suited to the production of dry crops like wheat, barley, millet and maize. They were grown only as minor crops supplementing the rice harvest but never as a substitute for it. Rice required a mean summer temperature of 75 to 77 degrees Fahrenheit, and preferably an annual rainfall of about 50" with 5" a month during the growing season. Rice was normally grown on low lands with a clayey soil retentive of moisture. These ideal conditions were found throughout the Province to a greater or lesser extent, particularly in north Bihar, which had an annual rainfall of 51" to 57", the Ganges Delta (i.e. Bengal proper, mainly the eastern districts of the Dacca-Chittagong Divisions), and the whole of Orissa. Though the natural conditions were not as favourable in south Bihar, which received an annual rainfall of about 43.3", they were sufficient to foster rice cultivation over a large area, which contributed positively to the agricultural productivity of this region.

Given the local conditions in Bengal, there was hardly any alternative to rice cultivation. Like the potato in Ireland, it had no equally cheap or effective substitute. Wheat, the most important staple in north India, had an entirely different range of environment, the conditions favouring rice cultivation being precisely those which hampered its growth.

Barley and gram, normally grown in the rabi harvest, as well as maize, an important crop in the kharif harvest, had a remarkably wide range of environment. Sugar-cane and oilseeds also grew in a wet climate. Yet the extent to which these crops were raised depended on the range of other more valuable crops,

[2] *Final Resolution of the Government of Bengal on the Famine of 1896–97* (Calcutta: Bengal Secretariat Press, 1898), p. 11.

which could be grown under similar conditions.[3] An important wet crop in the Ganges Delta, mainly in the eastern districts of Bengal proper, was jute, which was excellently adapted to the local climate, and was grown on the water-logged land in an extremely damp atmosphere. Here it supplemented rice as an important commercial crop in the bhadoi harvest. But jute cultivation exhausted the soil and was impossible on high lands without manuring. Hence, in western and central Bengal, it was confined to the highly manured lands near the village sites, while the low lands were devoted exclusively to rice.

On the whole, therefore, the options to rice cultivation were severely limited by the nature of the soil and climate in Bengal. Indeed, suitability to local conditions was a very important factor influencing the peasant's choice of crop, as it called for minimum investment in outlay. Since most of the big farmers and mahajans took no direct interest in agriculture, the final responsibility for preparing the fields fell on the raiyats, who could afford to spend little else besides their labour on the land. As rice thrived in the wet climate of Bengal, the cost of cultivation was low. It did not generally require any extra preparation except in special cases, such as terracing of the fields in the hilly regions of Chotanagpur and the Santhal Parganas.

[b] Extension of cultivation to marginal lands and new alluvial formations

Another factor which encouraged the growth of rice cultivation was the increasing pressure of population on the soil, leading, in turn, to the extension of cultivation from multi-crop to mono-crop regions which produced only rice. This was most apparent in the northward movement of agricultural settlements within the districts of north Bihar. The density of the agricultural population was highest in the districts of Saran, Muzaffarpur and Darbhanga, which had 930, 905 and 825 persons per sq. mile, respectively, in 1891.[4] Even in Champaran, Shahabad, Gaya, Purnea and Bhagalpur, where the density of population was much lower, there was practically no scope for new cultivation. This

3 Ganguli, *Trends of Agriculture,* p. 279.
4 *Bengal Census Report 1891*, para. 55.

increasing pressure in the old centres of population along the Ganges led to a gradual shift in agricultural enterprise away from the river, to the rice tracts in the extreme north along the Nepal border. This northern belt differed sharply from the south in terms not of the yield, but of the range of crops grown, for the soil, mainly *bangar* or hard clay, could produce nothing but aman rice. For example, rice was the only crop grown in the newly settled tracts of north Champaran, while the south of the district produced a variety of crops such as millets, pulses, cereals, oilseeds, opium and indigo. Similarly, the rice crop predominated in north Muzaffarpur, covering more than 73 per cent of the cultivated area, while the Sadar and Hajipur subdivisions in the south had only 35 per cent of the cultivated land under rice, the rest being occupied by a variety of other crops.[5]

Another area newly settled by immigrant Santhal labour was the vast tract in northern Bengal known as the Barind, covering the "Southern third of Dinajpur, the eastern half of Malda, the western half of Bagura and the northern half of Rajshahi".[6] Though the stiff clay of the Barind could grow mulberry and oilseeds, the Santhals were most interested in rice. The chief and indeed the only crop here was the *ropa* or transplanted aman rice, sown in mid-May and reaped in December–January.[7]

Cultivation was also extended into the freshly claimed tracts in the Sunderbans, mainly in Khulna-Bakarganj, and the alluvial formations in the eastern districts of Faridpur, Noakhali and Chittagong. These areas were exceptionally fertile due to inundations and rich salt deposits from the rivers, and the conditions were ideal for rice production. For example, in the comparatively new alluvium of the Meghna Estuary and the banks of the Meghna and Arial Khan in Bakarganj, the soil was a fresh deposit of sandy loam producing excellent crops of winter rice. In fact, rice covered 95.3 per cent of the net cropped area in Faridpur and 95 per cent of it in Bakarganj.[8]

5 Chaudhuri, "Agricultural Production in Bengal", p. 184.
6 *Bengal Census Report 1891*, para. 56.
7 Land Revenue Department Proceedings [hereafter LRP], Aug. 1896, pt. 1.
8 *Final Report on Survey and Settlement* [hereafter *SR*], *Faridpur*

Hence, though the quality of production in these newly reclaimed tracts was far superior to that of the marginal lands in the Barind and north Bihar, they had a common basis in the exclusive cultivation of aman rice.

[c] Growth of intensive farming

Population pressure was also responsible for the substitution of heavy-yielding food crops produced by intensive subsistence farming, for light-yielding crops suited to the methods of extensive cultivation. While in the Upper Ganges Valley this led to an increase in the area under rice, barley, maize and pure wheat, in the wet zone of Bengal-Bihar-Orissa the emphasis was most markedly on rice. Rice was a particularly heavy-yielding crop. Transplanted aman paddy had the highest yield: 1,000 lb. per acre on the average as against 906 lb. in case of aus rice.[9] To take a concrete example, in Murshidabad transplanted aman gave 1,265 lb. per acre on unirrigated land during 1898–1902, while the aus yield was only 614 lb. per acre.[10] The average yield of rice was remarkably high in certain districts, for instance, 1,394 lb. per acre in Hughli, 1,230 lb. in Murshidabad, 1,200 lb. in Rajshahi, and 1,230 lb. in Rangpur.[11] It amounted to as much as 21¼ *maunds* (md.) or 1,763 lb. per acre on first-class irrigated lands in Patna, Gaya and Shahabad.[12]

District, 1904–14, by J. C. Jack (Calcutta: Bengal Secretariat Book Depot, 1916), para. 29; *SR*, *Bakargunj* (1900–8), by J.C. Jack (Calcutta: BSBD, 1915), para. 64.

9 K. L. Datta, *Report on the Enquiry into the Rise of Prices in India, 1891–1911* (Calcutta, 1914), p. 74.

10 Ibid.

11 LRP, Nov. 1896, p. 309. Taken from Mr Mason's note dated 4 Feb. 1889, giving the results of weighments made of first-class crops on lands regularly irrigated from canals in the Patna, Gaya and Shahabad districts in 222 experiments made with transplanted aman. The yield averaged 33 md. of paddy, i.e. about 21¼ md. or 1,763 lb. of rice.

12 The standard weight measure of the time was expressed in maunds, *seers* and *chataks*, there being 16 chataks in 1 seer, and 40 seers in a maund. A seer was 930 grams, i.e., a little less than 1 kg in weight.

Wheat could not compete with rice in terms of yield anywhere in Bengal, except in parts of the Patna and Bhagalpur Divisions. Here, too, its importance was rather limited: it occupied no more than 6 per cent of the net cropped area even in Saran, where the proportion of winter rice was relatively low.[13] Cash crops like sugar-cane and jute, though lucrative and heavy yielding, had an entirely different rationale of production, that could not cater to the growing needs of a subsistence economy.[14] In fact, even when the cultivators grew valuable commercial crops like sugar-cane and jute from which they raised money for cash payments of their rent and interest, they had naturally to depend for their subsistence on the cultivation of heavy-yielding food crops like rice.

This intensive, subsistence cultivation exactly suited the changing needs of the peasant economy in this period, when distress sales, the splitting of family holdings, and the extreme pressure of population on land led to the subdivision and fragmentation of farms into small, uneconomic units. A heavy-yielding staple like rice—as in the case of the potato crop in Ireland—required very little in land or investment. Malthus notes that the "nourishing root", the potato, left the Irish peasantry with no other option but that of "immediate bare subsistence".[15] As Cecil Woodham-Smith comments on Irish agriculture: "Subdivision could never have taken place without the potato: an acre and a half would provide a family of five or six with food for twelve months, while to grow the equivalent grain required an acreage four to six times as large and some knowledge of tillage as well."[16] Similarly, peasants in large areas of Bengal managed to live on less than four *bigha*s of land, which fell far below the minimum subsistence level of an average peasant family.

[13] *District Gazetteer* [hereafter *DG*]: *Saran,* comp. L. S. S. O'Malley, 1908.

[14] LRP, Nov. 1896, p. 202.

[15] T. R. Malthus, *Essay on the Principle of Population*, 1798, quoted in David Arnold, *Famine* (Oxford: Basil Blackwell, 1988), pp. 56–57.

[16] Cecil Woodham-Smith, *The Great Hunger: Ireland 1845–9* (London: Hamish Hamilton, 1962), p. 35.

The frequent threats of famine from 1860 onwards further underlined this importance of rice as a heavy-yielding food staple. Besides the major famines of 1866–67, 1873–74 and 1896–97, local scarcities occurred in 1875–76, 1885–86, 1887–88, 1891–92, and 1895–96 in different parts of Bengal, Bihar and Orissa. Hence, the peasant hesitated to force any change in the existing pattern of the subsistence economy, or to switch over to cash-crop production to an appreciable extent, in order to ensure food supply for the lean years. For example, it was hoped that the introduction of the Sone Canal system would lead to an increase in the area under the rabi crops in south Bihar; in effect, however, "there was a tendency of the *kharif* to encroach on the rabi, directly a plentiful supply of water is procurable", despite the unsuitability of much of the land for rice. Indeed, there was an enormous increase in the production of the kharif crops, especially winter rice, which used up 70 per cent of the whole irrigation. Its average area during 1898–1903 increased to 334,565 acres, while that of the rabi crop was only 128,616 acres.[17] In Khurda, again, *saradh* (winter rice), which already covered 83 per cent of the cropped area, had now begun to encroach upon lands more suited to *biali* or the bhadoi crop.[18] Ironically, this urge to ensure against famine by producing a food staple led to over-dependence on a single crop, which increased agricultural insecurity.

[d] Limited applicability of commercialisation and the price factor

McAlpin, studying the famine conditions in western India between 1870 and 1920, suggested that the introduction of railways had considerably altered the situation. "Although the introduction of rail transport did not result in major shifts of land to growing non-food crops, some shifts did occur away from crops grown strictly for consumption, to those that could be

17 *Report of the Irrigation Department, 1879–80,* Revenue Report on the Sone Circle, para. 4; *Report, Irrigation Department, 1881–82*, para. 66; *Report of the Indian Irrigation Commission, 1901–3* (London: 1903), pp. 156–57.

18 LRP, Br. Land Revenue, Sept. 1900, p. 719, para. 11.

expected to command a good price in the market even though they were still 'food' crops. The rail lines which took away cotton, wheat and oil-seeds also brought in grain whenever a shortfall in the harvest began to push up prices."[19] But the famine experience in Bengal, Bihar and Orissa proved that the problem was more complex. The trend towards commercialisation in agriculture had no doubt set in, but was definitely contained along the fringes of the rice economy. Railway lines were few and far between, and had not yet penetrated to the interior. The Famine Commission Report of 1898 noted that the extension of railroads had considerably improved the situation in 1896–97, as compared to that in 1873–74. Yet, there was much to be desired, and most of the affected tracts suffered acutely due to lack of communication. The Bihar districts, in particular, had a distinct disadvantage in having no connection with the railway system of Bengal Province.[20] For example, the Ramnagar-Araraj-Madhuban tract in Champaran faced a deepening crisis in 1896, as the importation of foodgrains was checked by the high cost of carriage and the lack of "regular" communications.[21] Bhabhua in Shahabad was thirty miles away from the nearest railway station of Zamania. In Saran, railway communication was entirely confined to the southwestern corner of the district.[22] In Hazaribagh, all *thana*s except Giridih, Kharagdiha and Dumri were thirty to ninety miles away from any railway.[23] The distance from Daltonganj in the famine-prone district of Palamau was 101 miles from the nearest railway station of Gaya, and seventy-three miles from Barun.[24] In Orissa, land communications were submerged and the ports remained closed from July to October, which, being lean months, were crucial for the peasant. The early rice would not yet be ripe, and previous stocks would be drying up. The price

19 McAlpin, "Dearth, Famine and Risk", pp. 153–55.
20 *Selection of Papers*, vol. 4: p. 336.
21 Ibid., vol. 3: p. 303. Letter from Collector of Champaran, 10 Nov. 1896.
22 *SR, Saran District,* 1893–1901, by J. H. Kerr (Calcutta: BS Press, 1903).
23 *Selection of Papers,* vol. 4: p. 349. J. L. Herald, Dy. Comm. Hazaribagh to Comm. Chotanagpur Div., no. 1399 R, 20 Jan. 1897.
24 Ibid., vol. 4: p. 334.

mechanism, too, did not work so smoothly as to facilitate grain imports by rail "whenever a shortfall in the harvest began to push up prices". In fact, private trade in grain generally failed to bring in supplies effectively or adequately into the distress areas during the famine of 1896–97 in Bengal-Bihar-Orissa.

Faced with such threats of famine and scarcity, the peasant found it impossible to reduce the area under rice cultivation. In fact, between 1890 and 1905 there was a definite decline in Bengal Province in the percentage of all cash crops except jute, in relation to the gross area cultivated. Even the increase in jute cultivation was minimal both in north and east Bengal and in Bihar, while in southern and western Bengal there was a gradual shrinkage in the area under jute. The percentage of foodgrains, which in Bengal, Bihar and Orissa consisted of little else but rice, decreased slightly but was still incomparably high.[25]

In Bengal, Bihar and Orissa there was a distinct line between the rice area on the one hand, and the area under different crops, on the other, so that none of the latter could become an effective substitute for rice. Even in the jute districts of eastern Bengal, cheap cash crops of the rabi harvest, which could be grown as a second crop after the aman rice, sometimes replaced jute due to the lower cost of cultivation and the needs of a subsistence economy. For instance, though Dacca was a major jute-producing district, the thanas of Harirampur, Sealo and Manikganj had a rabi area of 45 per cent, 46 per cent and 58 per cent, and a jute area of 8 per cent, 11 per cent and 15 per cent, respectively.[26]

Even relatively high prices failed to attract the peasant appreciably towards cash-crop production. In north and east Bengal, jute did encroach on rice lands to some extent, as in Faridpur, where "jute is grown increasingly every year with far greater profit than was ever won from the crops which it has displaced".[27] But in Bihar and Orissa, jute was grown only in two districts, "in neither of which its competition with rice

[25] Datta, *Enquiry into the Rise of Prices*, p. 65.

[26] *SR, Dacca*, 1910–17 by F. D. Ascoli. Cited in Ganguli, *Trends of Agriculture*, p. 258.

[27] *SR, Faridpur*, p. 12, para. 27.

TABLE 1
Percentage of Crops to Gross Area Cultivated

	1890–91 to 1894–95	*1895–96 to 1899–1900*	*1900–01 to 1904–05*
Bengal, north & east			
Foodgrains	71.48	70.10	68.54
Jute	11.28	10.70	12.22
Bengal, south & west			
Foodgrains	85.34	84.88	85.04
Oilseeds	4.50	4.24	4.22
Sugar-cane	1.46	1.08	0.96
Indigo	1.02	0.82	0.12
Jute	1.42	1.14	1.28
Bihar			
Foodgrains	84.64	83.54	82.96
Indigo	1.72	1.64	1.16
Jute	0.46	0.04	0.72

Source: Datta, *Enquiry into the Rise of Prices*, p. 65.

assumes viable proportions. And outside of jute, the search for another crop remained unfruitful".[28]

In fact, higher prices generally failed to povide a strong motive to the peasant, for the simple reason that he did not operate in an open market. His stock of grain passed into the hands of the zamindar, mahajan and grain dealer in the form of rent and interest payments, rather than as market commodities governed by the price differential. Even those with a small surplus to sell found that the price of rice, though lower than that of cash crops in absolute terms, rose persistently from the last decade of the nineteenth century. This was an all-India phenomenon, the index number of the rupee prices of rice rising, after several fluctuations, from 96 in 1890–91 to 130 in 1905–06.[29]

The role of the price factor in fostering cash-crop production was further conditioned by the lower purchasing power of the masses, which limited effective demand. In this situation, rice, as

28 Dharam Narain, *Impact of Price Movements on Areas under Selected Crops in India, 1900–39* (Cambridge: Cambridge University Press, 1965).

29 Datta, *Enquiry into the Rise of Prices*, p. 113.

the main food staple, found a readier market than more valuable crops. This lack of purchasing power was one of the basic causes behind the persistence and spread of monoculture in the nineteenth century, for it lowered the rate of profitability, and hence of investment, in agriculture. In Khurda, for example, the raiyats did not like to grow two crops, where it had been the custom to grow one—for example, saradh rice—partly on account of the expenses of watch and ward, and partly to prevent exhaustion of the soil, which would call for the extra cost of manuring.[30] In the Sone Canal circle in south Bihar, peasants preferred rice to rabi, since rice, once assured of a plentiful supply of water, required much less labour and vigilance than rabi when the crop was growing. Another typical case was that of Midnapur in Bengal, where sericulture had been giving way to rice cultivation since the late eighteenth century. "Every natural disaster was followed by a steep rise in grain prices, and under the circumstances, it was more profitable for the raiyats to cultivate paddy rather than mulberry, which was expensive to cultivate."[31]

[1.2] Problems of rice cultivation

Thus, the raiyats in Bengal Province were almost totally dependent on the outcome of a single harvest of the rice crop, that is the winter rice or aman. Such extensive monoculture led to several problems: *(a)* rice, particularly the aman, was extremely susceptible to drought; *(b)* in case of crop failure during lean years, the exclusive rice tract had no other crops to fall back on; *(c)* even in double-cropped areas, the second crops sown after aman were invariably cheap cash-crops of inferior quality. This mono-crop pattern, therefore, had a close bearing on the vulnerability of certain regions to scarcity and famine.

[a] Susceptibility to adverse weather conditions

The rice crop required certain specific conditions as regards temperature and rainfall. Often the temperature was above

30 LRP, Br. Land Revenue, Sept. 1900.

31 Nag Chowdhury-Zilly, *The Vagrant Peasant*, p. 85.

normal, and hot winds quickly dried up the moisture near the surface of the soil. It needed heavy rains, preferably 50 inches or more per annum. Further, the distribution of rainfall was as important as its total volume. The winter rice required pre-monsoon showers in May and early June, heavy showers in late June and early July, and good rains in September or October, the last being most vital in determining the out turn. But weather conditions were always uncertain, and drought destroyed the rice crop over a wide region in 1866–67, 1873–74 and 1896–97. The potato famine in Ireland (1845–49) provides an exact parallel. Potato, like rice, was a cheap, heavy-yielding staple, and the most universally useful of foods; yet it was also the most unreliable and dangerous of crops. It would not keep, and was deeply affected by the slightest changes in weather conditions.

[b] Problems of insecurity in monoculture

The risk was even greater in that if the potato failed, neither meal nor any other crop could provide an equally cheap substitute. Potato cultivation could not be replaced, except after a long period, by the cultivation of any other crop. Likewise, in Bengal the failure of the rains naturally had a more serious and lasting effect in areas where winter rice was the sole or predominant crop, than in regions where the relative proportion of the three harvests was more balanced and equitable. In such districts, famine might occur only if the rains failed for two or three years in succession, for the peasant was compensated for the loss of one crop by another harvest reaped in the same year. In mono-crop regions, however, the cultivators were poor and had neither grain nor cash reserves to fall back on in a crisis; hence, a serious failure of the rice crop even in a single year would lead to acute distress.

Bihar

In the Patna Division, winter rice provided 48.33 per cent of the food crops, rabi 28.73 per cent and bhadoi only 22.52 per cent. While no region in Bihar in which the rabi and bhadoi crops were preponderant was ever seriously affected by famine, the new agricultural settlements depending on aman rice in north Bihar suffered acutely from the problem of monoculture.[32]

In Saran, winter rice was not confined to any one tract.[33] This, as pointed out by Mr Bourdillon, Commissioner of Patna, in his report on the famine of 1897, accounted for the "curiously variegated character of the Saran famine".[34] Yet the extensive rice tracts in Gopalganj thana in the north and the predominance of aghani crops in the Siwan and Darauli thanas (42 per cent and 43 per cent respectively) made them particularly vulnerable to famine.[35]

In northern Champaran, the bangar soil could grow nothing but rice and was entirely at the mercy of the winter rains, which in 1896 were severely deficient. In crisis years, as in 1897, two main areas in the north of the district were particularly hard-hit: a tract roughly corresponding to Dhaka thana, and a large area to the northwest of Bettiah, centring around Ramnagar, including the Bagaha and Shikarpur thanas.[36]

In Muzaffarpur, rice occupied as much as 73 per cent of the cultivated area in some parts, the largest portion of it being taken up by winter rice. Indeed, the weakness of Muzaffarpur lay in the concentration of rice cultivation in the Sitamarhi subdivision and the north of the district in general, which suffered most acutely during the famine of 1896–97.[37]

In Darbhanga, rice covered 61.39 per cent of the net cropped area, which was larger than in any other district of Patna Division north of the Ganges. Of this, 93 per cent was winter rice. The

32 For a more detailed study of the local cropping pattern during this period, see M. Chakrabarti, "The Lethal Connection: Winter Rice, Poverty and Famine in Late Nineteenth Century Bengal", *Calcutta Historical Journal* 18, no. 1, Jan.–June 1996, pp. 65–95.

33 *DG: Saran*, p. 71.

34 *SR*, *Saran*, p. 112, para. 396.

35 Ibid.

36 *DG: Champaran*, comp. L. S. S. O'Malley, 1907, pp. 81–82. Even by August 1897, when a plentiful bhadoi crop restored prosperity to the rest of Champaran, the Ramnagar tract remained unrelieved, as it had hardly any bhadoi crop. Also the crops in this area were always two to three weeks later than in the south, due to its climate and northerly position.

37 *DG: Muzaffarpur*, comp. L. S. S. O'Malley, 1907, p. 53.

tracts growing winter rice were mainly situated in the north of the district, where frequent inundations rendered the tracts unsuitable for the growth of bhadoi rice, except on the higher lands. With such a large area under winter rice—less than one-tenth of which was irrigated—Darbhanga, particularly the Sadar and Madhubani subdivisions in the north, became most liable to famine or scarcity, if the rains failed. Hence, it was not surprising that the distress was most acute in the Sadar and Madhubani subdivisions in the north, during the famine of 1896–97.

Moving within Bihar from Patna to Bhagalpur Division, one notes the same preponderance of rice. In the district of Bhagalpur, rice was almost as important as in Darbhanga. The *kharar* soil in the south was best suited for the growth of the aghani crop. North of the Ganges, the aman was less important, but was mainly concentrated in the vast rice tracts of western Supaul and Madhipura, which formed the traditional famine zone of the Bhagalpur district—50.55 per cent of the net cropped area in Supaul and 55.18 per cent in Madhipura were taken up by the aman. There was no other crop worthy of mention in this region; hence, it was liable to suffer from drought in the absence of artificial irrigation, and from floods of the Tilguja and Dhimra Rivers in case of heavy rains.[38]

In the Santhal Parganas, rice accounted for 47 per cent, or nearly half of the total cropped area, the proportion of autumn and winter rice being approximately 1:3.[39] Such excessive dependence on the aman in the whole district heightened the risk of famine. Moreover, the proportion of unprotected land was gradually increasing, due to the substitution of the aman for maize and millets which, though less lucrative than rice in good seasons, compensated the peasant for the loss of winter rice in years of drought. Thus, large areas of ridges and uplands—which formerly produced dry crops and were considered unfit for rice cultivation—were now turned into poor rice-lands liable to be hit by the slightest change in rainfall and weather conditions. In

[38] *SR, Bhagalpur* (1902–10), by P. W. Murphy (Calcutta: BS Press, 1911), p. 106, para. 193.

[39] *SR, Santhal Parganas* (1898–1907), by H. Mcpherson (Calcutta: BSBD, 1909), pp. 130–31, para. 115.

1896 the distress area lay mainly in Jamtara and Godda, where the proportion of upland rice was the highest.[40]

In Purnea, rice accounted for 73.47 per cent of the cropped area, of which winter rice alone covered 51.24 per cent. This was the highest percentage of rice land in north Bihar. The rice tracts lay mainly in the northeast, covering large parts of the Kishanganj subdivision.

Monghyr had only 30 per cent of the normal cultivated area under the aghani crop. Yet a broad tract in the south of the district, mainly comprising the thanas of Sheikpura and Sikandra, was liable to famine, because of the concentration of winter rice in this region. North Monghyr was almost immune, except for the extensive rice tract of Bakhtiyarpur in the Gogri thana, which suffered from the famine of 1874 and the scarcity of 1892.[41]

Thus in the Bhagalpur Division, the loss of aman rice would inevitably lead to a famine or near-famine situation, while the loss of aus, *janira, kulthi*, etc. could be compensated for by the aman.[42]

In the Chotanagpur Division of Bihar, rice constituted no less than 63.3 per cent of the food crops, the bhadoi 28.2 per cent and the rabi merely 8.4 per cent.[43]

TABLE 2

Percentage of Food Supply Contributed by the Main Harvests (Chotanagpur Division)

Crops	*Hazaribagh*	*Lohardaga*	*Palamau*	*Manbhum*	*Singhbhum*	*Divisional average*
Rabi	9.38	0.12	33.75	13.75	4.38	8.44
Bhadoi	28.12	38.76	26.25	11.25	15.62	28.19
Winter rice	62.50	61.12	40.00	75.00	80.00	63.37
Total	100.00	100.00	100.00	100.00	100.00	100.00

Source: LRP, Aug. 1898, pt. 2, pp. 612–13.

40 *Selection of Papers*, vol. 3: p. 250E.

41 *DG: Monghyr*, comp. L. S. S. O'Malley, 1909, pp. 104, 107.

42 W. W. Hunter, *Famine Aspects in Bengal Districts* (Simla, 1873), pp. 60, 63–64, 67, 71, 72, 74.

43 *Final Resolution*, p. 16.

The relative importance of these three principal crops in the different districts is especially interesting in a Division like Chotanagpur, where the food staples grown necessarily vary with the physical features of the country. It is also extremely important in gauging the effects of the failure of one or other of these crops on the economy of the different districts. Thus, while in Palamau an average rabi crop was equivalent to about four months' food supply (5.4 annas), in Lohardaga its yield was insignificant (0.12 an.). Again, in Lohardaga and Palamau, a good bhadoi harvest meant a four-and-a-half and a three months' supply of food (6.2 and 4.2 an.) respectively, while in Manbhum it would provide only a few weeks' supply (1.8 an.).[44]

The whole of Manbhum district was vulnerable to famine, winter rice being the predominant crop. Usually the problem tracts were Barabhum in the southeast, parts of Jhalda-Purulia in the centre, and Gobindapur in the north of the district, which depended almost exclusively on rice.

In Palamau, the crops were more evenly divided, though rice covered 56 per cent of the normal net cropped area.[45] The central and northeastern parts were most frequently affected by drought and famine. They were chiefly under rice and rabi crops, while the hill tracts to the south had comparatively little rice cultivation. In 1896–97, the most distressed area lay along a broad tract running from east to west through the centre of the district and consisting of parts of Garhwa, Daltonganj, Balumath, Latehar and Patan thanas.[46]

In Lohardaga, winter rice contributed 9.78 an. of the total food supply. Yet the plateau of Chotanagpur in Lohardaga, though

[44] *Divisional Commissioner's Annual Report* [hereafter *DCAR*], *Chotanagpur Division, 1897–98*, no. 247J, Ranchi, 18/19 July 1896, pp. 6–7, sec. 3, paras. 17–18. Contemporary crop measures followed the 16-anna concept, which also formed the basis of the indigenous currency system. The unit of currency (a rupee) consisted of 16 an., 1 anna thus being equal to 6.25 per cent of the rupee, 4 an. = 25 per cent, 8 an. = 50 per cent, 12 an. = 75 per cent, etc. In official terminology, the crop size or proportion was expressed in annas or fractions of an average out-turn, which was generally estimated at 16 an.

[45] *DG: Palamau,* comp. L. S. S. O'Malley, 1907, p. 78.

[46] Ibid., pp. 88–90.

equally subject to drought as the neighbouring districts of Manbhum, Hazaribagh, and Palamau, was almost immune to famine. This was due to the high proportion of low-lying (*garha*) rice-lands, which could retain moisture for long, and the light character of the soil, which was not beaten down and pressed in by the rains to the same extent as the heavier soils of Palamau.[47]

Singhbhum had 38 per cent of the net cropped area under winter rice. The northeast, especially Dhalbhum *pargana* (subdivision) adjacent to the rice tracts of Barabhum in Manbhum District, was most liable to famine. Dr Hayes, the Deputy Commissioner in 1866, pointed out that Dhalbhum suffered more than the other parts of the district, because "the people, who are of a better class, live chiefly on rice".[48]

Thus, in the whole of Chotanagpur Division there was no diversification of agriculture and no really important cash crop.

Orissa

Winter rice was even more vital to the agriculture of Orissa and central Bengal. In Bihar, if the aman was lost, the spring crop could afford partial relief, but in Orissa and the western and central parts of Bengal hardly anything was grown at this time. These regions thus continued to suffer until the next year's aus ripened in September, and the prospects of the aman were well assured.[49]

In Orissa, the saradh, or winter, rice amounted to 80 per cent of the total harvest in Balasore, 77 per cent in Puri, and 97.4 per cent in the Kanika Ward's Estate in Cuttack.[50] Hence, the failure of winter rice would invariably cause a widespread disaster in these districts. The report of the Famine Commission of 1866 showed that the mortality in Balasore was over 25 per cent from the famine.[51] In 1896–97, the effects of the famine were most

47 B. C. Basu, *Report on the Agriculture of the District of Lohardaga* (Calcutta: Bengal Secretariat Press, 1891), pt. 1, p. 125.

48 *DG: Singhbhum*, comp. L. S. S. O'Malley, 1910, p. 120.

49 *Famine Commission Report, 1880*, pt. I, p. 25.

50 *SR, Kanika Ward's Estate in the District of Cuttack* (Seasons 1889–94), by S. S. Hossein (Calcutta: BS Press, 1895), p. 33, para. 88.

51 LRP, Br. Agriculture, October 1900, p. 735, para. 5.

acutely felt in the tract around the Chilka Lake, and in scattered portions of the Khurda subdivision in Puri. Table 3 shows how greatly rice predominated in Puri, to the exclusion of other miscellaneous crops known as *baze-fasal*.[52]

Thus, practically the whole of the cultivated area was under winter rice, other crops being scarcely grown. Even autumn and spring rice were comparatively small crops. They did not exist at all in some parts and could nowhere compensate for the loss of saradh rice.

The famine of 1896–97 deeply affected Satpara and Balabhadrapur in the Khurda subdivision. Here the saradh occupied more than 85 per cent of the cultivated area, and was grown even on uplands more suited to biali. But the tract most severely affected by the floods and drought in that year lay around the Chilka Lake; it consisted of Bajrakote, Malud, Parikud, Andheri, Manikpatna, and parts of Chaubiskud and Serai in Puri subdivision. The percentage of saradh rice was highest in the parganas of Serai and Chaubiskud. Indeed, the Chilka tract was a sandy one-crop region without irrigation, where "the people live perpetually on the verge of famine". If the rains failed "there was more intense distress in Parikud than in any other part of Orissa".[53] It was here that the famine of 1866 first made its appearance. It was here, again, that relief measures were necessary in 1877–78, 1885–86 and 1888–89.[54] Significantly enough, it was precisely this region that had a remarkably high percentage of winter rice: 91.19 per cent, 83.42 per cent, 78.81 per cent and 78.19 per cent in Parikud, Malud, Andheri and Bajrakote respectively.[55]

Bengal

In north Bengal, the Barind tract in Rajshahi suffered likewise; it depended solely on aman unlike the *bil* (low-lying) and *deara* (river-side) lands, which also grew some aus and boro. In the

52 *DG: Puri*, comp. L. S. S. O'Malley, 1908, p. 151.

53 Note on Parikud in W. W. Hunter, *Orissa* (Calcutta: Thacker, Spink and Co., 1872).

54 *DG: Puri*, p. 164.

55 *SR, Jagirmahals in Puri* (1906–9), by S. Das (Calcutta: BSBD, 1910), p. 7.

TABLE 3

Crop Percentages in Puri

Crops	*Normal acreage*	*Percentage of the net cropped area*	*Crops*	*Normal acreage*	*Percentage of the net cropped area*
Aghani crops			**Rabi crops**		
Winter rice	548,700	77	Summer rice	9,300	1
Sugar-cane	3,100		Gram		
Total aghani crops	551,800	77	Other rabi pulses & cereals		
Bhadoi crops			Other rabi food crops		
Autumn rice	65,200	9			
Mandia	24,800	3	Linseed		
Indian corn	200		Rape & mustard		
Other bhadoi cereals & pulses	1,500		Til [rabi]		
Other bhadoi food crops	3,200		Other oilseeds		
Early cotton	2,300		Tobacco		
Til [bhadoi]	700		Late cotton		
Other bhadoi non-food crops	2,100		Other rabi non-food crops		
Total bhadoi crops	100,000	14	**Total rabi crops**		
Forest	310,691	43	Orchards & garden produce		
Twice cropped area	73,200	10			

Source: DG: Puri, p. 151.

western, central and eastern districts of Bengal, the deltaic action of the Ganges and its distributaries determined the agricultural conditions and cropping patterns to a great extent. East Bengal, as the new focus of the river's activity, began to benefit from its rich silt deposits and its system of natural flushing. The conditions were ideal for rice cultivation and the aman crop was supremely important. In Bakarganj and Noakhali, for example, cultivation had to depend on the success of the aman to a far greater extent than in the western districts of Bankura, Midnapur or Khulna. Yet the heavy local rainfall, along with inundations from the rivers, ensured an abundant harvest which was almost immune to the risk of drought and famine.[56]

Meanwhile, in the "moribund delta" of western and central Bengal where the river action had all but ceased, extensive rice tracts, particularly in the west, were very vulnerable to famine. This was due to the small amount of annual rainfall and the absence of irrigation facilities. In these regions the peasant had to choose between the bhadoi and the aghani crops, as the rainfall, soil conditions and timing of the agricultural seasons did not allow for the cultivation of both. The rabi crops were insignificant throughout the Ganges Delta.[57]

The aghani or the winter harvest consisted only of rice. In fact, the interite clay soil of the old alluvium in west Bengal was very difficult to work, and often could not grow any other crop but winter rice. This covered more than 70 per cent of the net cropped area in the districts of the moribund delta, listed below in table 4.

TABLE 4

Percentage of Net Cropped Area under Aman in the Moribund Delta

District	Percentage
Burdwan	83
Birbhum	78
Bankura	87
Midnapur	71
24 Parganas	77
Khulna	92

Source: Ganguli, *Trends of Agriculture*, p. 284.

56 Ganguli, *Trends of Agriculture*, p. 284.
57 Ibid.

As in the case of the new agricultural settlements in north Bihar, some of the blackest spots on the famine map of Bengal were those which relied most on the winter rice. Even within these districts, mono-crop tracts were the most vulnerable. The northern part of Sonamukhi thana in Bankura depended exclusively on winter rice, and suffered a deep crisis in 1896. Satkhira in western Khulna, which was one of the worst-hit tracts, grew winter rice in over 98 per cent of its total cropped area. Here, ill-distributed or scanty rainfall readily created famine conditions, for unless the rains sweetened the river water and washed out the salinity from the soil, the rice crop was liable to wither and die. Most of the bil areas in Magura and Bongaon in Jessore were single-crop regions sown with aman. In northwest Nadia, approximately 87.5 per cent of the entire area was occupied by winter rice in the low-lying tract known as the Kalantar, and by the bhadoi, usually aus rice, in the ex-Kalantar region.[58] Nadia was the only district in Bengal where aus rice predominated. Yet the large low-lying tracts in Gangni, Chapra, Nowpara and Karimpur, which were affected during 1896–97, were similar in nature to the Kalantar and were sown almost exclusively with aman.[59] In Murshidabad, too, the famine-hit tract in the southeast known as the Kalantar, was a continuation of the Nadia Kalantar and depended solely on winter rice.

[c] Problem of agricultural productivity in double-cropped regions growing winter rice

Rice cultivation involved problems not only of agricultural security, but also of double-cropping and productivity. The cultivation of rice contributed greatly to the agricultural productivity of a region where the increasing pressure of population on land was relieved by the development of intensive subsistence farming. Winter rice was often followed by a second crop as well. But the economic importance of double-cropping

[58] *Selection of Papers*, vol. 3: p. 221. The higher lands surrounding the low-lying Kalantar tract are referred to in official correspondence as the "ex-Kalantar" region.

[59] Ibid., vol. 4: p. 259; pp. 240–42.

depended not merely upon the area bearing more than one crop, but also on the nature and value of the second crop raised. Unfortunately, aman rice was almost always followed by cheap cash crops of an inferior quality, which could never compensate for the loss of the main harvest during lean years.

Bihar

In Bihar, the aghani crops were sown before the bhadoi harvest, and the more valuable rabi crops were sown before the reaping of the aghani. Hence, the aghani could not naturally be sown as a second crop after the bhadoi, while as the main harvest it could only be followed by the cheaper and inferior rabi crops like *khesari,* gram and linseed. The bhadoi, however, was followed by valuable rabi crops, which helped the raiyats tide over the crisis when the aman harvest failed.

Stevenson-Moore, in paragraph 721 of the Muzaffarpur Survey and Settlement Report, made the interesting suggestion that "by adding the bhadoi and rabi percentages of area and deducting the aghani, we get a fairly correct measure of agricultural prosperity" in north Bihar. This method, however, sometimes led to undependable results, though the trend was correctly reflected. As the rabi harvest was of little value unless sown after the bhadoi crop, the percentage of the latter was vital to the local economy; the larger the area under the bhadoi crops, the greater the contribution of double-cropping to the agricultural security of these regions. Hence, as suggested by B. N. Ganguli, a fair index of the economic significance of double-cropping in north Bihar may also be arrived at, by multiplying the double-cropped area by the proportion of the bhadoi area in relation to that covered by the aghani crops.

In the new agricultural settlements of north Bihar, i.e., the northern parts of Saran, Champaran, Muzaffarpur, and Darbhanga, both the extent and value of double-cropping were seriously limited by the overwhelming importance of winter rice. In Saran, the northern tract in general had a very small percentage of double-cropped area in relation to the south. On the basis of Stevenson-Moore's calculation, the thanas in Saran stood in the following order, as regards the index of prosperity:

TABLE 5

Index of Prosperity: Saran

Sonpur	123	Manji	64
Mirganj	87	Mashrakh	62
Gopalganj	79	Basantpur	56
Parsa	78	Siwan	46
Chapra	76	Darauli	32

Source: SR, Saran, pp. 111–12, paras. 391–95.

But these figures cannot be taken at face value in the case of Saran, due to the scattered nature of its rice-tracts. For example, though the crop averages in Gopalganj subdivision, that is the Mirganj-Gopalganj thanas in the north, register a high index of prosperity, it had vast rice swamps liable to famine, as was seen in 1896–97.[60]

In Champaran, double-cropping was not only more extensive but also more lucrative in the south, because the bhadoi harvest, unlike aman rice, was followed by the better varieties of rabi crops. The following figures illustrate this tendency.[61]

TABLE 6

Index of Prosperity: Champaran

Northern thanas		*Southern thanas*	
Bettiah	38	Sadar	57
		Adapur	77
		Dhaka	65

Source: Ganguli, *Trends of Agriculture*, p. 164.

The large tract to the northwest of Bettiah, comprising Ramnagar-Bagaha-Shikarpur and part of the Madhuban tract in the northwest, was most severely affected in 1896–97. In these regions rice was the principal crop, there being little of bhadoi and less of rabi.[62]

Likewise, in Muzaffarpur the contribution of double-cropping to agricultural productivity was much higher in the southern

60 *SR, Saran*, pp. 111–12, paras. 391–95.
61 Ganguli, *Trends of Agriculture*, p. 164.
62 *DG: Champaran*, p. 81.

thanas, as shown in table 7.[63] The Sitamarhi subdivision was most prone to famine and was severely affected during the famine of 1896–97.

TABLE 7
Index of Prosperity: Muzaffarpur

Southern thanas		*Northern thanas*	
Katra	58	Shinar	30
Muzaffarpur	44	Sitamarhi	30
Paru	41.5	Pupri	29
Hajipur	54	Belsand	31

Source: Ganguli, *Trends of Agriculture*, p. 164.

In Darbhanga, double-cropping was of little significance in the north, as the second crops invariably consisted of cheap rabi grains such as khesari, gram and oilseeds, which were grown on rice-lands. The northern and southern tracts stand in the following order as regards the indices of prosperity (table 8).[64]

TABLE 8
Index of Prosperity: Darbhanga

Northern thanas		*Southern thanas*	
Madhubani	13	Samastipur	28
Sadar	14		

Source: Ganguli, *Trends of Agriculture*, p. 165.

Thus it was only natural that the Madhubani subdivision in the north, which had an overwhelmingly large proportion of winter rice and the lowest level of prosperity, suffered most acutely during the famine of 1896–97.

In the Bhagalpur Division, one finds the same correlation between the extent of rice cultivation, double-cropping and the index of prosperity. The level of prosperity in the northern regions of Bhagalpur district was approximately seventeen or eighteen,

[63] Ganguli, *Trends of Agriculture*, p. 164.

[64] Ibid., p. 165. The indices are low in Darbhanga as compared to other districts, due to the predominance of aghani rice and the small importance of the bhadoi harvest in the district.

while in the southern subdivisions of Banka, where winter rice predominated, it dropped to four. Most of the double-cropped areas in the district lay to the north, where the bhadoi harvest was followed by valuable rabi crops. The famine zone of Supaul-Madhipura was an exception where, as in the south of Bhagalpur, the second crops were inferior grains sown on the rice-lands.

In Purnea the extent of double-cropped area was greater in the south than in the northeast, where the percentage of the aghani crops was the highest. Applying Stevenson-Moore's formula for estimating the general prosperity of the three subdivisions in the district on the basis of these figures, it may be concluded that Kishanganj subdivision in the north, especially Islampur thana where the double-cropped area was as low as 10 per cent, depended to a greater degree than was safe on the aghani crop.[65]

Table 9
Index of Prosperity: Purnea

Araria	+10
Sadar	+ 4
Kishanganj	–16

Source: SR, Purnea District, p. 101, para. 31.

In Monghyr, the balanced distribution of crops made the northern tracts almost immune to famine. In 1866 and 1873–74 only Gogri thana was affected, while in 1896 even this escaped. The double-cropped areas in Teghra, Begusarai and Gogri thanas were 31 per cent, 37 per cent, and 41 per cent respectively. But the larger extent of double-cropped area in Gogri did not have much economic significance. Here the percentage of rice was greater than in the other two thanas, and much of the second crops consisted of cheap rabi grains such as khesari, gram and kulthi, grown on the rice-lands. The indices of prosperity confirm these trends as to the relative immunity of the northern thanas to famine.[66]

65 *SR, Purnea* (1901–8), by J. Byrne (Calcutta: BSBD, 1908), p. 101, para. 311.

66 *SR, Monghyr North* (1899–1904), by H. Coupland (Calcutta: BSBD, 1908), p. 4, para. 10.

TABLE 10

Index of Prosperity: Monghyr

Teghra	93
Begusarai	87
Gogri	69

Source: SR, Monghyr North, p. 4, para. 10.

South Monghyr, however, depended mainly on aghani rice followed by cheap catch crops. Here the soil was dry, rainfall precarious, and double-cropping limited both in quality and extent.

The percentages of the total cropped area covered by rice in the Santhal Parganas are given in table 11. The area statistics also reveal certain interesting features (table 12). The index of prosperity, as obtained from this data, was 2.08 for Dumka, 1.81 for Deoghar, 0.60 for Jamtara, 1.52 for Pakaur, 3.36 for Rajmahal, and 3.35 for Godda.[67] Thus, Jamtara, which was severely affected in 1896, was without doubt the most famine-prone region in the district. It had the highest aghani and rice percentages, corresponding with the lowest percentage of cultivated and double-cropped areas. This region, along with Pakaur, had a remarkably low proportion of the rabi, so that there was less to depend on if the rice crop failed. Pakaur and Godda also had high percentages of the aghani crop, while the bhadoi in Godda was of very little importance. But, despite the large area under the aghani crop, Godda, after the Damin, had the lowest total percentage of rice in the district. Correspondingly, it had the highest proportion of the net cropped and double-cropped areas, and was by far the most advanced tract in the Santhal Parganas. Yet parts of it fell within the danger zone, for like Jamtara it had large tracts of upland rice. Deoghar, nearly the whole of which was included in the famine tract in the southwest of the district, had the smallest proportion of cultivated and twice-cropped lands after Jamtara, and a very low level of agricultural development. The Damin in Pakaur and Rajmahal was a backward tribal region, inhabited mostly by Santhals and Paharias. *Jhum* (slash and burn) cultivation exhausted the fertility of the soil in these areas. Double-cropping had little significance, consisting mostly of minor miscellaneous crops.

67 *SR, Santhal Parganas,* p. 129–31, paras. 114–15.

TABLE 11

Percentage of Rice in the Santhal Parganas

Crops	*Dumka*	*Deoghar*	*Jamtara*	*Pakaur*	*Rajmahal*	*Godda*	*District Total*	*Damin-i-Koh*
Bhadoi	16	16	16	15	8	4	12	9
Aghani	27	28	43	41	39	39	35	28
Rabi					1			
Total	43	44	59	56	48	43	47	37

Source: SR, Santhal Parganas, pp. 129–31.

TABLE 12

Percentage of Net and Double Cropped Areas

Subdivision	*Net cropped area*	*Twice-cropped area*	*Total culturable area*
Dumka	47	4	28
Deoghar	44	4	26
Jamtara	41	2	37
Pakaur	56	5	23
Rajmahal	56	7	15
Godda	59	16	17
Total district	50	6	24

Source: SR, Santhal Parganas, pp. 129–31.

Double-cropping played a very minor role in the tribal economy of Chotanagpur. Barabhum pargana in Manbhum had approximately 50 per cent of the cultivated area under the bhadoi crop, and 46 per cent under the aghani. In north Bihar such a high percentage of bhadoi, exceeding even that of aghani rice, would indicate a high level of agricultural security and prosperity. However, in Manbhum the bulk of the bhadoi rice was such a late crop that the conditions adverse to winter rice would similarly affect it. Its economic importance was also limited; being reaped in November, it could never be followed by a second crop of aghani rice on the same land, in the same season. The only true bhadoi rice was that known as *gora* (upland rice), which covered no more than 5 per cent of the total rice lands.[68] In Palamau, the northern and central parts inhabited mainly by Hindus contained fertile valleys growing rice and, to a lesser extent, sugar-cane and rabi crops, such as wheat, barley, gram and oilseeds. As elsewhere, the second crop grown on rice-lands were generally cheap catch crops like khesari and linseed.[69] The southern part, consisting of hill tracts mainly inhabited by the tribals, depended almost exclusively on the bhadoi crop. Double-cropping had very little importance in the southern tracts. However, in 1896–97 the famine zone lay mainly in the centre and the north, for the winter rice and rabi yielded only a 5-anna and 6-and-¾-anna crop respectively, while the bhadoi produced a 10-anna harvest.[70]

In Hazaribagh, rice-lands covered approximately two-thirds of the total cultivated area, and the second crops sown were invariably those of inferior quality. Double-cropping was insignificant in Singhbhum as well.

Bengal

In Bengal proper, the two important crops in the bhadoi harvest were aus paddy and jute, while the only crop in the aghani harvest was aman rice. The rabi crop was of very little significance

68 *DG: Manbhum*, comp. H. Coupland, 1911, pp. 121–22.
69 *SR, Palamau: Palamau Government Estate, Chotanagpur* (1894–5 to 1896–7) by D. H. E. Sunder (Calcutta: BS Press, 1898), p. 221, para. 75.
70 *DCAR, Chotanagpur, 1896–97*, sec. 3, pp. 6–8, paras. 18–19.

throughout the delta region. Hence, here the bhadoi was to be followed by the aghani crop on the same land in the same season, in order to ensure economic productivity. In statistical terms,the index of prosperity of the delta regions was found by deducting the percentage of the rabi from that of the double-cropped area. If the percentage of the double-cropped area exceeded that of the rabi crops, it showed that the bhadoi crops were followed by the aghani harvest on the same land, to the extent of this difference. On the other hand, if the percentage of the net cropped area covered by the rabi exceeded the percentage of the total double-cropped area, the difference indicated the extent to which the rabi crops grew independently. It also showed that the bhadoi crops were never followed by the aghani crops on the same lands in one season.

Double-cropping was obviously much more important in the eastern districts due not only to its greater exent, but also to its higher qualitative value; as much as 17.2 per cent of the net cropped area in the active delta grew aus or jute and aghani rice on the same land in the same season. This was sometimes followed by cold-weather crops as well.[71] In exclusive rice districts like Bakarganj, however, the heavy yield of aman rice reduced the economic importance of double-cropping.

Of the districts in western Bengal, the rabi area either coincided with or exceeded the percentage of the double-cropped area. This indicates that nowhere in this region was the bhadoi crop followed by the aghani harvest. Winter rice was generally grown, followed by inferior rabi crops.

In central Bengal, except in the 24 Parganas, Nadia and Khulna, the second crops were invariably rabi grains grown after the bhadoi or aghani crops.[72]

71 Ganguli, *Trends of Agriculture*, p. 257.

72 The excess of the percentage of rabi over the twice-cropped area also showed that in Bankura, Midnapur, Hughli, Howrah, Murshidabad and Jessore a certain area grew rabi crops independently. These were precisely the districts with a low level of material prosperity. In Nadia, 24 Parganas and Khulna, certain regions bore aus and jute crops followed by the aghani in the same season, which accounted for their relative prosperity. The percentages of double-cropping and of rabi crops were particularly high in Dacca, Faridpur, Murshidabad and Nadia. But the economic

TABLE 13

Percentage of Double-cropping in the Gangetic Delta

District	Percentage of rabi to the net cropped area	Percentage of double-cropped to the net cropped area	Index of contribution of double-cropping to agricultural productivity
Burdwan	14	14	0
Birbhum	3	3	0
Bankura	10	5	5
Midnapur	18	4	14
Hughli	11	9	2
Howrah	14	12	2
Average for western Bengal	**16.6**	**8**	**3.83**
24 Parganas	4	10	6
Nadia	56	64	8
Murshidabad	40	33	7
Jessore	21	17	4
Khulna	7	11	4
Average for central Bengal	**25.6**	**27**	**1.4**
Dacca	23	35	12
Faridpur	24	33	9
Bakarganj	7	13	6
Tipperah	18	38	20
Noakhali	14	50	36
Average for active delta	**17.4**	**33.8**	**17.2**

Source: Ganguli, *Trends of Agriculture*, p. 257.

Table 13 clearly indicates the extent and importance of double-cropping in the different parts of the Ganges delta.

Orissa

In Orissa, double-cropping had little relevance owing to the predominance of the saradh or winter rice. In Puri, especially in the Jagirmahals including the Chilka Lake tract, winter rice

value of double-cropping was relatively low, for the extensive cultivation of rabi crops, particularly in jute growing areas, was positively a sign of agricultural depression. Jute is a valuable crop with a higher cost of cultivation; hence the substitution of rabi crops for jute indicated poverty and stagnation in agriculture.

occupied 85.15 per cent of the total cropped area.[73] *Do-fasal* (double-cropped) lands receiving fresh silt deposits every year were only found along the banks in the upper parts of the Brahmani and Kharsoa Rivers. The crops grown on such lands generally followed the biali harvest.

TABLE 14

Double-cropping in Puri: Acreage

Crops	*Area under each crop (in acres)*
Kapa (cotton)	92.91
Moong	279.88
Birhi (lentil)	150.90
Khasa (sesamum)	139.59
Kulthi	10.00
Bargara	9.00
Wheat	Area not shown in Survey records. Grown along alluvial banks of fresh water rivers

Source: SR, Kanika Ward's Estate, District Cuttack, 1889–94, p. 33.

The average cost and yield per acre of these rabi crops were as follows:

TABLE 15

Double-cropping in Puri: Cost and Yield per Acre

Crops	*Cost (Rs.)*	*Yield (Md.)*	*Worth (Rs.)*
Birhi	4	4	7.0
Moong	6	3½	10.8
Barley	5	4	8.0
Wheat	7	4	10.0
Khasa	10	3	15.0

Source: SR, Kanika Ward 's Estate, Cuttack, 1889–94, p. 33, para. 86.

Thus, the *moong* (green gram) and *khasa*, which yielded a fair profit margin, covered a sizeable proportion of the double-cropped lands, i.e., 419.47 of 969.69 acres.[74] But do-fasal lands formed only a very small part of the total cropped area, while the saradh lands

73 *SR, Puri: Jagirmahals*, pp. 6–7, paras. 27, 31.

74 *SR, Kanika Ward's Estate*, p. 33, para. 86.

generally yielded no second crops at all. Of the entire cropped area of 125,880.78 acres, do-fasal lands constituted only 969.69 acres, i.e., 0.7 per cent. As saradh rice predominated throughout the Division, the level of material prosperity was remarkably low.

[1.3] The lethal connection: winter rice, poverty and famine

In conclusion, it may be said that winter rice, grown almost exclusively throughout the Province, generally led to a high degree of agricultural insecurity.

Rice cultivation, being eminently suited to the local conditions of rainfall, soil and climate, minimised the investment in outlay—a most important consideration affecting the peasant's choice of the crop. As cultivation reached its limit in the settled tracts, it extended into freshly reclaimed marginal lands and new alluvial formations, under a growing population pressure. This implied in effect a shift from multi-crop production to monoculture, for the new settlements produced almost nothing but rice. The changing land-to-man ratio and the constant threat of famines further emphasised the importance of rice as a heavy-yielding food staple. The growing needs of intensive farming thus reinforced the trend towards rice cultivation, to the extent that it covered even unsuitable tracts like the uplands in Chotanagpur and the Santhal Parganas, and canal-irrigated lands meant for valuable cash crops, as in the Sone Circle. The former heightened the risk of crop failure, while the latter reduced the level of prosperity in the regions concerned. Commercialisation and the price mechanism thus had little relevance in the local crop pattern, agriculture being conditioned by subsistence requirements rather than a price stimulus responding to market forces. The level of prices, in fact, fluctuated with the size of the harvest, which in turn was determined mainly by the rains—an uncertain variable at best.

Indeed, erratic rainfall and adverse weather conditions led to frequent failures of the rice crop. Rice was a delicate crop extremely susceptible to drought, with no effective substitute or second crop to fall back on except for a few cheap and inferior grains of the rabi harvest such as khesari, gram or linseed, which could never compensate for its loss in lean years. In fact, the higher the percentage of the net cropped area under winter rice in a particular region, the greater was the intensity of famine or scarcity in case of drought.

The following statistics (table 16) relating to the famine situation in north Bihar in 1896–97 distinctly emphasise this trend.

TABLE 16

Incidence of Famine in the Rice Tracts of North Bihar, 1896–97

District	*% of the net cropped area under winter rice*	*Highest no. of persons relieved on any one day during the famine of 1896–97*	*% of persons relieved to total population affected by crop failure*
Darbhanga	57.33	253,910	10.49
Muzaffarpur	42.35	139,355	6.93
Saran	29.11	85,173	5.75

Source: SR, Darbhanga, p. 122, para. 440.

The three districts of Saran, Muzaffarpur and Darbhanga were more or less similarly placed as regards pressure of population on the soil and the small scope for extension of cultivation. Yet the crop failure of 1896 affected them in varying degrees of intensity. Saran, with a more equitable distribution of the three harvests and less dependence on the aman, was not affected by the famine as severely as Muzaffarpur and Darbhanga, both of which had a much greater proportion of the net cropped area under winter rice.[75]

Likewise, in Orissa, the famine of 1896–97 struck hardest at the Chilka tract in Puri, which depended entirely on the saradh harvest. Table 17 shows the proportion of winter rice grown in the Jagirmahals and the Chilka region.

Significantly, it was here that distress was first felt and relief measures were necessary in 1866, 1885–86 and 1888–89. In 1896–97, too, the famine tract was most extensive, the affected population most numerous and relief measures most prolonged in the Chilka region.[76] This is apparent from table 18.

[75] *SR, Darbhanga* (1896–1903), by J. H. Kerr (Calcutta: BS Press, 1904), p. 122, para. 440.

[76] LRP, Aug. 1898, pt. 3, Br. Agriculture, p. 1619. From W. H. Lee, Officiating Collector, Puri, to Commissioner, Orissa Division, no. 2632, dated Puri, 2 Dec. 1897.

TABLE 17
Percentage of Winter Rice in the Chilka tract, Puri

Parganas	*Percentage of winter rice*
Bajrakote	78.19
Malud	83.42
Parikud	91.19
Manikpatna	67.96
Andhari	78.81

Source: Extract from app. 2, *SR, Puri: Jagirmahals,* 1906–9.

In Bengal proper, too, the exclusive rice-tracts were the first to suffer and the last to recover from the effects of drought in 1896–97. In Jessore, the worst tracts covered an area of 106 sq. miles in the northeast of Magura and 168 sq. miles in thana Bongaon. The population of the two tracts was about 163,000 and the all-important crop was aman.[77] In Khulna, the affected area covering 474 sq. miles with a population of 276,000, lay almost entirely in Satkhira and in Paikgacha thana in the Sadar subdivision. Practically the only crop grown was winter rice, the aggregate area occupied by other crops being, it was believed, not more than 2 per cent of the total cultivated area. In Nadia, distress was most prolonged and acute in Kaliganj-Nakashipara in the Sadar, and Tehatta in Meherpur. The entire area lay in the low-lying Kalantar tract, which, along with the distress areas in the Murshidabad Kalantar, was a mono-crop region producing winter rice.

Thus, the local crop pattern, which was marked by the predominance of winter rice throughout, had a definite role in causing and prolonging the famine situation in Bengal in crisis years like 1866 and 1873. Being susceptible to drought, rice failed frequently. The failure was most complete in mono-crop tracts. Even double-cropped regions growing winter rice invariably had a low index of prosperity, the harvest timings being such that it could neither be preceded by the bhadoi, nor followed by the more valuable crops of the rabi variety. Ironically, therefore, the intensive concentration on rice as an insurance against famine, in effect heightened the insecurity in agriculture. This correlation

[77] *Selection of Papers*, vol. 5: p. 6, para. 2.

TABLE 18

Intensity of Famine in the Chilka Tract, Puri

	Tracts	*Affected area Sq. miles*	*Population*	*Distress began to be felt*	*Relief was closed*
1	The shore of the Chilka, comprising Bajrakote, Malud, Parikud, Andheri, Manikpatna, Chaubiskud etc.	231	74,000	Feb. 1897	15.09.97
2	Rameswar and Kuhari in Khurda subdivision	20	10,000	"	29.09.97
3	Tract extending from east Ganjam Trunk Road to Aitpur in Khurda	9	2,000	"	"
4	Tract extending from shores of Chilka to foot of Bhalari Hills in Khurda subdivision	14	3,000	"	"
5	Sana and Bara Mals in Banpur, Khurda subdivision	68	2,000	15.04.97	19.06.97
6	Tract in Kuspalla near Baghmari in Khurda subdivision	10	4,000	11.04.97	"
7	Tract in Khurda and Dandimul on right bank of the Daya	23	7,000	29.02.97	"

Source: LRP Aug. 1898, pt. 3, p. 1619.

between rice cultivation, poverty and famine was vividly manifest once again during the great famine of 1896–97, which hit hardest at the rice tracts, both in terms of duration and intensity.

[2] *Rainfall: Volume and Pattern of Distribution*

The crop pattern in Bengal depended on the interacting influences of climate and soil, which together constituted the agricultural-economic environment. While the efficiency of rainfall depended on the nature of the soil, the fertility of the soil was largely determined by temperature and rainfall. In case of excessive rain, the low-lying tracts, as in many parts of the Ganges Delta, suffered from swamp and oversaturation due to defective drainage. Deficient rainfall and high temperature, on the other hand, led to rapid water loss outbalancing the absorption of moisture, so that the plants tended to wither and die.

Rice, the main crop and staple food in Bengal, required heavy rains and a high water table, preferably 50" annually, with 5" per month during the growing season. In normal years, this condition was fulfilled almost throughout the Province, as is evident from table 19.[78]

Even more important than the total volume of rainfall was the nature of its distribution during the agricultural seasons. The winter rice-crop required premonitory showers in May and early June, heavy showers in late June to early July, and, after an interval of comparatively fine weather, good rains in September–October. The September rains were most vital in determining the out-turn of aman rice.[79] Bhadoi or autumn rice was usually sown in May because it required light, intermittent showers between the months of April and May rather than heavy rains which would

[78] *Report, Indian Irrigation Commission,* p. 378.

[79] In north and east Bengal and the eastern districts of southwest Bengal, the preparation of rice fields began much earlier than in the rest of the Lower Provinces. Hence, the ante-monsoon showers in April, May and early June were more important here than in other areas where the lands were usually prepared after the monsoon showers started. These ante-monsoon showers in April, and in certain parts of lower Bengal as early as in March, were also essential for the preparation of the bhadoi lands.

TABLE 19

Average Annual Rainfall in Bengal Presidency

District annual rainfall	Average	District annual rainfall	Average	District annual rainfall	Average	District annual rainfall	Average
Burdwan	56.1	24 Prgs.	63.1	Dinajpur	69.9	Dacca	71.1
Bankura	55.3	Khulna	65.9	Rajshahi	57.1	Faridpur	65.4
Birbhum	59.2	Nadia	57.2	Rangpur	78.8	Bakargunj	85.1
Midnapur	59.9	Jessore	60.7	Bogra	66.5	Mymensingh	86.6
Hughli	59.0	Murshidabad	54.1	Darjeeling	132.5		
				Jalpaiguri	124.9	**Total Dacca Division**	77
Total Burdwan Division	57.9	**Total Presidency Division**	60.2	Pabna	61.4		
				Total Rajshahi Division	84.4	Hazaribagh	51.9
Tippera	75.6	Patna	45.2			Ranchi	56.8
Noakhali	113.0	Gaya	43.0			Palamau	48.1
Chittagong	111.8	Shahabad	43.5	Monghyr	49.0	Manbhum	52.2
		Saran	44.9	Bhagalpur	51.2	Singhbhum	58.3
Total Chittagong Division	100.1	Champaran	54.1	Purnea	72.5		
		Muzaffarpur	45.9	Malda	56.8	**Total Chotanagpur Division**	53.5
		Darbhanga	49.8	Santhal Prgs.	53.8		
Cuttack							
Balasore		**Total Patna Division**	46.6	**Total Bhagalpur Division**	56.7		
Angul							
Puri							
Total Orissa Division							

Source: Report, Indian Irrigation Commission, p. 378, statement I.

disturb the sowing operations. Rabi crops flourished when the monsoon rains ceased early in October, followed by light showers in late October and early November and occasional showers in December–January.[80]

The distribution of rains in each area thus determined the local crop pattern and out-turn. North Bihar, for example, received more rainfall than south Bihar between 1 March and 30 September, which covered the monsoon as well as the bhadoi season. Hence, here the bhadoi crops supplemented the aghani harvest to a much greater extent than in south Bihar, which depended almost solely on the out-turn of the winter rice. Again, the main crops in a monsoon region like the Ganges Delta were wet crops included in the bhadoi and aghani harvests. Dry crops of the rabi harvest occupied a comparatively small area, due to the heavy annual precipitation and excessive moisture in the soil. For the bhadoi crops, the showers in March, April and May were crucial. The "active delta" or eastern districts of Bengal received nearly double the amount of rainfall during these months than the "moribund delta" or the western parts. Likewise, the distribution of rains during the monsoon, as well as in September-October, which were essential for the winter rice, distinctly favoured the former. Hence, given a normal distribution of the rains, the eastern part of the Ganges Delta could produce three harvests during the year, while the western districts depended mainly on the aghani rice followed by a few cheap catch-crops of the rabi harvest.

[2.1] Deviations from the norm in crisis years

Agricultural operations were, in fact, so delicately adjusted to climatic conditions that insufficient or ill-distributed rainfall in any season would deeply affect the quality and size of the crop. This was evident in crisis years like 1866, 1873–74 and 1896–97 in various parts of Bengal, Bihar and Orissa. In all these years, the divergence of rainfall conditions from the normal were quite marked, both as regards volume and distribution.

[80] *Final Resolution*, ch. 2.

[a] Deficiency in total volume

Deficient rains in Puri throughout 1865 led to an agrarian crisis which deepened in 1866, followed by excessive rain and floods. This is apparent from table 20.

TABLE 20
Volume of Rainfall in Puri, 1865

Average annual rainfall	60 to 65 inches
Rainfall of 1864	41.8 inches
Rainfall of 1865	36.3 inches
Rainfall of 1866	77.2 inches

Source: Report on the Famine in Bengal and Orissa, 1866, p.16.

The mean actual rainfall during the monsoon period (1 May to 31 October) in comparison with the average is given in table 21.

TABLE 21
Distribution of Rainfall in Puri, 1865

Month	*Average fall in inches of the 13 years preceeding 1865*	*Fall in 1865*
May	2.1	13.0
June	9.2	5.6
July	12.2	4.3
August	17.3	5.6
September	16.8	5.2
October	9.4	0.0

Source: Report on the Famine in Bengal and Orissa, 1866, p. 16.

Thus, the total registered fall of the usual rainy season, June to September, was 20.7 inches, or an average of five inches per month. This might have sufficed in a cooler climate but was enough to cause an extreme failure in a hot rice country, even without the greater crisis of a total lack of rain in October.[81]

Likewise, the mean actual rainfall in the affected districts during the monsoon period of 1896, as compared with the normal fall

[81] *Report of the Commissioners appointed to enquire into the Famine in Bengal and Orissa in 1866* (Calcutta, 1867), p. 16, para. 56.

as well as with that of 1873 and 1895, was remarkably low (table 22).[82]

Thus, in the Patna Division the deficiency in 1896 as compared to that in 1873 was far greater in Saran and Champaran and somewhat more in Shahabad. It was about the same in Muzaffarpur but in Sitamarhi subdivision in this district, where there was a total concentration of rice production, the percentage of shortfall was 41.6 as against 25.3 in 1873. In Darbhanga the volume of rainfall was greater than in 1873, but the total lack of rain for six weeks since the beginning of July was most irregular and harmful to agriculture. In Bhagalpur and Santhal Parganas there was more rain in 1896 than in 1873, but the deficiency during two successive seasons in 1895 and 1896 more than marred its effects. Moreover, in Jamtara and Deoghar, the heart of the famine tract in the Santhal Parganas, the deficit in 1896 was 21 per cent as against 16 per cent in 1873. In the Chotanagpur, Burdwan and Presidency Divisions, the deficiency in 1895 was almost uniformly greater than in 1896, which made the shortfall in the latter year even more disastrous, for the carry-over stocks were very low.

[b] Divergence from the normal pattern of distribution

More important than the total volume of rainfall, however, was the nature of its distribution, because the entire prospect of the great winter rice crop depended on the September and October rains.

In 1865–66, for instance, there was a widespread failure of the rains in Puri during these crucial months, as given below.

	Average in inches	*1865 (in inches)*
September	16.8	5.2
October	9.4	0.0

In Cuttack and Balasore, the rainfall was 7.5" and 9.30" in September and 0.0" and 0.30" in October, respectively. Thus, in Puri, where the failure was the greatest, rice reached a famine

TABLE 22

Volume of Rainfall in the Affected Districts of Bengal in 1896

Districts	Normal	1873		1895		1896	
		Rainfall	*Percentage of excess or defect on normal*	*Rainfall*	*Percentage of excess or defect on normal*	*Rainfall*	*Percentage of excess or defect on normal*
Patna Div.							
Shahabad	40.15	30.19	-24.80	38.07	-5.18	29.47	-26.20
Saran	42.83	31.40	-27.70	44.24	-3.30	22.29	-47.96
Champaran	52.60	33.03	-37.20	57.34	+9.01	27.94	-46.80
Muzaffarpur	43.49	30.80	-29.18	47.73	+9.75	30.99	-28.74
Darbhanga	47.33	24.22	-48.80	42.08	-11.09	35.73	-24.50
Bhagalpur Div.							
Bhagalpur	48.68	30.27	-37.80	41.00	-15.70	37.27	-23.40
Santhal Prgs.	49.70	33.62	-32.30	36.74	-26.07	41.67	-16.15

Chotanagpur Div.							
Hazaribagh	50.05	53.72	+7.33	43.03	-14.02	47.04	-6.01
Palamau	46.46	39.11	-15.80	28.38	-39.90	32.71	-29.50
Manbhum	49.09	42.10	-14.23	39.86	-18.80	40.38	-17.70
Burdwan Div.							
Bankura	51.64	39.08	-24.30	43.57	-15.60	44.97	-12.90
Presidency Div.							
Nadia	50.24	39.21	-21.90	34.11	-32.10	38.94	-22.49
Murshidabad	48.89	31.86	-34.80	31.61	-35.30	39.15	-19.09
Khulna	57.30	50.22	-12.70	52.36	-8.90	47.07	-18.18
Orissa Div.							
Puri	52.33	50.41	-3.74	68.84	31.40	55.38	5.70

Source: Final Resolution, 1896–97, p. 14.

price (13¾ Calcutta *seers* per rupee) as early as September 1865, before there was any alarm in the country, generally.[83] By October, the deficiency in rainfall in all the three districts led to the first signs of crop failure and distress.

In 1873–74, again, the rains failed in September, and a severe famine prevailed throughout an area of 20,950 sq. miles, especially in north Bihar and north Bengal. In 1875–76, 1885–86, 1887–88 and 1891–92, early cessation of the rains and irregularities in the monsoon during September and October caused much damage to the winter rice. In 1896, too, the rains were remarkably ill distributed, as is apparent from chart I on page 54.[84]

Table 23, which gives the figures of the mean district rainfall in September–October 1896, as compared to that in normal years and in 1873, further illustrates the point.[85]

Actually, with the onset of the monsoon in 1896, a low-pressure belt was formed over the north of the Bay of Bengal, which deprived north Bengal and Bihar of a considerable portion of the rainfall during the most crucial phase of the rainy season.

Throughout the Patna Division there was a late commencement of the monsoon in June, heavy rains early in July, and two long periods of drought till mid-August and mid-September. The damage to the crops was severe: those which escaped the floods in July withered from drought later on, especially in the northern districts.

In Bhagalpur Division, too, the rains set in late, and the break from mid-July to mid-August ruined the bhadoi, while that from the end of September to December destroyed the prospects of the aman.

In Chotanagpur, the failure of the ante-monsoon showers in April-May hampered the preparation of the land, while the excessive fall in June-July damaged the weak seedlings. These were further affected by the premature cessation of rain in September and October.

83 *Famine Commission Report 1866* (Calcutta: Superintendent, Government Printing, 1867), pp. 16–17, paras. 56–58.
84 Bengal Revenue Proceedings, reg. no. 117, Apr. 98–450.
85 *Final Resolution,* p. 15.

TABLE 23

Distribution of Rainfall in the Affected Districts of Bengal in 1896

Affected districts in 1896–97	*N O R M A L*			*1 8 7 3*			*1 8 9 6*		
	Sept.	*Oct.*	*Total*	*Sept.*	*Oct.*	*Total*	*Sept.*	*Oct.*	*Total*
Shahabad	6.83	2.87	9.70	2.43	nil	2.43	2.30	Nil	2.30
Saran	7.60	3.49	11.09	1.12	nil	1.12	1.28	Nil	1.28
Champaran	9.50	3.31	12.81	0.51	nil	0.51	2.35	Nil	2.35
Muzaffarpur	7.57	2.64	10.21	2.85	nil	2.85	2.73	Nil	2.73
Darbhanga	9.91	2.10	12.01	3.87	nil	3.87	6.21	0,03	6.24
Bhagalpur	9.27	2.59	11.86	4.54	0.03	4.57	9.47	Nil	9.47
Santhal Prgs.	9.17	3.57	12.74	5.14	nil	5.14	7.97	0.10	8.07
Hazaribagh	8.51	3.44	11.95	9.06	0.20	9.26	6.47	Nil	6.47
Palamau	7.82	2.78	10.60	5.05	nil	5.05	4.28	Nil	4.28
Manbhum	7.79	2.62	10.40	6.48	0.07	6.55	5.20	Nil	5.20
Bankura	8.15	3.16	11.31	3.60	0.45	4.05	4.82	Nil	4.82
Nadia	8.12	4.12	12.24	3.28	0.81	4.09	8.45	Nil	8.45
Murshidabad	9.02	3.68	12.70	5.83	0.78	6.61	7.76	0.01	7.77
Khulna	8.85	4.94	13.79	6.59	0.50	7.09	10.46	0.14	10.60
Puri	10.74	1.91	17.65	9.61	8.02	17.63	7.48	0.37	7.85

Source: Final Resolution, p. 15.

Chart 1: Rainfall in the Fifteen Affected Districts during 1896–97

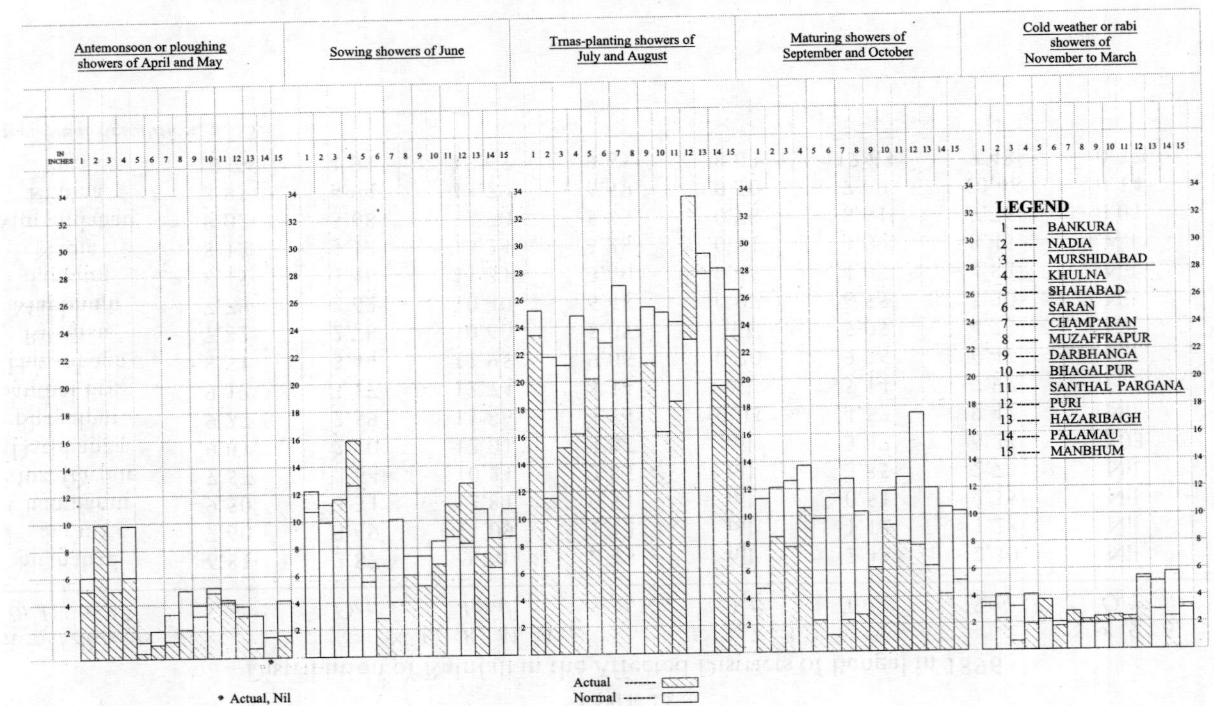

In the Presidency Division, Nadia suffered severely: the exclusive rice-tracts in the Kalantar, which depended entirely on inundations, were left without any irrigation when the rains ceased abruptly on 19 September. Elsewhere in Nadia, the aus crop which predominated was affected by the lack of rain in August. Khulna, generally considered immune from famine, might have escaped the crisis despite deficient rains in 1896, had it not been for the excessive salinity of the soil caused by a storm wave that hit the district in October 1895.

In Puri, where the total volume of rainfall was only a little below the normal, the failure of the September and October rains, both in 1865 and in 1896, caused the most terrible famines ever known in the district.[86]

Thus, both in terms of the volume or quantity as well as the timing or distribution of the rains, the season of 1896 was as unfortunate as that of 1873.

[2.2] No general change in rainfall pattern in the late nineteenth century

Rainfall statistics do not imply any marked change in climatic conditions or the rainfall pattern in Bengal during the late nineteenth century,[87] as seems to have been the case in western India between 1870 and 1920, according to the findings of Michelle Burge McAlpin.[88] Abnormal seasons as in 1873 and 1896 were the result of sporadic meteorological factors, which do not fall into any definitive pattern.

In explaining the crisis of 1896, Little, the Meteorological Reporter to the Government of Bengal, related it to the depth of sub-soil water, which was vital for crops whose roots pass only a

86 *DG: Puri*, p. 147.

87 Index numbers of rainfall in Bengal, Base: 100

1875	1876	1877	1878	1879	1880	1881	1882	1883	1884	1885	1886	1887	1888	1889
93	103	98	100	102	109	107	91	86	79	106	116	98	98	100

1890	1891	1892	1893	1894	1895	1896	1897	1898	1899	1900	1901	1902	1903	1904
110	87	89	129	104	83	81	104	112	118	110	94	100	88	105

Source: B. M. Bhatia, *Famines in India (1860–1965)* (Bombay: Asia Publishing House, 1967), apps., pp. 345–47.

88 McAlpin, "Dearth, Famine and Risk", p. 145.

few inches below ground surface. The sub-soil water level had been falling more rapidly than usual during the past two years in the drier months. Moreover, the hot westerly winds in October 1896 rapidly dried the surface layers of the soil, and the moisture necessary for the support of the crops was restored neither by occasional rainfall nor by capillary action from the sub-soil. In fact, the monsoon rainfall both in 1895 and 1896 was not sufficient to supply even what was lost in ordinary years, so that when the rains ceased prematurely in mid-September, the sub-soil was inadequately charged with moisture.[89]

[3] *Inundations or Spill Irrigation*

The level of sub-soil water was determined not only by rainfall but also by inundations or river floods, which provided the only other source of natural irrigation.

The laterite formations and *char* (riverside) lands above the reach of flood water usually depended on the rains, and transplantation was the rule. The laterite portion of western Bengal, i.e. parts of Midnapur, Bankura, Ranigunge and the Rarh tract in Burdwan and Murshidabad stretched out on the west into south Bihar and the Chotanagpur Plateau, and southwards to Angul-Khondmals and the tributary *mahal*s (estates) of Orissa. The char lands included the ex-Kalantar region and Meherpur in Nadia, Magura-Bongaon in Jessore, the Barind tract in Rajshahi, and the generally high-level lands in Bihar.

On the other hand, the districts in eastern Bengal and low-lying areas of bils like the Kalantar tract in Murshidabad and Nadia, Satkhira in Khulna, the *bilan* (low-lying) lands in Rajshahi, the rice belt in north Bihar and the greater part of Orissa depended on inundations. Here, the seeds were generally sown broadcast.[90] Indeed, in low-lying areas, the overflow of rivers during seasonal floods supplied the surrounding spill basin with moisture and silt, and hence ensured a satisfactory harvest. Again, when the floods ebbed away and the level of the river fell, its main channel and distributaries were flushed by the receding current of clear,

89 *Selection of Papers,* vol. 1, pp. 11–12.

90 Transplantation prevailed in north Bihar, though river floods were common.

silt-free water. Thus, an active river system, with its alternate functions of flood and flush, served the purpose of both irrigation and drainage.

[3.1] Ideal conditions for spill irrigation

Spill irrigation, in order to be really effective, had to meet certain specific conditions as to the level, timing and duration of the floods. If the land was too high or the floods too low, it had to depend solely on the rains, and was suitable only for growing dry crops. Conversely, if the land was too low or the floods too deep, it could not grow even long-stemmed rice, but only boro rice before the water rose. The lands lying between these two extremes received the full benefit of the floods and normally produced a fair crop of aghani or saradh rice in Bihar and Orissa, and both aus and aman in eastern Bengal.

The timing and duration of the floods were equally important. In the delta region, flood water was required to cover the land in June, rise gradually till September, and then slowly drain away. If the land was submerged too soon in the active delta, the sowing of the aus, aman and jute crops was delayed, while the late aus was destroyed by floods at harvest time. Again, in Orissa, when the floods occurred late or were of long duration so as to render re-sowing impossible, the crops sustained severe damage.[91] If the rise of the floods was too sudden or violent, the saplings were liable to be washed away, while a rapid fall in the water level caused the rice plants to lose support and collapse. Conversely, if the water had a slight fall and fairly swift current, it tended to deposit rather than excavate, the process of land formation continued, and the river system remained active.

Naturally, conditions were not always ideal, and the benefits of flood irrigation were often more than neutralised by certain characteristic problems.

[3.2] Long-term problems of drainage and sanitation

Long-term issues vitally connected with flood irrigation and the raising of embankments were those of drainage and sanitation.

91 *DG: Puri*, p. 147.

These were already jeopardised by the frequently changing course of the Ganges and its distributaries, and the decaying river system in a large part of west and central Bengal.

In some areas, as in Muzaffarpur and Darbhanga in north Bihar, the rivers served as drainage channels, though flowing on raised beds. The high river banks running parallel enclosed shallow depressions which, when filled with rain water, had no other outlet and opened out into the nearest rivers at relatively low points. In Saran, however, the Collector, E. F. Growse, noted before the Irrigation Commission in 1902, that the Saran embankment, though protecting the district from floods, upset the level of natural drainage. It choked up the spill channels, which deteriorated into "a series of malarious pools" and caused a distinct sanitary problem. Champaran, north Bhagalpur and Purnea all suffered from water-logging to a greater or lesser extent. Purnea was "singularly ill-drained", being full of shallow swamps generally along the old beds of the Kosi, which frequently changed its course.[92]

In the active delta, i.e. the eastern districts of Bengal, even lands which were fully raised and levelled up by silt did not suffer from problems of obstructed drainage and water-logging, as they had been elevated by a natural process. Even so, any interference with the drainage channels—for example by fishermen who bunded them up and laid fishing traps in every tiny rivulet and creek—led to the accumulation of silt, and large areas were thrown out of cultivation, relapsing into quagmires.[93]

It was in the "moribund delta" i.e. central and west Bengal, however, that drainage was a real and pressing problem. This was due to several factors: the eastward shift of the Ganges and the sluggish current of the silt-laden "dead rivers" which lost connection with it; the extreme flatness of the country, which caused a network of circuit and cross-dams, weirs and embankments to be thrown across rivers and drainage channels, or built around the fields in order to retain water (thus restricting the action of the tides); and the construction of railway lines and

[92] *Bengal Census Report 1891*, para. 147.

[93] LRP, Br. Land Revenue, March 1895, p. 1467.

feeder roads, which often ran across and obstructed the natural lines of drainage.[94]

Large areas in Orissa faced an identical problem. Parganas Behera and Ankura, lying in the affected areas of Bhadrak in Balasore in 1896–97, were protected from the influx of sea water by an the embankment extending from north to south. Bayang, situated along the Baitarni, had a continuous embankment running on its left. But, despite their protective function, embankments interfered with the natural drainage of the land. When the Baitarni rose in flood, the extensive rice-tracts in Bayang, Behera and Ankura lay submerged for days, as there were no outlets for it in the sea dyke.[95] Though erection of new *bund*s (embankments) was prohibited in most of these littoral tracts, they were still constructed under the pretext of repairing old ones. Such restrictions of the spill basin of rivers, besides obstructing drainage, also reduced the fertility of cultivated lands by shutting out the silt deposits required to sustain and enrich them.[96]

94 In Nadia, the Kalantar tract was too water-logged to bear any crop except the aman, which was liable to be swept away by heavy rains, or dry up in years of abnormally low floods. In Murshidabad, the construction of a marginal embankment (called the Lalitakuri or Nultakuri embankment) on the left bank of the Bhagirathi cut off its connection with the Jalangi, and made drainage extremely difficult in the country east of the Bhagirathi. In Jessore and Khulna, water did not move easily in the old alluvium due to silting up of the rivers which no longer received freshets from the Ganges, while in the littoral tracts the raising of embankments to keep out salt water resulted in a serious interference with drainage lines and the process of land formation. The construction of the bridge of the Eastern Bengal State Railway near Kushtia in Jessore contributed to the silting up of the Garai in its upper reaches. Much of the decay of the Nabaganga was attributed to the construction across its bed of the East Bengal Railway embankment north of Chuadanga; the Beng, formerly fed by the Nabaganga, lost its supply. The head of the Chitra closed up too, due to the silting up of the Nabaganga as well as the artificial disconnection caused by an embankment thrown across its off-take several decades earlier.

95 LRP, Aug. 1898, pt. 3, p. 1607. From B. De, Collector of Balasore, to the Commissioner, Orissa Division, no. 3308, Balasore, 10 Dec. 1897.

96 Ibid., Br. Land Revenue, May 1897, p. 1171. Memorial of the Landlords' Association of Orissa, to Sir Alexander Mackenzie, Lieutenant Governor of Bengal, para. 6.

Sanitation was a major problem in these ill-drained marshes along the moribund rivers, and it was precisely in these tracts that malaria was most rampant in the late nineteenth century.

In north Bihar, the fever epidemics were invariably linked up with floods and the problem of drainage. For example, in Muzaffarpur the Lalganj and Mahua thanas were submerged by a heavy flood in 1883, and fever prevailed epidemically. In Champaran, malaria was most severe in the notoriously unhealthy swamps of the Terai in Hardi thana and in Bettiah. Purnea, where cultivation suffered due to the frequent changes in the course of the Kosi, lived up to the proverb "*Marne chaho to Purnea jao*" (If you want to die go to Purnea).

The virulent outbreak of fever in south Bihar during the 1880s and early 1890s was generally connected with the "great extension of canals and distributaries from the Sone Irrigation Works at Dehri, which both raised the level of the sub-soil water and interfered by their embankments with the natural surface drainage of the country". The Civil Surgeon of Shahabad categorically stated in 1890 that this "interference with drainage and water-logging of the soil . . . had no doubt injuriously affected public health".[97]

Bengal was indeed the stronghold of malaria. In Hughli, the tracts worst hit by the fever were those lying between the Damodar and the Hughli, where numerous rivulets (*khal*s) had choked up due to the raising of embankments between 1853–63.[98] The outbreak of the fever in Jessore was linked up distinctly with various phases in the "drying up" of the Bhairab. A local indigo planter threw a bund across it, converting its clear water into a "filthy, floating morass . . . choked with weeds and

[97] *Bengal Census Report 1891*, para. 151. Monghyr had the highest mortality in the whole of Bihar. Some viewed it as a northward extension into Birbhum, south Monghyr and Bhagalpur of the Burdwan fever which, incidentally, was also a result of water-logging and drainage problems. In 1883, for example, when the Patna Municipal Agency registered the remarkably high death rate of 51.2 per 1000, the Assistant Surgeon of Bihar subdivision, Patna, wrote: "The malarious fever of Bengal has gradually established itself in this part of the country".

[98] Bengal Irrigation Proceedings, May 1872, no. 31.

mud".[99] Dr French, the Civil Surgeon of Rajshahi, agreed with local opinion that the fever was caused by a want of inundation.[100] Infrequent inundations also led to an acute scarcity of good drinking water, which was a potent cause for the persistence of the fever in Burdwan and Nadia. According to the Nadia Fever Commission (1881), "The water supply in Nadia is of the worst possible quality".[101] In Jessore, malaria was at its worst in those parts of Jhenida and Magura where there was a chronic shortage of drinking water.

While in the malaria-hit western and northern parts of Bengal the percentage of population growth during 1881–91 was only 4.1 and 3.4 respectively, in eastern Bengal it was 14.3, only a very small part of which was accounted for by immigration.[102] This depopulation was a crucial factor in the agricultural decline of this period, as the worst sufferers belonged to the poorest classes, i.e., the labouring and peasant communities. Fields reverted to waste in the absence of an adequate labour force. Even the survivors lost their efficiency. A Settlement Officer in Jessore wrote: "The agricultural population stricken by malaria have lost their physical vigour and energy . . . and are incapable of hard work in the field or at home".[103] Arrangements among the peasants for mutual help and exchange of labour during busy seasons (*ganta, badlan, humrul)* went out of vogue due to the frequent recurrence of fever and the uncertainty of labour agreements.[104] The problem was aggravated by the fact that the fever was at its worst during the harvesting of the aman rice in November–December, when the demand for field labour was greatest. Thus, in the last decades of the nineteenth century, fever greatly raised the death rate and devitalised the rural labour force. It retarded agricultural development in tracts cut off from the

[99] *Report of Sanitary Commission, 1868*; Report by McLeod, pp. 34 and 40, quoted by Chaudhuri, "Agricultural Production in Bengal," p. 154.

[100] Ibid., p. 173.

[101] *Report of Sanitary Commissioner, 1882*, para. 48.

[102] *Bengal Census Report 1891*, para. 70.

[103] *SR, Jessore* (1920–24), by M. A. Momen (Calcutta: BSBD, 1925), para. 21.

[104] Chaudhuri, "Agricultural Production in Bengal", pp. 164–65.

river floods, on which they formerly depended both for irrigation and drainage.

[3.3] Short-term problems: too-high or too-low floods

Of the immediate or short-term problems faced by lowlands depending on the overspill of rivers, the most frequent one was that of very high, violent and destructive floods sweeping across the fields and damaging the crops.

This was most apparent in Orissa, particularly in the Puri district. The basic problem in Puri lay in the limited capacity of the Koyakhai River and its distributaries, which in years of high flood, as in 1872, burst through the dams, swept away the crops on the surrounding lowlands, and converted the greater part of the district into a vast sheet of water.[105] The eastern parts of the Khurda and Sadar subdivisions were flooded annually by the Daya and Kushbhadra Rivers respectively, and the "protected" area lying between the embankments of the Daya and Bhargavi was also deeply affected when the rivers rose. The embankments, in trying to confine and hold back the river floods, only intensified their velocity and were frequently breached or overtopped by them. The dams, being ill-kept, easily gave way, as neither the zamindars nor the government were bound by the terms of settlement in Puri to maintain any of them, except one small bund on the Kushbhadra.[106]

Thus, in Puri protection from floods was a more urgent and pressing need than irrigation. Of the thirty-two years ending in 1866, twenty-four were years of flood, some being particularly severe. In 1866, 275 sq. miles were submerged for five to forty-five days, and the damage done to crops resulted in a prolonged famine. In 1888–89, the autumn and winter rice were severely damaged by floods in Khurda and the Chilka tract. In 1897 all the great rivers rose simultaneously to nearly unprecedented heights, and submerged the adjacent lowlands for the unusually

105 *DG: Puri*, p. 168.

106 LRP, Jan. 1894, no. 15, Simla, 6 Oct. 1893. From W. C. Macpherson, Officiating Director of Land Records and Agriculture, Bengal, to the Secretary, Board of Revenue, Lower Provinces.

long period of over a month. This ruined the crop, and much land was permanently thrown out of cultivation by sand deposits.

The effects of flood were usually least felt in the northern parganas where the rapid slope of the land helped to drain off the water. It was in the mono-crop regions in the south, particularly in Bajrakote, Malud, Parikud, Andheri, Manikpatna, etc. in the Chilka tract, that cultivation was most exposed to this risk. It is not surprising, therefore, that the effects of famine were first felt here during the crisis years of 1877–78, 1885–86 and 1888–89, and were most severe and prolonged in 1896–97.

Mr. W. A. Inglis, Chief Engineer to the Bengal Government, proposed to alleviate the problem by regulating the outflow of excess water from the channels. Such attempts met with a fair degree of success in Cuttack. In the Puri Delta, however, the channels were relatively small, and the floods could not be confined between embankments. The only outlets were the Chilka Lake and the small opening of the Kushbhadra, neither of which could be called an efficient estuary.[107]

But Cuttack was not free from the problem of floods either. The embanked or "protected" areas were particularly vulnerable. Embankments were not kept in proper repair. Act XXXII of 1855 providing for the maintenance of the Orissa embankments did not in this context clarify the role of the government, which intended to minimise its responsibility and abandon any embankment without compensation.[108] The state of negligence is revealed by the fact that during the floods of July 1894, part of the water escaped even to the south of the Pattamundi Canal, because some syphons under it (near Judpur) were left without gates![109] In fact, by confining the volume of water, the bunds intensified the force of the floods, so that when they gave way, the crops in the protected tracts were most severely damaged.[110]

107 Ibid., pp. 169–71.

108 Ibid., no. 104, Calcutta, 10 Jan. 1894. From C. E. Buckland, Secretary to the Govt. of Bengal, Revenue Dept., to the Secretary to the Board of Revenue, Land Revenue Dept.

109 Ibid., Sept. 1894. Br. Agriculture, nos. 1–2. no. 1476 G, Cuttack, 16 Aug. 1894. From G. Stevenson, Collector of Cuttack, to the Commissioner, Orissa Division, paras. 3–4.

110 Ibid., Sept. 1894, Br. Agriculture, nos. 1–2, 1476 G. This enhanced damage in protected areas during floods, which illustrated the

Champaran, Muzaffarpur and Darbhanga in north Bihar also suffered from frequent floods. In 1889 and 1893, for example, Bettiah and the Sadar subdivision in Champaran were severely affected by the overspill of the Sikrana and Bagmati Rivers.[111] Likewise, the river Kamla adversely affected the Madhubani subdivision in Darbhanga.

Similarly, in the western part of the Ganges Delta in Bengal, embankments running along the larger rivers increased the volume and frequency of floods. For example, the lands lying to the south of the Damodar in Burdwan as well as parts of Midnapur and Hughli were liable to widespread and severe inundations. Even in east Bengal, high floods occasionally tended to scour away the earth instead of enriching it with silt deposits.

In areas served by spill irrigation, cultivation suffered not only from too high, but also from too low floods. The floods, like the rainfall, were particularly precarious in 1896–97. While high floods caused much damage in Orissa, the flood level fell sharply in certain areas like Rajshahi and Nadia.

In Rajshahi the maximum height of the flood that year was 64", while in a normal year it would be 66" above the mean sea

---

disadvantages of damming up rivers, especially by "ring" embankments, was due to two causes: First, the lands behind the embankments were lower than those outside mainly due to the non-deposit of silt, and formed in case of ring bunds a regular basin which, once filled with water, practically remained so throughout the rains. Second, this not only ruined the crop on the ground but made further cultivation that season impossible which, considering that the bund-protected areas grew only saradh rice, totally blighted the prospects for local agriculture. The embankments maintained by estates were ruined along the right bank of the Brahmini River, as well as those along the rivers Hansua, Kharsua, and the extensive ring embankment called the Aul "Bherabund" covering the major part of Killa Aul. The river banks unprotected by dams, though subject to more frequent floods, could grow two crops: biali or early rice on the highlands, and saradh or late rice lower down. Unlike in protected lands, the water ran off soon, allowing for replantation of the rice if the first planting was damaged, and even a rabi harvest which would be all the finer, the heavier the floods and the greater the silt deposits.

111 Ibid., June 1894, Br. Agriculture, no. 582, Motihari, 30 Aug. 1893. From W. Dunbar-Blyth, Collector, Champaran, to Commissioner, Patna Division, paras. 1–10.

level. The abnormally low inundations of the Padma injured the winter harvests and prejudiced the rabi prospects.[112] In Pabna, too, the crop depended for moisture mainly on the floods, which fell unprecedentedly in 1896.[113]

In Nadia the lowest recorded flood level occurred in 1895.[114] The Kalantar tract in northwest Nadia typically illustrated the injurious effects of abnormally low floods on the local agriculture, as the system of water distribution in this region made it most vulnerable to drought and famine. In Nadia there was no other form of irrigation, as the bils were normally flooded during the monsoon. The Kalantar was inundated by the rivers, mainly the Jalangi, and was eminently suited for aman cultivation. During the rains, flood water rushed into the bils through numerous khals or inlets opening into the river, and the entire tract went under water usually from mid-July to late October.[115] Even after October, when the rains began to subside, bunds were very often thrown across the khals to hold in water for fishing. Thus, normally the rice fields were not completely drained of flood water till December, so that, unlike in other regions, the October rains were not vital in determining the aman prospects.

But the flood level here was unprecedentedly low in 1895, falling further in 1896. Hence, the bils got little or no flood water. In such a year, the rains were crucial in ensuring an average yield.[116] But in 1896, the rainfall was deficient throughout July–August and early September. The heavy showers in mid-September did not help, as the bils in the Kalantar, unlike other bils, were open to the river and could not hold the rain water for

112 *Selection of Papers,* vol. 3: p. 263.
113 Ibid., p. 280.
114 Ibid., p. 223.
115 Ibid., p.220.
116 According to an old saying, well-distributed rain in October–November was essential for the satisfactory growth of winter rice plants. *"Kurkut Bhurkut Shing Shukhana Kunnya Kannay Kan; Bina Baway Toola Bursay Kaha Rakhoga Dhan"* (If there be heavy showers in Sraban, slight or no rain in Bhadra, if the rice-fields be deeply covered by water in Aswin, and if the showers in Kartik be seasonable and well-distributed, without any high wind, the crops are so splendid that the cultivators have to enlarge their storehouses).

long. After September, no rain fell till January, so that the soil dried up quickly and the aman crop totally failed. The aus, grown to a small extent on the higher lands surrounding the bils, was always a precarious crop; the early floods often destroyed it, while in years of drought it withered from want of moisture.[117] This ruined the peasants, for the Kalantar had suffered from destructive floods in 1889–90 and 1894, and crops had failed in the region for the last four to five years.

Low river floods aggravated yet another problem in spill-irrigated areas along the seaboard, namely, that of salt-water intrusion into the fields. In 1896–97 this problem was most acute in the Satkhira Sunderbans in Khulna, and the Chilka tract in Puri, both of which were among the areas worst hit by the famine. For such areas, river inundation was essential to wash out the saline impregnation from the soil and so to neutralise the ill-effects of tidal floods.

Rice cultivation was almost entirely dependent on river water in the Satkhira Sunderbans in Khulna. The rivers Yamuna-Kalindi on the west, the Kholpetna running through the centre, and the Kabadak to the east of the affected tract in Satkhira, all flowed downstream from Jessore to the sea. But the rivers usually remained salty from December to the end of June. It was only after the rains set in that the drainage of the higher country to the north, combined with the local rainfall and the flood water of the Ganges flowing into the Yamuna-Kalindi, sweetened the river water and washed out the salt from the soil.

But during the previous thirty to forty years, the range of salt water had extended further north, as the silting up of the *par* (ridges) of the rivers cut off the Kabadak and Kholpetna Rivers from the Ganges and reduced the volume of fresh water from the Ganges and the Yamuna-Kalindi. In addition, the construction of canals like the Hasnabad and Boalia Khals—to shorten boat routes from Calcutta to the eastern districts—also diverted much of the sweet water of the Yamuna-Kalindi and the Kabadak from the Satkhira Sunderbans into other rivers. This problem of

117 LRP, Aug. 1898, pt. 2, p. 459. Report from the Collector of Nadia, as enclosed in letter no.128 G; SR, Calcutta, 7 Jan. 1898, from E. V. Westmacott, Commissioner, Presidency Division, to the Secretary to the Govt. of Bengal, Revenue Dept.

increasing salinity of the local rivers contributed indirectly to the crisis in 1896.[118]

The immediate cause of crop failure in Satkhira was excessive salinity of the soil from the beginning of 1896 on account of the storm wave on 1 October 1895 that had deposited a larger quantity of salt on the fields than was usual. To worsen the situation, the embankments and dams blocking the khals which connected the bil with the river gave way, as they always did, at the outset of the rains in May-June, before the water was sufficiently sweetened. As the river was particularly salty in 1896, especially as one moved south to the Sunderbans, it damaged the entire rice crop. But while heavier rains were required this year to raise the river level and wash out the salt from the soil, the rainfall turned out to be 22 per cent to 33 per cent short of the average. Hence, the soil remained impregnated with salt, and the river water failed to become sweet during and after the monsoon, except for a few days in August and September.[119]

Only the fully protected *astameshi abad*s (where sluices with self-acting valves let in rain water but kept out river water till it was fit for use), as in the newly reclaimed Sunderbans area and the fields removed from the influence of the tide (as in Nakipur and Mukundapur), escaped this fate.[120]

It is interesting to note why the rice crop was a total failure in the Satkhira Sunderbans, while Khulna Sadar and Basirhat in the 24 Parganas, which approximated closely to Satkhira, reaped a moderately good crop. The Sadar subdivision had better irrigation facilities from fresh-water rivers like the Sipsa, Bhadra and Pasar, while in the Satkhira Sunderbans, river water remained salty both in 1895 and 1896. As for the Basirhat Sunderbans, it was well protected from salt water and the rains were more abundant. [121]

Tracts lying within a belt of about five miles round the shore of the Chilka in Chaubiskud and Serai, and on the lower reaches of the Kushbhadra, Prachi and Kadua Rivers, and the tidal creeks of the Kodhar block in Puri, were also liable to salt-water

118 Ibid., pp. 185–86.
119 Ibid., p. 189.
120 Ibid., pp. 185–86, 189.
121 Ibid., p. 189.

inundation. The local rivers, whether opening out into the Chilka Lake or the sea, ran dry in the hot summer months when tidal action, helped by the strong south breeze, tended to force salt water up their channels. High tidal floods, backed up by the embankments running along the rivers, often overspilled and submerged the adjacent lands, damaging their crops and affecting their fertility for the next three to four years. Ironically, while the numerous distributaries and channels of the Koyakhai overflowed their banks, supply of river water was not available on the shores of the Chilka, where it was required to wash out the salt impregnation of the hot-weather tides.[122] This was precisely the case in 1896–97, when almost fifteen annas of the paddy crop were destroyed by the high floods of the Chilka. At the head of the lake, the embankment known as the Nuni Bund was breached by the high saline floods in August, and the loss to the paddy crop was immense. The floods were due to the filling up of the Chilka by the Mahanadi and Katjori Rivers, which had not risen so high for many years. Near the Nayapara Salt Works in Parikud, too, the great paddy fields were a scene of desolation, as the lands were broken and the tanks filled up with salt water.[123]

[4] *Canal Irrigation*

The effects of scanty rainfall and low floods could have been alleviated to a great extent by proper irrigation facilities. But there was hardly any large-scale, organised attempt in this direction, except in the specific areas covered by the Orissa, Midnapur and Sone Canal-systems. Of an average gross area of 63,665,027 acres annually under crop in the whole of Bengal, the government canals covered only 743,060 acres, i.e. no more than 1.16 per cent.[124] In fact, the government was of the view that irrigation was not such a boon here as in Punjab and the NWP for, due to heavy rains and inundation, it was only in years of drought that the raiyats would keenly avail themselves of water.[125]

122 *DG: Puri,* pp. 167–69.
123 *Selection of Papers,* vol. 4: p. 420.
124 *Report, Indian Irrigation Commission,* p. 378.
125 *Famine Commission Report, 1880*, pt. 2: p. 85.

[4.1] The Orissa Canal

The canal systems were not without limitations. In Orissa, for instance, water rates were found to be prohibitive in effect. A system of annual block leases was introduced in 1872, which was later modified to give long-term block leases, and to discriminate between the various classes of land forming a block. The lease system was well-suited to these canals, as it tended to prevent loss of revenue in seasons when irrigation was not required. But even by 1899 it had not been possible to induce the local peasants to pay more than Re. 1 and 5 an. on an average, while the corresponding rates on the Godavari and Krishna Canals in Madras varied from Rs. 4 to Rs. 4-12 an. per acre. Even the Midnapur Canal had a higher average rate of Rs. 1-9-6 per acre, as there were no special rates for lands which needed the canal water only in years of drought. Hence the working expenses were by no means covered, which explained the government's growing apathy towards any scheme for further extension of irrigation facilities in this region.[126]

On the other hand, during normal years when rainfall was heavy, the peasants were naturally reluctant to pay a separate rate for irrigation; protection from floods was locally considered to be a greater necessity. Rents could not be increased on account of irrigational facilities either, since the existing rates for ordinary occupancy raiyats were already too high, as admitted even by government officials in temporarily settled areas.[127] Much of the opposition to the canal assessment was, in fact, due to the "heavy rents demanded by *zamindars*".[128] The zamindars, too, actively opposed the levy of a water rate, in apprehension that the peasant might give priority to government dues over rent payments, and openly threatened their tenants with grave consequences if they took to using canal water.[129]

126 *Report, Indian Irrrigation Commission,* p. 152, para. 387.

127 Ibid., p. 245, evidence of J. M. Das, Deputy Collector, Cuttack, 11 Nov. 1902.

128 Bengal Irrigation Proceedings, Mar. 1891, no. 19, Deputy Superintendent of Canal Revenue to the Collector of Cuttack, 5 Mar. 1881.

129 Ibid., (Accounts), December 1877, App. A, J. Mukherji to Collector of Midnapur, 1 Aug. 1877.

Another major drawback of the Orissa Canal was that much of the water ran to waste, for want of proper channels to distribute it over the fields.[130] Of the gross area commanded by the whole project (approximately 820,000 acres excluding the Balasore section), only 264,000 acres were irrigable. Some of the remaining lands were uncultivable; others were too low to take irrigation without proper channels for distribution, or too high to be watered otherwise than by lift irrigation, which was hardly practised here.[131]

[4.2] The Midnapur Canal

The Midnapur Canal served about 100,000 acres of exclusively rice-growing tracts in the 1880s. Heavier rainfall in Midnapur than in south Bihar made the canal system less of a necessity for the peasant than in the Sone Canal region. The indebtedness of the local peasants was, however, the "most potent cause" of their reluctance to use canal water, except in case of a prolonged drought.[132] While collecting the water rate, officials had to wait till the debtor-raiyat returned after selling his rice, for even a day's delay may force him to give priority to the mahajan's demands.[133] Enhanced rents in the irrigated tracts tended to neutralise any benefits obtained by the peasant through the use of canal water. It is significant that in lands under the oppressive *sanja* system of produce rent, which required the raiyat to pay a certain quantity of grain irrespective of the size of the crop, no peasant applied for canal water. This was because the water rate and high sanja rent taken together would more than offset the value of any increased productivity resulting from canal irrigation.[134]

130 *Famine Commission Report, 1898*, H. C. 1899, vol. 31: p. 343.

131 *Report, Indian Irrigation Commission,* p. 151, para. 386.

132 Ibid., (Accounts), Dec. 1877, App. A, Deputy Revenue Superintendent of Canals, Midnapur, to Collector of Midnapur, 1 Aug. 1877, para. 9.

133 Ibid., Jan. 1874, App. B, 28 July 1873, para. 22. Deputy Revenue Superintendent of Canals, Midnapur, to Collector of Midnapur.

134 Ibid., Jan. 1873, no. 50, Collector of Midnapur to the govt. of Bengal, P.W.D. Irrigation Br., 18 Oct. 1872.

The increase in the extent of the irrigated area under both these systems was therefore negligible during the long period from 1874 to 1890, except for the quinquennium of 1879–80 to 1883–84. Only years of extensive crop failure would cause the peasants to make good use of the canal water. In 1876 the government noted with concern the "collapse of the fair prospects" of success of the Midnapur and Orissa Canals, especially in view of the positive results obtained in the Sone Canal region.[135]

[4.3] The Sone Canal

Frequent droughts in Bihar had made irrigation an urgent necessity, and the extensive crop failure of 1873 prompted the government to execute the Sone Irrigation Works and supply canal water on a regular basis from 1875–76. The Sone Canal played a decisive role in the agricultural economy of the south Bihar districts of Patna, Gaya and Shahabad.

Previously only small areas under special crops like poppy and sugar-cane adjacent to the Sone had benefited from the use of its water. In the period 1877–78 to 1891–92, however, the irrigated area increased by nearly 96 per cent.[136] An assured water supply increased production by encouraging the reclamation of arid lands. It also foced a distinct change in the quality and type of crops grown. The prolific kharif harvest replaced the rabi, which often consisted of cheap and inferior pulses. The area under sugar-cane—a most lucrative cash crop—the cultivation of which had previously been contained due to the high cost of well irrigation, was doubled since the construction of the canals.[137]

But these changes in the nature and range of crops grown in the canal-irrigated tracts ultimately contributed to a growing insecurity in agriculture. Instead of encouraging the growth of valuable rabi crops like oilseeds and barley, canal irrigation led

[135] Ibid., May 1876, no. 15. Despatch to Secretary of State, no. 43. Mar. 1876. para. 3.

[136] *Reports of Irrigation Department* for relevant years.

[137] *Report, Indian Irrigation Commission,* p. 210, evidence of J. H. Toogood, Superintending Engineer, Sone Circle, Bankipur, 25 Oct. 1902.

to a great increase in the cultivation of winter rice, which encroached on the rabi area and even took up lands which were most unsuitable for its growth.

Rice was a prolific crop requiring little care once assured of a steady water supply. Yet, as seen above, it fostered the growth of mono-culture and was most vulnerable to drought. Hence, when the supply of canal water fell short of the demand, the Irrigation Department was "compelled to discourage, as far as possible, the cultivation of rice, and encourage the growth of *rabi*".[138] Despite its efforts, however, the area under aman rice continued to increase at the expense of the rabi until, in 1898–1903, it covered as much as 334,565 acres as against the rabi area of 128,616 acres only.[139] Similarly, the cultivation of sugar-cane which had increased fast initially due to the Sone irrigation, received a check by the close of the century. Sugar-cane required water in the hot weather, before the rains started; but the Sone ran down to about 300 cubic feet in April-May, and the eastern section often had to be closed owing to dearth of water.[140] In fact, while commenting on the character of cultivation in the Sone Circle, the Irrigation Commission went to the extent of stating that "the work has been so far unproductive", though "its construction has been fully justified by its great potective value".[141]

The protective aspect of the Sone Canal in years of drought was indeed remarkable. Previously, the *ahar pyne* system of irrigation (rainwater reservoirs fed by artificial channels) totally depended on the rains, and hence failed to work effectively in periods of drought. Moreover, hill torrents coming down after heavy showers often swept away the embankments and let out the stored water, which was drained fast by the rapid slope of the country, especially in Shahabad and Gaya. The Sone system minimised the possibility of such a total collapse of the water supply, and ensured greater stability in agricultural production. The peasants appreciated the insurance of the irrigation and,

138 Ibid., evidence of J. H. Toogood, q. no. 26; evidence of D. B. Horn, q. no. 15, 1902.

139 Ibid., p. 160, para. 409.

140 Ibid., J. H. Toogood, Bankipore, 25 Oct. 1902.

141 Ibid., pp. 159–60, para. 409.

unlike in wetter zones like Orissa, came to regard the canal water as so essential a part of agriculture, that the supply fell short of the demand.

In fact, the effectiveness of the canals as a protection against drought was limited by the seasonal nature of this demand. For the peasants, it was of no use utilising canal water to their full capacity during the transplantation in June-July, if they could not water that area in the critical phase of the *hathiya* asterism (26 September to 10 October). Water was crucial at this time for the rice crop to mature. The fields also had to be moistened, due to the universal practice of draining them (*nigar*) earlier in September.[142] The peasants often waited till mid-October, and it was only when the rains definitely failed that they asked for canal water to fill their *ahar*s (rainwater reservoirs). If the water was too late to benefit the crop, remissions of water rate had to be given.[143] This put too great a pressure on the system, and applications for canal water had to be refused during the dry kharif season of 1899, and again in 1902.[144]

But these limitations of the Sone project, whether as a productive venture or protective measure, did not debar either the government or the landlords from trying to raise the water rates and rents respectively.

Produce rents naturally went up, for the increase in the size of the crop due to irrigation automatically raised the landlord's share. Even cash rentals which generally prevailed in the canal-irrigated tracts shot up fast despite government legislation, the landlords claiming that they could "drive a carriage and pair through the Tenancy Act".[145] Oldham, Collector of Gaya, cited cases in which rents had risen from Rs. 3 to as much as Rs. 5 and

142 For further details, see M. Chakrabarti, "Crisis in a Peasant Economy: A Study of the Famine of 1896–97 in Bengal" (Ph.D. diss., University of Calcutta, 1995).

143 *Report, Indian Irrigation Commission Report,* evidence of D. B. Horn, Chief Engineer to the Bengal Government, Darbhanga, 31 Oct. 1902.

144 Ibid., p. 212, evidence of J. H. Toogood, Superintending Engineer, Sone Circle, Bankipore, 25 Oct. 1902.

145 *Report of the Irrigation Department, 1885–86.* Collector of Gaya to Commissioner, Patna Division, App. p. 95, para. 4.

7 per bigha. The Executive Engineer of Buxar Division pointed out instances where the rent rose from a few annas to as many rupees, while the Superintending Engineer noted cases in which rents went up fourfold.[146] For this substantial increase in their income, however, the landholders paid nothing to the State; hence the entire burden of the water rates, which were by no means low—as admitted by Oldham before the Irrigation Commission in 1902—was passed on to the tenant-occupier.[147]

[4.4] The extent of canal irrigation

In spite of these distinctive local problems, however, canal irrigation had undoubtedly introduced a new and improved technique of water supply to the areas concerned. But, being extremely limited in scope and extent, it addressed only a fringe of the irrigation problem. The Orissa Canal was confined to Cuttack; hence, government works covered only 6.45 per cent of the gross area annually under crop in Orissa.

The average area irrigated annually by the Midnapur Canal was 73,280 acres; in the whole of the Burdwan Division, government works covered a mere 1.95 per cent of the gross cropped area. Actually such canal projects had little commercial feasibility in heavy-rainfall zones like Bengal, especially its eastern region. They were also difficult and impracticable owing to the uneven land surface and small catchment areas of most rivers in the laterite portion of west Bengal, and the extreme flatness of the country in the rest of western and central Bengal.

In the Patna Division, the Sone system annually irrigated no more than 3.16 per cent of the area under crop.[148] In fact, the Sone Canal was confined only to a small area in the west of south Bihar. There was little scope for the extension of canal irrigation in this region, since the rivers of south Bihar except the Sone could not be relied upon for a regular supply of water. They were mostly non-perennial streams depending on the rains,

[146] *Report, Indian Irrigation Commission*, pp. 156–57.

[147] Ibid., evidence of C. E. A. W. Oldham, Collector of Gaya, Bankipore, 24 Oct. 1902.

[148] Ibid., chart, p. 378.

and generally too small to feed a canal system.[149] Even in the canal-irrigated tracts, there were large areas outside the canal lease. In north Bihar, too, drought was most frequent and irrigation imperative, especially in the new agricultural settlements depending exclusively on rice.

The government, however, was reluctant to sanction projects like the Sone Irrigation Works in other parts of Bihar. It maintained that since in this region, irrigation primarily meant an insurance on the rice crop, those who benefited from the crop, mainly the landowners, should pay for that insurance. Thus, despite the extensive crop failure caused by drought in 1875, the government refused to finance the Bagmati and Kamla projects for north Bihar in 1876. The plans for the Tribeni Canal were greatly modified, and a much smaller project covering only a part of the original left bank canal was taken up as a famine-relief work in 1897.

[5] *Other Forms of Irrigation*

Other forms of artificial irrigation, apart from government canals, consisted of reservoirs, ridges (*ail*s) or terrace cultivation to hold in and percolate rainwater; private canals or channels drawing on river water; and wells, which tapped the level of sub-soil water for small areas producing special crops like vegetables, tobacco and sugar-cane.

[5.1] Terrace cultivation

Terrace cultivation was the outcome of attempts to store rainwater, and it provided a very common form of irrigation for the uplands of Chotanagpur, Santhal Parganas and the Rarh tract in west Bengal.

In the hilly regions of Singhbhum and Manbhum, for instance, the constant run of surface drainage down the slopes and hollows was broken by converting them, wherever possible, into terraces at different levels. They were then divided into smaller rice fields, each with its protective ridge or embankment, varying from a

[149] *Report of the Royal Commission of Agriculture in India*, evidence volume, p. 309, quoted in Ganguli, *Trends of Agriculture*, p. 180.

few inches to several feet in height. The rainwater was thus retained on each terrace and field; it gradually percolated from one level to another, thus making wet cultivation possible. The lowest slopes provided the most secure rice-lands.[150] In Palamau, too, terracing of the rice fields (*kerker, khundwat* or *ariab)* was a rather popular form of investment in agriculture, as the peasants could then hold these lands at a privileged rate of rent for a specific term.[151]

In west Burdwan, the hillsides were converted into tiers of rice fields, which were embanked along their lower edges. In the Santhal Parganas, the rice slopes were like a series of steps varying in height from one to five feet. They were flooded soon after the rains set in, the lowest levels retaining moisture until February–March. The latter constituted the first-class *dhani* (rice-producing) land called *awal* or *jol*, which was relatively immune to drought and was reserved exclusively for the growth of winter rice.[152]

Yet, even here the crops were liable to be damaged by the onrush of sand-laden water if the surrounding slopes were too steep. Elsewhere, terrace cultivation depended entirely on the rains. It was liable to be severely affected in years of drought except when protected by other means of artificial irrigation.[153]

[5.2] The ahar-pyne system

Such irrigation works mainly took the form of tanks or reservoirs (ahars), consisting of embankments thrown across any favourable dip in the general surface level. In hilly regions, ravines and hollows impounding the drainage water, or streams running along the bed of the valley, were dammed up to form reservoirs irrigating a series of terraced rice fields, which stretched away and widened as they receded from the dam. In the Rarh tract in Burdwan, embanked rice terraces, bils and *kandar*s (rivulets) served as irrigation tanks.[154] The smaller embankments called

150 *DG: Manbhum,* p.113.

151 *Report, Indian Irrigation Commission*, p. 227.

152 *DG: Santhal Parganas*, comp. L. S. S. O'Malley, 1910, pp. 157–58.

153 Ibid., p. 160.

154 Water was provided from them mainly by means of the *duni* or

*hir*s in the Santhal Parganas consisted of low banks around the depressions which dried up soon after the rains, but held enough water to tide over the critical months of October–November. They normally irrigated about five to ten acres of rice-land. The relatively high embankments or *bandh*s thrown across deep valleys sometimes served up to 100 acres of land, and had basins large enough to provide a continuous water supply from the end of one monsoon to the beginning of the next. In Manbhum, irrigation from bandhs was generally effected by percolation. In Singhbhum, 10 per cent of the cultivated area was irrigated from bandhs.[155] In Palamau, the tanks were provided with several outlets (*bhao*s) which were closed during the rains. After the monsoon, the water was drained off and the *dub* or bed of the reservoir was sown with cold-weather crops.

The main weakness of this system of tank irrigation was that, being monsoon-oriented, it was primarily designed to provide water for the transplantation of paddy if the rains failed in its later stages. The tanks offered no protection against long spells of drought in a drought-prone zone. In a dry year, the bandhs failed to irrigate cold-weather crops, as most of them retained little water after December. In fact, their utility diminished gradually with the extension of rice cultivation, which took up the lowest lands first; as the bandhs on the lower levels were themselves converted into rice fields unless too deep, the new bandhs constructed higher up received proportionately less water and had to serve a larger area. Hence, in districts like Manbhum, where practically all the lands suitable for rice had been brought under cultivation, bandh irrigation was of little value as a safeguard against crop failure in dry seasons.[156]

The water supply was uncertain as well as inadequate, for the catchment areas of ahars were generally small, and could not

bent trough with a closed end worked on the lever principle, and the *chheni* or a scoop of matting with attached slings worked by two men having the water between them. LRP, Br. Land Revenue, May 1894. From S. Halder, Settlement Officer, Burdwan Raj Khas Mahals.

155 *DG: Singhbhum*, p. 110.

156 *DG: Manbhum*, p. 117.

provide a continuous flow during the lean months. The general practice of nigar or draining the fields in September led to a very great demand for water if the hathiya rains failed. The pressure was felt most acutely in the tribal areas where, due to the ignorance of the peasants, the water was not always judiciously used. For instance, the unfavourable kharif out-turn in Lohardaga in 1896 was partly accounted for by a peculiar local custom among the Kols, which is thus described by Mr Streatfeild, Deputy Commissioner of Ranchi: "Owing to this rain (viz. the last fall in the middle of September) having fallen before the Karma Puja (a Kol agricultural festival), the water was, according to local custom, allowed to run off the fields instead of being kept in. Had this rain been three days later, or had the Karma Puja not happened to be late . . . the water would have been preserved, with, I believe, the result that the upland crops would have been considerably better than they turned out. As it was, the crop on the high lands was a very poor one indeed".[157]

Moreover, the tanks were liable to be breached or swept away by heavy rains and rendered useless just when it was most imperative to store rainwater, the problem being "fairly common". The ahars were generally rude constructions made merely to catch the surface drainage from higher lands, and as such were not provided with suitable escape weirs.[158] In fact, escape outlets big enough to be effective for the larger reservoirs would be expensive works, which the zamindar would not provide for.

In Chotanagpur, for instance, the zamindars, who were responsible for the maintenance and repair of the ahars and bandhs, took no interest in the matter; the raiyats had no incentive either, as any improvement on such works on their lands would immediately lead to a rent increase. F. A. Slacke, Officiating Commissioner of Chotanagpur, advised the Irrigation

157 *DCAR, Chotanagupur Division, 1896–97,* no. 262 J, dated Ranchi, 10 July 1897. From A. Forbes, Commissioner, Chotanagpur Division, to the Secretary to the Govt. of Bengal, General Department, Sec. 3, p. 7, para. 18.

158 *Report, Indian Irrigation Commission,* App. p. 207, evidence of C. E. A. Oldham, Collector of Gaya, Bankipore, 24 Oct. 1902; *DG: Palamau*, p. 74.

Commission in 1902 that unless the raiyats had better security against this, "no irrigation scheme would succeed".[159] Even rat holes in the embankments were left unrepaired, so that they were gradually enlarged and finally destroyed the bandh.[160] Due to joint control over property in large areas of the Patna and Presidency Divisions, no party was ready to bear the expenses of tank repairs. Difficulties were also placed in the way of the raiyats making or improving tanks, by the landlords' demand of *salami*s (fees or purchase money). In Darbanga, for example, the custom was to pay Rs. 250 as salami before a raiyat was allowed to dig a tank, which created difficulties during the scarcity of 1876. In Orissa, too, numerous tanks were silting up and neither the people nor the properietors took any interest in the matter.[161] The repairs of ahars could be taken up as famine works, but this also involved practical problems: petty irrigation works would not pay under supervision with an establishment, whether taken up by the government or the zamindars.

In some districts, as for example in Gaya, Patna and Monghyr in south Bihar, it was possible to heighten the effectiveness of ahars by channels or *pyne*s taking off from the nearest stream or water-course, some of which depended for their water not on local rainfall, but on the rainfall of the hilly regions where they had their source. The water flowing past the fields was thus diverted to the ahars, which became the receptacle of all the water available in the neighbourhood. Ahars were most suited to the highlands where pynes could not go; on lower lands there were both ahars and pynes, either working together or separately.[162] In Bhagalpur, too, irrigation from rivers was

159 *Report, Indian Irrigation Commission,* p. 227, evidence of F. A. Slacke, Officiating Commissioner of Chotanagpur, before the President of the Irrigation Commission, Purulia, 3 Nov. 1902.

160 Ibid., pp. 228, 231.

161 Jamini Mohan Das, Department Collector, Cuttack, to Irrigation Commission, Cuttack, 11 Nov. 1902.

162 A big pyne could irrigate from 100 to 200 villages. The ahar-pyne system attained its highest development in Gaya, where more than half the area, i.e., as much as 1,670,000 acres were watered in this way. *Report, Indian Irrigation Commission,* p. 161, para. 413, App. p. 208.

common through channels (*danrs*) and distributaries (*singhas*). The erection of pynes, however, depended on the level and current of the local rivers. In Manbhum and Singhbhum, for example, most rivers flowed rapidly, much below the general ground level; hence, in order to utilise their water, very long channels would have to be constructed through difficult country at prohibitive rates.

The ahar and pyne constituted, in effect, an ingenious empirical system conditioned by the distinctive problems of south Bihar. The rapid drainage of the country called for the storage of rain- and river water; the rocky soil prevented the growth of well irrigation; the rivers were too small and unreliable for canal projects; while the prevalence of produce rents (*bhaoli*) ensured the zamindars' interest in maintaining irrigation works as a form of investment to increase production.

The system, however, was far from perfect. The limitations of ahars or tanks have already been noted. The utility of pynes, moreover, could diminish due to lack of proper headwork to control the flow and the level of water at their entrance.[163] The erection of masonry heads on the pynes, however, was opposed by the owners on the ground that they would reduce the water supply. Moreover, the level of the rivers, except for those flowing down from the distant hills, fell sharply in dry years when they were not swollen by local rainfall. Many of the hill streams, again, were bunded up in Nepal during seasons of drought, so that their supply ran dry lower down.[164] Thus, irrigation from both

[163] Ibid., App. p. 216. In such cases, deepening of the mouth of the channel often caused the river to deflect from its original course into the channel of the pyne. The old bed thus silted up, leaving dry large tracts formerly irrigated by other pynes taking off from the river lower down. Meanwhile, the river, entering the artificial channel of the pyne, scoured and flooded the adjoining lands, covering them with sand deposits. It was due to this fact that R. S. King, Manager of the Darbhanga Raj, who had saved a considerable portion of the crops in 1896 with water from ahars and pynes fed by the Kamla, objected to putting a permanent weir across that river.

[164] M. Finucane, Commissioner, Presidency Division, to Irrigation Commission, App. p. 238, Calcutta, 8 Nov. 1902.

ahars and pynes tended to be uncertain when it was most needed in crisis years.

Finally, the efficiency of the system was greatly reduced by the lack of a rationalised control over the distribution of water. Joint control over these irrigation works made maintenance difficult. Disputes arose over the rights of water in various parts of the streams which ran through many villages, each in turn containing land belonging to several different proprietors. In parts of Bhagalpur, a working arrangement was attempted to decide the question of precedence in obtaining channel water. By the *banokhar* system, the village nearest the source usually had the first turn.[165] But the system did not always function smoothly. Bunds were sometimes made along the upper reaches of the river, shutting off the water lower down; people from below would then steal in quietly and cut the bunds, which often resulted in widespread riots. The peasant was naturally more anxious about the produce of lands which he held on cash rent, and control over irrigation was often used by proprietors as an instrument of oppression. Oldham, Collector of Gaya, even proposed a special legislation to enforce the zamindars' obligations in this context, which however was not feasible in practice. As the peasants' demands for cash commutation of their produce rents became more persistent towards the end of the century, the zamindars' interest in the maintenance and control of irrigation works visibly slackened.[166]

[5.3] Well irrigation

Well irrigation could hardly be an effective substitute for ahars, pynes or canals, as it could exist only under specific conditions

[165] Water flowed from the danr into the singhas within its area, while a dam was erected in the danr at its other end to prevent the water from flowing into the next village. Water from the singhas irrigated the adjacent lands within the village and was led into the fields lower down by cutting their ridges or ails. *SR, Bhagalpur District, 1902–10,* by P. W. Murphy, Settlement Officer, Bihar, p. 113, paras. 207–08.

[166] *Report, Indian Irrigation Commission*, App., evidence of Oldham, Collector of Gaya, 24 Oct. 1902, q. no. 75.

of the soil and water level. Wells could not work in Orissa, nearly the whole of Bengal, and the northern part of north Bihar, due to high floods. In some districts like Nadia, again, the heavy clayey soil made it difficult to sink wells.

It was only in the southern uplands of the north Bihar districts that it featured to a small extent. The exception was Saran, where the soil was suitable for well irrigation and the percentage was ten times that in adjacent districts. Attempts to encourage well irrigation in north Bihar during the famine of 1896–97 mostly proved abortive, the soil being so loose and sandy in many areas that wells tended to fall in. In the Sitamarhi subdivision of Muzaffarpur in 1896–97, for instance, water lay within 6 to 7 ft. of the ground level, while the crops withered on the surface.[167] In Saran, sub-soil water lay very near the surface, but even here the closure of the Saran canals brought it down at least by four to five feet all along this tract.[168] In many places, again, the constantly flowing high-level canals brought down the level of the sub-soil water, thus rendering well irrigation more difficult. In south Bihar and the Chotanagpur Plateau, too, the hard and uneven rock surface made well digging a difficult and expensive process seldom resorted to, except in south Bhagalpur and south Monghyr (1.21 per cent), where they watered special crops of the rabi harvest.

Wells could irrigate only a very small area and could not provide the volume of water required by the rice crop in dry seasons.[169] Moreover, their level fell in the summer months. According to the Commissioner of Chotanagpur, "wells always fail at the beginning of April". In Hazaribagh town, for example, all wells but one went dry in summer.[170] Roughly speaking, well irrigation stopped west of the river Gandak. The reason was

167 Ibid., p. 241, evidence of M. Finucane, Commissioner, Presidency Division.

168 Ibid., p. 214. evidence of E. F. Growse, Officiating Additional Commissioner, Patna Division, Muzaffarpur, 27 Oct. 1902.

169 A permanent or *pucca* well could water no more than a 5-acre plot, while temporary wells sometimes irrigated as little as $\frac{1}{20}$ of an acre. Ibid., p. 177, paras. 457–58.

170 Ibid., App., p. 228. F. A. Slacke, Commissioner, Chotanagpur; Purulia, 3 Nov. 1902, q. no. 30.

obvious. Well irrigation was ineffective and superfluous for a heavy-rainfall zone like Bengal, which depended almost exclusively on rice cultivation. It had a very limited use only in Bihar, mainly for irrigating garden vegetables, sugar-cane, poppy and similar valuable crops.

The labour and expenses of well digging further restricted its popularity. In Muzaffarpur, Darbhanga and Champaran, for example, the peasants, unlike in Saran, could not find the labour required for working the wells either by lever or lifts. Each temporary or *kaccha* well was worth about Rs. 2, while a *pucca* well could cost upto Rs. 200. Unless the site was well chosen, it would be a total loss. The peasants could seldom afford such risks and expense. Thus, even the bounties of Re. 1 per kaccha well, which were granted in north Bihar during the famine of 1896–97, did not lead to much except in Sitamarhi, Muzaffarpur.[171] In south Bihar and the Chotanagpur Plateau, well digging was particularly expensive due to the rocky soil and uneven surface. Besides, in Chotanagpur, peasants took little interest in such works, for any improvement on the land would call for an immediate rent increase, unless it was directly instrumental in enhancing the gross rental of the estate.[172]

In fact, there was a distinct local prejudice against well irrigation in large tracts of north Bihar, as revealed by inquiries initiated in 1896–97. In Champaran and Darbhanga, in particular, it was believed that well irrigation brought the salts to the surface, and that sandy soils would always require irrigation, once it was resorted to. In fact, it was true that in the soils of this region, irrigation did lead to a crust below the surface, which impaired the fertility of the land unless it was regularly continued.[173]

[6] *Soil*

The effectiveness of irrigation depended to a great extent on the conformation and composition of the soil.

171 Ibid., p. 225.
172 Ibid., p. 227.
173 LRP, Br. Agriculture, Nov. 1899, p. 513.

[6.1] Conformation of the soil

[a] Height

The relief, i.e., the height and slope of the land, was vital in determining its capacity to retain moisture and facilitate percolation, which was essential for the growth of plants. If the land was too high or too low, it invariably affected production. The district of Midnapur was a typical case in point. "A part of the district being high and undulating and a part flat and low-lying, most estates are liable to suffer to some extent from the vicissitudes of the season. If the monsoon sets in early with very heavy rains the crops on the lower lands cannot be grown at all or are damaged by submersion, while if it sets in late or ceases prematurely the crops on the high sites suffer from drought".[174]

Generally, the higher lands, depending almost entirely on rainfall, were more severely affected by drought than low-lying areas, which received the overspill of rivers and a greater share of the surface drainage. The risk was heightened in uplands formerly considered unfit for rice cultivation; they were converted into poor, unprotected rice-lands liable to be hit first by famine. The rice terraces on the higher slopes were worst exposed to drought in Burdwan, Bankura and Birbhum. In the Santhal Parganas, the distress area in 1896 lay mainly in Jamtara and Godda, where the proportion of upland rice was the highest.[175] In the Chotanagpur Plateau, the higher ricelands (*chaunra*) were invariably scorched in the event of a drought beginning in September, while the lower slopes or garha retained moisture for a considerable period after the rains.[176] Palamau was the worst-hit in Chotanagpur during the famine of 1896–97. A distinctive feature of its landscape was the preponderance of uplands (*tanr/piri*) over low-lying areas (*don/dohar*). Hazaribagh and Manbhum, too, faced this problem on a lesser scale.[177]

174 *DG: Midnapur,* comp. L. S. S. O'Malley, 1911.

175 *Selection of Papers,* vol. 3: p. 250.

176 Basu, *Report, Agriculture of Lohardaga*, pt. 1, p. 125.

177 K. Suresh Singh, *The Indian Famine, 1967: A Study in Crisis and Change* (New Delhi: Peoples' Publishing House, 1975), p. 6.

[b] Slope

The slope of the land was equally important. If it was too sharp or pronounced, as in Gaya, the rapid drainage of the country rendered it peculiarly unretentive of moisture. The greater part of south Bihar, including the Chotanagpur Plateau merging on the east with the laterite portion of west Bengal, was marked by an undulating surface broken up by low ridges, valleys and bils, partly covered with brushwood and jungle. It was very difficult to hold in rain or river water in these regions, while the uneven surface made canal and well irrigation impraticable. In the districts of Bankura and Midnapur in west Bengal, and along the shores of the Chilka in the Khurda subdivision of Puri, water was drained off too quickly for irrigation purposes, due to the high slope of the land. The first essential, therefore, for the cultivator was to break up this constant drainage and try to retain moisture by terracing and embanking the rice slopes.[178]

If, on the other hand, the level of the country was too flat, water did not move easily, leading to water-logging and drainage problems, as in the moribund delta. In west Bengal, the configuration of land varied distinctly from east to west. Unlike the laterite formations on the western fringe, the eastern and central parts of this region had too slight a slope; hence, canal irrigation was impracticable and embankments often had to be built around the fields for the purpose of retaining water, as in eastern Midnapur. Further southeast, even these slight differences of level practically disappeared. Here, larger embankments had to be built around entire villages of 5 or 6 sq. miles in area, within which there was not even a two-inch difference between one field and another.[179]

[6.2] Composition of the soil

[a] Texture

Cultivation was affected as deeply by the composition or texture of the soil as by its relief or conformation, for the proportions of

[178] *DG: Manbhum*, p. 113.
[179] *SR, Midnapur: Minor Settlements* (1907–13), by B. Sanyal (Calcutta: BSBD, 1916).

sand and clay in it determined the extent of percolation. In districts like Gaya in south Bihar and the westernmost districts of Bengal, the soil was thin, sandy and porous, leading to rapid drainage and percolation. Hence, whenever the rains were scanty or ill-distributed, large tracts in these districts dried up fast, such as Bhabhua in Shahabad, the southern part of Gaya, west Midnapur and the Sonamukhi thana in Bankura. Again, the black clayey soil as in the Nadia Kalantar was difficult to work. It grew sticky when wet and hardened quickly after the rains, cracking and splitting miserably, and causing the crop to wither and die. In Palamau, too, the soil, being heavy, was beaten down and pressed by the rains.[180]

[b] Salinity

Another factor affecting the productive power of the soil was excessive salinity in littoral regions like south Khulna and the Chilka tract in Puri. This problem has been analysed in some detail in section 3. As noted, the range of salt water in the Sunderban rivers had been extending further north since the last thirty to forty years. The gradual reclamation of land and clearing up of the jungles accentuated the process.[181] Hence, in dry years like 1896–97, when the volume of rainfall was not sufficient to sweeten the river water, the adjacent fields were covered with a saline efflorescence. Besides affecting production in dry seasons, this particular feature of the soil had a further disadvantage in limiting the choice and range of seed grains. In Satkhira, Khulna, for example, only grains from the district itself or from neighbouring areas like Bakarganj in the 24 Parganas could be used as seed, due to the excessive salinity of the soil.[182]

The problem of salinity was even more pronounced in Orissa. For example, the parganas of Behera and Ankura in the Bhadrak subdivision of Balasore, which were affected by the famine in 1896–97, could not grow vegetables due to excessive salt in the

180 Basu, *Report, Agriculture of Lohardaga,* pt. 1, p. 125.
181 *DG: Khulna*, comp. L. S. S. O'Malley, 1908, p. 90.
182 *Selection of Papers,* vol. 6: p. 223.

soil.[183] Similarly, the famine-prone "salt" tracts on the Chilka, namely, Manikpatna and Satpara, as well as Malud, Parikud and Bajrakote on the southern or sea face of the lake consisted of saline, sandy soil growing only rice.[184] Fields deeply submerged by salt-water inundations did not recover their fertility for a period of three to four years; the crop prospects were, therefore, precarious. Thus, whenever the rains were scanty and the overspill of rivers failed to counter the effects of tidal waves, large stretches of country would be impregnated with salt and lie waste around the Chilka.[185] In fact, "the almost incessant inundations to which the country is generally subject, and which are now augmented by the abolition of the embankment system, have changed cultivated lands into sandy tracts, the area of which largely exceeds the area of lands on which silts are deposited".[186]

[c] Swamp and infertility

Meanwhile, in west and central Bengal the moribund rivers deeply affected the fertility of the land due to water-logging, swamp, the lack of silt deposits and interference with natural drainage. In the Damodar Valley, productivity was reduced by about 42 per cent.[187] The Nadia Fever Commission (1881) confirmed the local belief that except for the lower lands growing winter rice, "there is a distinct decrease in the fertility of the soil of Nuddea". Apart from the fall in out-turn, another prominent feature of this decline was the substitution of inferior grains like the aus for superior ones like the aman, which had a finer quality and higher yield. This growing infertility necessitated fallowing and manuring; yet no lands except those under sugar-cane and tobacco

[183] LRP, Aug. 1898, pt. 3, p. 1607. From B. De, Collector, Balasore, to the Commissioner, Orissa Division, no. 3308, dated Balasore, 10 Dec. 1897.

[184] Ibid., p. 1620. From W. H. Lee, Officiating Collector, Puri to the Commissioner, Orissa Division, no. 2652, Puri, 2 Dec. 1897.

[185] *DG: Puri*, p. 167.

[186] LRP, May 1897, p. 1171. Memorial of the Landlords' Association of Orissa to Sir Alexander Mackenzie, Lieutenant Governor of Bengal, para. 6.

[187] A. Bentley, *Malaria and Agriculture in Bengal* (Calcutta: 1925), p. 44.

were ever manured.[188] Meanwhile, longer periods of fallowing led to a steady shrinkage in the net cropped area, which came down to 40 per cent of the total cultivable area between 1904–05 to 1908–09.[189] In parts of the district, land value depreciated by as much as 75 per cent. In Jessore, the decline was in the north and the northwest, the floods between the Kumar and Nabaganga Rivers having nearly ceased in the 1870s. In Jhenida, the absence of river floods during the past fifteen years caused a "permanent deterioration" of the soil and a contraction of the area under aman rice.[190] A similar decline in soil productivity and quality of the produce was noted by local officers in Khulna, Hughli and Burdwan.[191] In Orissa, too, it was reported that "on account of the embankment of irrigation and navigation canals and the canal drainage, the fertility of lands in many quarters has materially deteriorated". Valuable crops could seldom be produced on these lands. In fact, as mentioned by Toynbee in his history of Orissa, "wild gunja or pati, sugar cane, tobacco and other crops have all been 'officially cultivated' at various times, but none ever proved a success". The same applied to indigo cultivation.[192]

[d] Deforestation and exhaustion of the soil

In certain tracts, again, increasing pressure of the population upon the soil led to the denudation of forests, soil erosion and exhaustion, resulting directly in agricultural decadence. This was most apparent in the Bihar districts. There was a rapid growth of population there in the decade 1872–81, a smaller rate of growth in 1881–91, and a declining trend in some districts in

188 *Report of the Sanitary Commissioner 1882*, App. 3, p. 39, para. 74.

189 *Bengal Census Report, 1911*, para. 222.

190 *DG: Jessore*, comp. L. S. S. O'Malley, 1912, ch 5.

191 *Report of the Drainage Committee, Bengal* (Calcutta: Bengal Secretariat Press, 1907); Chaudhuri, "Agricultural Production in Bengal", p. 159.

192 LRP, May 1897, p. 1171. Memorial of the Landlords' Association of Orissa to Sir Alexander Mackenzie, Lieutenant Governor of Bengal, para. 6.

the next decade.[193] The scope for new cultivation, however, was severely limited. There were no new land formations brought into existence by river action to accommodate the growing population, as in east Bengal. Moreover, regional problems such as the general infertility and dryness of the land in south Shahabad and Gaya, the difficulties in drainage due to the vagaries of the Kosi in Purnea, and the unhealthiness of large tracts in Champaran prevented further expansion of cultivation.

Consequently, in districts like Saran and Muzaffarpur the practice of fallowing, necessary for recouping the fertility of the soil, had nearly disappeared. In Saran only 1.14 per cent and in Muzaffarpur a little over 1 per cent of the cultivated area was left fallow.[194] As wastelands were taken up for cultivation, the peasants encroached upon the pasture, which in turn affected the physique and well-being of their plough cattle. In some areas, as in the Hajipur subdivision of Muzaffarpur, the process was so advanced that the only lands available for grazing were the ails between the fields. Even the mango groves, which were considered sacred, were cleared in this "craze for extending cultivation". This led to deforestation and exhaustion of the soil. A local officer in Muzaffarpur wrote: "At the rate mango groves are being cut down, I am afraid the country will be bare in not many years".[195] In Saran, too, "the tendency in recent years is rather to cut down all that are not immediately profitable".[196] Other factors often quickened the process. In 1894, a complaint against the Opium Agency pointed out that in Bihar, 127,000

[193] *Census of India 1901,* vol. 4, U. 124. Referred by Chaudhuri, "Agricultural Production in Bengal," p. 171:

District	*1872–81*	*1881–91*	*1891–1901*
Champaran	+19.5	+7.9	-3.7
Muzaffarpur	+14.9	+5.0	+1.5
Darbhanga	+23.1	+6.4	+3.9
Saran	+10.5	+7.3	-2.2
Patna	+12.6	+0.9	-8.4
Shahabad	+13.9	+5 8	-4.7

[194] *SR, Muzaffarpur, 1892–99,* by C. J. Stevenson-Moore (Calcutta: BS Press, 1901), para. 686; *SR, Saran District,* para. 374.

[195] *SR, Muzaffarpur,* para. 688.

[196] *SR, Saran,* para. 377.

mango trees were felled to make opium and indigo chests every year.[197] In Lohardaga, "the rapid disafforestment of the country and the wholesale clearing of valuable sal trees" were attributed to the "indebtedness of the landed proprietors, who find in the sale of timber trees a ready means of satisfying their wants".[198] In tribal tracts, as in the Rajmahal Hills or Angul Khodmals, the wasteful practice of jhum or *toila* cultivation led to extensive deforestation. Here, the land could be cultivated only after every three or four years, or whatever time it required to recover from the ill-effects of the denudation of forests and erosion of the soil.

[e] Marginal lands

As the better types of soil were already taken up, this growing pressure led to the extension of cultivation into inferior, marginal lands. The reclaimed lands in the Sunderbans and the fresh alluvial formations in eastern Bengal were the only exceptions to this rule. In Faridpur, for example, the vast marsh in the south was converted into high-yielding rice-lands. But the Madhupur Jungle to the north of Dacca, which was a thinly populated tract reclaimed by "various mongoloid tribes", had an undulating surface and a stiff, hard soil deficient in clay—an ingredient necessary for rice cultivation. Though rice was cultivated by terracing the lands, no crops were obtained in winter and spring without liberal showers. Likewise, the newly settled Barind tract in north Bengal consisted of a quasi-laterite soil "covered by thick brushwood" unsuitable for the growth of cereals. But the Santhal cultivators here preferred to grow rice, and hence converted them into poor rice-lands most vulnerable to drought. In Midnapur, the Jalpai lands in Contai and Tamluk, where cultivation extended and population increased by 25.6 per cent and 23 per cent respectively between 1872 and 1901, were liable to salt floods.[199] In the overpopulated north Bihar districts, a "wave of agricultural enterprise, starting from the southerly thanas, has flowed

197 Editorial notes, *The Statesman*, 5 October 1894.
198 Basu, *Report, Agriculture of Lohardaga*, pt. 1, sec. 6, p. 22.
199 *Bengal Census Report 1901*, paras. 102–03.

northwards within recent years".[200] While in the Barind and the Madhupur Jungle, "the new cultivation was inferior in point of both productivity and security", the fresh agricultural settlements in north Bihar were not necessarily less fertile. Yet, there were certain distinctly arid lands which were particularly hard-hit during the famine of 1896–97. For instance, the Ramnagar-Araraj-Madhuban tract in Champaran was unfit for rabi cultivation, while in parts of Supaul-Madhipura in Bhagalpur, nothing but indigo would prosper. Generally speaking, however, the problem in north Bihar was primarily one of moving from a multi-crop to a mono-crop region, for the hard and clayey (bangar) soil, unlike in the south, could produce only winter rice. Though the yield was reasonably high, agriculture was naturally less secure; the crop, mainly dependent on the rains, failed frequently and had no substitute.

[7] *Plant Disease and Pestilence*

Plant diseases and pestilence often reduced the chances of a good harvest, the problem being aggravated by the lack of a sufficiently specialised knowledge of agricultural chemicals.

In the Dakhin Shahbazpur estates in Bakarganj, paddy was often damaged by the insects called *leda poka*. The chief enemies of the rice crop in this district, apart from wind and weather, were several insects and an aquatic weed called the *baicha*. Amongst insects, the *mewa* or rice hispa and the *brahmajal* fed upon the rice leaves, causing the plants to wither and die. Most dreaded of all was the *seni* or *pamari* insect, which did immense damage to the winter rice in the cloudy weather so common in late December. The insects crept up the plants after dark and could strip entire fields in the course of three or four nights, the loss being all the more bitter to the cultivator as it came within a few days of harvesting. Both the mewa and the pamari thrived when the rains were scarce, and hence added to the cultivators' distress in years of drought.[201] The *gaicha pharing, maricha*

200 *SR, Champaran* (1829–99), by C. J. Stevenson-Moore (Calcutta: BS Press, 1900), para. 63.

201 LRP, March 1898, p. 961, para. 155; *SR, Bakarganj District, 1900–*

pharing and *barsha poka* caused much damage to the rice plants in Faridpur, the last with its nightly attacks on the near-ripe corns of rice.[202]

In Palamau, rice was of little consequence, and wheat, an important rabi crop, often suffered from a disease called *harda* or rust and also the attacks of large crickets (*uchring* or *katoi*) and the *karup* worm. Linseed or *tisi*, a cash crop of the rabi harvest, also suffered from these problems.[203] In November 1896, large areas sown with wheat, barley and gram in Palamau, as well as those sown on the highlands in October, were attacked—some by rust and others by crickets and other insects; the result was that the rabi yield nowhere exceeded 6¾ an.[204] A particular type of caterpillar attacked the poppy and pea crops in Bhabhua in January 1897, thus cutting in further on the cash income of the local peasants in this year of crisis.[205] In 1894 the rabi out-turn in Gogri thana in Monghyr was no more than 4 an., owing to extensive damage by insects.[206]

The districts of the Orissa Division shared the routine problem of blights and insect attacks. In the Kanika Ward's Estate, for instance, pests called *rangi* and *kalimukhi* among others, appeared in August–September and seriously injured the crops.[207]

Conclusion

The wide range of problems relating to agriculture in Bengal in the late nineteenth century helps to specify the traditional famine

1908, by J. C. Jack, Settlement Office of Bakarganj, p. 25, para. 63; p. 29, para. 79.

202 *SR, Faridpur,* p. 11, para. 24.

203 *SR, Palamau*, pp. 49–50, paras. 218–19, 237. Tisi was an extremely delicate crop, which called for the saying: *"Jan jame, Goham ghare awe, Tisi ka tel pirawe,"* i.e., barley (*jaun*) is certain if it germinates, wheat (*goham*) when it is brought home, but tisi only when oil is obtained from it.

204 LRP, Aug. 1898, pt. 2, p. 768, para. 13.

205 *Selection of Papers,* vol. 6: p. 152, no. 8198 G, 3 Feb. 1897.

206 LRP, December 1894, p. 542, para. 3. From H. A. D. Phillips, Collector of Monghyr, to the Commissioner of the Bhagalpur Division, Monghyr, 30 Aug. 1898.

207 *SR, Kanika Ward's Estate,* p. 37, para. 99.

zones in the Province. As noted, conditions varied distinctly in the different economic regions: the marginal lands of north Bihar, the tribal areas in Chotanagpur, Bhagalpur and the Chittagong Hills, the quasi-laterite formations in the Rarh tract, the ill-drained marshes in western and central Bengal, and the large areas exposed to saline floods in the Khulna Sunderbans and the Chilka in Puri. The failure of the aman crop was, however, a common factor. A combination of untoward natural circumstances in the winter of 1896 brought into play the extreme fragility of the rice economy in Bengal. The all-important winter rice depended essentially on the rains and, occasionally, on inundations—both uncertain variables at best. The importance of irrigation in such an equation can hardly be overrated. However, the government canals and private irrigation works, drawing on the rains, floods or sub-soil water, were limited in scope and extent. Their efficacy was further frustrated by the problems of ecology, drainage and sanitation, soil texture, and conformation—all of which were intensified in a year of drought.

2

Institutional Framework of Peasant Agriculture

Crop failure and famine are not synonymous. An extensive failure of crops merely aggravates the basic conflicts and entitlement problems within the peasant economy, as a result of which the crisis may deepen into famine.

In Bengal, institutional anomalies—as in credit, rent, trade and labour relations—varied in intensity in different regions: (i) In the tribal tracts—Bhagalpur (especially the Santhal Parganas), Chotanagpur, parts of Birbhum, Bankura and the Jungle Mahals of western Midnapur, the Terai region in Darjeeling-Jalpaiguri, the Chittagong Hill Tracts and Angul-Khondmals in Orissa—the problem was most acute and sharply defined. Here the creditors, landlords and traders were generally alien intruders, who exploited the local people by taking full advantage of their backwardness and ignorance. (ii) In settled but poor districts, as in north Bihar and parts of the Orissa, Burdwan and Presidency Divisions, the creditors and proprietors were local mahajans and big farmers whose grip on the cultivators was equally rigorous and secure. (iii) In the relatively prosperous districts of the Rajshahi, Dacca and Chittagong Divisions, the wealthier agriculturists mostly functioned as mahajans and retailers, while the average peasant was more of a force to reckon with, and not so hopelessly involved in debt.

[1] *The Credit Mechanism*

[1.1] Penetration of alien credit into tribal areas

The tribal situation was brought into sharp focus in the Santhal settlements in various parts of the Bhagalpur, Rajshahi and

Burdwan Divisions.[1] The rent and credit problems, with minor variations, were essentially the same in all these regions. Moulded by the simplistic customs and traditions of a tribal society, the Santhal, like the Paharia, Bhumij, Munda or Bhuiya, had no aptitude for business deals and no knowledge of the technicalities of British law; hence, he was always at a distinct disadvantage in his relations with the crafty Marwari and Bengali creditor-proprietor, or with the mahajan-adventurer from Bhojpur.

In Chotanagpur, the northern parts were to some extent a continuation of the rich alluvial tracts of south Bihar, inhabited by high-caste Hindus and Muslims, while the tribal population was less numerous. In the south, however, the hill country was covered with brushwood and jungle, where the lower castes and tribes preponderated. At the end of the nineteenth century, the tribal belt in Chotanagpur was undergoing a distinct phase in the transition to early capitalism. With the introduction of the Permanent Settlement in 1895, and the opening of the Bengal-Nagpur Railway, Chotanagpur was integrated within the larger regional economy of Bengal, which already had a well-developed market for land. Simultaneously, there was a steady and secular rise in agricultural prices in the 1890s. The most obvious way in which capital could exploit these new opportunities in the agrarian sector, was through the credit mechanism.

The process was seen most clearly in the expropriation of land, labour and the grain surplus. In Kolhan in Singhbhum, for example, so long as the country was virtually inaccessible and not worth exploiting, foreigners kept away. But, as land acquired value in exchange, money was increasingly lent on the security of the holdings. "Bargains are made on most unequal terms between astute and unscrupulous capitalists from the outer world

[1] The Bhagalpur Division—Bhagalpur, Purnea, Malda, Monghyr and the Santhal Parganas—was inhabited by a great variety of aboriginal and semi-aboriginal tribes, such as the Dhangar, Kanjhar, Kherwar, Kol, Mal, Paharia, Pujahar, Naiya, Nat, Batar, Bhuiya, Gangaonta, Kadar, Markande, Musahar and Santhal. By the close of the nineteenth century, the Santhals had spread to the north, east and south of the Santhal Parganas, i.e., to the quasi-laterite Barind tract in Dinajpur, Rajshahi and Bogra, to the tea gardens in Darjeeling-Jalpaiguri, and to Burdwan, Birbhum, Bankura and Midnapur in west Bengal.

on the one side, and on the other a simple, . . . absolutely guileless and straightforward race, hitherto sheltered from such contests by their distance from civilization, and knowing little of money or of the equitable price of their property or its produce".[2]

Except for a few Telis and Sunris, most of the moneylenders in Lohardaga and Palamau, for instance, were Sahus or *bania*s (traders) by caste, consisting of first- or second-generation immigrants from Bihar, who settled in the relatively large villages. The petty Sahus were mostly shopkeepers or grocers, carrying on small-loan transactions ("len den") with the villagers. The richer Sahus dealt wholesale in all sorts of country produce, and gave out substantial loans. "A large portion of the landed property of the country has already passed into the hands of moneylenders, either by sale or mortgage. As landlords, they are proverbially grasping and avaricious, and their wealth enables them to make oppressive demands on the raiyats with impunity". The Hinduised tribes of Cheros and Kherwars in Palamau, for instance, lost nearly all their landed property, and a major portion of their produce to the Sahu in payment of his dues.[3] The expropriation of labour, based on debt bondage or the notorious kamia system so widely prevalent in Gaya, Manbhum and Palamau, followed in natural sequence. As described by Sudipto Mundle and, more recently, by Gyan Prakash, the "plains Hindus . . . used the nineteenth century instruments of land control and Kamiauti advances to make their intrusion more extensive and pervasive than ever before". In the absence of technical improvements, and with a deterioration in the existing irrigation facilities, the needs of agricultural growth and commercialisation could be met only by the intensification of labour exploitation.[4]

In the northeastern Terai regions, Marwari moneylenders economically exploited the Rajbansis and the Koches of

[2] LRP, Aug. 1898, pt. 1, nos. 56–57, p. 195. "Report on Land Transfers from the Agricultural to the Non-Agricultural Classes", para. 10, no. 834 A, Cal. 9 Sept. 1896. From F. A. Slacke, Offg. Secy. to the Board of Revenue, L.P., to the Secy. to the Govt. of Bengal, Rev. Dept.

[3] Basu, *Report, Agriculture of Lohardaga*, pt. 1, sec. 6, p.20; pt. 2, sec. 6, p. 11.

[4] Prakash, *Bonded Histories,* pp. 166, 169.

Darjeeling, British Sikkim and Jalpaiguri. W. B. Oldham, Deputy Commissioner of Darjeeling, noted in 1884 that when the Rajbansi *jotedar*s (landholders) of the Terai were sold up on default, the Marwari mahajans and traders of Darjeeling bought the *jote*s (landholdings) and settled them with the defaulters as sub-tenants, at exactly double the settlement rate of the jote.[5] Similarly, the Santhals, Meches and Garos were driven by the tea planters from lands cultivated by them in the Duars.[6]

In the Chittagong Hill Tracts, the hillmen were hopelessly indebted to the plainsmen. Missionaries from Haluaghat, Susang and other areas testified to the exploitation of the Hill Garos by moneylenders, causing many of them to lose their lands. Thereafter, Hindus and Muslims started coming "like the wave over the land of the Garos".[7] A large number of Garos who had settled at the foot of the Hills, as well as the Banuahs of Barisal and the Maghs in the Bakarganj Sunderbans, were firmly in the clutches of their mahajans.[8] The local Muslims, too, were exploited by their Hindu proprietors and mahajans. "There is a recklessness about the Muhammadans which places them, in respect to their patient and more capable Hindu neighbours, in something of the same position as the ignorant and improvident primitive races".[9]

Angul Khondmals, like extensive parts of Bhagalpur, Chotanagpur and Puri, belonged to the fringe of hill country

[5] LRP, Aug. 1898, pt. 1, p. 221, W. B. Oldham, Commissioner, Chittagong Div., to the Secy. to the Board of Rev., L.P., para. 15. Camp Feni, 6 Mar. 1896.

[6] *SR, Jalpaiguri* (1906–16), by J. A. Milligan (Calcutta: BSBD, 1919), p. 110, para. 109.

[7] Ibid., Sept. 1916. Rev. M. L. Barber, Baptist Mission, Susang, as quoted by J. Lang, Collector, Mymensingh, 15 Feb. 1915, para. 5.

[8] Ibid., Sept. 1916. F. D. Ascoli, Settlement Officer, Dacca to Commissioner, Dacca Division. no. 1403, 22 Dec. 1914, para. 3. Nomads among the Garos, Koches, Manipuris, Tipperahs and Rajbansis—who cleared small tracts in parts of the Bhowal, Kasimpur, Sasan, Basan, Durgapur and Talipabad parganas in the Madhupur Jungle of Dacca and moved to fresh patches every three or four years—were relatively immune to this problem, due mainly to the lack of credit.

[9] Ibid., para. 17.

inhabited by aboriginal or semi-aboriginal tribes.[10] It was a typically backward tract. In Saringia and Nuapada in Angul, the primitive forms of jhum and toila cultivation were followed to raise crops of *ato dhan, konga, jhulunga* and *kolka*, on which the Khonds lived. In Jehelingia, Patengia and Bakalmendi, large areas of jungle were never cleared for cultivation. This was an "index to the tracts liable to famine": Jehelingia and Petengia were locally known as the "famine country", and the people there were never free from distress. For instance, in 1898, Gochapara passed through a crisis though the crops of 1897–98 were nearly 16 annas in the entire subdivision.[11] Bordered by tracts which were more prone to scarcity than surplus, no substantial grain imports could be expected even in lean years.[12]

The problem was aggravated by poor communications. It took four days for a letter to reach Angul from Khondmals, and two to reach Cuttack.[13] Private trade in grain could not grow in the absence of big or regular grain dealers and mahajans. Those holding stocks were either *sarbarahakar*s (petty traders) or well-to-do tenants. As jungle roots and herbs largely supplemented the daily diet of the local people, the effects of crop failure were not felt until the crisis deepened into famine. Only then, the cultivators panicked and stopped employing labour or selling grain, while the grain holders withheld loans, which suddenly brought on distress.[14] There was no regular mahajani system. A large number of Khonds, however, lived as day labourers, and were deeply indebted to the local Sundi moneylenders, to whom

10 In the Khondmals, there were aborigines and Hindus such as Khonds, Savars, Taulas, Pans, Haris, Sudhas, Sundis and other Oriya castes. The Khonds, who were preponderant, held paddy lands and cultivated turmeric and oilseeds to a considerable extent. The Pans were mostly weavers with a dwindling income, the Gowalas lived by grazing cattle, Sudhas cultivated land, while the Sundis had liquor shops and moneylending interests.

11 LRP, Br. Agriculture, Oct. 1900, p. 597. Letter from Dy. Comm., Angul, to the Comm., Orissa Div., 31 July 1900.

12 Ibid., Feb. 1900, p. 233, no. 4. From F. A. Slacke, Offg. Secy. to the Govt. of Bengal.

13 Ibid., Nov. 1899, p. 600.

14 Ibid., Jan. 1900, p. 85. From E. Mc. L. Smith, Dy. Comm., Angul,, to the Sup., Tributary Mahals, Orissa.

they mortgaged or sold their lands.[15] Often their crops, too, were pledged to the *Mogulbandi* dealers, who functioned all the year round, making advances to cultivators and taking away the crops as soon as reaped.[16]

The predominance of alien creditors and proprietors in the tribal areas may be attributed to some "exceptional circumstances".[17] The inability of the Santhal, Paharia, or Kol agricultural settlements in wastelands to be self-sufficient, especially in view of the increase in land revenue and rentals, explained their growing dependence on outside forces able to cater to their needs. The hilly and barren lands, together with the wasteful methods of jhum or toila cultivation among the Paharias and Khonds, and the Kol practice of draining the fields at Karma Puja irrespective of the nature of the rains, made the tribal areas poor and backward. They were, therefore, easily infiltrated and controlled by alien capital.

Yet even in such backward tracts, local moneylenders, though relatively few, were no less influential. In the Santhal villages of the Rampur Hat and Suri subdivisions of Birbhum, for example, "the better-class raiyats combine with their cultivation the business of mahajani, and thereby constantly increase their holdings. Practically all the mahajans are resident within the villages under settlement, and belong to the cultivating classes".[18] In south Bihar, too, the rich Koeri peasants were the most stringent in their terms of kamiauti advances (under the bonded-labour contract system) to the local Bhuiya population. This was comparable to the situation in the eastern Mahals of Gujarat, where the resident Kanbi creditors were hated by the Bhils with even greater intensity than the alien Sahukars.[19]

15 Ibid., Feb. 1900, p. 221.
16 Ibid., July 1897, nos. 9–10, p. 41.
17 B. B. Chaudhuri, "Rural Credit Relations in Bengal, 1859–85", *Indian Economic and Social History Review* 6, no. 3, September 1969, p. 219.
18 LRP, April 1916. Final Report on the Survey and Settlement Operations in the Santhali villages of Rampur Hat and in several other villages in the Rampur Hat and Suri subdivisions, district Birbhum, sec. 10, para. 23.
19 Hardiman, "Bhils and Sahukars", pp. 17, 54.

In non-tribal areas, the creditors and proprietors were almost always local men, whose intimate knowledge of the *khataks*' (debtors') background and assets enabled them to pressurise the latter with even greater effect. The Commissioner of Burdwan wrote in 1884, "it is difficult to draw a distinction between a moneylender and an ordinary ryot. Any ryot who saves a little money . . . lends it in small sums to his neighbours so that almost every well-to-do ryot is a moneylender".[20] In north Bihar during 1885–95, much of the lands of Koeris, Kurmis and the lower cultivating classes were alienated, mostly by mortgage, to affluent raiyat-creditors to the extent of 83.9, 79.63, 79 and 55 per cent in Saran, Darbhanga, Muzaffarpur and Champaran respectively.[21] In the relatively prosperous districts of the Rajshahi, Dacca and Chittagong Divisions, too, the wealthier agriculturists mostly functioned as mahajans and retailers. The Commissioner of Chittagong noted: "What is meant by *mahajan*? Is it not the case that in many, if not most, cases the *mahajan* is also a person directly interested in agriculture? As soon as a ryot gets free from debt . . . does he not immediately set up as a money lender on his own account?"[22]

[1.2] Problem of rural indebtedness

In fact, the entire peasant economy in Bengal was enmeshed in a complex web of credit relations. The system was such that the peasant could seldom repay the principal: routine interest payments in cash or as a share of the produce often left him on the verge of starvation even in normal times. It was a perennial process. After paying off his rent and interest dues at harvest time, the peasant was soon obliged to borrow again to tide over the next season. Moreover, the accumulation of compound interest, the expense of social obligations, the demands of crisis years and the initial investment in case of commercial agriculture

20 *Report of the Government of Bengal on the Bengal Tenancy Bill 1884* (Calcutta, 1884), vol. 2: Burdwan Commissioner's Report of 8 Aug. 1884.

21 *SR, Saran,* paras. 531–35; *SR, Darbhanga*, paras. 429, 436.

22 *Report, Bengal Tenancy Bill 1884*, vol. 2: Chittagong Commissioner's Report of 10 July 1884.

increased his debt, so that gradually his produce, land and in the last resort, even his labour, were pledged and lost to the creditor. Thus, the average peasant, especially in the tribal regions, could seldom sell his grain, implements, land or labour in the open market.

It was due to this fact that calculations of the peasant's "surplus"—based on the "money value" of his aggregate production and the income, if any, from other sources, minus the cost of cultivation and the cost of living—were misleading. The concept of market value, familiar to capitalistic farming, was totally alien to an economy controlled by pre-existing credit relations. The peasant, after paying the rent and interest, consumed nearly all that was left of the produce, and borrowed on the security of the next crop. Hence, there was little basis for such statements of a fair profit-margin, as of 55 per cent for "pure cultivators" and 39 per cent for "cultivating labourers", as quoted in the Muzaffarpur Survey Reports, or for the Collector of Nadia's assertion that "if the prices are higher . . . the profit is large", since the second crop on the aus fields was "wholly a profit".[23]

The small number of mortgages and alienations of land in some parts of north Bihar and Bengal also led some district officials to conclude that rural indebtedness was not extensive there at the end of the nineteenth century. This was an illusion, for various reasons there were many forms of credit in which the peasant borrowed on securities other than land; the debtor often retained possession of the mortgaged land; and only a small number of mortgages and alienations were officially recorded.

The existence of debt, for instance, was much less obvious in cases where the debtor was too poor to offer any tangible form of security, and entered into a debt-labour contract which was, however, far worse in effect, and often continued for generations.

[23] *SR, Muzaffarpur*, paras. 925–26; *Report on the Condition of the Lower Orders of the Population in Bengal* (Calcutta: BS Press, 1888) (The report was ordered by Lord Dufferin; henceforth, the report will be referred to as the *Dufferin Report*.); A. Smith, Comm. Presidency Division, to the Secy. to the Bengal Govt., Calcutta, 17 May 1888, paras. 47–48.

Thus in Dinajpur, where indebtedness was stated by some to be "very small", it was noted that "the labouring classes are frequently weighted by debt, and continue in many cases servants for life to their creditors".[24] Oldham, the Collector of Burdwan, noted in his report on the "condition of the lower orders of the population" in Kaksa, a "typical" village in his district: "The disappearance of indebtedness, which was general in 1872, . . . is a remarkable circumstance. Most of the people whom I questioned owed nothing at all; others owed a rupee or two to a fellow labourer or . . . to their permanent employers. These employers still retain their field labourers by lending grain to them in the slack season without interest. These transactions are not regarded as loans; still less as mahajani". The observation hardly fits in with his "confirmed" opinion that "nowhere in the district is there a lower rate of income, a lower standard of ease, a narrower margin for subsistence, or a greater prevalence of poverty among the agricultural and labouring classes than at Kaksa".[25] The people here were perhaps too poor to offer any other form of security but their physical labour; and the grain "lent without interest" during the slack season was probably no more than part of the employer's obligation to feed and clothe his bonded labourers throughout the year.

Except for such occasional misconceptions and contradictions, the wide range and extent of rural credit have been universally noted in district reports, monographs and official enquiries on the subject (see appendix A). Poverty and the lack of credit could not eliminate the problem, as is proved by the widespread prevalence of indebtedness even in the remotest tribal tracts. B. C. Basu noted in his Report on Lohardaga: "The indebtedness of the raiyats of Lohardaga is a matter of proverb. Very few raiyats I did meet with, who did not owe a few maunds of paddy to their Sahus".[26] The Kol peasant was "obliged to stint

24 *Dufferin Report*, from P. Nolan, Secy. to the Govt. of Bengal, to the Secy. to the Govt. of India, Rev. and Agricultural Dept., para. 7, Darjeeling, 30 June 1888.

25 Ibid., Oldham's Report to the Divisional Commissioner of Burdwan, 16 April 1888, paras. 11 and 17.

26 Basu, *Report on Lohardaga*, pt. 1, Sadar subdivision, sec. 6, pp. 20–21.

himself for a few months before the bhadoi harvest and to borrow, whatever his credit will allow, from his Sahu at enormous interest". In Palamau, too, indebtedness was equally widespread, Hinduised tribes like the Cheros and Kherwars being entirely in the clutches of the Sahus.[27]

The Collector of Bhagalpur wrote in 1888: "figures were perhaps scarcely necessary to prove the melancholy fact . . . that the majority of our ryots live in debt and pay off one year in order to begin borrowing for the next".[28] In north Bihar, Tytler, the Sub-Deputy Opium Agent at Siwan, Saran district, noted: "95 percent of the *raiyats* live and die in debt".[29] The Collector of Patna, studying the condition of petty cultivators and labourers in a selected area in the district, considered it as "one of extreme poverty and indebtedness, those only being free from debt whom the *mahajan* will not trust".[30] In Puri, indebtedness was "pretty general".[31] In Parikud, for instance, about 90 per cent of the population were more or less permanently indebted to the mahajan, who was not usually a local man, but some affluent peasant from the Banpur side of the Khurda Khasmahal. In Jessore, "more than 50 percent of them (the agriculturists) are said to be in a state of chronic indebtedness to their *mahajans*".[32] Similar observations are numerous with regard to nearly all the districts in the Province, including the relatively prosperous areas like Rajshahi, Dacca and Chittagong.

[27] Ibid., pt. 2, sec. 6, pp. 10–11.

[28] *Dufferin Report*, Collector Bhagalpur to Comm., 7 April 1888, para. 12.

[29] *SR, Saran*, para. 556.

[30] *Dufferin Report*, from Quinn, Collector of Patna, as forwarded by J. Boxwell, Offg. Comm. of Patna Division, to the Secy. to the Govt. of Bengal, Rev. Dept., no. 286 G, dated Bankipore, 2 June 1888, para. 14.

[31] Ibid., Allen, Puri district, to C. F. Worsley, Comm., Orissa Division, dated Puri, 3 June 1888.

[32] LRP, Aug. 1898, pt. 2, p. 535. From L. F. Morshead, Collector, Jessore, to the Comm., Presidency Division, no. G/2230, Jessore, 12/13 Nov. 1897, para. 4.

[1.3] Forms of credit

[a] Grain loans

Grain loans for seed and food (*bij-khad*) were the most common form of credit transaction in rural society. The peasant's stock of rice was gleaned mainly from the aman crop in December. This stock, however, was largely depleted by the payment of the mahajan's interest and the largest instalment (*kist*) of rent which fell due in the reaping season, the lowness of post-harvest prices compelling the peasant to part with a greater share of the produce.

The remainder usually supported the peasant's family for about three to four months. Supplies ran out in mid-March/April, which marked the beginning of the lean season, when grain prices rose high. It was during this time, that is, from March (Chaitra) to July (Sravan), that the cultivator was obliged to borrow grain for food, seed and payments in kind for hired labour, often essential during the sowing (May–June) and transplantation (July–August) of the winter rice. In August–September, the bhadoi harvest eased the strain, except when and where it was scanty or unimportant, in which case the period of stress continued until the reaping of the aman crop in December.

Tribals like the Garos, Meches, Rajbansis, and others had little use for cash, and their debts were mainly in the form of grain loans. Even their rent very often had to be paid in kind. By the *tanka* system prevailing among the Garos in Susang, for instance, the rent was fixed at 10 md. of paddy per acre per annum, a fine of 4 an. in the rupee being demanded in case of money payment. Hence, in lean seasons, when their entire crop of paddy fell considerably short of this proportion, the Garos had to take substantial grain loans, first for their rent, and then for food and seed.[33]

Likewise, every Santhal had to borrow grain, usually no more than 5 md. of paddy a year, when supplies from the previous

33 LRP, Sept. 1916, report of Rev. Barber of the Baptist Mission, Susang, as noted in letter from J. Lang, Collector Mymensingh to Comm., Dacca Div., no. 475, Mymensingh, 15 Feb. 1915, para. 5.

harvest ran out. Compound interest was charged on these loans at exorbitant rates. Sometimes, grain could be borrowed in October on condition that for every 40 sr. lent, 50 sr. were repaid at the aghani harvest.[34] Generally, however, foodgrains were repaid at 50 per cent interest called *adhia* or *dera* at the time of harvest, while the loan of seed grains, which were expected to be of a finer quality, called for a 100 per cent interest or *dubra*. The unpaid amount of the year was carried on to the next year, until, at compound rates, even a petty loan was so inflated that the Santhal could hardly ever hope to repay it in full.

When the Santhal's accounts were made up at the end of the year, interest for the whole year was charged, irrespective of when he had taken the loan. The transactions were made by volume. As the Santhal repaid newly reaped paddy for dried paddy, the interest would work out to less than 50 per cent due to the shrinkage in size. But there was every reason to believe that the mahajans used different sets of weight measures for their receipts and disbursements. The Santhals were not generally aware of the exact extent of their debt, and took the mahajans' word for it. "In no case does the money lender give a receipt to the Santhal for the amount paid".[35] The accounts of the mahajan were extremely unreliable. Very often, even debts which were cleared and interests which were paid, were not entered as such into the mahajani *khata* (account book). As the marketable produce had to be rushed out before the rains and nothing more could be brought in during the monsoon due to defective communication, the mahajan could make his own terms with the debtors for food and seed grain.[36] If the creditor accepted the repayment of grain in instalments, the Santhal would stand some chance of clearing his debt. Frequently, however, the grain loan was converted into a money value far in excess of the actual debt.

34 *Dufferin Report*. From J. Beams, Comm., Bhagalpur Div. & Santhal Parganas, to the Secy. to the Govt. of Bengal, Rev. Dept., no. 7, Bhagalpur, 2 May 1888.

35 LRP, Nov. 1908. Report of Munshi Ekramuddin, Kanungo, 21 Feb. 1908.

36 *Dufferin Report*. From R. Carstairs, Offg. Dy. Comm., Santhal Parganas, to Comm., Bhagalpur Div. & Santhal Parganas, Doomka, 6 April 1888, para. 12.

The peasant was next induced to execute a registered mortgage deed in favour of the creditor, who could then file a suit and get a decree for possession of the Santhal's land on the basis of this document.[37] The Report on the Nayabasan Estate in Midnapur recorded numerous case histories of this type, while surveying the extent of transfers which occurred in the Santhal villages during the twenty years from 1889 to 1909.

In the backward tracts of Chotanagpur, grain loans were by far the most popular form of credit. The manager of Dhalbhum in Singhbhum stated:

> The mainstay of the ryot is the winter rice crop of December. After payment of rents and cesses by the sale of a portion of the crop, and returning the loan of grain previously taken from the mahajan with the usual addition of one-half of the advance, the portion of the produce left for the maintenance of the ryots and their families enable them as a rule to live upon it for only four months, namely from Aghran to Falgoon (December to March). With Chyte commences the strain. The raiyat again resorts to the mahajan for an advance of grain, and lives upon the advance, supplemented by mohua flowers and kenda fruits, till Bhadra, when the harvesting of the bhadoi crops viz. aus dhan or early rice, makoyi, marooa, etc. relieves the pressure and enables him to hold out till the next Kartic. The interval between Chyte and Bhadro is usually the hardest time for the bulk of the ryots, and during this period they can seldom afford to eat two full meals of grain a day.[38]

In Lohardaga and Palamau, too, grain loans were taken between Chaitra and Sravan at dera (50 per cent) interest for foodgrain (*khiyan*) and dubra (100 per cent) for seed (*beejan*). Cultivators were usually the largest borrowers.[39]

[37] LRP, Dec. 1914, no. 201, 5 Sept. 1913. From P. M. Robertson, Settlement Officer, Rampur Hat, Birbhum, to Director of Land Records, Bengal.

[38] *Dufferin Report*. Report by Manager, Dhalbhum, Singhbhum District, as forwarded by C. C. Stevens, Comm. Chotanagpur Div., to the Secy. to the Govt. of Bengal, Rev. Dept., no. 351 R, Ranchi, 31 May 1888, para. 19.

[39] Ibid., C. C. Stevens, Comm. Chotanagpur, to Secy. to Govt. of Bengal, Rev. Dept., no. 351 R, Ranchi, 31 May 1888, paras. 33, 43. In a selected village in Lohardaga, for example, 50 out of 129 cultivators and 25 out of 76 labourers and artisans, owed an aggregate of 32½ and 3 md. of *dhan* (paddy), respectively. In a

These grain loans were sometimes part of the *dadni* transaction with the mahajan, that is, advances on the security of the crop on the fields, both principal and interest being delivered at harvest time. As his dues were measured out before the grain was taken into the peasant's storehouse, the grain income of the raiyats in a year of deficient harvest was remarkably low, nearly the whole of the paddy going over to the mahajan. As in the Santhal Parganas, the principal, if not repaid in time, increased at compound interest every year. B. C. Basu, in his Report on agriculture in Lohardaga, observed: "This is a source of the most grievous oppression for the raiyats. Instances like the following are very numerous. A raiyat had borrowed 1 *maund* of paddy from the sahu, and at the lapse of four years, during which he was somehow unable to liquidate the debt, he was called upon to deliver 16 mds. of paddy. This latter it was beyond his means to meet, and accordingly he was obliged to sell off his cattle; or if he had any korkar or bhuinhari land, to give it away zaripeshgi to the sahu."[40]

In Angul-Khondmals, the wandering, aboriginal tribes had, by the 1890s, all taken to cultivation or labour in settled villages. But their methods of cultivation were backward and though largely supplementing their diet with jungle products, they could not do without paddy loans. The Pahi raiyats of Angul having holdings of three acres and under were particularly prone to this. As their income from land did not exceed Rs. 30, while the expenses of cultivation were seldom less than Rs. 10, they were forced to borrow rice for their subsistence.[41] This was supplied to some extent by the sarbarahakars and the Mogulbandi dealers who advanced grain on the security of the next harvest; but there was no regular mahajani system, the wealthier agriculturists withholding stocks at the first signs of crop failure.[42]

---

village in Palamau, all the twenty cultivating families owed 122 md. of grain, i.e., 6 md. per family on an average.

40 Basu, *Report on Lohardaga*, pt. 1, sec. 6, p. 21.

41 *Dufferin Report*. From A. K. Roy, Jt. Settl. Officer, to the Director of Land Records, Bengal, through the Supt., Tributary Mahals, Cuttack, no. 4T, Angul, 12 April 1888, para. 25.

42 LRP, Feb. 1900, p. 211. From the Supt. Tributary Mahals of Orissa; Ibid., July 1897, nos. 9–10, p. 41.

Grain loans were by no means confined to backward, tribal tracts. In lean years, dependence on the mahajan naturally increased. For instance, Tytler, the Sub-Deputy Opium Agent of Siwan in Saran district, wrote on 28 November 1896: "Nearly all agriculturists (excepting wealthy men) will run out of home stores by the middle of January". The banias, however, held large stocks. "Nearly all raiyats are carried on by their mahajans, and . . . 80 per cent will be so carried on with advances, if nothing goes wrong with the poppy or rabi".[43]

A most distinctive and widely prevalent form of grain loan was that given by a cultivator to his labourer, which was repaid by physical labour or, as in case of a sharecropper, from his share of the produce. As peasant holdings were very often too small to be self-sufficient, the great majority of these peasants had to supplement their income from land by hiring out their labour to a greater or lesser extent. As the professional mahajan seldom lent grain on such an intangible form of security as physical labour, peasants depended upon their cultivator-employers to advance them their requirements for food and seed. In Birbhum, for example, the employment of field hands was often based on such grain advances. "The cultivators take them on by the year to do the bulk of the work of cultivation under their own supervision. During the year before the crop ripens, these labourers live upon advances of grain given by the cultivators, which are deducted with 25 per cent interest from the labourer's share . . . Few of the labourers are free from debt". The same phenomenon was noted in the Santhali villages in Rampur Hat, Birbhum, nearly three decades later.[44] In Dacca, the *bargadar* or tenant on produce rent sometimes received "a portion of the necessary seeds" from his landlord. In Midnapur, seed grain to the bargadar "is often advanced in the first instance by the landlord, but simply owing to his being the most convenient person to borrow from and the advance is strictly a loan to be repaid at harvest time".[45]

43 LRP, July 1897, nos. 34–35, p. 202.

44 *Dufferin Report*. C. J. S. Faulder, Offg. Collector of Birbhum, to the Comm. Burdwan div., no. 205 G, Suri, 30 May 1888; *SR* of the Santhali village in Rampur Hat, Birbhum; LRP, April 1916, p. 13, para. 29.

45 B. B. Chaudhuri, "The Process of Depeasantization in Bengal

[b] Cash loans

Cash loans were less frequent in the peasant economy, and were required mainly for social ceremonies and the payment of rent. If the rent instalment was not fully paid up after the December harvest, the zamindar brought rent suits against the peasants in the period between March and April, i.e., precisely when their stocks were very low. Hence, they had no option but to borrow money from their mahajans in order to make good their rent arrears.

The Santhal, for example, usually took loans of Rs. 5 to Rs. 15 a year to pay his rent dues, or agricultural loans for which one of the kists for repayment fell in the lean summer months. The mahajan kept a running account of the loans. The rate of interest for money loans was generally 25 per cent (called *sikki*), and compound interest was charged. Sometimes, the rates were even higher. The extortionate interest allowed on debts under the provisions of the Civil Procedure Code (Act VIII of 1859) increased the rigour of the mahajans' demands in the Santhal Parganas. A full enquiry into the grievances of the raiyats led to the passing of Regulation III of 1872, which limited the interest on debts to 24 per cent per annum, and to a total amount not exceeding the principal. It also excluded compound interest.

But the laws had little effect in practice, and the moneylender's business continued to flourish.[46] At the turn of the century the rates were as follows: if the loan was taken in Magh, Falgun, Chait, Baisakh or Jeth, the rate charged for these months was 2 an. in the rupee (*korali*); but if it was not paid until later, 4 an. to the rupee were charged for the winter months, so that the total rate of interest worked out to 37.5 per cent or 6 an. in the rupee. If the loan was taken in Asar, Sraban, Bhadra or Aswin the rate was 4 an. per rupee (*barsali*). When cash loans were repaid in grain, the mahajan took care that the rate of valuation should be well in his favour; thus "he takes his interest and makes a second profit on the sale of grain at a good deal over the

---

and Bihar", *Indian Historical Review* 2, no. 1 July 1975, p. 162.

46 *SR, Santhal Parganas,* p. 40, paras. 31–32; p. 45, para. 37.

valuation on which he received it".[47] Two such types of interest on cash loans, viz., *chota* and *dhurta*, prevailed along the fringe settlements of Midnapur and Birbhum.[48]

When the Santhal's debts passed beyond the stage of the current account and were converted into money, a document was executed and the interest rates were supposed to fall; in fact, however, they still remained between 4 and 6 an. a rupee.[49] The case of the Santhals in Tappa Madhuban, south Bhagalpur, provided a typical example of the extent of fraud practised by alien mahajans even on petty cash loans. The *tappa* (land area) was reclaimed chiefly by the exertions of the Santhals, but during the 1890s large numbers were dispossessed by Babhans and Rajputs attached as peons to the Colgong Indigo Concern.[50]

47 H. Mosley, Collector of Monghyr, to Comm. Bhagalpur Div., no. 273 R, Monghyr, 3 May 1888.

48 LRP, Nov. 1908. From notes taken at a local inquiry in villages in west Rampur Hat regarding the alienation, etc. of lands by Santhals in Birbhum district, April 1908, p. 7, Report by Munshi Ekram-ud- din, kanungo, 21 Feb. 1908, sec. II. Here, urgent chota loans of money in Aswin-Kartik had to be repaid in grain during harvest time in Aghrahayan (mid-November to mid-December) or Pous (mid-December to mid-January) at an arbitrary rate fixed by the mahajan, with one *ari* (10 sr.) in the rupee as interest. Many Santhals, who had received loans at this rate in Aswin when paddy was selling at 2½ aris per rupee, were required to pay in Pous at 8 aris per rupee as fixed before hand, with one ari as interest per rupee. Thus, "practically the Santhal had to pay in four months 9 aris of paddy for every 2½ aris got, or more than treble. It is said that such is the case every year". In Narainpur, some moneylenders even deducted 4 an. per rupee while paying to the Santhal, who had to repay the full amount with interest. The second form of interest (dhurta) was fixed on small loans taken in Kartik for sacrifices. It was repaid in paddy in Pous-Magh at the proper price, with 1 ari in the rupee as interest.

49 M. McAlpin, *Report on the Condition of the Santhals in the Districts of Birbhum, Bankura, Midnapore and North Balasore* (Calcutta: BS Press, 1909).

50 As peons they were paid only two or three rupees per month, but were soon able to start lending money to the Santhals. "Once this began, the Santhals were doomed. A man borrowed 20 rupees, paid back 30 in the course of a couple of years in small sums of 1 or 2 rupees at a time, and was then informed that he still owed 25. Being unable to check the simplest calculation, the aborigines

The Garos and Meches, like the Santhals, sometimes contracted small cash loans, often with identical results.[51] The Paharias on the Rajmahal Hills paid 25 per cent interest for the whole year on money advanced only four to five months earlier. The Paharia was so much in the hands of the mahajans, that he would sign any document in order to secure a few rupees. The mahajans fully manipulated the situation, and produced bonds which were apparently records of lump sum payments, but actually were *hisabi* (running account) debts; in fact, no mahajan would advance without security such sums as Rs. 400 or Rs. 500, as noted in these bonds, in one instalment to a Paharia.[52]

Money loans on the security of their jote lands, likewise, enabled the tribals of Chotanagpur "to pay their rents on time and carry on their agricultural operations". Enquiries in Govindpur subdivision, the Bhumij country of Barabhum and the Santhal settlements of Tundi in Manbhum district, show that the raiyat was sometimes compelled to borrow money on *bhukta bandha* or usufructuary mortgage. This imposed "more usurious terms than the ordinary 60-odd per cent of the mahajans for a loan advanced on the security of a transferable *jote* and [the peasant] is reduced during its currency to practical penury".[53]

In Palamau and Lohardaga, however, this form of mortgage was not common. Here the usual means of raising money on landed property was *zaripeshgi* or usufructuary mortgage—by which the land was pawned to the sahu until it was released by paying up the capital—or the *mokarrari* lease, by which land was permanently leased out for an advance twenty to twenty-

---

were absolutely at the mercy of the money lenders. In a few years they had executed deeds of sale transferring their entire holdings to the latter in order to extinguish the debt". *SR, Bhagalpur,* para. 124.

51 LRP, Sept. 1916, nos. 57–58. From J. Lang, Collector Mymensingh, to Comm. Dacca Div., no. 475, Mymensingh, 15 Feb. 1915, para. 5.

52 LRP, Sept. 1909.

53 Ibid., Nov. 1907, nos. 66–67. Letter no. 1936 R, dt. 16 Dec. 1906, from H. C. Woodman, Dy. Comm., Manbhum, to Comm., Chotanagpur Div., paras. 4 and 7.

five times of the net profit that the lessee would earn on such land.[54]

Cash loans were more frequent in non-tribal areas. In Nadia, for instance, besides many debts for social ceremonies and lean seasons, many raiyats resorted to short-term cash loans for the payment of rent, at an interest rate of 24 to 30 per cent per annum. These were often post-harvest loans, when the raiyat was eager to hold back part of his stocks until the grain prices were higher, and yet was compelled to meet the pressing demands of the landlord.[55]

[c] Loan of cattle and agricultural implements

Another distinctive form of credit besides grain and cash loans was the loan of agricultural implements, mostly of ploughs and cattle. Indeed, the plough featured crucially in the peasant economy. The Presidency Commissioner noted in 1888: "The distinction between small cultivators and labourers lies in this, that a man who has a plough and oxen is called a *chasa* or cultivator, and he that has no plough or oxen for tilling his

[54] Basu, *Report, Agriculture of Lohardaga*, pt. 1, sec. 6, pp. 19–21; pt. 2, sec. 6, pp. 10–11. These money loans, however, could only be resorted to by the landed classes and, among the peasants, by the bhuinhars and a few chatisa raiyats alone. Most raiyats took petty cash loans such as the *karja, seri* or *chara*. Karja could be taken at any time of the year at stipulated rates of interest varying from 1 or 1/2 an anna per rupee per month in case of small loans, to 12 per cent per annum in case of larger ones. By the seri, a rupee borrowed in summer was repaid by 3 to 5 *kat*s of paddy, including interest, at harvest time. A chara loan of one rupee borrowed in summer was repaid by 20 to 25 *poila*s of rice as interest in Agrahayan, and by the principal in Magh. Dadni advances in cash were occasionally made in the lean months, by which the peasant undertook to deliver for every rupee borrowed, a fixed amount of the produce of his labour, such as cotton, ghee, lac or *tussar,* which worked out to a rate 25 to 50 per cent lower than the market price. Sometimes, the dadni advances were made at such "egregious rates of interest", that the actual cultivators got little more from the produce than the wages of their labour.

[55] *Dufferin Report*. From A. Smith, Comm. Presidency Div., to the Secy. to the Govt. of Bengal, Rev. Dept., no. 1M.A., Cal., 17 May 1888, para. 55.

small holding is known as a *mojoor* or labourer".[56] Considering the size of each family and the extent of land held by it, he concluded: "It does not appear that the number of members in a family much affects its prosperity: the prosperity of a family appears to be regulated by the number of ploughs it can afford to keep in work".[57] Hence, cultivators without ploughs were obliged to borrow them from their richer neighbours or landlords. Sometimes a bargadar was provided with bullocks and implements by the landlord. This was, however, strictly on a credit rather than capitalist basis.[58]

Such loans were widely prevalent in Nadia, Jessore, Khulna, the Santhal Parganas and other parts of Bhagalpur Division. E. W. Collin, Settlement Officer of the Raj Banaili and Srinagar Estate, wrote in 1888: "Generally the ploughs belong to a big raiyat who lends them to smaller raiyats in exchange for their services in driving them".[59] One day's use of the plough and bullock was allowed for three days' service as ploughman.[60] After the famine of 1896–97, this practice grew more frequent here as moneylenders in the Damin-i-Koh, Santhal Parganas, began to evade the exemption of plough cattle from attachment, by themselves becoming the owners and lending the cattle out.[61] As always, the creditor had the upper hand, and the cost of labour put in by the debtor was much more than the amount spent by the former on cattle feed and mid-day meals to the labourer.[62]

Yet the plough could never really be the absolute criterion of a peasant's prosperity: it had to be considered in relation to the size of his holding, which may nor may not have been sufficient

[56] Ibid., para. 60.
[57] Ibid., para. 29.
[58] Chaudhuri, "The Process of Depeasantization", sec. 13.
[59] *Dufferin Report*. E. W. Collin to the Collector of Bhagalpur, 13 April 1888, p. 6, no. 233, Camp Buloah.
[60] Ibid., no. 51, Camp Ekar, Circle Nauhatta, 24 April 1888. Babu Burhandeo Narayan, Asstt. Settlement Officer, Raj Banaili and Srinagar Estate, to the Collector of Bhagalpur.
[61] *DCAR, Bhagalpur, 1897–98*, p. 10, para. 62: Comments by the Comm.
[62] Chaudhuri, "Rural Credit Relations", p. 240. By the arrangement known as *adh-hali* (half-plough) in Jessore, the creditor often managed to get five bighas of land ploughed for Rs. 2-8 an., which normally would have cost him Rs. 7-8 an.

in supporting the peasant's entire family. In two selected villages in Nadia, 62.5 and 81.9 per cent of the peasant families respectively, had one plough each. The family unit normally consisted of four to ten members, and the size of its cultivation seldom exceeded ten to twelve bighas; even this land was not their own, and was generally held on *barga* (produce rent). Most of them had thus ceased to cultivate in their own right. They were generally indebted, and had to pay 25–37.5 per cent interest for advances.[63] In the final analysis, therefore, peasants without sufficient land had to depend on the more prosperous farmers for a loan of their land in return either for their services, or for a share of their produce.

[d] Loan of land

Due to the increasing pressure of population on the soil, resulting in uneconomic holdings and the extension of cultivation into marginal lands, such loans of land acquired greater significance. Regular systems like the bargadari drew on it. Often the new cultivation, too, was based on this form of credit, in which the rich entrepreneur, called the *hawaladar*, *jotedar*, *gantidar* or *aymadar*, financed the first work of reclamation and gave occasional loans to ensure its continuity. He settled some cultivators on the new land, and advanced money to build houses, buy ploughs and cattle, and obtain seed for sowing crops; the size and nature of the rent collected from these raiyats were determined essentially by credit considerations. The Collector of Noakhali noted: "The capital expended on the land is small, and on that capital an enormous interest is charged".[64] Sometimes these lands were reclaimed and worked by immigrant tribal labour, as for example in the Barind region of Rajshahi and Malda, and in the Jungle Mahals of western Midnapur and Bankura. They rarely obtained any rights in the lands cultivated by them, and the entrepreneurs, on the plea of raising a return

[63] Presidency Comm. to Bengal Govt., Cal., 17 May 1888, paras. 29–41.

[64] E. V. Westmacott, Collector Noakhali, to the Secy., Board of Rev., 30 April 1881.

on their initial investment, almost entirely appropriated the profits of the new cultivation.[65]

[1.4] Forms of appropriation by the creditor

[a] Labour bondage

The loan, whether of grain, cash, agricultural implements or land, was repaid in various forms. The poorest peasants, in the absence of other assets, repaid the creditor with their labour. The kamia system of debt bondage in Chotanagpur rested on this basis. As noted above, in backward tracts like Kaksa in Burdwan and parts of Dinajpur, indebtedness was less apparent, the only form of repayment being the debtor's labour.

[b] Share of the produce

The next and most obvious of the peasant's assets was the produce on his fields, a sizeable portion of which went to the mahajan in payment of interest, whether direct or in cash value. In Bhagalpur, for example, the Collector noted in 1888: "the large majority of them live in debt, and have practically mortgaged most of their crop before it is harvested". In Banka, the Subdivisional Officer found a considerable number of the peasant population indebted to the extent of more than one

[65] It is interesting to note the case of the Sahebganj traders and mahajans, who did not even reclaim wastelands, but merely financed the cultivation of *sabai* grass on the Rajmahal Hills, by converting the *kurao*s or food-crop lands of the Paharias into sabai lands. They arbitrarily fixed the price of the sabai at Rs. 8 to 10 per 100 loads, but kept back the greater part of the purchase money in settlement of their "old debts", i.e., the initial cost borne by the mahajan in clearing the sabai fields. The mahajans then sold this grass at a fair profit to large contracting firms like those of Ramgopal Sheo Dayal and Dina Nath Puri. Thus, while the sabai exports more than doubled between 1901 and 1908, and the mahajans fast extended their godowns in Sahebganj, the Paharias' entitlement was sharply reduced by the every-increasing burden of their "old debts". Bengal Revenue Proceedings: Sept. 1909, nos. 1–2, p. 136. From Patterson, S.D.O./Rajmahal, to the Dy. Comm. Santhal Parganas, 14 April 1908, para. 3.

year's yield of their land.[66] Extensive debt sales of grain were also noted by Taylor, the Collector of Bankura, in 1888. In a typical village in the 24 Parganas, the indebted families owed nearly the selling value of one year's crop on an average.[67]

The amount payable in grain was generally determined by its current money value. Hence, compulsory payments with interest at harvest time—when grain prices were lowest—inflated the mahajan's share. The creditors insisted on this condition of payment, and the lack of local markets and proper communication further forced the hands of the peasant.[68] Carstairs, the Deputy Commissioner of the Santhal Parganas, noted in this context: "The true power of the mahajan is, I think, his monopoly". The Collector of Monghyr reported: "crops are not sold to any extent . . . the mahajan takes payment in grain, taking care that the rate of valuation shall be well in his favour". Frequently, the liquor seller in Santhal villages was also a mahajan who credited drinks on the security of crops. During the dhan-cutting season he reaped a rich harvest, 4 an. worth of paddy being paid for two-pice worth of liquor.[69]

In Jessore, *bawardar*s (guards) were sent to keep a watch on the ripening crop. In the Pichasa estate of Bihar, the mahajans sent their bullocks to the threshing floor.[70] In Midnapur, officials collecting the water rate waited till the debtor-raiyat returned after selling his rice, for even a day's delay would oblige him to give priority to the mahajan's demands.[71] In the Rajmahal Hills, the mahajans sent outside labourers to cut and carry away the produce, i.e., the sabai grass grown by the Paharias. In the process,

66 *Dufferin Report*. From A. A. Wace, Collector of Bhagalpur, to Comm. Bhagalpur Div., dated Bhagalpur, 7 April, 1888.

67 Ibid., P. Nolan, Secy. to the Govt. of Bengal, to the Secy. to the Govt. of India, Rev. & Agri. Dept. para. 26. Darjeeling, 30 June 1888.

68 Ibid., From R. Carstairs, Offg. Dy. Comm., Santhal Parganas, to the Comm., Bhagalpur Div. and Santhal Parganas, Doomka, 6 April 1888, para. 12.

69 Ibid., Herbert Mosley, Collector Monghyr, to the Comm. Bhagalpur Div., no. 273 R, Monghyr, 3 May 1888, para. 3.

70 Chaudhuri, "Rural Credit Relations", p. 233.

71 Bengal Irrigation Proceedings, Jan. 1874, app. B, 28 July 1873, Dept. Rev., Superintendent of Canals, Midnapur, to Collector, Midnapore.

they grossly under–estimated and undervalued the produce in their *chukti* bonds (sale deeds of sabai grass) with the Paharias. Further profits were made by enlarging the sabai bundles with foreign substances when selling them to the Sahebganj contractors.[72] In Angul-Khondmals, the Mogulbandi dealers gave advances on the security of the crop, and carted it away immediately after reaping. In Parikud, one of the poorest tracts most liable to famine in the Jagirmahals of Puri, "the crops are generally forestalled. When they are harvested the creditors carry off the whole and the agriculturist has to begin again borrowing for his daily wants".[73] Where the creditor provided the land, the usual form of appropriation was a share of the produce or sharecropping, known as *adhiyari, bhagchash* or *bhagjote*. The creditor paid the rent and obtained generally a half share. In Birbhum, two-thirds of the produce was surrendered for the best lands. In this way, "a large amount of paddy comes into the mahajan's hand, nearly equivalent in value to the rental of the village".[74]

[c] Distraint of movable property

As the debt, accumulating with compound interest, began to exceed the peasant's meagre surplus, the form of appropriation changed. Besides the produce on his fields, the movable property of the peasant liable to be confiscated generally consisted of his agricultural implements, cattle and livestock, utensils and ornaments.

The problem was most acute in the tribal areas. For instance, the Santhals of the Damin-i-Koh, "under the police on the one hand and civil courts on the other, as manipulated by mahajan adventurers from Bhojpur in the Shahabad district, who

72 Bengal Revenue Proceedings, Sept. 1909, nos. 1–2. Report on the Petition of the Hill Manjhis of Parganas Teliagarhi and Tappa Madhuban Regarding the Dealings of the Mahajans in the Sabai Trade and proposals regarding the Future Management of the Trade, paras. 39 and 61.

73 *SR, Jagir Mahals, Puri* (1906–9), p. 8, para. 33.

74 *Dufferin Report,* From N. S. Alexander, Comm. Burdwan Div. to the Secy. to the Govt. of Bengal, Rev. Dept., no. 7 RG, Burdwan, 16 April 1888, para. 91.

systematically exploited them, were reduced to a condition of serfdom in which they could not call a bullock, a utensil, or even a grain of their produce their own".[75] The revised Civil Procedure Code of 1877, however, prohibited the attachment by creditors of the "implements of husbandry" and the "materials of an agriculturist's house or farm-building". Although the peasant could still be pressurised to sell or pawn the articles in order to pay his creditor, distraint of moveable property as a measure towards the recovery of debts became illegal and hence, risky. This, along with the growing land market and the rise in agricultural prices, shifted the focus to the debtor's land as the most valuable form of security.

[d] Sale or mortgage of land

The insatiable land hunger of the creditor, fostered by the ever-increasing debt obligations of the average peasant, led to a phenomenal increase in land sales at the end of the nineteenth century. It rose by about 500 per cent between 1885 and 1913, and by approximately 300 per cent between 1885 and 1904.

This upward trend in the sale and mortgage of raiyati holdings—whether at fixed rates or with occupancy rights—is reflected in the figures of the Registration Department, which show an increase of more than 50 per cent in the quinquennial period 1890–91 to 1894–95.[76] The total number of transfers in the Province increased by 166.3 per cent between 1883–93. It was least marked in the Presidency Division (41.8 per cent), and most so in Patna (626 per cent).[77] On the whole, the sale of raiyati holdings at fixed rates nearly doubled, and that of ordinary occupancy holdings nearly trebled, in the ten years preceding the famine of 1896–97.[78]

[75] LRP, Aug. 1898, pt. 1, nos. 56–57, "Land Transfer from the Agricultural to the Non-Agricultural Classes." W. B. Oldham, Comm. Chittagong Div. to the Secy., Board of Rev., Lower Provinces, 6 March, 1896.

[76] *Notes on the Administration of the Registration Dept. in Bengal, 1894–95* (Calcutta, 1895).

[77] LRP, Aug. 1894, Report on the Working of the Tenancy Act, pp. 5–6.

[78] *Triennial Report on the Administration of the Registration Dept.*

However, these and other statistics of the Registration Department regarding the sale and mortgage of peasant holdings are by no means precise.[79] They reflect the increasing trend, rather than the actual volume, of land sales and mortgages in Bengal in this period.

This trend, fostered as it was by secular forces such as the changes in the land-man ratio, the rising agricultural prices and the growing profitability of speculation in land, increased remarkably in years of scarcity and famine. For instance, though the number of registrations affecting immovable property went up successively throughout the 1890s, its rise was more pronounced (977,883 to 1,127,340) between 1895–96 and 1896–97 than in any previous year. This remarkable increase in land registrations in 1896–97 can be attributed to a great extent to the prevalence of the famine, and "affords some indication of the pressure felt by the people in the districts chiefly affected".[80]

---

in Bengal for the years ending 1898–99. Resolution of the Government, para. 12.

79 For instance, the number of sales and mortgages do not reflect the exact proportion of the lands transferred, in the absence of accurate information as to their size or area. Moreover, only a very small percentage of sales and mortgages were actually registered. In the tribal areas, the transfer of land to outsiders was illegal, and hence could not be registered. Even in the settled districts, as noted above, the transferability of land depended on 'local custom'. This was determined by the consent of the landlord—usually acquired by the payment of a considerable amount of purchase money, or salami. In cases where the landlord was particularly difficult and the demand for salami exorbitant, the purchaser often preferred to hold the land in *benami* (under a false name) instead of formally registering his name as the new owner. Registration was optional in case of transactions worth less than Rs.100 so that a large number of sales, especially of part-holdings, went unregistered. In case of remote villages, the expense and inconvenience of travelling to the Registration Office also acted as a deterrent.

80 *Notes on the Administration of the Registration Department in Bengal, 1896–97*, no. 497 P-D from C. W. Bolton, Chief Secy. to the Govt. of Bengal to the Secy., Govt. of India, Home Dept., Darjeeling. 24 Sept. 1897, paras. 3–6.

[1.5] Problem of land alienation to "non-agricultural classes"

This prolific increase in the transfer of raiyati holdings, most marked in years of scarcity and famine, opened up a very basic problem in agrarian relations regarding *(a)* the social composition of the new owners, and *(b)* the implications of the 'depeasantisation' process.

[a] The transferees: 'mahajan' or raiyat?

It was remarked that the power of alienation exercised by the raiyat was bringing in the moneylender or mahajan. Divisional statistics on the registered sales of occupancy holdings for the years 1883–84 and 1892–93, covering almost a decade, show the outlines of a distinctive pattern in the class composition of the new owners. Though the fixed-rate holdings were principally bought by the raiyats themselves, the mahajans also accounted for a considerable proportion of the purchasers, while they were second only to the raiyats in the purchase of occupancy holdings.[81] "Of these so-called mahajans however, but a small proportion were probably other than substantial raiyats themselves, for these are the chief moneylenders in rural Bengal".[82]

Indeed, the term 'mahajan' is rather vague. There was no clear line of distinction in effect between various social groups like the 'mahajans', 'landlords' and 'raiyats'. As noted earlier, many landowners and even raiyats with a small surplus lent grain or money to their tenants and neighbours, as it was the most profitable form of investment. "There is in such cases no sharp distinction between the raiyat who lends and the raiyat who borrows, and as a man's circumstances improve or deteriorate, he may pass year by year from the one class to the other".[83] The Collector of Noakhali notes the existence of resident raiyats

[81] Ibid., 1894–95, statement no. 13.
[82] LRP, Aug. 1894, p. 285, para. 14.
[83] Ibid. From E. V. Westmacott, Comm. Presidency Div. to the Sec. to the Board of Revenue, Lower Provinces, no. 53 R.L., Calcutta, 27 April 1893, para. 7.

"possessed of capital, who are partly actual cultivators and partly the suppliers of capital to dependent cultivators".[84]

These raiyat-mahajans found it much easier to conceal their purchases than the purely non-agricultural bania or trader, who would stand out more prominently in rural society and was much less likely to be permitted to remain unregistered.[85] Hence, for the latter "we may accept the registered transfers as including nearly all their transactions".[86] Meanwhile, even when the wealthy raiyats registered their purchase of occupancy rights, the stigma often attached to the term 'mahajan' induced many of them who lent money or grain as a side business, or even as the main profession, to define themselves as raiyats or proprietors, as long as they held some land in their possession. Inclusion among the group of 'raiyats' rather than 'mahajans' would also give them a better legal status in relation to their land. In fact, the unhindered right of subletting granted to occupancy raiyats by the tenancy legislation of 1859, was condoned and extended by implication even to non-resident holders of occupancy rights by the Act of 1885.[87] Hence, a large proportion of the purchasers were wealthy raiyat-mahajans, rather than traders or moneylenders belonging exclusively to the non-agricultural community. Even the statistics marginally reflect this trend, for between 1884–1893, the proportion of holdings transferred to mahajans proper fell from 14.2 to 12.8 per cent, while the transfers to raiyats rose approximately from 68 to 70 per cent.[88]

[b] The process of depeasantisation: eviction or social depression of the peasantry

The debtor raiyats were sometimes physically evicted by the new owners, but more frequently they remained as *burgadars*

84 Quoted by Ashok Sen, "Agrarian Structure and Tenancy Laws in Bengal, 1850–1900", in *Perspectives in Social Sciences* (Calcutta: Centre for Studies in Social Studies and Oxford University Press, 1982), 2: p. 65.

85 LRP, Aug. 1894, Report on the Working of the Tenancy Act, p. 5.

86 ibid. Letter from F. W. Duke, Offg. Collector of Hooghly to the Comm., Burdwan Div., no.127, Hooghly Collectorate, 20 April 1893, para. 8.

87 Ashok Sen, "Agrarian Structure", p. 24.

88 LRP, Aug. 1894, p. 286.

(sharecroppers) on their old lands. Often this practice was resorted to by the mahajan as a cover or a "protective measure against the zamindars attempting to oust him from the holdings".[89] This forced a distinct change in the social status of the peasant, and destroyed all incentives to expand or improve cultivation. His financial position naturally worsened as the purchaser, having to pay the full former rent, made more stringent terms with his under-tenants than before. These terms were generally batai, bhaoli or barga. Though agricultural prices soared, such produce-payments, unlike cash rents, were not subject to restraints; hence they suited the interests of the purchaser, who had bought the land as an investment. It would also relieve the non-resident owners from the onus of direct cultivation, while ensuring a sizeable share of the crop. As the Collector of Dacca noted, the increasing volume of rural indebtedness and the bargadari system were the twin evils which gnawed at the very basis of rural society in this period.[90]

This process of depeasantisation, i.e. the eviction or social depression of the average small peasant, was apparent in the different economic regions: (i) in tribal areas like the Chittagong Hills, Santhal Parganas, or the fringe settlements in Birbhum and Midnapur; (ii) in the settled but backward districts like Bhagalpur, Purnea or Champaran; (iii) and even in relatively prosperous areas like the Dacca and Chittagong Divisions.

(i) In tribal areas, it was most pronounced wherever the transactions were not inter pares (among equals), as between the plainsmen and hillmen of Chittagong; the Bhojpuris, bazaar-traders and the Santhals; or the Marwaris and the Rajbansis and Koches of British Sikkim and Jalpaiguri.

The Hindu proprietors and big farmers were fast usurping the lands of the tribals and Muslims of Chittagong, though never as actual cultivators. In March 1896, W. B. Oldham, Commissioner of the Chittagong Division, noted a case in which a well-known

89 Ibid., p. 314. Extract from the Progs. of the Managing Committee Meeting of the Rajshahi Association, 3 June 1893. Enclosure in letter no. 526, dt. Rajshahi Association, 6 June 1893. From Babu S. C. Moitra, Secy., Rajshahi Association, to the Collector of Rajshahi.

90 *SR, Dacca*, p. 76.

shopkeeper in Chittagong appealed to the Special Judge and acquired occupancy rights of some lands which he had never even seen. This process, as Oldham observed, "is in progress at an increasing pace".[91]

In the Santhal Parganas, land sales increased remarkably since Regulation III of 1872 recognised tenant rights, and guaranteed security of tenure and fixity of rent. Interest on debts was limited to 24 per cent per annum, and compound interest was abolished. Yet, occupancy rights became negotiable assets, with the help of which the village usurer could easily circumvent the new usury laws. In effect, it was "of no avail to restrict interest to 24 per cent if you allow a raiyat to part with his land in payment of his debts".[92]

Within ten years of the settlement, 10,000 court sales and 40,000 private sales of raiyati holdings were noted. Lands settled by Regulation III of 1872 with the Santhal headmen and cultivators were alienated to moneylenders from Bengal and Shahabad. In Pakaur subdivision, sales and mortgages increased fivefold between 1874 and 1879.[93] In 1882 the Deputy Commissioner, Oldham, observed that the bazaar traders of Dumka had gradually absorbed all the Santhal settlements in the area. A large tract of about 450 sq miles of raiyati land in Handwe, had also passed into the hands of their creditors. The "sale question" became one of grave political importance, especially in Deoghar subdivision, between 1878–86.[94] In the Damin-i-Koh, the raiyats, in collusion with the headman, sold out or sublet large portions of their lands to "foreigners".[95] All this demoralised the peasants, as noted in the Annual Reports on the administration of civil justice in the district since 1878.

Mr Barlow's letter no. 1164 R of 28 June 1877, para. 3, mentions a class of speculators who "take up villages solely to

[91] LRP, Aug. 1898, from W. B. Oldham, Comm. Chittagong Div., to the Secy. to the Board of Revenue, Lower Provinces, no. 2, Camp Feni, 6 March 1896, para. 17.

[92] *SR, Santhal Parganas*, para. 37.

[93] Bengal Survey and Settlement Proceedings, May 1880.

[94] *SR, Santhal Parganas*, p. 45, para. 37.

[95] LRP, Feb. 1894, no. 1363 R, Rajmahal, 27 Feb. 1893, from W. H. H. Vincent, S.D.O., Rajmahal, to the Dy. Comm., Santhal Parganas.

make money, and they have the ghatwals with them, as they pay large salaries". The raiyats were oppressed till they abandoned their lands, which were then sold to speculators. The settlement-holder sometimes enriched himself, but was more often a mere instrument in the hands of some moneylender for squeezing the village.[96]

Many of the mul raiyats, *manjhis* or *pradhans* (headmen) claimed lands on the basis of early investments as pioneers. Actually, the original settlers were mostly Santhals, who were driven out by the claimants, nearly all of whom were zamindar Babhans, and many of them moneylenders by trade. For instance, a large proportion of the lands registered at Deoghar were those of Tularam and Ananda Rai, who were very influential moneylenders. Any improvements made by them on the lands were no doubt effected by forced labour, rather than pioneering zeal.[97]

Numerous cases of sale and rack-renting of village lands by the mul raiyats, who held occupancy rights unlike the *thikadar* (lessee), came to light during the enquiry on the subject after 1886. The number of holdings transferred during the twenty-five years between the first settlement (1872) and the next (1898) was 212,476.[98] Sales were disguised mostly as mortgages in which the use of the land paid for the interest alone, or as a form of sublease, the raiyat having little hope of ever clearing his debt.

[96] A typical case was that of Mahta Manjhi Santhal, headman of village Nowka Chibutia, taluk Pathrol, Deoghar Subdivision. He sold six bighas of rice land, probably the pick of the whole village, along with 1¼ bighas of *bari* land (upland) to a Muslim outsider, Johardin Miya of Rampur, for Rs. 400; ignoring the interests of the sixteen Santhal raiyats and one kamar who inhabited the village. According to the *mul raiyat* (headman), "I offered land to the raiyats for sale, but they would not pay me for it. Therefore, I sold it to this Mussalman". But the raiyats were entitled to get settlement of the land sold, without cess or premium. The rental, Rs. 6 – 6 an., at fifteen years' purchase, was increased to four times the rate by the premium. (LRP Nov. 1894, nos. 9–10, no. 2010 R, Dumka, 13 Aug. 1894. From R. Carstairs, Dy. Comm., Santhal Parganas, to the Comm., Bhagalpur Div. & Santhal Parganas).

[97] Ibid.

[98] *SR Santhal Parganas*, p. 75, para. 67.

Both of these were as good to the mahajan as outright sales. It is significant that of the area covered by various forms of transfer—that is, sale, mortgage, re-settlement, relinquishment to headmen, sublease and new settlements—the percentage of eviction was 5, 100, 10, 25, 4 and 1, respectively.[99]

The Santhals numbered most in the districts bordering on Chotanagpur and the Santhal Parganas. In Midnapur, the Santhals and Kurmi Mahtos were the principal aboriginal and semi-aboriginal tribes. Though the statistics available can never be exact enough to show the full extent of lands lost, they definitely indicate a steady process of land transfers from the aborigine to the *dikku* (alien) or Bengali element in these regions during the twenty years from 1893 to 1913.[100] The total transfer of 20,892 bighas by the aborigine population, minus the transfers to them of 8,836 bighas, shows a net loss of 12,056 bighas, or 74.02 per cent of the total area transferred since 1893.[101]

These facts highlight several interesting aspects of the problem of land transfers in tribal areas. It is very dificult to gauge the enormity of land loss by the tribals, due to the simultaneous process of reclamation by them. Usually, the Santhals or other aborigines and semi-aborigines parted with the lands of superior quality, and retained the worst or marginal lands. In villages like Dharampur and Debdattapur, where the proprietor was also a mahajan , the degree of dispossession was particularly high. The mahajan coveted such conveniently located lands, as they lay close to his home base, or to the nearest market town. The Santhal sold his land at a very low price, generally between Rs. 10 and 20 per bigha. He had little idea as to the value of his land, and the mahajan invariably dictated the terms. The very low percentage of usufructuary mortgages, by which the land reverted to the mortgagor after a fixed period, clearly reflects the greed of the mahajan, who was intent on permanently possessing the land.[102]

99 Ibid., para. 71.

100 LRP, Dec. 1914, unofficial note no. 61/7 5238, dt. 27 June 1914, para. 12, apps. D and E.

101 Ibid., app. F.

102 For further details on land transfers in tribal areas, see M. Chakrabarti, "Alienation of Raiyati Holdings in Nineteenth

The Paharias inhabiting the Rajmahal Hills in Pakaur, Santhal Parganas, were even more ignorant and helpless in the face of outside intrusion. They were not conscious of their occupancy rights in the land, and considered them to be temporary holdings dependent on the will of the manjhi. The latter would appropriate their lands or sell them outright to alien mahajans and also to the Santhals, who had already reclaimed the foothills and were now fast encroaching on the lower slopes. In 1899 it was discovered, for instance, that about 35,000 acres planted with sabai were being worked by outside labour employed by the Sahebganj traders, to whom the hillmen had alienated their occupancy rights. No Paharia had ever reported or complained of this extensive alienation, which, therefore, went unnoticed. Faced with the problem of encroachment by outsiders, and hedged in by the forest conservancy rules which expressly discouraged their wasteful methods of jhum or *kurwa* cultivation, the Paharias existed almost on a starvation-level entitlement.[103]

Like the Santhals and Paharias, the Meches and Garos too were being driven from lands cultivated by them, as more and more areas in the Duars region were being taken up for tea plantations.[104] In 1915, the Rev. L. Barber of the Baptist Mission, Susang, pointed out that many Garo villages in which the mission had worked fifteen years ago no longer existed. The Hindus and Muslims coming from Dacca and beyond offered much higher prices for land than the Garos, and thus secured them. Meanwhile, the Garos, burdened by the high rates of interest charged by the moneylenders and weighed down by the pressure of the tanka system of produce rent, were often obliged to "throw up" their lands.[105]

Century Bengal", in *Retrieving Bengal's Past: Society and Culture in the Nineteenth and Twentieth Centuries,* ed. Ranjit Roy (Calcutta: Rabindra Bharati University, 1995), pp. 96–124.

103 LRP, Aug. 1899., nos. 148–49, 1614 R, dated Dumka, 1 July 1899. From R. Carstairs, Dy. Comm., Santhal Parganas, to the Comm., Bhagalpur Div. & Santhal Parganas.

104 Ibid., Aug. 1895, Br. Land Revenue.

105 Ibid., Sept. 1916. no. 475, dated Mymensingh, 15 Feb. 1915. From J. Land, Collector of Mymensingh, to the Comm., Dacca Div.

In the Terai region in Darjeeling, firms of Marwari mahajans and others acquired jotes from the Rajbansis not to cultivate the land, but to place "an agent in charge to screw as much rental as possible from their under-tenants". Studying a selected area in the Terai, it was seen that approximately one-eighth of the tract was owned by non-residents—mostly Muslims and mahajans.[106]

In 1885, Oldham observed that due to the sale by public auctions, "the purchaser, who thereby gets an indefeasible title and easy possession, has been a member of the foreign money-lending class in every case, and the cases have been numerous".[107]

The opening up of Chotanagpur by the land survey and settlement and the introduction of the Bengal Nagpur Railway was also marked, as has been noted above, with the intrusion of alien capital and the growth of a land market. In the Kolhan, for instance, the number of non-Kols more than doubled in the twenty-four years between 1867 and 1891.[108]

Alien credit gradually expropriated the land, labour and produce of the tribals. The persistent rise in agricultural prices further fostered this trend. In many cases, the mahajan financed the tenant to fight the zamindar's attempts in enhancing the rent by 5 per cent, only to attach, sell and purchase his holding and sublet it to him again at twice the rent. Thus, the problem of land alienation in its various forms depressed the raiyats to the status of under-tenants or even kamias, while the percentage of non-occupancy raiyats was already high due to their habit of shifting cultivation. The practice of alienating land to the mahajan took root so deeply, that even service tenures like *baigai* lands held by the village priest passed into the hands of the moneylender. Transfers were in fact much more extensive than noted, for they were mostly made on stamp paper or by verbal arrangements, and were rarely registered.[109] Under the pressure of circumstances, the raiyats, especially in the southern tappas,

[106] Ibid., Nov. 1894, p. 1202; note by Mr Morsehead, para. 64.

[107] Ibid., Nov. 1894; extract from no. 1449 G of 14 Feb. 1885, from the Dy. Comm., W. B. Oldham, to the Comm.

[108] Ibid., July 1894, Rev. Dept., Br. Land Revenue, no. 272 R, 25 July 1892. From R. H. Renny, Dy. Comm., Singhbhum, to the Comm. Chotanagpur Div., paras. 10–11.

[109] *SR, Palamau,* pp. 27–28, paras. 93, 94, 98.

absconded in lean seasons to Assam, the Duars and other regions, forfeiting even their occupancy rights.[110]

(ii) In the longer-settled but poor districts as in north Bihar and Orissa, the problem differed not in essence but only in emphasis, for here the raiyat-mahajans rather than alien credit played the crucial role.

In Patna Division, North Bihar, the increase in transfers of occupancy holdings is apparent from the following, which include the figures for 1883–84 and 1892–93 for each district.

TABLE 24
Number of Transactions

District	*1883–84*	*1892–93*
Patna	77	646
Gaya	173	232
Shahabad	73	28
Muzaffarpur	988	5224
Darbhanga	356	1368
Saran	39	152
Champaran	261	6599

Source: LRP, Aug. 1894, p. 286, para. 17.

Significantly, the registration figures are low for the southern districts of the division, in comparison with the famine-prone rice tracts of the north.

In Muzaffarpur, the landlords, especially those other than the landlords of the holdings sold, acquired more than three times the number of lands transferred to mahajans. This may partly be explained by the existence of a large number of indigo planters in the district, who were interested in buying up the occupancy holdings. However, at least some of these 'other landlords' and many of the 'raiyat' purchasers must have belonged to the "large class of small village mahajans—well-to-do cultivators, who gradually absorb their poorer neighbours' occupancy rights". The enormous increase in the percentage of sales and mortgages of properties below Rs. 100 (173 and 227 per cent respectively) between the quinquennial period 1880–

110 LRP, Jan. 1900, Br. Land Rev., p. 98. From Thomson, Dy. Comm. Singhbhum, to the Comm. Chotanagpur Div.

85 to 1887–92, further reflects the improverishment and declining entitlement-level of the lower class of cultivators.[111]

In Champaran, land transfers to non-agricultural classes had reached a "serious extent". The number of transfers "grew twenty-five fold in the ten years following 1883–84".[112] Here, unlike in Muzaffarpur, the moneylenders generally came from the non resident trading community.[113] Even the so-called raiyat purchasers were, almost to a man, the "*mahajan's* land grabbers, pure and simple".[114] It was noted in 1897 that out of 160,000 holdings attested, no less than 14,000 had within the past ten years been affected wholly or partially by sales and mortgages. Of the 14,000 purchasers, no less than 40 per cent belonged to the mahajan class, who did not directly cultivate the land but made their living mainly by moneylending and trading, and "let out any land they acquired to *raiyats* to cultivate for them".[115] They often operated through intermediaries who oppressed the peasants, and reduced the debtor raiyats to the condition of bonded labourers.[116]

Saran had a smaller number of land transfers in general. Yet, even within these limits, "it is evident that the tendency is for the land to pass from the hands of the purely agricultural classes, the Koeris and Kurmis and Ahirs, to the hands of the Brahmans and Rajputs and Banias, who, though agricultural, are more

[111] Ibid., Aug. 1894, no. 1089 R, dated Camp Muzaffarpur, 29 Jan. 1894. From A. Forbes, Comm., Patna Div., to the Secy. to the Board of Revenue, L. P., paras. 4, 6.

[112] Ibid., Aug. 1898, W. B. Oldham, Comm. Chittagong Division, to the Secy. to the Board of Revenue, P.P., no. 2, Camp Feni, 6 March 1896.

[113] Ibid., Aug. 1894, Report on the Working of the Tenancy Act, p. 8, para. 19.

[114] Ibid., Aug. 1894, no. 1089 R, dated Camp Muzaffarpur, 29 Jan. 1894. From A. Forbes, Comm. Patna Div. to the Secy. to the Board of Revenue, L.P.

[115] Ibid., Aug. 1898. Correspondence on Land Transfers from the Agricultural to the Non Agricultural Classes, no. 58. From M. Finucane, Secy. to the Govt. of Bengal, Rev. Dept., to the Secy. to the Govt. of India, Rev. & Agri. Dept., no. 2296 L.R., Calcutta, 30 July 1897, sec. 3, para. 13.

[116] Ibid., Aug. 1894, no. 25, dated Bethiah, 13 April 1893. From J. G. Cumming, S.D.O. Bethiah, to the Collector, Champaran.

prone to carry on their work by hired labour or to underlet their holdings".[117] Most of the important mahajans at Mirganj had acquired a great deal of land in this way.

In Bhagalpur, sales exceeded mortgages by 30 per cent, the area sold being double the mortgaged lands. Significantly, more than two-fifths of the total area transferred (50,000 acres) lay in Supaul subdivision. The moneylenders constituted 23 per cent of the purchasers in Supaul and 16.5 per cent in Madhipura, as against 13 per cent in the other thanas. These statistics reflect a distinct tendency towards encroachment by the moneylenders during lean seasons, as in the years immediately preceding the survey in Bhagalpur. Significantly, the raiyats were most deeply indebted to the moneylenders in Supaul-Madhipura, the traditional famine zone of Bhagalpur.[118]

In Purnea, mortgages and part-sales fetched a higher price than sales of entire holdings, as in the former case the creditor or buyer could choose the best lands, the raiyat preferring to raise as much money as he could by parting with the smallest possible area. Of the transferees, 9 per cent were moneylenders and 87 per cent raiyats, though, as noted, these class divisions were not mutually exclusive.

In Orissa, the problem of land sales was no less acute. In Puri district, it was seen that "many of the villages are bought up by large mahajans and by the land owners".[119] In the Jagirmahals, only a few of the transfers of raiyati lands were registered at the settlement in 1906, most of which passed on to the local mahajans. In Parikud, the sale of occupancy rights increased with the rising value of land.[120] In the Kanika Ward's Estate, Cuttack, the area of raiyati holdings sold increased more than two and a half times and four times in case of *thani* (resident) and *pahi* (non-resident) raiyats respectively, between 1882–90.[121]

(iii) Even in the third economic zone, that is, the most prosperous regions like Dacca and Chittagong, the sale of peasant

[117] Ibid., Aug. 1898. From the Settlement Officer, Saran, to the Director of the Land Records and Agriculture, Bengal, no. 381, dated Siwan, 16/17 Sept. 1895.

[118] *SR, Bhagalpur,* pp. 128–29, para. 238.

[119] *DG: Puri,* p. 214.

[120] *SR, Jagir Mahals in Puri,* p. 16.

[121] *SR, Kanika Wards' Estate,* p. 57, para. 150.

holdings increased fast. For instance, in 1896–97 and 1897–98, Chittagong registered the second-highest number of sales of fixed-rate holdings in the Province. Similarly, Tipperah had the highest number of sales of occupancy holdings, while Mymensingh came third in sequence. In fact, after the Presidency and Burdwan Divisions, the number of land registrations were highest in Dacca and Chittagong.[122]

The buyers were often professional mahajans and less-regular moneylenders, mostly Brahmins. Even more prominent were the rival landholders or talukdars who competed with each other in acquiring new properties and resettling them at enhanced rates. In Chittagong, Tipperah and Noakhali, the practice of such private creditors and landowners attaching and selling raiyati lands had become very common.[123] Transfers went on in many forms. In Bakarganj, for example, a peculiar kind of transfer was noted in the Tushkhali Estate. Usury being a vice according to Islamic Law, the Muslim mahajans here would only lend money if the debtor raiyat made a fictitious transfer of the whole or a part of his holding and paid interest for the loan under the name of rent, which often exceeded the limits imposed by section 48 of the Bengal Tenancy Act.[124]

[1.6] Need for socio-economic reform rather than legislation to avert land transfers

This problem of increasing sales and transfers of raiyati holdings had several interesting facets. The prohibition or restriction of such transfers except in tribal areas could be detrimental to the raiyat's interest, as it would impair his credit both with the mahajan and landlord. In fact, he might be better able to survive

[122] *Notes on Administration of the Registration Dept. in Bengal*, 1896–97, no. 497 P.-D. From C. W. Bolton, Chief Secy. to the Govt. of Bengal, to the Govt. of India, Home Dept., Darjeeling, 24 Sept. 1897, para. 6; Ibid., 1897–98, no. 429 P.-D. From C. W. Bolton to the Home Dept., Darjeeling, 24 Sept. 1898.

[123] LRP, Aug. 1898. From W. B. Oldham, Comm., Chittagong Div., to the Secy. to the Board of Rev., L.P., no. 2, Camp Feni, 6 March 1896.

[124] Ibid., Nov. 1899, Br. Land Rev., pp. 1729–31. *SR, Tushkhali in Bakarganj* (1894–98), by P. M. Basu (Calcutta: BS Press, 1898).

in years of stress with adequate loans or remissions of rent on the security of his land.

If, however, his credit failed despite such loans and remissions, the peasant in the last resort could either sell his land, or be evicted by the landlord. The raiyat would benefit if sale was allowed; he would then be able to realise the full value of his land minus the salami, and pay back his loan or rent arrears from it. Non-saleability, on the other hand, would reduce the value of the land to a great extent and force the peasant to give up a larger proportion of it. In case of eviction, the landlord would realise his dues, but the peasant would be left a pauper. Moreover, the real value of land would continue to rise, benefitting the new owner.[125] Thus, if the raiyati lands became non-saleable, "what they (the zamindars) now give a high price for, they will get for nothing by a right of lapse to be created by statute".[126]

Due to these reasons, attempts were made to restrict rather than totally prohibit the sale of peasant holdings. As noted, the sale of land was to be sanctioned by "local custom", in order to ensure that the practice was not introduced in areas where it was hitherto rare or unknown.

In effect, however, this would only deprive the raiyat of a considerable amount of the sale proceeds, which went to the zamindar in the form of a salami.

It was further suggested in bureaucratic circles that the right of land transfer be restricted by prohibiting only mortgages and part-sales of raiyati holdings. The indebted raiyat generally handed over to the mahajan the most fertile part of his holding, retaining only the inferior land from the income of which he was unable to pay his rent and interest, and was eventually sold

125 The returns given in the Board of Revenue's letter no. 800A, dated 20 June 1894, show that occupancy rights selling at 9.6 years' purchase in 1883–84 had risen to 13.5 years' purchase in 1892–93, and would go up to 15 years' purchase approximately by the end of the century.

126 LRP, Aug. 1898, pt. 1. Note on Land Transfers from the Agricultural to the Non-Agricultural Classes, no. 56–57. From P. Nolan, Comm., Rajshahi Div., to the Secy. to the Board of Rev., L.P., no. 1020 T, Camp Dankimari, Jalpaiguri, 12 Feb. 1896, paras. 5–6.

up.[127] Yet such a restriction would, in fact, force the raiyat to resort to the extreme measure of selling all his land. To allow a raiyat to sell his entire holding but not to mortgage or sell part of it, would be to prevent him from tiding over a temporary need or calamity except by selling all he had, and thus ruining himself for ever.[128]

Yet another suggestion was to limit all sales to the agricultural classes, so that there would be less scope for the ousting of peasants by moneylenders and absentee speculators.[129] Yet this would narrow the field of competition and deprive the peasant from getting the full value of his land, especially in lean seasons, when all agriculturists would be financially hard-pressed to a greater or lesser extent, and hence could not afford to buy land at its proper price.

In fact, the wealthy raiyats and landed proprietors often presented a greater threat to the small peasant, than the moneylender or purely non-agricultural class. Their encroachments on occupancy lands may be studied from different angles. In the settled districts of north Bihar like Saran and Muzaffarpur, for instance, the "de-peasantisation" process during 1885–95 was caused "not by an invasion of non-agriculturists, but by the natural increase in the population of landlords, who gradually crowd out their poorer neighbours".[130] In Saran, many petty landholders preferred to buy up occupancy holdings in lieu of their interests in revenue-paying estates, for the latter, often being shares in joint properties, were

[127] Ibid., Aug. 1894, no. 179 G., dated Motihari, 8 May 1893. From W. Dunbar Blyth, Collector Champaran, to the Comm., Patna Div., Bankipore.

[128] Ibid., Aug. 1898, nos. 56–57. From R. C. Dutt, Offg. Comm. of Orissa Div. to the Secy. to the Govt. of Bengal, Rev. Dept., no. 124 R, dated Cuttack, 1 Feb. 1896, paras. 20–21.

[129] Ibid., Aug. 1894, no. 179 G, dated Motihari, 8 May 1893. From W. Dunbar Blyth, Collector Champaran, to the Comm., Patna Div., Bankipore, para. 17. Dunbar Blyth went so far as to propose that occupancy rights be extinguished as soon as a peasant holding passed into the hands of the "non-agricultural classes—the *mahajan,* the *vakil* and the *mukhtar*".

[130] Ibid., Aug. 1898. From P. C. Lyon, Offg. Director of the Dept. of Land Records and Agri., Bengal, to the Secy. to the Board of Rev., L.P., no. 19235, dated Calcutta, 31 July 1896, para. 13.

threatened by the intrigues of their stronger partners.[131] E. V. Westmacott, Commissioner of the Presidency Division, noted in 1893: "I have found that *raiyati* holdings have been bought up by *zamindars,* especially by those who possess only a fractional share in *zamindari* estates".[132]

Rival landlords also vied for occupancy rights in order to spite each other. In Bakarganj, for example, landlords grabbed the occupancy rights of holdings under neighbouring zamindars, under cover of the infamous *"zimha"* system peculiar to this district.[133]

The zamindar was frequently a keener purchaser than the mahajan for, unlike the latter, it was often worth his while to buy the occupancy rights in order to extinguish them. In Muzaffarpur, for instance, raiyati holdings sold in execution of money decrees in the munsifs' courts went down from 59 to 25 between 1888–89 and 1891–92, while those sold out for rent decree increased from 153 to 384 in the same period. Landlords were frequent purchasers in the latter cases; in case of the former, they succeeded in preventing 95 per cent of the auction-purchasers, usually moneylenders, from taking possession of the land on the ground that there was no local custom of transferring occupancy rights.[134] In Burdwan Division, too, the returns for 1883–84 show that mahajans purchased no more than one in seven holdings, and were in most cases cultivators themselves.[135] The Collector of Mymensingh noted: "the *mahajan* is, in this district, driven into the background by the *zamindar.* The former

131 Chaudhuri, "The Process of Depeasantization," Sec. 4d, p. 134.

132 LRP, Aug. 1894, no. 53 R.L., dated Calcutta, 27 April 1893. From E. V. Westmacott, Comm., Presidency Div., to the Secy. to the Board of Rev., L.P.

133 By it, a landlord would win over some of his opponent's tenants, nominally buy their holdings, and resort to force in order to defend these tenants in refusing rent payments to their original zamindar, thereby hurting his prestige. LRP, Aug. 1894, no. 3855 L.R., dated Barisal, 31 March 1893. From H. Savage, Collector, Bakarganj, to the Secy. to the Board of Rev., L.P., paras. 10–11.

134 Ibid., Aug. 1894, no. 19, dated Muzaffarpur, 10 March 1893. From Babu Poorno Chundra Mitra, Roy Bahadur, Munsif, 1st Court, Muzaffarpur, to the Collector of Muzaffarpur.

135 Ibid., Aug. 1898. From R. C. Dutt, Comm. Orissa Div., to the Secy. to the Govt. of Bengal, Dept. no. 124 R., dated Cuttack, 1 Feb. 1896.

consequently frequently appears in the form of a mortgagee like the zarpeshgidar of Bihar, but not often as a purchaser of a *raiyat's* holding".[136]

The abolition of land transfers, especially to the non-agricultural classes, would further strengthen the landlords by removing the competition of the purely business interests. The risk would be particularly severe in certain areas such as the indigo-planting districts of Bihar, or districts in which the big farmers were responsible for the reclamation of new lands. The indigo factories, being cultivators themselves, would be able to buy up the raiyats' interests at a far cheaper rate than in a competitive land market. It stood to reason, therefore, that the Secretary to the Bihar Indigo Planters' Association was greatly in favour of giving all tenants a free right of transfer and of limiting the salami paid to the landlord.[137] Likewise, large landowners associated with the reclamation process reinforced their position as creditors with rights of occupancy in these lands. In Rangpur, for instance, "these big cultivators [chukanidars] are becoming worse than the ordinary middlemen. This new and growing class of big cultivators . . . is a greater menace to the agricultural community".[138]

[136] Ibid., 1894, no. 1828 G, dated Mymensingh, 12/14 Aug. 1893. From A. Earle, Collector Mymensingh, to the Secy. to the Board of Revenue, L.P.

[137] Ibid., Aug. 1894. Report on the Working of the Tenancy Act, p. 7, para. 18. Significantly enough, the transfers to "other landlords" was more than three times as numerous as the sales to mahajans in a district like Muzaffarpur, where indigo planters flourished. Under-raiyats in Muzaffarpur had part-interests in 5.3 per cent of the holdings, and held only about 4.1 per cent of the total occupied area. The Settlement Officer remarks: "These figures are low enough, but if it is further remembered that a considerable proportion of even this small number of under-raiyats are indigo factories who have taken land from *raiyats* on kurtauli leases for the cultivation of indigo, the dangerous inaccuracy of those who believe that land in Tirhut is to a large extent being absorbed by *mahajaṇs* and sublet to the real cultivators at rack rents, is clearly demonstrated". (*DG: Muzaffarpur*, p. 118.)

[138] *Report of the Floud Commission*, vol. 69 (Calcutta, 1940). Evidence of the Manager of the Estate of the Nawab of

Thus, abolition or restriction of the transfer of raiyati holdings was too simplistic a solution for such a complex problem. Whether the sale of their lands was legitimised or not, the peasants could not escape eviction and exploitation by the richer classes, as long as they were economically backward. In fact, non-saleability of their lands would further reduce their exchange entitlement, by depriving them of the exchange value of their prime asset. Not arbitrary regulations, but only subtle reforms from within could improve their economic status and give them the staying power necessary to retain their lands in years of stress.

[2] *Rent Relations*

[2.1] Subdivisions and fragmentation of land

The root of the problem went deep into the system of land tenure and rent. In the late nineteenth century, sales and laws of inheritance, especially in case of the Muslim community, led rapidly to the splintering of estates and the multiplication of shares in land.[139] This trend was fostered by a growing spirit of individualism, as opposed to the old system of joint control of property.

The following table for thirteen selected districts in Bengal indicates that the number of estates on the revenue roll more than doubled in the forty years between 1851 and 1891.

Murshidabad. Similar tendencies are seen in Chittagong, especially in newly cultivated tracts like the Noabad taluks of Old Thana Ramu, where the itmamdars controlled large tracts of waste lands, requiring heavy initial investments in terracing, embankments and drainage. (LRP, March 1894, no. 1803 G.S. Chittagong, 22 Sept. 1892. From C. G. H. Allen, Settlement Officer, Chittagong, to the Director of the Dept. of Land Records and Agriculture, Bengal.)

139 LRP, Aug. 1894, no. 3855 L.R., dated Barisal, 31 March 1893; from H. Savage, Collector Bakarganj, to the Secy. to the Board of Revenue, l.P.

TABLE 25

Fragmentation of Estates in Bengal, 1851–1891

District	*Total no. of estates on the revenue roll*		
	1850–51	*1871–72*	*1891–92*
1	*2*	*3*	*4*
Patna	4,777	6,220	9,984
Gaya	4,635	1,588	6,044
Shahabad	3,468	4,907	7,260
Saran	3,767	3,590	4,703
Champaran		896	1,173
Muzaffarpur	5,186	13,432	18,422
Darbhanga			11,425
Bhagalpur	3,007	4,422	4,551
Monghyr	3,563	4,156	7,072
Dacca	8,487	8,864	8,903
Cuttack	2,417	3,572	4,173
Faridpur	165	3,028	5,970
Mymensingh	5,377	6,307	7,357
Total	44,849	63,979	97,039

Source: LRP, April 1895, p. 1628.

The situation in parts of north Bihar most effectively illustrates the minute subdivisions of property being effected in the Province. In 1870, the average size of an estate in Tirhut was 303 acres, which came down to 93 acres in Muzaffarpur during the settlement of 1907. "The minuteness of proprietary interests does not end here, for innumerable sub-divisions of even these petty estates are common, many of them being split up among different sets of sharers according to a private partition". In one case, it was found that a village of 179 acres contained three estates partitioned by their 159 proprietors into 114 sub-estates.[140] Such private partitions, again, led to the splitting of properties in Saran to the extremely low average of 14 acres per sharer. There was a regular scale to determine the minutest interests held—the smallest fragment, a *khanwa*, was about 59-millionth part of the estate. Even smaller fractions, representing a *ken* or 1/73,728,000,000,000 of an estate, were noted during the attestation in 1896–97.[141] In north Monghyr, the splitting of

[140] *DG: Muzaffarpur,* p. 118.
[141] Ibid., *Saran*, p. 120.

estates reached a point of absurdity. Each square mile contained 1,361 plots and 400 holdings in Teghra, and 1,066 plots and 291 holdings in Begusarai, the smallest fraction registered being 1/2,480,000,000 of an anna. In a half-acre plot, there were 1,582 co-sharers, each share thus amounting to 0.00036 of an acre, or 7¼ sq ft. Comparing the above statistics, it appears that "in respect of the minute sub-division of proprietory interests, Teghra and Begusarai easily surpass the rest of North Bihar".[142]

Subdivisions of land led not only to fragmentation, but also to the complex and scattered nature of landed property in general. Shares of estates were bought or inherited piecemeal, little attempt being made to ensure compactness or cohesion in the process. This involved pattern is most apparent in the survey records of Bakarganj and Faridpur. In Bakarganj, "it is rare for any village, however small, to be included in a single private estate, while many villages contain a portion of a large number of estates".[143] Within each village, again, lands belonging to different estates were not "geographically compact"; they consisted, rather, of a collection of "detached parcels" at distant points. Moreover, only a few estates held all their lands in severalty: some possessed only an undivided fractional interest in their entire area.[144]

[2.2] Effect on the landed interests

Such minute, ad hoc subdivisions of an estate adversely affected both the proprietor and the tenant.

[a] It would place the owner of a very small share in the position of a mere cultivator. "His actual landed property is so small, that unless he draws from it the entire profit of the produce, without the intervention of a tenant, he cannot both pay his revenue and support his family".[145] As in most districts, the extension of cultivation had reached the limit while subdivisions of property continued, so that the position of the

142 *SR, Monghyr, North*, p. 24, para. 73; p. 90, para. 288.
143 *SR, Bakarganj*, p. 61, para. 160.
144 Ibid.
145 LRP, April 1895, p. 1524. Note by Mr. Lane, Junior Secy. to the Board of Revenue, paras. 31 and 32, dated 4 May 1864.

petty proprietor became increasingly "serious".[146] They could neither afford any improvements on their land, nor withstand the effects of even a single crop failure.

Threatened by these problems and by the intrigues of their stronger co-sharers, the petty proprietors were often sold up, thus being reduced to the position of under-tenants, or migrating to towns in search of other professions. Sometimes, again, they disposed of their lands in favour of occupancy holdings, as seen most frequently in the districts of north Bihar. Sharers of zamindari and hereditary tenures also tried to supplement their dwindling income from land by directly encroaching on raiyati holdings, or by raising their rents. The Collector of Monghyr wrote: "Directly petty maliks are put in possession of their putties by partition proceedings, they try and convert it all into khud kasht or kamat, ejecting right and left. This minute subdivision is a positive curse to the tenantry".[147] In fact, these petty proprietors and tenure-holders were more often a greater threat to the small peasant than the trader or moneylender. This reminds one of the greater intensity with which the local Kanbi peasant, rather than the alien shahukar, was hated by the Bhil agriculturists in eastern Gujarat. The former had an eye on the peasants' land, while the latter was a "relatively distant figure" confining his interests to credit transactions.[148] The Darbhanga Gazetteer notes: "it is a proverb in the district that the small proprietor is the harshest landlord".[149] In south Bihar, too, the resident Koeri maliks, being in greater need of kamia labour, used their local influence and proximity to practise the most systematic forms of exploitation.[150]

[b] Proprietors with a larger share and a slight surplus margin most often let out their lands in barga, to maximise their income from land, while avoiding the responsibilities of direct cultivation.[151] Indeed, "the growth of this class [of petty sharers] had

[146] *DG: Darbhanga*, comp. L. S. S. O'Malley (Calcutta: BSBD, 1907), p. 121.

[147] LRP, Oct. 1894, Revenue Administration Report 1893–94, p. 38, paras. 143–152.

[148] Hardiman, "Bhils and Sahukars", p. 14.

[149] *DG: Darbhanga*, p. 121.

[150] Prakash, *Bonded Histories*, p. 188.

[151] Significantly, the extension of the barga system coincided with

tended . . . to cause a general enhancement of rents. The old, well-to-do *zamindar* has in many villages been replaced by a number of petty proprietors who are always endeavouring to extort more rent from their tenants".[152]

[c] Meanwhile, a large section of the big landlords, i.e., the stronger partners in zamindari properties and the new owners or purchasers of land, migrated to the cities. They were attracted by the prospect of Western education, government jobs, and the luxuries and amenities of urban life in general. The insanitary conditions, swamp and malaria in some backward districts of western Bengal reinforced this tendency, inducing "the well-to-do people to desert villages and live in town".[153]

The scattered nature of their lands further inconvenienced the owners, as each part of the property was split into multiple shares. "In fact, many of the new proprietors became absentee landlords, mainly because of the way in which they had acquired their property. The estates, bought piecemeal, were located in different places, often far apart, and were not the result of a growth around a given nucleus over a period of time".[154] The problem was particularly acute in districts like Bakarganj, where

---

the increase of the parasitical *bhadralok* class in villages. Thus in Bakarganj, where produce rent was an exceptional feature of land tenure, it thrived precisely in that portion of the Gournadi thana where large colonies of bhadraloks—Kayasthas, Vaidyas and Brahmans—had settled. This class increased from 15,000 to 23,000 between 1872–1901. Meanwhile, raiyati holdings were also being split up by similar processes of partition and sale. In 1909, J. C. Jack, Settlement Officer of Faridpur and Bakarganj, calculated on the basis of these facts that, "[i]t is apparent that there are now 28 men for every 18 in 1872, who are to be supported by produce rents, while the family who from 5 acres in 1872 might have had surplus rice with which to contribute to the support of 15,000 idle bhadralogs, have now only 3 acres to meet an increased burden of 23,000 drones". *SR, Bakarganj*, app. G, sec. 5, p. xlvii. letter no. 937 from J. C. Jack to the Comm., Dacca Div., 13/20 June 1909.

152 LRP, April 1895, p. 1628, para. 6.

153 Ibid., April 1915, no. 2, Letter to the collector, 16 July 1913, para. 102.

154 B. B. Chaudhuri, "Movement of Rent in Eastern India, 1793–1930", *Indian Historical Review* 3, no. 2, Jan. 1977, p. 363.

reclamation was most extensive and difficult; in Chittagong, where small estates were continuously being splintered into minute fragments, making direct management a definite ordeal; or in south Bihar, where the difficulties of joint control often led to violent disputes over water rights.[155]

[2.3] Sub-infeudation of tenures

The co-sharers of zamindari estates considered their lands no longer as the ancestral base of power and responsibility, but merely as the source of a fixed rental income. Likewise, the new owners or purchasers of land, often belonging to the non-resident trading community, were primarily interested in it as a lucrative form of investment. This approach was nurtured, as noted, by the lure of urban life and the health hazards and administrative problems involved in the direct management of their joint properties. Hence both these classes of big proprietors generally assigned their managers and tenure-holders with the task of rent collection, and took little interest, active or otherwise, in works of reform and maintenance. The indigo-planters' need for tenurial jurisdiction furthered the process of sub-infeudation. The road

155 Of the total registered perpetual leases in Bengal in 1896–97, Chittagong accounted for no less than 1 per cent. (*SR, Chittagong*, 1888–98, by C. G. Allen [Calcutta: BS Press, 1900], paras. 102, 258). In Bakarganj too, "the interests in land spread out like a fan, the holders in each grade dividing their tenancies amongst a more numerous body of sub-lessees, until the cultivators who are the ultimate sub-lessees form the most numerous body of all". J. C. Jack, the Settlement Officer of Bakarganj, traces the reason for this to the "historical accident" of absenteeism among landowners during the process of reclamation. This, in turn, was caused by a "geographical circumstance". The waste lands were covered so extensively by dense forests and a network of streams that it was impossible for the owners to directly supervise the work of reclamation or rent collection over large areas (*SR, Bakarganj*, p. 43, para. 126; p. 45, para. 129). The direct management of joint properties also led to distinct administrative problems whenever the need was felt for collective enterprise in agriculture. This was most clearly reflected in the neglect and decline of the ahar-pyne system of irrigation in south Bihar, particularly in Gaya district.

cess valuation statistics show that in the 1870s, more than 60 per cent of all tenures in Bengal were sub-infeudated.[156]

The process of sub-infeudation of land thus had its rationale in absentee ownership. The original tenures were held by the *talukdar*s directly from the zamindar. Below the talukdars were a class of tenure-holders known variously as jotedars in northern Jessore, gantidars in southern Jessore and west Khulna, and haoladars in eastern Khulna and Bagerhat. They probably had their origin in the *haola*s (tenures) of Bakarganj.[157] Variations of similar tenures were seen in those of the *makaddam*s and sarbarahakars of Orissa. Sub-infeudation went beyond the fourth level in Jessore and the 24 Parganas. The tenure system of Bakarganj illustrates the phenomenon of sub-infeudation in its extremest form, there being eight to twenty grades of intermediate holders on every piece of land, between the revenue-paying proprietor at the top and the cultivator at the bottom.[158]

Financial pressure and absenteeism forced most of these tenure-holders to delegate some of their rights and responsibilities to *ijaradar*s (lessees) and their sub-lessees (*dar-ijaradar*s), who held farming leases by which an annual rent was fixed for a specified term, on expiry of which they were not entitled to renewal. Zar-i-peshgi and *katkina* ijaras were leases of land on usufructuary mortgages. This system was most common in north Bihar, where the indigo concerns almost invariably held lands on lease (*ijara* or *thika*) from the local proprietors. As the thikadars had no permanent interest in the land, their system of land management "proved the veritable curse of the province and has been no less effective as a means of rack-renting, than as a method of keeping wages down to starvation level". It tied down the peasants to the unprofitable system of indigo cultivation, which yielded only a net gain of Rs. 3 to 7 per bigha, as against Rs. 10 for other country crops and Rs. 30 or more for paddy.[159] Indeed, "the cancer which has eaten into the

156 Ashok Sen, "Agrarian Structure", p. 4.

157 Satish Chandra Mitra, *Jashohar Khulnar Itihash*, ed. S. S. Mitra (Calcutta: S. S. Mitra, 1965), 2: p. 715.

158 For further details on the nature and stratification of tenures, see Chakrabarti, "Crisis in a Peasant Economy", pp. 147–48.

159 LRP, Nov. 1894; *SR, Muzaffarpur*, p. 15, para. 55.

vitals of Bihar is this thikadari system, especially in its combination with indigo planting".[160]

Special tenures appeared and changed with the distinctive needs of each region. The *lakhiraj* or rent-free grants, known as *tanki* in Orissa, and the *chakran* or service tenures prevailed widely, yet differed in emphasis from district to district. The *ghatwali* tenures in Burdwan, for instance, created originally as service tenures for the defence of the ghats or hill passes, later formed part of the rural police system and were finally terminated in 1894.[161] Again, the lack of facilities for the formal partition of tenures led to the creation of the *aliquat* tenures, based on private partitions in Bakarganj.

[2.4] Fluidity of tenures in the tribal belts

The situation was most fluid in the tribal tracts, and was systematically exploited by the village headmen and interested outsiders. This is seen in several cases, as of the jotedars in the Terai region, the non-resident Hindus in the Garo and Susang Hills, the mul raiyats in the Santhal Parganas, and the *tikri manjhis* (headmen) in the Paharia settlements of Damin-i-Koh.

The Rajbansis of the Terai were Koches belonging to the same stock as in the Duars and Coochbehar. Yet the development and crystallisation of tenures was slowest in the Terai, and it was "to the obvious interest of the jotedars to use their influence to prevent further progress".[162]

Though the jotedar held a heritable and transferable tenure in most cases between the government and the direct cultivator, he claimed occupancy rights, thus preventing those lower down like the thikadar, *dar-thikadar* and *chukanidar* from acquiring similar rights. The claim, however, was open to question, for land rights in the Terai were developing along the lines laid down in Coochbehar and the Duars, where "occupancy rights" could be acquired by every grade of cultivator, down to the *adhiyar* (sharecropper). There was thus scope for confusion in this

[160] LRP, Nov. 1894, p. 1250.
[161] *DG: Burdwan*, p. 157.
[162] LRP, no. 1894, p. 1201, para. 59.

context, as "the raiyat of the rest of Bengal is an elusive body in the Terai", and the jotedars took full advantage of the situation.[163]

The terms of a typical lease (appendix B) show how hard the jotedars of the Darjeeling Terai were on their chukanidars, and how systematically they curtailed any rights of occupancy that the latter might have claimed. Thus, for the chukanidars and those lower down, a record of rights was immaterial, like the "present of a patent safe to a pauper who has nothing to lock up".[164]

In the Chittagong Hill tracts, as noted earlier, the hillmen were at a distinct disadvantage in relation to the plainsmen, both Hindu and Muslim, who encroached systematically on their lands. At the foot of the hills, the raiyats were seen to be unaware of their rights and entirely at the mercy of the *itmamdar*s (tenure-holders), found mostly in newly cultivated tracts like the Noabad taluks of Old Thana Ramu.[165]

The Paharias in Damin-i-Koh were subjected to similar exploitation by their headmen, known as tikridars or tikri manjhis. Large portions of the hills were held by the tikridars.[166] There were several *kurna*s (tenant holdings) within each tikri, cultivated by different tenants, each of whom paid rent to the tikridar. Besides taking rent, the tikridars often sold their tikris to Santhals for nominal sums. For instance, in 1894, the Subdivisional Officer of Pakaur found that two large tikris called Perpara and Kerma in Kuarpal were occupied by Santhals. The

163 Ibid., pp. 1200–01, paras. 54, 57–59.

164 Ibid., Nov. 1894, nos. 113–14; The Terai Settlement, pp. 1183–84.

165 The *itmam* was a tenure like the haola of Bakarganj and Noakhali, and the chukan of Jalpaiguri. But while the chukanidars were depressed to the level of tenants-at-will, the itmam was mostly held by capitalists who added new dimensions to it. They frequently changed tenants for higher rents, thus denying them rights of occupancy while forcing up the rent level. (LRP, March 1894, no. 1803 G.S., Chittagong, 22 Sept. 1892. From C. G. H. Allen, Settlement Officer, Chittagong , to the Director of the Dept. of Land Records and Agriculture, Bengal, para. 3.)

166 *Tikri* was derived from the Hindi word *tukra*, meaning "piece", and was equivalent to the word *chak*. There may be several tikris on a hill, the man on whose tikri the hamlet existed being recognised as village headman.

settlement records proved beyond doubt that the tikri manjhi had of late sold the land to the Santhals, though he initally denied it. The tikridars not only exercised the right of sale, but in some hills of Rajmahal also changed the lands of their tenants periodically, to prevent them from acquiring occupancy rights. Thus the Paharias appeared to hold their lands not in freehold but as tenants, with the manjhis operating in effect as lakhirajdars.

There was, however, no real basis for any such tenure in the hills. In paragraphs 32 and 33 of a resolution dated 17 July 1823, the government clearly recorded the hill people as being its direct raiyats, there being no intervening tenures. Hence the tikri manjhis were not constituted as proprietors of the hills, but shared the freehold rights to the land equally with all. They could take a *dasturi* or allowance from the hillmen for the exercise of police duties, but the claim to rent was a gross abuse of power. Moreover, they could not evict the tenants at will, or sell their lands to outsiders. In fact, "the practice of buying and selling of tikris, even among their own community, is injurious to the interests of the tenants".[167]

Village headmen were almost always in a position of advantage in tribal societies. For instance, "representative raiyats", such as the mul raiyats in the Santhal Parganas, or the pradhans, *manki*s and *munda*s (headmen) in Chotanagpur, had occupancy rights in their land; yet unlike the thikadar, they were merely rent collectors and not tenure-holders. However, the mul raiyat often sold land to outsiders at rack-rents, thus ignoring the rights of the Santhals in the village, who were entitled to get settlement of the land sold, without cess or premium.[168]

[2.5] Increasing complexity of tenures: Widening gap between tenure-holders and actual cultivation

While the fluidity of tenures was thus deftly and rigorously exploited, especially in tribal societies, their complexity very often

167 LRP, Oct. 1894, nos. 3–4 (File 16–S 1/15), p. 589–91. Report on the Paharia Settlement, Damin-i-koh, by the S.D.O., Pakaur.

168 Ibid., Nov. 1894, Nov. 9–10, no. 2010 R., Dumka, 13 Aug.

removed the tenure-holder as far from the soil as the proprietor. By the aliquat tenure in Bakarganj, for instance, the tenure-holder collected and paid his share of the rent separately—sueing, selling and subletting without reference to the other partners in the undivided land. Yet he could not claim any specific portion of the land solely as his own, but had an undivided share in the entire land and in every field. The system was further complicated by the distinct bias in this district against the merger of tenures, even if held by the same person. In fact, "the buying and selling of tenures have become as common as the buying and selling of shares, and the purchaser has very often been content, as in the case of shares, to take his dividends in the shape of rent from the undertenants and forego all further knowledge of the land which produced them".[169]

This growing apathy of the proprietors and tenure-holders and the lack of resources among the sub-lessees led to a gross neglect of works of reform and maintenance. Link roads, tanks and dams consequently fell into disrepair. The problem was particularly apparent in years of famine and scarcity, when the need for such works was most acutely felt. The behaviour of the zamindars and tenure-holders in various parts of Jessore, Khulna, Nadia, south Bihar and the Chilka tract during the famine of 1896–97, "illustrates the evil of the tenure intermediate between a *zamindar* and the cultivators".[170] A typical case was that of Babu Girija Nath Raychaudhuri, zamindar of Satkhira in Khulna, who in 1896 passed on the entire responsibility of supplying seed to cultivators, to the gantidars in his estates. He also refused to repair the dams and embankments, so vital in protecting the rice crop in Satkhira from salt-water incursions, particularly when the rains were too scanty to sweeten the river water, as in 1896. As the gantidars did not generally have the sort of resources needed for such extensive repairs, they failed to relieve the raiyats in this crisis. The Collector of Khulna proposed government advances to the cultivators for such purposes through their respective zamindars; but E. V. Westmacott,

---

1894. From R. Carstairs, Dy. Comm., Santhal Prgs., to the Comm., Bhagalpur Div. and Santhal Prgs.

169 *SR, Bakarganj*, p. 55, para. 148; p. 57, para. 152; p. 54, para. 147.

170 *Selection of Papers*, vol. 8: p. 291.

Commissioner of the Presidency Division, had grave reservations about the success of such a plan "in view of the chain of subinfeudation".[171] Large and fertile areas in Nadia and Khulna thus reverted to jungle, while tanks went dry in Kaliganj, Nakashipara, Shyamnagore and Paikgacha, due mostly to the apathy of the non-resident owners.

The decay of the ahar-pyne system of irrigation in south Bihar, especially in Gaya, illustrates in detail how joint control and sub-infeudation frustrated all attempts at collective enterprise in agriculture. As noted earlier, the pynes or river channels flowed through several villages under different owners. The working of the system was thus extremely complicated, and depended on the local rules (*parabandi*) regulating water rights. There were several ways by which any one of the owners of the pyne could easily take more than his share of the water: by enlarging the channel at the head, which had no masonry sluice; by putting a bund in the pyne below his own fields; by raising the height of the dam across the river; by holding up the water longer than permitted; or by making a new pyne to divert the supply of the owners further downstream. Hence, the regulation of water rights was "a fertile source of dispute" between proprietors and co-sharers of adjoining lands, leading frequently to violence and litigation.[172]

Yet the system survived, for the owners had a share in the increased crop returns under the prevailing system of produce rents. Gradually, however, they lost the interest or ability to maintain these works due to the endless partitions of estates, which cut in both on their resources and unity. Thus, "owing to the sub-division of the land in recent years, and to the total want of any power of combination on the part of the land-owners, these simple but valuable irrigation works are falling year by year into disrepair".[173]

Lands let out on the thika or lease system in Bihar suffered most acutely from such neglect. The thikadar or temporary farmer was intent on maximising his income from land by rack-renting his tenants, as a result of which they could not afford to

171 Ibid., no. 40 G-S.R. dated Calcutta, 26 May 1897. From E. V. Westmacott, Comm. Presidency Div. to the Secy. to the Govt. of Bengal, Rev. Dept., para. 30.

172 *Report, Indian Irrigation Commission*, sec. 3, para. 416.

173 Ibid., para. 414.

undertake any works of reform or maintenance. The thikadar himself did not invest on improvements either, for his tenure was too short for him to reap the dividends.

Works of reform suffered further, as any improvement on the land by the tenant on his own initiative would immediately call for a higher rental or levies. The Bengal Tenancy Act of 1859 did not prevent the landlord from claiming a share of such "unearned increments". In Chotanagpur, for instance, the proportion of irrigated lands was very low, especially in the tribal belts in the south. Here, ahars were formed by surrounding the low-lying lands in the villages by a succession of bunds needing regular repairs. Yet the raiyats neglected these, as any improvements of this kind on their lands would immediately raise them to a higher rent-level. F. A. Slacke, the Officiating Commissioner of Chotanagpur, advised the Irrigation Commission in 1902 that unless the raiyats had better security against this, "no irrigation scheme would succeed".[174] Similarly the Santhals, who were pioneers in extending cultivation to wastelands, "have now become resigned . . . as soon as the lands have become valuable, landlords and money lenders combined dispossess them of their holdings [by pressing high rent claims] and make them move on to some other jungly tract".[175] In Bakarganj, there were fines (*nazar*) on the excavation of tanks and ditches, as well as a cess calculated per acre covered by the tank. This was always very high, sometimes even more than the purchase money of the land, in addition to which the rent was to be paid. The effect of this tax was to so reduce the size of tanks, that drinking water became unnecessarily scarce, especially in areas where the rivers were brackish or saline.[176]

[2.6] Stratification of peasantry

Even the occupancy raiyats were gradually losing touch with the soil. The tenancy legislations of 1859 and 1885 underlined

174 Ibid., p. 227. Answer to Q. 2 by F. A. Slacke, Off. Comm. of Chotanagpur, to the President of the Irrigation Commission, Purulia, 3 Nov. 1902.

175 *SR, Bhagalpur*, p. 65.

176 *SR, Bakarganj*, p. 80, para. 195.

the position of occupancy raiyats as a privileged class among the peasantry, holding their land directly from a landlord or substantial tenure-holder. At the highest level, this protected class held up to 100 bighas of land—the line of demarcation between the tenure-holders and occupancy raiyats. The lower limit remained vague and undefined, consisting of the mass of under-raiyats, including sharecroppers and tenants-at-will. The latter had no security or legal protection against rent increase, as the implementation of such a measure would overstrain the administrative machinery and deprive the favoured class of occupancy raiyats of a lucrative source of income. Thus, the Tenancy Acts "supported a particular status of landholding, and went by no clear definition of the same status in terms of their role in actual cultivation . . . [t]here was no safeguard against the danger that an occupancy ryot might convert himself into a rent-receiver and an oppressor of the worst kind".[177]

The full implication of this was brought out by the development of the land market. Indeed, it was in this context that such "prescriptive rights" determined the pattern of rural stratification: the tenure-holder with more than one hundred bighas (thirty acres); occupancy raiyats holding not more than thirty and not less than six acres; non-occupancy tenants enjoying some protection but no hereditary rights; unprotected tenants-at-will, under-raiyats, etc. subsisting on three to six acres; subtenants and sharecroppers, who had to supplement their income from land by hiring out their labour.[178]

[2.7] Rent increase: background

Partitions, sub-infeudation and subletting of lands thus raised rents rather than the level of administrative efficiency. There was a considerable increase in the gross rental in the last quarter of the nineteenth century, as indicated by the road cess statistics. Yet, this amount should not be equated solely with rent payments made by the peasants. It had other components, too, such as the

[177] Ashok Sen, "Agrarian Structure", pp. 12–13.

[178] Dietmar Rothermund, *Government, Landlord and Peasant in India: Agrarian Relations under British Rule, 1865–1935* (Wiesbaden: Steiner, 1978), pp. 94–96.

zamindars' income from the expansion of the rural grain markets, exploitation of mining resources and revision of the rent demand on different grades of tenure-holders. Due to insufficient data, however, the relative size of these variables in relation to the total rent cannot be determined with precision.

The increase in rentals was not entirely arbitrary or unreasoned. It was often determined by (i) changes in the level of agricultural resources brought about by an increase in the extent and intensity of cultivation in many regions; (ii) the secular and steady rise in agricultural prices; and (iii) a rapid growth of population, which naturally forced up rents in a competitive land market.

(i) The percentage of cultivated area at the end of the nineteenth century was seldom less than 75 to 80, except in some districts like Nadia, Bankura and Champaran. In Champaran, where there was still scope for expansion, "the rent roll has mainly developed as a result of new assessment on extended cultivation".[179] In north Monghyr, about 77 per cent of the increase in rent which occurred during the 1890s was allowed on the basis of "excess holding".[180] In north Bhagalpur at the turn of the century, "nearly 80 per cent of the increase in rent was due to assessment of excess areas".[181] In Shahabad, "the greatest extension of the cultivated area occurred after the introduction of canals".[182]

Cultivation increased not only in extent, but also in intensity. It became more stable, particularly in areas like south Bihar where the Sone Canal extended irrigation facilities, while the pressure of population led to the shortening of the fallow periods. Again, in districts like Bakarganj, low-lying lands were sometimes raised and enriched by "fluvial action".

However, this basis of a demand for enhanced rentals was qualified by several factors. Rent enhancements did not always correspond to the size of the increased cultivation. In Darbhanga, for instance, the road cess returns show that "in the 17 years between 1876 and 1893 the rental . . . had increased by over 25 per cent, though there could have been but little extension of

[179] *DG: Champaran*, p. 90.
[180] *SR, Monghyr, North*, paras. 156–58.
[181] *SR, Bhagalpur*, paras. 79, 152–55.
[182] *DG: Shahabad*, comp. L. S. S. O'Malley, 1906, pp. 80–81.

cultivation during that period". In Chittagong, too, the new rates involved an increase of 19.5 per cent of which 3.5 per cent only was due to assessment of new cultivation, 16 per cent being "pure enhancement".[183]

Besides, "the increased cost of cultivation and the diminished fertility of the soil from constant croppings and from extended cultivation over inferior soils, is to be taken into account".[184] Indeed, the 'new agriculture' had a distinct difference in quality. As cultivation reached its limits in most districts and shifted to single-crop, marginal lands, it became a high-risk venture due to the heavy initial outlay and the extreme vulnerability of monoculture to the vagaries of the weather.

It is further doubtful whether cultivation in the canal-irrigated lands, though intensive, was secure or valuable enough to merit the phenomenal rise in rent rates. Contrary to expectations, the Sone project could not force any distinct change in the quality and type of crops grown in south Bihar. Instead of replacing the cheap and inferior pulses of the rabi harvest by valuable cash crops, canal irrigation only led to a voluminous increase in the cultivation of winter rice, which was most vulnerable to drought.[185] Canal water, as noted earlier, was not an effective substitute for rainfall in dry seasons. Yet rents soared high, often rising from a few annas to as many rupees in parts of Gaya, Patna and the Buxar division.[186] Produce rents went up naturally with the increase in crop returns on irrigated lands. Even cash rentals shot up in occupancy and non-occupancy lands despite government legislation, the landlords claiming to "drive a carriage and pair through the Tenancy Act".[187] This substantial increase in their income was received gratis by the landowners, the sizeable burden of water rates being passed on entirely to the

[183] *DG: Darbhanga*, p. 82; LRP, March 1894, Note by W. C. Macpherson, Offg. Director of Land Records and Agriculture, Bengal.

[184] LRP, Nov. 1894, p. 1044; *SR, Muzaffarpur*, p. 20, para. 71.

[185] *Report, Indian Irrigation Commission*, evidence of J. H. Toogood, Superintending Engineer, Sone circle, Bankipore, 25 Oct. 1902.

[186] Ibid., p. 156–57.

[187] *Report, Irrigation Department*, 1885–86, Collector of Gaya to Comm. Patna Div., app. p. 95, para. 4.

tenant-occupier.[188] In fact, much of the opposition to the canal assessment was due to the "heavy rents demanded by the *zamindars*" in Orissa and the oppressive sanja rent in Midnapur, which would totally offset the value of any increased returns resulting from canal irrigation.[189]

(ii) One must next consider whether the effect of rising prices on the peasant economy justified the rent enhancements in this period. The rise in agricultural prices could not create a substantial profit margin for the peasant, as the subdivision of holdings simultaneously cut in on the size of the crop per average peasant family. The price rise partly neutralised this effect by raising the exchange value of the reduced crop, and to that extent helped the peasant to maintain, rather than enhance, the level of his income. For instance in Orissa, where the population was almost wholly agricultural, the area required for the support of one person decreased from 1.15 to 0.77 acres, that is, by about one-third.[190]

Even this limited gain should be determined in relative terms, i.e. only in relation to the cost-of-living index. In the absence of precise data, one might refer to the broad comparison of index numbers for agricultural income and prices of necessities bought by the peasant, as attempted by the Datta Committee for the period between 1895 and 1912 in Bengal and Bihar. According to Datta, during 1894–1904 the farmer increased his income by a mere 2 per cent while commodity prices went up by 10.5 per cent. This proved that "the rise in the cost of living has been all along more than the rise in the agricultural income, showing that the cultivators in these parts have been adversely affected by high prices".[191]

This had special relevance to subsistence agriculture or foodgrain production, which covered more than 85 per cent of

188 *Report, Indian Irrigation Commission,* evidence of Oldham, Collector of Gaya, Bankipore, 24 Oct. 1902.

189 Bengal Irrigation Proceedings, Mar. 1891, no. 19, Dy. Supdt. of Canal Revenue to the Collector of Cuttack, 5 March 1881; Ibid., Jan. 1873 no. 50. Collector of Midnapur to the Govt. of Bengal, P.W.D. Irrigation Branch, 18 Oct. 1872.

190 LRP, April 1898, p. 1089.

191 Datta, *Enquiry into the Rise in Prices*, pp. 183–84, paras. 435–36.

the total cropped area. Unlike in cash-crop sectors, a sizeable portion of the crop here was consumed rather than marketed.

Even the alleged "surplus"—so reduced by the fragmentation of land units, the rise in the cost of living and the peasant's own food requirements—was not drawn to the market by a wholesome price stimulus. Rather, the 'surplus' was extracted in the form of compulsory rent and interest payments to the zamindar and mahajan, who ultimately benefited from the price rise. The landlords deftly exploited the situation and, in their keenness to profit from the rise in agricultural prices, exerted a steady pressure for the commutation of cash rentals. Produce rents like the *mankhap* in Bhagalpur and Monghyr and the sanja in Midnapur minimised the peasants' share in the price rise, for he was to surrender not simply a portion of the crop raised, but the market value of a fixed, bulk amount of grain at the time of harvest. The low harvest rates forced the peasant to yield a larger share of the produce, while the zamindar reaped the full benefit of rising prices by re-selling the grain as the season advanced. These rents were fixed irrespective of the crop out-turn: hence, in lean years the effects of a poor yield were not mitigated by scarcity prices. Further, when the kist payment was timed just before the harvest, the crop was hypothecated by the peasant and sold for a pittance, "as the disparity between the prices of hypothecated and free crops is large".[192]

Thus the rural power structure rather than open market conditions determined the flow of the peasants' meagre surplus. Even if the residue arrived at the *hat*s (village markets), it fetched a much lower price than in the organised grain centres of the nearest towns. But in these town markets, the primary producer or seller was always at a distinct disadvantage in relation to the brokers and agents of big buyers; he could not grasp the market mechanism or verify the prevailing prices in bargaining with them. The prevalence of different weights and measures in

[192] K. K. Ghosh, *Agricultural Labourers in India: A study in the history of their growth and economic condition,* Indian Publications Monograph Series no. 7 (Calcutta, 1969), pp. 65, 264. For instance, the price of 82 lbs. of jute in a market near Calcutta was quoted as Rs. 5–8 as. to Rs. 6 in case of a mortgaged crop, while a free crop fetched as much as Rs. 8–10 as. to Rs. 9.

different localities and the practice of additional weights further reduced his sale proceeds. The primary producer also had to pay for the transport, octroi and levies, so that "the marketing cost is one of the most important hindrances to the cultivator's reaping the benefit of the price rise".[193]

Hence, "it appears that the increase in the price of staple crops is not sufficient to account for the ascertained increase in the average rates of rent. The increase of prices since 1840 has been at most 32 per cent (gleaned from the jail statistics regarding the cost of rations per prisoner), whereas the average increase of rents has been over 110 per cent".[194] Only in exceptional cases, as for instance in the rich and fertile tracts of Bakarganj district, did the rise in agricultural prices appreciably lighten the rent burden.

(iii) By far the most potent cause for rent enhancements was the growing pressure of population on the soil. This was used most effectively by the landlords and even occupancy raiyats as a lever for extensive subletting at rack rents. "The circumstances which cause a rise in rents are those which increase the demand or limit the supply. Thus, increase in population brings about enhanced demand, and . . . produces increased competition".[195]

Many of the newly reclaimed lands initially enjoyed concessional rates of rent—the criterion being the demand for them, rather than their level of productivity. In Bakarganj, for instance, heavy enhancements occurred in the last quarter of the nineteenth century, as the need was no longer felt to keep the rents particularly low in order to attract colonists to the forests and newly formed char lands. In north Bhagalpur large tracts were previously held at *kamdar* or low rates of four to eight annas per bigha. The reason why the very low rates lasted longer in north Bhagalpur than in the other north Bihar districts is probably due to the fact that a considerable portion of area consisted of wasteland and jungle. So long as this area remained available for cultivation, the landlords were unable to raise the

193 Ibid., p. 64.

194 LRP, no. 1894, Report on the Survey and Record of Rights in Muzaffarpur, p. 20, para. 71.

195 Ibid., April 1898, p. 1088, Note by Mr. D. H. Kingsford on "Competition Rents".

rents to any considerable extent. Changes in the land-man ratio altered the situation: illegal enhancements were forced on nearly 40 per cent of the villages and the kamdar were revised to *purdar* or full rates by 1885.[196] Similarly, the *chakband* tenures on low rents in parts of south Bhagalpur and Monghyr, under which the Santhals had reclaimed large areas of wasteland, gave way since the 1880s to the *mustagiri* or thikadari system at enhanced rates of rent.

[2.8] Occasions for rent increase

Rents were generally raised at specific points in time, as for instance (i) when the whole or part of an estate or holding changed hands through partition or sale, or during (ii) re-settlement, (iii) the reclamation of wastelands, and (iv) pre-settlement surveys.

(i) "Rents are affected most materially by the partitions of estates". As soon as the division was complete, each shareholder tended to disregard all previous rates and proceeded to reassess his lands according to his own estimates of their productivity. The raiyat, whose lands often lay scattered in several estates, was unable to resist the pressure of these different proprietors and submitted to a new rent roll. Sometimes the lands were resumed after partition by the landlord, and subsequently let out at enhanced rates.[197] "Government sales for arrears of revenue have also been almost invariably followed by an enhancement of rent, and the ryots have seldom made any effort to resist this, the belief being universal that the purchaser starts with a 'tabula rasa' and can levy any rent he likes".[198]

(ii) When a new peasant replaced another, or when new land was available for cultivation, the proprietor demanded a considerable salami or entry fee, and sometimes in return granted perpetual leases, amounting in effect to a "freezing of rent".[199] Generally, however, any fresh settlement called for enhanced rentals. P. W. Murphy, Settlement Officer of Bihar, noted during

196 *SR, Bhagalpur*, p. 37, para. 79.

197 Ibid., Nov. 1894, p. 1046; *SR, Muzaffarpur*, p. 22, para. 78.

198 *DG: Saran*, p. 84.

199 Chaudhuri, "Movement of Rent", sec. 18, p. 367.

the survey operations in Bhagalpur: "When new settlements of land are being made, or when purchased or abandoned holdings are being resettled, the rate of rent is generally increased and a *salami* is also taken". According to him, the average enhancement obtained in this way since 1885 amounted to three to four annas in the rupee in north Bhagalpur and between two to three annas in the south.[200] In Deoghar, numerous cases of sale and rack-renting were brought to notice since 1886.[201] In Orissa, abandoned *thani* (resident) holdings were let out at *pahi* (temporary) rates, which saw an increase of 40 per cent between 1836 and 1896. Extension of the thikadari system, and of the *zirat* or *khas* (demesne) lands of the proprietor also called for settlement of peasant holdings at enhanced rates.

(iii) The reclamation of wastelands led to assessment for rent after the initial phase, and to resettlement at higher rates when cultivation was stabilised. As noted, extensive wastelands reclaimed by the Santhals in the Barind tracts and in Bhagalpur were assessed at a rate beyond the means of the original settlers, who then moved on to fresh jungle tracts, while their holdings were resettled at higher rents.[202] After 1875, rents were enhanced on the chars and wastelands in Bakarganj. In Singhbhum, the gora or unembanked uplands were assessed to a rent of one anna per local bigha for the first time in 1897.[203] By the settlement of 1896–97 in Palamau, the *pariadari* system of exempting uplands (tanr) from rent gave way to the *uttakar* system, by which all lands were assessed for rent.[204] In some cases, where there was no wasteland for extending cultivation, the landlord increased his income by exacting rent for some fictitious land, commonly known as *kaghazi zamin* (literally land on paper).[205]

(iv) During the survey and settlement proceedings in the different districts, the persistent aim of the zamindars was to

200 *SR, Bhagalpur*, p. 125, para. 230.

201 LRP, Nov. 1894, no. 2010 R, Dumka, 13 Aug. 1894. From R. Carstairs, Dy. Comm., Santhal Prgs., to the Comm. Bhagalpur Div. and Santhal Prgs.

202 *SR, Bhagalpur,* para. 79.

203 *DG: Singhbhum*, pp. 126–27.

204 LRP, March 1897, p. 673.

205 *DG: Champaran*, p. 129.

legalise all increases in rent effected by them since the time of the last settlement, and to press for a further rise on various grounds. During the assessment of the Terai jotes in 1894, for instance, it was noted that in twenty-four jotes selected for survey, there had been an average enhancement of 180 per cent since the last settlement in 1879.[206] In Muzaffarpur, again, the average rent in thirty-three villages increased by 137 per cent and that in thirty-six others by 116 per cent since 1843 when the first survey began. The greater part of the increase occurred in 1874–1880, just before the second settlement was undertaken. Attempt was naturally made to incorporate these new rates into the survey papers in 1894.

[2.9] Grounds for further enhancements

Further enhancements were claimed either *(a)* by the assessment of excess holdings and increased cultivation, or *(b)* by raising the rent rate on various grounds.

[a] Assessment of excess areas

In the case of districts which still had land for reclamation, as in north Bihar and Bhagalpur, rents were enhanced by 77 to 80 per cent by the assessment of excess areas. In 1892–99 in Muzaffarpur, "nearly the whole of the enhancement made during the settlement was due to the assessment of excess area to rent, and there was practically no enhancement of rent rates throughout the proceedings".[207] As noted, this increase in rent did not always correspond to the size and quality of the new cultivation, which extended mostly over marginal lands.

A distinction was clearly made between increases in the quantum of rent by the assessment of new lands or excess areas, and an increase effected by raising the rent rates. The Champaran raiyats, for example, were ready to pay for excess lands, but not for the old lands at enhanced rates.[208] The zamindars, however, persisted in their claims. It was noted during the settlement

206 LRP, Nov. 1894, p. 1203; Note on Terai region, p. 17, para. 66.
207 *DG: Muzaffarpur*, p. 119.
208 *DG: Champaran*, p. 90.

operations in Muzaffarpur, that "though the increase of zamindari assets had been largely obtained by the reclamation of waste and the expansion of cultivation, there can be no doubt that enhancement of rent rates has been also an important factor leading to this result".[209]

[b] Enhancement of rates

Rates were raised on the basis of: (i) the rise in agricultural prices; (ii) improvements effected on the land; and (iii) higher rates allegedly prevailing in neighbouring lands of similar quality.

(i) It has been shown in some detail that any gains made by the peasant from the rise in foodgrain prices were more than offset by the percentage of increase effected in rent rates.

(ii) Higher rates were also claimed on the basis of "improvements" made on the land, mainly in irrigation works, by the proprietor. In the produce-paying lands, the proprietor's interest in repairing and maintaining irrigation works was stimulated to some extent by the prospect of better crop returns; but many cash-paying lands benefited from the pynes as well, and it was here that the problem came into sharp focus. Generally, however, the apathy of the proprietors and tenure-holders in undertaking works of reform has already been noted. Most of these alleged improvements amounted in effect to no more than the ordinary annual and decennial repairs, which were usually fixed as the landlord's responsibility at the time of determining the rent, as proved by his *gilandazi* (agreement) papers. Hence, enhancements on this basis were illegal, as the Bengal Tenancy Act allowed an enhancement of up to 2 an. in a rupee, only for improvements to which the raiyat was not originally entitled.[210]

(iii) Most often, however, higher rates were obtained arbitrarily, and on no fixed principle. As noted by L. S. S. O'Malley in the *Muzaffarpur District Gazetteer:* "The other great cause of enhancement has been the way in which zamindars have been able to tamper with rent rates, enhancing them at their own pleasure and in a purely arbitrary way".[211] A favourite method

209 *DG: Muzaffarpur*, p. 81.
210 *SR, Bhagalpur*, p. 68, para. 128.
211 *DG: Muzaffarpur*, p. 81.

was to demand higher rentals on the basis of the prevailing rates of rent (*pargana nirik*) in lands of similar quality in adjacent villages. Obviously, these had no relevance for the new cultivation. For other lands, too, rates were not easy to verify due to the variety and complexity of rent rates in different regions, there being no uniform criteria for assessment. In Bengal, in particular, soil productivity had seldom been the standard for fixing rent rates.[212] Reference to the old rates for comparison was almost impossible, as past records, even when available, were obsolete and liable to manipulation by the zamindars, who were no longer so familiar with the details of their tenant holdings. Sometimes the rate was left intact, the classification of the land being changed to obtain higher rents.[213]

[2.10] Response of the tenants

The tenants did not accept such increases without resistance. In fact, higher castes like the Brahmins, Kayasths, Babhans and Rajputs, who formed a large proportion of the cultivators in the north Bihar districts, "are not easily coerced into agreeing to enhancements".[214] In Champaran, the higher-caste raiyats, who were most vocal in opposing the demand for free labour (*beth-begar*) and enhancement, generally held their lands at privileged rates. "The almost invariable reason for this is that they have been able to resist the landlord's efforts to enhance their rent, while the Kurmi or Koeri have consented to enhancements".[215] In Muzaffarpur, it was noted that the increase in rent for the higher castes was minute, while that for the others was considerable. The Settlement Officer of Muzaffarpur thus defines the problem: "The general impression is that the tenantry of Bihar are . . . in complete subservience to their landlords, who evict and enhance their rents at pleasure. The impression, however, is only partially true. Like most things in India, it is largely a question of caste. I believe this impression to convey a correct idea of the condition of low-caste ryots, such as Dusadhs, Kurmis,

212 Chaudhuri, "Movement of Rent", p. 358.
213 *DG: Singhbhum*, p. 129.
214 *SR, Bhagalpur*, p. 37, para. 79.
215 *DG: Champaran*, p. 89.

etc. but cultivators of higher caste, like Babhans, are usually quite prepared to fight their landlord if he attempts to oppress them".[216]

As implied above, the aborigines and lower castes were most susceptible to pressure by the landlords. Competitive rates and rack renting were noted specifically in areas where there was an influx of tribal migrants. For instance, in Malda the average rate of Rs. 2 per acre went up to Rs. 3 and more in the Barind tract, which was colonised by the Santhals and other tribals. The Deputy Commissioner of the Santhal Parganas wrote in 1888: "The district [Santhal Parganas] has now been filled up, and is overflowing into Maldah. Symptoms of pressure are appearing as inferior land is being taken up".[217] Evictions and abandonment of land was not infrequent among the backward communities. The Subdivisional Officer noted about the Paharia settlements in the Damin: "as soon as a tikridar has parted with his tikri, the Paharia tenants are expected to shift, especially if their Kurnas can be furrowed by the plough".[218] In the Susang Hills, too, Garo villages began to disappear, as the pressure of debts and the tanka system of produce rent obliged many Garos to "throw up" their holdings.[219]

In the lands reclaimed by the Santhals in south Monghyr and Bhagalpur, the original tenures (chakband) at concessional rates systematically gave way to the mustagiri or thikadari system by which outsiders, usually moneylenders and Hindu cultivators, replaced the tribal headmen (*chakbanddars*). Unlike the chakbanddar, the thikadar or mustagir was a temporary lessee of the land. "The Santhals (or other tribals) as a rule do not remain long in the village after it is handed over to these thikadars. The latter take their best lands, settle them with outsiders, and demand high rents for the remaining lands. . . . when it reaches a certain pitch, the whole community often abandon their lands and set out for some other

216 *DG: Muzaffarpur*, p. 120.

217 *Dufferin Report*. Letter from R. Carstairs, Offg. Dy. Comm., Santhal Prgs., to the Comm. Bhagalpur Div. and Santhal Prgs., dated Dumka, 6 Apr. 1888, para. 4.

218 LRP, Oct. 1894, Report on the Paharia Settlement, Damin-i-koh, by S.D.O. Pakaur, p. 2, para. 5.

219 Ibid., Sept. 1916, no. 475, dated Mymensingh, 15 Feb. 1915. From J. Lang, Collector Mymensingh, to the Comm., Dacca Div.

place to begin again their work of reclaiming the jungle". The pattern was the same in all tribal areas.[220]

[2.11] Adverse effects of thika or ijara on the tenant and landlord

In fact, the thikadari or ijara system "is in the hands of a grasping landlord a most effective means of procuring regular enhancements of rent", not only in tribal settlements but in other areas as well.[221] As a temporary lessee, the thikadar was not interested in works of reform or maintenance, which were unlikely to pay dividends within the short period of his lease. Hence, the purely farming system increased the pressure of rent on the peasant, while reducing the size and quality of his crop. The system was so unpopular with the peasants, especially in its combination with indigo planting as in north Bihar, that the very threat of leasing out lands on "thika" was generally sufficient for the raiyats to submit to rent enhancements.[222]

In some districts as in Manbhum, *bemiadi* ijaradars, who held the land indefinitely rather than on leases of fixed duration, posed a distinct threat to the zamindar. Here the ijaradar got the benefit of all newly assessed lands and settled them on his own terms, depriving the landlord of any share in the profits. If on detection the landlord pressed for enhancements, his claim, unsupported by relevant papers as to the area and pattern of the new holdings, would be held invalid.[223] In such cases, the malik could not collect his rent except through the middleman or ijaradar. Hence, he was obliged to settle amicably with the local middleman of influence, and even employ him as *tahasildar*

220 *SR, Bhagalpur*, p. 77, para. 141.

221 Ibid., pp. 76–77.

222 During the survey in Muzaffarpur in 1894, it was found that at least three villages had yielded to the imposition of a cess on the understanding that their lands should not be leased to any indigo factory. Yet it was precisely this that the proprietor did after three or four years, when it was too late to deny payment of the enhanced rental. (LRP, Nov. 1894; *SR, Muzaffarpur*, p. 22, para. 77).

223 *DG: Manbhum*, pp. 206–7; *SR, Purnea*, comp. L. S. S. O'Malley (Calcutta: BSBD, 1911), pp. 53–54, para. 178.

(village accountant/revenue official) for areas beyond the purview of his lease.

Thus, whether it be lease or tenure, "the landlord loses and the tenant suffers while the middleman grows rich".[224] The following table of rent rates of thirty-nine villages of thana Araria in Purnea district is an instance in point.

TABLE 26

Rent Rates in Thana Araria, Purnea (in Rs.)

Raiyats to patnidar	*Under-tenure -holders to patnidar*	*Raiyats to under-tenure-holders under patnidar*
1.44	1.09	3.26

Source: SR, Purnea, p. 115, para. 356.

The rent commitments to the under-tenure-holders were thus more than twice that to the *patnidar*; again, the net gain of the under-tenure-holder after payment of his dues to the patnidar was Rs. 2.17 per acre, i.e., Rs. 1.08 more than the gross amount received by the patnidar.[225] Hence, the raiyats preferred to hold under patnidars than under petty, subordinate tenure-holders who, like the peasant proprietors of Muzaffarpur, were harsher in dealing with their tenants. In the Presidency Division, the so-called raiyats who had ceased to cultivate their lands directly, extorted more than the zamindars.[226] In Bakarganj, the tenure-holders had six times the extent of land held by the cultivators, though each acre held by the raiyat was worth 57 annas in rent to the proprietor, as against 19 annas for each acre held on tenure. "Had they eschewed middlemen and dealt only with the cultivator, the owners would reap a profit of 50 lakhs from their estates, where they now reap a profit of only 16 lakhs".[227] In south Bhagalpur, the rise in agricultural prices caused a

224 *SR, Purnea*, p. 56, para. 181.

225 Ibid., p. 115, paras. 356–57.

226 *Report of the Land Revenue Administration, Lower Provinces 1895–96*, p. 40.

227 *SR, Bakarganj*, p. 63, para. 164.

widening gap between produce and cash rentals, the difference being appropriated mostly by the tenure-holders. Hence the strongest opposition to the commutation of produce rentals came from the "intermediary agents, who intercept a large proportion of the produce rent".[228]

[2.12] Expansion of khas lands by the landlord

Instead of letting out lands on thika, ijara or even ordinary tenures as a means of forcing up the rental, the landlord often preferred to extend his khas or demesne (known variously as *nijchash* or *nijjote* in Bengal and Orissa, *bakasht*, *sir*, *khamar* or zirat in north Bihar, and *kamat* in Bhagalpur, Purnea and Monghyr), which could be resettled directly as produce tenancies at enhanced rates.

It has been remarked that except in case of the indigo interests, as in Champaran and Muzaffarpur, the proprietor in general was not keen to add to his responsibilities by retaining the holdings of defaulting peasants which passed into his hands.[229] Yet, the district survey reports have dealt exhaustively with the zamindars' intent to increase their demesne in every possible way, and with the extent of this increase in the period under review.[230]

Indeed, the process was not unreasoned. The Settlement Officer of Bihar noted during the survey operations in Monghyr in 1899–1904: "In specific areas the rent question was mixed up with that of 'kamat' or proprietors' private land, failure to enhance rents successfully having led to attempts, often successful, to oust *raiyats* from their holdings, and either hold them in khas cultivation or lease them out at higher rates to other tenants".[231] As direct cultivation would bring increased liabilities, produce tenancies were generally preferred. They fetched a good return on the proprietor's initial investment in purchasing raiyati lands,

228 *SR, Bhagalpur*, p. 5, para. 16 in the forwarding letter by McPherson, Dir. of the Dept. of Land Records, Bengal, to the Secy. to the Board of Rev., L.P., dated Calcutta. 15 Dec. 1911.

229 Chaudhuri, "Movement of Rent", p. 364.

230 For detailed case studies, see Chakrabarti, "Crisis in a Peasant Economy", pp. 168–70.

231 *SR, Monghyr (North)*, p. 32, para. 98.

especially in case of valuable crops like tobacco and chillies, while preventing the acquisition by tenants of any right therein. This explains the unusually large percentage of lands held on produce rents in certain areas like Teghra and Beguserai in north Monghyr, and Dalsinghserai and Bahera in Darbhanga. They were inhabited mostly by petty, resident proprietors, who were better able to supervise their interests in produce-paying lands.[232]

Hence, every effort was made by the proprietor to increase this area, and to get it sanctioned during the traverse surveys. Mr Lyon, the Settlement Officer of Muzaffarpur, graphically describes the process:

> If a mukarrari lease is granted over a large area of land, the mukarraridar proceeds to carve his zirat out of the tenants' holdings, giving them lands in exchange elsewhere. If a partition is made in a village, the owner of each of the newly formed estates takes up a large area within his estate as zirat. All lands taken up in blocks by ticcadars for indigo or other cultivation are termed zirat, and most of the lands left by dying or absconding raiyats are held by the malik as his zirat until such time as he may see fit to settle it with someone else. . . . and the anxiety of the zamindars to use the present survey as a means for increasing the area of the zirat lands has . . . been shown in a hundred cases.[233]

In legitimising such extensions of their zirat, the zamindars fully exploited the elasticity and ambiguity of its definition as noted in section 120 of the Bengal Tenancy Act. The landlords' definition of 'zirat' covered every piece of land cultivated by a zamindar, thikadar or rent-free tenure-holder within his estate or tenure. It was further extended to all lands which, previously held as khas, had been let out on produce rents without being officially entered into the *jamabandi* (rent roll) on the basis of a formal agreement with the tenant. Lyon, the Settlement Officer of Muzaffarpur, reported in May 1894: "The term zirat bears a meaning in Muzaffarpur which is wholly distinct from that given it in the Bengal Tenancy Act".[234] Babu Sosi Bhusan Chowdhuri, a Munsif of Chittagong, noted that

232 *DG: Monghyr,* p. 125.
233 LRP, Nov. 1894, no. 59, dated 9 May 1894. Enclosure in the letter of the Dir. of Land Records, no. 20305, dated 11 June 1894.
234 Ibid.

"the local definition of zirat lands seems to differ very widely from that which obtains under Section 120 of the Bengal Tenancy Act".[235] Macpherson, the Director of Land Records, agreed with the Settlement Officers in different districts, as to "the conflict on the one hand between popular usage in Bihar of the words sir, zirat, khamar, and the legal sense of these words as defined in Chapter XI of the Tenancy Act".[236]

Indeed, the ambiguity of this definition in the Bengal Tenancy Act left enough scope for misrepresentation and wrangling on vital legal points. Under section 120 of the Act, only two classes of land could be entered as zirat, that is, lands in the continuous cultivating possession of the proprietor for twelve years or more; and lands recognised to be zirat by local village usage. The former was relatively well-defined and could be tangibly proved or disproved. But, the demarcation of village 'sir' lands was imprecise. If they were to be taken to cover all lands loosely termed 'sir' or 'zirat' in each village, there would be an enormous increase in the proportion of such lands, with a corresponding shrinkage in that of raiyati holdings. Hence, the local usage of these lands would have to be ascertained precisely by going far back in point of time, in the process of which several problems arose. As to zirat lands subsequently occupied by peasants, it might be argued that the zamindars had neglected their duties as defined in section 116. They thus forfeited their zirati rights in the land by allowing it to drift back into the common stock of village lands, thereby enabling the raiyats to acquire occupancy rights in them. Further, it was almost impossible to prove the exact status of these peasants in relation to the land, for it was seldom based on written leases or pattas, annual or otherwise, as required implicitly by the Act in case of zirati lands. Yet the assumption that the peasant had occupancy rights in the land in the absence of such specific leases, was actively opposed by the proprietor. This problem was particularly acute in Bihar where, unlike in Orissa, there were no previous settlement papers for reference, in verifying the areas claimed as zirat during the current survey.

235 Ibid., no. 929 A, From M. Finucane, Offg. Secy. to the Board of Rev. L.P., to the Secy. to the Govt. of Bengal, Rev. Dept., dated Calcutta, 24 July 1894, para. 8.

236 Ibid., p. 6, Letter no. 103 T.S., dated 25 June 1894.

The ignorance of the peasants and the dishonesty of the local *amin* (surveyor) and inspector were fully and effectively exploited by the proprietor in controversial cases. Colvin, the Settlement Officer of Champaran, wrote in 1894:

> The tenant, being accustomed to hear the land called 'zirat' and unaware of the effect of the entry 'zirat' in the survey papers, would very possibly raise no dispute, and thus, in mere ignorance, contribute to the destruction of his own occupancy rights. . . . If every inspector were honest there would still be numerous mistaken decisions, through ignorance, and if any inspector were dishonest there can be no doubt that the power of writing down lands as 'zirat malik' might be very seriously abused".[237]

[2.13] Methods of effecting increase in rent rates

Yet cases of eviction and settlements with new tenants were presumably limited in number, and "it was through increasing the rent rates of the old peasants that the *zamindars* derived the largest advantage from the increased demand for land".[238] This might have been achieved by (i) forced agreements, (ii) false suits for rent arrears, (iii) changed entries in the jamabandi, (iv) withholding of rent receipts, and (v) contraction of the local land measure during the assessment of peasant holdings. None of these methods being strictly legal, "the change is rarely effected in an open and undisguised manner".[239]

(i) "The commonest method of raising the rents is by inducing the *raiyat* to consent to the enhancement by the process of free contract".[240] Most often, however, such agreements (*ikrarnama*s) did not stand the test of scrutiny.[241] In March 1894, for instance,

237 LRP, Nov. 1894, no. 929 A, no. 201C, dated 14 May 1894, enclosure in the letter of the Dir. of Land Records, dated 11 June 1894. The nature of such abuses are described in some detail by Babu Sosi Bhusan Chowdhuri, Munsif of Chittagong (Ibid., Note by Babu Sosi Bhusan Chaudhuri, Munsif of Chittagong, circulated in Nov. 1893, para. 9.).

238 Chaudhuri, "Movement of Rent", p. 361.

239 *SR, Bhagalpur*, p. 79, para. 142.

240 LRP, Nov. 1894, Report on the Survey and Record of Rights in Muzaffarpur, sec. 2, p. 20, para. 72.

241 Ibid., p. 1232. Collin's letter no. 4J, dated 17 Nov. 1893, appended to the Dir. of Land Record's Annual Report, 1893. Collin noted:

a group of raiyats in Muzaffarpur denied any knowledge of a *sharahnama* (rent agreement) drawn up in their names, the *patwari* (village official) having signed in their absence. Collin wryly commented: "This is perhaps as good an instance as any that could be given of the option of free contract, by which the *raiyat*, in his generosity, voluntarily consents to forego part of the profits of his land. . . . it is extremely dangerous to allow the exercise of free contract when the circumstances of the parties are so unequal".[242]

(ii) Direct suits for enhancement were rarely brought, only twenty-five such cases having come up in five years in the Munsif's court in Muzaffarpur. The usual method was to effect an increase indirectly, by suing for arrears of rent at enhanced rates, and filing fictitious rent rolls in court, as was seen in the villages of Sirsia, Muhammadpur, Moshtaq and Roshanpur in Muzaffarpur. Sometimes rents were inflated indirectly, by the addition of *abwab*s (extra-legal impositions). The amount paid as rent was credited to abwabs, suits then being filed for the resulting rent arrears.[243]

(iii) Some cases of tampering of rent rolls, as by Udit Narain Singh of Chakrakhaira in Monghyr, were more complex and interesting.[244] In order to keep settlement rates very low for his estate, he forced the raiyats to state their rents at the absurdly low rate of 8 an. per bigha. He deliberately neglected to repair the embankments in order to prove that the land was submerged and of poor quality, and so to account for the low rates claimed. Thus, while his lands would be lightly assessed, he could use his influence over the tenants to go on collecting rents at the old

---

"The principle of free contract . . . is much abused . . . . This consent must always have been obtained by concealment of fact, and by ignoring the rights of the *raiyats*, or by improper pressure upon them". For various instances of this, see Chakrabarti, "Crisis in a Peasant Economy", p.172.

242 LRP, Nov. 1894, pp. 20–21, paras. 72, 74.

243 Ibid., p. 21, para. 75. In one instance in Muzaffarpur, fictitious rent rolls for fifteen years were filed, in order to exclude mention of the abwabs.

244 *SR, Monghyr (North)*, pp. 38–39, paras. 120–21.

rate (Rs. 2–8 to Rs. 3 per bigha) in spite of the attestation.[245] The Settlement Officers in Bhagalpur noted numerous cases "in which there is grave reason to suspect that documents produced in evidence before them are forged. . . . the record of rents laboriously collected at first hand from landlords and tenants, is frequently set aside by the civil courts on compromises wrung from intimidated *raiyats* on forged papers and perjured evidence".[246]

(iv) The withholding of rent receipts was easy as these were seldom, if ever, granted to the raiyats, especially for produce rents. Sometimes, *dakhila*s (receipts) were withheld till the abwabs were paid in full. Often, only *parkhai*s (temporary receipts) and not dakhilas were granted even on full payment of the rent, no mention being made of the amount paid.[247] The raiyats most often did not know their rentals, and being only too glad to get any form of receipt, failed to scrutinise them carefully.[248] When suits were filed for rent arrears after several years, "the *raiyat* cannot give any satisfactory documentary evidence of payment, while the landlord can very easily file some 'tuck' lists and 'hishab' prepared . . . to suit his own purpose".[249] The zamindar

245 In Bakarganj, many estates like Marichbonia and Kakrabonia "adopted this fraudulent method of deflating their receipts from rent, while at the same time they swell their income from the tenantry". The original jamabandis were not produced for fear of detection of such illegal enhancements. The Settlement Officers in Bakarganj felt that "Kabuliyats could be obtained with the greatest difficulty". (*SR, Bakarganj*, app. 8 p. xciii). In Darbhanga, it was noted that "the canker which has mainly affected agricultural prosperity, is the constant tampering with rent rolls and consequent uncertainty as to rents" (*DG: Darbhanga,* p. 83). In Bhagalpur, the landlords of Sabalpur and Panjwara avoided submitting their jamabandis during the attestation, on the plea of their having been destroyed by floods and fire respectively, in 1899. Even the imposition of fines under the Survey Act could not make them produce the documents (*SR, Bhagalpur*, p. 73, para. 136).

246 *SR, Bhagalpur*, p. 5, para. 15.

247 *SR, Bakarganj*, app. 18, p. cxii, Mauza Patuakhali (2925), estate no. 4645, Settlement with Durga Prasanna Roy Chowdhury.

248 LRP, Nov. 1894, Report on the Survey and Record of Rights in Muzaffarpur, p. 21, paras. 75–76.

249 *SR, Bakarganj*, app. 19, p. lxiv.

often denied the validity of the parkhais granted by his own agent. As in many cases such parkhais and even rent receipts were not acknowledged by the courts, tenants usually preferred to execute *kistibandi* bonds (contract for instalment payment) for any rent arrears claimed by the landlord, rather than to fight suits with him on the strength of such unreliable documents.

(v) In certain regions like Bhagalpur and Monghyr, demands for higher rent were made by diminishing the local land measure known as the *laggi.* The size, location and quality of the lands were noted in detail in a *khasra* or *laggit* (record) kept by the landlord. In effect, however, the initial measurements were made very roughly, the area being understated but overassessed. After a while the land was accurately re-measured, the excess area thus discovered being made to pay the same high rates. When a fairly accurate area had been detailed in the laggit, the unit of measurement was diminished; hence the area again increased in theory, and the application of the previous rates further inflated the rental. An elaborate local system of survey and assessment was thus converted by the landlords into "a method of making illegal enhancements".[250]

The process was facilitated by the absence of a standard unit of measure (*pargana laggi*): different lengths of the laggi were used, varying from village to village, and even from landlord to landlord within a single village. Different standards were used to measure rent-paying and *brahmottar* lands (granted rent-free to Brahmins) belonging to the same landlord.[251] Sometimes the land was not initially measured at all, so that there were no previous records to go by.[252] The case laws on the subject were imprecise, and the settlement courts left the parties to contend among themselves, to the great disadvantage of the raiyats.

250 *DG: Monghyr,* p. 124.

251 For diverse methods of measurement, as of fractional units of the laggi in Bakhtiyarpur in North Monghyr or the *kamarband* system in South Bhagalpur, see Chakrabarti, "Crisis in a Peasant Economy", p. 175.

252 LRP, Nov. 1894, no. 929A, File 22R/12, para. 5.

[2.15] Produce rents

The rent burden increased in real terms in case of produce payments, as they reduced the peasant's share in the profits of rising agricultural prices, while denying him the rights of occupancy in his land.

The produce-rent system had its rationale in the maintenance and upkeep of large-scale irrigation works required for subsistence cultivation, like the ahars and pynes in south Bihar. As noted earlier, rents in kind ensured the zamindar's participation, so essential for the smooth working of this system. In fact, in the early nineteenth century, the zamindars insisted on cash payments for their superior lands, as they entailed no such obligations on their part. Buchanan found cash rents were "much higher than the share which the landlord receives on the division of crops". Rents in kind fell easier on the raiyats, and related more closely to the varying levels of cultivation. Rents were more flexible on the whole in the first half of the nineteenth century: tenants were often allowed to choose between payments in cash and kind, and in case of the latter, between divisions of the actual produce (*batai*) and of the estimated out-turn (*danabandi*).

With time, the produce-rent system lost much of its relevance and dynamism. The endless partitions of estates depleted the resources of the zamindars, and minimised their involvement in works of reform or maintenance. Their attitudes hardened, and the system gradually underwent a deep, qualitative change in three distinct phases: *(a)* the replacement of the principle of batai or actual division of the crop by appraisement and fixed grain payments; *(b)* the payment of produce rent in terms of money; *(c)* and the commutation of cash-paying lands into produce tenancies.

[a] Replacement of batai by appraisment or fixed grain payments

Initially, the most significant change was the gradual replacement of the batai or *aghorebatai* (a simple division of the actual crop) by the danabandi system of dividing the estimated out-turn. Unlike batai, it ruled out the possibility of pilferings by the peasant from the crop on the field. Indeed,"danabandi is the system which is most in favour with the landlords, who, by means of various abwabs or cesses and over-appraisement, manage to secure a very large proportion of the out-turn – as much as 27 *seers* in the *maund* in some cases". Instances are noted where the danabandi estimate was further inflated by the amalgamation of *amla*s' dues (*bhaoli nausat*) with it, though the amlas continued to claim their share separately from the raiyats.[253] Such estimates gradually became a most effective lever against recalcitrant raiyats. As land prices rose in the later years of the nineteenth century, distraint was often made on the strength of false rent suits based on over-appraisement of the crop. The batai, varying between one-third, two-fifths and half the produce in different regions, was known as *adhiyari*, *bhag* or barga in Bengal, and as *dhulibhag* in Orissa. A variation of the dhulibhag based on appraisement corresponded to the danabandi system.

The gradual change from batai to danabandi was noted in the Bisthazar estate as early as in 1835, during the survey proceedings in south Monghyr. The change became widespread during the next three decades. In 1849, P. Taylor, Collector of Gaya, found that the "just and simple system which formerly prevailed all over has now given way almost universally to that of danabandi".[254] In 1862, the Collector of Shahabad observed that "the old system almost universally in vogue" had been "gradually superseded by the danabundee system".[255]

An even more oppressive form of produce rent consisted of fixed grain payments irrespective of the crop size, such as the sanja in Midnapur and Orissa, the *dhankarari* in Faridpur and Bakarganj, and the *manhunda* in Bhagalpur and Monghyr. It required the peasant to surrender a specific quantity of grain whether the season was favourable or otherwise, and laid the greatest pressure upon him in lean years, when he was least able to bear it. For instance, in Nij Khurda, Banpur and other parts of the Puri district, the sanja usually amounted to about six

253 *DG: Monghyr*, p. 126; *SR, Bhagalpur*, p. 122, para. 227.

254 Bengal Board of Revenue Proceedings, 10 July 1849, no. 21, Taylor's letter to the Comm., Patna Div., 19 May 1849, para. 5.

255 Ibid., 24 July 1863, no. 149; Report on the Working of Act X of 1859 and Act VI of 1862 of Bengal Council, app., Letter of the Collector, Shahabad, 16 Dec. 1862, para. 73.

maunds per acre, which would fetch Rs. 6 in a good year and Rs. 9 during a lean season.[256] The landlord thus profited from scarcity prices, to the acute distress of the peasant. Instances are known of raiyats starving, yet buying grain at exorbitant rates during famine years, in order to pay their rents under this system.[257] The situation was comparable to Ireland, where the small peasant could not consume his grain, which was to be sold for rent. "If the people are forced to consume their oats and other grain, where is the rent to come from?" wrote the Commissariat Officer at Westport in 1846.[258] In Faridpur, dhankarari was common in certain regions like Kotwalipara and Gopalganj, where "the rent is much severer than the prevailing cash rents".[259] It was of recent origin in parts of Bakarganj where, "owing to difficulties in measuring the crop and to the fluctuations in its amount with the varying seasons, the landlords subsequently devised a new system, —the dhankarari". It maximised the share of the growing class of bhadraloks in the rising foodgrain prices, while minimising the expenses of cultivation. The landlords neither bought the seed nor supplied the plough and cattle, so that "both the burden and the hazard of cultivation were taken by the tenant". Hence, if the barga tenancies were disliked by the raiyats, the dhankarari was detested by them.[260] In Bhagalpur and Monghyr, raiyats paying in such fixed, bulk amounts of grain (manhunda) were deepest in debt to their landlords, the arrears of each year being carried forward in their names, irrespective of famine or scarcity.[261]

[b] Produce rent in cash terms

Having secured a sizeable proportion of the produce whether by appraisement or fixed payments in place of a simple division of the actual crop, the landlords next tried to make their own terms

256 *DG: Puri*, p. 174.

257 *DG: Darbhanga*, p. 81.

258 Capt. Perceval to Trevelyan, 14 Aug. 1846. Quoted in Woodham-Smith, *Great Hunger*, pp. 76, 122.

259 *SR, Faridpur,* p. 32, para. 75.

260 *SR, Bakarganj*, p. 168, para. 332.

261 *DG: Monghyr*, p. 127.

in determining the form of this payment. In fact, a further change in the danabandi or manhunda systems occurred in the form of *mankhap* rents, by which the zamindars began to insist on the payment either of their share of the produce in terms of cash, or an inflated money value of this share. The former was a further means of increasing their share, for it would fetch a larger amount of the grain in money terms at the time of the kist payment, when low harvest prices prevailed. The latter was favoured by the smaller, resident zamindars in remote areas, where the problems and cost of carriage made them eager to avoid the trouble of directly marketing their share of the produce. The low post-harvest prices often forced the peasant to hypothecate his crops, which went at far cheaper rates than free crops that were sold in the open market.[262] In some districts like Bakarganj, four kists were fixed instead of the two recognised by government. If the tenant failed to clear his dues in any of these kists, a *kist-khelapi* interest on the arrears was realised at 25 to 50 per cent and sometimes to the extent of 60 per cent.[263] From the peasant's viewpoint, it thus "embodies all the vices of the cash rent system without any of its advantages".[264] This system, resorted to temporarily by the zamindars in the late eighteenth century only to dispose of their grain during short spells of low agricultural prices, became widely accepted by the mid-nineteenth century. Taylor, Collector of Gaya, went to the extent of stating that "rent is hardly ever, if ever, paid in kind in Bihar", the danabandi system being "in fact a nugdee one of an arbitrary and fluctuating nature, only ostensibly based upon division of crops".[265]

The arbitrariness of the system was heightened in cases where the zamindar specified not only the amount, but also the type of crop to be given in rent. For instance, it was found during the survey proceedings in north Monghyr in 1899–1904, that in the village of Rani in Teghra thana, the tenants holding an area

[262] Ghosh, *Agricultural Labourers,* pp. 263–64.

[263] *SR, Bakarganj,* app. 18, p. cx.

[264] *DG: Bhagalpur*, p. 3.

[265] Bengal Board of Revenue Proceedings, 4 Jan. 1850; no. 30, Taylor's letter to the Comm., Patna Div., 22 Nov. 1849, para. 6; Ibid., 6 Nov. 1849, no. 43, Taylor's letter of 13 Oct. 1849, para. 2.

of 677 bighas on batai for six years were forced to execute *kabuliyats* (contracts with tenants) agreeing to pay mankhap rents at 5 or 6 md. per bigha according to the *paseri* (list) of the malik's *cutcherry* (office), in terms of special crops like chillies, tobacco, wheat and maize. Even if the peasant did not grow these crops, payment was still to be made in their market value, subject to a maximum of Rs. 50 per bigha. The peasant's choice of crops was thus restricted by the landlord.[266]

[c] Conversion of cash rents

The third and most radical change attempted by the landlords was the outright conversion of cash to produce rents in many areas. The move was not unreasoned, for it enabled them to share in the benefits of the rising agricultural prices. It became a distinct feature in the 1890s, when a steady and secular rise in foodgrain prices also became apparent. The produce-rent system further helped them to avoid the various restraints imposed on the enhancement of cash rents by Act X of 1859 and the Tenancy Act of 1885. Indeed, produce tenancies seldom enjoyed a fixity of rent or security of tenure. In most districts, "the idea is prevalent that occupancy rights do not accrue in lands held on produce rents".[267]

266 *SR, Monghyr (North)*, pp. 36–37, paras. 113–14. The mankhap kabuliyat of one Daho Paswan, a Dosadh tenant of Rani, clearly illustrates this: "without written permission of the said maliks, I have no power to grow in these lands any other crops than *mirchai*, wheat, rahar and *makai*, . . . the said maliks shall receive from me 2 *maunds mirchai*, 1 *maund* 10 *seers* wheat, 6 *paseris rahar* and 1 *maund makai* year by year. If I fail to deliver these crops at the appointed times, then I shall pay their value at the market rate".

267 *DG: Monghyr*, p. 125. This belief might have originated in a confusion between two groups of peasants paying rents in kind: the sharecroppers and a section of occupancy raiyats. The fact that the former had no legal or customary rights of occupancy in their land might have encouraged the notion that no peasant paying his rent in produce was entitled to such rights. J. C. Jack, Settlement Officer of Bakarganj, noted during the survey operations in the district between 1900 and 1908: "Whatever their legal incidents, barga tenancies are locally regarded as

In fact, the produce rent under systems like the *jaedadi* and *halhansali* in the Kishanganj and Supaul thanas and the *bhushan* and *patwan* rates in Colgong thana in Bhagalpur, the *birahwari* in southeast Purnea and the *utbandi* in Nadia, varied from year to year according to the area or type of crops sown. In these districts, where the sown area was liable to change every year due to floods and fluvial action, continuous possession of the same land for twelve years was impossible. Hence there was neither any fixity of rents, nor occupancy rights of any kind in these lands, while the annual measurements of the sown area provided an excellent source of threats and bribery for the landlord's amla. Moreover, discriminatory rates on the basis of the crops grown, such as the patwan in Bhagalpur, went against section 23 of the Tenancy Act, for it curbed the peasant's right to use and cultivate his land as he chose. Systems like the utbandi sharply reduced the value of even lakhiraj lands in Nadia; they would fetch only Rs. 3 or 4 per bigha as against Rs. 50 or 100 elsewhere, so that the peasant in these regions had little to fall back on, in years of stress.[268]

Produce tenancies thus gave the landlords several advantages over the tenants. Hence they tried to convert *nagdi* (cash lands) into bhaoli (produce tenancies) in various ways: by purchasing occupancy holdings at distress sales and settling them on rents in kind at higher rates; by extending their khas lands in every conceivable way, only to let them out on produce rents; by sometimes converting the nagdi lands to bhaoli and reconverting wholly or partly to nagdi, the second rate of cash rent far exceeding the first.

Complaints poured in from all over the Province against landlords converting cash into produce rents by force and threats of eviction, rather than by any process of law.[269] "From the point of view of the cultivator there is no problem in the district so urgent or so important as that of produce rent, as the land under

tenants-at-will or, in the most advanced areas, as mere agricultural labourers". (*SR, Bakarganj*, p. 71, para. 180).

268 *Selection of Papers*, vol. 3: p. 230.

269 For case instances from various districts, see Chakrabarti, "Crisis in a Peasant Economy", pp. 180–81.

produce rent is continually increasing and the dimensions of the problem are continually growing".[270]

The peasants' reaction to the problem came in sporadic acts of resistance and in an increasingly vocal demand for the commutation of produce to cash rents, since the 1890s. The process was stimulated by section 40 of the Bengal Tenancy Act (1885), which for the first time permitted commutation on applications by the peasants. The zamindars made every effort to frustrate such moves. Most of the suits were decided in their favour, and the commutations granted were annulled on the ground that the attestation officers were authorised only to record and not to settle rents.[271] Gradually however, such technical confusions were cleared, and the raiyats began to overcome their initial fear and hesitation. The number of applications increased rapidly, and the Settlement Officer of Patna found that commutation under section 40 of the Tenancy Act was the "heaviest item" in the case work.

[2.16] Abwabs

In 1886, the Collector of Gaya noted: "At present the struggle is centred round the bhaoli sections [of the Tenancy Act] and what are abwabs, and till these points are definitely settled, a certain amount of friction between landlord and tenant is inevitable".[272]

Indeed, the abwabs or cesses could not be ignored when considering the actual rent burden on the raiyat. In some districts like Purnea they more than doubled the nominal rates, while in Bakarganj they covered 25 per cent of the entire rental. Though the imposition of fresh abwabs was forbidden at the time of the Permanent Settlement, the zamindar persisted in collecting them, as he valued the abwab as an assertion of sovereignty over his tenants. Being thus extra-legal in nature, they were not subject to constraints, and hence had an unlimited potential for increase. For this reason the zamindar's agents, too, had a direct interest in realising the abwabs, in which they had a share. Yet, though formidable in their total impact, each of these impositions was

270 *SR, Faridpur*, p. 32, para. 75.
271 *SR, Bakarganj*, p. 168–69, para. 332.
272 *DCAR, Patna 1886–87*, para. 88.

too small in itself to provoke any organised resistance as in case of a direct enhancement of rent. Besides, the peasant did not object as strongly to the imposition of an abwab as to a rent enhancement, for the former, unlike the latter, was not formally recognised or legally recoverable, and hence was not considered a permanent addition to his burdens.

Annual levies for the payment of the landlord's collecting staff were universal under the names of *tahuri*, *mamuli*, *rashami*, *tahsilan*, *rajdhuti*, *pyadgan*, and so on. Levies for special purposes, as for roads and embankments (*khal bandi*), bridges (*pol kharach*), postal services (*dak kharach*), markets (*bhandari kharach*), rent receipts (*dakhila kharach*) and marriages (*sadiana*) were realised, besides annual charges (such as *punya* or *nazarana*), *bhet* (gifts in kind), and *begar* (forced labour) for a fixed number of days.

The last (begar) was very unpopular with the tenants, as it interfered with the work on their own fields during the peak season. Indeed, the beth-begar or predial services connected with the land, which prevailed extensively to the south of Hazaribagh in the Chotanagpur Division, became a focal point of dispute between landlords and tenants in the 1890s. As the raiyats pointed out, the custom of fifteen days' labour on the landlord's manjhihas (demesne) was levied per family or holding. But, while the landlord's manjhihas gradually expanded with the addition of khas lands (*rajhas*), the peasant's holding was being continuously split up into smaller fragments. Hence, the pressure on each unit increased with time, until it became oppressive. The zamindars refused to accept the tenants' demand for commutation of the beth-begar or *rakumat* into a cash payment, amounting to about Rs. 1–8 an. for fifteen days' labour.[273] In some areas, however, where the begar was less oppressive, as in the kar mahals of Dhalbhum in Singhbhum, such services were commuted to Rs. 2 per *hal* (plough-measure) of land as *betherkshati*.[274] In Manbhum, too, beth-begar on the khas lands was gradually reduced.

[273] LRP, Dec. 1894, no. 35, Letter from Rev. F. Hahn, German-Evangelical Lutheran (Gossner's) Mission, to Sir Charles Elliot, Lt. Gov. of Bengal, para. 3.

[274] *DG: Singhbhum*, p. 131.

The abwabs differed in implication from district to district. In Faridpur, Tipperah, Pabna, Dacca and Rajshahi they were confined mainly to the annual levies. These, even when high were at least certain and calculable, while "the peculiar vice of the chanda, fine and salami is that they are arbitrary, incalculable and an infringement on the liberty of the subject".[275] In Bakarganj, for instance, the *chanda* or subscription was raised on the flimsiest of pretexts, as for any function in the family of the zamindar, his *naib*s (estate manager) or *amla*s, for his pilgrimages, pleasure trips and visits to the tahsil cutcherry.[276] In Purnea, all subscriptions were incorporated into one demand called *babat*, i.e., "concerning" or "regarding". It was noted during the attestation in Surjapur: "The word 'babat' – (on account of) – by itself is suggestive of untold imposts. The tenant is content to pay babat and what the babat is for, he does not often care to philosophise over . . . it is babat and simply babat, leaving the unfortunate tenant . . . to devise the rest".[277] Another lucrative source for raising money was the salami amounting in effect to a bribe. The zamindar demanded a salami as the price for his recognition of land sales and transfers, as well as the appointment of village officials. In addition to these, diverse fines were collected on the pretext of dispensing justice.[278] J. C. Jack, in his Survey Report on Bakarganj, quotes thus from the diary of a landlord on a tour of his estate: "2nd Feb - from 4.10 p.m. the tenants began to come and paid naẓar . . . Retired for the night. God save me from all troubles in the night and bless me for the next morning, so that I may realize money in abundance as miscellaneous receipt".[279]

The abwabs were in effect incorporated into the rent, so that often the peasant, in his ignorance, failed to distinguish between

275 *SR, Bakarganj*, pp. 79–83, paras. 195–99.

276 Ibid., app. 7, p. 1xxxix; app. 17, p. ciii.

277 *SR, Purnea*, p. 122, para. 376.

278 *SR, Bakarganj*, app. 17, p. cvii. The papers for Mauza Girakhali in Bakarganj show that a certain Nadoo, son of Intoo of Pakshya, was fined Rs. 25 for quarrelling with his stepmother. Again, Asakali of Girakhali was fined Rs. 10 for failing to invite the *peadas* and *mridhaas* (village officials) on the occasion of his sister's marriage.

279 Ibid., p. 81, para. 197.

the two. This was specially true of north Bihar, where the peasants had little idea as to the extent of their rights and liabilities in the land. Landlords urged that since the tenants consented to the cesses, these should properly be considered part of the rental. But a contract to pay them was obviously void, as the law did not recognise them.[280] To neutralise this, even mortgage deeds and kabuliyats often contained stipulations regarding the payment of various dues or *kharchas*.[281] Payment was ensured by first crediting the money paid for rent against these heads, and later suing the peasant for rent arrears. The dakhila or rent receipt was withheld, until both rents and abwabs were paid up in full. The zamindar could also enforce such payments by social ostracism (*samaj-band*), or by coercion through his agents like the *paik, peada, mridha,* and others.

[2.17] Falling entitlement-level of the small peasant

The pressure of rent was felt more acutely with the fragmentation of peasant holdings into small, uneconomic units by the law of succession, the diminishing land-man ratio, the distress-sales of occupancy rights, and the extensive subletting of occupancy holdings as ratified by the tenancy legislation of 1859 and 1885. Subletting was not explicitly banned even at the level of non-occupancy raiyats and under-raiyats. The increase in subsistence cultivation fostered this trend, for rice, being a heavy-yielding staple—like the potato crop in Ireland—required very little in land or outlay. The conditions of Irish culture, i.e., "the whole of this structure, the minute subdivisions, the closely-packed population existing at the lowest level, the high rents, the frantic competition for land, had been produced by the potato".[282] Similarly, rice cultivation determined the size and pattern of peasant holdings in Bengal. Due to the high yield of rice, the tendency of the peasant was to eke out a living, however meagre, from a holding which could not otherwise support his family.

[280] LRP, Nov. 1894; Report on the Survey and Record of Rights in Muzaffapur, p. 23, para. 79.
[281] *SR, Bakarganj*, app. 17, p. civ; app. 18, p. cix.
[282] Woodham-Smith, *Great Hunger*, p. 35.

For instance, in 1888, 40 per cent of the peasants in selected areas of Patna, and 60 per cent in Darbhanga were seen to hold less than four bighas of land, while the minimum size of a subsistence holding was seven bighas for an average peasant family of five members.[283] In Gaya, 48 per cent of the peasants had holdings of five bighas, which could not support a cultivator and his family.[284] In Dholla in Birbhum, only one out of thirty peasant households had lands which could support a family of three by local standards.[285] The result was a starvation-level entitlement even in normal times, consisting largely of khesari *dal* (a variety of lentil) and only one meal a day.[286] Such uneconomic holdings obliged many of the small peasants to supplement their income from land, by working as agricultural labourers.

[3] *De-industrialisation and the decline of traditional rural crafts*

The growing labour surplus in agriculture could not be absorbed in the rural trades or crafts, as the economics of colonial exploitation checked industrialisation, urbanisation and capitalist development. Even the linkage effects of jute production, plantations, and extractive industries were not locally felt. The growth of the jute economy, for instance, fitted in neatly with the commercial needs of the British empire, and "worked against the interests of the bulk of the peasantry through a market mechanism subject to gross imperfections".[287] The limited demand for labour in these new fields could not absorb even a fraction of those displaced by the decline of traditional handicrafts. For instance, in 1892 the total number of workers employed in the organised sectors and plantations came to no

283 *Dufferin Report*. Comm. to the Govt. of Bengal, Rev. Dept., 2 June 1888, paras. 15 and 18.

284 Dr Grierson, *Note on Gaya District* (Calcutta, 1893), p. 94.

285 *Dufferin Report*. Collector, Birbhum, to Comm. Burdwan Div., 30 May 1888.

286 Ibid., Comm. Patna Div. to Govt. of Bengal, Rev. Dept., 2 June 1888, para. 17.

287 Ashok Sen, "Agrarian Structure", p. 60.

more than 500,000 approximately, which was less than those previously supported by indigenous salt production alone.[288]

The decline of certain indigenous industries was a most persistent feature in this period. The rudiments of the problem did not go unnoticed in contemporary journals and newspapers. *The Statesman* noted in its editorial of 22 August 1888: "The weavers can neither employ machinery, nor have they probably the ability to learn its use, or to betake themselves to other fields of labour. . . . The same story is being repeated all over the country . . . let no one imagine we pay a small price in India for the unquestioned advantages of free trade, since it costs us the exasperation, the despair, and finally the ruin of a large section of the industrial population".

[3.1] Decline of cotton weaving

There was still a local demand for coarse cotton cloth like the *gamcha* (cotton piece used as a towel), *masari than* (cloth for mosquito nets), or *pagri* (cloth for making turbans) among the poorer classes of the population. This was specially noted in tribal tracts like the Santhal Parganas, Chotanagpur, Angul Khondmals or the Garo Hills, where such cloth was preferred to the more finished but less durable products of foreign mills. But there was no organised trade in these coarser manufactures, which were limited to those areas where they were in demand. Sometimes the coarser cotton cloth was made on contract as in case of the Santhals, who supplied the weaver with *kapas* (type of cotton) grown in their fields and paid him the wages for his labour annually, in grain.[289] As many Santhals emigrated to Malda and the jungles of Dinajpur, a demand for coarse cloth developed in these regions.[290] Similarly, in Paharpur in the Raj Banaili and Srinagar Estate, the villagers supplied the thread to the weavers, who were paid a contract rate of one pice per yard for a particular

288 Ibid., p. 72.

289 LRP, Apr. 1898, no. 4, Note on Cotton Industries of Bengal, by Rowland Nogendra Lal Chandra.

290 Ibid., nos. 70–71, no. 1416 R, dated Dumka, 25 June 1897. From R. Carstairs, Dy. Comm. Santhal Parganas, to the Secy. to the Govt. of Bengal, Rev. Dept., para. 10.

type of cloth. About three to seven yards of this cloth could be woven in a day by one man.[291] However, this limited local demand for coarse cloths, and even the silk industry thriving in certain areas, could not sustain the class of weavers.

The roots of the problem lay in: *(a)* a growing attraction for the fine but flimsy imported fabrics sold by Marwaris in the local bazars even in backward districts like the Santhal Parganas; *(b)* the failure to develop subsidiary occupations like spinning or dyeing; *(c)* the purely seasonal demand for coarse cloths; and *(d)* the rising cost of production.

[a] Indeed, the indigenous cotton industry was almost ruined by the intrusion of machine-made piece goods from Lancashire and Manchester, which were finer and cheaper than the local manufactures, and had greater variety and range of colour. The lowest price of a locally made *dhoti* or *sari* was between Rs. 2 and Rs. 3, while a mill-manufactured dhoti or sari cost only 10 to 12 annas. Cotton weaving also faced competition from the silk industry. Many cotton growers took to mulberry cultivation and cocoon rearing, and a large number of the Jolas and Jugis were employed in the manufacture of silk and *tussar* (coarse silk) fabrics.[292]

[b] Some hill races like the Tipperahs and Manipuris increased their scope for employment by dyeing homespun yarns of the hill cotton. Sometimes the dyes of the Manipuris were so brilliant as to excite the envy even of leading British dyers like Messrs. Wardle and others. This, however, was an exception rather than the rule. In Angul and Singhbhum, for instance, there were no professional dyers, and the weavers bought dyed yarns. In Singhbhum, the Kols spun two kinds of thread, which were used by the Pan tantis in manufacturing coarse cloth; all the other weavers generally used imported thread numbers 10, 12 and 16

291 *Dufferin Report*, no. 51, dated Camp Ekar, Circle Nauhatta, 24 Apr. 1888. From Baboo Burhandeo Narayan, Asst. Settlement Officer, Raj Banaili and Srinagar Estate, to the Collector of Bhagalpur, para. 21.

292 LRP, April 1898, nos. 18–19, no. 1474 R, dated Hazaribagh, 1 Feb. 1897. From J. L. Herald, Dy. Comm. Hazaribagh, to the Secy. to the Govt. of Bengal, Rev. Dept. Report on Cotton Fabrics, paras. 8–12.

for weaving coarse cloth, and number 20 for fine cloth.[293] In Hazaribagh, though cotton was grown and collected locally, imported yarn was used for the manufacture of cotton fabrics. "The use in handlooms of home-spun twist is exceedingly rare, for cotton-spinning . . . does not exist in this district". No oil was pressed from the cotton seeds, nor were the seeds crushed for cake.[294] In Patna, twenty-five years earlier, women of small means spun thread from the local cotton, but this industry was "almost extinguished by the importation of cheap thread made by machines".[295] Hence, weaving was the only form of employment relating to the indigenous cotton industry.

[c] The weaver found work mainly during the four months of the cold weather, when thick, handwoven cloth was much in demand. This coincided with the harvesting season, so that the slack period for the weaver was also that of a minimum demand for field labour, except during the rabi harvest or transplantation of the aman rice. The average monthly earnings of a fully employed weaver could be around Rs. 6 as estimated in Burdwan, and between Rs. 4–8 to Rs. 5 in Singhbhum. Yet, due to such under-utilisation, "few weavers are in full work", and it was difficult to estimate their actual earnings.[296]

[d] Even the few months' work proved unremunerative, for the cost of production had gone up appreciably for the weaver, while the price of cloth could not keep pace with it. In fact the demand and price of cotton fabrics fell: a five-*hath* (hand-measure) dhoti which cost five to five-and-a-half annas forty years ago in Murshidabad, sold for only four annas in 1888.[297]

293 Ibid., nos. 5–6, no. 967 R, dated Chaibassa, 20 Jan. 1897. From the Dy. Comm. Singhbhum, to the Secy. to the Govt. of Bengal. Note on Cotton Fabrics in the district of Singhbhum, para. 3.

294 Ibid., nos. 18–19, no. 1474 R, dated Hazaribagh, 1 Feb. 1897. From J. L. Herald to the Secy. to the Govt. of Bengal, Rev. Dept. Report on Cotton Fabrics, paras. 8–12.

295 Ibid., no. 69, no. 541R, dated Bankipore, 18 June 1897.

296 *Dufferin Report*, no. 351. R, dated Ranchi, 31 May 1888; no. 7RG, dated Burdwan, 16 Apr. 1888. From N. S. Alexander, Comm., Burdwan Div., to the Secy. to the Govt. of Bengal, Rev. Dept.

297 Ibid., no. 1 M.A. dated Calcutta, 17 May 1888. From A. Smith, Comm. Presidency Div., to the Secy. to the Govt. of Bengal, Rev. Dept.

In Angul, the price of an ordinary handloom used by the Pans was about Rs. 5–8, the depreciation on which, along with the cost of repairs and interest on capital, would be about Rs. 1–8 per annum. As the market price of a sixteen-hath piece of cloth, which took about four days to weave, was Rs. 1–8, minus Rs. 1–2 (as the value of the cotton to be exchanged for thread), a weaver's earnings were not much more than one anna and six pice per day.[298] In Bhagalpur, their earnings were about two annas a day.[299] Weavers engaged in the manufacture of silk and tussar fabrics, though better off, were not free from these problems. The tussar weavers of Hasimpur in Midnapur, for instance, formerly turned out one tussar piece for Rs. 5, minus four annas for selling the refuse tussar, i.e., Rs. 4–12 net. In 1888, a piece of tussar cloth cost Rs. 6–11, the net cost after deducting five annas for the shoddy being Rs. 6–6. But the price of finished tussar, which was also affected by the market for European piece-goods, did not go up in proportion. It sold at Rs. 8 at most, as against Rs. 7 per piece in former times. Considering the rising cost of production, the net profit of the weaver went down from Rs. 2–4 to Rs. 1–10 per piece, while the cost of living had doubled in the last two decades. Moreover, malarial fever had considerably reduced their working capacity in these areas. Hence, "the weavers cannot save anything. . . . Having no capital, they borrow Rs. 20 or Rs. 25 at a time from their majahans, and by selling cloths repay them gradually".[300]

Due to these diverse problems, the community of weavers gradually dwindled. This was most marked in specific areas, as in case of the tussar industry in Bhagalpur, where the number of looms in 1888 was only half of what it was ten years earlier.[301] A study in selected areas of Hazaribagh showed that between 1860 to 1896, weaving as an industry ceased to exist in 234 out of 483, i.e., in 48.4 per cent of the weaving villages. During this period, the number of handlooms dwindled down from 3,340 to 1,013, i.e., by about 30 per cent. Assuming that the same number of persons were employed at each hand-mill throughout

[298] Ibid., no. 4T, dated Angul, 12 April 1888, para. 19.
[299] Ibid., no. 8, dated Bhagalpur, 5 May 1888.
[300] Ibid., Midnapur, 13 April 1888.
[301] Ibid., no. 3, 10 April 1888, para. 16.

the period, the number of weavers should have fallen from 8,650 to 2,920. However, only 1,298 weavers were actually employed at the looms in 1896. If the numbers are approximately correct, the loom that supported 2½ persons in 1860 could not support more than 1¼ persons in 1896, which amply reflects the miserable condition of the cotton industry at the close of the nineteenth century.[302]

Some of the weavers clung tenaciously to their hereditary profession, while others sought new forms of employment. The process was not easy. As the editor of *The Statesman* noted in the issue of 22 August 1888: "The conditions of an almost wholly agricultural country and the force of caste render absolutely impossible any speedy shifting of skill from one employment to another". Even the social standing of the weavers began to change with the times. The Tanti usually stood higher than the Jugi in the social scale, while the Muslim Jola was placed very low even in his own community. "At the present day, however, the industrial position of all three classes is pretty nearly equal. It is very low, being nearly equivalent to that of a day labourer".[303]

As a sizeable proportion of the weavers took to agriculture and field labour, the resulting pressure on land was acutely felt in many districts. In Midnapur, the Settlement Officer of Bogri and Kesiari noted in April 1888: "The absence of grazing-grounds is due to weavers and other castes who used to follow other professions before, having now taken to agriculture for their subsistence. The margin of cultivation has thus been extended far into the Khas palit lands of the village".[304] In Bhagalpur, the Collector observed about the weavers: "Imported cloth has ruined this industry and . . . about half of this class have taken to field labour".[305] In Burdwan, "most of the weaver class supplement their earnings . . . by working as agriculturists or agricultural

302 LRP, April 1898, nos. 18–19, no. 1474 R dated Hazaribagh, 1 Feb. 1897. Report on Cotton Fabrics, para. 14.

303 Ibid., paras. 16–17.

304 *Dufferin Report*, Midnapur, 13 April 1888. From B. Banerjee, Settlement Officer, Bogri and Kesiari, to the Director of Land Records and Agriculture.

305 Ibid., no. 3, 10 April 1888. From A. A. Wace, Collector

day-labourers". As Oldham, Collector of Burdwan, noted: "few weavers are in full work. . . . But the labour market, with its minimum rate of 10 *pice* a day all the year round, is open to them".[306]

[3.2] Decline of other trades and industries

Of other artisans and small traders in the peasant economy, the potters suffered in many districts due to the replacement of earthenware vessels by brass and bell metal to a considerable extent. In Nadia, the earthenware *sanki* (plate) for eating rice gave way to brass and bell-metal *thali*s (metal plates).[307] In Angul, the grant of jagirs to potters declined in the 1880s, "the one great reason being the increased demand for brass vessels". Moreover, in the potter's trade the risk of fire was high, recurring every five to six years and causing damages of at least Rs. 20.[308] In Bhagalpur the potter earned only about one and a half to two annas a day, which was no more than half the income of an ordinary village carpenter. In this district, the goldsmith was said to get less work than his father did, due to less spare cash among the raiyats.[309] Salt manufacture, which was an important industry in the coastal regions of Orissa, as near the Chilka Lake and Devi River, was paralysed by government regulations. Cocoon rearing and sericulture, which employed a large number of Pans and Haris in Angul, declined due to the extensive reclamation of jungle lands. The *asan* tree, upon which the silkworms were chiefly reared in this estate, were all but driven into the reserved forest, and the silkworm rearers dwindled down to a very small number.[310] In Murshidabad, too, the silk industry was passing

---

Bhagalpur, to the Comm. Bhagalpur Div., dated Bhagalpur, 7 April 1888, para. 16.

306 Ibid., no. 7RG, dated Burdwan, 16 April 1888, paras. 4, 21.

307 Ibid., no. IMA, dated Calcutta, 17 May 1888, para. 64.

308 Ibid., 4T, dated Angul, 12 April 1888. From Baboo A. K. Roy, Jt. Settlement Officer, to the Director of Land Records, Bengal, para. 21.

309 Ibid., no. 3, 10 April 1888. From A. A. Wace to the Comm., Bhagalpur Div., dated Bhagalpur, 7 April 1888.

310 Ibid., no. 4 T, dated Angul, 12 April 1888, para. 23.

through a depression during 1886–96, there being frequent silkworm epidemics. Carpenters and blacksmiths were better off, though they usually found difficulty in obtaining work during the four months from September to December.[311] Iron manufacturers were often reduced to starvation, as in Angul, where they could earn no more than six pice a day. Naturally, they sought relief by working as day labourers.

[4] *Depression in the Labour Market*

Indeed, the mounting pressure of the population on land, together with any fluctuation or depression in the various trades and services in a rural society, immediately caused a surplus in the agricultural labour market, which was open to all. "They [the agricultural labourers] constitute a large body, probably a fourth of the whole population, and their numbers are everywhere recruited from cultivators having holdings too small for their support".[312] In the agrarian sector, not all could acquire or inherit land; hence, they swelled the ranks of the agricultural labourers. Simultaneously, the decline in many industries such as weaving, ivory carving and salt manufacture, and temporary setbacks in other trades (as in those of the potter, goldsmith or cocoon rearer in specific areas), put further pressure on the land. In fact, "the continual tendency of events has been to turn the people more and more towards agriculture, and less and less to manufacture".[313] Thus, the labour market absorbed and offset the pressures and strains in the peasant economy to a considerable extent. Due to this elasticity and the constantly changing size and pattern of field labour in rural society, agricultural labourers were not recognised as a distinct class in the census returns, and there was no definite information as to their numbers.[314]

[311] Ibid., no. 351R, dated Ranchi, 31 May 1888, para. 21.
[312] Ibid., no. 87 T-R. From P. Nolan, Secy. to the Govt. of Bengal, to the Secy. to the Govt. of India, Rev. and Agri. Dept., para. 25.
[313] Ibid., no. 109 M, dated Rampur Boaleah, 30 April 1888.
[314] Ibid., Agri. no. 87 T-R, 30 June 1888, p. 12, para. 25.

[4.1] Factors affecting wage rates

[a] Size of surplus labour

This constant and growing pressure on the agricultural labour market by the small peasants and artisans in distress made for a ready surplus and directly affected wage rates, in keeping with the principles of demand and supply. The government enquiry on the lower orders of the population in Bengal, based on detailed district reports, thus concluded in 1888 that "the pressure of population on natural resources has a decisive influence on the rate at which labour is remunerated throughout the Lower Provinces generally".[315] Thus in the extreme east, where the land was most fertile and labour relatively scarce, the demand for labour was greater and wages were high. The daily wage of an agricultural labourer was about four annas in Chittagong, four to six annas in Bakarganj, and four annas and two meals (worth another two annas) in Khulna. As one moved westward, the pressure on the soil increased, while wage rates dropped in inverse ratio. They varied between three and four annas in Rangpur, Dinajpur, Purnea and Malda, coming down to two to three annas in Murshidabad and three annas in Midnapur. In parts of the Rajshahi and Burdwan Divisions wage rates were stabilised to some extent by the unhealthy climate of the region, which did not permit the number of labourers to rise to a point where they would press too hard on the local resources. In the north Bihar districts of Bhagalpur, Monghyr, Darbhanga, Muzaffarpur and Saran, as well as in Gaya and Patna, wage rates were as low as five or six pice to two annas per day. Further west, in Chotanagpur, a study of selected areas showed an average daily income of no more than six pice.[316] The comparative lowness of rates in Bihar was widely recognised. In the Commissioner's Report for the Patna Division (1874–75), the Deputy Magistrate of Bihar noted: "For what we pay 6 *annas* in Eastern Bengal, 8 *annas* in Calcutta, for that we pay 3 to 4 *pice* in Behar. . . . The

[315] Ibid., no. 87 T-R, Darjeeling, 30 June 1888. From P. Nolan to the Secy. to the Government of India, Rev. and Agri. Dept., para. 14.

[316] Ibid., para. 21.

lower classes of labourers, as coolies ploughing in the fields, digging earth, carrying grain, are paid not more than 3 to 4 *pice*, or 2½ *seers* of paddy or *janera* when they are paid in kind, which is generally done".[317] The reason for such low rates was that, except in parts of Champaran, the pressure of the population was excessive in Bihar, ranging between 500 to 750 persons per square mile.

[b] Social composition of labourers

The social composition of the population was as important as its volume. As John Boxwell, Officiating Commissioner of the Patna Division, observed in 1888, "we must not trust too much to the calculations from density".[318] A study of selected areas in neighbouring districts like Nadia, Jessore and Khulna showed a considerable disparity in wage rates, on account of the varying proportion and composition of agricultural labourers. In northwest Nadia, about one-fifth to one-third of the population consisted of landless day labourers, while there were few of this class in Satkhira or eastern Jessore. The only day labourers in Jessore were recruited from among the "Bunas" of aboriginal descent and some low castes like Bagdis and Kahars.[319] Even within a single district like Murshidabad, some regions like the Bagri and Kalantar in the east suffered more during lean seasons, for they had a labouring population of 30 per cent, as against only 10 to 15 per cent in the Rarh tract on the west.[320] In Bihar, the population was almost wholly agricultural, with a large proportion of small peasants and labourers.

Low-wage pockets usually had a greater concentration of female labourers, unskilled workers or "general labour" without any fixed avocation, as well as tribals and depressed classes, many of whom were bonded labourers working for one-third the rate of a free labourer. These were, in fact, the "built-in pressures" in the

317 Ibid., para. 12.
318 Ibid., no. 286G, Bankipore, 2 June 1888.
319 *Selection of Papers,* 6: p. 229; 4: pp. 257, 307, 313.
320 *Dufferin Report*. Letter no. 1 M. A. From A. Smith, Comm., Presidency Div., to the Government of Bengal, Revenue Department, Calcutta, 17 May 1888, p. 29.

agricultural labour market, which pulled down the general wage level.[321] The Commissioner of Chotanagpur observed: "In the parts most inhabited by aboriginals they [wage rates] are still very low, and often the wages of one or two members of the family are regarded merely as supplementing the general resources".[322]

Like the bonded labourers, female workers were mostly of tribal origin. No women of the ordinary cultivator class in Bengal, including low castes like the Bauris, would work in the fields except under extreme pressure. But in districts like Midnapur and Bankura, where the people were of a semi-aboriginal stock, women were found to husk paddy or carry in the harvest. However, they did not work regularly in the fields as day labourers. These women were recruited almost invariably from migrant tribals like the Nagpur Kols, Dhangars and sometimes, the Santhals.[323] Similarly, in the tribal tracts of Manbhum, a study of 157 labouring households showed that there was one female labourer for every two males.[324]

The tribals also worked as "general labour", who had no specific area of work; they laboured on the fields in the peak seasons and took to road repair, earthwork, construction work, etc., in the lean periods. This fluid nature of their work prevented them from asserting themselves in the labour market, and forced them to accept lower wage rates.[325]

In case of bonded labourers like the kamia, *musahar* or *jan* employed by zamindars and affluent raiyats, "the credit basis of the labour was reinforced by caste coercion".[326] However, in Gaya, land control rather than casteism accounted for the maliks' power over the kamias, who constituted 56 per cent of the agricultural labourers, and 11 per cent of the local rural population in 1898.[327] Even if the money value of the kamia's labour far exceeded the

321 Ghosh, *Agricultural Labourers*, p. 128.
322 *Dufferin Report*, no. 351R, Ranchi, 31 May 1888, para. 54. From C. C. Stevens, Comm. Chotanagpur Div., to the Secy. to the Govt. of Bengal, Rev. Dept.
323 Ibid., no. 7RG, Burdwan, 16 April 1888, para. 7.
324 Ibid., no. 351R, Ranchi, 31 May 1888, para. 7, quoted from the Notes of Mr Baker, Dy. Comm. of Manbhum.
325 Ghosh, *Agricultural Labourers*, p. 127.
326 Chaudhuri, "Rural Credit Relations", p. 241.
327 Prakash, *Bonded Histories*, pp. 168–69.

amount originally borrowed by him, the fiction of his debt was kept up and he was paid a meagre amount in coarsest grains, just enough for sustenance. The proportion of bonded labour was high in the tribal areas of Chotanagpur and Bhagalpur. In Palamau, the bulk of the people belonged to the labouring classes: Ahars, Dosadhs, Chamars, Bhuiyas, Kahars, Gareris and others of the kamia class.[328] In Bhagalpur, an enquiry in 1888 showed that 50 per cent of the labourers in Banka, 60 per cent in Madhipura and 42 per cent in Supaul always worked for one raiyat, presumably in this capacity.[329] Debt labour was widely practised in other regions as well, most notably in Dinajpur, Birbhum, Bankura, Midnapur and Orissa.

[c] Level of agricultural development

Besides the pressure of population on the soil and the distinctiveness of their social composition, wage rates were also related to the level of agricultural development in different regions. Indeed, labour conditions varied with the locality, "as the rate of the agricultural labourer's wages is always an index to the degree of prosperity enjoyed by the working classes in a Bengal district".[330]

The income level of the farmer determined the wage rates of the farmhands. Hence, low productivity per acre due to the minuteness of holdings (as in Bihar) or primitive methods of cultivation (as among the Kols, Paharias, Garos and Meches) would basically limit the peasant's income to a very low level. Moreover, in drought-prone, mono-crop regions like north Bihar, Bankura or the Chilka tract in Puri, the insecurity in agriculture was reflected in lower wage rates. Contemporary officials like D'Oyly clearly recognised the relative instability of the rice-tracts of Bihar: "Seetamarhi appears to be worse off in all respects

328 *Selection of Papers,* vol. 4: p. 328.

329 *Dufferin Report*. Letter no. 3 from J. Beames, Comm., Bhagalpur Div., to Secy. to Government of Bengal, Rev. Dept., 10 April 1888, p. 3.

330 Ibid., no. 87 T-R, Darjeeling, 30 June 1888. From P. Nolan, Secy. to the Govt. of Bengal, to the Secy. to the Govt. of India, Rev. and Agri. Dept., para. 25.

than the rest of Mozufferpore, just as Madhubani is worse off than the rest of Durbhunga".[331]

The varying levels of agricultural prosperity and disparity in wage rates in the different districts came into sharp focus in crisis years like 1896–97. In famine-prone regions like Nadia and the Chilka tract, people were used to government relief, and more ready to work at the low famine rates than in well-off districts like Khulna, Jessore, Pabna or Rajshahi. Indeed, the frustration of accepting employment at the relief works on a daily wage of one and one-fourth annas would naturally be much greater in Pabna (where the usual wage was four annas) than in Bihar, where it seldom rose beyond two annas a day even in years of plenty.[332]

[d] Seasonality in agricultural employment

The district rates as noted by local officials, however, cannot be taken to prevail uniformly during the whole year. Due to the purely seasonal nature of agricultural labour, employment could be found only for a maximum period of six to eight months, so that the yearly average would be much lower. The labourers got almost daily employment during the three months of the rainy season, i.e., from mid-June to September. The bhadoi crop was weeded in July and cut in August and September. Work on fields was most intensive during the two months of the aman harvest, in December and January. Cereals of the rabi harvest were cut within one month, in March-April. For the remaining six months, the agicultural labourers did not get daily or even frequent employment. Assuming that they could take up various other work during two months, the duration of their employment would be for a maximum period of eight months in the year. At harvest time, however, they earned almost double their usual payments in grain.[333]

[331] Ibid., no. 286G, Bankipore, 2 June 1888, quoted by John Boxwell, Offg. Comm. Patna Div., to the Secy. to the Govt. of Bengal, Rev. Dept.

[332] *Selection of Papers*, vol. 3: pp. 229, 282.

[333] *Dufferin Report*, no. 51, Camp Ekar, Circle Nauhatta, 24 April 1888, para. 27.

Conditions differed from region to region. In indigo-growing districts, workers found employment nearly all the year round. Indigo cultivation was labour intensive, requiring four and a half times as much labour as other crops—an acre under indigo giving employment to 172 labourers, as against 39 persons being employed on an acre under ordinary cultivation. But indigo cultivation shrank greatly at the end of the nineteenth century. The decline of the industry seriously affected labour wages in districts like Muzaffarpur. While the number of workers in indigo factories there increased between 1891–96 and then began to fall sharply, wages for agricultural labour rose correspondingly until 1896, falling since then from Rs. 4 to Rs. 3. Between 1901–1911, a decrease of more than 100,000 acres in indigo cultivation and the closure of indigo factories in south Bihar laid off about 50,000 labourers.[334]

The problem of off-season unemployment was naturally more acute in mono-crop areas than in multi-crop regions having two or three harvests in the year. The plight of exclusively rice-growing tracts like the northernmost parts of Bihar running along the Nepal border, the Barind lands in Rajshahi, the Kalantar in Nadia and Murshidabad, or the Chilka region in Puri was reflected in the growing volume of emigration. The labourers there were well off only during the first three months after the harvesting season, and felt the pinch during the remaining nine months of the year.[335] The Collector of Bankura observes: "At the seasons of sowing, transplanting and cutting paddy they are fully employed, but at other times they suffer much for want of employment and are reduced to one meal a day".[336]

These busy months, too, did not imply continuous employment, but "clusters of time when work was available".[337] During the peak seasons in agriculture there were intermittent

334 Ghosh, *Agricultural Labourers*, p. 168; *DG: Muzaffarpur*, p. 84.

335 A. Smith, Comm., Presidency Div., to the Secy. to the Govt. of Bengal, Rev. Dept. no. 1, MA dated Calcutta, 17 May 1888, para. 20.

336 N. S. Alexander, Comm., Burdwan Div., to the Secy. to the Bengal Govt., Rev. Dept. no. 7RG, Burdwan, 16 Apr. 1888. From the Report of Mr Taylor, Collector Bankura, para. 31(b).

337 Prakash, *Bonded Histories*, p. 170.

periods of unemployment or under-utilisation of labour, depending on the vagaries of climate and rainfall, and the natural processes of agricultural production. Though not long in themselves, these gaps between the different field operations added up to a considerable proportion. Moreover, this intra-seasonal unemployment could not be relieved by alternative work, as the labourer would have to be ready at hand to take up the next operation at the most opportune moment.

[4.2] Mitigating factors.

[a] Alternative employment

There was no systematic solution to these problems of unemployment and underemployment of labour in agriculture. Sporadic attempts were made to earn from other sources during the lean months—as from fishing, lumbering, ferrying and cutting of *golpatta* (leaves used for thatching) in the Sunderbans; weaving and bamboo-work in the Khondmals; collecting *ber* fruit, honey and other jungle produce in tribal areas like Chotanagpur and parts of Bhagalpur; or manufacturing salt in Puri and Balasore. In fact, due to the abolition of salt production, thousands of men in the coastal regions lost an employment opportunity for three to four months during the slack season.[338] Women supplemented the family income by husking rice, spinning cotton yarn, or collecting and selling snails, shell and firewood.

[b] Emigration

Emigration, whether seasonal or permanent, relieved the pressure on land to some extent in many parts of Bihar, Chotanagpur and Orissa. Saran was "the first district in Bengal to come to the point where it cannot maintain its population", so that emigration became a necessity.[339] Both in Saran and Chotanagpur, the steady flow of money remitted by the emigrants helped greatly

338 C. F. Worsley, Offg. Comm., Orissa Div., to the Secy. to the Bengal Govt., Rev. Dept., 20 PT, Camp Puri, 3 June 1888.

339 *DG: Saran*, p. 87.

in sustaining the local population. Emigration exercised a "powerful influence" in the tribal tracts, especially among the Oraons and Mundas in Chotanagpur, who were mobile, industrious and highly valued as labourers in the tea gardens of Assam, Jalpaiguri and the Duars. Emigrations to Assam were of a more permanent nature, but from the Duars about 10,000 people returned every year, bringing back a saving of approximately one lakh rupees.[340] The Bengal-Nagpur Railway and the coal mines of Jharia, Raniganj, etc. were also expected to attract a large number of workers.

Emigration to the eastern districts of Bengal was widespread and more effective. Here, the transplantation and harvesting of winter rice absorbed a large amount of immigrant labour. Upcountry men from north Bihar, Chotanagpur and the Santhal Parganas, as well as labourers from Orissa and the western and central parts of Bengal, caused an annual exodus from late November to January into the plush, aman-growing districts of the Dacca, Chittagong and Mymensingh Divisions. The volume of this emigration from west to east was reflected in the statements of the census of 1881, which showed that in Bengal proper there were 47,548 persons from Saran, 40,536 from Patna, 38,220 from Shahabad, 36,235 from Gaya, 25,481 from Muzaffarpur, 18,167 from Monghyr and 12,958 from Bhagalpur.[341] In neighbouring districts where the aus or boro rice predominated, as in Nadia and Satkhira (Khulna) respectively, the small peasants and labourers could reap the local harvest and later emigrate eastwards to participate in the harvesting of the aman rice.

Intra-district migrations were also common. In Khulna, for instance, many of the farmers in the north of the district also had *abads* (large clearings) in the Sunderbans in the south. Hence, many cultivators and labourers worked on their home fields during March to May, spent the next three months preparing the land in the Sunderbans, arrived in the north to reap the rice crop which matured earlier than in the south, and again went to

340 *Dufferin Report*, no. 351R, Ranchi, 31 May 1888.

341 Ibid., Darjeeling, 30 June 1888, para. 19. From P. Nolan, to the Secy. to the Govt. of India, Rev. and Agri Dept.

the southern abads for a second harvesting season. Work was thus plentiful in Jessore-Khulna. The danger here lay in the fact that scanty rains paralysed all agricultural operations, for the crops not only withered, but were subjected to saline floods.

On the whole, emigration had a limited and temporary effect in relieving pressure on the agricultural labour market. The migrations eastward would have assumed new dimensions of a more permanent nature with the work of jungle clearing, which would provide enough employment for migrant labour in the Sunderbans, Chittagong and the extensive wastes of Assam and Burma. The Santhals in particular were renowned for their pioneering efforts in clearing forests and settling down (as in Malda, Dinajpur, the Barind lands in Rajshahi, or the jungles of Madhupur in Dacca) until the pressure of rent forced them to move to new jungle tracts. But the upcountry men from the congested Bihar districts proved unsuitable for the work of reclamation, as they could not withstand exposure to swamps and malarial fever.[342]

[c] Long-term or permanent attachment of labour

Labourers worked in the field on a daily, seasonal or yearly basis. The second group would thus be able to avoid intermittent unemployment during the agricultural season, while those working throughout the year, mainly bonded labourers, could hope for protection from off-season unemployment. In fact, the high seasonality of agriculture in south Bihar accounted largely for the growth of the local kamia system. As Gyan Prakash noted: "the land holders' need for an assured labor supply during the peak periods of agricultural activity and the laborers' need for support during lean months were combined in the Kamia labor system".[343] The classification of 'day' and 'seasonal' labourers was confusing, in as much as all workers, including seasonal and even bonded labourers, received their wages daily in grain. The distinction lay, rather, in the fact that the duration of employment of a 'day' labourer, which might well be for the

342 Ibid., para. 19.
343 Prakash, *Bonded Histories*, p. 170.

whole season, was casual, and not specified clearly by any agreement between the employer and the labourer.

[d] Payments in grain

As noted, payment in kind was almost universal, the money value of the grain paid being recorded in calculating wage rates for the different localities.[344] Hence, no direct comparison of rates could be made until the grain payments were converted to their money value according to the varying levels of foodgrain prices in different regions. Almost everywhere, there was a separate standard of rates for the harvesting season, when instead of daily wages, the labourers received a share of the quantity of crops reaped by them. In the Banaili and Srinagar Estate, they were given one-tenth of the crop reaped, which came to "about double the amount of their ordinary daily wages". In other parts of Bhagalpur, they received one-sixteenth of the grain in the bhadoi harvest, and payments by the sheaf from the rabi crop, the rate being about double the general wage. Labourers engaged by the year got more liberal terms, receiving one out of every eight or ten sheafs during the rice harvest.[345] In the Sunderbans, the rate was one for every ten or eleven bundles reaped. In Burdwan, the Collector, Oldham, noted in 1888 that "in the height of the field season (from August to December), labour is at a premium and special rates have to be given".

Grain payments benefited the labourer in several ways. The rise in foodgrain prices did not affect them to any great extent, as the quantity of grain paid remained the same, irrespective of prices or out-turn. It thus served as an insurance against famines,

344 For instance, an adult male in 1888 received five cutcha or four pucca seers of unhusked rice in the Banaili and Srinagar Estate in the Santhal Parganas, two to three seers of rice or cheaper grain in Hazaribagh and Manbhum, three seers of dhan in the Kolhan and four in Porhat, three local seers of grain and one seer *sattu* (gram flour) in Saran, two to two and a half seers of the coarsest and cheapest grain in Patna, four seers of dhan or five seers of makai in Muzaffarpur, and five seers of dhan and a meal in Burdwan.

345 A. A. Wace, Collector, Bhagalpur, to the Comm., Bhagalpur Div. 7 April 1888, para. 14.

especially for the kamia, musahar, *baramashiya* and other bonded labourers, who were to be fed and clothed by their masters throughout the year, even in seasons of drought. Besides being thus protected from the effects of price rise and famine, the labourers could even make a marginal profit from the secular rise in foodgrain prices, to the extent that the surplus grain after consumption could now be sold for a higher price, in order to buy other necessities of life.

Yet, grain payments disguised low wage rates, for they remained static while cash wages went up to some extent, though not in keeping with the rise in prices. In Bihar, wages had not risen for twenty years and more. As regards Orissa, O'Malley noted in 1907: "Measured by the quantity of grain given, there does not appear to have been any increase in wages paid to agricultural labourers during the last 30 years".[346] True that the rise in foodgrain prices automatically raised the money value of the payments made in kind. Yet, it should be noted that higher prices did affect the quality, if not the quantity of the grain paid, for the cheapest and coarsest of grains began to replace those of a better variety.

Wage rates in the peasant economy were determined by the force of custom and habit, which sought to maintain the status quo and checked any sharp fluctuations in the income level of the agricultural labourer. Payments in kind reinforced this tendency, and made it difficult for the labourer to raise his standard of living. The grain given was in most cases barely adequate for the consumption of the labourer and his family, consisting of four to five members on an average, so that the question of selling the surplus did not arise at all. Even if there happened to be a surplus at any time, it was almost impossible, in the existing market set-up, for the rural labourer to sell this small amount at a profit.

In fact "these grain payments, though they suit the rural economy of the country, are of course the real danger to the population".[347] By supplying ready food for the labourer in

346 *DG: Balasore,* comp. L. S. S. O'Malley (Calcutta: BSBD, 1907), p. 121.

347 A. A. Wace to the Comm., Bhagalpur Div., 7 Apr. 1888, para. 15.

normal times, they made him oblivious to the price situation, or the need to provide for lean seasons. As soon as the crop showed signs of failure, the farmer tried to economise as far as possible and many of the labourers were undoubtedly underfed. Gradually, employment opportunities were minimised as agricultural operations shrank considerably: a large number of labourers thus found no work in the face of the impending crisis and rising food prices. The experience of 1896–97 showed that even the kamias were left to drift by their masters, in gross violation of the terms of their contract. In the famine tracts of Bihar, as the Lieutenant Governor noted, "one can feed himself for an anna a day, but the usual agricultural labour by which landless classes earn wages is mostly at a standstill, and they have to resort to relief works to earn that anna".[348]

[4.3] Moving towards a starvation-level entitlement

The agricultural labourer thus lived perpetually on the brink of starvation. Contrary to the conclusion of the Datta Committee Report, his wages did not keep pace with the rising level of prices. Datta dealt only with the rates in money wages, which prevailed in the more developed sectors covering no more than a fringe of the peasant economy in Bengal. He also failed to consider the pressures within the labour market, viz. the effect of lower wages for bonded, "general" and female labour, as well as the seasonal nature of agricultural operations, which naturally pulled down the average daily rates. Datta's conclusion is thus vitiated by the limited representativeness of his data. Besides, even his table on agricultural real wage in Bengal shows a rise of only 6 per cent between 1891 and 1901, while prices rose by 18 per cent.[349] The Labour Enquiry Commission understated the problem when it wrote in 1896: "though the price of food has risen very much in recent years, the wages of the labourer have not always varied to the same extent".[350] The per capita availability of foodgrains

348 *Famine Commission Report, 1898* (London, 1898), ch. 2, para. 52.

349 Ghosh, *Agricultural Labourers*, pp. 129–30, 166.

350 *Report of the Labour Enquiry Commission, 1896* (Calcutta: BS Press, 1896), p. 8, para. 14.

declined by 9 per cent, while the population rose by 7 per cent in India between 1893 and 1915.[351] Due to the anomalies in the system of exchange entitlement, as noted above, the effect of this decline was felt most deeply by the agricultural labourer, who was thus least able to withstand any crisis in the peasant economy. "Spending what he earns from day to day, he has very little to pawn or sell in times of distress: he gets no credit from the mahajan; and he is the first to succumb if the crops fail and he cannot get labour".[352]

[5] *Peasant Society in Terms of Proneness to Famine*

The entitlement pattern in the different economic zones was thus determined by the complexities of credit, rent, trade and labour relations. It is evident that the sections of rural society most prone to famine were the under-raiyat*s*, tenants-at-will, sharecroppers and labourers, especially in tribal regions. The vast and unspecified class of agricultural labourers, in particular, absorbed much of the strains and pressures of rural society, as this sector provided the main outlet for dispossessed peasants and displaced craftsmen. The actual cultivator, often distinct from an occupancy raiyat, most keenly felt the real burden of the rent which, along with the decreasing size of his holding, pushed him towards eviction and a bleak future either as a landless labourer, or as a bargadar on the land he once held. The rural craftsmen (most notably the weaver), faced with the decline in their respective trades largely as a result of colonial exploitation, further swelled the ranks of the agricultural labourers. This growing surplus and other constraints depressed labour wages to a near-starvation level. Simultaneously, the web of credit relations so enmeshed the small peasant, artisan and labourer, that they were unable to sell freely their land, assets, produce or labour, which were pledged and lost to the creditor.

351 Daniel Thorner, "Long Term Trends in Output in India", in *Economic Growth: Brazil, India, Japan,* ed. S. S. Kuznets, W. E. Moore and J. J. Spengler (Durham, N.C.: Duke University Press, 1964), p. 123.

352 *DG: Muzaffarpur*, p. 87.

The following chapters will show that the famine raged in its greatest intensity in areas with the highest concentration of under-raiyats and rural labourers, especially in the tribal regions.

3

Famines in Bengal during 1866–96: Availability or Exchange Crisis?

The broad outlines of the famine map of Bengal emerge distinctly from the preceding analysis of the local problems. They were confirmed by the pattern of famines and scarcities which occurred in the region between 1866 and 1896.

As seen earlier, certain natural and ecological factors explained the high incidence of crop failures in Bengal in the late nineteenth century; entitlement problems in rent, credit, trade and labour relations transformed such a deficiency into famine. The purpose of this chapter is to analyse the interplay of these two factors, i.e., crop failure and exchange failure, in causing or prolonging the famine situation at various points in time during the thirty years prior to the great famine of 1896–97 in Bengal.

Three major famines affected Bengal, Bihar and Orissa with varying intensity in 1866, 1873–74 and 1896–97. Besides, partial crop failures led to acute local scarcity and distress in different regions of the Province in 1875, 1884–85, 1888–89 and 1891–92.

[1] *The Orissa Famine of 1866*

The famine of 1866 intensively affected a long stretch of land along the eastern coast, including a large part of Madras and Orissa, and several districts in western Bengal and Bihar.

Though the crops were deficient in central Bengal, distress was not deeply felt except in the western districts of Bankura, Burdwan, Hughli, and to a greater extent, in Nadia. Due to its easy accessibility and proximity to Calcutta, even Nadia managed to escape the extremity of the famine situation.

It was only further west, i.e. in Cuttack, Puri, Balasore and the Tributary Mahals, and in the adjoining region of Midnapur in Bengal, that the famine raged in all its intensity, so much so that the famine of 1866 is generally termed the "Orissa Famine".

The devastation was also felt in large parts of Manbhum and Singhbhum in Chotanagpur, and in Saran, Champaran and Tirhut in north Bihar. In fact, in the dry, laterite tract extending from the north of Balasore to the higher plateaus of Chotanagpur, the famine reached an intensity second only to that in Orissa.[1] The impact was less severe in the south Bihar districts of Shahabad, Gaya, Monghyr, Bhagalpur and the Santhal Parganas.

Out of a total affected area of 67,013 sq. miles, the famine was intense in 11,966 sq. miles in Orissa, western Bengal and Chotanagpur, and severe in 11,450 sq. miles in the rest of Bihar.[2]

[1.1] Food Availability Decline

The famine of 1866 in Orissa was marked by a most severe manifestation of Food Availability Decline or FAD, as indicated by an extensive crop failure for two successive years. This resulted in low carry-over stocks, and the total inability of the local traders to cover even a part of this deficiency by substantial foodgrain imports. There was thus an almost complete failure in the supply and availability of foodgrains, which was reflected in the following: frequent closures of the grain marts; the purely nominal or fictitious nature of the price roll at the later stages of the famine, as no grain was available even at these high rates; higher prices of the foodgrains in the interior than in the coastal towns, indicating an acute local shortage and the extreme urgency of imports from outside; the futility of money wages at government relief works; the belated decision at some private relief works to make part payments in kind; and the inability of their contractors to arrange for such payments for their labourers, as no steady or assured supplies of foodgrain were available at any stage of the famine.

[1] *Famine Commission Report, 1866*, p. 7, para. 25.
[2] Ibid., pp. 6–7; *Famine Commission Report, 1880*, pt. 3, pp. 41, 68.

Orissa, and in fact the whole of the Lower Provinces, had a very low reserve of foodgrains in the beginning of 1865. The stock position in each district was determined by a number of variables, such as the current yield, the absolute food requirements of the people between one harvest and the next, the provision for seed, and the precise extent of the export and import trade in foodgrains.

[a] Low reserves due to deficient harvests

The size of the reserves or the stocks in hand in any year was most closely determined by the nature of the harvest in the preceding year. Indeed, a shortfall in agricultural production leading to a diminished surplus, would naturally reduce the level of the reserves. The Famine Report of 1866 states that on an average, the crop out-turn had not been very large in the Province of Bengal for the past few years. In Bihar, the yield was low for the two preceding seasons; a large tract in Midnapur and the 24 Parganas was devastated by the cyclone of October 1864; further west, the laterite districts of Singhbhum and Manbhum, falling within the famine tract of the second degree, suffered from scanty harvests since 1861. The stock of grain in Singhbhum, never very substantial, began decreasing since 1862. Manbhum suffered from short crops in 1863 and 1864, while the early rice in 1865 was damaged by an excess of rain. The crop in Puri was considerably below the average in 1864, though Cuttack and Balasore had a satisfactory yield. Throughout 1865, the strain was felt in Puri due to the depletion of stocks, prices rising instead of falling as the crop matured. Rice, which sold at 35 sr. per rupee in July 1864, went up in value to 18¾ sr. in July 1865.[3]

[b] Excessive exports

There is, however, scope for doubt as to whether the low carry-over stocks in 1865–66 resulted mainly from deficient harvests or from a rise in demand, as indicated by the growing

3 J. C. Geddes, *Bengal: The crops of 1865–66 for comparison with those of 1873–74, compiled from extracts from official papers* (Calcutta,1873), pp. 8, 14.

volume of exports. The export fund in foodgrains might have been drawn primarily from the grain sold by the peasants to pay their rent, which brought an assured supply to the market at low rates at a fixed time of the year. Yet, as the demand grew, high export prices also cut into the surplus stocks, which were largely controlled by the zamindars and mahajan traders in the form of produce rents, debt payments and a host of other levies determined by the rural set-up. Indeed, "the questions of export trade and of reserves re-act on each other so far that, generally speaking, increased exportation means diminished reserves, and increased reserves connote a falling off in the export trade".[4]

Mauritius, Burma, Ceylon and various other countries in Asia and Australasia had begun to draw heavily on the rice reserves of Bengal in the 1860s. Within India, too, areas growing commercial crops like the cotton districts in the west imported foodgrains on a large scale from Bengal and Orissa. The upcountry merchants bought grains for export as soon as they were reaped, and sold a part of it later at enhanced rates.[5] Though cash crops could never really encroach upon the rice economy of Bengal, in certain areas as in the rice-growing district of Monghyr the best lands were under indigo. This was a potent cause of distress, especially in view of the increasing outflow of grain.

In November 1865, it was noted that though Monghyr and Bhagalpur had enough grain in stock, a fortnight's continued exportation would completely alter the situation.[6] Prices rose mainly due to a keen competition among the grain dealers in supplying the markets of the North–West. In fact, in 1858 even a greater deficiency in crop out-turn did not raise the price of rice to more than 15 sr. a rupee (as against 10 sr. in 1865), precisely due to the absence of exports to the North–West. Distress

[4] *Report on Foodgrain Supply and Statistical Review of the Operations in the Districts of Bihar & Bengal during the Famine of 1873–74* by A. P. Macdonnell (Calcutta, 1876), p. 12, para. 53.

[5] Geddes, *The crops of 1865–66*, S. Misser, zamindar of Toolsipore, Monghyr, in reply to the Memorandum of Questions on the Famine of 1866.

[6] Ibid., A. Money, Comm., Bhagalpur Div. and Santhal Prgs., to the Secy. to the Board of Revenue, Lower Provinces, no. 148, dated Bhagalpur, 6 Nov. 1865.

deepened in the northernmost parts of Bhagalpur, Darbhanga and Champaran adjacent to Nepal, as grain flowed into the North–West and Nepal, far in excess of that in normal years. Meanwhile, an important source of supply was shut off, as the Nepal government strictly forbade exportation in view of the crop failure in the *terai* region. In Burhait in the Santhal Parganas, the Santhals, frustrated by government inaction, kept prices down by combining not to sell grain for export to the North–West.[7] The Deputy Magistrate of Banka notes:"I believe the general outcry at present is not of bad crops, but of scarcity of grain caused by export".[8] The quantity of rice and paddy exported from Calcutta and the outposts increased from 9,475,637 and 23,439 md. respectively in 1855–56, to 19,186,522 and 264,860 md. in 1864–65: an increase of more than 100 per cent in the case of rice, and eleven times in the case of paddy within a decade![9]

Exports from Orissa were particularly attractive, for in spite of an increase in the price of rice, the price in Orissa was still rather low compared to most other provinces until the end of 1864. The Telinga Koomtees of Madras and the French trading house of Messrs. Robert, Charriol and Company, and later the Nakodas or Bombay merchants, were most actively engaged in this export trade. False Point recorded an increasing outflow of foodgrain. Exports grew in volume from southern Orissa to Ganjam and Gopalpur (where the Koomtees cornered large stocks), and from northern Balasore to Midnapur, Hijli and Calcutta.[10]

The following statistics show that exports from Orissa had increased more than six fold in the decade between 1855 and 1865, and 1.7 times in the year preceding the famine.[11]

7 Ibid.

8 Ibid., H. Metcalfe, Dy. Magistrate of Banka, to Offg. Collector and Magistrate of Bhagalpur, no. 182, 23 Oct. 1865.

9 Statistics of the Board of Revenue, noted in the *Famine Commission Report, 1866*, p. 5, para. 19.

10 *Famine Commission Report, 1866*, pp. 5, 6, 13, paras. 19, 23 and 47.

11 Ibid., p. 13, para. 47.

TABLE 27
Export of Rice and Paddy from Orissa, 1855–56 to 1864–65 (in md. of 80 lb.)

Year	*Balasore*	*Cuttack*	*Puri*	*Total*
1855–56	142,616			142,616
1856–57	188,658			188,658
1857–58	34,232			34,232
1858–59	52,970			52,970
1859–60	536,382			536,382
1860–61	354,074	23,044	83,936	461,054
1861–62	327,504	69,880	46,780	444,164
1862–63	407,622	36,696	4,816	449,134
1863–64	520,052	29,464		549,516
1864–65	806,576	72,128	58,824	937,528

Source: Famine Commission Report, 1866, p. 13, para. 47.

This growing volume of the export trade in foodgrains thus had a distinct role in bringing down the reserves in the Province, just before it was struck by the famine of 1865–66. For instance, though Puri suffered from such an extensive crop failure in 1864 that the pressure was felt throughout the next year, it did not prevent a sharp rise in exports (58,824 md. in 1864–65 as against 4,816 md. in 1862–63). This factor was as much responsible as the deficient harvest, for doubling the price of rice in Puri in 1864–65. The growing demand for foodgrain exports thus became a most persistent feature of the local economy since the 1850s and "may be said to have reached its utmost height in the early part of 1865".[12]

[c] Crop failure in 1865–66

It was against this background of low reserves that the crops failed extensively in the autumn of 1865, leading to a total breakdown in the supply of foodgrains.

12 Ibid., p. 16, para. 55.

The rains were erratic and ill-distributed during the monsoon, and altogether deficient in the winter months. For instance, Puri had a total rainfall of about 36.3 inches in 1865, as against the yearly average of 60–65 inches. After an unusual and useless rainfall of 13 inches in May, it fell to 5 inches per month during the monsoon and ceased altogether in the crucial months of October and November. In Cuttack, too, there was no rainfall at all in October–November, while in Balasore the rain stopped in November–December, with a meagre fall of 0.30 inches in October.[13] The strain was felt earliest in Puri, severe distress spreading first over the traditional famine zone of Malud, Parikud and the Chilka tract, covering the southwestern, central and eastern parts of the district approximately. In October, the Collector of Balasore reported that the rice crop did not promise to reach even one-eighth of the previous year's yield. In Cuttack, too, there was widespread panic by mid-November, when reports of a large-scale crop failure were confirmed. The Orissa Commissioner's estimate of the Divisional average at half of the usual out-turn in November 1865, was deemed too optimistic by the Famine Enquiry Commission.

Distress, though less intense, spread over the rice belt of north Bihar, part of the moribund delta in western Bengal, the laterite tract stretching from Birbhum, Bankura and Midnapur across south Bihar, and up to the Chotanagpur plateau in the west. Not more than half of the crop could be saved in Nadia and the 24 Parganas, while in areas of severe drought it would not exceed one-eighth of the average out-turn.[14] Prices rose sharply in Bankura in September, in apprehension of scarcity. In western Midnapur, the Jungle Mahals adjacent to Orissa produced only one-third of a full harvest, while the usual cold-weather crops completely failed. In large areas of the Patna, Bhagalpur and Chotanagpur Divisions, sowing was delayed due to the arrival of the monsoon very late in June. In July, however, the rains were so excessive as to injure the early rice. The rains ceased abruptly in September–October, causing a widespread failure of

[13] Ibid., paras. 56–58.

[14] Ibid., District Narratives, p. 40, para. 4; Bluebook on Orissa and Bengal Famine 1866, Enquiry Commission, paras. 3–4 on Presidency Division.

TABLE 28

Course of Price during the Period of Greatest Pressure in Each District of Bengal, 1866 (Quantities per Rupee)

Division	*District*	*Period of greatest pressure*	*Price movement (sr.)*	*Highest price (sr.)*	*Average 10 years*
Burdwan	Burdwan	June–Oct	7¾–9	Aug., 7¾	23.6
	Bancoorah	June–Sept	6–7½	Aug., 6	25.5
	Beerbhum	June–Oct	8–9½	July, 8	–23
	Midnapore	May–Sept	6–9	Aug., 6	24.7
	Hooghly	June–Oct	7–9½	July, 7	19½
	Howrah	June–Oct	8–10	July, 8	18.6
Presidency	24 Parganas	June–Oct	7–10	Aug., 7	16.8
	Nuddea	June & July	8–9¾	July, 8	–19
	Jessore	June & July	8–9	July, 8	18.5
Rajshahye	Moorshedabad	June–Sept.	8–9	July–Sept., 8	21.8
	Dinagepore	July–Sept.	11–11½	Sept., 11	26
	Maldah	April–Oct.	10–11½	July, 10	29.7
	Rajshahye	Aug. to Oct.	9–12	Sept., 9	21.2
	Rungpore	July–Sept.	10–11½	Sept., 10	23.7
	Bograh	July–Oct.	10–11	Aug., 10	26.7
	Pubna	May–Oct.	9½–11¼	June, 9½	22.6
Dacca	Dacca	June–Sept.	10–10½	Sept., 10	24
	Furreedpore	June–Oct.	8½– 9½	Sept., 8½	29
	Backergunge	June–Oct.	8½–11	Sept., 8½	29
	Mymensing	Aug & Sept.	–8¾	Aug., 8¾	23
	Sylhet	April–Oct.	8–11½	June, 8	25
	Cacher	May–Oct.	4¼ –9	June, 4¼	23.6

Division	*District*	*Period of greatest pressure*	*Price movement (sr.)*	*Highest price (sr.)*	*Average 10 years*
Chittagong	Chittagong	Sept & Oct.	11–13	Sept., 11	21.9
	Noakhally				
	Tipperra	May–Oct	11–14	Aug., 11	24
	Hill Tracts				
Patna	Patna	April–Oct.	8½–11	Aug., 8½	28
	Gaya	May–Oct.	7¾–10	Aug., 7¾	23.8
	Shahhbad	April–Sept.	7½–10½	Aug., 7½	19
	Tirhoot	April–Oct.	8–9½	Aug., 8	19.6
	Saran	June–Aug.	9½–11	Aug., 9½	17.9
	Champaran	April–Aug.	6¾–9	Aug., 6¾	17
Bhagalpur	Monghyr	April–Oct.	7½–10	July, 7½	23.5
	Bhagalpur	June–Oct.	8–10	July/Aug./Sept, 8	18.8
	Purneah	April–Oct.	8–12	Aug., 8	25
	Sountal -Pergunahas	April–Oct.	7½–10	Aug., 7½	20
Orissa	Cuttack	April–Oct.	4¼–8	June & July, 4¼	24.5
	Pooree	Feb–Oct.	5–9½	June/July/Aug., 5	22
	Balasore	April–Oct.	5¼–9¼	Aug., 5¼	28.8
Chotanagpur	Hazareebagh	May–Oct.	6½–9	Aug., 6½	18.6
	Lohardaga	July–Sept.	8–10½	Aug., 8	19
	Singhbhoom	June–Oct.	5–10	Aug., 5	30.6
	Manbhoom	June–Oct.	4–8	Aug., 4	17.8

Source: Geddes, *Administrative Experience*, p. 258.

the winter rice and other crops growing on the highlands. In Manbhum, the cold-weather crops were estimated to be between one-third and half, and in some areas as low as one-fourth, of a full harvest. In north Bihar and Bhagalpur the unseasonable nature of the rain, more than its deficiency, caused intensive damage to the crops. The yield in 1864 and 1865 varied between two-thirds to one-third, and in vulnerable areas like northern Tirhut and Champaran, did not exceed one-fourth of the average out-turn.[15]

[1.2] Supply crisis as reflected in the price movement

The phenomenal rise in foodgrain prices reflected the supply crisis in the most real and absolute terms, there being a three- to four-fold increase in the normal price range in most districts, during the lean months of 1866.

As seen in table 28, the longest duration of famine rates is recorded in Puri.[16] The weekly returns in Orissa between October 1865 and December 1866 (table 29) show that for the space of five months in the best supplied markets the price of food (supplied erratically), ranged from five to ten times the average rate.[17]

TABLE 29

Prices of common rice in seers per rupee: weekly returns in Orissa (Oct 1865–Dec 1866)

		Puri	*Cuttack*	*Balasore*	*Average*
Latter part of Oct 1865		8 to 13	8 to 15	11 to 16	12.00
Week ending					
1865	13 Nov.	8.00	12.00	15.00	11.67
	20 Nov.	10.00	11.00	15.00	12.00
	27 Nov.	11.50	10.50	16.00	12.67

[15] Geddes, *The crops of 1865–66*, p. 45, para. 129, Extract from Mr Cockerell's Retrospect, 1867, on the Patna and Bhagalpur Divisions in 1865–66.

[16] J. C. Geddes, *Administrative Experience Recorded in Former Famines* (Calcutta,1874), p. 258.

[17] Ibid., p. 246.

		Puri	*Cuttack*	*Balasore*	*Average*
	4 Dec.	12.00	11.25	16.00	13.25
	11 Dec.	12.00	11.25	16.00	13.25
	18 Dec.	13.00	13.00	16.00	14.00
	28 Dec.	14.00	14.00	14.00	14.00
1866	1 Jan.	14.00	14.00	13.00	13.67
	8 Jan.	13.50	14.00	13.00	13.50
	15 Jan.	12.50	12.00	13.00	12.50
	22 Jan.	10.00	12.00	11.00	11.25
	29 Jan.	8.75	11.25	10.00	10.00
	5 Feb.	8.75	9.50	11.00	9.75
	12 Feb.	9.25	8.50	9.00	9.00
	19 Feb.	8.50	9.00	9.00	9.00
	26 Feb.	9.50	9.25	9.50	9.33
	5 Mar.	8.25	9.25	9.50	9.00
	12 Mar.	8.00	9.75	10.00	9.25
	19 Mar.	8.25	9.25	10.00	9.25
	26 Mar.	8.00	8.75	7.50	8.25
	2 Apr.	7.50	7.50	7.50	7.50
	9 Apr.	6.50	7.50	7.50	7.25
	16 Apr.	7.75	6.25	8.50	7.50
	23 Apr.	6.50	6.00	8.50	7.00
	30 Apr.	6.25	6.00	8.00	6.75
	7 May	6.25	6.25	8.00	7.00
	14 May	6.75	6.00	8.00	7.00
	21 May	6.75	5.00	6.75	6.25
	28 May	6.00	4.75	6.00	5.75
	4 Jun.	6.00	4.75	6:50	5.75
	11 Jun.	5.25	4.50	6.00	5.25
	18 Jun.	5.75	4.00	5.50	5.00
	25-Jun.	5.75	4.00	5.00	5.00
	2 Jul.	6.25	4.00	5.00	5.00
	9 Jul.	6.25	4.00	5.50	5.25
	16 Jul.	5.75	4.50	5.50	5.25
	23 Jul.	5.75	4.75	6.00	5.50
	30 Jul.	5.50	5.00	4.75	5.00
	6 Aug.	5.50	5.50	4.50	5.25
	13 Aug.	5.75	5.00	3.50	4.75
	20 Aug.	5.75	4.88	4.75	5.25
	27 Aug.	5.50	4.50	4.50	4.75
	3 Sep.	5.50	5.00	5.00	5.25
	10 Sep.	6.50	5.50	5.00	5.67
	17-Sep.	7.75	6.00	6.00	6.50
	24-Sep.	7.75	7.00	6.00	7.00

	Puri	*Cuttack*	*Balasore*	*Average*
1 Oct.	7.25	7.00	7.00	7.25
8 Oct.	8.75	7.00	8.25	7.75
15 Oct.	7.25	7.00	9.00	7.75
22 Oct.	7.75	7.00	9.00	8.00
29 Oct.	7.25	8.25	9.00	8.25
5 Nov.		8.00	11.00	9.50
12 Nov.		11.00	17.50	14.25
19 Nov.		13.75	17.00	15.50
26 Nov.		15.75	20.00	17.88
3 Dec.		15.00	20.00	17.50
10 Dec.		15.00	19.00	17.00

Source: Geddes, *Administrative Experience,* p. 246

The price movement in Orissa had several distinctive features, suggesting a total exhaustion of foodgrain supplies in the region. Its sharp edge was felt most keenly by the poor, since the proportion of rise was the greatest in case of the coarser foodgrains such as common rice in Bengal, and *jowar* and *bajra* in the North-West Provinces. The problem was particularly acute in districts with cheap grain and low wage levels. The rate of increase in such cases could be correctly gauged only in relation to the local range of prices. Yet the Board of Revenue, viewing the problem from a metropolitan angle, often failed to allow for the extreme cheapness of grain normally prevailing in certain districts; prices were reported to be reasonable, when in fact they were alarming by local standards.

This was most relevant in Orissa, where the price of rice was generally low compared to other parts of the Province. For instance, on 24 January 1866, the Board of Revenue described the prices in Puri as being "happily insufficient to tempt exporters from the opposite coast", implying the existence of adequate reserves which kept the rates down.[18] Yet the Collector of Puri mentioned that rice was not generally procurable. The prices current of the weeks ending 23 and 29 January show rice selling at 10¼ and 8¾ sr. per rupee respectively (table 29), which was four times its average price in the district.[19] Allowances also had

[18] *Famine Commission Report, 1866,* p. 44, para. 141.
[19] Geddes, *Administrative Experience,* p. 245.

to be made for seasonal variations in the price of rice, for the cheap post-harvest rates invariably rose as the season advanced. Any contrary movement of prices would imply a major change in the supply position, as had happened in Puri when prices rose instead of falling as the crops ripened in 1865.

Grain prices in the interior, as compared to those in the coastal towns and cities, further indicated the extent of shortfall in agricultural production. In normal times, the price of rice was always lower in the interior, and rose in the cities due to a complex of factors such as cost of carriage, middlemen's profits and greater purchasing power. Any reversal of this trend, as in January 1866, indicated a most serious exhaustion of stocks in the Province. According to Mr Barlow, the Magistrate of Puri, "it is one of the features observable in the famine" that "the city is the only place where a certain supply (small though it be) of grain is to be found, while in various parts of the interior, none at all is procurable".[20] Between October 1865 and December 1866, food, rarely available in the interior of Orissa, sold for upto thirty-five times the normal price.[21] No stocks existed in the localities of Nubbah, Gope and around the edge of the Chilka via Haridas and Boosoonpur; while no rice was sold at the large mart of Lattaharan in Kodhar, indicating "the nakedness of the land".[22]

The price quotations showed sharp fluctuations and discrepancies, due to the lack of any assured supplies. This was most apparent in the Cuttack returns, the prices varying "from hour to hour and from one street of Cuttack to another".[23]

[1.3] Response failure of the market

The supply crisis was accentuated by a total failure of the market to respond to the price stimulus. As noted earlier, a distinctive feature of this famine in Orissa was the frequent closure of the grain marts rather than price hikes by the local traders, reflecting an acute shortage in the availability of foodgrains. The Report

20 *Famine Commission Report, 1866*, p. 45, para. 147.
21 Geddes, *Administrative Experience*, p. 287.
22 *Famine Commission Report, 1866*, p. 27, para. 87.
23 Geddes, *Administrative Experience*, p. 244.

of the Famine Enquiry Commission in 1866 notes this point: "Throughout this famine, from the very first, it was symptomatic of its character as rather due to scarcity of grain than scarcity of money, that each fresh accession of alarm consistently took the shape of stopping sales at the regular marts altogether, rather than of mere sudden enhancements of price".[24]

In Cuttack, rice selling at eight sr. per rupee on the morning of 21 October 1865 was no longer available at noon, all the grain markets being shut down. Assured that the government would not under any circumstances try to fix rates in the bazaar, the dealers opened their shops the next day and proposed to sell rice at twelve sr. per rupee. But since the 22nd, the prices began to soar, and on 26 October the grain market was closed down once again. On 23 October, supplies to Ganjam from Puri via the Chilka ceased entirely, resulting in a general closure of all the grain stores there.[25] On 26 October, Mr G. N. Barlow, Magistrate of Puri, wrote that while "dundeedars have combined, so as to altogether close the modees' shops [in Cuttack] we are so far better off at Pooree, that rice is being sold there, though at enhanced rates".[26] Yet on 27 October, Ravenshaw, the Officiating Commissioner of the Cuttack Division, mentioned reports of a closure of the grain stores in Puri.[27] Even Barlow was concerned enough to write in a postscript to his deputy: "Write to me demi-officially always about this, and tell me if you see any indication of the buniah and dokandars closing their shops altogether. Try and persuade people to send out into the mofussil to buy in their own rice".[28]

24 *Famine Commission Report, 1866,* p. 26, para. 86.

25 *Minutes on the Famine in Bengal and Orissa, 1866–67,* by Sir Cecil Beadon, app. to para. 6. From T. E. Ravenshaw Esq., Offg. Comm. Cuttack Div., to the Offg. Secy. to the Govt. of Bengal, no. 407, dated 27 Oct. 1865, paras. 2, 4.

26 Geddes, *The Crops of 1865–66,* p. 21. Demi-official letter from G. N. Barlow Esq., Magistrate of Puri, to Baboo Ramakhoy Chatterjee, Dy. Magistrate of Puri, dated 26 Oct. 1865.

27 *Minutes on the Famine,* app. para. 6. T. E. Ravenshaw, Offg. Comm. Cuttack Div., to the Offg. Secy. to the Govt. of Bengal, no. 407, dated 27 Oct. 1865, para. 5.

28 Geddes, *The Crops of 1865–66,* p. 21, G. N. Barlow to Ramakhoy Chatterjee, 26 Oct. 1865.

Official reports tended to dismiss this trait as the usual dealers' combine in a lean season, to raise the price by holding back supplies. Thus, Ravenshaw believed: "There are large stores in the hands of dealers probably enough to supply the market for a couple of years. In hopes of gain the dealers . . . agreed to keep all grain out of the market until the price rises to 8 annas per seer". Yet, the belief that a free flow of trade would eventually enable the demand and price stimulus to regulate supplies was belied by the sporadic closures of the market. Even Ravenshaw admitted that "the total closing of shops is a somewhat peculiar feature in the present crisis, which I am quite at a loss either to account for or explain. The very fact of the exceedingly high prices now ruling . . . ought to operate as an inducement to sell".[29]

The behaviour of the market, though apparently confusing, was not unreasoned, for the price quotations had little relevance in Orissa in 1865–66. In fact, the weekly returns from Puri and Cuttack were more nominal than real, for grain was not available there even at these high rates.

The problems faced by the civil servants, jail authorities and others in feeding their staff and inmates, amply illustrate the point. In October 1865, the Judge, the Magistrate, the Commanding Officer, the Superintendent of the Light-House, and others in Cuttack complained of the difficulty experienced by their establishments in procuring rice.[30] T. E. Ravenshaw, the Officiating Commissioner of Cuttack, reported to the Secretary to the Bengal Government, on 27 October, 1865:

> I have this morning received a letter from Colonel Owen, noting the difficulty he finds in obtaining grain for the troops and camp-followers in cantonments. The Judge writes that the vakeels of his court have petitioned, stating that they were unable to get rice. . . . My own office people tell the same tale; and my servants draw their daily rations from a few maunds of rice I happened to have in hand.[31]

29 *Minutes on the Famine,* app. to para. 6. T. E. Ravenshaw to the Secy., Govt. of Bengal, no. 407, dated 27 Oct. 1865, paras. 8 and 10.

30 Geddes, *The crops of 1865–66*, p. 24.

31 *Minutes on the Famine,* app. to para. 6; Letter from T. E.

The Deputy Magistrate of Puri wrote on 25 October 1865: "It is to be regretted that we have no stock of rice in the jail at this time, and I am at a loss how to procure rice for more than eighty prisoners".[32] Even at the government relief works, where payments were never made in kind for fear of disrupting the private trade in foodgrains, the labourers could not obtain rice for their money. This was a case of "response failure" being greater than "pull failure" in the market, where cash wages could not bring relief.

Amartya Sen remarks: "The rationale of cash relief rests on the assumption that 'pull failure' is the main problem to deal with, and that the problem of 'response failure' will not provide a barrier to curing the entitlement problem through regenerating purchasing power. This need not always work, and the possibility of using this type of relief must depend to a great extent on the nature of the markets as well as the limits of bureaucratic management".[33] In Orissa in 1866, the market was too imperfect and the traders too apathetic to respond to any "pull" provided by the government, while the bureaucrats vied with each other in emphasising the principle of laissez faire, and would have nothing to do with the import or distribution of food.

On 15 January 1866, Barlow spoke of "a danger likely to interfere materially with, if not actually put a stop to, the works", viz. the want of food.[34] The labourers were extremely anxious to receive their daily wages in kind, rather than cash wages for task work. Yet the suggestions of Ravenshaw and Barlow to this effect were ignored by the Board of Revenue, lest grain payments should interfere with the flow of private trade. Even when part of the wages were paid in kind, as in the private relief works at Kendrapara in Cuttack, rice for payment was almost impossible

---

Ravenshaw, Offg. Comm. Cuttack Div. to the Offg. Secy. to the Govt. of Bengal, No. 407, dated 27 Oct. 1865, para. 3.

32 Geddes, *The Crops of 1865–66*, p. 20, Baboo Ramakhoy Chatterjee to G. N. Barlow Esq., no. 68, dated 25 Oct. 1865.

33 Amartya Sen, "Hunger and Entitlements: Research for Action", from monograph based on the WIDER (World Institute for Development Economics Research) study and conference paper presented at Helsinki in Aug. 1986.

34 *Famine Commission Report, 1866*, p. 45, para. 147.

to procure and was mostly imported from Calcutta.[35] Thus, the Orissa famine of 1866 was a stark manifestation of FAD, resulting primarily from a lack of food rather than money.

Yet, the undertones of 'exchange' or 'pull' failure could not be altogether ignored, for they highlighted another facet of the problem, viz. that of effective demand. Since the Province was drained of stocks, the only way the market could respond to the situation was through an active import trade in foodgrains. The government remained firm in the belief that "If the market favours imports, rice will find its way to Pooree without government interference".[36] Prices in Orissa, however, were generally so low compared to neighbouring states, that even the prevailing famine rates were not attractive enough to draw supplies from outside. The Board's description of the prices in Puri as being "happily insufficient to tempt exporters from the opposite coast" has a mistaken emphasis, for the low prices implied a poor level of purchasing power, rather than self-sufficiency in stocks.[37] It failed to realise the magnitude of the problem, as prices considered alarming by local standards seemed reasonable in comparison with other parts of the Province. The exchange entitlement of a section of the population had fallen further in 1863 with a total cessation of the government manufacture of salt on the coasts of Orissa, which had given employment to many. As their holdings were not sufficient to support them, the *molunghee*s (salt manufacturers) relied mainly on their wages of labour, the loss of which forced them to swell the ranks of the already large class of agricultural labourers in Orissa. Some of them went to distant works and to Calcutta in search of employment, and mostly worked as ordinary coolies to supplement their meagre earnings from land. This class was thus most susceptible to famine, for the slightest derangement of the agricultural economy would throw them out of employment and reduce them to starvation.[38] As Mr Barlow noted, the real state of affairs could not be determined "until

35 Ibid., p. 52, para. 166.

36 Ibid., p. 48, para. 154, telegram from the Board to T. E. Ravenshaw, Comm., Cuttack Div., 1 Feb. 1866.

37 Ibid., p. 44, para. 141.

38 Ibid., p. 14, para. 49.

you examine further down, and remember that there is a large class of people, the bouries, coolies and chasees, to whom the prohibitive rate is equally starvation with the altogether non-existence of grain".[39]

The problems of exchange failure were of a deeper shade in Bengal and Bihar, where food could still be had at exorbitant rates. In the famine-affected regions of north Bihar, some of the classes which felt the severest pressure were the Dosadhs, Ahirs, Domes, Kurmis and Nooniahs. The Nooniahs were the worst hit, one-third of whom were believed to have perished during the famine. The manufacture of salt petre could no longer sustain them due to high export duties and the competition of substitutes from Europe. Hence, being thrown onto the general labour market where the demand was naturally slack during a lean season as in 1865–66, the Nooniahs were left with hardly any means of subsistence. Another group suffering from exchange failure was the large community of weavers in Hughli, Birbhum and Midnapur. As the terms of trade moved against them, the weaving centres of Bishnupur, Jehanabad and others gradually declined, and the tantis shut their looms to wander about in search of food and labour. For instance, while the Jehanabad subdivision had turned out cloth valued at Rs. 765,000 in 1864–65, the estimated out-turn in 1865–66 was only worth Rs. 625,812.[40]

[1.4] The crisis deepens into famine

The first signs of famine became apparent late in 1865. When mid-October passed without rain, the situation became serious. The country ceased to supply the towns, and the grain marts in Cuttack and Puri were shut down. Prices of common rice soared from 13 to 8, and 15 to 8 sr. per rupee in Puri and Cuttack, respectively.[41] Even in Nadia, where the famine was less intense, people who normally ate thrice a day could now afford no more

39 Ibid., p. 27, para. 87.

40 Geddes, *Administrative Experience*, pp. 368–69; extract from Mr Cockerell's Report on Tirhut and Champaran, paras. 13 and 44; *Famine Commission Report* 1866, vol. 1, pp. 327–28, para. 18.

41 Geddes, *Administrative Experience*, p. 246.

than one meal.[42] The government remained complacent in the belief that reduced consumption, rather than importation of grain, was a more practicable method of relief during famines.[43] Distress forced a change not only in the quantity, but also in the quality of food consumed: in the interior of Orissa as well as in the famine belt in north Bihar, people took to eating roots, wild fruit and berries.[44] In Chotanagpur and portions of laterite western Bengal, the forest products normally supplementing the poor man's diet now became the sole means of subsistence. Predictably, malnutrition and unwholesome food led to a spurt of diseases, mainly cholera. As the Famine Commissioner remarked, it was "quite impossible to distinguish between the mortality directly caused by starvation and that due to disease, directly or indirectly connected with starvation, want, and bad food".[45] Cholera constantly accompanied want, breaking out first in southern Puri and then in Gope, eastern Cuttack and Balasore—in keeping with the progress of the famine. C. O. Woodford, Police Surgeon in London, remarked on the "immense mortality" in the Police Hospital as being the result of "dire destitution . . . and, in nearly every instance, of actual starvation".[46]

A natural corollary to starvation and disease was an alarming increase in the incidence of crime, especially in "grain plunder". In the Jungle Mahals of Midnapur during the first part of 1866, twenty-one out of twenty-five cases of dacoity involved grain looting.[47] The neighbouring tract of Balasore was also subjected to lawlessness and the plunder of grain, as starving migrants from Mayurbhanj swelled the ranks of the destitutes.

Panic gripped the public mind, and rumours began to circulate. At Dantoon, on the borders of Balasore, the lower castes were said to be eating raw cow's flesh and human corpses. The story was probably baseless, but its very circulation reflected the

42 *Minutes on the Famine,* app., letter from R. Harvey Esq., Khalbolea, to the Collector of Nadia, dated 10 April 1866.

43 Ibid., app., p. 32.

44 *Famine Commission Report, 1866,* p. 27, para. 87.

45 Ibid., p. 23, para. 75.

46 *Minutes on the Famine,* From C. D. Woodford Esq., M.D., F.R.C.S., London, Police Surgeon, to James Anderson, Esq., M.D., Dy. Inspector General of Hospitals, Presidency, no. 2466, dated 5 March 1866.

47 Ibid., app., p. 107, para. 11.

growing fear psychology of the local people.[48] The intensity of distress caused many to violate age-old social customs and accept cooked food at the government *unnochutter*s (relief kitchens), though often at some distance from their homes, the Cuttack *pandit*s (priests) demanding merely the payment of a few annas in redemption.[49] In Parikud, the chashas were burying instead of burning their dead in December 1865— a sure sign of distress.[50]

[1.5] The policy of laissez-faire

While the crisis thus deepened into famine, the government remained largely inactive. As noted, its policy of rigid adherence to the principle of laissez-faire, or non-interference in private trade, was based on a firm belief that the price stimulus would naturally draw supplies from surplus to scarcity areas, through the channels of private trade. Having full faith in the political economy of John Stuart Mill, it maintained that "though a Government can do more than any one merchant, it cannot do nearly as much as all merchants".[51] Hence, it refused to disrupt private trade by importing any foodgrains into the Province, making no allowances for the exigencies of the local situation, and relenting only when it was too late to be effective.

The outlines of this policy were emphasised throughout the history of the famine. On 31 October 1865, Muspratt, Collector of Balasore, reported to the Commissioner that the merchants had no large stores in hand. In fact, the Telinghee merchants from the south, who had carried off the previous year's crops, causing a sharp price-rise, had to return from Orissa without any cargo this season.[52] The Collectors of Balasore, Puri and Cuttack applied for permission in very clear terms, during

[48] Ibid., app., pp. 111–12, From W. J. Herschel, Magistrate, Midnapur, to the Comm., Burdwan Div., no. 52, dated 25 April 1866.

[49] Geddes, *Administrative Experience,* Note of Mr Kirkwood on the Recovery of Caste after Partaking of Cooked Food at a Poor House.

[50] *Minutes on the Famine,* app., p. 49.

[51] *Famine Commission Report, 1866*, app., p. 137, Extract from Strachey's Paper on Famine Relief.

[52] Ibid., p. 28, para. 90.

October-November 1865, to make enquiries in their districts, regarding the areas and extent of shortfall. The applications, however, were summarily rejected, the Commissioner and the Board concurring in opinion.[53]

In January 1866, the engineers of the PWD found it impossible to procure rice for the *coolies* on relief works, in return for their cash wages. Mr Ravenshaw, learning of the situation from the District Collectors, sent the following telegram, of a most "important and emergent character" to the Board of Revenue on 31 January: "Famine relief is at a standstill. Public Works Department refuse to advance money to Collectors to purchase rice. Pooree must get rice from elsewhere. May I authorise advance for this purpose for Cuttack, Balasore or Pooree". The Board's answer of 1 February was short, sharp and decisive: "The Government decline to import rice into Pooree. . . . All payments for labour employed to relieve the present distress are to be in cash". Mr Ravenshaw conveyed the instructions to Mr Barlow in Puri, pointing out that "to supply grain will interfere with legitimate trade".[54]

The beginning of February 1866 was a crucial point when government should have undertaken to import foodgrains into Orissa, or at least to enquire into the nature and extent of the shortfall. Works suitable for famine relief, such as raising of embankments, road repair and collection of metal could at this stage have been undertaken extensively and fruitfully, if the workers had received payment in kind. As the Famine Commissioners remarked, "The whole question, therefore, is in this instance narrowed to one of food".[55] If the problems had been so viewed by the authorities in February, the crisis could perhaps be resolved and provisions made for the monsoon months, when the greater part of Orissa became virtually inaccessible both by land and sea.

It was only in mid-June, when the monsoon was in full force, that the government woke to the realities of the situation, and suddenly commenced imports. As late as 26 May 1866, the Superintending Engineer in Cuttack was still complaining of

53 Ibid., p. 35, para. 116.
54 Ibid., p. 48, para. 154.
55 Ibid., p. 63, para. 207.

labourers leaving the works throughout Balasore, Cuttack and Puri, as food was not procurable for their money. On 28 May, the Lieutenant Governor requested the Board to "give their renewed and immediate attention to the question of importing rice into the distressed districts" and for the first time questioned "their confident opinion that such importation is unnecessary".[56]

On 29 May, the Lieutenant Governor telegraphed to his Secretary in Calcutta, requesting the Board to send rice worth Rs 1 lakh (100,000) at once from Calcutta to Balasore, Dhamrah and False Point, and, if necessary, to "indent on a second lakh for the purchase of rice".[57] Importation now commenced on an emergency basis. On 10 June, additional cargoes were accepted for Orissa. On the 11th, the Board was authorised to spend the whole balance of the North Western Fund on rice imports. A government steamer arrived before the end of the month, with a cargo of rice from the Madras coast to Puri. The Government of India sanctioned an advance of twenty lakh rupees for the importation of foodgrains into Orissa.

Yet these belated efforts were largely frustrated by the extreme difficulty of landing supplies at the coast and conveying them to the interior of Orissa at the height of the rains, no pre-arrangements having been made for their storage or transport. As the monsoon advanced, problems in communication forced several cargoes to be diverted elsewhere. The light government steamer, *Nemesis*, could carry only about 8,000 md. of rice up the Balasore River till late in July. Supplies of rice from False Point took as much as five to six weeks to reach Cuttack. At Puri, the landing was so difficult that apart from a small supply obtained from the Arracan, it took seven weeks (9 July to 30 August) to unload one steamer, the *T. A. Gibb*. The government vessel *Tubal Cain*, carrying the large cargo sent from the Madras coast, found it impossible to unload and, being caught in a gale, was forced to throw over part of her cargo and divert to the rice port of Akyab.

Balasore, deprived of these supplies, suffered from extreme want, rice being sold at less than 3 sr. per rupee. In Puri and Cuttack, too, supplies of rice into the interior were cut off by unusually high floods. Private steam tugs and sloops, if pressed

56 Ibid., app., p. 248, no. 769 T.
57 Ibid., p. 89, para. 283.

into government service, could have been of some help in drawing and unloading rice, especially in the country around Dhamrah, which was one of the worst affected and least relieved tracts in Orissa. False Point, too, was much closer to Calcutta by sea, than to Cuttack by land, and landing arrangements made with greater insight would perhaps have alleviated the distress to some extent. Yet, due to its total obsession with the laissez-faire theory and fear of unprofitable expenditure, the government failed to do the needful during the crucial pre-monsoon months.[58]

[1.6] Reasons for the failure of the laissez-faire policy

[a] Decline in foodgrain availability

During the Orissa famine, the government insisted on too rigid an application of the general principle of laissez-faire, without adapting it to the specific needs of the local situation. Sir Cecil Beadon, later reviewing his policy in 1866, realised the grave error made by the administration in declining to import foodgrains into Orissa: "I am free to confess that in deciding not to recommend the adoption of this measure, I relied too much both on the resources of the Province itself and on the ability of the private enterprise to supply a possible deficiency from other quarters, and that I believed that in Orissa (as in Bengal and Behar) the question was one of money rather than of food".[59]

The first premise of the official policy, that is, that the province was not lacking in resources or foodgrains, was based on a misconception of the level of local reserves. The officials in Orissa were not to blame, for their warnings went largely unheeded. In October 1865, Baboo Ramakhoy Chatterjee, Deputy Magistrate of Puri, had apparently been misinformed about the stocks held by local zamindars and math chiefs, which were thought sufficient to supply the district for two years. However, he entirely changed his opinion after personal inspections and called for immediate action by the government in apprehension of famine.[60]

58 Ibid., pp. 91–92.

59 *Minutes on the Famine,* p. 9, para. 15.

60 Geddes, *The crops of 1865–66*, p. 20, Baboo Ramakhoy Chatterjee

Mr Barlow, Magistrate of Puri, distinctly mentioned to the Commissioner that the sort of stocks supposed to be held in Cuttack had no existence in Puri. The Collector's telegram from Puri on 24 November 1865, was more explicit: "Starvation at Parikood, Malood; deaths increasing . . . Grain shipped to Metacooah better than money".[61] Mr Muspratt, Collector of Balasore, apprehended that the rice would yield no more than one-eighth of last year's crop, and categorically denied the existence of any large stocks with the local traders. He further describes how the Telinghee merchants, who had carried off most of the previous year's rice, failed to obtain cargoes this year.[62] In fact, the Collectors of Puri, Cuttack and Balasore had applied in clear and unequivocal terms during October–November 1865, for permission to make enquiries in their respective districts, regarding the areas and extent of shortfall. The applications, however, were rejected by the Commissioner and the Board.[63] At the end of October, the Commissioner received letters from the Judge, Magistrate, Commanding Officer, Superintendent of the Lighthouse and others, noting their inability to procure rice for their establishments. They were duly informed that trade could not be interfered with. The government remained complacent in the belief that the dealers were withholding stocks, which would be drawn into the market by the price stimulus at the right moment.

This, in fact, was the most vital premise in the philosophy of laissez-faire, applied in rigid uniformity by the British government to famine situations whether in Ireland or Orissa, without regard to local circumstances. According to this theory, the price differential would naturally draw supplies into the famine zones through a free flow of private enterprise, undeterred by official interference or regulations of any sort. Yet, contrary to all expectations, the behaviour of the market did not conform to this pattern during the Orissa famine of 1866. The reasons were complex.

to G. N. Barlow Esq., Magistrate of Puri, no. 68, dated 25 Oct. 1865.

61 Geddes, *The crops of 1865–66*, p. 22.

62 *Famine Commission Report, 1866*, p. 28, para. 90.

63 Ibid., p. 35, para. 116.

[b] Absence of big traders or import-base in foodgrains

The trading community in Orissa was neither large, nor resourceful. There were hardly any big grain merchants, and the existing volume of the local trade was definitely export-oriented. While the export structure grew more elaborate and dynamic with the increasing outflow of grain in recent years, Orissa had hardly any machinery or network for the import of foodgrains. Grain-importing districts like Saran in Bihar were always at a distinct advantage in lean seasons, for it was realtively easy to widen the existing channels of foodgrain imports. Without any established trade base or organisation, however, it was almost impossible to improvise on these lines in Orrisa, especially in the midst of a crisis. Even European mercantile houses like Robert & Charriol, or Gisborne & Company failed to bring in supplies to any appreciable extent for, as the Famine Commission noted, "Trade does not very easily adopt new channels".[64]

In fact, to move against the established currents or directions of trade within a dateline was almost an impossible feat. In districts which normally exported foodgrains, the outflow persisted irrespective of scarcity and rising prices in the local market. The lack of import or storage facilities and distributing agencies, as noted above, as well as the need to honour previous contracts, prevented the merchants from diverting grain from the export fund into the distress zones. "The consequence is an apparent reversal of the law of supply and demand, — grain leaving a dear market for a cheaper one".[65] Conversely, an import network could hardly be established in a year of crisis, for the surplus districts constituting the sources of supply would likewise have prior commitments, and were often reluctant to export in new directions in lean seasons. In 1866, for instance, distress was initially feared on a wider scale than had actually occurred, and a distinct tendency was noted in many areas of eastern Bengal and Bihar to withhold stocks in apprehension of scarcity. The rapid extension of cotton cultivation leading to an increasing demand from western India reduced the reserves of grain and enhanced its price in large areas of NWP. In the Punjab,

64 Ibid., p. 60, para. 197.

65 *Report on Foodgrain Supply*, p. 157, para. 56.

meanwhile, the size of the surplus was too small for the Lower Provinces, and difficult to convey over so long a distance.

[c] Lack of free access

The physical difficulties of transport and communication were largely aggravated by the advent of monsoon, when Orissa became virtually isolated and inaccessible both by land and sea. On the land side, there was hardly any source of supply, and the Mahanadi would be closed for several months to come. To the south, there was famine in Ganjam, itself an importing district. Puri could not be called a port, and there were no ships. In Balasore the traders were inactive till March, when the surf became heavy and access difficult from the north and east, so that local trade ceased altogether along that coast. European merchants, even big houses like Messr. Robert & Charriol, who had formerly exported by way of False Point, would not risk unaccustomed import operations on such a coast; the risk multiplied greatly with the advent of the rains, and became overwhelming when the monsoon proper burst forth in mid-June.

[d] Lack of effective demand

The pattern might have been different to some extent, had the pull factor been stronger. As it happened , however, Orissa had a low level of prices and purchasing power, and even the local famine rates were not sufficient to justify such high-risk ventures. In fact, the very wide range of the escalation in foodgrain prices during 1865–66, prevented the inflow of rice into Orissa at the outset. As noted, the Board rested complacent in the knowledge that prices in Puri were "happily insufficient to tempt exporters from the opposite coast", without going into the depth of the problem of exchange and entitlement relations.[66] Though Sir Cecil Beadon later admitted his mistake in believing that "the question was one of money rather than of food", neither the level of grain reserves nor that of purchasing power was closely enquired into. The rates in Puri were not high or stable enough to attract imports till the end of February when the southwest winds dislocated trade along its coast. Balasore,

[66] *Famine Commission Report, 1866,* p. 44, para. 141.

the only port where imports could have comenced to some extent, was the last to experience the extreme rise in prices. The price quotations, moreover, were largely nominal due to the non-availability of rice in general. Even in cases where it could be obtained, effective demand was severely limited by the low purchasing capacity of the local people. This pull failure was a most potent factor in the market mechanism, due to which the famine zones in Orissa could neither draw in supplies from other regions, nor divert grain from the local export fund.

[1.7] No critical analysis either of availability or exchange crisis

The policy of laissez-faire in Orissa seems all the more futile, in view of the problems noted. As the Famine Commissioners remarked in 1866, "In truth all question of interfering with private trade is set at rest by the simple fact, that there was at this time none to interfere with". The government failed to step into this void, and the toll was heavy in terms of lives lost. The urgency of FAD was ignored, while the issue of exchange entitlement was not considered in the proper perspective. The administration professed the need to generate purchasing power by opening relief works, but failed to pay for labour in the form most effective for the purpose, viz. in foodgrain. The Secretary of the PWD wrote to the Superintending Engineer on 30 December 1865: "the payments should be made in coin at the usual rates, and anything that may be necessary to enable these wages to purchase food advantageously will be carried out under local arrangement".[67] As noted earlier, this proved impossible and the non-availability of rice almost brought relief to a standstill. Another feature making government works unpopular was the attempt at task payment, for a starving and enfeebled population—whether in Ireland or in Orissa—would naturally prefer daily wages to the enforcement of task works.

[67] Ibid., app., p. 92.

[2] *The Famine of 1873–74*

In 1873–74, famine again raged over several districts in north Bihar and Bengal, viz. Saran, Champaran, Tirhut, Bhagalpur, Purnea, Dinajpur and Bogra. It was less intensive in south Bihar and parts of northern and western Bengal, including Shahabad, Gaya, Monghyr, Santhalia, Manbhum, Rajshahi, Malda, Pabna, Jalpaiguri, Murshidabad and Burdwan. The former covered an area of 26,950 sq. miles and the latter came upto 19,159 sq. miles, affecting a population of 10,700,000 and 7,064,650, respectively.

[2.1] Crop failure

The bhadoi crop had been indifferent in 1873, while the crucial hathiya rains failed over large areas in the Province, reducing the out-turn of winter rice to about 37.5 per cent of the normal in Bengal, and 21.87 per cent of the usual out-turn in the Bihar districts.[68] The shortfall was estimated at 3.75 million tons, the extent of loss being greater than in 1865–66.[69]

In north Bihar, Saran suffered from a more extensive crop failure, the yield being 66.66 per cent and 10 per cent of the average bhadoi and winter rice, respectively. In Champaran, the bulk of the bhadoi crops were damaged severely. In Darbhanga and Muzaffarpur, the shortfall in agricultural production caused deep anxiety, in view of the abnormal weather conditions of the past three years. The failure of winter rice in Bhagalpur was most complete in Supaul subdivision, the yield nowhere exceeding 12.5 per cent of the average. The food supply was reduced by about 70 per cent in Purnea, the bhadoi and winter rice yielding one-half and one-fifth of the normal out-turn, respectively. Manbhum had only a 6-8 an. crop of winter rice in the central regions, while the eastern parts had no more than 4 to 6 an. Kurthi and oilseeds were a total failure, except in the west. Other cold-weather crops being far more

68 Famine Proceedings Dec. 1876, Reports of J. C. Geddes and A. P. Macdonnell, app. C.

69 *Special Narrative of Drought in Bengal and Bihar, 1873–74, together with Minutes* by the Hon. Sir Richard Temple (Calcutta, 1874), p. 4.

deficient in 1874 than in 1866, the stock position in general was no better than in the latter year.[70]

In north Bengal, the unseasonable rains of 1873 caused widespread damage to the crops. The aus or autumn harvest was half of the usual out-turn in Rangpur and Rajshahi, only 6 an. in Malda, and a total failure in Dinajpur. Winter rice, coming after such a bleak season, yielded no more than 25 per cent of the average in Malda, 37.5 per cent in Rajshahi and Bogra, and 50 per cent in Pabna. In Rangpur, it varied between total loss and 12.5 per cent of the normal in the central tracts, and nowhere exceeded 50 per cent of the average yield.[71] In the famine tracts of western Bengal, the aus and aman amounted only to 56.25 per cent and 37.5 per cent of the average in Birbhum, and 50 per cent of that in Bankura, respectively. The Collector of Bankura compared the winter of 1873 with that of 1865, thus: "The crop this year in Moheshra is about one-half that of 1865–66, and . . . in the rest of the district the two years give about an equal out-turn".[72] Burdwan reaped half of the aman crop, which constituted the principal food supply of the district. The Collector of Burdwan, comparing the shortfall with that of 1865, concluded that they were "about the same".[73] In Murshidabad, the aus crop in the lowlying eastern regions had an average 12 an. yield as in 1865, while the aman was only one-third of the average, i.e., 40 per cent of the out-turn in 1865–66.[74] Nadia had an average crop of the main staple or aus rice, while the aman came upto one-third of the usual out–turn, the former being better and the latter deficient compared to the harvest of 1865–66. On the whole, the Collector thought that the district would be better off until March but worse since then, as compared to 1866. Lord Ulick Browne, Commissioner of the Presidency Division, wrote from Nadia in February 1874: "taking crops all round, the general prospects are much the same".[75]

70 *Report on Foodgrain Supply*, pp. 204–5, paras. 21–22; p. 358, para. 15.

71 Ibid., p. 237, paras 25–26, p. 251, para. 22.

72 Ibid., p. 322, para. 29.

73 Ibid., p. 337, para. 25.

74 Ibid., p. 267, para. 31, Extract from the Report of the Collector of Murshidabad, 11 Dec. 1873.

75 Ibid., p. 350, para. 21.

[2.2] Supply failure and the price movement

The magnitude of the loss was reflected in the price indices. In Shahabad, for instance, prices continued to rise, until in February 1874, common rice sold at 12 sr. to the rupee, which was 8 to 16 per cent dearer than in February 1866. In Saran, market conditions in January 1874 were more stringent than in January 1866, with grain dealers hoping to reap an even greater profit than in the latter year, when rice and Indian corn sold at 300 per cent above normal rates. In Darbhanga, the price of common rice reached the famine rate of 10 sr. per rupee as early as in January 1874, while in 1866 this stage had not been reached till in April. By April 1874, the price rose by another 20 per cent, after which price quotations were merely nominal, no rice being available in the market. A similar trend is seen in the case of Indian corn, which formed the staple food of the labouring population. It sold at 18 sr. to the rupee in January 1866, while the quotation for January 1874 was 13.9 sr. It rose to 14 sr. in April 1866, while for the corresponding period in 1874, the price moved as high as 12.9 sr. to the rupee, which was thrice the normal rate prevailing at this time of the year.[76] In Champaran the food staples sold at more than double the usual rates, the quotations provided by Mr Cockerell proving without doubt that the prices of rice and Indian corn were on a level with those prevailing in 1866. Thus, "in 1873 the failure in the crops was much greater than in 1865", so that "notwithstanding all the aid given by government till it commenced supplying the market, prices ranged as high in the first quarter of last year as they did in 1866".[77] Mr Macdonnell's calculations showed an absolute deficiency of 227,000 tons of foodgrain in the Patna Division, which would go up to 370,000 tons with the usual allowance for wastage.

In Monghyr, the prices of rice and Indian corn were double the normal rates in January 1874, and even higher than those prevailing in January 1866, Likewise, in Santhalia, the prices current in the first quarter of 1874 were higher than in the

[76] Ibid., p. 21, para. 81; pp. 39–40, para. 44; pp. 68–69, paras. 71–72.

[77] Ibid., pp. 108–9, para. 36.

corresponding period of 1866. The price quotations for common rice in Manbhum during the first four months of 1874 were as high as those for the same period in 1866, the downward trend since May resulting largely from the inflow of government grain.[78]

In Rangpur, rice sold at Rs 5-8 an. per md. in April, which was four times the normal rate, while in the interior it rose to Rs 6. The price of rice rose to three or four times the normal rate in Dinajpur during the lean months of May and June. In Malda it was selling at the prohibitive rate of 9 sr. to the rupee at the end of April. Famine rates prevailed all over Rajshahi district in June, with rice being sold at 7¼ sr. per rupee. The price of rice at Bogra rose to 13½ sr. for the rupee in January 1874, which was two and a half times the usual rate. By June, it went upto 10 sr. in distressed tracts like Sherpur. Grain marts in the affected regions of western Bengal show the same stringent conditions. In Birbhum, for instance, rice sold at double the usual rates in January 1874, the tension in the market continuing throughout the year. Relatively low rates in Burdwan led to excessive exports, though the prices were high enough by local standards to "cause sustained pressure on the people".[79]

[2.3] Response failure

While the crop failure was thus more extensive and prices mostly higher in Bengal and Bihar during the famine of 1873–74 as compared to the year 1865–66, private trade was almost equally ineffective in supplying the deficiency. Once again, the movement of the grain trade disproved the government theory that high prices would naturally attract supplies from surplus to scarcity zones. As in 1866, private trade in the famine tracts was hindered at various points by the physical difficulties of transport and communication; the underlying problem of exchange failure and the lack of effective demand; and the persistence of the prevailing trade pattern, which made it almost impossible to cut through the existing lines of inflow and outflow, or to improvise a system of imports in the face of a crisis for normally surplus districts.

[78] Ibid., p. 358, para. 17.
[79] Ibid., p. 337, para. 26.

While in 1866 all these points were brought to a sharp focus in Orissa, in 1873–74 the affected districts in Bengal and Bihar felt the problem in varying degrees of intensity.

The location of the affected tracts determined to a great extent the volume of their imports, as remoteness from the main channels of trade would heighten the merchant's risk and expenses, and hence lower his profit margin. For instance, Tajpur in Darbhanga attracted a steady flow of foodgrains for, unlike the Madhubani and Darbhanga subdivisions, it had a favourable trading position with easy access to Patna. Hajipur on the left bank of the Ganges, enjoyed the same advantage in relation to Sitamarhi in Muzaffarpur. Similarly, Saran and Champaran were commercially better placed than Muzaffarpur and Darbhanga. Saran could draw on the foodgrain traffic from the NWP and Nepal, while Champaran on the river Gandak was approachable from Patna, the great trade centre of Bihar. Significantly, private trade was brisk in Saran in the early part of 1874, and showed a degree of vitality in Tajpur, Hajipur and Champaran, unmatched in the rest of north Bihar.

As in 1866, the existing lines of the traffic in foodgrains persisted with great tenacity. Exports flowed unchecked from the distress zone of Sitamarhi, which failed to hold on to any of the grain passing through it from Nepal. In Bhagalpur, the surplus produce from Madhipura, instead of being drawn into the affected regions of Supaul where famine rates prevailed, flowed out of the district to their usual destination. In November 1873, the Collector remarked on the "great exportation of rice that has been, and is, going on" from Madhipura, while famine loomed large over Supaul.[80] Monghyr, though blessed with a relatively satisfactory harvest, disposed of grain according to prior commitments rather than the exigencies of the local situation. Ironically, in 1874 the lowering of railway freights by the government as an incentive to importation only succeeded in enlarging the volume of rail-borne exports. It was largely due to this that the export stream in Monghyr was fuller in 1874 than in ordinary years. The outflow of grain was "very general and heavy" in the Santhal Parganas during October–November

80 Ibid., p. 157, para. 55.

1873, and even in February 1874 the export of janera (the chief bhadoi crop) continued.

Sometimes, exports went on to such an extent from districts with a reasonable yield, that the balance was overturned and famine rates prevailed. For instance, prices of rice in Jalpaiguri would never have reached 8 or 6 sr. for the rupee by May 1874, but for the unprecedented scale of exports by traders coming in from Purnea, Rangpur, Dinajpur and Darjeeling. Rice being generally very cheap in the district, the local traders were so attracted by the high prices they received from exporters, that even men from other professions, such as cloth merchants and farmers, began to function as grain dealers.[81] Similarly, an excess of foodgrain exports from Burdwan raised its relatively low rates to such a level as to cause a persistent pressure on the local population.

Except for normally importing districts like Saran or regions like Tajpur in Darbhanga, which produced only about half of its food requirement even in ordinary years, private trade hardly opened up any new lines of foodgrain imports to meet the demands of the famine situation. Even the established import trade in Saran found it difficult to attract the necessary supplies in 1873, as it normally drew upon distant regions like the NWP which, being harder hit by the famine that year, were apprehensive of exporting foodgrains. Again, in April 1874, the entire import trade in north Bengal from the Brahmaputra to the Ganges collapsed suddenly, as grain stopped flowing from its normal sources of supply in Assam, Coochbehar and Dacca. Caused probably by the prohibitive rise in prices in the latter regions due to excessive exportation, the closure of this trade led to a total cessation of grain movements in Rangpur-Dinajpur, and their partial paralysis in Rajshahi and Malda. Distress thus deepened into famine in the north Bengal districts, as indicated by a three- or fourfold rise (7½ to 9 sr. for the rupee) in foodgrain prices between April and June 1874.

In fact, the extent of the rise in Dinajpur and Rangpur was unmatched in any other district but the very core of the famine zone in north Bihar, where private trade hardly functioned. A

81 Ibid., pp. 367–68, paras. 9, 11, 14.

strategically located district like Dinajpur had a most active export trade in grain, with easy access to the up-country areas and the west through the Punarbhaba and Mahanadi rivers, and to Calcutta and the south through the depots on the Atreyi, Karatoya and Yamuna. Yet private trade failed to utilise this network to bring in supplies in a crisis. As Mr A. P. Macdonnell comments in his Report on the foodgrain supply in the districts of Bihar and Bengal during 1873–74, "There is perhaps no more curious phenomenon than this in the history of the famine—the tenacity with which regions that usually export held to accustomed trade routes, and the incapacity of local grain merchants to grasp their opportunity".[82]

Yet this relentless, persistent feature of "grain leaving a dear market for a cheaper one" becomes less of an enigma, on analysing the effectiveness of the demand and the relevance of the prevailing rates in the affected tracts. For instance, it was due to the low level of prosperity in Darbhanga, that grain continued to leave the district despite acute local scarcity in 1874, northeast Tirhut being by far the largest exporting tract in Bihar. Significantly, Tajpur drew in supplies on the strength of its valuable tobacco and potato crops. Likewise, Saran had greater resources than its neighbours, in the form of lucrative harvests of oilseed, opium and indigo, and the cash remittances sent home by the remarkably large number of its migrant labourers. Even so, as prices slackened in June in anticipation of the bhadoi harvest in Saran, the rates for wheat and bajra in the Benaras and Allahabad Divisions of the NWP went up to a level which made exports to Saran unprofitable. Similarly, imports into north Bengal stopped when prices rose to a higher level in Dacca, Coochbehar and Assam, which normally supplied it with grain.

[2.4] "Pull" failure

The basic question was thus one of purchasing power, as private traders could not be expected to import foodgrain into the famine tracts, unless the local people could afford to pay the prevailing high rates. In Jalpaiguri, for instance, excessive exports

[82] Ibid., p. 157, para. 55.

led to the establishment of "an abnormal and fictitious market rate" much beyond the reach of the common people. Similarly, the Santhal Parganas failed to hold on to its bhadoi crop, which was whisked away in 1873, as in 1865, to more affluent regions with an effective demand. Supplies in the Sadar subdivision in Muzaffarpur were drained by a continuous export trade to a point when the market rate "placed them out of the reach of large numbers of the community". In April 1874, the quotations for rice were merely nominal in large areas of Darbhanga, no local transactions being made at this price. In his Report on the foodgrain supply in Bengal and Bihar in 1873–74, Mr A. P. Macdonnell expressed grave reservations on the question whether the Patna Division possessed enough resources to raise its foodstocks from a two to a six months' supply, had private trade been able to make good the deficiency.[83]

The question becomes particularly relevant during famines, due to the problem of exchange failures in a crisis. A shortfall, whether in cash or food crops, caused a sharp dip in the purchasing power of the agrarian community, and had a far-reaching impact not only on the fortunes of the peasant and agricultural labourer, but also on a wide range of rural crafts and services. The Collector of Burdwan, during a tour of of the affected areas in April 1874, found the labourers in a wretched condition due to lack of employment. The more affluent classes like the goldsmith (*sonar*) and barber (*napit*) also complained of a severe depression in their trade, the priest's services were required by few or none, while the weaver did not receive advances, and the *chaukidar* (guard) his money dues.[84]

[2.5] Government policy in 1873–74

The facts noted are enough to show that at the point when government decided to intervene in resolving the crisis, the crops were more deficient and the prices higher almost everywhere than in 1866. Government action proceeded along two main lines, viz. the sale of grain at fair rates in distressed areas, and

83 Ibid., p. 90, para. 48; p. 137, para. 35.
84 Ibid., pp. 338–39, para. 29.

the opening of relief works where payment was most often made in kind. The former countered the problem of FAD, or non-availability of foodgrains. It raised the public morale by neutralising the effects of inactivity and hoarding by private traders, and by stabilising foodgrain prices in the famine zones. Meanwhile, the latter tried to generate purchasing power and create direct entitlements to food for the local population. But for this government action, Macdonnell maintains, the Darbhanga subdivision alone would have had a mortality figure of 100,000. Mr Steuart Bayley, the Commissioner of Patna, endorsed his estimate, stating that "for the whole division, these figures may be multiplied, in my opinion, by four or five". If, in 1865 the mortality had reached 132,307 in this region, as mentioned in Mr Cockerell's Report, the above estimate does not seem far-fetched. In Darbhanga, for instance, government action helped to prevent "a calamity far more ghastly than that which befell the district in 1866", as the range of prices was much higher in 1873–74.[85] Again, it was primarily due to government intervention that the population of Champaran were saved from a fate worse than in 1865, when an admittedly conservative estimate put the mortality figure at 56,000. Saran, too, drew heavily on government stores since June, when private importations visibly slackened. Of the total deficit of approximately 370,000 tons allowing for wastage in the Patna Division, the government supplied about 205,323 tons of grain and Rs. 87 lakhs in cash, the remainder being the measure of the people's suffering.

While south Bhagalpur was served by private trade, it never extended to the distress zones in the north, which depended entirely on government aid. Meanwhile, heavy exportation from Monghyr necessitated government action, but never to the extent provided in more remote areas. It was more moral than material in its impact, for the very willingness of the administration to release grain into the market when prices were prohibitive, and to provide relief in other ways, eased popular apprehensions in the face of the crisis.

As imports ground to a halt in north Bengal during the first week of April 1874, government action varied in nature and

[85] Ibid., p. 139, para. 39; p. 69, para. 73.

extent in the different districts of the region. In Rangpur, where the suddenness of its impact caught the administration unawares, the aid provided was more remedial than preventive in nature, unlike in Dinajpur, where the officials had some inkling of the crisis. In Malda, government intervention had more of an indirect effect: the timely sales of government grain helped to break the traders' combine in north Bengal by easing prices in Dinajpur, and so ensured a steady flow of supplies into the dearer markets of Malda.

The affected district of Manbhum in Chotanagpur showed a price level similar to that of 1866 until April 1874, when the first consignments of government grain reached Barakar. Moreover, it was precisely at this time of the year, both in 1866 and 1874, that the drain on local reserves from other famine-hit regions with greater resources brought the people to the brink of starvation. The situation in 1874 was thus similar to that of 1866, as indicated by the crop size, price indices and movement of the grain trade. Yet the district managed to avert the extreme suffering and mortality of the previous famine year, due primarily to the prompt action of government in importing foodgrain.

Yet the government policy in 1873–74 did not escape criticism in bureaucratic circles, though it had successfully averted a repetition of the disaster of 1866. The crisis of 1873–74 was described as a "scare" rather than a "famine", although it had the potential for greater misery over a more extensive area than in 1865–66. It was ironical that the danger, when averted by timely government action, was underestimated, and the administration criticised for blowing it up beyond proportion. As Sir Richard Temple wrote later, "By irony of fate, it was actually argued that the danger of famine could not have been extremely urgent because it was successfully overcome".[86] The real cause for concern was the expenditure incurred by government on the sale of grain at low rates, and the liberal wage scales at relief works. The Famine Commission of 1880 estimated that had relief been given on this scale during earlier famines from 1803 to 1873, the cost of relief would be 34

[86] Sir Richard Temple, *Men and Events of my Time in India* (London: John Murray, 1882), p. 405.

million pounds sterling, as against the 4½ million actually spent. However, it was seen that the reduction of wages and raising of the "task" on relief works, as recommended by the Central Relief Committee in April 1874, caused 350,000 labourers to leave the works, about 100,000 of whom edged dangerously towards starvation.[87] This proved that if the relief works were to be effective, the scale of wages would have to be determined by the current prices and daily food requirements of the labourer, rather than by budgetary considerations. A total of 6,615,601 persons were employed on relief works from November 1873 to September 1874, the cash wage bill amounting to Rs. 12,840,000 while Rs. 60,401 were spent on grain.

The government sales of grain at fair rates was criticised not only on financial grounds, but also from the viewpoint of economic policy. This criticism of government interference as a hindrance to private trade was, however, unjustified, as it confused cause with effect—it was only when private trade dwindled or ceased to operate that government importations commenced, as for example in Saran in June, and north Bengal in April 1874. That private traders had no intention of bringing in supplies into famine zones, is apparent from the fact that the reduction of railway freights, introduced by government to encourage imports, was seized by them to subsidise and enlarge the volume of exports from distressed areas to more affluent regions with greater purchasing power. In fact, the government was too conservative in not prohibiting exportation from famine tracts, which partially neutralised the effects of its import policy.

The import of government grain, even in small quantities, gave a great boost to the public morale at such times, by making it evident that the administration was ready to undertake the responsibility during a crisis. As Richard Temple noted, even before April 1874, when "not a single public granary had been opened and not a pound of grain had been issued, [the mere sight of] the long convoys of the government grain threading the way over the country [exercised] a potent effect on the public mind".[88]

87 *Minutes* by Richard Temple, p. 39.
88 Ibid., ch. 2, p. 21.

Unfortunately, much of the goodwill was lost later due to the strictness with which government enforced the repayment of its loans, often causing great distress to the people in the post-famine situation. Moreover, Indians were seldom associated with famine administration, and the lack of agricultural statistics hampered relief work in many areas. Yet, in spite of these relatively minor flaws in policy and administration, the government action in 1873–74 was undoubtedly successful in preventing much misery and loss of lives.

[3] *Local Scarcities between 1875 and 1896*

The early cessation of rains in 1875–76 caused a serious failure of the winter rice over a large area in Dinajpur, throughout the Sitamarhi and Madhubani subdivisions in Tirhut, and in the extreme north of Supaul in Bhagalpur. Though relief was ultimately required only in Madhubani and Supaul, the crop failure, coming so soon after the famine of 1873–74, dealt a severe blow to the local peasant economy.

In 1884–85, distress was felt once again in the famine tracts of north and west Bengal: Bogra, Burdwan, Bankura, Nadia and Murshidabad. The deficiency of the winter rains considerably damaged the rice crops in these districts, as well as in parts of Gaya, Patna, Darbhanga and Chotanagpur. The crisis was not serious, the provision of relief measures being mostly limited to the old and infirm. In August–September 1885, floods in Nadia and Murshidabad and a cyclone in Orissa necessitated relief in the form of loans. In Burdwan Division the problem was of greater magnitude, affecting about 600 sq. miles in Burdwan, 200 sq. miles in Birbhum and 170 sq. miles in Bankura, with a total population of 472,000. Yet the distress did not deepen into a famine due to a satisfactory monsoon in 1885, and by November, relief measures were closed throughout the Division.

Lack of purchasing power was a basic problem throughout the course of this scarcity. Stocks were available and prices stable, due, perhaps, to the limited area affected and its accessibility by rail, as well as to the fall in exports from India to Europe in 1884–85. It could not, however, prevent the inevitable crisis in exchange relations caused by the dislocation of agricultural functions and the consequent fall in the wages of unskilled labour, as seen most vividly in the districts of the Burdwan Division in the lean season of 1885. The road repairs and earthworks started in the form of relief measures by the District Boards in the affected areas were unpopular, a sizeable section of the labourers preferring to migrate to neighbouring industrial areas in search of employment. Hence, help was required mainly in the form of gratuitous relief to non-labouring classes—especially to aged persons, widows and children, who, as victims of the existing value system in rural society, were hardest hit by famines and scarcity.[89]

The distress in Bihar and Orissa in 1888–89 illustrated the problems of crop failure in two typically vulnerable tracts: part of the rice belt running along the Nepal border in north Bihar, and the relatively inaccessible tribal regions of Angul in Orissa.

A failure of about 50 per cent in the crucial hathiya rains in September–October 1888 caused extensive damage to the rice crop in Champaran, Muzaffarpur and Darbhanga. As little else but winter rice was grown here, widespread distress was felt, especially in a strip of land over 1,000 sq. miles in area, extending for about 90 miles along the Nepal frontier through the three affected districts. Prices soared in consequence, rice selling at 11 to 12 sr. to the rupee in January 1889. The need for relief among the poor was "quite unmistakable", and the District Boards opened relief works in January, supplemented later on by works conducted by the revenue authorities. Heavy rains in June caused a decline in the numbers on relief, due to resumption of field operations. In July, however, floods dislocated grain traffic, rice sold for as high as 9 sr. to the rupee, and relief works could not be finally closed down until the crops ripened in October. The crisis was thus averted by prompt government action, and was neither so extensive nor so severe as in 1867 or 1874. Yet, as the Secretary of State noted, "in such a thickly populated region any serious failure of crops gives cause for anxiety".[90]

The same promptitude, however, was not seen in dealing with the situation in Angul and the Tributary States in Orissa. Angul, a tributary state confiscated by the Birtish in 1847, was remote and

[89] Greenough, "Indian Famines and Peasant Victims".
[90] *Famine Commission Report,* 1898, p. 12.

difficult of access from Cuttack, being cut off on all sides by hills and unbridged rivers. Rice was the sole crop, carried on by toila cultivation (with the hoe) on the uplands. The population, about 100,000 in number, consisted of aboriginal hill tribes and semi-Hinduised castes such as Khonds, Savars, Santhals, Kols, Gonds, Pans and Bhuiyas, who subsisted mainly on forest products, temporary cultivation, and occasional field labour in the more open tracts. The problems of tribal economy surfaced during agrarian crises, as in 1888–89. As in the Santhal Parganas, the uplands, though not very suitable for rice cultivation, were persistently being converted into rice-lands, and hence were most vulnerable to drought. Again, like the Paharias in the Rajmahal Hills, the method of agriculture of the Angul hill tribes was primitive and wasteful, and gradually had to give way to plough cultivation by the superior castes, who began to encroach on the uplands. The loss of these lands forced the aborigines into field labour, the scope for which, however, was sharply reduced in case of crop failure. Simultaneously, the stringency of the new Forest Laws denied them access to jungle fruits and products, which had supplemented their diet for ages, particularly in lean seasons. They were thus perched too precariously on the brink of starvation, to sustain the pressure of crop failure. After two deficient harvests in succession in 1887 and 1888—when the yield was less than half of the average—distress was widespread, calling for quick relief measures. No effective action was, however, undertaken, until Sir John Edgar, Chief Secretary to the Bengal Government, visited the area in July and advocated immediate and extensive relief measures. The cost was estimated at Rs. 41,000, while Rs. 15,000 were spent on the purchase and supply of unhusked rice from Cuttack. Though these measures and favourable rains finally eased the situation, it was more difficult, as the Bengal Government remarked, to "overtake a famine which has been allowed to get out of hand than to prevent starvation by timely measures".

A scarcity recurred in 1891–92 in the Patna, Rajshahi and Bhagalpur Divisions. Though a crisis was initially feared throughout these Divisions, it ultimately narrowed down to the districts of Muzarffarpur, Darbhanga, Bhagalpur, Monghyr, Purnea and Dinajpur. In the affected parts of Bihar, the rice crop nowhere exceeded 50 per cent of the normal output. Due to the deficient rains in September–October 1891, the crop totally failed on the higher lands, as in large areas of Muzaffarpur and Darbhanga. The winter rains, too, did not fall until February 1892, causing extensive damage to the rabi crop. Yet a full bhadoi crop reaped in 1891, coupled with the generally good harvests of 1890, mitigated the distress in the regions of north Bihar where the bhadoi was largely sown. Prices of the chief staples rose to 11 to 12 sr. to a rupee for rice, and 12 to 13 sr. for wheat. However, commoner bhadoi grains could still be had at 16 to 20 sr. per rupee, thus preventing a total crisis. Though the deficiency in the affected districts was almost as severe as in 1873, the cost of relief was about Rs. 4 lakh, as compared to more than four times the amount spent on the same tract in 1873–74. The lack of purchasing power was a persistent problem. The Lieutenant Governor remarked after a tour of the affected areas in April, 1892: "The present condition of things may be described by saying that there is apparently food in the country, and that anyone can feed himself for an anna a day, but that the usual agricultural labour by which the landless classes earn wages is mostly at a stand still and they have to resort to the relief works to earn that anna".[91]

[4] *Conclusion*

The above analysis of famines and scarcities in Bengal in the thirty years prior to the great famine of 1896–97, confirms the fact that FAD and FEE did not always flow in cross-currents. An agrarian crisis caused by a shortfall in production usually deepened into famine due to the failure in exchange relations. With the advent of railways and the penetration of the market economy into agriculture in the late nineteeenth century, the effects of crop failure became less intense, but more extensive in nature. A famine or scarcity now came more often in the form of a sharp price rise, causing distress over a wider area as in 1873–74, 1884–85, 1888–89 or 1891–92 in Bengal, rather than absolute want, starvation and mortality in the famine tracts alone, as had largely occurred during 1866–67 due to the inaccessibility and distinctive trade problems of the affected

[91] Ibid.

regions in Orissa. Mr R. Carstairs, Deputy Commissioner of the Santhal Parganas, wrote in October 1897: "although facilities for communication and freedom of trade have, as was hoped, eased the strain where famine was acute, they have been enabled to do so by spreading it over regions which, in former circumstances, would have escaped, or suffered little".[92]

In this changing context, the problem of FEE assumed a new dimension, though mostly as a sequel to the decline in food availability. A crop failure, for instance, caused an immediate shrinkage in field operations, and to that extent reduced the exchange entitlements of the small peasant and agricultural labourer. Again, a sharp rise in food prices was not offset by a corresponding rise in the value of other items, which adversely affected the dealers in those particular commodities. In fact, an agrarian crisis would naturally cause an overall depression in rural trades and services, by reducing the purchasing power of the peasant community. The uncertain weather conditions causing a food-crop failure often damaged commercial crops like mulberry, mango or opium, thus closing a lucrative source of income in the cash-crop sector. Apart from such linkage effects of an agrarian crisis, FEE could also be caused by extraneous factors unrelated to any shortfall in agricultural production. The depression of the coal and lac industries in Chotanagpur in the late 1890s, or the decline in indigo cultivation in Muzaffarpur since 1896 due to keen competition from artificial dyes, are manifestations of this type of exchange crisis, though they were by no means typical of the regional economy in this period.

The famine of 1896–97 makes an interesting study in this context, both as regards the failure of crops, as well as in exchange relations. The decline in food availability was very real, affecting not only Bengal, but nearly the whole country to a greater or lesser extent. The exchange crisis changed connotation in the different economic zones in keeping with their relative crop size and 'pull' capacity, and the terms of trade moved accordingly.

92 LRP, Aug. 1898, pt. 1, p. 355, R. Carstairs, Dy. Comm., Santhal Prgs., Dumka, 29 Oct. 1897.

4

Nature and Impact of the Shortfall in Agricultural Production (1896–97)

[1] Magnitude of the Problem in 1896

As noted earlier, scanty and unseasonable rains, the unusually low flood level and an abnormal fall in the depth of subsoil water in the drier months during the past two years, accounted largely for the extensive crop failure in Bengal during the winter of 1896.

The problem manifested itself in various forms in the different economic regions. In the marginal lands of north Bihar—Saran, Champaran, Muzaffarpur and Darbhanga—the kharif crop, so vitally dependent on the hathiya rains, withered for want of water, as did the upland rice in the tribal tracts of Bhagalpur and Chotanagpur. The Barind and deara lands in Rajshahi faced the same problem.

In certain other areas, the flood level, rather than rainfall, was crucial in determining the extent of crop failure. In Orissa, the rivers rose in spate and high floods caused much damage to the winter rice, while the inundations in Karimpur and Chapra in Nadia washed away a major portion of the crops.

Elsewhere, the extreme lowness of rivers was equally devastating in its impact on agriculture. The abnormally low inundations of the Padma injured the winter harvest and prejudiced the rabi prospects in Rajshahi.[1] The maximum height of the flood this year was 64 ft., while in a normal year it rose up to 66 ft. above the mean sea level. In Pabna, the crop

[1] *Selection of Papers*, vol. 3: p. 263, para. 6. The average height and duration of the floods of the Padma during the past three years was as follows:

depended for moisture on the floods as well as on rain, and "it is notorious that the supply from the former source was never so scanty as in 1896. . . . The lowness of the rivers is due to the fact that the drought is more general throughout India than any hitherto known".[2] The aman cultivation in Nadia and Murshidabad, concentrated in the "Kalantar", failed as the bil (lowlands) could not retain moisture, as in normal years. This was due to the unprecedentedly low flood level in 1895 and 1896 and the lack of an alternative method of irrigation. In the Sunderban tracts of Khulna and Jessore, the sea water entering the rivers forced open the dams and impregnated the soil with a saline efflorescence. The local rivers usually remained salty from December to June, when the monsoon rains, together with freshets from the Ganges flowing into the Yamuna-Kalindi, diluted the salt in the water. During the last three to four decades, however, the range of salt-water had extended further north due to reasons discussed earlier. In 1896 the problem was aggravated by the storm wave of 1 October, which led to a larger volume of salt-water penetration in the fields, while the scanty rains and low flood level failed to sweeten the river water and wash out the salinity from the soil. Likewise in Orissa, the high salt floods of the Chilka in the Puri district breached the embankment known as the Nuni Bund at the head of the Lake, and entirely submerged the paddy fields in the surrounding region, leading to a loss of more than 15 an. (93.75 per cent) of the rice crop. Ironically, while the Koyakhai and its tributaries overspilled their banks and created havoc elsewhere, the supply of river water on the shores of the Chilka was not sufficient to wash out the saline impregnation from the fields.

Years	*Average height of the flood above sea level*	*Duration of flood*
1893	63.46'	89
1894	64'	103
1895	63'	45
1896	62'	29

2 Ibid., vol. 3: p. 280, para. 2.

The effects of scanty rainfall and low inundations were accentuated by the abnormal meteorological conditions of the year. The soil failed to retain moisture for the usual length of time, due to the rapid fall in the depth of subsoil water during the past two years, and the hot westerly winds which quickly dried the surface layers in October 1896. The problem was particularly acute in areas like Gaya, where the slope of the soil was very pronounced, or in Karimpur and the Kalantar tract in Nadia, where the stiff clay could not hold water for long even in normal times. Hence, the soil dried up too soon in 1896, the moisture necessary for the support of crops being restored neither by sufficient rainfall, nor by capillary action from the subsoil.

[2] *District Surveys regarding Crop Out-turn, Reserves and Trade Balance in Foodgrains in the Famine Zones*

The magnitude of the problem was reflected in the crop size and extent of deficiency, as compared to normal years, in the fifteen districts most severely affected by the famine: Shahabad, Saran, Champaran, Muzaffarpur, Darbhanga, Bhagalpur, Santhal Parganas, Manbhum, Hazaribagh, Palamau, Nadia, Murshidabad, Khulna, Bankura and Puri. The significance of this shortfall in agricultural production can be realised in full only in relation to the crop pattern, stock position and balance of trade in foodgrains in each of the districts concerned.

[2.1] Patna Division

[a] Shahabad

In the Patna Division, the southern district of Shahabad had an out-turn of 7an. (43.75 per cent) of the bhadoi crop, 4 an. (25 per cent) of the aghani, and between 9 to 11 an. (56.25 to 68.75 per cent) of the rabi in 1896–97. The total out-turn was 45.35 per cent of the normal, the deficiency thus being 54.65 per cent. The failure was much greater than in 1873–

74, when the crop output came up to 52.42 per cent of the average, the deficit being 47.58 per cent.[3]

The bhadoi amounted to 11.19, the aghani to 68.59 and the rabi to 20.21 per cent of the total crop out-turn in the district in a normal year. Indeed, Shahabad had comparatively little deara or riparian land suitable for bhadoi cultivation. The richer rabi crops, too, could not be grown after the winter rice, which inevitably covered all irrigated lands under the Sone Canal system and came up to nearly seven-tenths of the total harvest.

The failure of the monsoon rains, however, could be fatal for the rice-lands not thus insured by irrigation, as in the southwestern corner of the district consisting of Bhabhua and part of the Sasaram subdivision. Much of this unirrigated and inaccessible tract, covered by the Kaimor Range and Valley, suffered from a widespread failure of its sole crop—winter rice—due to lack of the monsoon showers. In Bhabhua the rice crop of 1896 was an absolute failure, the out-turn being reported as "nothing". The existence of rabi-producing tracts in the Chenari outpost of Sasaram partly mitigated the distress there, but even the rabi was damaged by caterpillars, and produced no more than a 6 to 7 an. (37.5 to 43.75 per cent) harvest. It was this total loss of the aghani crop in the affected regions that brought down the district average of rice production in 1896 to as low as 4 an. (25 per cent of the normal), in spite of the protection given by the Sone Canal to a considerable proportion of the areas under winter rice.

As 1895–96 had not been a good year for the Patna Division, especially for Shahabad and the north Gangetic districts, the carry-over stocks were low. The yield of winter rice in 1895 was only 10 an. (62.5 per cent); the yield of rabi in 1895–96 was 11 an. (68.75 per cent); and that of bhadoi in 1896 was 7 an. (43.75 per cent of the average). The total crop out-turn in Shahabad had been 61.66 and 45.35 per cent of the normal in 1895–96 and 1896–97, respectively, the deficiency thus increasing from 38.34 per cent in 1895–96 to 54.65 per cent in 1896–97. Expressed more tangibly, Shahabad suffered from a total

[3] LRP, Aug. 1898, Pt. 2, pp. 916–19, Final Report on the Famine and Relief Operations (FRFRO), Patna Division, ch 2., para. 59.

deficiency of 8,580,624 md. of foodgrains in 1895–96 and of 12,231,901 md. in 1896–1897. The total deficiency was 46.50 per cent, the out-turn being only 53.50 per cent of the normal for the two years taken together.

From October 1896 to September 1897, 529,053 md. of foodgrain were imported and 523,628 md. exported by rail, leaving a net balance of 5,425 md. The river-borne trade showed an excess of exports by 71,834 md. These statistics, however, are based on widely varying ratios, none of which can be regarded as even approximately correct, so that the result is more a "feat of arithmetical calculation" than a record of facts.[4]

In the affected area, food stocks were soon exhausted, prices of common rice in Bhabhua going up from 11 sr. per rupee in the first half of October 1896, to 9 sr. in the second half and 8 sr. at the end of December. From June to August 1897, the price of rice rose to 7 sr. for a rupee. Such prices were unheard of in this purely agricultural, backward and remote tract inhabited mainly by Kherwars, Dhangars and Ahirs. The region lacked resources even in normal times, and the incidence of land revenue (paid in kind) was higher in proportion to the rental than in any other pargana of the district. Indebtedness being general, the rabi harvest of the famine tract was largely exported by the mahajans, who had bought up the crop before it was reaped. A police estimate of food stocks gave about two months' supply in hand on 1 April 1897.[5] Rice was imported in small quantities from Sasaram, and principally from Burma via Howrah. For the district as a whole, import of rice from Calcutta between January and September 1897 was recorded as 133,003 md. No figures, however, are available for the famine tracts, where the condition worsened and the crisis persisted until the bhadoi season in August 1897.

[b] Saran

The crops in Saran, too, were severely affected by the scanty and ill-distributed rains in 1896, the deficiency amounting to 48.9

[4] Ibid., ch. 3, paras. 9, 11.
[5] Ibid., paras. 10, 11.

per cent of the normal fall. The bhadoi and aghani in consequence gave only a 6 and 1¼ an. (37.5 per cent and 7.81 per cent) out-turn respectively, while the rabi, helped by the winter rains, came up to 12¾ an. (79.68 per cent). The total out-turn of foodgrains in the district was 42.28 per cent of the normal in 1896–97, the deficit being as much as 57.72 per cent. As in the case of Shahabad, the out-turn was much lower than in 1873–74, when the total yield had been 50.22 per cent of the average, and the deficit no more than 49.78 per cent.[6]

The bhadoi, aghani and rabi crops took up 32.58, 28.73 and 38.67 per cent of the acreage under food crops in an ordinary year, yielding 31.73, 28.35 and 39.90 per cent of the total harvest, respectively. Rabi was thus of most value, and aghani rice of least importance in terms of output, in Saran. No other district in the Patna Division except Champaran had such an equitable distribution of crops throughout the year, which greatly mitigated the distress in lean seasons. This balance in the proportion of crops was accounted for largely by the conformation of the land in Saran, which consisted of large rice swamps interspersed with higher lands and riverside dearas suitable for maize and millets in the autumn, and cold-weather crops of a large variety.

The experience of stress was greatest in the swamps scattered throughout the district, which grew little else but winter rice. This explains the "curiously variegated character of the Saran famine map".[7] The Gopalganj subdivision was the most severely affected, for it contained many large rice tracts in the southeast, north and northwestern parts of both its thanas. Two-thirds of Siwan and about half of the Sadar subdivision also fell within the famine zone. The floods of 1890 and 1893 had inflicted great hardships on the people of this region, from which they had barely recovered. In Basantpur thana, 15 per cent of the highlands were under indigo, while the soil was better adapted to the bhadoi than the rabi. The recurrence of the floods in June, however, destroyed nine-tenths of the indigo, and the whole of

6 LRP Aug. 1898, pt. 2, p. 909, para. 24; pp. 919, 921, paras. 59, 66.

7 Ibid., p. 910; Report on Famine in Patna Div. 1896–97, ch. 1, para. 25.

the germinating bhadoi. Meanwhile, large areas of rice in the Sadar subdivision had not been sown at all for want of rain, the remainder producing only fodder for cattle. When the stress eased a little, relief was first felt in the tracts growing bhadoi crops, while in the rice-lands the crisis continued until the end of September.

Grain reserves were always low in Saran, which even in normal years could not support itself and supplemented its food supply by substantial imports. Moreover, the previous season had been less than satisfactory, leaving a deficiency of 18.60 per cent. Expressed in maunds, Saran had a crop deficiency of 3,540,852 in 1895–96, and 10,984,589 in 1896–97, as compared to a normal harvest. In these circumstances Mr Earle, the Collector of Saran, was unable to ascertain with any degree of accuracy the quantity of foodstocks existing in the district, if any. He tried, rather, to estimate the requirements of the district, the deficit in normal years and the increase in deficiency caused by crop failure, which would have to be covered by importation. According to his report dated 5 February 1897, the total deficit in Saran was 244,261 tons in an ordinary year, while in 1896–97 it was 410,525 tons; the latter amount, equalling 11,494,700 md. had, therefore, to be imported. The eventual net imports amounted to 1,888,345 md. leaving a deficit of 9,606,355 md. It was roughly estimated that at the beginning of the scarcity, the district had about nine weeks' food supply in hand.

The extent of shortfall in Saran would have led to deeper distress over a longer period, had it not been for certain factors peculiar to the district. As noted, the relatively proportionate distribution of the three harvests in Saran enabled it to avoid overdependence on a single crop; elsewhere, an average aghani harvest of 1¼ an. (7.81 per cent) would have spelt disaster, but Saran managed to survive on hopes of a fair rabi prospect, boosted by substantial imports. Indeed, the very fact that the district had an active import trade in normal years became an asset in times of crisis, for the grain merchants merely had to extend their operations rather than to improvise new trade connections. The extension of the import trade, however, was only possible due to the relatively high level of purchasing power in Saran, resulting partly from its opium and indigo cultivation, and mainly from the substantial cash remittances from the large number of its emigrant labourers.

Yet, the fact remains that in 1896–97 Saran had a net deficit of 9,606,355 md. due to crop failure, which could not be made good by importation, while exports of the bhadoi and rabi crops to the NWP increased by 20,000 md. by rail alone, compared to the previous year. As to imports, the increase was mainly in rice and paddy supplies throughout the famine, while other grain imports decreased slightly, thus indicating once more the complete failure of the rice crop.[8] The usual sources of supply to the district were Muzaffarpur, Champaran, Darbhanga, Purnea and Bhagalpur, which even in 1895–96 provided 97 per cent of its total imports of rice, maize, and other crops. In 1896–97, however, imports fell off considerably from these famine-hit districts, causing acute distress in Saran, where the pressure of population was the most intense. Monghyr, Murshidabad, Birbhum and Burdwan supplied it with rice this year, but the price level had to be consistently high in order to draw grain from these new sources and to divert them from flowing into the markets of the NWP. Cash crops did not effect any substantive increase in local resources, as indigo covered only 0.59 per cent of the total bhadoi acreage, while for the past nine years there had been a succession of partial failures of the poppy. Besides, both opium and indigo cultivation were carried on in the areas chiefly dependent on the bhadoi and rabi harvests, and hence provided little relief in a famine which affected mainly the rice-lands. In fact, the crop failure in Saran led to famine so far as it formed part of a general failure throughout north and central India, ending in a sharp price rise. Prices in Saran had been high for years, and in 1894–95 nearly touched the famine rate. This overpopulated district always depended on outside supplies both of food and wages; in 1896–97, with famine raging over a vast area, the critical question for Saran was whether either of them would be sufficient for it to tide over the crisis, while the NWP drew upon its rabi and bhadoi resources with unrelenting force.

[8] Ibid., pt. 3, p. 1151–52, FRFRO, Saran, ch. 3, paras. 24–25.

[c] Champaran

In Champaran, the rainfall was only 44 per cent of the normal, causing the out-turn of the bhadoi, rice and rabi harvests to be no more than 8, 3½ and 12 an. (50, 21.87 and 75 per cent) of an average crop, respectively. The total foodgrain production was 44.5 per cent, the deficiency amounting to 55.5 per cent. In the famine year of 1873–74, the situation was far better, the out-turn being 52.95 per cent of the normal, and the deficiency 47.05 per cent.

There was an equitable distribution of crops, as in Saran, the bhadoi taking up 36.98 per cent, the aghani 38.41 per cent and the rabi 24.59 per cent of the cultivated area in an ordinary year. In terms of output, these three crops amounted to 33.13, 39.75 and 27.12 per cent respectively, of the total yield. Thus in Champaran aghani rice was the most important (as the rabi was in Saran), forming about 40 per cent of the entire foodgrain production. When the monsoon rains were scanty and ill-distributed as in 1896, Champaran suffered more than Saran, for it had relatively little rabi to fall back on, the bhadoi and winter rice accounting for nearly 73 per cent of the harvests of the district.

Though the proportion of crops determined to a great extent the fate of the district in general in years of famine, it had little relevance for the affected tracts, which were normally inaccessible regions depending most often on a single crop of rice. In Champaran two main areas were always worst off when the rains failed—a portion of the Dhaka thana and a large tract to the northwest of Bettiah, with its centre at Ramnagar. Both depended solely on winter rice, which was a total failure in 1896. The soil was poor and communications difficult in the Ramnagar tract, there being no railway line or proper road beyond Bettiah, which lay 28 miles from Ramnagar and 21 miles from Shikarpur. One of the worst tracts to the north of Bagaha thana was 50 miles away from the railway. This situation made imports almost impossible, while locally, "owing to the failure of all crops no one had any stock for sale".[9] In August 1897, a good bhadoi

[9] Ibid., p. 1275, FRFRO, Champaran, ch. 3, para. 51, by D. J. Macpherson Esq., Collector of Champaran; extract from accounts

crop ended the crisis in other parts of the district. The Ramnagar tract, however, remained unrelieved, as it had little or no bhadoi and the deficiency of rainfall continued there for a longer period; while due to its climate and northerly position, the harvests came in two to three weeks later than in the remainder of Champaran.

With this widespread failure of crops, so complete in the affected tracts, the most potent question was how long the district reserves could feed the local population. The out-turn in 1895–96 had been 83.82 per cent, the shortfall amounting to 16.18 per cent. In 1896–97 the deficiency rose to 55.5 per cent. Taking the two seasons together, Champaran had an out-turn of 64.16 per cent and a deficiency of 35.84 per cent. The winter rice, covering about 40 per cent of the total foodgrain production in the district, was specially hard-hit by the vagaries of the weather during the last three years. The aghani crops of 1894 and 1895 had been deficient by 10.4 and 20.8 per cent respectively, while in 1896 it was 81.9 per cent below the normal, taking into account a contraction of about 16.5 per cent in the area sown. Expressed in maunds, the total deficit in foodgrains in 1895–96 and 1896–97 were 3,308,740 and 11,350,271, respectively. Moreover Champaran, unlike Saran, was an exporting district in normal times; hence, in a year of widespread crisis in north and east India as in 1896–97, the outflow persisted and even increased in volume, until by April 1897 the stocks were reduced approximately to 1,076,590 md., i.e., less than one and a half months' supply in hand. The deficiency to be made good by imports in the next six months was more than 3,300,000 md.

In an ordinary year, Champaran exported 450,000 md. of foodgrain approximately to Saran and Muzaffarpur, 150,000 by rail and the rest by road and river. An equal amount of Nepal rice was re-exported from this district to Saran, 150,000 md. by rail and 300,000 by road. Exports from Champaran continued in full volume due to a higher level of purchasing power in the NWP up to the first half of November 1896, when local prices rose by 16 per cent and the current was reversed. The export fund of foodgrains until then must have drawn upon the relatively good crop of 1895–96, as well as a sizeable portion of

---

of Charles Still, Relief Superintendent of Hardih.

the bhadoi harvest of the current year held by the dealers as a result of hypothecation. The returns, however, were only for the railborne trade in foodgrains, estimates of the traffic by road and river, especially that of smuggled rice from Nepal, being largely speculative. By mid-March, the district reserves were seriously reduced, and prices made it remunerative to import Burma rice and paddy from Calcutta, which accounted for 85 per cent of the total importation by rail into Champaran. The total inflow during the year of famine amounted to about 1,200,000 md. against an export of only 150,000, leaving an excess of 1,050,000 md. in the district. Very little of the rabi harvest came into the market in mid-March, increased importations after the harvest proving once again the minor importance of the crop in this region. A monthly balance sheet of foodstocks shows a deficit in current supplies during January, February, July and August, when 1,282,818 md. were estimated to be brought out from old reserves. Imports and previous stocks drawn upon throughout the year thus covered less than two-thirds of the total deficit during the six months from April to December 1897.

Though calculations of the district reserves and the balance of trade in foodgrains were no doubt speculative in nature, the existence of a serious shortfall in supplies cannot be ruled out. Even official estimates, generally optimistic, warned that the scarcity would deeply affect 9.6 per cent of the population by mid-November 1896, 57.1 per cent by the end of December, 71.1 per cent in mid-February of the following year, and as much as 79 per cent by the end of April.[10] The estimates tally with the fact that the maximum numbers on relief were found in mid-March and June 1897, while prices reached the peak at the end of December, February and July. Mr Macpherson, the District Collector, noted: "so far as the District of Champaran is concerned, a comparison of all available relevant facts leads me to regard the present famine, in intensity combined with duration, as more grievous than those of 1866 and 1874, or than any that have occurred during the present century".[11]

10 LRP, Aug. 1898, pt. 3. FRFRO, Champaran, ch. 3, para. 57.
11 Ibid., ch. 16, para. 186.

[d] Muzaffarpur

Though the deficiency in rainfall ultimately amounted to less than 25 per cent of the normal in Muzaffarpur, its erratic distribution severely damaged the crops. The bhadoi gave only a 5 to 6 an. (31.25 to 37.5 per cent) out-turn, the rice 3 an. (18.75 per cent) in all subdivisions, and the rabi 11½ an. (71.87 per cent) of the average. Subdivision returns are unfortunately not available for the bhadoi and rabi crops. The total foodgrain production in 1896–97 thus came up to 41.20 per cent and the deficiency to 58.80 per cent, as against an output and shortfall of 62.71 and 37.29 per cent respectively, in 1873–74. Of all the districts in the Patna Division, Muzaffarpur seems to have suffered the most serious shortfall in 1896–97. As to commercial crops, the district stood lowest among those that received anything from opium, while the indigo out-turn was roughly two-thirds of that in the previous year.

Of the total cultivated area, 28.02 per cent was covered by the bhadoi, 40.63 per cent by the aghani and 31.34 per cent by the rabi crop. Of the total output, in a normal year, the aghani, rabi and bhadoi harvests represented 45.65, 30.21 and 24.11 per cent, respectively. Though the proportion of the aghani rice was only about 5 per cent higher than in Champaran, the weakness of Muzaffarpur lay in the fact that rice cultivation was so exclusively concentrated in one part of it. Consequently, its loss brought great distress to a relatively large area unrelieved by the prospect of a second crop.

In fact, aghani rice was the chief crop in the district due to the great extent of rice cultivation in the Sitamarhi subdivision. Distress was most severe in this tract, as well as in the north of the Sadar subdivision at the end of 1896, gradually spreading over the entire district except the southernmost tip of Hajipur. The north of the district, especially Sitamarhi, was very prone to famines: it suffered acutely in 1866 and again in 1873–74. In 1875–76 and 1888–89, distress was felt in the north of Sitamarhi, while in 1891–92 it was particularly severe in the Belsand and Shiuhar thanas of the subdivision. The winter of 1895 was not the best of seasons for this region and gave no more than 12 an. (75 per cent) of the average aghani crop, so that it was ill-prepared to face the crisis in 1896. Whatever little of rabi and bhadoi existed also yielded poor crops this year, the strain being felt as early as in July.

Stocks were low throughout the district in 1896–97, the total output of foodgrains in the previous year being 69.77 per cent and the deficiency 30.23 per cent. The deficit in maunds is roughly estimated at 6,272,417 and 12,240,283 respectively, for 1895–96 and 1896–97. Taking the two years together, Muzaffarpur seems to have obtained 55.48 per cent of an average crop, the shortfall being 44.52 per cent. Direct enquiries indicated that the foodgrain reserve in December 1896 amounted to only 1,450,000 md., which could not feed the district even for a month. Dismissing the figure as absurdly low, the Collector, Mr Hare, estimated the stocks in the district to be around 7,000,000 maunds during the five months from 1 April to 31 August 1897. According to his calculations the requirements during this time would be 8,250,000, so that 1,250,000 md. would have to be imported to keep the district going. The import of foodgrains far exceeded the exports in 1897, reaching the peak in May. Yet the net balance in favour of the district came to no more than 842,211 md., leaving a deficit of 400,000 md. between 1 April and 1 September 1897.

[e] Darbhanga

Darbhanga suffered less from the deficiency of rainfall than from its ill-distribution during the crucial months of August, September and October, which severely damaged its main crop of winter rice. The bhadoi gave a 10 an. (62.5 per cent) out-turn, the aghani a mere 5 an. (31.25 per cent), and the rabi 14½ an. (90.62 per cent) of an average crop. The percentage output of all the crops taken together came to 43, with a deficiency of 57 per cent as compared to normal years. The situtation had been marginally better in 1873–74, the percentages of the total yield and shortfall being 45 and 55, respectively.

The shortfall is significant in the context of the crop proportions of the district. Of the entire cultivated area, aghani rice normally took up as much as 54.26 per cent, the bhadoi 24.02 per cent and the rabi merely 21.71 per cent. As to output, about 57.71 per cent of the total foodgrain production was contributed by the aghani, 21.33 per cent by the bhadoi and

21.05 per cent by the rabi. Since the aghani rice thus accounted for more than half the total harvest in the district, a loss of more than two-thirds of it, as had occurred in the winter of 1896, would obviously lead to a crisis.

The figures noted above were for the district as a whole, and could by no means reflect the extent or intensity of distress in the worst affected parts, where the yield was bound to be lower. The problem was aggravated in Darbhanga by the close concentration of the rice tracts in the northern half of the district, stretching in a broad belt across the north of the Madhubani subdivision, along the Nepal border. The district depended entirely on the rice crop, which was mostly grown on fairly high lands whence the rain water ran off quickly, unless the rivers were in high flood. In the southern tracts of Samastipur and Dalsinghserai, however, the main staples were provided by the bhadoi and rabi, while rice was grown in large *chaur*s which held the rainwater throughout the winter. Indigo, tobacco and oilseed plantations were also concentrated in the south. Hence, in normal years the import of foodgrains in these tracts far exceeded the exports, which stood them in good stead in times of drought and famine. The affected tracts in the Madhubani and Sadar subdivisions, however, had little experience in importing foodgrains, as they normally had a surplus of rice and were rather remote from the railway.

Stocks ran low in Darbhanga, as the crops had been consistently below average from 1891 to 1894. In 1894–95, the bhadoi and winter rice yielded bumper crops, but again in 1895–96 the bhadoi was just about normal, while the winter rice was poor and the rabi much below average. The total deficiency in 1895–96 was stated to be 37.13 per cent, which, added to the shortfall in 1896–97, rose to 47.07 per cent for the two years together. According to the Collector's estimate, the deficit in maunds for 1896–97 was 16,802,550. Including the indifferent rice and rabi crops of 1895–96, there was a total deficiency of 20,969,524 md. in the crops harvested from December 1895 to March–April 1897. During April to September 1897, the net imports in maunds were 1,001,616; the returns, however, were for railborne trade alone, to the exclusion of cart and boat traffic. Deducting the amount required for food and seedgrain during these six months from a total stock of 27,192,315 md., Mr Carlyle arrived at a net surplus of 1,165,340 md., i.e., barely a month's supply, before the harvesting of the bhadoi in 1897.[12]

[f] Total deficit in the Patna Division

By a very general estimate—admittedly speculative in nature—the positions as regards supplies from 1 April to 1 October 1897 in the five affected districts in the Patna Division were as shown in table 30.

TABLE 30

Foodgrain Deficit in Patna Division

Districts	*Estimated stock in hand on 1 April 1897(md.)*	*Number of months' supply*	*Deficiency to be made good by 1 Oct. 1897 (md.)*
Shahabad	3,486,055	4.28	1,389,971
Saran	950,637	0.97	4,475,411
Champaran	1,076,590	1.47	3,316,435
Muzaffarpur	226,678	0.21	6,182,447
Darbhanga	2,045,905	1.85	4,573,712

Source: FRFRO, Patna Div., 1896–97, paras. 107–9.

The estimates are based on the assumption that in October 1896 each district had about half the bhadoi crop in reserve. The total is arrived at by adding to it the produce of the aghani and rabi harvests for 1896–97, plus or minus the net excess of imports or exports by rail, as the case may be. Deducting from this amount the quantity required for seed and foodgrain consumption (at the rate of ½ seer per head per day), the figures obtained as above were taken to represent the available reserve in each district before the harvesting of the bhadoi in 1897. According to this estimate, the Division had, on the whole, a stock for 1.75 months, or fifty days, on the average. Though

12 Ibid., pp. 1453–54. R. W. Carlyle, Esq., Collector of Darbhanga, to the Comm., Patna Div., dated 8 Dec. 1897, ch. 3, paras. 52–55.

the data are very imprecise and the Collectors' reports often grossly contradictory, the calculations, for all they are worth, broadly indicate a real deficit both in old reserves and current stocks. Neither could it be made good by the import of foodgrains which was, after all, "a mere trifle", equivalent only to thirty-three days' food requirements of the Division.[13]

[2.2] Bhagalpur Division

In the districts of the Bhagalpur Division, the total food produce was about half of the average in 1896–97 (table 31).[14]

TABLE 31

Foodgrain Out-turn in Bhagalpur Division

District	*Percentage of average crop out-turn*	
	Bhadoi	*Winter rice*
Monghyr	65.62	52.06
Purnea	53.12	52.06
Malda	60.93	25 to 37.5
Santhal Parganas	62.50	50.00

Source: Figures taken from Final Reports of the Directorate of Land Records and Agriculture, as noted in *DCAR, Bhagalpur Division, 1896–97,* sec. 3, para. 28.

Winter rice was everywhere affected by the want of moisture. Important non-food crops like tobacco and jute in Purnea were below average. Indigo, grown extensively in the Sadar and Araria subdivisions in Purnea, came only up to 10 an. (62.5 per cent), partly due to the Kosi floods. Ill-distributed rains severely injured the mango crop in Malda, which also suffered from the low yields of mulberry, jute and indigo. The damage done to cash crops throughout the Division naturally lowered the level of purchasing power, thus deepening the crisis arising from food shortage.

[13] LRP, Aug. 1898, pt. 2, p. 933, FRFRO, Patna Division, 1896–97, ch. 3, paras. 107–9.

[14] Extract from *DCAR, Bhagalpur Division, 1896–97,* sec. 3, para. 28.

[a] Bhagalpur

The Bhagalpur district had a bhadoi and aghani out-turn of 9 and 8 an. (56.25 and 50 per cent) respectively, in 1897. In fact, the good bhadoi crop of 1895 had been followed by five indifferent crops, the aghani and rabi coming up to 11¾ and 10 an. (73.43 and 62.5 per cent) respectively in 1895–96, followed by the three deficient harvests of 1896–97. In the affected area in north Bhagalpur, covering a large portion of the Supaul and Madhipura subdivisions, the situation was even worse. Its poor soil was most suited for the cultivation of indigo, which had also declined in recent years. The famine tract lying in the western side of north Bhagalpur, adjacent to Darbhanga, suffered from distress throughout the year, the crisis being severest in pargana Kabkhand in the Bongong thana.

Relatively low reserves and a poor output, combined with excessive exportation, aggravated the problem in Bhagalpur. The district usually exported rice, and the poor crop this year was no deterrent. "Excessive and vigorous exportation of grain to regions affected by famine has been the most pronounced feature of the year, and it is due to this cause very much more than to local failure of crops, if not entirely so, that prices were forced upto famine rates, that scarcity and distress appeared, and that the introduction of measures of relief was found to be required".[15] The Collector estimated a surplus of 4,000,000 of mds. in foodgrain even in this year of famine, but it flowed out of the district incessantly, instead of being channelised to the distress areas within.

As soon as the bhadoi was reaped in 1896 and a famine became imminent in other parts of India, an immense activity in grain dealing began. The standing crops were gathered and stocks bought up in all directions, local middlemen competing with buying agencies of large firms in other districts. During October 1896 to September 1897, exports by rail exceeded the imports by 2,336,013 md., and in not even a single month did the imports ever exceed the exports.

[15] LRP, Aug. 1898, pt. 1, p. 311, Report on Famine in Bhagalpur district, p. 13, chs. 2 and 3, paras 12–13.

From October 1896 to March 1897, trade was most brisk. The exports were 1,901,106 md. in excess of the total imports during this period, the latter amounting to no more than 49,323 md. Anxiety was heightened during the lean months from April to July, the stocks being depleted and prices reaching the peak. The highest price of common rice was 7sr. 12 ch. per rupee in August in Madhipura, and 7½ sr. throughout July in Banka. In 1873–74, the highest price ever reached was 10 to 11 sr., though allowance should be made for the general rise in prices during the last two decades. The imports from April to July 1897 rose to 204,222 md., i.e., more than six times the previous rate, yet exports were still in excess by 180,874 md.

[b] Santhal Parganas

Due to the increasing pressure of population in the Santhal Parganas, large tracts of uplands previously producing dry crops like maize and millets were turned into poor-rice lands, to increase food output and to share in the larger profits yielded by rice. The old rice tracts in the ravines, being extraordinarily fertile, produced an average crop. As the same family did not often hold both types of land, the lines of division and distress were deeply marked. The district had been better situated in 1873–74, as the rice crop was less extensive and less precarious. The fast spread of upland rice cultivation, with its inherent risks, in the next twenty years intensified the problem in 1896–97. The bhadoi gave 10 an. (62.5 per cent), and the aman only 8 an. (50 per cent) of an average crop for the whole district this year.

The stress was severest in the Jamtara and Deoghar subdivisions, which had a smaller proportion of bhadoi than elsewhere and hardly any spring crops. The distress in these subdivisions was attributed by Mr Oldham "to the failure of the upland rice and other upland crops which could not be artificially irrigated except at prohibitive cost".[16] The crop deficiency in these two subdivisions was as follows:

16 Ibid., Aug. 1898, pt. 1, p. 299. Mr Oldham's forecast survey, Kharagpur, 1 January 1897.

TABLE 32

Foodgrain Deficit in Famine Zone of Santhal Parganas

Subdivision	*Normal in md.*	*1895–96 in md.*	*1896–97 in md.*	*Percentage of deficiency in 1896–97*
Deoghar	2,440,000	1,500,000	1,266,000	48.11
Jamtara	1,318,000	1,000,00	712,000	45.97
Total	3,758,000	2,500,000	1,978,000	47.36

Source: LRP, Aug. 1898, pt. 1, p. 342.

Taking the average food consumption at 12 ch. per head, the entire out-turn which in normal years covered the requirements for food, rentals, and exports against cloths, groceries, etc., was in both years insufficient for food alone. As the uplands and fertile tracts were held by different people, the deficiency was felt more acutely than mere averages would show.[17] As to the rest of the district, Rajmahal, especially the Damin, was in deep distress, while Godda, Dumka and Pakaur subdivisions were less severely affected.

The sole great industry throughout the Santhal Parganas was the production of foodgrain, on which the bulk of its 1.75 million inhabitants relied. The district needed about 12 million md. of grain to feed its population, the normal out-turn being about 15 million. The loss in 1896–97 was estimated at 6.5 million, leaving a deficit of 3.5 million md. in the food reserves. As it was generally an exporting district, grain continued to flow out, though on a moderate scale.

A limited quantity of Burma rice was imported into Deoghar, the total inflow of grain from without being negligible. Locally, however, some amount of foodgrain moved from the south-centre of the district towards the centre and west, where supplies were running out fast, grain being practically out of the market for a long time in many places. So far as prices went, the year 1896–97 was the hardest on record, common rice rising up to 6¾ to 7 sr. per rupee, which was much higher than in 1873–74. The district failed to hold in an adequate supply of grain at such high rates, the purchasing power being low due to the falling

17 Ibid., p. 324, Report on the Famine in the Santhal Parganas, 1896–97, ch. 2, p. 45, paras. 6–7.

demand for labour in mines and stone quarries, and the reduced rates for reaping in the neighbouring areas where the crops had also failed.

[2.3] Chotanagpur Division

Though the Divisional averages in Chotanagpur show that the winter rice gave about two-thirds or 10.14 an. (63.37 per cent), the bhadoi a little over one-fourth, i.e., 4.51 an. (28.12 per cent), and the rabi not more than 1/12 or 1.35 an.(8.43 per cent) of the total food supply, the importance and proportion of each harvest varied from district to district. While an average rabi crop gave about four months' food supply in Palamau, in Lohardaga its yield was most insignificant; again, a good bhadoi harvest may have been equivalent to a four and a half and four months' supply of food in Lohardaga and Palamau respectively, while in Manbhum it would signify no more than a five weeks' reserve. In addition to the usual foodgrains the poorer sections in the wilder parts of this region resorted largely to the use of edible forest products, particularly in years of scarcity. The most important of these was the flower of the *mahua* tree, grown in equal profusion in cultivated as well as forest tracts in all parts of the division. Seeds of the *sal* tree, the fruit of the banyan and *peepul* tree, mangoes, wild yams, the *bhẹlwa, piar,* ber, and a wide range of jungle fruits and roots supplemented the common man's diet, especially in lean seasons. However, such scanty meals of forest produce, if taken continuously without a cereal base, weakened their physique and made them most vulnerable to prevailing disorders like cholera and dysentry.[18]

From 1893 to 1896, the total out-turn in the districts of Hazaribagh, Manbhum and Palamau, which were hit hardest by the famine of 1896–97, amounted to 12.56, 14.33, 11.20 and 7.69 an. (78.5, 89.56, 70 and 48.06 per cent) of a full crop. The collective deficit was thus 21.5, 10.44, 30 and 51.9 per cent for 1893, 1894, 1895 and 1896, respectively. This very sharp fall of nearly 22 per cent in agricultural production in 1896, combined with the indifferent harvests of the three

[18] Ibid, Aug. 1898, pt. 2, p. 613, paras. 7, 8.

previous seasons, naturally had a grave and penetrating effect on the economy of the region.

In order to sustain themselves until the next bhadoi season after a widespread failure of the aghani rice, the people relied heavily on the approaching rabi harvest as well as the mahua, mango and other edible forest products. As noted, the rabi was of little consequence except in Palamau, where it provided approximately one-third of the total food supply. The normal acreage was further contracted due to the premature cessation of the rains in 1896, which did not leave sufficient moisture in the soil for the rabi sowings. In Hazaribagh, for instance, they came up to only one-fourth of their usual extent. Showers at the end of November led to later sowings, but these, being out of season, yielded poor results and could not compensate for the shrinkage in the original area of the regular crop. As a result, the crop estimates were only 10, 6¾, 6 and 5 an. (62.5, 42.18, 37.5 and 31.25 per cent) for Hazaribagh, Palamau, Lohardaga-Singhbhum and Manbhum, respectively.

More important as a food staple was the mahua flower, a full crop of which reaped in March–April was estimated to provide two to three months' food supply in each of these districts. But severe storms and rain at a crucial time when the trees were in full bloom at the end of March, caused considerable damage to the crop, which in consequence gave only a 6 an. (37.5 per cent) out-turn in Palamau, 8 an. (50 per cent) in Manbhum, and from 10 to 12 an. (62.5 to 75 per cent) in the other three districts. It was reported from Lohardaga that even the sal fruit and *sarai* (wild plum), as well as other edible roots and leaves, were unprecedentedly scarce this year. The wind and rain in March also destroyed the mango blossoms, causing a total failure of the mango crop, which in normal years considerably augmented the food supply during May and June.[19]

The cash-crop sector was affected as well by adverse weather conditions. The lac industry suffered due to the dullness of the Calcutta market and the local failure in produce. Sugar-cane yielded three-fourths of the average in Hazaribagh and Palamau, and only half a crop in the other three districts. Tobacco and

[19] Ibid., p. 741, para. 9.

jute gave 8 an. (50 per cent) of the normal out-turn, while oilseeds and tea plantations also suffered in Hazaribagh and Lohardaga, as the weather in 1896 was not conducive to the growth of the tea saplings. Opium alone did reasonably well, though it was grown only in Hazaribagh and Palamau, where it gave an out-turn of 14 and 13 an. (87.5 and 81.25 per cent), respectively.

The crisis in 1896 may be compared to that of 1873–74, in which case also a year of poor crops was followed by famine:[20]

TABLE 33

Foodgrain Deficit in Famine Zone of Chotanagpur Division

Districts	*Percentage of bhadoi*		*Percentage of winter rice*		*Percentage of rabi*	
	1873–74	*1896–97*	*1873–74*	*1896–97*	*1873–74*	*1896–97*
Hazaribagh	31.25	53.12	62.50	50.00	not given	62.50
Manbhum		50.00	50.00	43.75	40.62	31.25
Palamau	Failed	62.50	28.12	31.25		42.18

Source: DCAR, Chotanagpur Division, 1896–97, sec. 5, para. 24.

The bhadoi seems to have yielded a better crop in 1896–97. Yet the principal harvest of winter rice, occupying two-thirds of the acreage in Hazaribagh and covering 81.25 per cent of the cultivated area in Manbhum, was definitely worse. The mahua and mango, so vital in years of scarcity, provided much relief in 1874: the former yielding a bumper crop and the latter at least an average one. In 1897, however, the mahua did not anywhere give more than a 10 an. (62.5 per cent) out-turn, while the mango crop failed completely. In 1873–74 the lac industry was very active and the yield exceptional, while in 1896–97 the *baisakhi* lac was almost a total failure. Thus, the shortfall in agricultural production in the districts of Chotanagpur in 1896–97 affected both the food- and cash-crop sectors, which substantially reduced the local level of grain reserves and purchasing power. Due to the lack of effective demand and big

20 *DCAR, Chotanagpur Division, 1896–97,* sec. 5, para. 24.

grain dealers in the region, the volume of foodgrain imports could not make good the shortfall in agricultural output.

In order to analyse the nature and extent of shortfall in each district, the figures for the famine-hit regions of Hazaribagh, Palamau and Manbhum are the most relevant in 1896–97. The proportion and size of each harvest in Lohardaga and Singhbhum are also of interest, to the extent of their bearing on the inter-district trade and the supply position in the Division as a whole. Though Singhbhum with 10 an. (62.5 per cent) and Lohardaga with 8 an. (50 per cent) of an approximate total food supply, as compared with a year of full crops, managed to escape acute distress during the famine, they were hardly in a position to reinforce the dwindling supplies in the neighbouring districts.

[a] Hazaribagh

The available figures relating to the proportion and average out-turn of the three main crops in the district of Hazaribagh in 1896 show a vast deficit, as compared to the preceding seasons of 1893 to 1895 (table 34).

TABLE 34

Foodgrain Deficit in Hazaribagh, 1896

Food crops	*Percentage of area under each kind of food crop to total cultivation*				*Percentage of out-turn of each food crop*			
	1893	*1894*	*1895*	*1896*	*1893*	*1894*	*1895*	*1896*
Rabi food crops	8.12	8.12	8.12	8.12	87.50	75.00	90.62	73.75
Bhadoi food crops	28.12	28.12	28.12	28.12	53.75	70.00	95.00	53.12
Winter rice	63.75	63.75	63.75	63.75	87.50	100.00	62.50	50.00
Approximate total food supply compared to normal. Total annual out-turn obtained by multiplying the respective crop areas by the corresponding crop out-turns, and adding the results.					78.12	89.37	73.75	52.50

Source: Ibid., p. 9, para. 21.

Thus, the bhadoi and winter rice in Hazaribagh yielded no more than an 8.5 (53.12 per cent) and 8 an. (50 per cent) crop respectively, while the rabi, though yielding 11.8 an. (73.75 per cent) of a full out-turn, covered only 1.3 an. or 8.1 per cent of the total cultivated area. Though the mahua crop was relatively good, the total out-turn of food crops was only 8.4 an. or 52.5 per cent, as compared to a year of full crops. This, together with the indifferent harvests of the previous year (11.8 an. or 73.75 per cent), resulted in acute food shortage and soaring prices.[21]

The estimated quantity of the local stocks for 1897 was about five million maunds of paddy and four million maunds of other foodgrains. This could just about meet the consumption requirements of the district, leaving out the quantity needed for sowing the next crop. Besides, a sizeable amount of the stock was not available in the market, being kept in reserve for paying the labourers during the cultivating season. The price index for rice corresponded with the stock position, moving up from 8/9 sr. to the rupee in March 1897, to less than 8 sr. in April, and a minimum of 6 sr. in September, after which it again fell to 8 or 9 sr. in October 1897. Mahua sold at 30 to 19 sr. between April and August, while the rates for marua and makai rose from 12 and 11 sr. respectively in November 1896, to 9 and 7 sr. per rupee in June 1897, after which they fell again due to the new crops reaped.[22]

In Hazaribagh, the figures for the rail-borne imports of foodgrain passing through Giridih show a distinct increase in the monthly average from January to May 1897, when it rose to more than 40,000 md., as against the ordinary rate of 16,000 md. per month approximately. However, it fell lower than the regular monthly imports in August-September, due to the reaping of a bumper bhadoi harvest and the prospects of a good aman crop.

21 Ibid., para. 21.

22 LRP, Aug. 1898, pt. 2, no. 1474 R, dated Hazaribagh 24 Nov. 1897, from J. L. Herald, Dy. Comm. Hazaribagh, to the Comm., Chotanagpur Div, ch. 3, paras 11–13; and ch. 4, para. 15.

[b] Palamau

The proportion and out-turn of the food crop in Palamau were as shown in table 35:

TABLE 35

Foodgrain Out-turn in Palamau 1893–96

Food crops	*Percentage of area to total cultivation*				*Percentage of out-turn*			
	1893	*1894*	*1895*	*1896*	*1893*	*1894*	*1895*	*1896*
Rabi	26.25	26.25	24.37	18.12	78.12	75.00	84.37	50.00
Bhadoi	16.87	13.12	16.87	32.50	33.75	26.87	68.75	62.50
Winter rice	56.87	60.62	58.75	49.37	125.00	118.75	62.50	31.25
Approximate total food supply as compared with year of full crops.					96.87	95.00	68.75	44.81

Source: DCAR, Chotanagpur Division, 1896–97, p. 9, para. 21.

Palamau had a better balance in terms of the contribution of the three main harvests to the total food supply. The area under rabi and winter rice had been reduced by 6.25 per cent and 9.37 per cent respectively in 1896, while the bhadoi acreage was extended to cover this gap of 15.62 per cent. Yet the bhadoi food crops still amounted to only about one-third (32.5 per cent), while the winter rice took up half (49.3 per cent) of the total area under food crops. Hence, a 5 anna (31.25 per cent) crop of winter rice inevitably led to a crisis, which could hardly be resolved by drawing upon the reserves of an indifferent (62.5 per cent) bhadoi out-turn.

Expressed in maunds, the average out-turn in a normal year would amount to 835,030 md. of bhadoi, 1,255,680 md. of winter rice, 1,757,952 md. of rabi and 791,077 md. of double-cropped rabi crops, with a total of 4,639,739 md. Taking the district population at 620,640 and allowing an average of ¾ of a seer of food per head per day, as suggested by Macdonnell in his Report on Foodgrain Supply in Bihar and Bengal, the annual food consumption would amount to 4,247,505 md. The district requirements for seed being 400,718 md., the total quantity of grain needed would be 4,648,233 md. in a year. Hence, even in a normal year the out-turn of foodgrains in the district was deficient by 8,484 md.

Indifferent harvests in 1895 and the large-scale crop failure in 1896–97 greatly increased the deficit. Ill-distributed rains led to an 11 an. (68.75 per cent) bhadoi,10 anna (62.5 per cent) winter rice, and 8 an. (50 per cent) rabi crop in 1895. In 1896 these crops came up to 9½, 5 and 6¾ an.(59.37, 31.25 and 42.18 per cent) of the normal out-turn, respectively. The rabi crops on the threshing floors rotted to a great extent, as did the mahua flower on the trees. Hailstorms and rain were frequent. Hailstones the size of betel nuts fell in the eastern part of the district in early March and the temperature dipped to twenty degrees below normal at the end of the month. Lightning being very injurious to mahua, the inclement weather in early March reduced it to a 6-anna (37.5 per cent) crop, nearly all of which had been consumed by the end of April. Comparing the rainfall returns of the past seven years for March, Mr Renny found that the conditions in 1897 more nearly approached those of 1891, when the mahua gave only a 5-anna (31.25 per cent) yield. Yet that year the situation was saved by an early yield of a 12-anna (75 per cent) rabi crop. In 1897, however, rains on and off since November last greatly delayed the rabi harvest. Apart from being affected by adverse weather, the late rabi sowings as well as those sown on higher lands in October, were seriously damaged—wheat and barley by rust (*harda*), and the gram by insects (*ghungri).*[23]

Extensive local enquiries were made in November 1896, at important trade centres of the district such as Daltonganj, Leslieganj, Balumath and Garhwa to ascertain the local stock position and to estimate the probable deficit in foodgrains. The result of the enquiry showed that the local reserves in the beginning of December 1896 amounted to about 300,000 md., i.e., approximately a month's supply.[24]

23 *Selection of Papers,* vol. 6: p. 279, para. 12; p. 307, no.IR, Daltonganj, 1 April 1897, from R. H. Renny, Dy. Comm. Palamau, to the Comm. Chotanagpur Div., paras. 5–8; vol. 8: p. 403, no. 263 R., Daltonganj, 30 April 1897, Renny to the Comm., para. 5.

24 LRP, Aug. 1898, pt. 2, p. 765, no. 322 F, dated Daltonganj, 5 Nov. 1897, From R. H. Renny, Dy. Comm. Palamau, to the Comm., Chotanagpur Div., ch. 3, paras. 17 to 22.

The yield of the ensuing rice and rabi crops was estimated to be 392,400 and 1,274,514 md., respectively, the former being calculated at 5 an. (31.25 per cent) and the latter at 8 an. (50 per cent) of the usual out-turn. In fact it was even lower, the rabi harvest yielding no more than 6.75 an.(42.18 per cent) of the average, which amounted to 1,075,371 md. approximately. Adding another 300,000 md. from the mahua harvest, the total food supply in the district would amount to 2,067,771 md. The total quantity of food and seedgrain required from the beginning of December 1896 to the end of August 1897, would amount approximately to 3,589,256 md., thus leaving a deficit of 1,521,485 md. in the food supply of the district during these nine months.

Allowing for the large number of children under fourteen among the rural population of Palamau (40 per cent according to the Census of 1891), and the reduced rate of food consumption in general during years of scarcity and famine, the average rate of food intake may be calculated at half rather than three-fourths of a seer per head per day.[25] This would bring down the food and seedgrain requirements of the district from 3,589,256 to 2,524,470 md., during the nine months from December 1896 to 31 August 1897. However, as Mr Renny noted, "It is very difficult to compute to what extent the consumption of food can be curtailed without endangering life and health, or to what extent it was curtailed in the present year: but that it was curtailed was very evident from the emaciated condition of the poorer classes during July and August". It possibly fell to less than half a seer per day, which according to the scale of ration prescribed in the Famine Code and in Macdonnell's Report, would be "inadequate to sustain life for any length of time".[26]

Even this reduced rate of consumption, however, would leave a deficit of 456,699 md. approximately, for nine months. This was more than fifty times the total annual deficit in normal years (8,484 md.), to be made good by importation. The full implications of the crisis are realised only on considering the

[25] *Census Report, 1891*, vol. 3, table V, para. 217.
[26] LRP, Aug. 1898, pt. 2, Renny to Comm., para. 23.

peculiarly unfavourable position of the district as regards trade and communication. Palamau was "probably the most isolated district in the whole province of Bengal—a district which in a time of scarcity . . . may not ineptly be compared, in the words of the late Sir George Cambell, to 'a ship at sea running short of provisions'".[27] It had neither railways, nor metalled roads or reliable water communication. Daltonganj was over 100 miles from the nearest railway station of Gaya, the journey by bullock cart being extremely slow and expensive. There were no big grain merchants in Palamau who could face such a challenge in the midst of a crisis, local dealers normally carrying on a petty barter trade in foodgrains, involving little capital or knowledge of inter-district trade.

With the closure of the normal sources of supply in Lohardaga, Sirguja, Gangpur and Jashpur, the crisis deepened into famine. The low level of stocks was evident from a statement on the quantities of rice exposed for sale at the grain marts of the district in February, March and April 1897 (table 36).

TABLE 36

Rice Supplies in Palamau, 1897

Date of report 1897	*Quantity exposed for sale, in md.*	*Number of markets reporting*
13 Feb.	3,652	91
20 Feb.	2,548	90
27 Feb.	3,270	83
6 Mar.	3,099	88
13 Mar.	2,751	88
20 Mar.	2,094	84
27 Mar.	2,066	86
3 Apr.	1,717	94
10 Apr.	1,827	91

Source: LRP, Aug. 1898, pt. 2, para. 25.

The supply of rice in each market thus dwindled from an average of 40 md. on 13 February to 31 md. on 13 March and

27 Ibid., no. 322 F, dated Daltonganj, 5 Nov. 1897, Renny, to the Comm., Chotanagpur Div., FRFRO, Palamau District, 1896–97, Ch. 3, para. 24.

20 md. on 10 April—a decline of about 25 per cent in every four weeks.[28]

The acute scarcity was reflected in the price index, which moved up from 66 per cent above the normal rate in October 1896 to 144 per cent in August 1897, rice selling at a little over 5 sr. to the rupee. According to Renny, Deputy Commissioner of Palamau, "the prices in the district during the present famine rose to double the prices that ruled in any previous famine, and . . . were higher . . . than anywhere else in India".[29] The high rates prevailing for the rabi just harvested was an ominous sign, as also the price for mahua, selling at 30 sr. per rupee.[30]

The demand, however, was not always effective when prices went beyond a certain level. The local level of purchasing power, in fact, was not such as to induce outsiders to invest in such expensive and risky ventures. Of Rs. 25,000 sanctioned by the government for payment of an 8-anna bounty on every maund of Burma rice (and later on all rice) imported into Palamau, only Rs. 9,895, 10 an. and 10 paise could be expended. The total quantity of rice brought into the district by private trade until June 1897 was 23,692 md., while the government directly imported 15,000 md. for supplies to relief works between June and August 1897. The entire amount thus covered only 8.4 per cent of the total deficit in the district from December 1896 to August 1897, leaving a shortfall of approximately 418,007 md.

[c] Manbhum

The crop proportions and out-turn in Manbhum are indicated in table 37. Though in Manbhum the rabi yielded a 13-anna (81.25 per cent) crop in 1896, its acreage had been reduced by 15 per cent. The proportions of bhadoi and winter rice were increased by 1.88 and 13.12 per cent respectively, yet the yield was no more than 8 to 7 an., i.e., 50 and 43.75 per cent of a full out-turn.[31] The winter rice in some areas came down to a 5-

[28] Ibid., para. 25.
[29] Ibid., ch. 4, para. 36.
[30] *Selection of Papers,* vol. 7: p. 375.
[31] *DCAR, Chotanagpur Division., 1896–97,* p. 9, sec. 5, para. 21.

TABLE 37
Foodgrain Out-turn in Manbhum, 1893–96

Food crops	*Percentage of area to total cultivation*				*Percentage of out-turn*			
	1893	*1894*	*1895*	*1896*	*1893*	*1894*	*1895*	*1896*
Rabi	21.25	21.25	21.25	21.25	50.00	50.00	75.00	81.25
Bhadoi	10.62	10.62	10.62	12.50	32.50	56.25	87.50	50.00
Winter rice	68.12	68.12	68.12	81.25	68.75	100.00	62.50	43.75
Approximate total food supply as compared with a year of full crops					96.87	95.00	68.75	44.81

Source: DCAR, Chotanagpur Division, 1896–97, p. 9, para. 21.

anna (31.25 per cent) crop, while the rabi in 1897 gave only 3½ an.(21.87 per cent) of the average. The mahua was severely damaged by untimely showers. Coming after the generally poor harvests of the preceding year (with winter rice yielding 62.5 per cent and the rabi 75 per cent), this extensive crop failure in 1896–97 considerably reduced the level of the local reserves.

Almost the entire district was affected. The worst tracts were purely agrarian, with one-fourth of the population subsisting on unskilled labour and hence liable to be hit hard by any contraction of the agricultural operations or by a shortfall in output. In 1896, the normal sown area of the bhadoi and winter rice were reduced by 24,000 and 41,100 acres, respectively, leading to a corresponding cut in the size of labour required.[32] Under the circumstances, many small farmers were unable to feed or utilise the services of their bonded labourers or kamias. The latter, left to fend for themselves, swelled the ranks of the agricultural labourers. Moreover, due to the plague in Bombay and the general slackness of trade following the poor harvest, a large number of those employed in the coal trade were discharged. The lac trade was dull too, as was usually the case in such years.

Though Mr Luson thought that the food supply in the district would suffice until August 1897, his calculations of the reserve of paddy and old rice (2,500,000 md.), as well as the out-turn of the new winter rice and rabi (3,733,359 and 134,062 md. respectively), were based on mere guesswork. The price range

32 LRP, Aug. 1898, pt. 2, p. 840.

seems to indicate an acute shortage. The rates for rice and makai spiralled from 11¼ and 14 sr. per rupee in the beginning of October 1896 to 7 and 8 sr. respectively, in July–August 1897. Even in the straitened circumstances of 1895, their prices had not risen above 17½ and 20 sr. per rupee, respectively. Considering the condition of the labour market, as noted, this steep rise in food prices was shattering in its impact.

Though foodgrain imports increased in 1896 and surpassed the exports in 1897, the deficit remained. Moreover, the figures for 1897 represented the trade in all foodgrains, as against that of rice alone for the other years. Besides, much of the quantity imported was re-exported to Lohardaga, for which no statistics are available.

[2.4] Presidency Division

In the Presidency Division, the out-turn of the staples in the affected districts during 1895–96 and 1896–97 was as follows:[33]

TABLE 38

Foodgrain Out-turn in Presidency Division, 1895–97

Districts	*Year*	*Percentage of*		
		Aus	*Aman*	*Rabi*
Nadia	1895–96	68.75	46.87	50.00
	1896–97	42.18	15.62	28.12
Murshidabad	1895–96	62.50	50.00	66.25
	1896–97	53.12	43.75	33.75
Jessore	1895–96	62.50	53.12	73.75
	1896–97	56.25	18.75	58.75
Khulna	1895–96	75.00	71.87	65.62
	1896–97	56.25	37.50	60.93

Source: LRP, Aug. 1898, pt. 2, p. 378.

[a] Nadia

In Nadia, the affected tract consisted of two distinct divisions: the black, clayey soil of the low-lying Kalantar in the centre and

[33] Ibid., p. 378, From E. V. Westmacott, Comm. Presidency Div., to the Sec. to the Govt. of Bengal, Rev. Dept., para. 5.

north (subject to inundations mainly from the Jalangi, and growing only aman rice), and the ex-Kalantar or light, sandy soil of the higher char lands (lying along the Bhagirathi and Jalangi, which grew mainly aus and rabi crops). The distress was initially felt in the Kalantar, covering about half of Kaliganj thana, one-third of Nakashipara and half of Tehatta, the first two forming part of the Sadar subdivision, and the third a part of Meherpur. It spread later to the Daulatpur, Karimpur, Meherpur and Gangni thanas. The total area affected was 1,182 sq miles, the effects being felt most severely over 503 sq miles, more than half of which fell within the Kaliganj and Karimpur thanas.

Aus rice was the main staple in the district except for the Kalantar, where the aman predominated. The percentages contributed by the aman, aus, and rabi crops were 9, 44 and 47 in the ex-Kalantar, and 71, 8 and 21 in the Kalantar, respectively.[34]

In 1896–97, the absence of the usual inundations in the Kalantar and the total failure of rains from September onwards, caused extreme dryness of the soil precisely at a time when moisture was most needed for the grain to form in the ears. Hence the crop, which had initially seemed promising, came to no more than one-eighth of the average, i.e., 2 an. (12.5 per cent) and even 1 anna or 6.25 per cent in the worst affected regions. In fact, the district average of aman rice in 1896–97 was no more than 2¾ an. (17.18 per cent), being 2 an. (12.5 per cent) in the Sadar, 4 an. (25 per cent) in Kushtia, 1 an. (6.25 per cent) in Meherpur, and 4 an. (25 per cent) in Ranaghat.[35] The aus, most important in the rest of the famine tract, yielded no more than 37.5 per cent, or 6 an. of the average, due to failure of the rains in August 1896.

Carry-over stocks were low in the Kalantar, due to recurring floods in the recent past. The average out-turn of the aman in

34 *Selection of Papers*, vol. 3: p. 221, From B. C. Basu, Asst. Director of the Dept. of Land Records and Agriculture, Bengal, to the Director of the Dept. of Land Rec. and Agri., Bengal, Cal., Jan. 1897. A Note on the Out-turn of Crops in the North-western thanas of Nadia, para. 8.

35 LRP, Aug. 1898, pt. 2, p. 466, para. 45C.

the district for the preceding nine years was less than 8 an. (50 per cent), i.e., nearly 3 an. (18.75 per cent) lower than in any other district in Bengal. In 1894 and 1895, the yield was 12½ and 7 an. (78.12 and 43.75 per cent), respectively. The aus crop, too, had been indifferent for the last decade, being only 10 an. (62.5 per cent) only in 1895.

Parts of the district, especially the Kalantar, suffered from problems typical of the moribund delta. The productive power of the soil, which could grow little else but aman rice (in the bils) and aus (in the surrounding char lands), declined further as it was no longer enriched by fresh silt deposits. Neither jute, which was a lucrative crop in the eastern half of the district, nor sugar-cane were grown in the affected tract to any appreciable extent. Date trees were scarce too, not to mention their regular plantations as in Ranaghat and Chuadanga east. Moreover, the soil in the Kalantar and Bonaj failed to nurture indigenous fruit trees like the mango and jack, which usually supplemented the diet of the poorer classes in years of scarcity and famine.

Not only the quality, but also the size of the crop was affected as the floods became erratic, with the clogging up of the water channels and offshoots carrying freshets from the main rivers into the bils. Formerly the floods rose gradually, in pace with the growth of the rice saplings. However, with the choking of the access lines, the floods were shut out till they rose to a dangerous height, and burst through the channels with great force and suddenness, submerging the bils and sweeping away the crops, as in Karimpur and Chapra in 1896. The affected tract was very vulnerable to inundations from the Ganges and more particularly, the Bhagirathi. Sometimes, the floods were abnormally low as in the Kalantar in 1896. This, together with scanty rainfall, caused the crops to wither and die.

In January 1897, the stock of foodgrains available in the district was calculated to be 2,985,425 md. by the Collector, the reserve being estimated at 2.1 million md. and the aman and rabi out-turn at 228,125 and 657,800 md., respectively. The total population of the district being 1,644,108 and assuming the average rate of consumption to be ½ sr. of rice per person per day, the total requirement for the next nine months was calculated to be 5,548,770 md. The deficit, according to this estimate, was 2,563,345 md., exclusive of seeds.[36] Considering that the rabi estimate included other food crops besides rice, the total deficiency in the rice stock was likely to be even greater.

Imports could not be relied upon to supply the deficiency in foodgrains, as the silting up of the principal water routes in the famine tract was a "powerful factor" in the decline of trade in this region.[37] During the nine months till September 1897, the exports and imports for Nadia were recorded to be 807,970 and 721,095 md., respectively. Though the imports of rice and paddy far outweighed the quantities exported, there was a great increase in the outflow of wheat, gram, pulses, sugar and linseed. In the Kalantar, however, the only imports consisted of supplies brought in from Rarh in Burdwan by cart men and petty traders.

[b] Murshidabad

In Murshidabad, the affected area in 1896 lay mainly in the east and southeast of the district, unlike in 1874 when the aman-producing Rarh tract to the west of the Bhagirathi felt the severest strain. The Rarh fared better this year, though it produced only a 9-anna (56.25 per cent) crop due to scanty rains and was saved from greater loss by the showers in mid-September. The average out-turn of winter rice in the district was no more than 7 an. (43.75 per cent) of the normal. The famine-hit tract of the Bagri, covering the part of the Sadar subdivision lying to the east of the Bhagirathi, grew mainly aus rice followed by the cold-weather crops. On the extreme southeast lay the Kalantar, continuous with the Nadia Kalantar to its south, and growing solely aman rice dependent on the floods.

In 1895, the scanty rain and lowness of the rivers led to a partial failure of the autumn and winter crops. In 1896, again, the early cessation of the rains caused the aus to be only 8 an. (50 per cent) of the average, while in parts of the famine zone it was a total failure. Low floods, on the other hand, completely damaged the aman crop in the Kalantar, though it was marginally better than in the adjacent tract in Nadia. To worsen the situation, the mango crop this year yielded no more than 2 an.(12.5 per

36 Ibid.

37 Ibid., p. 462, para. 24.

cent) of the average out-turn, while the failure of the March *bund* (out-turn) led to the closure of many of the silk filatures in the affected area.

The export and import of foodgrains in the district over a period of eight months in 1897 amounted to 372,535 and 63,643 md., respectively. The reserves were thus very low, due to successive crop failures in 1895 and 1896, as well as a large trade deficit in terms of imports.

[c] Jessore

Jessore, too, felt the impact of the famine, though it was not officially included in the list of the affected districts in 1896–97. Distress first appeared in January 1897 over a tract of about 106 sq. miles on the northeast of the district in Magura subdivision. By July 1897 it had spread to the whole of Magura; a quarter of Bagerpara and four-fifths of the Kesabpur thana in the Sadar; Narail and Lohagara in Narail; and Jhenida and Sailkopa in the Jhenida subdivision.

The problem was most acute in the northeast of Magura and western Kesabpur in the Sadar, areas growing aman rice and consisting largely of char lands.

In spite of scanty floods, the winter rice fared better in the lowlying bils rather than the higher char or riverside lands depending solely on the rains. The western part of Kesabpur thana bordered on the river Kabadak, and consisted mostly of high lands. In Magura too the winter rice practically failed except in limited bil areas or swamps.

Even in the bils, the higher lands on the edges yielded a poor crop, as seen in parts of Mamudpur. Narail suffered less, as it differed from Magura on two vital points: the greater proportion of bil land; and the relative importance of boro rice, which was often followed by a continuous harvest of summer til, aus , paddy and jute.

The intensity of the distress thus varied according to the crop proportions in various parts of the district. Aman or winter rice was the main staple, followed in order of precedence by aus rice, jute, indigo, oilseeds, pulses, millets and tobacco. Though the extraction of date juice featured prominently in the economy of the Sadar, Bongaon and Jhenida subdivisions, it made hardly any contribution in Magura and Narail.

The level of reserves went down in Jessore, due to erratic rains and an extensive crop failure in the preceding season, followed by the deficiency in 1896. This is seen clearly in the summary of the main crop out-turns in percentages for the Sadar and Magura subdivisions, which felt the severest strain.

TABLE 39

Crop Out-turn in Affected Areas, Jessore

	1894–95	*1895–96*	*1896–97*
Sadar subdivision			*[up to July]*
All crops	71.87	68.75	43.75
Aus paddy	112.50	50.00	50.00
Aman paddy	100.00	50.00	25.00
Magura Subdivision			
All crops	71.87	62.50	56.25
Aus paddy	93.75	62.50	37.50
Aman paddy	100.00	68.75	12.50

Source: LRP, Aug. 1898, pt. 2, p. 537, FRFRO, Jessore, p. 3 para. 3.

Thus, the aus and aman cultivation, on which the people depended chiefly for food, suffered a major setback in 1895, followed by a more complete failure in 1896. Even jute, which had replaced paddy to a limited extent, yielded no more than an 8-anna (50 per cent) crop. Though the produce of the date palm provided some relief in the Sadar, it was of little consequence in Magura, as noted earlier.

In January 1897, the official estimate of rice stocks in the district was about 3.3 million md., which was deficient by about 1.6 million md. for local consumption during the seven months from February to August. The balance of trade in foodgrains during this period favoured the district by 200,000 md., i.e., only by one-eighth of the total deficit.[38]

38 Ibid., p. 537–38, From I. F. Morshead, Collector of Jessore, to the Comm. Presidency Div., no. G/2230, dated 12/13 Nov. 1897, ch. 2, para. 3; ch. 3, para. 2.

[d] Khulna

In Khulna, aman rice was the main staple, aus and boro paddy as well as jute being grown only on the highlands. Other crops such as kalai, khesari (both lentils) and mustard were grown in negligible quantities. Hence, a good harvest of winter rice was crucial to the economy of the district.

A distinctive feature of this region was a network of tidal rivers and channels intersecting it in every direction. The river water remained salty from December to June, when the low volume of fresh rain water and drainage drove it beyond the limits of cultivation. Hence, the two essential preconditions for a satisfactory yield of the aman rice were: dams and embankments strong enough to shut out the salt-water tides; and sufficient rainfall to sweeten the river water for irrigation purposes. Khulna was usually immune from famine, weather conditions generally favouring a prolific yield of aman rice.

Yet, an unusual combination of adverse circumstances in 1896 led to partial but acute distress. As noted earlier, the salty spring tides were in recent years penetrating further inland. The rivers also remained salty for a greater part of the year, as the silting up of the Bhairab and Bhagirathi cut off freshets to the tidal creeks and reduced the volume of the sweet water floods. Due to lack of proper maintenance, the dams gave way before the tidal incursions, allowing the salt water to percolate into the land, to its lasting detriment. Moreover, the storm wave of 1 October 1895 covered the fields with a saline efflorescence, which could not be washed away by the scanty rainfall of 1896. Nor were the rains sufficient to sweeten the river water. The result was an immediate shrinkage in the sown area, and the complete failure of the only local staple, winter rice, over a tract of approximately 474 sq. miles, falling almost entirely in the Satkhira subdivision and in Paikgacha thana in the Sadar.

In 1893 and 1894, aman rice yielded a 14- and 16-anna (87.5 and 100 per cent) out-turn, respectively. Though the storm wave and erratic rains led to a 10-anna (62.5 per cent) harvest in 1895, carry-over stocks from the two preceding seasons helped to tide over the crisis. However, the strain felt due to this deficient out-turn early in 1896 deepened into distress as the monsoon showers failed, retarding transplantation and drying up the area sown. The rivers were brackish throughout, except for a short spell in August–September. In consequence, the winter rice came up to hardly 2 an. (12.5 per cent) of the average in the great rice-producing tract of Satkhira, verging on the Sunderbans. The portion of Paikgacha thana to the left of the Kabadak river was similarly affected, distress being severest in north and south Assasuni, and north Kaliganj.

The crop failure in 1896–97, combined with the shortfall in the previous season, led to an acute, localised deficit in stocks: 600,000 md. according to the Subdivisional Officer of Satkhira. Though precise figures for the trade in foodgrains are not available, especially for the considerable boat traffic of the district, the trade lines with Calcutta were open throughout.

[e] Total deficit and trade balance in foodgrains in the Presidency Division

On the basis of the shortfall in out-turn, the stock of foodgrains in each famine-hit district in the Presidency Division was thus assessed at the end of 1896, determining the size of the deficit to be made good by importation (table 40).[39]

TABLE 40

Foodgrain Deficit in Presidency Division

District	*Total stocks (md.)*	*Total out-turn (md.)*	*Grand total (md.)*	*Probable requirement (md.)* *	*Percentage of surplus or deficit* **
Nadia	2,100,000	885,425	2,985,425	5,548,770	46.19 D
Murshi -dabad	2,405,810	976,427	3,382,237	4,032,000	16.11 D
Khulna	628,034	5,775,000	6,403,034	4,500,000	42.28 S
Jessore	1,779,013	1,541,475	3,320,488	4,958,172	33.02 D

* As per Sir A. P. Macdonnell's calculations

**Marked S or D accordingly

Source: LRP, Aug. 1898, pt. 2, nos. 42–43, p. 379, FRFRO Presidency Div., p. 3, para. 8.

39 Ibid., p. 379, From E. V. Westmacott, Comm. Presidency Div., to the Secy. to the Govt. of Bengal, Rev. Dept. ch. 3, paras. 7 and 8.

TABLE 41
Trade Balance in Presidency Division

Districts	*Excess of imports or exports (Marked I or E accordingly)*
Nadia	86, 865 E
Murshidabad	249,281 E
Jessore	195,261 I
Khulna	15,275 E

Source: Ibid., para. 7.

The net balance of imports or exports in each of these districts is indicated in table 41. Though the statistics were far from precise, especially in relation to the road and river traffic in foodgrains, the trend clearly shows a persistent outflow from the three districts officially included in the famine zone. While the problem touches on a wide range of issues relating to local trade and exchange failure which have been dealt with elsewhere, its relevance here lies in the fact that the shortfall in agricultural production was rarely, if ever, made good by the importation of staples.

[2.5] Burdwan Division

Moving westward to the Burdwan Division, the focus is inevitably on the drought-prone districts of Birbhum and Bankura, the latter falling within the famine zone in 1896–97. It was essentially a rice famine, winter rice occupying 87.46 per cent of the cultivated area in Bankura.

[a] Bankura

The out-turn of aman rice was only 4 an. (25 per cent) in the western part of Gangajalghati thana and its outposts (Saltora and Mejhia), north Sonamukhi, Raipur and Simlapal. The output came to 5 an. (31.25 per cent) in the Chatna outpost and 6 an. (37.5 per cent) in Taldangra and Barjora. The great rice-producing thanas of Indas and Kotalpur in the Vishnupur subdivision had an aman crop of 10 an. (62.5 per cent) each. The bhadoi gave a full crop of 16 an., while the rabi yielded a 7-anna (43.75 per cent) crop. The bhadoi and rabi, however, had little importance in Bankura, the former occupying only 8.4 per cent and the latter 7.2 per cent of the total area under food crops.

The extensive crop failure in 1896 was preceded by a year of shortfall, the district averages for the aman, bhadoi and rabi harvests in 1895–96 being 9½, 10 and 12½ an. (59.37, 62.5 and 78.12 per cent), respectively.

Grain continued to flow out of the district, despite low reserves due to successive crop failures. In fact, there was an abnormally heavy drain to other districts as early as in September 1896, even from famine tracts like Sonamukhi and Gangajalghati. As a result, prices soared high in Bankura where they were normally low, the region being cut off from the railway routes by the river Damodar. Before the end of October 1896, common rice was selling for 10/11 sr. to the rupee in Bankura as against 16¼ sr. in September 1896, 17¾ sr. in October 1895, and 18¾ sr. in 1894. Imports were nominal, police returns from January to September 1897 showing only 35,454 md. of pulse imported as against 420,554 md. of rice exports.

[2.6] Orissa Division

[a] Puri

Further to the southwest, in the Orissa Division, the worst-affected area lay in Puri. It consisted of a tract in the Sadar subdivision running along the northern, eastern and southern shores of the Chilka, and certain scattered areas in different parts of the Khurda subdivision. They included the parganas of Malud, Parikud and Bajrakote on the southern or sea-face of the lake, which along with Manikpatna and Satpara were generally known as the "salt parganas". The soil was mostly sandy, the principal crop of rice being dependent solely on the rains. Communication was difficult even in normal times, while during the rains the tracts became veritable islands. The Chilka region was notorious for salt floods and crop failure, while the affected area in the Khurda subdivision was most liable to drought.

Of the different varieties of rice—*dalua* (summer rice), biali (autumn rice) and saradh (winter rice)—the third predominated throughout the district. Besides the main rice crop (bara) reaped in December-January, saradh rice had two earlier varieties, *laghu* and *majhila,* maturing in September-October and November-December respectively, and requiring correspondingly less water. The heavier saradh rice was grown chiefly in the southern portion of the Sadar subdivision which, being on a lower level, was more subject to inundations, while the higher lands in the north were suited to the cultivation of the biali and laghu. The most striking preponderance of the saradh was in parganas Chaubiskud and Serai on the east and northeast of the lake, which were subjected to severe river floods and also deluged by the brackish waters of the Chilka when the southerly winds blew. Hence, it was dependent essentially on the rains. In Khurda subdivision, the saradh, occupying 85 per cent of the cultivated area, extended even to the uplands more suitable for the biali rice, which was less dependent on the later rains.[40]

The rains were very heavy until mid-August in 1896, after which they stopped suddenly and were most inadequate. Serious floods were thus followed by drought, while an insect blight spread over large parts of the district. These combined causes reduced the all-important saradh crop to less than half the average. The percentage of shortfall in agricultural production may be noted (table 42) in comparison with those of the two preceding years:

TABLE 42

Crop Deficit in Puri, 1896–97

Crop	*Percentage of out-turn* 1894–95	1895–96	1896–97
Biali	75.00	81.25	50.00
Saradh	87.50	93.75	43.75
Pulses	81.25	75.00	50.00
Cotton	75.00	81.25	68.75
Oilseeds	68.75	81.25	43.75
Laghu	87.50	93.75	50.00
Sugar-cane	75.00	81.25	50.00
Mandia	62.50	75.00	31.25
Dalua	81.25	75.00	75.00

Source: DCAR, Orissa, 1896–97, sec. 3, para. 43.

40 *DG: Puri,* p. 152.

While the out-turn of bhadoi and winter rice was estimated at 50 per cent for the Sadar subdivision, the saradh crop in Khurda was about 62.5 per cent. These estimates, however, were for the subdivisions as a whole, the actual distress being mostly localised due to the inaccessibility of the tracts affected.[41] Owing to the splendid out-turn of 1895–96, stocks from the previous season helped the people to a considerable extent in the early phases of the crisis. However, acute distress was felt in the lean period, the crime returns showing that a large section of the poor in the district went without a full meal a day, for several months in 1897.[42]

According to the calculations made by the Commissioner on 5 January 1897, the probable stock of rice from the past year could not be more than 1.2 million maunds, allowing for the consumption rate of two-thirds of a seer per head per day. This would leave a real deficit of 0.3 million md., to be made good by importation.

Statistics of foodgrain traffic by sea and rail, imperfect as they are, indicate a two-thirds reduction in the total volume of exports in comparison with 1895–96, i.e., approximately 108,000 md. as against 362,647 md. the previous year. Imports were minimal. In the Chilka tract there was no local trade, people growing paddy for their own consumption. A few wealthy raiyats in Chaubiskud sold their stocks to the Ganjam and Bombay merchants, attracted by the high prices offered. Deducting the amounts imported from the total volume of grain trade, the net export of foodgrains from the Division was 4,086,096 md. in 1896–97, as against 3,887,769 md. in 1895–96.[43]

41 *DCAR, Orissa, 1896–97,* sec. 3, para. 43.

42 LRP, Aug. 1898, pt. 3, no. 2069, dated Puri, 2 Dec. 1897, from W. H. Lee, Offg. Collector of Puri, to the Comm., Orissa Div.; FRFRO, District of Puri during 1896–97 and 1897–98, chs. 2 and 3.

43 *DCAR, Orissa, 1896–97.*

[3] Main Trends

The district-to-district survey, as collated above, brings to the surface certain salient points on the implications of the agricultural crisis this year.

It is evident that the famine of 1896–97 in Bengal was essentially a rice famine caused by the failure of the great winter rice crop. The tracts which suffered most were inevitably the marginal lands and other mono-crop regions with an exclusive concentration of rice, such as Siwan-Gopalganj in Saran, Ramnagar-Araraj-Madhuban in Champaran, Muzaffarpur-Sitamarhi in Muzaffarpur, Madhubani in Darbhanga, and parts of the Bhabhua subdivision in Shahabad. A similar plight is seen in Supaul-Madhipura in Bhagalpur, the uplands of Jamtara and Godda in the Santhal Parganas, Barabhum in Manbhum, and Kota-Pundag in Palamau. In northwest Nadia, approximately 14/16 of the entire crop area was occupied by winter rice in the Kalantar; the large, low-lying tracts in Gangni, Chapra, Nowpara and Karimpur were similar in nature to the Kalantar, and were almost exclusively sown with aman. The deficit amounted to 86 per cent of the average in the Kalantar, while Karimpur suffered crop failures five times in the last twenty years. Magura in Jessore was in a worse plight than Narail for unlike in Magura, which depended almost solely on the aman, boro rice predominated over a large part of Narail. Satkhira in western Khulna which exclusively grew winter rice (98 per cent of the total crop area), had hardly a 2-anna (12.5 per cent) out-turn of the crop and suffered from crop failure in three of the previous five years. The Chilka tract, exclusively dependent on the saradh rice, lost 15 an. (93.75 per cent) of the crop in the winter of 1896.

As the failure of the winter rice became apparent, the anxiety of the peasant to produce food crops of any kind led in many cases to a temporary change in the traditional crop pattern. For example, in the affected areas in Murshidabad, the land sown with boro dhan and aus in 1897 was considerably in excess of the average.[44] In Satkhira, jute, along with the aus crop which normally had little importance here, was grown in larger

[44] *Selection of Papers*, vol. 10: p. 315.

quantities than usual, thus providing the raiyat with some credit.[45] In Rajshahi the boro was sown over an unusually large area: 77,000 acres as against the normal 15,000 acres, as both the aus and aman had been below average in 1896.[46] In the exclusively rice-growing tract in Sitamarhi in Muzaffarpur, yam was cultivated to a much greater extent than usual, and efforts were made to encourage rabi cultivation by means of wells.[47] In Cuttack, a larger area than usual was sown with the biali crop in 1897.[48]

The problem was less acute in regions with a more equitable distribution of crops. The most typical example is provided by Saran, where all the crops were of more or less equal value, so that whatever happened, one-third of its food crop was nearly always safe.

The pattern of distribution of the different crops over the year was also an important factor to be considered in lean seasons. For instance, if the late monsoon showers and the winter rains failed in Shahabad as in 1896, they would affect both the kharif crop and the rabi sowings.

The district, in such years, had no relief until the reaping of the next year's kharif, the bhadoi being of little consequence here. In Champaran, again, the rabi was of relatively little value, and this consideration lent additional gravity to the situation: with the failure of the monsoon rains, two crops of the year had passed, one with half and the other with only one-fourth of the average out-turn. There being no substantial crop to fall back on in spring, the district would thus have to survive on its reserves until the next autumn harvest in August. The bhadoi crop being late by two to three weeks in the affected tract of Ramnagar in Champaran, the crisis there continued well into September. In the districts of Chotanagpur, the rabi was of little consequence except in Palamau. The mahua reaped in March–April provided two to three months' food supply, supplemented by the mango crop in May–June. The failure of both in 1897 left the people to

45 Ibid., vol. 10: p. 335; vol. 11: p. 330.
46 Ibid., vol. 3: p. 260.
47 Ibid., vol. 2: p. 4.
48 Ibid., vol. 10: p. 611.

fend for themselves until the reaping of the next bhadoi harvest. Again, the bhadoi in Palamau and Lohardaga would provide enough food for four months, until the aghani harvest in December; in Manbhum, however, the bhadoi rice was a very late crop reaped in November, so that the conditions adverse to winter rice would similarly affect the bhadoi as well. The crisis was thus prolonged for a year in Manbhum, little dependence being placed on the rabi.

The out-turn sometimes varied widely in tracts closely adjacent to each other, as in the Nadia and Murshidabad Kalantars, or in the Satkhira Sunderbans and Khulna Sadar. The crops were worse in Nadia than in the Murshidabad Kalantar due mainly to unequal distribution of the flood waters of the Bhagirathi. Again, the rice crop was a total failure due to salt-water infiltration in the Satkhira Sunderbans, while the Sadar and Basirhat reaped moderately good crops owing to greater protection from saline floods, and irrigation facilities from fresh-water rivers like the Sipsa and Bhadra.

Some parts of the famine zone, particularly the extensive tribal tracts in Chotanagpur and Bhagalpur, had a distinct advantage in that they had an abundance of jungle products to supplement the meagre foodgrain supply. In Palamau, Lohardaga and Manbhum, mahua was being very generally eaten in place of rice in 1896–97, as shown by the fact that it sold at 20 to 40 sr. a rupee instead of about 2 md. as in ordinary years.[49] This year, however, the mahua and mango crops failed largely, and the sal fruit and edible roots were also scarce. It was this combination of untoward circumstances which had created a degree of scarcity not known before.[50]

The existence of cash crops sometimes brought partial relief to the affected areas. Regions which lacked cash crops, such as northwest Nadia, were definitely in a worse position than areas where the raiyats could tide over the crisis—as with jute and sugar-cane in other parts of Nadia, and jute and jaggery in Jessore-Khulna.

49 Ibid., vol. 7: p. 427.
50 Ibid., vol. 11: p. 393.

In northwest Nadia, jute was grown in very small areas only for local consumption. Sugar-cane had no importance, except in parts of Daulatpur and Meherpur. Mulberry cultivation centred round an European silk-reeling factory at Plassey and was confined to a few villages in north Kaliganj. Besides, the Aghani and March bunds were very poor, and the Maghi bund was not taken in Nadia. Though parts of Jessore were single-crop regions approximating closely to the Nadia Kalantar, it had one distinct advantage over northwest Nadia in that the affected areas here had several important cash crops like jute, date palm and tobacco, which compensated the raiyats to some extent for the failure of the rice crop. In Magura, jute fetched a good price in 1897, while the existence of date trees on high-lying villages where the crop failure was most extensive kept the raiyats going until the end of the tapping season in mid-March.[51]

But for the jute and date trees, the greater part of Bongaon too would have been in much the same position as northwest Nadia. Here jute took up one-ninth of the estimated area under aus rice, and yielded a good crop fetching high prices in 1896. The yield of juice and jaggery, however, was somewhat deficient this year, and prices were lower by 8 to 12 an. per maund.[52] Yet Sarsa thana, containing the most important date-growing area in the subdivision, was better off than other parts. Generally speaking, the rest of the subdivision was more vulnerable to famines than the east, due mainly to the comparative sparseness of date trees there. Tobacco, which gave a good crop in 1896, was as important in mitigating the distress in a portion of southwest Bongaon, as date trees were in the east. In Satkhira, Khulna, crops other than aman rice did not occupy more than 2 per cent of the total cultivated area. Date trees, however, grew

51 Ibid., vol. 4: p. 306; From B. C. Basu, Asst. Director of the Dept. of Land Records and Agriculture, Bengal, to the Director, no.7, dated Calcutta, 4 Feb. 1897: A Note on the Out-turn of Crops and the Present Condition of the People in the Magura and Narail subdivisions of Jessore, para. 8.

52 Ibid., vol. 5: p. 226. Note by B. C. Basu on the Out-turn of Crops and the Present Condition of the People in the Bongaon subdivision of Jessore, para. 6.

in small numbers and provided an alternative source of income for the raiyats, though perhaps not to the extent as in Jessore.

In Bihar too, the well-irrigated cash-crop lands, though very limited in size, compensated the raiyats to some extent. The *rahar* (type of pulse), sugar-cane and opium were expected to give a reasonable yield this year, while the indigo payments brought some cash relief to the districts of north Bihar.

Where the cash crops also failed, the situation was disastrous. In Bongaon, for instance, the rice crop hardly came up to 2 an. (12.5 per cent), while the failure of the later rabi crops such as gram and linseed which, all taken together, formed the most important item of income to the raiyats, severely affected them. The affected areas in Murshidabad too grew some cash crops like jute, indigo, mango and mulberry. In 1896–97, however, the mango crop was below 2 an. (12.5 per cent) of the average, while the complete failure of the March bund caused the vast majority of the silk filatures to be closed until July, greatly increasing unemployment.[53] The failure of sugar-cane, jute, tobacco and oilseeds in Chotanagpur likewise caused a sharp fall in the level of purchasing capacity.

Contrary to the general view that the cash-crop sector was fast swallowing up the area under foodgrains and hence contributing to the famine situation, the effects of 1896–97 tend to show that cash crops still covered only a very small part of the total cultivated area; and that they alleviated the distress during famines, by providing an alternative source of income to the raiyats.

Admittedly, the database for the foodstock position in this year of famine was very imperfect. The crop statistics were widely variant. Grain trade returns were equally unreliable due to: the large segment of trade, especially by road and river, that went unregistered in every district; the frequent absence of the inter-district returns in the Annual Divisional Reports; and the disparity between the district figures of railborne traffic and the trade returns of the affected tracts which were often remote,

[53] Ibid., vol. 6: p. 230–31, From E. V. Levinge Esq., Collector of Murshidabad, to the Comm. of the Presidency Division, no. 2204 G., dated Berhampore, 17 March 1897, para. 2 (a) and (b).

inaccessible and untraversed by the railways. Yet, though vague and imprecise, the statistics are sufficient to warrant the conclusion that the decline in food availability was both real and determinate. The failure of the winter rice crop was evidently a common factor throughout the famine zone in 1896–97, the yield varying between 56 per cent (as in Puri), and 6.25 per cent (as in the worst-hit tracts of Nadia). In certain areas, the crisis was aggravated further by the failure of the bhadoi or rabi crops (as in parts of north Bihar), of jungle products like mahua (as in Chotanagpur), and a variety of cash crops (as in Nadia, Murshidabad and Jessore).

5

The First Signs of Scarcity and Entitlement Failure

[1] The Price Movement

The advent of the crisis was marked by a phenomenal rise in foodgrain prices. Indeed, as soon as the September rains failed in 1896 and the aman prospects grew uncertain, agricultural prices showed a sharp and unprecedented rise, compared to normal years as well as previous crisis years like 1873–74. The price movement in 1896–97 had a higher range and greater duration than ever before; it did not conform to the normal pattern of fluctuations in the post-harvest and lean seasons; it was remarkably extensive, covering the whole Province and beyond in area, and nearly every description of foodgrain in degree.

A distinct sign of strain was the approximation in the prices of finer and coarser foodgrains in 1896. Rice, the staple food of the people in Bengal, Orissa and the Bhagalpur Division in eastern Bihar, was not eaten by the masses in the districts of north Bihar and Chotanagpur, except what little they got while harvesting it. The common people in these parts generally lived on maize, *marua* (small-grained cereals), makai and various kinds of cheaper millets and pulses, such as janera, bajra, kurthi or khesari, supplemented by jungle produce. In famine years, however, the tendency was for all types of grain to approach very nearly the same price level, the percentage of increase thus being greater in case of the cheaper foodgrains.

The price movement in Darbhanga in 1896–97 typically illustrates this point. At its highest, the price of common rice in June and July this year was 7 sr., Indian corn 8½ sr. and marua 9¼ sr. There was thus a difference of only 2¼ sr. per rupee between the prices of the dearest and cheapest of these three foodgrains, as against a difference of about 9½ sr. in normal times. Coarse foodgrains were thus catching up with finer grains by 78.31 per cent.[1] Similarly, while the price of common rice in Palamau rose from 66 per cent above the normal in October 1896 to 101 per cent in April 1897, the rise in the case of makai was from 65 to 123 per cent during the same period. The average percentage rise throughout the year was as much as 99 for makai, as against 87 for common rice. Compared to the price of rice in October 1873, that in October 1896 rose by 26 per cent, i.e., by less than half of the rise in the case of makai, which shot up by 54 per cent.[2] The crisis in 1873–74 was a rice famine in a more literal sense of the term, coarser foodgrains like maize generally not rising over 15 sr. to the rupee.[3] The highest rates for these crops in 1873–74 barely touched the lowest price levels of 1896–97 as early as in September, when the new bhadoi crops were still coming in.of Charles Still, Relief Superintendent of Hardih.

Rice was in fact the most commonly available foodgrain throughout the famine zones in 1896–97, the main sources of supply such as eastern Bengal, Burdwan, Bhagalpur, Orissa, Burma or Nepal being able to provide little else but rice. In Champaran, for instance, no less than 85 per cent of the food imported by rail consisted of common rice, the people having "to feed on so expensive a commodity, because outside markets supplied nothing else".[4] Burma rice was practically the only grain available in the famine tract of north Bettiah. Hence, rice stocks were the last to run out, while in 1897 first maize, and then marua, disappeared from the market. In Patna and Saran, their supplies ran out as early as in March 1897, and in Darbhanga makai or maize was hardly procurable from March to July.

Of rice, too, the cheaper varieties flowing into the famine

1 LRP, Aug. 1898, pt. 3, p. 1443. Famine Report, Darbhanga. From R. W. Carlyle, Collector of Darbhanga, to the Comm., Patna Div., 8 Dec. 1897, para. 63.

2 FRFRO, Palamau, 1896–97, no. 322 F, dated Daltonganj, 5 Nov. 1897; from R. H. Renny, Dy. Comm. Palamau, to Comm., Chotanagpur Div., paras. 35, 37.

3 LRP, Aug. pt. 3, p. 1154.

4 FRFRO, Champaran, para. 67.

Price of Common Rice and Maize during the Famine of 1896-97

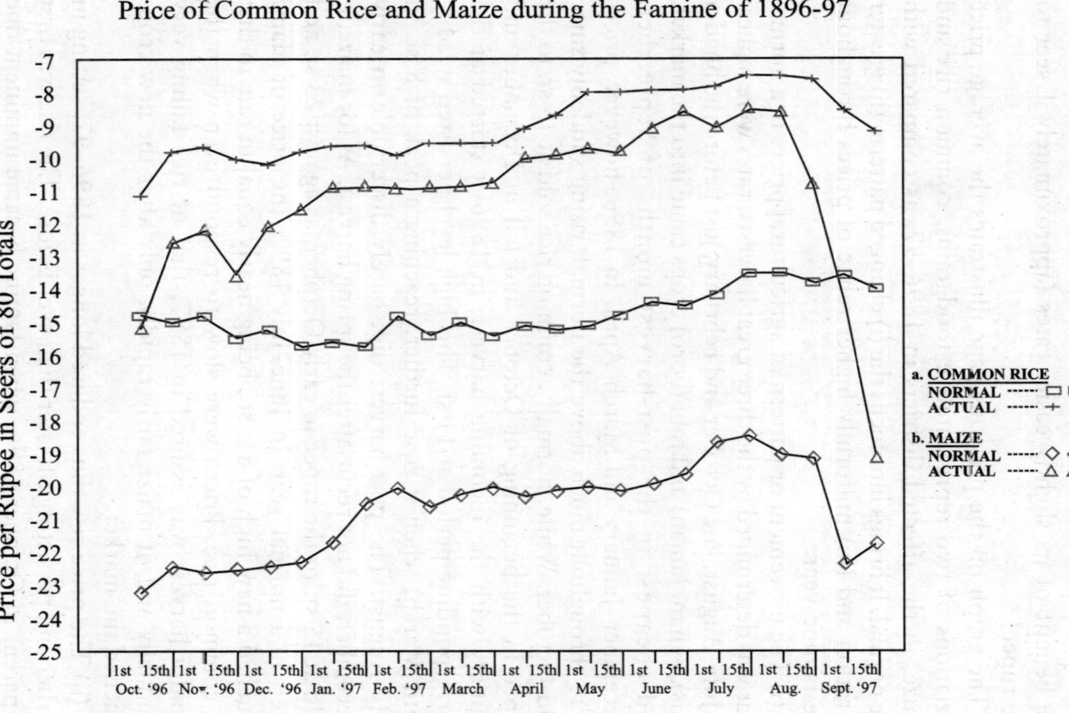

Source: Reg. No. 112, Bengal Rev., Apl. 98-450

tracts invariably consisted of the newly reaped grain and Burma rice, which were often less in bulk weight and nutritive value. A standard complaint against Burma rice in all districts was that it was less palatable and substantial, which somewhat neutralised the benefit of its slightly easier rates (approximately 1 seer to the rupee).

The graph on the previous page illustrates the average price variations of two representative foodgrains: common rice and maize, in the affected districts in 1896–97, as compared with the normal. It brings into focus the (i) changed pattern, (ii) greater duration and (iii) uniformly higher range of prices throughout the famine year.

(i) The movement or pattern of agricultural prices in a normal year was determined by the three great harvests: rates were highest in July–August, late October and February, just before the bhadoi (aus), aghani (aman) and rabi (boro) crops came into the market, and cheapest in the post-harvest months of September, December–January and March–April. In 1896, however, prices were throughout much above the normal, rising suddenly since mid-October. While, normally, common rice sold at 15 sr. to the rupee in the beginning of October and fell in December and January with the incoming harvest, in 1896 it started at the corresponding period at 11 sr. This high level persisted steadily until March, when it rose further, reaching a peak of 8 sr. in July–August. The post-harvest dip, barely discernible in early December, did not recur after the spring harvest. As for maize, it sold at 15 sr. to the rupee in early October, as against 23 sr. and over, in a normal year. In June–July 1897, the price of maize touched a new high of 8½ sr., being nearly equal in rate to that of common rice. Prices were slow to respond even when the bhadoi harvest was assured in 1897, that of rice falling very gradually and of maize fairly rapidly, only after the new crops reached the market.

(ii) The price rise thus endured longer in 1896–97, setting in earlier and persisting till later than ever before. The rise was first apparent in October 1896, when famine became imminent due to the failure of the rains in September and October. The market, already unsettled by the indifferent bhadoi out-turn, felt the increasing pressure of exports, as apprehensions of loss of the winter harvest were confirmed not only in Bengal, but throughout India. The prices of common rice in the affected districts from 30 September to 31 October 1896, reflect these stringent conditions:[5]

TABLE 43

Prices of Common Rice in the Affected Districts, Oct. 1896 (in seers and chataks to a rupee)

	30 Sep.		*15 Oct.*		*31 Oct.*		*% price rise*
	Sr.	*Ch.*	*Sr.*	*Ch.*	*Sr.*	*Ch.*	
Shahabad	11	0	10	0	8	8	22.72
Saran	12	0	10	0	9	0	25.00
Champaran	14	0	1	4	1	4	19.64
Muzaffarpur	10	0	9	0	8	4	17.50
Darbhanga	12	0	11	0	10	0	16.66
Bhagalpur	11	6	11	4	9	6	17.24
Santhal Prgs.	12	4	10	0	9	4	25.00
Hazaribagh	11	8	9	0	8	12	23.91
Palamau	11	4	9	0	8	7	25.06
Manbhum	14	0	11	8	12	4	12.50
Bankura	15	4	13	0	11	0	26.56
Murshidabad	12	0	11	0	9	8	20.83
Nadia	12	0	11	0	8	5	30.75
Khulna	9	8	9	14	9	0	5.26
Puri	17	0	16	0	11	13	30.52

Source: Final Resolution, p. 71.

A sharp rise is thus noted in every district without exception in September–October 1896, when the bhadoi crops had just come in. It marked the beginning of a trend which hardened and persisted throughout the lean season of 1897, with little relief even in the post-harvest months. As noted by the Collector of the Santhal Parganas: "The rise in prices began early, and was not materially checked by the harvest".[6] There were minor regional variations—in Bankura, for instance, the crisis set in as late as May and lingered until mid-October for, unlike in Bihar, the bhadoi was of little consequence here and did not come into the market until the end of October.[7] Elsewhere, the rise persisted

[5] *Final Resolution*, p. 71.

[6] FRFRO, Santhal Prgs., para. 2.

[7] *Selection of Papers*, vol. 11: p. 509, no. 144T , dated Camp

well into September 1897. Prices were "disappointingly high" in Hazaribagh at the end of August, when the bhadoi harvest would bring them down in normal years.[8] On 31 July, rice was selling at 4 sr. and under, per rupee in twenty-nine grain marts in Lohardaga, while in Palamau it sold for below 5 sr. in eleven hats as late as mid-August. It was abnormal for "such high prices to continue upto the very commencement of the bhadoi harvest".[9] The Collector of Champaran noted in the last week of August: "Prices instead of falling, as usual, in this fortnight, have continued to rise".[10] Early in September, prices in Champaran were still 85.7 per cent higher than the average of recent years. The mean price of foodgrains at Motihari was 10 7/16 sr. to the rupee, as against 15 sr. in the corresponding period of 1874. In fact, during the previous famine year of 1873–74, prices in all districts were "both later in rising and earlier to fall", not going up appreciably until November 1873, and beginning to ease by July next.[11]

(iii) Expressed in tabular form, the enormity and range of the rise in foodgrain prices come into sharper focus. Table 44 shows the percentages of increase in 1896–97 over the normal, and over the prices of 1873–74, in the market rates for common rice during each quarter of the agricultural year in the fifteen affected districts.[12]

The magnitude of the rise was shattering. As the Collector of Muzaffarpur remarked, "The figures are very instructive to anyone who believes, as I do, that prices are the chief gauge of the pinch

Dalpur, 3 Sept. 1897. From G. E. Manistry, Collector of Bankura, to the Comm., Burdwan Div., para. 3.

8 *Selection of Papers*, vol. 11: p. 428. Memo. by J. L. Herald, Dy. Comm. to Comm., Chotanagpur Div., no.1072 R., dated Chotanagpur, 1 Sept. 1897, para. 1.

9 A. Forbes, Comm. Chotanagpur Div., to Secy. to the Govt. of Bengal, Rev. (Famine) Dept., para. 4, no. 760 F., Ranchi, 22 Aug., 1897.

10 *Selection of Papers*, vol. 11: p. 73, para. 9.

11 *Final Resolution*, p. 73, para. 74.

12 Ibid., p. 72.

13 FRFRO, Muzaffarpur, para. 23. From W. Maude, Collector Muzaffarpur, to the Comm., Patna Div.; no. 849 F.R., Muzaffarpur, 9 Dec. 1897.

TABLE 44

Increase in Market Rates for Common Rice during 1896–97

Districts	*31 Oct. (% rise over normal)*	*31 Oct. (% rise over 1873–1874)*	*31 Jan. (% rise over normal)*	*31 Jan. (% rise over 1873–74)*	*30 Apr. (% rise over normal)*	*30 Apr. (% rise over 1873–74)*	*31 Jul. (% rise over normal)*	*31 Jul. (% rise over 1873–1874)*
Shahbad	52.0	56.9	58.3	34.7	59.5	30.1	70.6	56.8
Saran	60.9	43.0	61.6	31.3	47.6	25.1	47.3	40.4
Champaran	44.6	67.7	77.7	37.8	76.0	14.5	77.2	69.1
Muzaffarpur	69.5	97.1	68.4	10.5	77.9	14.1	92.2	55.5
Darbhanga	56.6	73.6	67.5	190.0	90.7	195.3	90.0	181.8
Bhagalpur	84.2	84.2	91.3	18.5	97.8	30.0	112.5	57.8
Santhal Prgs	54.2	46.4	75.8	46.4	91.7	32.3	106.0	27.3
Hazaribagh	52.4	46.8	60.5	66.4	108.8	70.7	113.8	115.8
Palamau	66.9	30.2	91.4	59.7	134.7	87.7	88.8	71.9
Manbhum	42.8	49.1	76.5	65.8	94.1	47.0	89.1	73.3
Bankura	18.4	20.3	44.4	36.0	55.7	30.9	86.5	49.2
Murshidabad	33.5	77.0	59.4	81.1	69.2	70.0	75.8	83.3
Nadia	48.3	37.3	50.3	19.2	59.7	38.1	80.7	61.3
Khulna	45.0	140.0	35.5	65.6	62.1	56.7	74.1	68.3
Puri	42.0	178.5	70.9	114.5	34.2	111.9	52.9	144.1

Source: Final Resolution, p. 72

of famines, such as those experienced in 1874 and last year".[13] The prices in nearly every district climbed to a successively higher level before each harvest, the climax being reached in July–August 1897, when the bhadoi crops were reaped. Saran was an exception, for here the impact of the rabi harvest, covering 40 per cent of its total foodgrain output, lingered well into July, lowering and steadying prices until the new bhadoi crops came in. Though the district average for Puri was seen to be lower at the end of April, the percentage of increase in the Chilka tract in March–April was more than 50 per cent over the prices prevailing in the same period last year. As regards Santhal Parganas, "So far as prices went, this was the hardest year of which we have record in this district".[14] R. H. Renny, the Deputy Commissioner of Palamau, noted: "the prices in this district during the present famine rose to double the prices that ruled in any previous famine, and . . . were higher . . . than anywhere else in India".[15] Here the price of common rice in Occober 1896, ruling 66.9 per cent above the normal and 30.2 per cent above the prices in October 1873, rose to 134.7 and 87.7 per cent, respectively, on 30 April 1897. In fact, in nearly every district the highest price recorded for any month of 1873–74, was close to the lowest price noted for the same month in 1896–97. In considering the relative price levels, however, one must allow for the general increase in prices during the twenty-three years between the two famines and the beneficial effect of foodgrain imports by the government in 1873–74.

Moreover, the wider area covered by the famine in 1896–97, along with the development of trade and communications, led to the equalisation and rise of prices to a level and extent hitherto unknown.

[1.1] Determinants of the price movement other than crop out-turn

The price movement may be viewed from different angles in the

14 LRP, Aug. 1898, pt. 1, p. 343.

15 Ibid., pt. 2, p. 773. From P. H. Renny, Dy. Comm. Palamau, to the Comm., Chotanagpur Div., no. 322 F, dated Daltonganj, 5 Nov. 1897, para. 36.

TABLE 45

Price of Rice in Post-harvest Period

	1896–1897				*1895–1896*				*% of price rise*	
	31 Dec.		*31 Jan.*		*31 Dec.*		*31 Jan.*		*31 Dec.*	*31 Jan.*
	Sr.	*Ch.*	*Sr.*	*Ch.*	*Sr.*	*Ch.*	*Sr.*	*Ch.*	*1896*	*1897*
Surplus districts										
Burdwan	10	8	9	12	17	0	16	8	38.23	40.90
Tipperah	8	6	10	10	16	0	15	0	40.62	40.00
Gaya	9	8	9	0						
Scarcity districts										
Champaran	9	0	9	0	14	0	14	0	35.71	35.71
Muzaffarpur	9	0	9	0	16	6	19	0	45.02	52.63
Palamau	8	11	8	11						
Nadia	9	2	9	2	16	0	16	0	43.00	43.00
Khulna	10	14	11	3	16	12	17	0	35.10	34.23
Rajshahi	9	6	9	12	16	0	16	0	41.43	39.06
Pabna	9	6	9	6	13	8	13	4	30.59	29.28
Santhal Prgs.	11	0	10	0	23	0	23	10	52.17	57.66
Puri	11	0	10	8	13	4	14	8	16.98	27.58

Price of Rice in Lean Period

	1897				1896				% of price rise	
	30 Apr.		31 May		30 Apr.		31 May		30 Apr.	31 May
	Sr.	*Ch.*	*Sr.*	*Ch.*	*Sr.*	*Ch.*	*Sr.*	*Ch.*	1897	1896
Surplus districts										
Burdwan	8	7	9	0	16	4	16	0	48.12	43.75
Tipperah	9	0	8	0	12	1	10	7	28.57	23.29
Gaya	7	12	7	12	16	0	14	0	51.56	44.64
Scarcity districts										
Champaran	8	12	7	12	17	4	17	0	49.27	54.41
Muzzaffarpur	8	0	7	8	14	8	13	0	44.82	42.30
Palamau	6	14	7	5			13	5		45.07
Nadia	8	3	8	4	14	8	12	13	43.58	35.59
Khulna	9	4	8	12	14	8	13	0	36.20	32.69
Rajshahi	8	1	8	1	13	14	12	12	37.99	32.54
Pabna	9	0	8	0	15	0	12	14	40.00	37.83
Santhal Prgs.	8	2	7	12	16	8	16	0	50.78	51.56
Puri	11	13	11	13	23	10	21	0	50.00	43.76

Source: Data gleaned from relevant volumes of *Selection of Papers*, 1896–97.

context of the famine. Some distinctive trends are evident in table 45, which shows the quantity of common rice sold per rupee in certain surplus and scarcity districts in 1896–97, both at the post-harvest time when prices normally fell, and in the lean season when they reached the peak.

Prices could not in all cases be connected directly with crop out-turn. For instance, in Tipperah the prices were 17 sr. 12 ch. of common rice for a rupee in 1873, 16 sr. in 1888, and 13 sr. 14 ch. in 1891. Though the out-turn in 1896–97 was 62.5 per cent as compared to 75 per cent in 1873 and 87.5 per cent in 1888 and 1891, the price had nearly doubled in 1896. In fact, in Tipperah and Gaya (both surplus districts), prices were higher than in many of the scarcity tracts. Again, in Nadia and Jessore prices were low in relation to Khulna, though in these districts the winter rice out-turn was estimated to be only about 15.6 per cent and 9.3 per cent, respectively, as against 62.5 per cent in Khulna. There was also a considerable difference in price rates between Khulna, on the one hand, and 24 Parganas-Hooghly, on the other, though all of them were close to the Calcutta market. The interaction of grain trade might, to some extent, explain these price differentials.

Contrary to expectations, the price stimulus seldom attracted supplies from surplus to scarcity, and scarcity to famine tracts. Due to excessive exportation and greater purchasing power, the usually surplus districts often showed a higher price rate than the scarcity districts. The tables show, however, that in the lean months, prices in the surplus districts steadied down even where they were exceptionally high earlier in the year; but in the scarcity tracts they rocketed still further, thus proving that here the deficiency was real.

[a] Trade pattern and export of foodgrains

The large volume of exports from Tipperah, which had more than a 10-anna out-turn of winter rice, pushed up the price of common rice to 7 sr. 10 ch. a rupee as early as in September 1896—a rate higher than in the affected areas in Bengal. Again, Gaya, which enjoyed the full benefit of the Sone Canal system and had the best yield in the Patna Division, consistently showed a higher price rate than elsewhere. Grain flowed in a steady stream from Gaya to the

NWP, affected areas in the Patna Division, and even to Palamau in Chotanagpur via Daltonganj. Singhbhum in Chotanagpur, which had a good out-turn in 1896, showed a price rate of 8 sr. per rupee at important hats, which was higher than in all scarcity areas except Palamau. In the interior, however, rice still sold at 10 sr. and over. Obviously, continued exportations (amounting to 5,911 maunds to north Bihar, Hazaribagh and Asansol in April 1897) were sending up prices, especially in trade marts near the railway.[16] A continuous flow of exports from the Rarh tract in Burdwan and Murshidabad depleted the local stocks and doubled the price of common rice (8 to 9 sr. per rupee) by April–May 1897. Exports from the normally surplus rice-producing districts of Bhagalpur and Bankura too, continued despite the low out-turn in 1896. The Collector of Bhagalpur noted: "Extensive and vigorous exportation of grain . . . has been the most pronounced feature of the year, and it is to this cause very much more than the local failure of crops, if not entirely so, that prices were forced upto famine rates."[17]

[b] Purchasing power

The level of purchasing power was a vital factor in regulating prices and the flow of trade. Due to lack of effective demand, grain was very often drained out from scarcity areas to those with greater resources as from Bihar to the NWP, or from Puri to Bombay and Ceylon. Acute scarcity areas like Champaran, Muzaffarpur and particularly Saran, which imported even in normal years, failed to hold in grain even as late as November 1896, which led to grain riots and widespread panic. It was not that prices were low in north Bihar; in fact they rose to unprecedented heights. The problem, however, was that very few of the local people could afford to buy rice at the prevailing rates, and the NWP agents outbid them.

A variation of the problem is seen in Bankura, which had a habitually low price and wage level. Here, the danger point of 10 sr. to the rupee was reached in May 1897, when prices in most districts of Bihar, Chotanagpur and the Presidency Division ranged between 7 and 8 sr. Hence, the crisis deepened within, while exports went

16 *Selection of Papers,* vol. 7: p. 402.
17 FRFRO, Bhagalpur, paras. 13–14.

on in full volume.

[c] Inaccessibility and transport expenses

Remote tracts in the famine zone suffered from unusually high prices, more due to the cost of carriage than to a deficient harvest. Palamau, for instance, was probably "the most isolated district in the whole province of Bengal".[18] Here, despite the grant of a government subsidy of 8 annas per maund on importations of rice, the difficulties of carriage by road and the scarcity of carts were so great that the trade response was most disappointing throughout. Similarly, Shikarpur and Ramnagar in the centre of the famine zone in Champaran were 24 and 28 miles, respectively, from the railway, the severely distressed tracts extending for 10 to 12 miles further north. One of the worst tracts to the north of Bagaha was about 50 miles from the railway. Macpherson, the Collector of Champaran, remarked: "The most remote parts (such as Ramnagar and Bagaha) were thus those in which prices rose highest of all, and there they were generally almost 2½ times the normal rate for these parts". In May, the price of common rice rose to 6 sr. and in July that of Burma rice to 7 sr. per rupee in Ramnagar, while in Bagaha it sold at 6¾ sr. to the rupee in mid-August.[19]

Yet the very problem of inaccessibility, which raised prices in the remote tracts in times of famine by making relief difficult, kept them down by minimising exports when the out-turn was normal. In fact, lower prices in the interior showed that the district was not yet devoid of grain. The hinterland usually supplied the grain, which increased in price due to the retailers' profits, cost of carriage, etc. as it flowed towards the grain marts near the coastal towns or railway lines. Fluctuations of the inter-district trade, as well as the pressure of exports further raised prices in the major hats and towns, while the relative lack of transport deeper in the interior shut out these influences and generally accounted for a lower and more even range of prices.

Even during the famine of 1896–97, prices in the interior of surplus districts often remained lower due to defective

[18] LRP, Aug. 1898, pt. 2, p. 773. R. H. Renny to Comm., Chotanagpur Div., No.322 F, dated Daltonganj, 5 Nov. 1897.

[19] FRFRO, Champaran, paras. 17 and 68.

communication. Raipur in Bankura was so badly off in terms of communication that export of rice was apparently nil. This resulted in a peculiar situation in which the price of common rice rose from about 12 to 12½ sr. per rupee in January 1897 to 10 sr. in May in Bankura and Bishnupur, whereas the price in Raipur and Simlapal did not fluctuate during the same interval, having remained constant at 10¾ sr. Conversely, Gangajalghati and Sonamukhi, both situated near the East Indian Railway, had their stocks reduced by export, and prices rose earlier.[20] Again, in Singhbhum, rice sold at 8 sr. per rupee in the larger marts due to brisk export activity, while it remained at 10 sr. deeper in the interior.[21]

Any reversal of this trend was a sure sign of impending scarcity or famine, as had been apparent in Orissa during the crisis of 1866. In the Barind in Rajshahi, the cultivators had kept sufficient stocks of aman rice in 1896 to last until mid-January 1897. This was confirmed by the fact that in the interior of the Barind the price of paddy was easier than in the exporting hats, such as Godagari. In the deara lands, however, there was a depletionof paddy stocks to an alarming extent. In the interior of this tract, the price of rice was higher than at Charghat hat.[22] Similarly, in July 1897 the Deputy Commissioner of Chotanagpur noticed that the price rise in Hazaribagh was more remarkable in the smaller than in the larger marts, which showed that the cultivators' stocks were fast running out. In famine-hit districts like Hazaribagh, which depended largely on imported rice from Calcutta in 1896–97, prices were most often higher in the interior, where the people had to pay Calcutta prices plus the mahajans' and retailers' profits.[23] Transport problems, as noted, further raised prices in the remote tracts of Saran, Champaran, Palamau, the Nadia Kalantar, or Bhabhua in Shahabad, which lay thirty miles off from the nearest railway station of Zamania. In Saran, prices were "curiously equal" except in an area

20 *Selection of Papers.*, vol. 8: p. 522.
21 Ibid., vol. 7: p. 402.
22 Ibid., vol. 3: p. 265.
23 Ibid., vol. 7: p. 421; vol. 9: p. 436.

stretching from Barauli outpost in the Gopalganj subdivision to Cheyton Parsa in the Sadar, the area most remote from the railway: here foodgrains sold throughout at rates 1 to ½ sr. higher than in the rest of the district.[24]

Champaran, normally an exporting district, had to import largely to all parts in 1896–97, the divergence in prices as compared with the normal being much greater in the interior of the district than at Motihari. Macpherson observed: "In ordinary years prices in the interior are much lower, but in this year were much higher, than what they are near the line of rail".[25]

[d] Manipulations of the market

In many instances, prices were arbitrarily pushed up by hoarding and rigging on the part of the traders, which led to a widespread apprehension of grain riots in the Patna Division during the winter of 1896. These events and similar tendencies in other parts of the famine zone have been dealt with in some detail in chapter 8.

Not content with rigging the market, the merchants exploited the problems of transport and communication by organising carters' combines to further push up prices, as in Puri. In Palamau, independent combinations of the *thakurs* (cart owners) in the trade marts had a similar effect.[26]

Thus, in 1896–97 the behaviour of prices in relation to crop out-turn was far from being simple and direct. It was a problem of many dimensions, which did not always conform to preconceived patterns.

[2] *The Psychology of Scarcity: Dissolution of the Existing Patterns of Entitlement*

The various manifestations of this abnormal rise in foodgrain prices, led in logical sequence to the second distinctive feature marking the advent of famine: the growth and development of

24 LRP, Aug. 1898, pt. 3, p. 1154, para. 31.

25 FRFRO, Champaran, para. 68.

26 W. H. Lee to the Comm., Orissa Div., no. 116, Puri, 20 Jan. 1897, para. 5; *Selection of Papers,* vol. 8: p. 416.

a psychology of scarcity. Several factors contributed to this. As soon as the rains failed in September 1896, rural credit was paralysed and stocks went out of market, so that the average cultivator was left without adequate provisions for foodgrain or seedgrain. There were numerous instances of zamindars refusing to make advances to their tenantry and of mahajans to their khataks, while the banias exploited the situation by hoarding stocks and selling them off to export agents.

This freezing of rural credit and disappearance of grain from the market naturally led to a feeling of widespread panic. In the Nadia Kalantar and Satkhira in Khulna, rumours were current about another year of scarcity and peasants began to sell off their meagre belongings in alarm. In Patna, the public mind was weak and pessimistic as late as in mid-1897. The haze which followed the floods at this time, was looked on as a portent, which was a sign of the existing tension.[27] In Lohardaga, too, the Brahmins were prophesying another year of scarcity and prices rose far above the usual famine level. The rains were erratic in June–July, and "preconceived fears being thus confirmed, a regular panic ensued".[28]

The peasants' apprehension was not unreasoned; rather, it reflected a keen and almost intuitive awareness of the impending crisis, based on long experience. Their observations and deep anxiety about weather and crop prospects found expression in a host of agricultural proverbs and predictions, which were often remarkably astute. In the Kalantar, for instance, cultivators attached great importance to the significant adage, *"Kurkut bhurkut shing shukhana kunnya kannay kan; bin boway toola bursay kaha rakhoga dhan"* (If there be adequate showers in Sravan, slight or no rain in Bhadro, the rice fields are inundated in Ashwin and the Kartik showers be well-distributed and free of high winds, the cultivators have to enlarge their granaries to store the abundant crops).[29] Indeed, sayings attributed to the legendary Kshana (*"Kshanar bachan"*) were adhered to all over Bengal. They were remarkably precise, as, for instance, about

27 *Selection of Papers*, vol. 10: p. 31.
28 Ibid., vol. 10: p. 451; H. C. Streatfeild to the Comm., Chotanagpur Div., no. 409 F, Ranchi, 12 Nov. 1897, para. 9.
29 LRP, Aug. 1898, pt. 2, p. 459, para. 10.

the pre-harvest rains in February–March: *"Jodi barshe Magher shesh, dhonyo rajar punyo desh"* (if it rains in mid-February, blessed are the king and his country); or *"Jodi barshe Phagune, raja jay magune"* (Showers in late February to mid-March make a pauper of the king). As the rains failed throughout the Province in September–October 1896, followed by erratic spring showers in 1897, the worst fears of the peasants were confirmed.

This sharp deviation in rainfall and weather conditions in 1896 was followed by a shake-up of the normal obligations and relationships in rural society, as between the landowner and the labourer, the creditor and the debtor, the customer and the producer, the grain dealer and the consumer, and the pater familias and his female, minor, old and ailing dependants. In view of the looming subsistence crisis, a subjective value system was applied to each of these areas by the dominant groups concerned, in order to determine their respective obligations and the right to survive.

The zamindar or landowner was traditionally viewed as the village patron (malik or *annadata*) who had an enduring relationship with his attached labourers (like the kamias in Gaya and Chotanagpur, the low-caste bondmen of the Utkal Brahmins in Bankura, or the *pannaiyal*s in the south), and with certain occupational groups like the washerman, barber, musician, and others, who were annually offered fixed proportions in kind for the services rendered through several generations. This seemingly permanent relationship, viewed in terms of "reciprocity", emphasised the patron's moral obligation to protect the client in return for his services, acknowledging in the process his "right to subsist".[30] In reality, however (as seen in the previous sections on rent, credit and labour), the patron-client relationship, with rare exceptions, was in each case a working arrangement between two unequal classes with conflicting interests, which could not bear the strain of an economic crisis. The class of exploiters, i.e., the landed and mercantile interests with their gradual encroachments on finance and the mahajani business, were not creations of the British; they

30 Scott, *Moral Economy of the Peasant;* Greenough, "Indian Famines and Peasant Victims", 205–35.

were, however, nurtured by colonial rule and given a new force and direction in the changing context of a growing market economy.

Such a relationship, based on self-interest, almost invariably broke down in times of stress. For the labourer, the expectation of getting food during a scarcity was an important consideration in such relationships. Greenough and Epstein cite instances in Andhra Pradesh and Mysore where labourers were willing to accept lower wages in kind from their customary employers, in the hope that when drought set in they could turn to them for help.[31] Often, however, there was bitter disillusionment, for the landlord did not feel bound to feed him in a year when there was little work and lesser grain in store. David Arnold describes the strain bearing down on this system, when famine became imminent in Madras in 1876.[32]

In a similar situation in Bengal in 1896, a considerable proportion of the kamias in Palamau and Manbhum, numbering thousands, were cast off by their masters and left to fend for themselves, many of the lesser zamindars pleading to have run out of cash and grain.[33] In Manbhum alone, the kamia population numbered 263,000 persons approximately.[34] This system of debt bondage, so effective to the landowner in normal times as an instrument for attaching labour in the face of increasing migrations from Chotanagpur, could not thus guarantee sustenance for the labourer in the face of a crisis. The employer, however, tried to retain his permanent farmhands wherever he could on considerations of expediency rather than philanthropy, for he would need their services again, once the famine was over. In Raipur and Simlapal in Bankura, for instance, many of the Utkal Brahmin employers retained their labourers in 1896, which partially accounted for the better conditions of these tracts, compared to Sonamukhi and Gangajalghati.[35]

[31] Greenough, "Indian Famines and Peasant Victims", 205–35; Scarlett Epstein, "Productive Efficiency and Customary Systems of Rewards in Rural South India", in *Themes in Economic Anthropology,* ed. Raymond Firth, pp. 229–52 (London: Tavistock, 1967).

[32] Arnold, "Famine in Peasant Consciousness", 79–80.

[33] *Selection of Papers,* vol. 10: p. 461; vol. 12: p. 340.

[34] LRP, Aug. 1898, pt. 2, p. 612, para. 5.

[35] *Selection of Papers,* vol. 8: p. 522.

There was no such binding force or consideration, however, in case of hired or seasonal labour, viewed by Greenough as a "casual" form of the patron-client relationship. As the sown area shrank considerably in 1896–97, the contraction of agricultural operations led in natural sequence to a fall in the demand for field labour. In Khulna, agriculturists that year were employing few or no *thika* (casual) labourers, "contrary to their usual customs". Wages fell to the minimum, till jute cutting and transplantation of the aman in August–September 1897, once again raised the demand for labour.[36] In Rajshahi there was practically no work in the fields from mid-October to late November, wages falling as low as 1 anna per diem in the Boalia and Durgapur outposts.[37] Grain payments made to hired farmhands throughout the year, as in Bhagalpur, were a potential source of danger, for in lean seasons the labourer's food entitlement was automatically and drastically cut.[38] In tribal areas like Angul and Tundi, cultivators stopped employing labour in "sudden seizures of panic".[39]

A similar impasse was seen in credit relations. Satkhira in Khulna is a typical case in point. In 1895, too, the crops here were very poor and the raiyats were obliged to borrow heavily for their maintenance. Being unable to repay these debts, their credit with the mahajans was gone. Smaller zamindars, tenure-holders and mahajans were supposed to have exhausted their resources in maintaining the raiyats. For example, Maulvi Abdul Aziz of Sriula, who had a grain and moneylending business, was said to have become bankrupt. He kept a reserve of 2,000/3,000 maunds of paddy, which had fallen now to a mere 100 maunds. Mahajans being few and far between, people in Satkhira looked mainly to the zamindars for advances. But the landlords, mostly gantidars, were generally impoverished and were unwilling to make further advances to their tenantry. Even larger zamindars

36 Ibid., vol. 10: p. 336; vol. 12: p. 279.

37 Ibid., vol. 3: 263–64.

38 *Dufferin Report,* A. A. Wace, Collector Bhagalpur, to the Comm., Bhagalpur Div., Bhagalpur, 7 April 1888.

39 LRP, Jan. 1900; E. Mc. L. Smith, Dy. Comm., Angul, to the Supdt. of the Tributary Mahals in Orissa, Revenue Proceedings, Aug. 1898, pt. 2, p. 841.

refused to take the risk of granting loans which may never be repaid. For instance, Babu Hari Charan Chaudhuri of Nakipur, who had already lent a large sum of money (about Rs. 45,000) to his tenants in the last few months, would not lend further, for he did not expect to get back a farthing of the money he had already given out. Girijanath Ray Chaudhuri, zamindar of Satkhira, took a similar stand.[40] Such instances abound in all the districts falling within the famine zone in 1896–97. This freezing of rural credit, however, was a purely temporary phenomenon: as soon as the bhadoi crop was assured in 1897, normal lending operations were resumed.[41]

Unfortunately, tracts like Satkhira or the Kalantar had no large traders. But, even where trade was brisk, stocks went out of market as soon as the crops failed and a crisis ensued. In the Patna Division, for example, from 30 September onwards in 1896, repeated complaints of hoarding by grain dealers were received from Phulwari, Barh, Maner, Bihar, Dinapore, Naubatpur, Khagole, etc. A general wave of alarm also led to the near-complete locking up of stores in Lohardaga and Palamau since January 1897.[42] In November 1896, local merchants in Hazaribagh bought up all the foodgrains in the market at prices slightly higher than the current rate, thus laying in stocks while raising their own prices. A feeling of anxiety and uneasiness was apparent, popular "demonstrations" calling in vain upon the district authorities to reduce the price of food.[43] The traders acted contrary to the public interest not only by withholding supplies, but by siphoning off these stocks into the export fund. Thus, there was a constant outflow of grain from famine districts like Bhagalpur, Nadia, Bankura, Champaran or Puri, large consignments being sold off at a profit by the banias to outside agencies, while the local people suffered from want of food. Appeals to the government to restrict such exportations from

40 *Selection of Papers,* vol. 3: pp.199–204.

41 For a parallel case-study during the famine of 1899, see Hardiman, "Bhils and Sahukars", 37–50.

42 *Selection of Papers,* vol. 1: p. 216; vol. 12: p. 334.

43 LRP, Aug. 1898, J. L. Herald Esq., Dy. Comm., Hazaribagh, to the Comm., Chotanagpur Div., para. 16, no. 1474 R., dated Hazaribagh, 24/27 Nov. 1897.

the famine tracts met with no response, the principle of laissez faire being strictly followed with regard to the private trade in foodgrains. As the crisis intensified, the bania*s* profited even from government relief contracts. According to the Famine Report on Saran, "they were constantly using short weights, issuing short doles, or doles of grain mixed with earth".[44] The Report on Shahabad stated: "The prices in 1896–97. . . show how terrible was the strain upon the people . . . the bania alone thrives at such a time".[45]

The relationship of the bania with the average consumer in rural society, though theoretically perhaps a "market" tie, was in reality a further manifestation of the rural power structure. The banias were a superordinate class vis-à-vis the producer or consumer, grain dealing often being an extension of the mahajani business, or of proprietory interests in land. The peasant did not operate in an open market, his surplus, if any, being transferred in the form of rent and interest payments to the granaries of the zamindar and raiyat-mahajan, many of whom directly dealt in grain or had close links with the grain market. During a crisis, the bania used this tremendous influence to further his own interests, at the cost of the producer-consumer. He suspended his normal operations, hoarding large quantities of grain either for export or for local sales when prices rose higher. This further diminished supplies, while panic created an abnormal demand. The psychology of greed and fear, thus reinforced, pushed up prices to unprecedented heights all over Bengal in 1896–97.

As to the trade in other articles and rural services, however, the seller was at a distinct disadvantage in relation to the consumer—the "market" aspect of the patron-client relationship, according to Greenough. The advent of famine was characterised by a general trade depression due to lack of purchasing power, and the abrupt rise in the price of food staples in relation to that of other commodities. This reflected an exchange crisis which, by restricting effective demand, forced a change in normal market ties. For instance, in Murshidabad the price of vegetables, fish, milk and fruit did not rise proportionately with the rise in the price of rice, thus adversely affecting the dealers in these particular

44 FRFRO, Saran, para. 83, point 6.
45 FRFRO, Shahabad, para. 13.

commodities.[46] At Naubanki, a fairly large hat in Satkhira, all shopkeepers and traders complained in December 1896 that business was extremely dull. Every kind of trade had suffered from the existing depression. The fishermen said they could sell very little fish and that too at ruinously cheap rates. The vegetable growers and the itinerant dealers in piece goods who roamed in bodies from one market to another faced a similar plight. The *gowala*s (milkmen) who had come to sell *dahi* (curd), the *moira* or confectioner and the trinket dealer (*manohari*) found their business all but gone.[47]

At Jadavpur Bazaar near Bongaon, the books of a cloth dealer showed a sale of goods to the value of Rs. 320 during Pous in 1896–97 as against Rs. 497 in the same month the previous year, thus showing a falling off in his business to the extent of nearly 40 per cent. In Lakshmipara, Jaipur and Lohagara in Magura, too, the purchasing power of the people was reduced, and general trade suffered in consequence. The books of a cloth dealer and a confectioner in the local bazaar showed that the former had sold piece goods to the value of Rs. 180 in the first twelve days of Magh in 1897 against Rs. 240 in the same period the previous year, while the business done by the latter during the 4½ months from the beginning of Aswin last amounted to Rs. 178 against Rs. 290 in the same period the year before. The falling off in business thus amounted to nearly 25 per cent in one case and 40 per cent in the other.[48] In regions with greater resources the effects of depression were naturally less pronounced. For example, in Satrujitpur hat near Magura where the bhadralok class predominated, the sale of such articles as oil, fish, jaggery, piece goods, etc. did not register such a large-scale decline.[49]

As the crisis deepened into famine, the growing strain was felt even in family relationships. It revealed an active discrimination in the pattern of food consumption within the average family unit, based on established social norms evaluating the role of the different members. In November 1896, it was reported from Hatia and other distressed areas in Noakhali-Chittagong, that whatever rice could

46 *Selection of Papers,* vol. 10: p. 380.
47 Ibid., vol. 3: p. 200.
48 Ibid., vol. 5: p. 230; vol. 4: p. 316.
49 Ibid., vol. 4: p. 313.

be scraped up or obtained by alms, was consumed by the pater familias, at the cost of the female, minor, old and infirm members of the family.[50] In Hatia alone there were three or four cases of husbands divorcing their wives, and two or three instances of desertion of families by former breadwinners.[51] Emigration to the tea gardens of Assam and the Duars from Hazaribagh and its neighbouring districts was abnormally large this year, the able-bodied males leaving the weaker members of the family to fend for themselves.[52] Likewise, as a result of large-scale male emigrations from Bhabhua in Shahabad and from Saran towards the east, "it is found that the number of women and children left by their husbands and fathers is very large indeed".[53] Such short-term migrations by men, combined with a high proportion of paralysis (said to arise from eating khesari), accounted for the large percentage of those on gratuitous relief (6.35) in the affected tracts of Shahabad. Men on the government relief works in the Chilka tract in Puri complained that they could not support their wives and children on the low wages offered, thus making their priorities clear in the matter of food entitlement. This "amounts practically to taking the adult female population of the whole area on a modified form of gratuitous relief to which they do not appear to be entitled".[54] The Famine Report of 1896–97 remarked on the caste-conscious raiyats sending their wives and children to bear the social disgrace and

[50] For an extensive empirical investigation on the nature and persistence of gender bias in intrafamily food distribution in South Asia in modern times, see Barbara Harriss: "The Intrafamily Distribution of Hunger in South Asia", in *The Political Economy of Hunger*, ed. Jean Dreze and Amartya Sen, vol. 1, 351–424 (Oxford: Clarendon Press, 1990).

[51] LRP, Nov. 1896, Branch Agri., nos. 34–35. Note on distress in Hatia, Noakhali, Chittagong Div.

[52] LRP, Aug. 1898, pt. 2, no. 1474 R., dt. Hazaribagh, 24/27 Nov. 1897, from J. L. Herald, Dy. Comm., Hazaribagh, to the Comm., Chotanagpur Div.

[53] *Selection of Papers*, vol. 7: p. 5, para. 9, Rev. Dept. Agri., no. 299 T. R./Fam., Darjeeling, 19 May 1897. From M. Finucane, Secy. to the Govt. of Bengal, to the Secy. to the Govt. of India, Rev. and Agri. Dept.

[54] Ibid., vol. 6: p. 396.

[55] Ibid., vol. 1: p. 148.

hard labour at the government relief works.[55]

TABLE 46

Recipients of Gratuitous Relief in Patna Division (1896–97)

District	*Lunatic/ Idiot*	*Cripple*	*Blind*	*Decrepit from age*	*Purdan women*	*Orphans and destitutes*	*Other causes*
Shahabad	0.42	8.76	3.29	40.97	10.22	10.5	25.81
Saran	1.36	3.17	4.07	32.15	7.62	6.95	44.65
Muzaffarpur	1.11	7.47	6.22	35.56	8.25	6.99	34.3
Darbhanga	0.62	3.25	3.66	32.56	6.44	2.88	50.56

Source: Final Resolution, p. 51.

The social composition of those on gratuitous relief in the affected districts of the Patna Division is highly suggestive.[56] The group under "other causes", constituting nearly 39 per cent of the total average, consisted almost entirely of children. As distress deepened, a considerable deterioration was noticed in the children's physique, the inference being that their adult relatives were appropriating their doles, and turning them adrift to pick up food for themselves in the jungles.[57]

Though many of the children were taken back into their homes from the poor houses once the crisis was over, the rehabilitation of widows as well as aged and infirm dependants presented more of a problem. They were the ones with "no margin, or but the slenderest margin".[58] One of the first signs of strain was the increasing number of beggars and vagrants on the streets, for "in every family there are helpless people who are tolerated in times of plenty, but cast adrift as soon as scarcity or famine appears".[59]

Thus the underlying tensions of the rural society, tempered

56 *Final Resolution,* p. 51.

57 Ibid., p. 53; *Commissioner's Report*, Chotanagpur, 1896–97, p. 2, para. 27.

58 *Dufferin Report,* Oldham, Collector of Burdwan, Rev. Dept. Agri. No. 87 T-R, Darjeeling, 30 June 1888 to Comm., Burdwan.

59 Ibid., No. 1 M.A., Cal., 17 May 1888. From A. Smith, Comm., Presidency Div., to the Secy. to the Govt. of Bengal, Rev. Dept.

down in ordinary years, floated to the surface in times of stress like a famine, war or revolution. As famine was imminent in October 1896, there was a crisis of identities and loyalties, when the landowner virtually disowned his farmhand, the mahajan his khatak, the bania his client, and the breadwinner his dependants. Existing relationships and socio-economic functions were thus transformed and suspended until the return of normalcy, when the bhadoi prospects were assured in August–September, 1897.

[3] *Changes in the Pattern of Foodgrain Consumption*

One of the immediate responses of the rural population to the crop failure of 1896 was a substantial cut in their foodgrain consumption. The Malthusian theory of the beneficial effects of such a cut in conserving food for a longer period and so in reducing the intensity of the famine, may be dangerous when applied to poor regions like the affected tracts of Bengal, where a sizeable section of the population lived perpetually on the brink of starvation. Macdonnell in his Report on foodgrain supplies in Bengal and Bihar takes the average foodgrain consumption of an adult male at $^2/_3$ of a seer per day, which is brought down by official estimates to ½ seer during a scarcity or famine. While precision is impossible in such estimates, it was, however, proved beyond doubt even from official reports and tour diaries that malnutrition and partial, if not total, starvation did exist on a large scale during this year of famine. In such times the poorer classes went without food for one or two days in a week, and generally had one instead of two meals a day. The daily ration fell to well below half a seer, which was "inadequate to sustain life for any length of time".[60]

There was also a qualitative change in local food habits in the famine tracts: a temporary switch from rice and wheat to coarser foodgrains, indicating great distress. In January 1897, it was reported from Jaipur in Cuttack, Orissa, that people were living on kulthi and birhi grains, not generally used for human

[60] FRFRO, Champaran, para. 42; Palamau, para. 23.

consumption, and some did not get a sufficient quantity even of these. From Puri, too, there were "reports of people living on short meals or inferior food obtained from the jungle". In Malud and other areas in the Chilka tract, Puri, poorer people—especially backward tribes like the Bauris, Kaudras and Pans—were largely eating forest products, the roots of the *kanika* or tuber grass, and a weed known as the *doanna sag* that they picked in the fields.[61] The aborigines in Angul consumed even the bamboo seeds.

Even in districts outside the famine zone proper, as in Rajshahi, boiled *kachu* (arum) was being eaten in January 1897 with a proportionately small amount of rice. Melon, *kaon* (millets) and Indian corn, which had yielded good harvests, were of service to the poor, as well as grass seeds and other makeshifts.[62] In September–October 1896, people in parts of Bagerhat, Khulna, were living on aquatic plants. In the Satkhira Sunderbans fish was being eaten in place of pulse to a much greater extent than was usual. Food crops called *kawoon* and *bhoora* were sown very largely all over the distressed area in Meherpur and Kushtia in Nadia district. Everywhere in the Nadia Kalantar there were destitute women and children (including even Brahmin women) clamouring for food. In this region kalai was largely being substituted for rice. There was a strong prejudice against the sole use of kalai, as the village hakims (doctors) thought that it engendered various diseases. It was probably on account of this that the grain was deemed impure for religious purposes, and the fact that it was being so used despite this prejudice, was significant.[63] In desperation people in the Kalantar also ate a grass seed called *shama.* It grew in the aus fields and bils to an unprecedented extent this year, and in normal years was considered unfit for human consumption.[64]

In Shahabad, Patna Division, people supplemented their foodgrain by a fruit diet to a larger extent than usual, including the *tean* and *bel* (both wild fruit), wild vegetables like *bhatua*

61 *Selection of Papers,* vol. 4: pp. 412, 414, 420.

62 Ibid., vol. 3: p. 258; vol. 10: p. 594.

63 Ibid., vol. 1: p. 315; vol. 3: pp. 215, 230, 234.

64 LRP, Aug. 1898, pt. 2, p. 465. Famine Report, Nadia, para. 43.

65 *Selection of Papers,* vol. 4: p. 151.

and *nakti*, ber and the mahua in April.[65] People in the Bettiah rice-tracts in Champaran began to curtail their foodgrain consumption as early as in August 1896, many of the poorer classes by then eking out a subsistence on wildgrass seeds, such as they never did in normal years. Thousands fed on roots and berries, and often a sugar-cane crop in the immediate vicinity of a relief work would be almost entirely appropriated by the labourers, as it stood. There being a scarcity of food for the fowls, Muslims and lower-caste Hindus fed largely on them and on their eggs, instead of keeping the latter for hatching.[66]

In Chotanagpur as well as the Santhal Parganas and other tribal belts in the Bhagalpur Division, people depended largely on jungle produce even in ordinary years, which would be deleterious if not accompanied by more nourishing food. By November 1896 the protected forests of Chotanagpur, Santhal Parganas, Puri and Angul were thrown open for people to collect edible forest products free of charge.[67] In these poverty-stricken districts where the people were in the habit of supplementing their food supply with articles of jungle produce, the problem was how far the supplemental supply could still further encroach upon the supply of cultivated produce. When rice and makai sold at 8 and 12 sr. a rupee, as in 1896, people could not afford more than half the supply of cereals usually consumed. There was also no doubt that without supplies in the hats of rice, makai, marua or wheat, public health would be injured by a continuous intake of insufficient or semi-nutritious foods like *sag* (spinach) and mahua, which should always be supplemented by a proper cereal base.[68] The Deputy Commissioner of Manbhum reported having seen "a collection of fangs enough to poison a regiment, which some Santhals had collected for food".[69] In November 1896, it was remarked that a large population in Hazaribagh town will eat nothing but rice; by April 1897, however, many of them were switching to "coarser foods". As the months advanced, distress areas like the Santhal Parganas, Palamau, Manbhum and Hazaribagh depended mostly on jungle

66 FRFRO, Champaran, paras. 42, 46.

67 *Selection of Papers*, vol. 2: p. 7.

68 Ibid., vol. 4: p. 348; vol. 7: p. 422.

69 Ibid., vol. 11: p. 418.

roots, sags and berries, sarai or sal fruit, makai, marua, *gondli* (wild fruit) and most important of all, mahua. But the mahua crop was a partial and, in some places, almost a complete failure in 1897, which greatly intensified the problem. In Lohardaga the failure of mango, mahua and sarai, and the scarcity even of the usual edible roots and leaves that year led to an unusually difficult situation.[70]

[4] *Problems in the Supply of Seedgrains*

Since the bij-khad loans had ceased with the advent of scarcity, the need for seedgrain too was acutely felt after the aman had been reaped. As stocks were depleted, "the provision for seed is also reduced. . . . there is no doubt that the usual seed reserve was trenched on to some extent".[71]

Zamindars refused to advance seedgrains to their tenants, and mahajans to their clients until they were assured of a good crop prospect. In Nadia, for example, the mahajans' attitude would depend on how the preparation of the land for the next aus crop proceeded. In Jessore the mahajan might advance money and seedgrains to the raiyats only on the security of their lands and future crop. In Satkhira, Khulna, where there were few mahajans, even big zamindars like the Roy Chaudhuris threw the entire responsibility of supplying seed to the cultivators, on the gantidars who were themselves impoverished.[72]

Any assistance on the part of the government was too limited in scope to be of much use. Government officials always preferred to hand over the loans for the purchase of seed paddy to substantial landlords or mahajans instead of tenants, the latter being more likely to use up the money as consumption loans. The zamindars and mahajans, however, were often reluctant to guarantee the raiyat's security and might appropriate the money in lieu of rent or debt arrears, while most of the gantidars were themselves insolvent. Besides, seed loans were to be given only to the really needy, and not to those who could borrow from the

70 Ibid., vol. 1: p. 335; vol. 11: p. 393.
71 FRFRO, Champaran, para. 46.
72 *Selection of Papers*, vol. 5: p. 243; vol. 6: p. 264; vol. 7: p. 291.

mahajans. This distinction was not always easy to make. The mahajans also feared government interference, and were afraid of lending to those who might again borrow from the government, thus causing a conflict of interests in which they were likely to suffer.[73]

Sometimes red tape and bickering among government officials delayed seedgrain advances until the sowing season was over. For instance, Mr W. H. H. Vincent, Collector of Khulna, maintained that the amount allotted for seedgrains was insufficient. He insisted that the grant of this money, to be of use, should not be delayed for submission of balance sheet and expense accounts lest the sowing season should pass, as did happen in Khulna. But it was pointed out from higher quarters that Vincent had not been able to account for the money spent, and that when he refused further advances, transplantation was still in progress in many places.[74] In Jessore, too, the sowing season had rapidly progressed before an adequate amount was sanctioned as loans for seedgrain.[75] In the Santhal Parganas many of the raiyats had consumed their seedgrain and the allotment of Rs. 30,000 came too late for the professed object of purchasing seed. Besides, as the Deputy Commissioner complained, it was not large enough to meet the needs of the raiyats, but enough to give them false hopes and prevent them from approaching the moneylenders for the usual supplies of seedgrain.[76] Official correspondence on the matter of granting loans for seedgrain in Palamau makes interesting reading. The Charge Superintendent of the Western Circle, Maulvi Yusuf Ali, reported from Garhwa on 29 September 1897 that money would hardly be required any longer for the large areas lying unsown, as the sowing season was over. This was construed by the Lieutenant Governor's Office to mean that the Deputy Commissioner was exaggerating the distress in Palamau, there being "no want of money for the

[73] Ibid., vol. 3: p. 204; vol. 4: pp. 308, 315; vol. 5: p. 205.
[74] Ibid., vol. 9: p. 316; vol. 11: p. 330.
[75] Ibid., vol. 8: p. 302.
[76] Ibid., vol. 9: p. 513.
[77] Ibid., vol. 10: p. 486. Agr. no. 1607 (Fam.), Cal, 18 Aug. 1897. From M. Finucane Esq., Secy. to the Govt. of Bengal, to the Comm., Chotanagpur Div.

purchase either of seed or cattle".[77]

There were also certain regional problems in the matter of procuring seedgrains. For example, due to the salinity of the soil in Satkhira, Khulna, only grains from the district itself or from neighbouring areas like Bakarganj in the 24 Parganas could be used there as seed.[78] In Jessore again, there was a particular scarcity of aman seedgrains. Due to these reasons, very little land in Khulna, and only 40 per cent of the total cultivable area in Jessore, could be sown that year.[79] In Nadia "as a general rule the fields, owing to lack of seed, have been very thinly sown".[80] Parts of the Nowada, Barua and Saktipur thanas in Murshidabad remained unsown, not for lack of seed but because the raiyats had not the means to purchase it.[81]

[5] *Sale or Mortgage of Capital Assets*

As prices soared high and all sources of rural credit dried up, the raiyats, pressed by the acute shortage both of food and seedgrains, resorted to the sale of their meagre belongings in a desperate bid to survive. Paul Greenough has referred to a controversy among historians as to whether the peasants "plan for crop failures in the midst of good harvests or plan for good harvests in the midst of crop failures". In other words, the question was whether they sold or pawned their capital assets in order to tide over the crisis in a famine year, or merely curtailed their food consumption, saving these resources for agricultural investments in the next season.[82] As noted, however, the average peasant hardly had any surplus, and the limit was soon reached when a further cut in their food intake would be fraught with grave risk.

As the crisis worsened into famine during 1896–97, the sale of ornaments, utensils and even agricultural implements became a common feature in most districts. This was remarkable in Khulna, where a great majority of the peasants sold off their metal utensils and ornaments, mostly of silver, at half to two-

[78] Ibid., vol. 6: p. 223.

[79] Ibid., vol. 8: pp. 290–91.

[80] LRP, July 1897, nos. 112–13, pp. 415–17.

[81] *Selection of Papers*, vol. 8: p. 346.

[82] Greenough, "Indian Famines and Peasant Victims", 205–35.

thirds their real value. This was followed by the sale of cattle on an extensive scale. As a direct indication of pressure from scarcity, even well-to-do raiyats sold off their plough cattle to *beparis* (traders) mostly from Calcutta, at cheaper rates than usual. The fear expressed on every side was that the following year there would not be enough cattle left to plough up the rice-lands. This was a most serious feature of the scarcity, and was seen also in Jessore, and in western Athaisi and Banchas in Orissa.[83] Agricultural loans by the government were a mere drop in the ocean and were hedged in by too many restrictions to be of any use.[84] In Chotanagpur and Orissa, too, people were selling off their brass and bell-metal utensils and trinkets. In Athaisi and Banchas, people were said to "have already parted with their all" by February–March 1897.[85] Credit was also raised on the security of the crops on the ground, as on the rabi foodgrains in the famine tract of Shahabad, and on the aus and jute crops in Khulna. Along with the sale of ornaments, utensils and plough cattle, the registration of bonds and mortgages on land showed an alarming increase.

There was a steady growth in the registration of land sales and mortgages in normal times, which leapt up sharply in crisis years as after 1891–92, and in 1896–97(table 47).[86]

TABLE 47

Registrations of Immovable Property

Year	*Registrations*		*Total*	*% increase or decrease*
	Compulsory	*Optional*		
1891–92	659,026	173,701	832,727	
1892–93	732,259	207,395	939,654	+12.84
1893–94	771,531	227,377	998,908	+6.30
1894–95	793,837	238,115	1,031,952	+3.30
1895–96	762,304	215,579	977,883	–5.23
1896–97	865,587	261,753	1,127,340	+15.28

Source: Report of Registration Dept., Bengal, 1896–97: Minor Statement no. I.

83 *Selection of Papers*, vol. 3: p. 233; vol. 6: p. 404.
84 Ibid., vol. 3: p. 199.
85 Ibid., vol. 5: p. 363; vol. 7: p. 427.
86 *Report of the Registration Department, Bengal, 1896–97:* Minor Statement no. I.

The total number of registrations affecting immovable property thus went up from 977,883 to 1,127,340 (over 15 per cent) in 1896–97. The number of sales rose from 291,581 to 336,615 (over 15 per cent) and the number of mortgages from 304,821 to 361,620 (nearly 19 per cent). Mortgage was often preferred to sale, as it held a prospect, however remote, of redemption in the future. In case of deeds of optional registration, instruments of mortgage valued less than Rs.100 show a large increase, as expected, on account of the famine. The number of transactions dealing with the sale of raiyati holdings increased by 19 per cent.[87]

Though the entire Province thus suffered from the prevailing high prices, the signs of stress were most visible in the statistics of sales and mortgages in the famine-hit districts (table 48).[88]

TABLE 48

Increase in Land Sales & Mortgages in the Famine-hit Districts

Districts	*Sales* *% Increase in 1896–97*	*Mortgages* *% Increase in 1896–97*
Shahabad	18.10	11.23
Saran	31.80	40.36
Champaran	52.13	51.84
Muzaffarpur	73.73	82.77
Darbhanga	36.40	35.00
Bhagalpur	22.22	15.14
Santhal Parganas	15.60	27.97
Hazaribagh	27.50	17.17
Palamau	20.27	14.78
Manbhum	28.13	30.79
Bankura	9.73	9.80
Nadia	4.99	11.50
Murshidabad	3.58	11.69
Khulna	12.21	24.42
Puri	8.75	13.65
Total	**26.80**	**33.26**

Source: Report of the Registration Dept., Bengal, 1897–98, no. 429 P. -D.

87 Ibid., no. 4122 from Khan Bahadur Delawar Hosaen Ahmed, I.G. of Registration, Bengal, to the Chief Secy. to the Govt. of Bengal, Cal., 27 July 1897.

88 Ibid., 1897–98, no. 429 P.-D. From C. W. Bolton, Chief Secy. to

The increase in the number of registrations during 1896–97 thus "affords some indication of the pressure felt by the people in the districts chiefly affected".[89] In the Patna Division, the districts of Saran, Champaran, Muzaffarpur and Darbhanga, where the distress was most severe, show the largest percentages of increase in sales and mortgages. In Satkhira, Khulna, government loans were being issued only on the security of landed property and general revenue-paying estates or *gantis*.[90] In Jessore, particularly in the Magura and Narail subdivisions, there was a definite increase in the number of mortgages registered, though at the same time the increase in the number of registered bonds showed that the people were still able to obtain loans for maintenance from mahajans without offering any landed security.[91] In Nadia, even the middle classes were trying desperately to obtain government loans under the Agriculturists' Loans Act on the security of their lands. Due to the utbandi system of tenure, however, land (even lakhiraj) had little value in these parts and proved an impediment in the way of issuing advances.[92]

[6] *Growing Intensity of the Famine as Reflected in Crime Returns*

In the face of the impending disaster, the inequalities in rural society became painfully evident, and the myth of "reciprocity" vanished. However, as David Arnold observed: "The poor did not accept the denial of their entitlements without contest". Famine crime was seldom widespread or organised. Amartya Sen notes, "Despite this important causal link (between famine and violence), the exact period of a severe famine is often not one of effective rebellion".[93] Yet, the association of famine and an

---

the Govt. of Bengal, to the Secy. to the Govt. of India, Home Dept., Darjeeling, 24 Sept. 1898.

89 Ibid., 1896–97. No. 497 P. - D. From C. W. Bolton, Chief Secretary to the Govt. of Bengal, to the Secy. to the Govt. of India, Home Dept., Darjeeling, 24 Sept. 1897.

90 *Selection of Papers,* vol. 6: p. 221.

91 Ibid., vol. 4: p. 307.

92 Ibid., vol. 3: p. 230.

93 Jean Dreze and Amartya Sen, *Hunger and Public Action* (Oxford: Clarendon Press, 1989), p. 22.

increase in sporadic crime was no new phenomenon. Crimes against property increased three-fold in 1846 during the course of the Irish famine, while the Orissa famine of 1866 and the Madras famine of 1876–78 produced the highest level of agrarian crime in these regions during the entire period from the 1850s to 1940.[94]

As the crisis deepened into famine in Bengal in 1896–97, there was a phenomenal increase in grain-related crimes. In some districts like Nadia, Murshidabad and Jessore, there was no striking difference in crime rates between the affected and the unaffected areas, which led the Collector of Jessore to conclude that the increase in crime was not essentially connected with the famine, there being "so many other causes at work in the production of crime figures that the part played by scarcity is obscured".[95] In Jessore, which fell outside the famine zone proper, the increase in crimes aginst property was not proportionately greater in 1896–97 as compared to 1894–95 or 1895–96. In Murshidabad, too, the crime rate did not rise very greatly, as the distress was slight beyond the Kalantar. These, however, were exceptional circumstances, not applicable to the famine-hit regions in general. In fact, the crime statistics in the affected districts from October 1896 to September 1897 may be taken as an index to the growing distress arising from scarcity. As stated in the Final Resolution of the Bengal Government on the Famine of 1896–97: "the relation between hunger and rioting, and theft, with its kindred offences of dacoity, burglary and robbery, is nowhere more clearly exemplified than in the crime statistics during the period of the recent scarcity".[96]

[6.1] Volume and pattern of increase in crime

As the pressure of hard times increased, there was a corresponding rise in the number of grain thefts, burglaries, etc., with a significant decline in noncognizable offences involving litigation,

[94] Arnold, *Famine,* pp. 85–86.
[95] LRP, Aug. 1898. pt. 2, nos. 42–43, No. 128 G - S.R. dated Cal., 7 January, 1898. From E. V. Westmacott, Comm., Presidency Div., to the Secy. to the Govt. of Bengal., Rev. Dept., para. 44.
[96] *Final Resolution,* p. 78.

in which the mass of the people could not now afford to indulge. The total number of offences against property in general, i.e., cases of theft, burglary, robbery and dacoity in the affected districts, rose from 19,942 and 20,865 in 1894–95 and 1895–96 respectively, to 34,952 in 1896–97, the increase being no less than 71.3 per cent over the average of the two preceding years. The increase in burglary and theft for the entire Province, from October 1896 to September 1897, was 43.47 and 31.19 per cent, respectively, over the mean of the corresponding periods of the two previous years.[97] The percentages of increase in the affected districts are given in table 49.

TABLE 49

Percentage of Increase in Crime

Districts	*Burglary*	*Theft*
Shahabad	48.10	29.84
Saran	27.73	58.09
Champaran	91.12	72.43
Muzaffarpur	95.47	133.40
Darbhanga	74.74	74.11
Bhagalpur	69.80	26.90
Santhal Parganas	113.80	73.77
Hazaribagh	93.10	69.50
Palamau	112.10	95.30
Manbhum	214.40	102.70
Bankura	216.50	37.20
Nadia	12.90	72.20
Murshidabad	36.70	10.80
Khulna	67.00	214.00
Puri	78.20	52.71

Source: Final Resolution, p. 78.

There seems to be a significant correlation between the increase in crime rate and the extent or intensity of distress experienced during the famine. Thus, in the Patna Division the incidence of crime was highest in the worst-affected districts of Champaran, Muzaffarpur and Darbhanga. Similarly, the large increase in offences against property in Chotanagpur and the Santhal Parganas coincided with the severity of the famine in these regions,

97 Ibid.

and reflected the growing sense of misery and frustration among the tribals. In Murshidabad, the percentage of crime was relatively low, as the distress was more or less contained within the affected tracts of the Kalantar. In Khulna and Nadia, parts of which were more seriously affected, the figures for cattle and grain thefts rose sharply.

The pattern of increase in the crime rate was as essentially connected with the famine, as its volume. The number of offences against property rose graphically in each succeeding quarter of the famine year. In nearly every district there was a sharp rise in crime, as apprehensions of scarcity were confirmed during October to December 1896. The number of offences rose further almost without exception in the three months from January to March 1897, which coincided with the period of greatest pressure on the relief works, as the contraction of the sown area cut down abruptly on employment opportunities in agriculture. In the following quarter, the rise in crimes continued except in the districts of the Patna Division, in Palamau, and in Puri, where it was temporarily arrested due to the reaping of the rabi harvest. The highest level, however, was reached everywhere in the last quarter from July to September 1897, when foodgrain prices in all the districts had also reached the peak.

[6.2] Nature of crimes committed

"Famine crime assumed many forms", from petty thefts to looting and riots.[98] An analysis of the nature of the offences committed in 1896–97 shows that the greatest increase occurred in crimes involving burglary, theft or pilfering, most notably of foodgrains, rather than crimes with an undertone or overtone of violence, as in cases of robbery, dacoity, loot, riot or arson. In the affected districts, the rise in the percentage of burglary and theft over the mean of the two preceding years amounted to 90.11 and 74.86, respectively. It was one of the earliest signs of distress. In Champaran, for example, the percentage of burglaries and corn thefts went up as early as in June 1896, when the rains were delayed. After a temporary abatement in July, when good showers fell, they became more pronounced and, with the serious break in the rains in August,

[98] Arnold, *Famine*, p. 85.

reached alarming proportions. Thefts of property, especially of corn, were much above the average in January 1897, while in early February there were no less than 217 cases as compared with only 81 in February 1896, 56 of these being grain thefts as against only 23 during the same period the year before.[99] Similarly in Magura, Jessore, the number of thefts and burglaries recorded until November 1896 was 303 as against 176 the previous year: an increase of more than 72 per cent in the earliest phase of the famine.[100]

The districts of the Patna Division and the tribal belt of Bhagalpur and Chotanagpur also registered an increase in the number of dacoities and robbery. This is evident from the crime statistics for the Patna Division in 1896–97, as compared to the mean of the two preceding years.

TABLE 50

Percentage of Increase in Crime, Patna Division

Nature of crime	*1894–95*	*1895–96*	*1896–97*	*Percentage of difference*
Dacoity	34	30	63	+96.87
Robbery	38	38	62	+63.15
Burglary	9,656	9,382	13,754	+44.48
Theft	4,365	4,325	7,274	+67.41
Total	14,093	13,775	21,153	+67.97

Source: Famine Report, Patna Div, 1896–97, para. 370.

Thus, the percentage of dacoities rose at more than double the rate of the burglaries committed, while the increase in robberies was nearly equal to that of thefts. The most noticeable increase in dacoities occurred in Shahabad (13 per cent) and Champaran (17 per cent).[101] The grain dacoities in the Bhabhua subdivision during October–December 1896 afforded one of the earliest signs of unrest in the district of Shahabad. In Bhagalpur and the Santhal Parganas, too, dacoities showed a significant increase. In the latter district, there were thirty-one cases against four, the mean of the three preceding years.[102] The affected areas

[99] *Selection of Papers*, vol. 5: p. 63.
[100] Ibid., vol. 4: p. 298.
[101] FRFRO, Patna Division, para. 370.
[102] FRFRO, Santhal Parganas, para. 23.

of the Chotanagpur Division recorded an increase of no less than 336.8 per cent over the average figures for dacoity in the two previous years. Of the total number of eighty-three cases, the majority were loots of grain. In Lohardaga, the Deputy Commissioner maintained in April 1897: "The most serious sign of the times is the increase of crime, which has been very marked during the past two months". There were several house dacoities, a crime almost unknown in this district in ordinary years. Of these, more than one case had occurred of *bhandar*s (granaries) being broken into by gangs of villagers. Crime was most common in the tract lying in the south of Lohardaga and north of the Toto and Sesai thanas, and also to the north and east of Lohardaga, where the people were in considerable distress and were anxious for work.[103]

Violence was generally contained, most of the crimes committed being thefts or seizure of foodgrains by a desperately hungry people. No riots are reported from the Presidency Division, while there was a decrease in riots by 4.45 per cent in the Patna Division. The Famine Report for the Patna Division explains this as being due to the absence of riots over the share of crops, as there were fewer crops to cut than usual.

Yet, sporadic cases of grain riots, loot and arson did occur, especially in Chotanagpur and the north Bihar districts. On 3 October 1896, a mob of some two hundred people looted four or five *gola*s (granaries) in Dinapur, in Patna, the value of the grain and cash looted amounting to about Rs.1,387. On the 4th, riot was apprehended at Khagole; it was, however, averted as the police persuaded the Marwaris to sell retail. The atmosphere was also tense at Barh, Maner, Phulwari and Naubatpur, as the local people seethed with resentment against the banias who were hoarding foodgrains.[104] In June–July 1897, reports of violence began to pour in from Rajshahi. Minor disturbances and grain looting near Rampur-Boalia on 10 and 12 June and on 3 July culminated in a "serious grain riot" on 11 July. On the 14th, another case of grain looting was reported from here, and tension continued.[105] Cases of arson were numerous, especially

103 *Selection of Papers,* vol. 7: pp. 426–27.

104 Ibid., vol. 1: p. 216.

105 Ibid., vol. 9: pp. 593–94.

in Champaran and Darbhanga. In a majority of instances, the fires were intentional, the idea being to draw out and steal hoarded stocks in the ensuing melee.[106]

[6.3] Resentment rather than starvation as motive force

It is interesting to note the social composition of the classes against whom such offences were generally committed. The targets were inevitably men of substance, usually mahajans or banias, and, in fewer cases, zamindars with large hoards of grain. These crimes were the results not of frenzied violence, but of a sense of betrayal and moral outrage, sharpened by the keenness of hunger. As the classes concerned refused to perform their normal functions of lending or selling grain, while the *sarkar* (government) was content to remain a passive onlooker, a feeling of deep resentment naturally overcame the starving villagers. As David Arnold has observed, "Sometimes the purpose was more to make a protest than to satisfy the 'instincts' of hunger by simply grabbing food for consumption". In Orissa in 1866, for instance, raiders often disclosed their identities and hardly ever harmed the inmates.[107] Similarly, in eastern Gujarat in 1899, "the Bhils rose not because they were then starving—though clearly they anticipated it—but because they considered that their *shahukars* had violated a moral code" by refusing credit and hoarding grain for export, even after receiving their dues from the Bhils.[108]

The growth of such a feeling is seen in the popular "demonstrations" held against the export of foodgrains by mahajans in Hazaribagh in 1897, and repeated requests for government interference. In a village in the Burmu outpost, seventeen miles north of Ranchi, the local people looted the stocks of a bania who had angered them by refusing to lend grain as usual. According to H. C. Streatfeild, Deputy Commissioner of Lohardaga, this was an act of pure vengeance rather than desperation, for most of the accused still had paddy in store. He feared that if the zamindars and banias refused to

106 FRFRO, Patna Division, ch. 15, para. 372.
107 Arnold, *Famine,* pp. 84–85.
108 Hardiman, "Bhils and Sahukars", p. 43.

lend grain for long, instances of grain looting and riots would not be uncommon in these parts.[109] In Shahabad, several cases of arson occurred where the fire was "directly traceable to revenge", the victims having refused to give loans or sell grain at the rates demanded.[110] In Rampur-Boalia, Rajshahi, several instances of grain loot and robbery were reported from the houses of local dealers. Eleven persons looted grain from the house of one Jabdi Paramanik on 10 June 1897. On 12 June, another mahajan had complained that some nineteen persons seized from him foodgrains worth Rs. 170, while Mamat Mollah on 3 July lost twenty rupees worth of grain to a gang of thirty-five. To his protests of being ruined, the rioters replied that he might as well live on purchased rice now, as they had been forced to do throughout the year of famine. The climax was reached on 11 July with an organised raid on the houses of influential local grain dealers like Chandra Nath Sarkar, Khudi Mollah and Binod Mandal, by an armed mob several hundred strong. The indifference of the government was a major irritant. However, the disturbances made no dent in the official policy of *laissez-faire.* Nolan, the Commissioner of Rajshahi, instructed the District Magistrate "not to give any advice to grain-dealers while investigating these offences, as to lending more freely now that rain has fallen".[111]

[7] *Changes in the Pattern of Migrations*

A year of scarcity and famine was almost invariably marked by an exodus of people in search of food and work from affected areas to other districts, 1896 being no exception to the rule. An early indication of distress was the increasing number of vagrants in the district towns, and an abnormally large flow of travellers moving eastward along the Grand Trunk (GT) Road. On

[109] *Selection of Papers*, vol. 7: pp. 426–27, no.141 R., dated Ranchi, 1 May 1897. From H. C. Streatfeild, Dy. Comm., Lohardaga, to the Comm., Chotanagpur Div., para. 2.

[110] FRFRO, Patna Div., ch. 15, para. 372.

[111] *Selection of Papers,* vol. 9: p. 593, no.402 Jet, dated Camp Rampur-Boalia, 18 July 1897. From P. Nolan, Comm. Rajshahi Div., to the Chief Secy. to the Govt. of Bengal, paras. 1–2, 4.

comparing the distinctive features of the permanent, long-term and short-term influxes in 1896–97 with those in normal years, one notes an increase in volume rather than any basic change in the pattern of migrations.

[7.1] Emigration and resettlement

In some cases, the pressure of hard times induced the people to shift permanently from their original homes to new settlements with better prospects. Such instances were admittedly few in number compared to the other types of migrations, and consisted both of intra-district and inter-district movements. Khulna provides typical examples of movements within the district. Here large numbers of cultivators, mostly of the *Pod* caste, absconded altogether from their holdings and emigrated to their newly reclaimed settlements or *abads* in the Sunderban area of east Khulna, which was a freshwater country *(mitha desh).* Numerous deserted abads in Paikgacha and Shyamnagore testified to this. Such abandonments threatened the interests of the landlords and mahajans to whom these peasants were indebted for rent and loans.[112] Emigration from the Santhal Parganas to Malda and other districts north of the Ganges for permanent settlement had been less extensive during the past few years. Under the pressure of scarcity, however, a stream of Santhal and Garos did move to the Duars and the jungle tracts of Dinajpur, Rangpur and Pabna. In Champaran, there had in recent years been a large permanent immigration, especially from Saran, Muzaffarpur, Gorakhpur and Nepal. At the census of 1891, the male immigrants from Saran alone numbered 50,000. The next decade, however, saw a check in this process largely due to the famine of 1896–97, which affected nearly the entire district. Thus, in the census of 1901, Champaran seems to have suffered a loss in the percentage of population by 3.72.[113] On the whole, no permanent demographic changes of any magnitude occurred as a result of the famine.

112 *Selection of Papers,* vol. 3: p. 192.
113 *Census Report 1911,* p. 125, para. 300.

[7.2] Long-term migrations

Long-term and annual migrations to the tea districts and the colonies took place on an organised scale in normal years from the Santhal Parganas, Bankura, and the districts of Chotanagpur Division.

The Santhals emigrated extensively to the northern districts for wood cutting and jungle clearance, and to the tea gardens in Darjeeling and the Duars, generally on one-year assignments. The exodus to Assam occurred for a longer period of two to three years. Table 51 shows the emigrations under Act I of 1882 and the Santhal Emigration Scheme, as well as those of government coolies sent to Chittagong that took place between January and September in the three years from 1895 to 1897.[114]

TABLE 51
Emigrations, 1895–97

	1895		*1896*		*1897*	
	Adults	*Dependants*	*Adults*	*Dependants*	*Adults*	*Dependants*
Act I, 1882	28	9	193	132	567	449
Santhal Emigration Scheme	736	116	814	79	1,729	1,035
Chittagong	440	...	611	...	467	...
Total	1,204	125	1,618	211	2,763	1,484

Source: Famine Report, Santhal Parganas 1896–97, para. 23.

The bulk of emigration cases, however, consisted of "free" emigrants who were not registered. Relative familiarity and easier access to Assam had of late increased the volume of such free migrations. Though no reliable statistics are available for such unregistered cases, the total emigration to Assam for the three years mentioned above may have been approximately 5,000, 6,000 and 12,000 respectively.[115] The scarcity gave an added impetus to this increasing outflow. As is evident from the above table, excluding the Chittagong coolies who went in such numbers as the government cared to engage, the volume of migration

114 FRFRO, Santhal Parganas, para. 23.
115 Ibid.

increased by 37 per cent in 1896, and as much as 158 per cent in 1897. The 61 per cent increase in the number of dependants migrating in 1897 was a further manifestation of the deepening crisis within.

Increasing emigration to Assam from the Chotanagpur districts of Lohardaga, Manbhum, Singhbhum and Palamau, indicated the extent of distress being felt.[116] From Hazaribagh and Manbhum, registered emigration increased more than three and four times respectively, in 1896 and 1897. The majority of cases, however, went unregistered.

In Bankura the number of registered emigrants in 1896–97 was 471 as compared to 264 and 209 in the two previous years, respectively. The increase was mostly from affected areas in Gangajalghati and Chatna, due to the pressure created by the abnormally high prices of cereals. Free emigration was unusually brisk, as many as 6,234 and 2,243 people having emigrated from the Raipur thana and Simlapal outpost alone.[117]

Due to the unusual abundance of labour from the tribal belts in the famine-hit districts this year, the tea gardens could afford to be more selective in recruiting coolies. The depot keepers at Jamtara and Karmater in the Santhal Parganas reported that the tea districts were very particular as to the class of labourers sent up in 1896–97, there being no demand for low-caste Hindus like the Bauris, Domes and Haris.[118] Similarly, the distinct preference for "free" labour could be indulged more easily this year, probably accounting for the very marked fall in the recruitment of registered coolies, as in the Burdwan Division (from 3,333 in 1895–96, to 922 in 1896–97). Under the free-emigration system, however, the number of coolies passing through Burdwan to the tea districts increased by more than 25 per cent, mainly in apprehension of scarcity in the surrounding tracts. Coolies brought in by the tea garden *sardars* were preferred

116 *Selection of Papers,* vol. 1: p. 335.

117 *Commissioner's Report*, Burdwan Division, 1896–97, Sec. 4, para. 49.

118 *Selection of Papers,* vol. 7: p. 473, no.81 R., dated Jamtara, 27 April 1897. From A. W. Stark Esq., S.D.O. Jamtara, to the Dy. Comm., Santhal Parganas.

to those recruited by professional *arkatis*, only 21 of the 471 emigrants from Bankura being of the latter class.

[7.3] Short-term or seasonal migrations

The temporary or seasonal migrations had a south-eastward trend, as from Bihar and the NWP to Bengal and Orissa, and towards the Sunderbans and eastern Khulna within Bengal.

In normal years, immigrants from Bihar to Bengal came mostly in the lean months after the rabi harvest, returning to work on their own lands before the monsoon. In 1896–97, however, the annual exodus from the Patna Division to the rice-growing countries and for service in Calcutta and its suburbs, had set in earlier than usual. In Gaya, the flow of coolies along GT Road to Calcutta and Purulia was unusually large. Labourers from Champaran went for harvesting operations to Nepal and north Bengal. An unprecedentedly large number of males left for the eastern districts from Saran and Shahabad. This was proved directly by the observation of local officials and corroborated indirectly by the great increase in the number and amount of money orders sent from without. In 1896–97 there was an increase of Rs. 10 lakhs in the amount of remittances sent to the districts of the Patna Division, that in Saran alone accounting for 3.5 lakh rupees.[119]

From the NWP, an extraordinarily large number of people moved eastward in search of work through Chotanagpur and the northern districts of Bihar to Bengal, Assam, and even to Cuttack in Orissa. Along with the increasing volume of migrants on GT Road, another stream of travellers passed down the riverside road to the right of the Ganges, from Benaras and Ghazipur through Buxar to Monghyr, and eastwards into Bengal.

In Chotanagpur, the movement of people in search of work to Giridih and the Jharia mines, and the increased number of wanderers on the roads and in Hazaribagh Town, indicated that the pinch of high prices was beginning to be severely felt by those who had no grain of their own, and were not regular agricultural servants.[120]

[119] FRFRO, Patna Div., para. 84.

[120] *Selection of Papers*, vol. 2: pp. 192–94.

In Bengal, large-scale migrations occurred from Nadia and Jessore to Calcutta, the Rarh tract in Burdwan, and the Sundarbans in Khulna. From western Khulna and the 24 Parganas too, there were seasonal migrations to east Khulna in search of work, mainly for reaping paddy. To take an example, a number of people from Basirhat who had been engaged to reap paddy in an abad to the south of Nakipur, found on arrival that the prospective employers had left home in search of employment in east Khulna.[121]

Thus, though the advent of the crisis in 1896 was not marked by any permanent or significant shifts in the demographic pattern, there was a definite increase in the size and duration of the normal migrations, whether long-term or casual.

[8] *Public Health and Mortality*

Demographic changes in a year of famine occurred not only from large-scale migrations of the classes affected, but also from their enfeebled physique and lower birth-rates; deaths from starvation; and diminished resistance to disease due to the weakening of the constitution by prolonged hunger and malnutrition. The "lethal connection" between epidemics, on the one hand, and famine or insufficient food intake even in normal times, on the other, has been sufficiently established. Deaths from disease rather than starvation feature more prominently in the assessment of famine mortality. In fact, migrations, overcrowding, and insanitary conditions at famine-relief works led to a rapid spread of diseases caused initially by under-nourishment.[122] During the Irish famine, deaths from actual starvation were only 5.8 per cent of those from fever, dysentery and dropsy. Of the three million deaths during the Bengal famine of 1943–44, only about 5 per cent were caused directly by hunger, the rest being traced to cholera, smallpox and malaria epidemics.[123] Habitual and long-term under-nourishment was cited as a possible cause of the Black Death in

[121] Ibid., vol. 3: p. 202.

[122] Elizabeth Whitcombe, "Famine Mortality", *Economic and Political Weekly* 28, no. 23, 5 June 1993, pp. 1169–79.

[123] Arnold, *Famine,* pp. 22–23.

TABLE 52

Mortality Statistics in the Affected Districts, 1896–97

District	*Whole district* Average of 5 years ending 30 Sept. 1895	1895 – 96	1896 – 97	*Affected tract* Average of 5 years ending 30 Sept. 1895	1895 – 96	1896 – 97
Shahabad	32.80	39.53	33.30	34.87	30.50	38.22
Saran	31.88	34.99	38.43	34.90	32.59	27.73
Champaran	36.07	40.92	34.60	.34.20	41.40	34.08
Muzaffarpur	38.28	47.90	30.53	38.28	47.90	30.53
Darbhanga	32.00	48.90	28.20	32.00	48.90	28.20
Bhagalpur	34.09	37.80	27.03	30.25	40.00	24.82
Santhal Parganas	22.36	25.57	25.18	25.77	28.49	33.13
Hazaribagh	33.32	37.37	43.83	32.95	36.12	48.35
Manbhum	25.35	29.24	31.39	21.77	24.76	27.78
Palamau	33.91	31.21	36.40	33.91	31.21	36.40
Bankura	26.37	32.64	27.17	25.96	29.11	29.41
Nadia	24.76 *	48.25	26.57	N.A.	47.52	23.32
Murshidabad	33.18	37.70	27.26	31.13	38.14	24.02
Khulna	31.42	39.53	34.09	33.03	41.29	33.17
Puri	30.11	27.44	24.81	32.81	28.21	25.00

Source: Final Resolution, p. 50. * Figures for 9 months only

Europe in the fourteenth century, and the ravages of malaria in western and central Bengal in the late nineteenth century.[124]

The famine of 1896–97, too, resulted in a spate of deaths from fever, cholera and enteric diseases in the affected districts, particularly in the tribal belts of Chotanagpur, the Santhal Parganas and Bankura. This is confirmed by the mortality statistics of the affected districts in 1896–97, which show a significant increase in death rates precisely in these regions. As to the rise in mortalities in Shahabad, it is noted that the physical condition of the population in the affected tract was always very low, a debilitating disease resulting from the consumption of khesari grain being widely prevalent.[125]

124 Chaudhuri, "Agricultural Production in Bengal", p. 155.
125 *Final Resolution*, p. 50.

There were fewer deaths resulting directly from starvation, than those caused by a persistent weakening of the constitution by malnutrition. Moreover, the eating of unwholesome food without a proper cereal base made the system most vulnerable to attacks of cholera and other gastro-enteric disorders. In fact, it has been observed that the decline in cholera mortality in India since 1908 was due not only to bacteriological change, but also to improved sanitation and medication, as well as the lower incidence and severity of famines in this period.[126] Malaria epidemics and fever deaths in the Punjab since 1868 have also been linked with a combined rain-prices factor, by applying modern methods of regression analysis.[127] As noted earlier, the poor in the tribal areas, who supplemented their diet even in normal years by a wide variety of jungle produce, subsisted almost entirely on them in a year of scarcity, as during the crisis of 1896–97. Local officials, however, were not overly concerned about this. The Deputy Commissioner of Manbhum reported having seen "a collection of fangs enough to poison a regiment, which some Santhals had collected for food", in support of his theory that they were well accustomed to eating such unwholesome products. He attributed the growing cholera epidemic in the district to a "microbe entirely propagated by water".[128]

Conclusion

All these signs indicated that the crisis had deepened into famine. As the price of cereals touched an all-time high, it had an erosive effect on rural society. Lending operations were stopped, grain disappeared from the market, breadwinners deserted their families, and an exchange crisis ensued. It forced a change in the

126 David Arnold, "Cholera Mortality in British India, 1817–1947", in *India's Historical Demography: Studies in Famine, Disease and Society,* ed. Tim Dyson, pp. 261—83 (London: Curzon Press, 1989).

127 For a distinctive analysis of acute and chronic hunger, see Sheila Zurbrigg, "Hunger and Epidemic Malaria in Punjab, 1868–1940", *Economic and Political Weekly* 27, no. 4, 25 Jan 1992, PE 2–26.

128 *Selection of Papers,* vol. 11: p. 418.

people's food habits, while the fields remained fallow for lack of seedgrain. Farmhands were laid off due to the contraction of the sown area, and an exodus began from the famine zone to other districts in search of food and employment. Distress sales of ploughs, cattle and land heightened the bleakness of agricultural prospects in the near future, and led to a further pauperisation of the peasantry. Their sense of desperation showed in the increasing crime returns, while the mortality statistics were a grim reminder of the intensity of their misery.

6

Increasing Intensity of the Famine: The Behavioural Pattern of the Superordinate Groups

[1] Heightening of Underlying Tensions in Rural Society

It has been seen how various anomalies in the peasant economy were accentuated during famines. As the existing pattern of entitlements began to collapse under pressure of the crisis, the superordinate groups in rural society perfected their mechanism of control over the surplus grain in the districts.

Even in normal times, absenteeism among zamindars and the sub-infeudation of tenures led to various complications in rent relations. More remarkable were the basic contradictions in the rural economy bound to the moneylenders' credit. The mahajan or moneylender did not belong to any distinct social class. Grain dealers including dadni merchants also functioned as mahajans, but could not make much headway if they were pure traders without local connections. In rural Bengal, as in Madras, the trading connections followed closely those of debt, so that the rural economy rested firmly in the hands of the few peasants with a surplus. Thus, the professional moneylenders were gradually being supplanted by big farmers who might also operate as graindealers-cum-mahajans and, in smaller villages, by anyone with a surplus to lend.

The zamindars, particularly smaller proprietors like the thikadars in Bihar, could also function as moneylenders, and the zamindar-creditor, by virtue of his local standing, was in a stronger position than professional mahajans or even the big farmers. In Nadia, for example, the peasants were seen to have little self-reliance during the crisis in 1896, as many of the zamindars acted in the threefold capacity of landlord, indigo planter and mahajan. The grain and cash loans were made on the security of crops and land, and, in case of landless labourers, on the basis of sharecropping (usually for half the produce) or bonded labour by the kamia, musahar, jan, etc. Due to the piling up of compound interest, the debtor, usually illiterate, continued to pay up indefinitely, the money worth of the kamia's labour or the interest payment in grain and cash far exceeding the borrowed amount. In fact, interest on loans by mahajans followed no fixed or uniform rate, but depended on their relationship with the debtor and the creditworthiness of the latter. The aim was usually not to recover the principal with interest, but to keep the debtor in perpetual dependence, perhaps with the ulterior motive of appropriating his land.

The bania or grain dealer, too, was most intent on extracting as large a share of produce as possible from the raiyat, especially in his capacity as mahajan. Indeed, the profits of the middlemen, retail dealers, etc., and the zamindars' levy of tolls over the local hats, always placed the seller-producer at a distinct disadvantage in relation to the bania. In fact, large parts of Nadia were held by the "shop-keeper" zamindars, who were Sahas, Tambulis or Telis by caste, and acquired land by speculation over three generations.[1]

Yet, in normal times a working arrangement was arrived at between the landlord and tenant, the creditor and debtor, and the grain dealer and producer.

The zamindar made advances to his tenants both in grain and cash when the agricultural season commenced. He employed a large number of raiyats and labourers on his lands, the kamias being provided for throughout the year. The zamindar was supposed to repair dams and embankments and the larger irrigation works like the ahar and pyne system in Gaya, which could not be managed without his intervention.

The mahajan was even more indispensable in the existing social set-up, for few others would risk giving loans to the cultivator, in view of the severe fluctuations in agricultural seasons. He had an intimate local knowledge of the khatak's background and capacity

[1] LRP, April 1900, Land Revenue, no. 138–39, p. 873.

to pay, and did not take recourse to law as long as faith was kept. The creditor did not insist strictly on the letter of the bond to recover his dues and would rather accept *panchayat* (village forum) decisions, for he did not wish to incur the opprobrium of society by defying the panchayat. The moneylenders' role in the peasant economy was all the more vital in view of the absence of any other credit agency which could finance agriculture in the way they did. Instances of *taqavi* advances by zamindars (usually without interest, repayable after the harvest) were becoming increasingly rare. No cooperative credit societies worth the name existed in this period. Government occasionally provided credit, but on conditions too rigid to have been acceptable to peasants. Besides, the sums allotted for the purpose were often inadequate, and official red tape further marred their effectiveness.[2] Hence, the moneylender was essential for the small peasant economy, and in single-crop regions like Satkhira and Bagerhat in Khulna, his absence was deeply felt, especially in a crisis year like 1896.

The grain dealer too had his usage, for in remote areas in the interior, the peasant could neither sell nor buy the required amount of foodgrain except through the agency of the bania-mahajan, or the beparis or itinerant traders. The absence of traders proper was keenly felt in remote areas like the Palamau district, the Ramnagar-Araraj-Madhuban tract in Champaran, the Kalantar in Nadia, and the Chilka region in Puri in 1896, when the need to import grain was imperative.

With large-scale crop failures as in 1896, however, the activities of these various groups tended to become antagonistic to the small peasant economy.

[1.1] Role of the zamindars in 1896–97

In regard to tenure and rent relations, the evils of absenteeism and sub-infeudation became evident in crisis years like 1896. For example, in Satkhira the greater portion of the permanently settled area was no longer in the direct possession of the zamindars, but was in the hands of a class of petty tenure and under-tenure holders, such as patnidars, gantidars, lakhirajdars

[2] Chaudhuri, "Rural Credit Relations".

and the like. The gantidars were very numerous in the Satkhira subdivision and owned the greater portion of the country. Their counterparts in north Jessore and in Bagerhat in eastern Khulna were known as the jotedars and hawaladars, respectively. In fact, the Simon Commission pointed out that in some places there were fifty or more intermediate interests between the zamindar at the top and the cultivator at the bottom.

So far as the lands in the possession of the gantidars were concerned, the zamindars had no interest except in the collection of rent, and did not consider themselves responsible for the welfare of the cultivators residing in their respective properties. The gantidars as a class were too poor to undertake costly works or to assist the raiyats in crisis years.[3] In 1896 Babu Girija Nath Raychaudhuri, zamindar of Satkhira, threw the entire responsibility of supplying seed to cultivators on to the gantidars in his estate, which, as the Commissioner pointed out, "illustrates the evil of the tenure intermediate between a zamindar and the cultivators".[4] The repairs of dams and enbankments in Satkhira were vital for protecting the rice crop from salt-water incursions particularly this year, when the rains were too scanty to sweeten the river water. But even rich zamindars like the Satkhira babus refused to take action in this matter, staunchly maintaining that it was the duty of the gantidar to repair the works. They held that it was the gantidar who dealt directly with the raiyat, and hence was immediately responsible for his welfare. Mr B. C. Basu, Assistant Director of Land Records and Agriculture, thus noted the hopelessness of the case: "The minute subdivision of property cannot but be a greater evil in a country where agriculture would be impossible but for an elaborate system of embankments and dams requiring a comparatively large outlay and constant care".[5] Indeed, due to joint control over property, no party was ready to bear the expenses, and large areas of fertile land reverted to jungle through the apathy of the landlords, most of whom resided in Calcutta and had no knowledge or interest in local problems. For example, two large bils in

3 *Selection of Papers,* vol. 3: p. 187.
4 Ibid., vol. 8: p. 291.
5 Ibid., vol. 3: p. 187.

Mukundapur and Dudhil near Kaliganj, the first containing more than 5,000 bighas of land, had reverted to jungle in the last few years due to the apathy of the zamindars Peary Mohun and Hari Mohun Roy of Calcutta, grandsons of Raja Rammohun Roy. A part of the land was held by lakhirajdars who were not willing to share the expenses of embankments with the zamindars. The local people repeatedly appealed to the zamindars to repair the dams in order to save whatever crops were on the ground this year, but to no effect.[6]

Government offered advances for the repair of dams in 1896, but the zamindars as a rule did not come forward to take loans: they left it to the tenure-holders and raiyats. The Panchberia bil was an instance in point. It contained some five to six thousand bighas and required embanking; but the managers of the zamindars, the latter being absentees, would not move in the matter though empowered to act in such cases. In fact, Aghor Nath Banerjee, the manager of Babu Kailash Chandra Pal, would not even see the Sub-Divisional Officer (SDO) or write to him, though he lived only three miles away from the SDO's office.[7] The raiyats, on the other hand, did not have a sufficient stake in the land to make the embankments themselves.

Hence, as a result of the apathy of the absentee landlords and the reluctance or inability of under-tenure holders like the gantidars to undertake repairs of the dams and embankments, many of the raiyats began absconding from Satkhira to southeast Khulna, and the newly reclaimed settlements in the Sunderbans. In January 1897, the SDO himself saw numerous deserted abads in Shyamnagore and Paikgacha, which testified to this.[8] This abandonment of holdings by tenants threatened the interests, not only of general cultivation, but also of the landlords and mahajans to whom they were indebted for rent and loans. But as government officials pointed out, it was punishment well deserved for so neglecting their duties towards the tenants.

In the Patna Division, too, violence often erupted over the question of water distribution from irrigation systems running

6 Ibid., p. 203.
7 Ibid., vol. 4: p. 240.
8 Ibid., p. 239.

through the properties of several landlords. Naturally, these issues were all the more vital in crisis years like 1896, when irrigation was most required. Similarly, in Malud in the Chilka tract in Puri, nothing was done to excavate tanks, though a terrible water famine was imminent in January 1897, as the estate suffered from all the disadvantages of absentee landlordism.[9]

Certain systems of tenure which made the raiyats' position particularly insecure were all the more disadvantageous in years of extensive crop failure. For example, the utbandi system of tenure in Nadia required one-fourth of the total cultivable area to remain fallow every year. This intensified the problem in northwest Nadia in 1896, as the deficit in total crop out-turn had amounted to 86 per cent in the Kalantar and 67 per cent in the surrounding regions this year. Under the utbandi system, the raiyats had no occupancy rights in practice and were at the mercy of the zamindar.[10] Due to these conditions, land, even lakhiraj, had little value in these parts, for the people did not set much store on occupancy holding. In fact, lakhiraj land was selling here for Rs. 3–4 per bigha, while elsewhere it would fetch between Rs. 50 and 100. This prevented the raiyats in Nadia from getting loans on the security of land in 1896–97.[11]

When the zamindar combined two or more functions in his person, the raiyats' dependence on him greatly increased. For example, in Nadia the zamindar acting in the threefold capacity of zamindar, indigo-planter and mahajan, left little freedom to the tenant. He even controlled the local hats as at Tehatta and Gotpara. Similarly, the absence of mahajans in Satkhira in Khulna, made the zamindar indispensible and all-powerful in these regions.

The usual advances of grain and cash by the zamindars to their tenants were all but stopped in 1896–97. Taqavi loans had long become obsolete, and in 1896, landlords refused to make advances even at reasonable rates of interest. In December 1896 Babu Hari Charan Chaudhuri of Kaliganj, Khulna, claimed to have given out some Rs. 45,000 to his tenants in the last few

9 Ibid., p. 421.
10 Ibid., vol. 3: p. 229.
11 Ibid., p. 230.

months and refused to issue further loans until past debts were cleared. His tenants were absconding or selling off cattle, and as a result, much of the land was likely to remain fallow next year. Girija Nath Raychaudhuri, who owned the 10-anna Satkhira estate, took up a similar stand with identical results.[12] In May 1897, the Collector of Khulna reported that despite personal appeals by him to Girija Nath Raychaudhuri for supplying seedgrain to his tenants, he refused point blank and threw the entire responsibility of supplying seed grains on to the gantidars.[13] As there were practically no mahajan*s* in Satkhira, the people had to depend almost entirely on the zamindar for advances. It was only in July–August that some zamindars started advancing money. Girija Nath Raychaudhuri was said to be issuing loans at the usurious interest of six pies per rupee per month. From these loans, he was also deducting the interest due on previous loans.[14]

The Pal Chaudhuris of Nadia, too, would not lend grain to their tenants until the agricultural season had commenced. Though they held about 55,000 md. of grain, half the people in their zamindari were subsisting on half-rations by December 1896. The zamindar of Sonadanga in Nadia, Babu Jatindra Nath Sinha Roy, proclaimed his intention of ceasing advances from January 1897, i.e., precisely the time when the people, due to the extensive failure of the winter rice, would feel the first pangs of hunger.[15]

Government tried to issue loans in some cases to the raiyats through and on the security provided by the zamindars, but the Collector of Khulna reported in June 1897 that the gantidars were instigating the raiyats to complain of distress. From the beginning of trouble in Khulna, he had noted that the class of petty rent receivers were exaggerating the distress, in order that money may flow into affected tracts, and eventually find its way into their own pockets. The Collector of Nadia reported in June 1897 that a certain zamindar in his district recently applied for a large sum to be divided among the considerable number of

12 Ibid., pp. 202, 204.
13 Ibid., vol. 8: p. 312.
14 Ibid., vol. 10: p. 354.
15 Ibid., vol. 3: p. 228.

his raiyats, on their joint security, for agricultural purposes. But since he received information that the money was intended principally to enable the raiyats to pay their rents, he declined to make the advances. Indeed, there was always this objection to advancing money to zamindars, or even village panchayats.[16]

As the Presidency Commissioner pointed out, "They [the zamindars] think far more of their own rents than of any starvation among the people".[17] The Satkhira Babus managed to collect two annas of rent by April–May 1897. But this figure supplied by their naib was probably a gross under-estimation. Mr B. C. Basu, Assistant Director of Land Records and Agriculture, suggested in December 1896 that the revenue be suspended this year in case of resident zamindars in Khulna district, so that they did not have to press their raiyats for rent.[18] In Nadia and Jessore, rent collection went on as usual in many places. By February, Mahendra Roy, zamindar of Samta in Bongaon, had already collected 12 an. of his rent and hoped to realise the rest by the end of the agricultural year. The same was reported from the Jadabpur cutcherry belonging to Babu Gurudas Das of Jaunbazar, Calcutta. They, along with the tahsildars of a small estate owned by Mathura Nath Pal Natuda, hoped to realise the full rent by the end of the agricultural year. The Dey Chaudhuris of Ranaghat greatly pressurised their tenants at Irshaldanga, and had already realised their full dues. Peasants pledged or sold off their ornaments to pay the rent. At Nawadagram, the zamindar had recovered every pice of the rent due. The raiyats had to take advances from jaggery dealers for the purpose, but both the yield and the price of jaggery were lower than usual, so that they were unable to repay their loans to their beparis. In Bongaon zamindars in their eagerness to collect the rent, favoured the cultivation of jute. This brought ready cash to the raiyat, but tended to disregard the SDO's order prohibiting the steeping of jute in water intended for drinking purposes.[19] In Azimpur, Amilaish, Dolu, Rupkania, and other

16 Ibid., vol. 9: p. 349.
17 Ibid., p. 351.
18 Ibid., vol. 3: p. 196.
19 Ibid., vol. 5: p. 225.

places in Chittagong, people were borrowing money at a high rate of interest for paying their rent.

The scenario was no different in Bihar or Orissa. In the Santhal Parganas, government officials appealed to local zamindars not to compel the raiyats to sell grain to pay their rents, as this drained the district of its foodgrain supply. Payment of the bhaoli system of rent, as in south Bihar, benefited the zamindars, but further depressed the peasants in such a year of crop failure and high foodgrain prices.

In the Chilka region in Puri, which was badly affected in 1896–97, the Khandait of Narsingpatna said: "the people had to pinch and save to collect the revenue which they would have to pay". In Puri, the Assistant Settlement Officer in Kotdesh, thought that "no relief operations will be necessary if the mahajans and zamindars are a little generous towards the poor". In the Kanika estate of Cuttack, it was remarkable that out of a total demand of Rs. 60,330 for the 8-anna kist in January, no less a sum than Rs. 51,882 was collected.[20]

The smaller zamindars, especially in Bhagalpur and Chotanagpur could not provide for their kamias this year, who were left to fend for themselves. Some of the zamindars like Kamaleshwari Prasad Singh of Monghyr, who owned the Bilputta estate, promised to do much work to employ people in that area, but did nothing in effect.[21] In Palamau, however, zamindars were less apathetic, and opened a number of relief works in the district.

[1.2] Activities of the mahajans during the famine

With large-scale crop failures, the activities of the mahajans, like those of the zamindars, tended to be antagonistic to the small-peasant economy. The mahajans were by no means 'rural capitalists' who would finance agriculture under all conditions, as implied by W. W. Hunter. Rather, as soon as the first signs of scarcity became apparent, they temporarily dissociated themselves from rural credit transactions. The zamindar-creditor, as noted

[20] Ibid., p. 367.
[21] Ibid., vol. 8: p. 483.

above, stopped advances in the famine year. Hence, dependence on the mahajan increased. But in 1896, the mahajans closed their golas all over the Patna, Chotanagpur and Bhagalpur Divisions. The same story was repeated in Orissa and other parts of Bengal.

In Jalpaiguri and Bogra, the raiyats still hoped to get advances from the mahajan against their aus dhan and jute crops in 1897, but the latter refused to lend until January–March of the following year, when crop prospects could be determined. The few mahajans in Satkhira, for example, stopped lending to their clients since September 1896, when it was realised that the crops would fail successively for two years. As a result, people sold off their ornaments, cattle and utensils, and even absconded to the southeast of the district.[22] In Nadia and Jessore, too, rural credit was paralysed. The smaller creditors went down with their clients as in many parts of Narail and Magura, while substantial mahajans, mostly big farmers or grain dealers, refused to risk issuing further loans unless past debts were cleared. In Bongaon, where the people were comparatively poor and hence depended more on the mahajans than in Magura or Narail, loans from the latter were essential during the slack season from Chaitra to Sravan. This year, however, loans were not granted, leading to despair and intense resentment among the raiyats. The golas of mahajans who refused to lend were often looted, as in Patna at the end of 1896, in Lohardaga in April 1897, and in Rajshahi in June 1897. In Bihar subdivision, Patna, the mahajans were enforcing their claims on the cultivators and demanding their "pound of flesh".[23]

This refusal on the part of the mahajans to issue loans was all the more significant, as there was no alternative source of credit for the raiyats. Taqavi, as already noted, had long become obsolete. There were no cooperative credit societies. Government sometimes issued loans, but the amount was inadequate and the terms too rigid to be of much use to the raiyat. In February, the Collector of Khulna complained that many applicants had to be refused loans on account of insufficient security, and also for

[22] Ibid., vol. 3: p. 196.
[23] Ibid., vol. 4: p. 22.

want of funds.[24] The security taken was always landed property, and general revenue-paying estates or gantis. In some cases, *mukarari mukarari jamas*, in which the applicants had heritable and transferable interest, were accepted. Before the loan was sanctioned, it was ascertained that the applicant was not in arrears with his landlord and the properties were not mortgaged. Few raiyats could fulfil all these terms and conditions. Mahajans and zamindars seldom guaranteed security of the raiyats. Sometimes, when loans were distributed through the local mahajans, they even deducted from this money the sum due to them in debt arrears from their clients. There was also danger in advancing money to gantidars, lest they should become insolvent. In Nadia, the application for loans on the security of land were turned down because even lakhiraj land had little value in these parts, due to the utbandi system of tenure. Red tape and bickerings among officials often delayed the issue of loans, particularly of seedgrains, which, to be of use, ought to have been granted before the sowing season was over.

Further, government loans were to be granted only to those who could not get advances from the mahajans. This distinction was not easy to make. Government officials faced another great problem in issuing loans, due to the interference it caused with the operations of private capitalists. To take only one example, Mr B. C. Basu, Assistant Director of Land Records and Agriculture, was told during his tour in Magura and Narail in January 1897, that in Mamudpur the mere rumour of government being about to give loans to raiyats had caused a temporary lull in private transactions. From all parts of the Damin in the Santhal Parganas, reports came in that the local mahajans had refused to grant any loans on the ground that advances were to be made by government. Mahajans were afraid of lending to those who might again borrow from the government, thus causing a conflict of interests, in which those of the private individual were more likely to suffer.[25]

As the aus and aman prospects were assured in 1897, mahajans recommenced their lending operations. In Nadia and Magura-

[24] Ibid., vol. 6: p. 22.

[25] Ibid., vol. 3: p. 230; vol. 5: p. 308, 315.

Bongaon in Jessore, small advances were being made by February 1897, in the hope of an average aus yield this year. Even in April, the loans were being made cautiously and to selected men, as in Bongaon. Most of the mahajans were renewing their old bonds only, but were not giving out fresh loans. In Nadia, they were advancing money only to the very few comparatively well-to-do cultivators who could afford to pay for the weeding of their fields.[26] Peasants did not gain from the high famine prices of foodgrains in 1896–97, for they hardly had any stock left after repaying their loans to the mahajans. As the rains set in and the agricultural season commenced with the preparation of the lands for the aman harvest, credit relations were more or less normalised. But the rates of interest were high and usurious in 1897. In Hazaribagh and Lohardaga, grain loans were made on ruinous terms. In many cases, loans were granted on the security of crops, to the distinct disadvantage of the raiyat-producer. For example, the imminence of the aus and jute harvests in Khulna in August–September 1897 made it possible for the cultivators to borrow money on the crops. However, they lost a great deal by selling their jute on the ground and taking part of the price in advance, for such deals inevitably resulted in lower prices.[27] Besides, the mahajans were naturally trying to make use of this opportunity to lend money on the security of land, in the hope of ultimately obtaining possession of it.

The result was seen in the increasing number of mortgages being registered in all districts in 1897. Moneylenders in the Santhal Parganas had less security for their loans than elsewhere, as the court would not allow them to attach either cultivated holdings or the crops there.[28]

[1.3] Response of the grain dealers to the growing subsistence crisis

The activities of the grain dealers, most of whom combined trade with moneylending and grain lending, were also harmful to the people in many parts of the famine zone in 1896–97. For

[26] Ibid., vol. 7: p. 302; vol. 9: p. 353.
[27] Ibid., vol. 9: p. 330, 420, 428.
[28] Ibid., p. 500.

example, exports from regions with low purchasing power, as from Bihar—especially the northern districts of Patna Division—went on unrestricted until early 1897 despite acute local scarcity, sometimes resulting in grain riots. Similarly, exports from Nadia went on as usual, though the northwestern part of the district was most severely affected. Even Garrett, the Collector of Nadia, failed to understand or explain this 'mystery', as he called it. Grain flowed out of Bhagalpur district but did not enter the Madhipura-Supaul area which was in acute distress. In the Chilka tract in Puri, the export trade was well organised but there were no corresponding imports. Moreover, despite repeated efforts by the government, private traders could not be induced to import grain into remote areas like the Palamau district, Ramnagar-Araraj-Madhuban in Champaran, the Kalantar in Nadia or the Malud and Chilka tract in Puri. Hoardings by grain dealers as in Barh, Maner, Bihar, Khagole and Phulwari in Patna, and the rigging of the market as at Manatu in Palamau, further intensified the problem. These activities of the grain traders during the crisis will be seen in greater detail when discussing the directions and problems of grain trade in 1896–97.

[2] *Mechanism of Surplus Control*

Subsistence requirements rather than a profit incentive on the part of the peasants, accounted for most of the surplus controlled and marketed by grain dealers. The peasants' stock of grain did undoubtedly pass into the hands of the grain dealer, but this did not come about through the agency of the price system. Rather, the moneylenders and the zamindars, through their demands, were the main agents for extracting the marketable output from the traditional peasant economy. It was thus conditioned more by the rural power structure, than by secular market forces. The mechanism by which the zamindars, mahajans and banias controlled the surplus grain in the district took several different forms which, however, interacted so closely, that they can hardly be split in analysis.

[2 .1] Traders' direct control over a share of the produce

[a] Hypothecation

A sizeable part of the raiyats' produce went to the dadni merchant. By the late nineteenth century, the system of hypothecation was well-entrenched in the cash-crop sector. The new credit agencies tried to control the production process, for unlike the local moneylender practising usury, they were connected with trade organisations and were primarily interested in the secure supply of a certain portion of the peasant's produce. Even in case of rice cultivation, which was the usual preserve of local moneylenders, the new credit agency became active, particularly as the rice market tended to expand. After the 1873–74 famine, MacDonnell, Collector of Darbhanga, wrote of the Bihar District: "In point of fact, a large portion of the crop—the rice crop particularly—is hypothecated from year to year; advances are made on it and it is exported as soon as reaped". But this system was not entirely new to grain trade, though it is uncertain as to whether and how far the merchants controlled the production process. In fact, the Proceedings of the Grain Department of the Government of Bengal (1794–1801) show that about 25 per cent of the cultivation in some districts depended on *dadan* (advances). This contradicts the general impression that the role of grain merchants in rural credit and the system of hypothecation against advances were much later developments. In the context of the extremely limited market for peasants' land in this period, the crops, apart from small movable assets, were the most important form of security.

This role of the grain merchants was considerably modified at the end of the century, with the growth of the land market and the emergence of a powerful community of big farmers as intermediaries between them and the actual cultivators. Yet, part of the grain was still marketed by dadan merchants even in famine years. For example, it was reported during the famine of 1896 that in the Angul district, Orissa, the Mogulbandi dealers stayed all the year round, making advances to the cultivators for the produce actually on the ground and taking away large quantities of grain as soon as it was reaped. In the famine tract of Parikud in the Chilka region, crops were "generally forestalled". In Khulna, Jessore and other districts, too, this system existed, though in 1896–97 grain merchants refused to make the usual advances in view of the extremely low credit of the raiyats.[29] When the situation improved in August–September 1897, peasants in Khulna were taking advances from the traders and mahajans on the security of the aus crop which was still on the ground.[30] In fact, the large-scale operations of grain trade in Bengal in this period required a system of secure and steady supplies as the dadan for, like the millers in Burma, rice merchants had to honour their "forward contracts".

[b] Post-harvest sales of grain by the peasants

Post-harvest sales of grain by peasants for the payment of cash dues to the mahajan and zamindar accounted for much of the stocks in the hands of the dealer. For example, in the scarcity areas of Santhal Parganas in December 1896, the peasants repeatedly pressed for "leisure" from their landlords and mahajans so that instead of selling what grain they had to pay their dues, they could keep it for food. The Rajas of Baneli, Hitampur, Pabia and Gidhour were warned by government officials that nothing would prevent the drain of foodgrains from the Santhal Parganas, unless they stopped compelling their raiyats to sell it to pay their rents. The Collector of Patna reports in November 1896 that as soon as the rice-crop prospects were assured, cultivators began to sell, calculating the extent of their transaction on the prospect of the paddy or the spring crops. The process would be repeated as soon as rabi prospects were assured, but not in the same degree. Rice being the staple food, they would not part readily with the crop they were now reaping. The peasants of Bihar had realised in the last quarter of a century, that grain once sent out of the country came back at an enhanced price. Even in December 1896, they were reported to be holding their stocks and sold only to meet the landlords' or mahajans' demand. In Bogra, Pabna and Rajshahi, however, relatively high prices in 1896 led to a greater volume of post-harvest sales.

29 *Selection of Papers,* vol. 3: p. 233.
30 Ibid., vol. 11: p. 330.

Obviously, open-market conditions did not prevail, and the peasant was forced to part with a greater portion of his crops than was necessary in order to pay his dues. The grain dealer exerted his local influence and took full advantage of the peasant's compulsion to sell, to further lower the rates which were already low during harvest time. As the peasant could not afford the cost of carriage to town markets, he had to depend for the disposal of his crops on local dealers and beparis, who naturally kept a margin for themselves. Such itinerant traders were active in the Satkhira and Bagerhat Subdivisions of Khulna. Bardal, the largest market in Satkhira, was reported to be well stocked with rice and paddy in December 1896, brought by a large number of itinerant traders roaming from hat to hat throughout the Sunderbans. In Palamau, too, beparis in bullock carts went from village to village, picking up supplies at a cheap rate and then taking them from one bania to another, until they could dispose of it at a small profit. Next, the dealers of Maharajganj bought the paddy in bullock-loads and retailed their purchases at a higher rate in the form of rice.[31] In Hazaribagh, too, the mahajan and the retail dealer made a considerable profit. In fact, even if the peasant gained access to the nearest hat, he could not hope to bypass the middlemen. This was particularly evident at Tehatta, Gotpara and other hats in Nadia, as noted by B. C. Basu, Assistant Director of Land Records and Agriculture, during his tour of the district in January 1897. Here the manner of sale was rather novel and was anything but free bargain. At each hat, a middleman (*mahaldar*) was appointed by the zamindar and paid rent to him for the privilege of collecting a small tax on each bargain. He also functioned as a *kayali* or licensed measurer, who measured every ounce of rice sold, and could alone fix the rates. Kayalis were met with everywhere in Bengal, but it was rather novel for them to determine grain rates, which were often arbitrary, and seldom to the advantage of the seller-producer.[32]

[31] Ibid., vol. 4: p. 335.

[32] Ibid., vol. 3: p. 231.

[2.2] Surplus control by mahajans, through interest payments in kind

Besides such sales of grain for paying his cash dues, direct payments in kind to the mahajan covered a very large part of the peasant's total produce. In fact, after paying off the grain loans the peasant had hardly any stock left so that, as local officials pointed out, the exportation of grain was not really in the hand of the raiyat, but that of the local *moody* (grocer). "The moneylender's control over much of the local stock of grain was a direct consequence of his role as a creditor".[33]

The range of variations in the interest rates on grain or bij-khad loans was smaller than on cash loans. According to custom, it was *bhojer dery bijer dwigun*, i.e., 50 per cent on grains lent for food and 100 per cent on seed grains, provided the loan was paid off at the following harvest. The rate of interest rose sharply with the failure of the debtor peasants to repay the loan at the agreed time. When the loan was a grain loan merely in form but a cash loan in content, peasants were worse off. Due to the low post-harvest prices, they had to surrender a much larger quantity of grain than they had received. The principal amount of the loan was not the quantity of grain loaned, but its money value at the market price when it was loaned; the quantity returned was what the principal plus interest brought in the market after the harvest. Besides, an inferior quality of grain was often repaid by a higher-priced variety. The creditor might also take advantage of his client's illiteracy to record a greater amount than was actually given out. Moreover, few checks could be kept on the debtor's 'account' with the zamindar-mahajan, who mixed up the banking and rent accounts. He credited receipts to the former and showed the balance due under the head of rent-arrears, for the custom of changing peasant holdings to cover rent arrears had gained legal recognition, unlike land sales to pay debt or interest dues. As crops were harvested, the zamindar-creditor often used coercive methods to carry off his dues before the crops left the field. By these various means, the moneylender managed to control an even greater portion of the produce than was strictly his due. As N. S. Alexander, Commissioner of the Burdwan

[33] Chaudhuri, "Rural Credit Relations", p. 253.

Division, wrote to the Secretary to the Government of Bengal on 16 April 1888: "a large amount of paddy comes into the mahajan's hand, nearly equivalent in value to the rental of the village".

At Assasuni in Satkhira in mid-December 1896, all the grain golas were reported to be empty except one belonging to a mahajan-cultivator who had grain to last him for five to six months. In Sriula a mahajan-dealer, Abdul Aziz, had only 100 md. left out of his reserve of 2,000 to 3,000 md. of paddy. Hari Charan Chaudhuri, a zamindar of Satkhira and the largest grain-holder in these parts, is said to have lent Rs. 45,000 to his tenants and his golas were reportedly empty. Zamindars like Girija Nath Raychaudhuri of Satkhira, the Pal Chaudhuri brothers of Nadia and Jatindra Nath Sinha Roy of Sonadanga were said to be in a similar plight. In fact, the mahajans, gantidars and zamindar-creditors in Khulna, Nadia and Jessore unanimously complained of being ruined due to non-payment by debtor raiyats. Yet it seems more than likely that only a part of their huge stock was denuded in this way, the rest being hoarded or marketed.

[a] Hoarding and exportation by the mahajans

Numerous sale transactions were noted on the part of the mahajans, including zamindar-creditors. In Nadia, the Collector reported that many mahajans were induced by high prices to sell their stocks of paddy as well as other foodgrains to outsiders. In late November they still had stocks sufficient for two months' consumption by the whole population of the tract. But they had now stopped advancing or selling paddy in the hope of a further price rise. Traders received stocks from the interior, mainly through local mahajans. In Bongaon, Jessore, raiyats were poorer than in Magura-Narail and so depended more on the mahajans. The lean season when the peasants borrowed was from March to July, i.e., till the reaping of the aus which was the main crop here. The mahajans realised all their dues from the last aus harvest (1896) which had been a good one, but refused to make fresh advances from March 1897 as this year's aus prospects were uncertain.

Besides, most of the mahajans were big raiyats themselves. They, therefore, had a larger stock in hand, sometimes consisting even of aus paddy from the 1894 crop, as in case of the Sadgop mahajans in Belta. At Sherpur near Nalta, there was a large stock of paddy in about thirteen golas, all in the hands of the mahajans. At Garapota, too, the mahajans had plenty of stock. In Samta, the three principal grain-lenders had sufficient stocks, but were holding them back for obvious reasons. Most of these mahajans were selling off part of their stocks while prices remained high. For example, Srikanta Roy, a wealthy mahajan at Samkur, sold off a large part of his stock. In Irshaldanga, there were three mahajans with about 400 md. of paddy in their hands. The chief grain-lenders here were the Biswas family at Sunderpur, whose operations as mahajan and dealer covered a wide area; their local *gomasta* (agent) was told to assess the requirements of Irshaldanga, whereupon the grain would be brought in from their stores elsewhere. At Sibchandrapur, the mahajans sold stocks and had none even to lend to their own raiyats. There were some big mahajans in a neighbouring village, but they refused to lend to outsiders and preferred to sell at high prices. The raiyats asked the government to interfere, which, of course, it would not.[34] In Murshidabad, mahajans held grain for sale when prices rose further. They sold out only in apprehension of the safety of their stocks, as repeated fires occurred in the godowns. Hence in April 1897, the local mahajans like Rani Mena Kumari of Jeagunj and Babu Narpat Singh of Azimganj were selling rice at 10 sr. a rupee.[35] Exports from Katwa in Burdwan ceased in mid-April, as the mahajans were getting no supplies from the interior. In Satkhira, Khulna, things were similar, for mahajans refused to advance seedgrains to their clients. In parts of Nadia, Khulna and Rajshahi, where there was no organised trade in grain, affluent peasants who controlled a large part of the surplus engaged in petty retail trade.

In November 1896, the mahajans raised prices by exporting large stocks in Pabna, Bogra, the Santhal Parganas, Hazaribagh and Singhbhum, while in Cuttack, Puri and in north Bihar many held back in the hope of a further price rise. In the Santhal Parganas, in particular, the mahajans would not reveal the state

34 *Selection of Papers,* vol., 5: p. 233–35.
35 Ibid., vol., 7: p. 324.

of their reserves lest they should have to advance to their clients. Many of the substantial Brahmin and Rajput raiyats in Bhagalpur had profited from the famine prices.[36] In fact, the Collector of Bhagalpur and the Deputy Commissioner of the Santhal Parganas both dilated on the profits made by grain dealers, especially as the terms of credit or sale were entirely dictated by them that year.[37] In Chotanagpur, grain was very unevenly distributed, being held mainly by mahajans. In Lohardaga, the main cause of distress was the failure of the mahajans to grant the usual loans owing to the greater and surer profits obtainable from selling at present high prices. As the bhadoi prospects were assured, mahajans in Hazaribagh complained that they could not get rid of their large hoards due to a fall in prices.[38]

In January–February 1897, Earle, the Collector of Saran, noted that stocks were sufficient not in the hands of the raiyats, but in those of the mahajans who supplied them.[39] Tytler, the Sub-Deputy Opium Agent of Siwan in the Saran district, wrote on 28 November 1896 that though nearly all agriculturists would run out of stocks by January 1897, "the banias will always have grain to sell if the people have the money to buy it with".[40] The Famine Report on Saran stated: "The greater part of the stock lay in the hands of two per cent of the population, [some of whom are] professional lenders pure and simple, and others are prosperous agriculturists".[41] The October grain riots in Patna were triggered off by a large-scale hoarding on the part of local banias. In the famine district of Champaran, which had no large traders, government favoured importations by the local mahajans. Unlike in Muzaffarpur, where affluent raiyats served as moneylenders, the mahajans of Champaran belonged to a non-resident, non-agriculturist community.[42] They held almost all the surplus grain, due to the general indebtedness and excessive prior hypothecation of crops prevailing in the district. The entire

36 Ibid., vol. 4: p. 387.
37 Ibid., vol. 8: p. 483.
38 Ibid., vol. 11: p. 429.
39 Ibid., vol. 4: p. 160, 53F–G, 4 Feb. 1897.
40 LRP, 1896, nos. 34–35, p. 202.
41 FRFRO, Saran, 1896–97, p. 9, paras. 27–28.
42 LRP, March 1899, nos. 14–15, p. 351.

export fund of grain in Champaran between September and November 1896 consisted, in fact, of the bhadoi crops already in the hands of the dealers. They had, as usual, prior contracts to fulfil, and in any case naturally sought the best markets open to them for the time being. There was, moreover, a good chance of making a double profit by re-importing the same amount when local prices rose to a remunerative level.[43] In Orissa, too, the mahajans were in the habit of storing surplus paddy for years together. Due to the high prices offered by the exporters that year, a large part of it was sold to outside agents.

Thus most of the produce collected by mahajans against loans and advances ultimately reached the grain-dealer: it was either sold to the grain merchant, or retained by the mahajan in his capacity as a dealer in the hope of a further price rise, especially during famine years, as in 1896.

[2.3] Zamindars' control over the surplus through the system of produce rents

Produce rents paid to the landlord (i.e., the zamindar, lakhirajdar, gantidar or mere occupancy-holders renting out their land on barga) were partly marketed as well, though the zamindar had to reserve a greater part of his stock than the raiyat-mahajan for the support of his tenantry and dependants. In Orissa, the *amar*s or the granaries of the zamindars did not depend on the harvests of one year, but on those of many years. The dhulibhag system of rent in Parikud and the salt parganas of the Chilka often ensured more than half of the produce for the landlord. In bhaoli areas, as in south Bihar, especially under the danabandi system, the zamindar's share was very large, raiyats seldom getting more than 35 to 37.5 per cent of the gross produce. With the rising price of rice, payment in kind at the market rate was favoured by many zamindars, especially where thikadars (farmers), with whom peasants had to deal directly, were also grain dealers. Zamindars fixed the timing of kists for revenue payment at harvest time, so that crops would be carried off from the fields

43 FRFRO, Champaran, 1896–97, by D. J. Macpherson, Magistrate and Collector, vol. 2: para. 34; ch. 3, para. 43.

of the tenant in order to cover the rental. In view of the low market prices at the time of the harvest, peasants had to surrender a much larger quantity than if they paid later, when prices tended to rise. Again, insistence on a pre-harvest kist in November, as at Parikud, obliged the peasant to borrow cash, which he paid back in February-March with interest in kind at the rate of two *gounies* (measures) of paddy per rupee of the loan.

[a] Accumulation of stocks and sale of grain by the zamindars

In 1896, the zamindars of Satkhira and Nadia were reported to be generally the largest stock-holders in the area. Even at the end of the lean year of 1896, the Pal Chaudhuris of north Nadia held 53,000 md. of grain, a considerable part of which was to be sold. As noted earlier, the Roy Chaudhuris of Satkhira in Khulna, the Dey Chaudhuris of Ranaghat and the zamindars of Samta and Jadabpur in the Bongaon Subdivision of Jessore, also held sizeable stocks, most of which would be sold when prices reached the peak. The zamindars were probably eager to make the most of their stocks while the prices remained high, which partly accounted for their insistence on quick payment of the rent. In the Santhal Parganas, too, the zamindars pressed for rent in view of the high market price of rice. In October–November, the zamindars' stocks in Orissa were very large despite frequent sales, for they stored the surplus for years together. One of the informants, Raja Baidyanath in Cuttack, himself had paddy worth Rs. 25,000. In Kodhar and Koralo in Orissa, zamindars and mukaddams having a large stock of paddy refused to lend that year.[44] In Palamau and Manbhum in Chotanagpur, the Deputy Commissioner could arrange to open relief works only by borrowing 2,400 md. of rice for the purpose from leading zamindars. H. Luson, Deputy Commissioner of Manbhum, noted that foodstocks were very unevenly distributed. It was held mainly by the zamindars and substantial cultivators, who would keep most of it for sale outside the district.[45] The zamindar of

[44] *Selection of Papers,* vol. 6: p. 404.
[45] Ibid., vol. 4: p. 373, no. 1356, 19 Jan. 1897.

Untari, who was in possession of a large stock of paddy, was secretly exporting grain to Mirzapur in the NWP, while prices were still high.[46] In Hazaribagh in May 1897, enormous local stores still existed in the golas of the mahajans and landowners, which would soon be available in the bazars.[47] In Biru Pargana in Lohardaga, rice was selling cheaper than elsewhere, as the local zamindars had stopped exporting grain. In March April 1897, raiyats in Lohardaga had mostly sold their surplus produce, while the zamindars and banias having large stocks still held off in anticipation of a further rise in prices.[48] Though hoarding by zamindars and affluent peasants was common in bhaoli areas like Patna and Jahanabad, a large part of the produce rent paid to the landlord ultimately found its way to the market.

This extortion of the small peasant was completed by the activities of the grain dealers. While the zamindar and mahajan siphoned off his meagre surplus into the market, the bania controlled its flow and distribution in such a way as to preclude any possibility of his buying back grain for his own consumption.

46 Ibid., vol. 5: p. 309.
47 Ibid., vol. 8: p. 400.
48 Ibid., vol. 6: pp. 296, 329.

7

Pull Failure and the Generation of Purchasing Power

The progress of the famine was marked by a deepening exchange crisis. As seen earlier, food shortage did not lead directly to famine, but merely intensified the existing tensions, inequalities and entitlement problems within the peasant economy. It affected the supply position, while the shift in exchange relations reduced the purchasing power or effective demand of a large section of the community. While a decline in food supply would thus lead to starvation, the change in entitlement values determined the pattern of that starvation, for a famine seldom, if ever, affected all groups within a given society.

[1] *The Exchange Crisis*

[1.1] Long-term entitlement failures during the 1890s

As noted in chapter 2, certain long-term developments other than food shortage were persistently reducing the production-, labour- and trade-based entitlements of various sections of the rural population throughout the last decade of the nineteenth century.

The secular rise in agricultural prices in this period neither benefited the average peasant, nor effected a corresponding rise in labour wages. Since open-market conditions did not prevail, the small producer and the labourer hardly had any share in the rising profits of the grain trade. The marketable surplus of the peasant, if any, was controlled by the rural power structure rather than the price mechanism. The growing insistence of the landlords on the commutation of cash into produce rentals is significant in this context. According to K. L. Datta, the index of agricultural income registered an increase of a mere 2 per cent during 1894–1904, while that of commodity prices went up by 10.5 per cent. Despite the limited representativeness of the data used, the Datta Committee Report concluded on the basis of this broad trend, that "the rise in the cost of living has been all along more than the rise in the agricultural income, showing that the cultivators in these parts have been adversely affected by high prices".[1]

Meanwhile payments in grain, the existence of bonded labour, and the complicated working of the system of compound interest ruled out any chances of a wage rate based rationally on agricultural price indices. According to one estimate, real agricultural wage in Bengal and Bihar moved up by a mere 1.5 per cent during 1896–1901.[2]

Simultaneously, several rural trades and industries such as weaving, ivory-carving, pottery-making and sericulture suffered from a variety of reasons discussed earlier. The profits of the silk industry, for instance, had fallen so low due to foreign competition, frequent silkworm epidemics in Murshidabad, and the reclamation of the asan forests where the cocoons were reared in Angul, that they could hardly finance the high mulberry rentals.

These broad trends caused much regular starvation among certain sections of the rural society during the last decade of the nineteenth century, and made them particularly vulnerable to famines. It was against this background that the linkage effects of a widespread crop failure in 1896 caused an exchange crisis of grave dimensions.

[1.2] 1896–97

[a] The crop-related failures in exchange entitlement

Of the crop-related failures, the most obvious were in the meagre surplus or share of the small peasant and bargadar, which were

1 Datta, *Enquiry into the Rise in Prices*, ch. 13, p. 183, para. 435.
2 Ghosh, *Agricultural Labourers*, p. 173, table 6.25.

directly and immediately hit by the reduction in crop size. Distress sales of land increased by 26.8 per cent and mortgages by 33.26 per cent in this year of famine, affording some indication of the pressure felt by the raiyats in the districts affected. In case of deeds of optional registration, instruments of mortgage of a value less than Rs. 100 showed a large and significant increase.[3]

Simultaneously, the contraction of field operations in a lean season abruptly reduced employment opportunities for the agricultural labourers, and also the numerous class of small peasants who supplemented their income from land by working as hired farmhands. Due to the poor yield in 1896, the latter pressed down with increasing force on the rural labour market. Faced with this labour surplus and a fall in demand, wages went down visibly by 33 to 50 per cent in most of the famine-hit districts.

Trade-based entitlements sank low as well, since the weather conditions affecting foodcrop production in 1896 had an equally disastrous effect on large areas of the cash-crop sector. The mulberry cultivation in Murshidabad, the lac industry in Manbhum, as well as the production of sugar-cane, tobacco, jute and oilseeds in all the districts of Chotanagpur, of date juice and jaggery in western Jessore, and of mango in Nadia suffered a severe setback, adversely affecting the foodgrain entitlement of all those who dealt in them. Moreover, a crop failure naturally reduced the level of purchasing power in an agrarian society, causing an overall depression in rural trades and services. The trade situation in Khulna-Jessore in 1896 was typical of this slump. Rural services such as those of the barber, washerman, boatman, blacksmith, priest and chaukidar suffered as well, as the average consumer had to cut down on other necessities, to be able to buy food at famine prices.

In fact, the fear psychosis which enveloped the entire peasant economy in a season of scarcity or famine, eroded the very basis of the existing patterns of exchange entitlement. It temporarily suspended all normal socio-economic functions and obligations between different groups in the rural society. Various

[3] *Report of the Registration Department*, no. 497 P.-D. from C. W. Bolton, Chief Secy. to the Govt. of Bengal, to the Secy. to the Govt. of India, Home Dept., Darjeeling, 24 September 1897.

manifestations of this phenomenon in 1896 have been noted in chapter 5. In the redefined pattern of entitlements which emerged under pressure of the crisis, the subordinates suffered almost in every instance.

Thus, the exchange failure in 1896–97 was primarily due to the linkage effects of a shortfall in agricultural production.

[b] Exogenous factors aggravating the exchange crisis in specific areas

Certain coincidental factors intensified the exchange problem arising from food shortage. These, however, were purely localised phenomena, affecting only the areas concerned.

The indigo industry in Muzaffarpur, for instance, suffered a sharp decline which first set in during this year of famine, though it took nearly a decade for the full results to show. Indigo cultivation being labour-intensive, the decline in this industry had a close bearing on the local problems of unemployment and exchange failure.[4] Lac and mica production declined in 1896–97, while stringent market conditions hit hard both at the lac and coal industries in Chotanagpur. In eastern Bengal, fishermen had a difficult year, as the rivers remained saline due to scanty rainfall. Manjhis (boatmen) suffered, as high winds and northwesters made navigation perilous. The filatures in Murshidabad closed down after the failure of the March bund in 1897, thus laying off a large number of workers during the worst months of famine. Meanwhile, the effects of the prohibition of salt manufacture were being deeply felt precisely during this time by the molunghee population in the Chilka tract.

4 *DG: Muzaffarpur*, p. 84.

[2] Government Response to the Exchange Problem in 1896–1897

[2.1] Context and principles of the famine relief policy

There was a sharp drop in the agricultural wage rates all over Bengal in 1896. In Nadia the labourers usually received 1 to 2½ an. and one meal per day in the paddy-cutting season, whereas in 1896–97, the poorer cultivators forming the mass of the population had practically no crops and hence could not afford to employ outside labour.[5] At Magura in Jessore, the usual rates of 4 an. a day had been reduced to 13 pice, i.e., a fall of 25 per cent, while at Lohagara too, the wages of agricultural servants fell by 25 per cent, from Rs. 4 to Rs. 3 per month.[6] At the prevailing prices of rice, the current wages were insufficient for the maintenance of the day labourers. There was no appreciable reduction in wages in places with a relatively good out-turn or access to important trade centres, as at Polta, Nalta and Garapota in Bongaon, Jessore.[7] In south Khulna paddy-cutting rates had been reduced to 33 per cent of the normal, as men from Nadia, western Khulna and other regions prone to scarcity crowded there in search of work this year. At Bardal in Satkhira, Khulna, about 50 per cent of the usual wages were given for the little field work available; instead of 3 an. and a meal a day, the men were content to work for 2 an. and no meal. A few months earlier, District Board contractors paid 5 an. to each coolie per diem in Khulna, while by November 1896, forty coolies were working for 2½ an. per diem, a 50 per cent cut, pointing to great distress.[8] This continued in Khulna until September 1897, by which time the promise of a good aman crop once again raised the labour wages to their normal level. In Rajshahi, at the end of September 1896 the price of rice was phenomenally high, but the wages of labour were almost the same as in an ordinary year. The average rate in the most acutely affected area was from 1 anna 6 pies to 2 annas 6 pies, while in the Barind and bilan

5 *Selection of Papers*, vol. 2: pp. 182–3.
6 Ibid., vol. 3: p. 205; vol. 4: p. 316.
7 Ibid., vol. 5: pp. 232–34.
8 Ibid., vol. 3: p. 180, 204.

lands it ranged between 3 and 4 an., so that labourers from the first tract flocked there in search of work.[9]

In Bihar, wages were particularly low and had remained static for the last twenty years; they were further depressed as elsewhere in 1896–97, leading to acute distress, especially in the rice belt along the Nepal border. In Palamau and Manbhum, pressure on the relief works despite unprecedentedly low rates testified to the prevailing distress. In Malda, the normally high wage rate of 4 an. a day fell by 30 to 40 per cent.[10]

In the face of this deepening exchange crisis throughout the Province in 1896–97, the administration sought to *(a)* generate purchasing power by offering employment upon test works—later converted to full-fledged relief works either under the control of the civil officers or of the Public Works Department, and following various work and wage systems; and *(b)* to create a direct entitlement offered in the form of grain or money doles or of cooked food for the weak, infirm and needy, who could not come on to these works.

The basic principle of government relief was thus to prevent loss of life by providing the bare means of subsistence, either through wage labour or by gratuitous relief to those physically incapable of labour in any form. Indirect measures such as occasional remissions of land revenue and the offer of loans and advances were mere appendages to these two forms of relief, which together constituted the essence of the government's response to the problem of entitlement failure.

[2.2] Organisation of famine relief

The broad outlines of famine relief were laid down at the Sonepur Conference of 20 November 1896, attended by the Lieutenant Governor himself. The details were worked out on this basis at the Muzaffarpur Conference of 4–5 December by Mr Glass, Chief Engineer and Secretary to the Bengal Government in the Public Works Department, the Commissioner and Collectors of north Bihar, and other local officials. The affected areas of the Patna Division were to be divided into charges of approximately 300

9 Ibid., pp. 263–64.
10 Ibid., vol. 8: p. 482.

miles in extent, each under a superintendent. A charge was generally subdivided into ten circles, each under a circle officer. As distress deepened into famine in other parts of the Province, the system adopted in north Bihar was extended elsewhere. The final structure of relief administration in each affected district is shown in table 53.[11]

For supervision of the charges and circles, the three sources of official, military and non-official agencies were drawn upon. Initially, all works were under civil agency in the Patna Division, a fully organised work usually consisting of an officer in charge, a sub-overseer, a cashier, a gang of *muharrirs* or mates in charge of labour gangs, as well as peons, water carriers and treasure guards. In districts less severely affected, the organisation was not so elaborate as in Bihar. Yet the principle everywhere was the same, except in the Santhal Parganas, where the local village agency was employed in place of circle officers.

[a] Relief works: labour and wage systems

The works undertaken were primarily meant to test the necessity for relief, while ensuring at the same time the maximum permanent benefit they could bestow on the country. The number and nature of these works were conditioned by the specific requirements of the area affected, as is apparent in table 54.

Thus, 92 per cent of the works were tanks and reservoirs, or earthwork on roads. The District Board in Champaran could not afford to take on the maintenance and bridging of expensive embanked roads, the emphasis being on the excavation of tanks. The embankment of the Bettiah-Bagaha railway line and work on the Tribeni Canal progressed. A distinct prejudice against tank and well irrigation in Saran, and the urgency to improve communications in Muzaffarpur, led to a stress on road works in these districts. In Darbhanga, the work on roads and tanks struck a more even balance. In Chotanagpur, irrigation projects were largely adopted, as for instance the scheme from the Nadaura river in Palamau. In Bankura, where the lack of communication was being deeply felt, the construction and

11 *Final Resolution*, p. 30.

TABLE 53

Relief Administration in the Famine Zones

Division	*District*	*Number of charges*	*Number of circles*	*Average area in square miles of each*		*Average population of each*	
				charge	*circle*	*charge*	*circle*
1	2	3	4	5	6	7	8
Patna	Shahabad	5	21	326	78	76,400	18,100
	Saran	7	63	332	37	321,862	35,762
	Champaran	8	71	410	46	232,433	26,189
	Muzaffarpur	11	94	242	28	209,727	24,542
	Darbhanga	12	90	245	33	201,465	26,862
	Total	**43**	**339**	**298**	**37**	**214,397**	**27,195**
Bhagalpur	Bhagalpur	2	6	250	83	162,500	54,166
	Santhal Parganas	4	64	330	20	942,79	5,892
	Total	**6**	**70**	**303**	**26**	**117,019**	**10,030**
Chotanagpur	Hazaribagh	5		1404		232,864	
	Palamau	4	24	1226	204	149,192	24,865
	Manbhum	4	12	843	281	248,774	82,925
	Total	**13**	**36**	**1,177**	**229**	**212,014**	**44,218**
Burdwan	Bankura	4	7	263	150	103,225	58,986
Presidency	Nadia	5	17	236	69	125,168	36,814
	Murshidabad	1	5	205	41	120,000	24,000
	Khulna	2	9	237	53	138,000	30,666
	Total	**8**	**31**	**232**	**61**	**128,355**	**33,124**
Orissa	Puri	2	8	182	45	59,500	14,875

Source: Final Resolution, p. 30.

TABLE 54

Nature of Relief Works

Relief works	*Patna*	*Bhagalpur*	*Chotanagpur*	*Burdwan*	*Presidency*	*Orissa*	*Total*
Wells	1		7				8
Tanks & Irrigation reservoirs	404	34	235	2	62	28	765
Roads	416	24	98	32	79	2	651
Railway embankments	2						2
Embankments	13			5	1	11	30
Roads on which metal collected			4	1	1		6
Canals & irrigation channels	43		1		2		46
Other works	22					1	23
Total	901	58	345	40	145	42	1,531

Source: Ibid., ch. 6, p. 38.

upkeep of roads were mainly undertaken. In the Presidency Division, especially Khulna, attention was focussed on the problems of water supply: the excavation of the Bhairab Canal was expected to improve the water supply of a large portion of Meherpur subdivision. Tanks and embankments, rather than the bridging of roads, were also resorted to in the Chilka tract of Puri in Orissa, keeping in view the problem of saline infiltrations which breached the bunds in the famine year, destroying the crops and causing an acute scarcity of sweet water in the region.

At the test works, attempts were initially made to form large gangs of sixty to seventy members, the task being worked out for the gang as a whole after taking into consideration the lengths of lift and lead. On being found unwieldy, the "pit gang" of about four diggers in a pit, with a suitable number of carriers, was introduced as the unit of the work system since mid-March, 1897. The standard tasks as finally prescribed were 200, 125 and 85 cubic feet per digger in soft, medium and hard soil, respectively. The carriers' tasks were regulated by the horizontal distance of the pit from the spoil-bank, that is, the lead, and the vertical height to the spoil-bank from the centre of the pit, i.e., the lift.

The wage system varied with the system of work adopted. At the outset, attempts were made to set out the individual tasks to each member of the gang, the task of each digger being measured and the wages calculated on a daily basis. The total aggregate earnings of the gang were then paid in a lump sum to the headman. This system, however, proved impracticable (as the measurement of individual tasks was time consuming) and tended to drag interminably; payments to the gang thus fell into arrears, leading to fraud and discontent.

Next, the work of the gang was measured as a whole, the total wages being made over to the muharrir or gang mates for distribution. But, though time was saved on measurement, ample scope was still there for malpractices over wage distribution by the headman. Besides, those working hard were fined alike with the idle members of the gang for failure to perform the daily task. If the digger alone was tasked, the carriers were fined along with the digger.

This problem persisted with the introduction of the small pit gang, though measurement was greatly facilitated. The power of the muharrir to inflict fines was finally reduced by the adoption of the Blackwood system, by which gangs were paid at the end of the task rather than the day. If the gang worked well, the task was completed and paid for within the day; if it was lax, the task may drag on to two days, the full wage for one day alone being nevertheless paid. The system was practically one of piecework, with a maximum payment not exceeding one day's wage.

At the height of the crisis, since May 1897, piecework was adopted extensively as a more efficient and workable system, which would also enable the worker to support his dependants. Yet even in such cases, the weak and the feeble stood the risk of being edged out by professional labourers, while the petty contractor often crept in by influencing the mate of a gang.

Full or minimum wages were calculated either by adding the money value of the different items in a full or minimum ration as quantified in the Famine Code, or by taking the money value of the "grain equivalent", i.e., the amount of grain which was in normal times equal in cash value to the total items of the ration.

The average maximum ration of an adult male and female consisted of 16.5 and 15 chitaks respectively by the standard weight, with 7.5 and 6 ch. for big and small children. The minimum entitlement for these different categories would be 14, 13, 6 and 6 ch. respectively.[12] The inter-district and intra-district wage level varied according to the different staples which were taken as the grain equivalent. The average relief wages paid throughout the famine differed little in the different districts:

TABLE 55

Average Relief Wages per Head

District	*Annas*	*Pies*
Shahabad	1	3
Saran	0	11
Champaran	1	2
Muzaffarpur	1	2
Darbhanga	1	3

12 *Final Resolution*, p. 36.

Bhagalpur	1	1
Santhal Parganas	1	7
Hazaribagh	1	8
Palamau	1	8
Manbhum	1	8
Bankura	2	6
Nadia	1	9
Murshidabad	2	1
Khulna	1	2
Puri	1	10

Source: Ibid., ch. 6, p. 36.

[b] Gratuitous relief

With the deepening distress, pressure increased both upon relief works and gratuitous relief, though the pattern was not identical. The average daily numbers on gratuitous relief exceeded those at the works since May 1897 until the end of the famine. While attendance at relief works fell off with the breaking of the monsoon, the number of those gratuitously relieved remained almost constant, the maximum numbers amounting to 25 per cent and 90 per cent respectively of those in 1873–74; this was because the latter represented more or less a fixed percentage of the population, largely the sick and disabled, the aged and the destitute, who even in normal times were dependent upon others. As the deepening crisis caused the sources of private charity to dry up, this segment of the population, their numbers reinforced by the respectable poor and families deserted by their menfolk, drifted on to the government lists and were obliged to remain there till the return of normalcy. It thus reflected a change in the entitlement pattern of certain groups, due to the temporary suspension of normal social ties and obligations in the face of a crisis.

The highest percentage of those on gratuitous relief to the total population of the affected area amounted to 3.92, 1.79, 1.13, 10.43, 2.91 and 3.83 on an average in the Patna, Bhagalpur, Chotanagpur, Presidency, Burdwan and Orissa Divisions, respectively. The average for the Presidency Division was raised greatly by the exceptionally high percentage of the gratuitously relieved in Nadia (13.27 per cent) and Khulna (3.99

per cent) while in Patna Division, Shahabad recorded a high of 6.35 per cent.[13]

In the Presidency Division, the disinclination of women, especially the Muslims, to come on relief works accounted for the great pressure on gratuitous relief; in the Patna Division, it was largely due to the high incidence of male migrations, and the spread of a debilitating disease attributed to the eating of khesari grain. The pattern is corroborated by the percentage of women and children to the total number gratuitously relieved (Table 56).

TABLE 56

Women and Children on Gratuitous Relief

Division	*Percentage of women & children to total gratuitously relieved*
Patna	82.06
Bhagalpur	81.90
Chotanagpur	79.58
Burdwan [Bankura District]	79.80
Presidency	91.12
Orissa [Puri District]	84.50

Source: Ibid., ch. 7, p. 51.

The Presidency Division stands out prominently in the list, due to the peculiar circumstances of the Nadia and Khulna districts, as noted above.

[2.3] Role of the government relief measures in generating purchasing power

The actual as against the estimated cost of relief, as sanctioned by the government, indicates a measure of the purchasing power created. The net result of relief operations throughout the famine, reducing the persons relieved to terms of one day, shows that in the fifteen affected districts 61,018,611 people were relieved for one day on works, and 70,783,120 gratuitously. The average daily cost per head of expenditure on the wages of workers, excluding contingencies, amounted to 1 anna, 4.9 pies per diem,

[13] *Final Resolution,* ch. 7, pp. 50–51.

and the average daily gratuitous dole to 8.6 pies per head; the total daily cost per person relieved, exclusive only of the compensation paid for land and crops, amounted to 1 anna 3 pies. Even the Lieutenant Governor admitted that the cost per head per day was "very moderate". The net expenditure was nearly Rs. 55 million less than that spent by the government during the earlier famine year of 1873–74.[14]

TABLE 57

Famine Relief Expenditure (1896–97)

	Estimated (Rs.)	*Actual (Rs.)*	*Saving (Rs.)*
Relief works, gratuitous relief, salaries & establishment	11,293,093	10,961,981	+ 331,112
Advances under Land Improvement Act	1,192,522	282,566	+909,956
Bounties for wells	4,467	7,458	–2,991
Total	12,490,082	11,252,005	1,238,077

Source: Ibid., p. 58.

Even this moderate volume of purchasing power created, was not always effectively circulated. The impact of the measures, whether in generating purchasing power through payment of wages at the relief works, or in creating direct entitlements to food through gratuitous relief, was marred by *(a)* the stringency of wages and rigour of the tasks, especially at the test works, which often proved too much for a starving and enfeebled population; *(b)* manipulation by contractors, gang mates and local distributive agencies.

[a] Stringency of wages and rigour of tasks

Private relief works were as a rule preferred to government works, largely on account of the rigorous exaction of tasks at the latter. In the affected tracts of Muzaffarpur, for instance, the numbers at the works rose very slowly in spite of acute distress, partly owing to the high tasks set by the Collector on roads, and partly due to his decision not to employ labour on tank-digging as a

[14] Ibid., ch. 9, pp. 57–58.

means of relief.[15] Again, when there was intense pressure at the works in Manbhum, ordinary full work was expected for test purposes, instead of the 3/5 prescribed in Mr Glass's standard tables.[16] Failure to consider either the distance of the works from the affected villages, or the distinct local bias against earthwork in certain districts like Jessore and Khulna, acted as further deterrents.[17] The duration of the works was also a vital factor, for they were expected to cover the periods of acute distress. The hurried and injudicious closure of the works in Manbhum, for instance, at the end of August 1897, invited criticism even from the Commissioner, Mr A. Forbes.[18] As he pointed out, Manbhum contained a large kamia population who were out of work at the time. They had nothing to fall back on, as the crops in this district were reaped later than in Lohardaga and Hazaribagh, while it lacked the forest resources of Palamau.

The wages paid at the government test and relief works were as a matter of policy kept at the very minimum, i.e. barely at the subsistence level. They did not often take account of the current prices of food staples, in calculating the subsistence requirements.[19] For instance, in Bankura the average earned by each individual at the government test work in May 1897 was 1 anna, 6 pies to 1 anna, 9 pies. With rice selling in the tract at 8 sr. for the rupee, this earning was not sufficient. It would buy scarcely three-fourth sr. rice, leaving no provision for pulses or

15 LRP, Aug. 1898, pt. 2, Report on the Operations for the Prevention and Relief of Famine in the Patna Div., 1896–97, p. 8, para. 35.

16 *Selection of Papers*, vol. 12: p. 302.

17 The unpopularity of task works in famine tracts was no new feature. During the potato famine in Ireland, tasks were so "furiously disliked" in Limerick, that the County Surveyor "dreaded an outbreak", which did occur at Ballingarry on 27 October 1846 (Woodham-Smith, *Great Hunger,* p. 127).

18 *Selection of Papers*, vol. 11: p. 444, no. 824 F, Calcutta, 8 Sept. 1897. Memo by A. Forbes, Esq., Comm., Chotanagpur Div.

19 A similar situation existed in Ireland in 1846, hostile demonstrations following low rates of payment at the relief works. Father Mathew wrote from Cork: "a shilling a day or even one and sixpence is nothing to a poor man with a large family if he has to pay 2 d. a lb. for Indian meal" (Woodham-Smith, *Great Hunger*, p. 127).

vegetables, or for more than one mouth to feed.[20] The Collector of Bankura admitted that the wages paid were about 25 per cent lower than the rates sanctioned by Mr Glass.[21] Again, in Champaran the conversion rate remained at 9½ sr. of rice per rupee from 21 January to 27 July 1897, though for most of this period almost the entire population had been living on Burma rice at about 7½ to 8 sr.—a difference of 2 sr. per rupee, or 26.6 per cent. A still lower or penal wage was devised, and no task could earn more than the prescribed daily wage. In Palamau, rates were reduced on road works in April 1897. Though piecework rates were raised throughout the Division by June, they still did not conform to the current grain prices.[22] The test rate enforced at the relief works in Manbhum was 25 per cent lower than any rate previously known in the district.[23] In the Santhal Parganas, the local people boycotted the test works in protest against their rigour and low wages in May, 1897, apprehending that the acceptance of such terms would permanently lower the customary rates.

[b] Manipulation by contractors and gang mates

There was ample scope for manipulation by the contractors and gang mates, in the measurement of tasks and payment of dues at the relief works. The systematic exploitation of the tribals might have accounted for the unpopularity of the government relief works in Chotanagpur, Bhagalpur and Bankura. In a comparable situation in Ireland in 1846, tickets were bought and sold freely for admission on to relief works, landlords and the clergy vying with each other to enter the names of their own men on the rolls.[24] The role of the middlemen and local distributive agencies was even more vital in case of gratuitous relief. For instance, the panchayats often included all residents

20 *Selection of Papers*, vol. 8: p. 518.
21 Ibid., vol. 9: p. 537, no. 545, Bankura, 17 June 1897. From G. E. Manisty Esq., Collector, Bankura, to the Comm., Burdwan Div.
22 Ibid., vol. 7: p. 403; vol. 8: p. 415; vol. 11: p. 394.
23 Ibid., vol. 12: p. 339.
24 Woodham-Smith, *Great Hunger*, p. 146.

of their respective villages in the lists of recipients, to the exclusion of the really needy. Village chaukidars entrusted with the relief of *pardanashin* women entered fictitious names on the rolls, and misappropriated funds. The banias were another potent source of trouble, for "they were constantly using short weights, issuing short doles, or doles of grain mixed with earth".[25]

[3] *Response of Labour to Government Relief Measures: Socio-economic Determinants*

The wage rates in different regions and the labourers' response and attendance at the government relief works were determined by several factors, both sociological and economic.

[3.1] Drought-prone or surplus disticts

There was a basic difference in the people's attitude towards relief in the typically drought-prone and normally surplus districts. In the famine-prone regions like Nadia, people were used to relief and more ready to work at low famine rates than in the normally well-off districts like Khulna, Jessore, Pabna, Rajshahi or Manbhum. In the affected tract in northwest Nadia, ordinary wages were very low, varying from 6 to 10 pice per diem with or without the midday meal, the average daily wage being 8 pice without a meal. Hence, earnings at the relief works were higher than normal agricultural wages. This attracted a much larger number of persons to the relief works than would be the case if the ordinary wages of day labourers were a great deal higher than the relief wages, as in Satkhira. Besides, there was a visible difference between the people of Nadia and those of Satkhira in their attitude towards government relief. In Nadia the people were quite used to relief and would flock to the test works on feeling the slightest pinch.[26] In Murshidabad and Bankura, likewise, the works attracted a large number of people. In Satkhira, however, the cultivators were more self-reliant and independent, and many of them would sooner sell off their cattle

25 LRP, Aug. 1898, pt. 3; FRFRO, Saran, ch. 5, para. 83.
26 *Selection of Papers*, vol. 3: p. 229.

or leave their homes, than resort to the relief works. Long accustomed to years of prosperity and a relatively comfortable life, people in this district were unable to take the same stand against distress as those living upcountry. Even Pods, Kamars, Muchis and other relatively inferior castes would not come on relief works, though evidently suffering for want of sufficient food.[27]

In Rajshahi, similarly, the inhabitants of the Gangetic tract were somewhat above the average of Bengal with regard to wealth, and local labourers refused to work at the famine rate of 2 an. a day.[28] The same was the case in Bogra and Pabna. The sacrifice of accepting employment at the relief works on 1¼ an. a day was much greater in Pabna (where the usual wages were 4 an.) than in Bihar where they were about half that amount, the fall being 62 per cent and 38 per cent, respectively.[29] At Sirajganj in Pabna, the coolies were clamouring for higher wages although they were being paid at the high rate of four to five rupees per thousand cubic feet.[30] The Malda peasantry were also relatively well-off and hence averse to attending relief works.

In Chotanagpur, especially Manbhum and Singbhum, peasants were drawing on the resources of the forests, and were selling off ornaments to buy food.

In Orissa, however, as in Nadia, the raiyats, being used to relief, were more dependent on the government works whenever crops failed.[31]

[3.2] Social composition of local population

The social composition of the bulk of the local population also determined wage rates and the demand for labour. For example, unlike Satkhira, a large population in northwest Nadia (about one-fifth to one-third) was composed of landless labourers or petty cultivators who depended mainly upon the wages of day labour, which accounted for the low wage rates even in ordinary

27 Ibid., vol. 6: p. 250.
28 Ibid., vol. 3: p. 261.
29 Ibid., vol. 3: p. 282.
30 Ibid., vol. 8: p. 554.
31 Ibid., vol. 4: p. 419.

times. Even people of the middle classes here mostly lived on the produce of the lands, and the labourers depended chiefly on the agriculturists for employment. Successive crop failures during the last few years had therefore equally affected almost all classes in this tract and thrown them upon the hands of the government for maintenance. There were comparatively few day labourers in east Jessore, that is, in Magura and Narail. The local population thought it degrading to work as day labourers. The only day labourers were the Bunas (descendants of aboriginal coolies, originally brought into these parts by indigo planters), and occasionally some other low castes like the Bagdis and Kahars. Owing to the paucity of day labourers, the wage rates had not substantially fallen, except in instances where the number of such men happened to be large, as at Satrujitpur, where it fell from 4 to 3 an. per diem, i.e. by 25 per cent.[32]

In Bankura, the affected areas in Raipur and Simlapal were better off than Gangajalghati. The Santhals who were numerous in the first two tracts migrated freely, while the Bauris, who formed the bulk of the population in Gangajalghati, did not emigrate and were mostly lepers and, therefore, beggars.[33]

In the northern districts of Bihar, particularly in Saran, almost the entire population consisted of labourers. In Palamau the bulk of the people belonged to the labouring classes (Ahirs, Dusadhs, Chamars, Kherwars, Bhuias, Kahars, Gareris and others of the kamia class) who were usually fed by their employers during the slack season. They were left to fend for themselves in 1896–97, which greatly increased pressure at the relief works.[34] Manbhum, too, contained thousands of labourers who were out of work that year, thus causing widespread distress. The abundant supply of field labourers here was increased in 1896–97 by the kamias whose masters could not feed them, and by the colliery coolies who had been thrown out of work by the slackness of the coal trade. Of the labourers in these parts, the castes that predominated were the Bauris, Bagdis, Santhals, Haris, Mals (snake charmers), Koras (diggers), Bhuiyas, Sunris and Jolahas.[35]

32 Ibid., vol. 4: pp. 307, 313.
33 Ibid., vol. 8: p. 532.
34 Ibid., vol. 4: p. 328.
35 Ibid., vol. 11: p. 444; vol. 12: pp. 340, 358.

[3.3] Scope for employment outside agriculture

Where there was any scope for employment besides agriculture, the pressure on land might be temporarily relieved and the fall in wages less pronounced. In Satkhira, for example, labourers tried to supplement their income by mat-weaving from aquatic sedge, extracting date juice, fishing, boat rowing and woodcutting in the Sunderbans. But the manufacture of *gur* (jaggery) from date juice was nearly over by March 1897. The *meha* reed from which mats were made could not now be had, for it was procurable only in September–October. The fishermen were comparatively well off and a new industry in fish had sprung up: drying of prawns for the Calcutta market. But the fishermen complained of very low prices this year, and fish was getting scarce day by day, as the water was becoming more salty and the rivers more rough on account of high winds. Fuel sold cheap, and the woodcutters in the Sunderbans had no capital to pay the forest dues. The Muslims of Magura and Narail in Jessore were expert boatmen, largely employed in the internal river traffic of Bengal. But, due to the northwesters, navigation was more perilous, and the boatmen felt the strain just as the effects of famine were first being felt in March–April 1897. Salt manufacture would have been a lucrative trade in Satkhira, but this was ruled out as a matter of government policy. In Nadia some of the labourers were trying out new types of work, such as the sale of dry aman straw.[36] The excavation and re-excavation of tanks due to a local water famine also provided some relief. In Jessore, rearing of date trees and cattle gave the people some alternative source of employment. Bongaon in Jessore formed the westernmost part of the important date-palm tract of central Bengal. But the tapping season, normally continuing until mid-March, ended early this year, for the weather was already warm by February. Due to the dry nature of the soil in 1897, the yield of juice and jaggery proved deficient, prices ruling about 8 to 12 an. lower per md. than usual. In parts of Bongaon, poorer people took part in the ragpicking business. The ragpickers took advances from the traders and supplied them with rags, which

[36] Ibid., vol. 3: pp. 200, 203, 228; vol. 5: pp. 204–5; vol. 6: p. 220.

were taken to Calcutta and sold to Bally and other paper mills.[37] In Murshidabad, the problem had been accentuated by the general depression in the silk industry and the all but absolute failure of the March bund. This led to the closure of the numerous silk filatures from mid-March to July 1897, thus laying off a large number of labourers at the height of the famine.[38]

The situation was better in north Bengal, as the silk industry and indigo cultivation provided some relief in Malda, while in Rajshahi there were reasonable prospects of employment in connection with jute, silk, indigo and other industries, the mulberry and jute crops being particularly good this year.[39]

In Orissa, the mass of the population were hit hard by the famine, as they were largely employed in agricultural pursuits. The prohibition of salt manufacture intensified the problem in the affected regions along the Chilka. The railways, however, drew away a sizeable percentage of labourers who would otherwise be dependent on relief.

The decline of the labour-intensive indigo industry had a close bearing on the wage problem in north Bihar, particularly Muzaffarpur, which already had a labour surplus of 68 per cent.[40] In Chotanagpur, the labouring classes were better off in ordinary years, due principally to the growth of the coal and mica mining industries, and the lac trade in Manbhum. There was a rise in the wages of the unskilled labourers during the past five years largely due to employment opportunities in the lac industry, and ordinary coolies were not often available for less than 3 an. per diem. There was a further demand for labour in the newly opened coal mines and the tea districts, the construction of the Bengal-Nagpur Railway and the Jharia extension line having facilitated transit to such new fields of employment.[41] In 1896, however, the shrinkage in the coal trade and depression in the important lac industry in Manbhum, increased pressure at the relief works. About forty collieries and 25 per cent of the lac factories employing a large number of Kols and Bhuiyas, were

37 Ibid., vol. 5: pp. 226, 232.
38 Ibid., vol. 6: p. 230.
39 Ibid., vol. 3: pp. 248, 261.
40 *DG: Muzaffarpur*, p. 84.
41 *Selection of Papers*, vol. 4: p. 351.

shut down. Mica production declined by 12 per cent, tea by 47 per cent, while no copper and tin mines were worked this year.[42] Although emigration increased, the closure of alternative fields of employment in such a year forced down wages, especially due to the simultaneous growth of the floating kamia population. This explains the large attendance at the road works in Palamau in April 1897 despite reduced rates, or the pressure on the test works in Manbhum, even when the wage offered was 25 per cent lower than any rate previously known in the district.

[3.4] Migration

Migration relieved pressure in certain areas and partially checked a further fall in the local wage rates. For example, due to large-scale migrations from western Khulna to the southeast of the district, particularly to the newly reclaimed abads in the mitha desh or Sunderbans area, there was not enough local labour available for repairing embankments in Satkhira. Almost all the professional labourers of the affected tracts in Nadia (as in the Karimpur-Daulatpur tract) had migrated by January 1897 to Calcutta, the Rarh (Burdwan), Barind (Malda-Dinajpur), and the Sunderbans in search of work; hence those attending the local relief works in Nadia were mostly unprofessional. From Jessore, a larger number of men than usual had migrated to cut paddy in the Sunderbans, and also to serve as coolies and hawkers in Calcutta, and an unusually large number of petty money orders were being received in the district. The exodus from Midnapur to the *Namal Desh* (new settlements in the Sunderbans) was abnormally large this year.[43] Parts of Bankura, like the Raipur and Simlapal thanas, were particularly fortunate in having a large proportion of Santhals who migrated freely to work on railways and agriculture in other districts; Gangajalghati, in contrast, was burdened with a Bauri population who refused to move, and only added to the local beggar class.[44]

[42] *DCAR*, Chotanagpur, 1896–97, pp. 15–16, paras. 46–49.

[43] *Selection of Papers*, vol. 3: pp. 199, 202, 238; vol. 4: pp. 237, 257, 307, 404.

[44] Ibid., vol. 8: p. 522; vol. 10: p. 555.

In Saran, Muzaffarpur, Shahabad and Champaran, it was feared that the absence of a very large proportion of the adult male population who emigrated to lower Bengal and elsewhere earlier than usual this year, would weaken the gangs when relief works began in earnest. Their families, particularly the weak and infirm, were left without proper support, and were thrown on to government relief. The volume of the exodus from the north Bihar districts in 1896–97 may be gauged from the proportion of women and children on relief, and the increase in remittances from the emigrants. The amount paid by money orders (from without) in Shahabad, Saran and Muzaffarpur rose by 3 per cent, 15 per cent and 18 per cent respectively.[45] The remittances were for small amounts of Rs. 5 on the average, and were obviously not enough for the maintenance of their families, as indicated by the growing pressure on government relief. The proportion of women and children at the works in the districts of Shahabad, Saran, Champaran, and Muzaffarpur came up to 63.2, 71.7, 58.3, and 48.7 per cent respectively, while they constituted 80.8, 84.1, 77.9 and 83.2 per cent respectively, of those gratuitously relieved.[46] Thus, the migrations in north Bihar led to a difference in quality rather than the size of the labour on relief works, for the decrease in the number of male workers was more than neutralised by the increasing dependence of women and children on government relief.

Simultaneously, the influx from the North-West Provinces into the Patna Division was so great that the proportion of local men on the relief works was remarkably small in some areas. For example, of about four hundred labourers between Sasaram and the Kudra river in Shahabad, there was only one gang of local workers not exceeding thirty, all the rest being from the North-West Provinces.[47]

Due to population pressure, the Santhals in the Santhal Parganas were more ready to emigrate in 1896 than in earlier years. They usually migrated to the tea gardens in Assam. The annual Kol migrations from Lohardaga to Burdwan, Hughli

[45] LRP, Aug. 1898, pt. 2, p. 926; FRFRO, 1896–97, p. 22, para. 23.

[46] *Final Resolution*, pp. 41, 51.

[47] *Selection of Papers,* vol. 6: p. 128.

and the 24 Parganas increased greatly due to the scarcity this year.

In Orissa, the migrations to Calcutta and elsewhere in search of work were larger than usual. Interestingly, about 70 per cent of the people trekking into Cuttack in March–April 1897, came from the North-West Provinces.[48]

Thus, the migration of labourers was not an unmixed blessing: to a certain extent it relieved pressure and prevented a further fall in local wage rates; but where the proportion of adult male labourers declined sharply, their dependants were left without support while people from other districts crowded at the local relief works.

[3.5] Seasonal nature of agricultural labour

Due to the seasonal nature of agricultural labour, pressure increased at the famine works in certain periods of the year. For example, private individuals conducting works in Manbhum exploited the cheapness of labour which was a regular feature before the mahua harvest in April. On the other hand, the number of relief works fell in Hazaribagh, Lohardaga and Palamau despite higher rates in June–July 1897, as ploughing and preparation of the land for the next season had begun.[49] In Bongaon, Jessore, wages fell very low from mid-March to the end of May, when the date-tapping season was over and the weeding operations were yet to commence. Excavation of tanks by private individuals this year were carried out at very low rates during these months.[50] The low wages in Khulna in 1896 persisted until August–September 1897, when jute cutting and transplantation of the aman once again raised the demand for labour. In Rajshahi there was practically no work in the fields from mid-October to end-November, and the price of agricultural labour fell as low as 1 anna per diem in the Boalia and Durgapur outposts.[51] Relief works were deserted in Bhagalpur in March when the mahua harvest was ready for picking, while numbers

48 Ibid., vol. 7: p. 537.
49 Ibid., vol. 9: pp. 394, 428, 435.
50 Ibid., vol. 5: p. 229.
51 Ibid., vol. 3: p. 263–64.

increased at the works from April onward when field operations were over.[52] The earnings of the piece-workers in Bhagalpur were small because piece-work was introduced at a period of transition when the rains fell, so that the labourers stayed at the relief works for only part of the day and devoted the remainder of their time to agricultural operations.[53] In the Patna Division, November to mid-March was the slack season for labour. During November–December, labourers lived on the produce of their own bhadoi fields and on their earnings from working in those of their masters. During the following two and a half months they lived on the earnings from paddy cutting and had difficulty in getting along despite exchanging paddy for cheap foods like yam. This year paddy had to a large extent failed and the yam crop was scanty, so that the pressure at the relief works increased since January 1897.[54]

Ignoring these local variations caused by special influences, and considering the figures broadly for the entire famine zone, the effects of the seasons are clearly manifest. The following table brings out the pattern of the daily average number of labourers on relief works during each month of the famine year:

TABLE 58

Average Daily Labour on Relief Works (Nov. 1896–Oct. 1897)

Month	*Average daily labour*	*Increase (I) or decrease (D) per cent*
November	3,893	
December	21,990	I 465
January	157,235	I 615
February	254,531	I 61
March	264,670	I 4
April	309,365	I 17
May	376,295	I 22
June	360,698	D 4
July	218,181	D 40

52 Ibid., vol. 4: pp. 362, 373; vol. 7: p. 459.
53 Ibid., vol. 9: p. 501.
54 Ibid., vol. 1: p. 258.

August	109,402	D 50
September	35,426	D 68
October	8,672	D 75

Source: Final Res., ch. 6, p. 40.

The phenomenal increase by 615 per cent in January and a further 61 per cent in February 1897 was due to the cessation of field employment—the reaping of the winter rice was nearly over, while little could yet be done to the rabi. In March, the harvesting of the rabi checked this increase, though deepening distress prevented the figures from falling. The reaping of the spring crops was followed by a steady rise in numbers throughout April–May. The turning point came in June, though the fall in numbers was slight, due to the delayed monsoon. From then on, attendance at the works rapidly dwindled, as normal field operations were resumed and new crops came into the market.

[3.6] Social restrictions and prejudices

Social restrictions and the stigma attached to certain kinds of work often determined wage rates and the type of labour available. In many districts of central and eastern Bengal, few women came to the relief works. In Khulna, it was remarkable that no women attended the works. Here, as in the rest of east Bengal, the women, even of the lowest castes (except Chamars) were debarred by custom from appearing in public and would sooner die than come to the relief works. Hence, gratuitous relief was more essential here than in other parts of Bengal, where women of the lower classes were used to working for wages. It was suggested that some kind of light labour was suitable for the women here, such as jute-twisting or rice-husking, but no organised attempt was made to introduce this on a large scale. In Jessore too, the women were not allowed to work outside and would never attend earthworks, as they did upcountry and in west Bengal.[55] In the affected area in Nadia, it was significant that Muslim women were coming to work, which indicated real distress. In this part of the country, Muslim women had never before been known to work outside, particularly on earthwork,

[55] *Selection of Papers*, vol. 3: pp. 194, 203; vol. 4: pp. 7, 299.

which was considered most degrading. At Kaliganj in Nadia, it was reported in December 1896 that many Brahmin women had left their seclusion to come to the police station to ask for relief.[56]

Similar restrictions prevailed in north Bengal. In Rajshahi the families of both Muslims and Hindus, belonging to both higher and lower classes (with the exception of banias and fisherwomen) did not do outdoor manual work. They may come on relief works when starvation became imminent, but at that stage they would be fit only for gratuitous relief. During the famine of 1873–74, the females who came to relief works mostly belonged to the bania class. The other females in receipt of gratuitous relief were employed in cleaning Burma rice imported by government, in jute and cotton spinning, and in collecting *kunkur* (pebbles). Cotton spinning was not feasible in 1896, as the indigenous spinning wheel was now a thing of the past. Jute spinning was highly unremunerative, and kunkur could be gathered only from one or two bils in the Baghmari thana. The only work which was both remunerative and congenial to the females in this district was paddy husking. However, as no paddy would be imported this year by government, there was considerable difficulty in finding work for them.[57] The appearance of women at the test works in Pabna in May–June 1897, indicated severe distress. The lower class of Muslim women in Pabna cared very little for *purdah* (seclusion) and this was true of the country generally. Yet it did not follow that they had no objection to earthwork: their abstention in Rajshahi, where identical social conditions prevailed, pointed to the contrary.[58]

Despite reduced rates at the Pakhuria camp in Manbhum, women from respectable families were seen on relief works, indicating real distress.[59] In the Chilka tract in Puri, government officials met with similar prejudices. The mass of the population were a casteless race with the functional designation of chasa or agriculturist, probably below the Kaibartas of Bengal in race and social prestige. They obstinately refused to let their women come

56 Ibid., vol. 3: p. 230.
57 Ibid., p. 285.
58 Ibid., vol. 10: p. 575.
59 Ibid., vol. 12: pp. 301–2.

on relief works, though they gathered roots and herbs in the fields to supply themselves with food. The men demanded higher wages to support their families, which in effect implied taking on the entire adult female population of the region on a form of gratuitous relief. They were not entitled to this by the terms of the Famine Code, as they were not debarred by custom from appearing in public, which was a condition of gratuitous relief under section 43–B. It was suggested to the relief officers that if the Brahmins of Puri assured them that no loss of caste or other religious penalty would result from these women coming on to relief works with their own castes, it may influence them to do so. In fact, the officers intended to approach Rai Hari Ballabh Bose and Babu Gokulanand Chaudhuri, who possessed special influence at Puri, to obtain a *byabastha* (arrangement) giving such dispensation as was required.[60]

The men too had a distinct bias towards certain types of work, most notably towards earthwork. In Satkhira, though there was very little of field work that year and only half the usual wages were being paid, even lower castes like Pods, Kamars and Muchis could not be persuaded to attend earthwork for wages.[61] In Jessore, especially in the eastern subdivisions of Magura and Narail, the Muslims and Chandals (Namasudras), who formed the bulk of the population, considered it degrading to dig earth. The poor among them would rather accept service as agricultural servants or *krishan*s, and the smaller cultivators would sell off their cattle and ploughs and mortgage their land to avoid it. None but the aboriginal Buna coolies, and occasionally the Bagdis and Kahars, would do earthwork even at 4 an. a day.[62] Government officials maintained that these social restrictions would have been swept away if the scarcity had been really acute. But the people in these parts would undergo great privation before giving in, for they were not used to relief, unlike their counterparts in Nadia or Orissa. Even when they consented to do earthwork or to serve as coolies, they did not do so in or near their villages. Hence very little local labour was available for

60 Ibid., vol. 6: p. 396.

61 Ibid., vol. 3: p. 204; vol. 6: p. 237.

62 Ibid., vol. 4: pp. 298, 307, 311.

earthworks in Jessore and Khulna.[63] In Magura and Narail, all kinds of work for wages were looked down upon, with the sole exception of house-building (*gharami*) work. Sometimes, however, distress forced people to overrule custom and tradition. For example, in Nadia the earthworks were attended by Muslim women and unprofessional men and boys belonging to the cultivating classes, who in normal conditions would never agree to do such work. Again, many of the labourers working on a tank near Assasuni in Khulna were cultivators of the better class, some of them owning as much as thirteen or twenty bighas of land which lay fallow this year for want of seed and plough cattle.[64] Usually, however, people preferred to work for men of local standing, and were inclined to be suspicious about the nature and aim of government relief. For instance, the artisans of south Kaliganj in Nadia discouraged attempts by the government to set up an organisation for their employment, in apprehension that it might monopolise their trade.[65] The landless Brahmins, Kayasthas and men of other high castes who suffered acutely, would on no account come on to relief works. Consequently gratuitous relief had to be provided for the bhadralok community in Khulna. In Orissa, particularly the Chilka tract in Puri, people professed their willingness to do earthwork, and the repair of embankments was the readiest and most profitable form of relief work at the time.

In Chotanagpur Division, local circumstances caused the gravest concern to the government, for though the numbers at relief works were never large, there was constant anxiety due to the scattered nature of the population in the tribal belt. Government relief works were never popular in the tribal belts, whether in Chotanagpur, Bhagalpur or Bankura. Reports poured in from Lohardaga, Hazaribagh, Manbhum and other places that people inspite of acute suffering, would not come to relief works. Even if they agreed to attend, they were averse to working very far from their villages. Similarly, the local people in Santhal Parganas were boycotting the test works in protest against their

63 Ibid., pp. 299, 304.
64 Ibid., vol. 4: pp. 257, 266, 314.
65 Ibid., vol. 5: p. 208.

rigour and low wages even at the height of the famine in May 1897. The Bauris, Goalas and other half-Hinduised aboriginals of Jamtara had resisted throughout on this issue. These people, particularly the Bauris, declared they would rather die than work on government relief.[66] In Bankura, too, Santhal labourers refrained from attending test and relief works, lest the low rates offered should permanently reduce the customary wage rates.

The Famine Report of 1896–97 attributed this strong bias against government works to the aversion of the tribals towards hard labour and discipline. This interpretation, however, is hardly feasible, for the normal life of the aborigines was one of privation, involving as much, if not more, of tough routine work. A more likely explanation would be that the tribals, being liable to be exploited more systematically by the contractors and the muharrirs at the relief works, preferred to stay away from them and subsist on jungle products. The relatively high rates of mortality in Chotanagpur and Bhagalpur testify to this.

Caste and class consciousness was another vital problem faced by the government in arranging relief. In Bongaon, Jessore, the condition of the Muchis and Domes was deplorable. Most of them were day labourers, but were not employed as long as Muslim labourers were available. They did bamboo work and a little weaving, but could derive very little income from these sources this year. For tank work they were not taken, as Muslims considered it degrading to work side by side with Muchis and Domes, who were despised alike by all.[67] In Khulna there was a tendency in many of the local committees to relieve only two or three of the better castes, and to leave out the others. As the Commissioner of the Presidency Division pointed out, this was naturally to be expected, as the bhadralok were not distinguished for their sympathy with the classes which they considered below their own. Again, it was reported from Jamtara in the Santhal Parganas that owing to the abundant supply of migrant labour, the tea gardens in Assam this year were more particular as to the class of labourers sent up, and in consequence there was no

66 Ibid., vol. 8: p. 450.
67 Ibid., vol. 5: p. 230.

demand for low-caste Hindu coolies, such as Domes, Haris and Bauris.[68]

The crisis compelled people to overcome many of their social prejudices in regard not only to relief works, but to normal field operations as well. In Khulna, agriculturists this year were employing no thika labourers, or as little as possible which, as the Collector pointed out, was "the exact contrary to their usual customs".[69] As noted earlier, even cultivators owning thirteen to twenty bighas of land were seen working on a tank near Assasuni, as their fields lay unsown for want of seeds and plough cattle. In Jessore, social bias was more pronounced and agriculturists would engage farm labourers, though stinting themselves of the necessaries of life. The Muslim cultivators of Narail seem to be more aristocratic than their confrères in Magura. Very few of them would hold the plough with their own hands, and this was looked down upon by the rest. The agricultural labourers here were all men from Jhenida or Magura.[70]

In the Patna Division, especially in Gaya, the large class of kamias or bonded labourers who were bound to work for the same employer all the year round, were to be provided for by their masters. In Raipur and Simlapal in Bankura, substantial cultivators of the Utkal Brahmin caste did not work themselves, but employed low-caste labourers who were fed by them throughout the year. According to the Collector of Bankura, the existence of this form of labour here and in Gaya accounted for the better position of Raipur and Simlapal in relation to Gangajalghati, and also partly explains why distress did not occur in Gaya, though there the food prices had risen higher than in the famine districts.[71] But many of the agriculturists were unable or unwilling to provide for the kamias in a year of crisis. For example, a considerable proportion of the kamia population in Palamau and Manbhum, numbering thousands, were cast off by their masters and left to shift for themselves in 1896–97, many of the lesser zamindars having run out of cash and food.[72]

68 Ibid., vol. 7: pp. 326, 473.
69 Ibid., vol. 10: p. 336.
70 Ibid., vol. 4: p. 317.
71 Ibid., vol. 8: p. 522.
72 Ibid., vol. 10: p. 461; vol 12: p. 340.

In Malda and Purnea, most of the substantial farmers, specially the more conservative and lethargic among them, employed outside labour for work on their fields. But in 1896–97 the upcountry labourers returned from these districts without finding work, which the agriculturists would have to do themselves this year.[73] In Bhagalpur social conditions largely affected the economic situation. Here the population was wholely agricultural and fell into three classes: the Brahmin and Rajput raiyats; middle-class raiyats; and the farm labourers who were mostly Jolaha, Musahar and Dosadhs. The social pretensions of the north Bhagalpur Rajputs were higher than those of their kinsmen elsewhere in Bengal. They, along with the Brahmins, would not work with their hands, their commonest complaint being that their labourers had left them and gone to earn elsewhere the wages which they could no longer afford to give. In districts like Jessore and Bhagalpur, where social prejudices were so pronounced, agricultural loans and grain advances were perhaps more essential than relief works. Significantly, during the previous famine of 1874, the grain loans in Bhagalpur district had been threefold the amount of grain spent in wages of labour.[74]

To sum up, the wage rates, nature of relief works and the type and extent of surplus labour available in the different regions were determined by their own distinctive socio-economic problems and conditions. Of these, the most remarkable were: the difference between famine-prone and normally surplus districts in determining people's attitude towards relief and wage labour and the prevailing wage rates; the social composition of the bulk of the population and the proportion of professional labourers among them; the existence, if any, of alternative sources of employment; the unusually large volume of migrant labour in 1896–97; problems arising due to the seasonal nature of agricultural operations; and finally, the social prejudices of the people in the different parts of Bengal, with regard both to relief works and to field work in general.

73 Ibid., vol. 3: pp. 248–49.
74 Ibid., vol. 4: pp. 386–87.

8

The Response Failure in 1896–97: Directions and Problems of Grain Trade

The rationale of cash relief during a famine assumed that "pull failure" was the basis of the entitlement problem; it did not assess the strength or ability of the market to respond to the "pull" provided by the regeneration of purchasing power. The year under review, however, saw a "response failure" of grave dimensions, caused largely by the imperfections of the market and the misconceptions in government policy.

[1] *Directions of Grain Trade*

[1.1] Deviations from the normal pattern

As the famine of 1896–97 was unprecedented in dimension and extent, panic was widespread and the terms of trade went against the affected districts in the Province of Bengal.

The most acutely affected tracts appear to have been in the Patna and Presidency Divisions. Parts of the Chotanagpur and Rajshahi Divisions (the Barind, deara and bilan lands in Rajshahi district, and the Padma-Burrul areas in Pabna) may be included in the next category, where distress and scarcity were being felt, though not to the extent as in the Patna and Presidency Divisions. The problems were slightly different in Bhagalpur and Orissa, which, though not suffering from such a shortfall in agricultural production as the above regions, were fast being drained of their stocks by excessive exports. Finally, the normally surplus districts of the Dacca, Chittagong and Burdwan Divisions apprehended scarcity, but, except in Bankura, actual distress was probably not felt. Here, the main impact lay in the new directions of their grain trade.

In 1896, the areas which normally supplied foodgrains held back in apprehension of scarcity. Hence, the usual sources of supply were closed this year: from the North-West Provinces to south Bihar; from Nepal to north Bihar; from Lohardaga, Udaypur, Gangpur and Jashpur to Palamau; and from the surplus districts in East Bengal (Dacca-Chittagong Divisions) to Rangpur, Bogra, Rajshahi, Khulna, Nadia, Jessore, and even parts of Bihar. Second, instead of exporting, these normally surplus areas began to import actively in 1896, and, having greater purchasing power, succeeded in attracting supplies even from the scarcity districts. For example, agents of the North-West Provinces were busy buying up local stocks in Patna, Gaya, Shahabad, Saran and Champaran. This led to scarcity, causing grain riots and widespread panic in the Patna Division at the end of 1896. In January 1897, traders from the North-West Provinces outbid the local people and carried off grain even from Palamau, which suffered from acute scarcity. Similarly, Mymensingh and the eastern districts imported grain from Rajshahi Division. The Nakodas or Bombay merchants exported actively from Puri in Orissa. Grain also flowed from Khurda to Madras. Third, though with the progress of the famine imports increased in volume, especially in the Patna Division, it was not always possible for the scarcity districts to seek new sources of supply. The latter usually had prior commitments, and did not find it profitable to divert their stocks to areas with low purchasing power. For example, attempts by the government to encourage imports from Gaya to Palamau failed repeatedly, as people in Palamau could not buy rice at less than 9 sr. a rupee.

[1.2] Comparison with grain trade in 1873–74

Thus, the movement of grain trade showed several changes this year, some of which may be compared to those of the crisis year 1873–74.

South Bihar generally imported large quantities of foodgrain from upcountry provinces, which further increased in times of stress. In 1873–74 the southern districts of Patna Division, especially Shahabad and the northern district of Saran, had been largely saved by the unprecedented activity of private traders, supplemented by government efforts in importing grain from the North-West Provinces. But in 1896 the effects of drought were felt in nearly the whole of India; this not only closed the normal sources of supply, but also filled the local markets with competitors. The North-West Provinces, for example, required all that they could produce, and were actively importing from Bihar. Bourdillon, Commissioner of Patna Division, reported a sharp price-rise throughout his districts at the end of September 1896. It was due mainly to the failure of the hathiya rains and heavy exportations by agents of the North-West Provinces, who were busy buying up local stocks in Patna, Gaya, Shahabad (Arrah, Buxar), Saran and Champaran. This led to scarcity, hoarding, grain riots and widespread panic in the Patna Division throughout October. In early November, the panic subsided and exports slowed down, for the upcountry markets were overstocked. In fact, the agents of the North-West Provinces in Patna district were asked to stop purchases and sell the stocks in hand. Exports from Champaran dropped as the late November rains had improved prospects upcountry. Yet the outflow of grain to the North-West Provinces, though fluctuating, continued throughout the year. In late November, exports again increased from Patna, Shahabad, Saran and Darbhanga. Exports from Champaran went to Gonda and Gorakhpur. Whereas in ordinary years a large part of the grain in Saran came from the west down the Gogra and Ganges, most of it in 1896–97 came upstream from the east. Imports to Saran from the stricken districts of Champaran, Darbhanga, Muzaffarpur and Purnea fell off considerably. A substantial increase occurred in supplies from Monghyr and Murshidabad, while Birbhum and Burdwan assumed the role of supplying districts for the first time.

Thus, instead of bringing grain from the North-West Provinces, Patna Division in 1896–97 sent out large supplies there. It imported, rather, from the east and south, as from Orissa to Patna and Saran, Bengal to Bhabua in Shahabad, Midnapur to Siwan in Saran, and Bhagalpur and Burma to Champaran. Muzaffarpur and Darbhanga drew most of their supplies from the Burdwan Division and adjoining tracts in the Bhagalpur district, where the crops were relatively good. In fact, Burma rice was all that could be had in the affected tracts of the Bettiah Subdivision, and became the staple food of the people during the famine.

In the northern districts of Patna Division rice imports from Nepal were considerable in ordinary years. Champaran imported largely from Nepal. In Muzaffarpur, the influx from Nepal was between 700,000 to 800,000 md. per year. Darbhanga imported 374,000 md. in 1894–95 and 387,000 in 1895–96.

But in 1896, the Nepal government prohibited exports in apprehension of scarcity. The import trade in north Bihar, active in September–October, therefore came to an abrupt stop. Soon, however, considerable amounts of smuggled rice from Nepal began to flow into Champaran, Muzaffarpur and Darbhanga. There was brisk activity at the stations on the Bairagnia extension in Muzaffarpur, which tapped the rice exports from Nepal. Darbhanga, too, received not less than 1,000 md. a week in early December. Yet, being a smuggling trade, this could not be relied upon, nor could the size of the imports be even approximately assessed.

In Bhagalpur in 1873–74, large-scale government and private importation had begun by November–December, in sharp contrast to the exports in November–December 1896. In 1873–74 there was an influx of grain in Monghyr and south Bhagalpur, and also from Jalpaiguri to Purnea, and from Dinajpur to Malda.

Bhagalpur was a rich food-producing district which normally exported its surplus; in 1896, however, there was a large increase in the volume of its outflow, so that prices rose sharply despite a good harvest. In the Santhal Parganas, landlords were asked to forego the rent, so that cultivators were not forced to sell grain to export dealers in order to pay their dues. Imports from Purnea and Dinajpur to Malda were not unusual, and had occurred in 1874. But simultaneous exports to Patna, Dacca and Mymensingh in east Bengal might indicate new problems. Grain also flowed from north Bhagalpur to Darbhanga and Champaran in late November, 1896.

In Chotanagpur, foodgrains were exported to Bankura in 1873–74. In Manbhum, exports continued throughout, but there were no imports except on government account. The local authorities in Palamau encouraged private import of grain from

Sambalpur, Lohardaga and the Tributary States of Sirguja, Gangpur and Jashpur.

In 1896 an important change occurred, for the sources of supply dried up. Palamau did not receive grain from any of the states which had supplied it in 1874. In ordinary years, it drew its grain from the Lohardaga plateau, the neighbouring Tributary States and, to a small extent, from the Gaya and Shahabad districts. Lohardaga supplied it with about 43,000 md. of rice up to mid-January 1897, and with another 10,877 md. by June. The flow then stopped, 4,500 of the pack-bullocks being sent back empty to Palamau. It obtained very little grain from the Shahabad and Gaya districts too, in view of the prevailing scarcity. Meanwhile, the Tributary States prohibited exports, and Palamau received not a grain from them. The local authorities wondered whether, in view of the existing state of affairs, they would be justified in interfering.

Export activity in Orissa was remarkable in 1896. In 1873–74, Orissa was not affected; yet there is no mention of any large-scale exports to scarcity areas. In October 1896, however, one notes the hectic activity of the Nakodas in Cuttack and Puri in exporting rice. Exports also went on from Cuttack to Patna and Saran in late October and early November. The outflow of grain from Chandbali this year was unprecedented, while that from False Point was greatly above the average until the end of October. Cuttack imported mostly from the Tributary States of Orissa, which would have stopped these supplies but for the intervention of the Deputy Commissioner. Meanwhile, Bombay merchants continued to buy rice in Puri, though to a moderate extent. This carried on throughout November–December 1896 and well into 1897, when local distress was most acute. In fact, there was an organised export trade but no corresponding import activity in the Chilka region in Puri, which fell within the famine zone. Most of the rice exported by sea went from Puri Port to Colombo in Ceylon, and from Banpur into the Ganjam district. The Bombay export had an important effect in keeping prices high in Puri town and raising them all over the district. Export activity was no less marked in Balasore and Angul. In Angul, Mogulbandi dealers stayed all the year round, buying up supplies for export from local markets and villages, and making advances to the cultivators for the produce on the ground.

Rajshahi district had to import about 110,000 md. of Burma rice during the famine of 1873–74. Rangpur imported foodgrains from Coochbehar, Assam and the districts of the Dacca Division. But much of the grain so imported passed into Dinajpur, which, in turn, exported most of the supplies derived from Rangpur. The import trade in Rangpur collapsed in 1874, the impasse being finally broken by foodgrain consignments brought into the market by the government. Export activity was considerable in Pabna and unprecedented in Jalpaiguri, the latter sending supplies to Purnea, Rangpur, Dinajpur and Darjeeling. Bogra exported to Rangpur and Dinajpur, and later, due to high prices, imported from the eastern districts of Bengal.

In 1896, prices shot high in Bogra and Sirajganj (Pabna) due to failure elsewhere, and in Jalpaiguri and the Terai due to local shortfall. Cultivators in Rajshahi took their carts to Tarash in Pabna, Nitpur in Dinajpur and elsewhere, to return laden with dhan. In the Barind regions there was yet no alarm, for prices in the interior were lower than in the exporting hats, such as Godagari. In the Charghat region, however, the situation was reversed, rice being imported mainly from Dinajpur and occasionally from Calcutta by local mahajans.

Even if the aus gave a full crop, Pabna had to live on rice imported from Rangpur, Dinajpur and Bogra at this time of the year, i.e. in November, when the aman was yet to be reaped. In 1896, its main supplies were derived from Bogra and Dinajpur, and were supplemented by imports from Goalando and Kushtia, as well as Saran, Rajshahi and Nawabganj in Malda. The main problem for Pabna now was whether Rangpur, Dinajpur and Bogra could spare this quantity of rice after satisfying their own needs. Bogra exported largely, which led to exceptionally high prices locally despite a good harvest, and old rice disappeared from the market by November. As there was no sizeable surplus, even a moderate demand for export led to great stress. Failure had been general throughout India, and when one district in the course of trade relieved the greater necessities of another, it was out of stocks which in ordinary years would be consumed at home. Thus, to feed its own population properly Bogra required more than three-fourths of the crop it was likely to get. Further, prices there would have had to rise high indeed before they drew away what could be dispensed with only by reducing consumption.

The most remarkable feature of the trade in the Rajshahi Division this year was that the drain was not to Calcutta or Bihar and the North-West Provinces, but to Mymensingh and the east.

In the Presidency Division, surplus districts like the 24 Parganas and Murshidabad exported grain to affected areas in Jessore and Khulna-Nadia respectively, in 1896–97. Export of rice and paddy from the 24 Parganas (for example, from Basirhat, Haroa and the Sunderbans to Bongaon in Jessore) might have been greater than in normal years, but it could not compare with the drain on Rarh in Murshidabad. In 1897, the Rarh tract lying in the western parts of Murshidabad and Burdwan was the main source of supply for the Kalantar in Nadia and famine areas in east Murshidabad. These exports, together with those to Calcutta and the North-West Provinces, were unprecedented. In ordinary years the affected areas in Murshidabad drew their supplies from the Rarh and from Malda, Rajshahi, Dinajpur and Rangpur. No imports could be expected from these districts this year, so the drain on Rarh was most severe and unusual.

In this Division the stress lay mainly in Khulna and Nadia. It was not difficult for private traders to supply the needs of Khulna, as it lay on the water routes from Calcutta to the eastern districts. Since the eastern districts did not export much this year due to shortfall in production, large supplies poured in from Calcutta and Midnapur. But as the people lacked credit and purchasing power, traders and mahajans failed to operate effectively in these regions. Meanwhile, in the Kalantar tract in Nadia, there was no organised private trade in rice, for this region did not normally export or import much rice. The cultivators themselves acted as petty traders; until mid-April, they brought in and sold paddy by cart, mainly from the Rarh tract in Burdwan and Murshidabad. But when the roads became impassable with the first showers in May, they would not be able to finance imports by boat. It was also indefinite as to how long Rarh could continue to supply them with paddy. In fact, after April stocks in Katwa fell very low and grain dealers there refused to sell rice to anyone except their regular customers, underlining the fact that imports from Rarh into Nadia were not a regular feature in normal years. The proximity of Nadia to the eastern districts, which proved such an advantage in ordinary years as well as in 1873–74, could not ease the situation this year.

The Burdwan Division normally sent out large supplies to neighbouring tracts. Throughout 1873–74 prices in Burdwan were lower than elsewhere, so that exportation never ceased. Foodgrains flowed out from Birbhum, Midnapur and from Bankura via Ranigunge. In 1896, the strain on its resources was much more pronounced. As imports from the eastern districts were cut off, Khulna and even Saran in Bihar drew upon supplies from Midnapur, while Nadia-Jessore imported actively from the Rarh in Burdwan. In January–February 1897, Patna and Shahabad received a large proportion of rice from Burdwan Division. Stocks were being depleted fast and it was doubtful whether Rarh could meet these demands much longer.

The changes in the direction of the grain trade in Dacca-Chittagong Divisions were most significant. As seen above, in normal years and especially during agrarian crises, certain areas drew upon supplies from the eastern districts of Bengal: the northern districts like Rangpur, Bogra and Rajshahi; Khulna, Nadia and Jessore in the Presidency Division; and even parts of Bihar. This year, however, Khulna and Nadia had to find other sources of supply in Midnapur and Rarh, while Rajshahi, instead of importing from Dacca, sent grain there. Jessore normally imported rice from the eastern districts, and continued to do so until May 1897, when supplies from that direction fell off. Since then, the importation of Burma rice from Calcutta commenced and persisted until mid-August; this was entirely a feature of this year of scarcity, rice never having been imported before from Calcutta to any large extent.

[1.3] Main trends

Thus, there were several changes in the direction of the grain trade in Bengal in 1896–97; Patna Division (especially south Bihar), instead of importing from the North-West Provinces, sent large supplies there. It now imported from the south and east, that is, from Orissa, Midnapur, Burdwan, Bhagalpur and Burma.

The rice imports from Nepal into north Bihar were officially stopped, though a considerable amount was still smuggled in. In Chotanagpur, the normal sources of supply to scarcity tracts like Palamau were fast drying up. Exports were unprecedented in Bhagalpur and Orissa, the Nakodas being most active in Puri and Cuttack. Rajshahi, instead of importing rice from the eastern districts and sending out supplies to Calcutta for Bihar and the North-West Provinces, was exporting, rather, to districts in Dacca. Khulna and Nadia, being deprived of rice from Dacca-Chittagong, imported largely from Calcutta and Midnapur, and from the Rarh tract, respectively, draining the resources of the latter.

[2] *Problems of Grain Trade*

The private trade in foodgrains during the famine of 1896–97 in Bengal involved several critical problems. First, excessive exports disturbed the trade balance and depleted stocks, as in parts of the Patna, Bhagalpur and Orissa Divisions, which might otherwise have staved off the crisis. Second, lack of adequate imports heightened the distress in problem areas like Champaran, Palamau, Satkhira in Khulna, Kalantar in Nadia and the Chilka region in Puri. Finally, hoarding and rigging of the market by private traders and mahajans was a common complaint, especially when the first signs of famine became apparent in September–October 1896, leading to widespread grain riots in the Patna Division.[1]

[2.1] Persistent outflow of grain from scarcity regions

As noted, there were heavy exportations from the Patna Division to scarcity areas in the North-West Provinces, which in normal years was the main source of supply for south Bihar. Bourdillon, Commissioner of Patna Division, reported a sharp price-rise due to this throughout his area at the end of September 1896. Distress was reported from Shahabad—where in the Arrah Subdivision the price of grain rose suddenly on 30 September and 1 October, owing especially to the hectic export activity of agents from the

[1] FRFRO, Patna Div., ch. 15, para. 372.

North-West Provinces—and grain riots were apprehended. Under the circumstances, Egerton, Collector of Shahabad, banned grain exports by an order under Section 144 of the Criminal Procedure Code, dated 2 October. Bourdillon immediately cancelled his order by wire, rebuked him for his "unwise" step, and "impressed upon him that no direct interference with trade can possibly be allowed". The government approved of this measure, and condemned Egerton's action as "both ill-advised and illegal". Even in the third week of October, exports continued from Arrah and Buxar in Shahabad. Large amounts of grain flowed quietly into Chapra, where most of the local banias had golas. Saran and Champaran were the worst affected in Patna Division. Yet, exports were brisk in Champaran and even in Saran which imported extensively in normal times. Bourdillon notes that applications were made to the Collector to interfere, "which he has of course declined to do". Similarly, the Collector of Patna was asked by a mob on 4 October to fix a rate and prohibit exportation. Even in Bihar Subdivision of Patna District, which lay farthest from the railway, export of foodgrains continued. Inglis, Collector of Patna, reported in early November that prices would have risen anyway due to a deficient harvest. Yet, even this local scarcity could not curb the export activity, and led to widespread panic.

In early November the exports slowed down and panic subsided, for the markets upcountry were satiated and agents were asked to stop purchases and sell the stocks in hand. But in late November the outflow again increased from Patna, Shahabad, Saran and Darbhanga. In early December there were no exports, mostly westward from Patna, Shahabad, Gaya and Darbhanga. But the distress in Palamau caused a drain on the outlying parts of Gaya in January–March 1897, as the tendency among traders was to buy supplies as close at hand as possible. Thus, export of foodgrains from the Patna Division, though fluctuating in volume, continued throughout 1896 and well into 1897.[2]

[2] *Selection of Papers,* vol. 4: p. 336, letter from A. Forbes, Esq., Offg. Comm. of the Chotanagpur Div. to the Secy. to the Govt. of Bengal, Rev. Dept., Calcutta, 8 Feb. 1897, para. 8, point 4.

Traders may have been compelled to honour prior contracts despite local shortage or the prospect of higher prices, as was often the case with rice traders and millers in Burma. But a considerable part of the exports from the Patna Division were not made in keeping with prior commitments. The North-West Provinces normally did not import from Bihar, and the agents sent there in apprehension of scarcity in 1896 probably attracted supplies not by virtue of forward contracts, but merely by outbidding local purchasers. Likewise, Gaya did not normally export so much rice to Palamau; Lohardaga and the neighbouring Tributary States were, according to the Commissioner, the "only sources" from which Palamau drew its food supply in ordinary years.[3] It was only in early 1897 that imports increased in Patna Division by more than 50 per cent and exports fell by 8.74 per cent. In Gaya, however, exports still largely exceeded imports.[4]

In the Bhagalpur Division, too, the export trade in foodgrains was unusually large. Even a rough estimate of food stocks in the Division could not be arrived at, as they fluctuated sharply due to the relatively good means of exportation by road, rail and water. It had been a prosperous year on the whole for Bhagalpur. Even for the three Subdivisions of Bhagalpur district for which anticipatory Famine Reports were submitted, it was estimated that local stocks would be ample until the following September, despite the exportation which took place. Yet, so good were the communications, and so dead had been the level of prices since last August, that even if the Division had produced a bumper harvest of autumn and winter rice, famine rates would still have prevailed in view of the circumstances elsewhere. The enormous export trade from Bhagalpur this year was, in fact, due to the general failure of crops in other parts of India.

As noted by the Collector of Bhagalpur in December 1896, "The cause of trouble is not so much the local failure of crops,

3 Ibid., vol. 4: p. 340, Agriculture (Famine), no. 381, 11 Feb. 1897.

4 Ibid., p. 134, letter no. 283F-G, Bankipore, 6 Feb. 1897, para. 58, from J. A. Bourdillon Esq., Offg. Comm. Patna Div., to the Secy. to the Govt. of Bengal, Rev. Dept.

as high prices caused by circumstances existing in other parts of India".[5]

By July, prices had peaked, due mainly to increasing exports and decreased imports. All the old rice had disappeared in the south Gangetic country; this was a most unusual and disturbing factor, as the poor did not eat rice so new as this. In Malda the export warehouses at Nawabganj and Rohanpur on the Mahananda were absolutely empty at the end of November 1896. In fact, as soon as the bhadoi harvest was reaped, and apprehensions of a famine turned to certainty in various parts of India, an immense activity in grain dealing was displayed in Bhagalpur. Existing stocks and even the standing crops were bought up in all directions, local middlemen and dealers competing with the agents of large firms sent here to purchase all they could. A heavy flow of exports commenced and persisted throughout, from October 1896 to September 1897. During this year the exports by rail exceeded the imports by 2,336,013 md. Simultaneously, strings of carts laden with grain passed from north Bhagalpur into Darbhanga, though the total volume of the outflow by road and river cannot be assessed in the absence of reliable statistics.[6]

Meanwhile, exports upcountry continued relentlessly from the Santhal Parganas. Here, the Commissioner tried to impress upon the landlords the fact that once foodgrains got into the dealers' hands, it would be impossible to restrict exportations. The landlords could help the district to hold its stocks by easing the pressure on their raiyats, who were selling it to pay their rents.

In Chotanagpur, too, grain flowed out of the Division despite acute local scarcity in Palamau, Manbhum and Lohardaga. For example, the *bhaiya saheb*, or zamindar of Untari was exporting 484 pack-bullocks of paddy to Mirzapur in the NWP in February 1897, when Palamau was in great distress due to want of supplies.[7]

5 Ibid., vol. 4: p. 390, no. 1874 G, Bhagalpur, 21 Dec. 1896, para. 6, from H. J. McIntosh, Esq., Collector of Bhagalpur, to the Comm., Bhagalpur Div.

6 FRFRO, Bhagalpur District, ch. 3, para. 14.

7 *Selection of Papers,* vol. 5: p. 309.

The process was similar in Orissa, where the Nakodas made large purchases for export in Cuttack and Puri. Most of the rice exported from Puri by sea went to Ceylon. In Cuttack, exports from Chandbali this year were unprecedented, while those from False Point up to the end of October were considerably above the average. On 25 November, the price of export rice fell due to rainfall in Bombay and the Deccan. But in early 1897 considerable quantities were still being exported, 40,000 cwt. of rice flowing out from False Point to Mauritius within one week in January. As the Collector noted, "Exports must go on and the government forbids interference! At the same time there is absolutely no machinery for imports. In this respect Orissa compares most unfavourably with other parts of the province".[8]

Purchases by the Nakoda merchants continued in Puri despite scarcity in the Chilka tract, and served to raise prices all over the district. Indeed, the export from Puri town by sea to Bombay was drawing a large quantity of rice from the district. The export agents even colluded with the carters in order to corner supplies. The Collector of Puri wanted to break through this and also to stop the exportation of rice by rail from the government Khas Mahal, which would otherwise be the direct cause of famine in June, down to the Banpur region.[9] Stocks were low in Balasore after the unusual export activity of the last nine months. In Angul, the system of exportation was very effective; here the Mogulbandi traders bought up supplies from local markets, and advanced money to cultivators for the produce on the ground.

Heavy exportation also took place from parts of Rajshahi Division, and from the Rarh tract in Burdwan to Nadia and Jessore. Exports from Bankura, where low prices normally prevailed, were "abnormally large" in the lean months of 1897.[10] Moreover, exports from Katwa and the Rarh in Burdwan continued unabated into the affected regions of Nadia from late

8 Ibid., vol. 4: p. 418–19, from E. F. Growse, Collector, Cuttack, to the Comm., Orissa Div., 24 Jan. 1897, para. 12.

9 Ibid., p. 421, no. 116, Puri, 20 Jan. 1897, para. 5, from W. H. Lee, Offg. Collector, Puri, to the Comm., Orissa Div.

10 LRP, Aug. 1898, pt. 1, p. 225. FRFRO, Bankura, from G. E. Manisty, Esq., Magistrate and Collector, Bankura, to the Comm., Burdwan Div. no. 1595, Bankura, 30 Nov. 1897, ch. 3, para. 4.

1896 to mid-April 1897. In his tour notes Mr B. C. Basu, Assistant Director of the Department of Land Records and Agriculture in Bengal, emphasised the importance of the supplies from Rarh into the affected areas of Nadia. However, as Mr J. H. E. Garrett, Collector of Nadia, stated:

> Mr. Basu in his note styles the present system of importation as an admirable one; no doubt it might be so called if the stocks in the Rarh were unlimited; but as that stock must fall short within a very few weeks, I am of opinion that the present system of importation is a very unfortunate one, as it leads the people to believe that they need to have no fears for the future. . . . So far as I can see, there must be very serious trouble in the Kalantar when the supply of rice from the Rarh suddenly ceases.[11]

Already, in early February 1897, the Collectorate of Nadia doubted the belief of the Katwa SDO that the local surplus in Katwa would hold out for another two months, and asked him to report to them immediately as the exportations from Katwa began to flag.

Exports from Murshidabad Rarh, too, were excessive. In February, the Collector of Murshidabad reported that the price of common rice had averaged 10 sr. per rupee since December last, as compared with 16 sr. in the preceding year, and a further rise was probably causing great distress, especially among smaller cultivators and the landless classes.He also apprehended that the stocks in hand would not be sufficient to meet local requirements up to September. The statistics for grain trade in Murshidabad during February and March 1897 amply illustrate this point.

[11] *Selection of Papers,* vol. 4: p. 235, no. 2619 G. Krishnagar, 3 Feb. 1897, para. 2, from J. H. E. Garrett, Collector, Nadia, to the Comm., Presidency Div.

TABLE 59
Grain Trade in Murshidabad

	Import *md.*	*Export* *md.*
3rd week February	Nil	14,800
4th week February	200	10,100
1st week March	1,700	17,100
2nd week March	100	21,100
3rd week March	566	18,120
4th week March	20	7,192

Source: Selection of Papers, vol. 4.

Thus, exports were already falling off by the end of March, probably due to depletion of stocks, though there was still very little of imports. By April, the price of common rice rose to 8–9 sr. a rupee in different parts of Murshidabad, and in some hats the supply of grain was insufficient to meet local demands. Yet exports rose to 15,522 md. in the first week of April and 14,661 md. in the second, as against 781 md. and 1,325 md. of imports, respectively. This temporary rise was due to the late rabi harvest, especially of gram and arhar, which was sent to Calcutta and the NWP, after which exports decreased again. After mid-April, exports to Nadia ceased. By mid-May imports increased, and Burma rice was being sold in the principal bazaars, which was an indication that the resources of the district were being taxed to the utmost. At the end of the month, however, mahajans had brought out their hidden stocks, and the local food supply appeared to be better than was apprehended. Exports once again increased, and rice flowed into Nadia.

Nadia, while importing from Rarh into the Kalantar region, exported largely from other parts. In early March, exports greatly exceeded imports by rail. Even considering the imports from Rarh, and those from the northern districts by boat, there is no doubt that Nadia sent out far more than it took in. In fact, it shows a net loss of nearly 100,000 md. in the second fortnight of March 1897. In April prices shot high and food stocks were very low throughout Rarh. Yet, exports still exceeded imports by rail and river, though to a lesser extent. Early in May, imports for the first time exceeded exports by 14,000 md., owing to acute local shortage. By the end of the month, the district was almost entirely dependent upon the inflow of grain, which was now nearly double the exports. Yet the Collector was faced with a crisis: "The stock of food grains is practically exhausted. . . . The efforts which I have made to stimulate importation have to a great extent failed. . . . It is a mystery to me that the exports should be as large as they are".[12]

The affected region in Satkhira (in Khulna) had almost no stock as early as February 1897. The eastern part of Khulna, the 24 Parganas and Backerganj supplied it with grain. Taking the district as a whole, however, there were practically no imports, while exports were considerable, especially from Bagerhat. The same state of affairs continued until May, when 1,086 md. of rice were exported by rail, while there was little importation of foodgrains. Burma rice was being imported and sold at 8 sr. a rupee at hats in affected areas. In the interior the price of rice was higher (7 sr. per rupee), which indicates that there were still no local stocks in the famine tract and the condition of the people was worse.

Thus, exports from the Rarh tract in Burdwan and Murshidabad, and from unaffected regions in Nadia and Khulna continued unabated, despite acute local scarcity. Rarh and east Khulna, however, exported not only outside the district but also supplied grain to affected areas within, though not to such an extent as to avert failure of supplies in these regions, especially in April–May.

But the case of Nadia was exceptional; it went on exporting large amounts of foodgrain throughout, while draining the Rarh for supplies to the Kalantar tract.

The excessive exports thus led to two types of problems: they either accentuated local scarcity, or raised prices to famine rates even in areas which had a relatively good harvest. The most typical examples of the former were in the North Patna Division (i.e., Saran, Champaran, Muzaffarpur and Darbhanga) and, to a lesser extent, Jamtara-Godda in the Santhal Parganas and the Chilka tract in Puri. As for surplus areas, such as parts of Orissa and the greater part of the Bhagalpur and Burdwan

12 Ibid., vol. 8: p. 333, no. 473F., Krishnagar, 4 June 1897, para. 4, point 2, from J. H. E. Garrett, Offg. Collector, Nadia, to the Comm., Presidency Div.

Divisions, the equalisation of prices with those prevailing in the scarcity tracts need not be regretted; in fact, it was the guarantee against starvation in famine areas, as provided by improved communications. But there were several instances where prices in surplus districts shot higher than in scarcity zones, due to excessive exportation. For example, in Gaya, which was the only district more or less unaffected by scarcity in the Patna Division, prices were higher than elsewhere except in Mirzapur. In Bogra, which had perhaps the best harvest in the Rajshahi Division, rice sold at 9 sr. 12 ch. per rupee in September, which was much more than in Jalpaiguri, Darjeeling and even the scarcity district of Pabna. Again, in the surplus region of Tipperah the price was 7 sr. 10 ch. a rupee as early as in September—a rate higher than those in the affected areas of Bengal.

[2.2] Feeble response of the import trade in foodgrain

While the outflow of grain thus went on unchecked, the level of imports fell far below expectations in the affected districts. Though there was a distinct increase in foodgrain imports in the Patna Division this year, they were unremarkable in Bhagalpur, Chotanagpur, Orissa and Burdwan.

As the railways had "largely absorbed" the foodgrain trade of the Patna Division, the following returns submitted by them from April 1895 to September 1897 reveal the general pattern of this trade, and the deviations in the year of famine.[13]

These figures for the successive half-years are extremely significant. It is clear that for the greater part of the year from 1 October 1895 to 30 September 1896, grain poured out of the Division, mainly westward, the excess of exports over imports being 2,154,653 md. Grain exports in the Patna Division had, in fact, received a great impetus from the rapid extension of the railways in the last two decades. Darbhanga, Champaran and, to a lesser extent, Muzaffarpur exported on a large scale in ordinary years. Shahabad and Gaya, too, became important export centres of grain, due to the opening of the Patna-Gaya Railway and the Sone Canals respectively. However, once the

[13] LRP, Aug. 1898, pt. 2, p. 929.

TABLE 60

Net Imports or Exports of each District in Maunds

District	*Apr. 1895 to Sep. 1895*	*Oct. 1895 to Mar. 1896*	*Apr. 1896 to Sep 1896*	*Oct. 1896 to Mar. 1897*	*Apr. 1897 to Sep. 1897*
Patna	I 49,571	E 681,447	E 1,054,281	E 551,608	I 333,279
Gaya	E 117,979	E 18,149	E 69,229	I 12,651	I 264,580
Shahabad	I 230,354	I 78,393	E 283,357	I 17,791	E 84,200
Saran	I 65,190	I 8,171	I 29,840	I 747,688	I 1,005,294
Champaran	E 8,531	E 7,220	E 5,681	I 80,163	I 407,867
Muzaffarpur	E 24,379	E 14,755	E 6,039	I 329,195	I 663,521
Darbhanga	E 64,579	E 90,174	E 40,725	I 31,005	I 1,124,127
Net Total	I 129,347	E 725,181	E 1,429,472	I 666,885	I 3,711,468

Source: LRP, Aug. 1898, pt. 2, p. 929.
Note: I = imports, E = exports

implications of crop failure in Bihar became apparent, the tide turned and the excess of imports came up to 666,000 md. During April–September 1897, when the famine reached its climax, the net imports rose to 3,712,500 md. In the twelve months ending on 30 September 1897, the export excess of the previous year (2,150,000 md.) had been wiped off, with a balance of more than 4,300,000 md. in the nature of imports. Thus, "The direction of the trade turned completely round and imports exceeded exports by 4,378,353; the measure of the revolution in the trade was thus 6,533,006 md."[14]

A very large proportion of the grain imported was rice, partly because it was the rice crop which failed completely in Bihar, and also because it was the grain most commonly grown in the two tracts which chiefly supplied Bihar this year: the Burdwan Division and Burma. Some rice also flowed in from Bhagalpur, eastern Bengal and Orissa.

The swing towards imports, however, seems less marked on considering several qualifying factors, such as the large volume of grain trade that went unregistered; the absence of inter-district returns in the Annual Divisional Reports, which therefore left out vital links in the trade pattern, such as the brisk exports from Champaran and Muzaffarpur to Saran; and the disparity of the district figures of railborne traffic with the trade returns of the affected tracts, which were often remote, inaccessible and untraversed by the railways.

It was indeed difficult to obtain accurate statistics of the total volume of this traffic, for in every district there were important segments of the grain trade beyond the purview of the railway returns. Patna had a large boat traffic as well as cargoes sent on steamers of the India General Steam Navigation Company. Gaya exported by carts and pack bullocks down the GT Road and into the Chotanagpur Division, and also across the Sone and up the Sone Canals. Much of the traffic from Shahabad went to Zamania, beyond the border of Bengal, whence trade flowed both ways across the Ganges with Ballia in the NWP. Saran imported largely down the Gogra from the NWP. Champaran and Muzaffarpur exported a sizeable amount of grain westward

[14] Ibid., Aug. 1898, pt. 2, p. 930. FRFRO, Patna, ch. 3, para. 92.

across the Gandak, while Muzaffarpur and Darbhanga, especially the latter, had a considerable traffic down the Ganges to Monghyr and Bengal. The three most northerly districts also had an active rice trade with Nepal, much of which went unregistered.

Even on analysing the figures for railborne trade alone, to the exclusion of this vast area of river and cart traffic, the imports do not seem to have satisfied the demand for foodgrains. From October 1896 to September 1897 the railborne trade in foodgrains in Shahabad left a balance of merely 5,425 md. in favour of the district, while the boat traffic gave a balance against the district of 71,834 md. Imports in Saran increased by 91,440 md. in 1896–97, as compared to the previous year. Yet even here, though the local traders were familiar with every aspect of the import trade, supplies dwindled in February and March due to the failure of a leading Chapra firm, while the falling off in May was due to a block in the traffic over the railway Ghat. As to the Maharani outpost, which eventually proved the worst-hit region in the district, it was far removed from the sources of supply and a cul-de-sac from the trader's point of view.[15] In Champaran, exports persisted until mid-November 1896, when a 16 per cent rise in prices gave a boost to the imports. The inflow of grain was feeble at first, as the local merchants "were not accustomed to this form of trade". It became more assured in the first quarter of 1897 due to a sudden price-rise in mid-March. However, supplies ran out again in the middle of May. This was because of the failure of the Bengal and North-Western Railway Company to bring in grain consignments from Mokama Ghat on the Ganges with reasonable despatch, and its inability to prevent pilfering during transit. An attempt made to open a steamer line from Patna up the Gandak—in apprehension of a further breakdown in the railway arrangements—was also frustrated by the problems of navigation when the water was low.[16] In Muzaffarpur, the exports by rail exceeded the imports by 10,000 md. in October 1896. By November, however, the situation was altered, the excess of imports over exports rising steadily until it amounted to 63,587 md. in May 1897. In

[15] FRFRO, Saran, ch. 1, para. 12.
[16] FRFRO, Champaran, ch. 3, paras. 49, 51.

Darbhanga, the thrust towards imports was restricted by the large cart-traffic to Muzaffarpur, Saran and Bhagalpur, as well as the river trade from Roserah in the south of the district down the Gandak, consisting almost entirely of exports.

Despite these reservations, it may on the whole be concluded that in 1896–97 the north Bihar districts imported a far greater amount than was usual, which is much more than can be said about the Bhagalpur Division. The district of Bhagalpur normally exported in large volume both within and without the Division, and the year of famine saw no exception to this rule. A vigorous outflow of grain began as soon as apprehensions of scarcity were confirmed late in 1896, and persisted throughout the year without interruption. Between October 1896 and September 1897, the exports by rail greatly exceeded the imports every month. By March 1897, the stocks were depleted. "Everything was exported, little or nothing being imported".[17] During the six months from October 1896 to March 1897 the imports were only 49,323 md., as against the export figure of 1,950,429 md. During the lean months from April to July, stocks were exhausted and imports went up to 204,222 md., or more than two-thirds of the total imports of the year. Even so, the exports exceeded the imports by 180,874 md. By August, good crop prospects led to a sharp drop in imports. In the Santhal Parganas, exports were below normal this year but did not cease, while the imports were negligible. A mere trickle of grain flowed into Jamtara and Sahebganj, while a very limited quantity of Burma rice was imported into Sahebganj and Deoghar.

In Hazaribagh, the normally small amount of foodgrain imports rose to nearly thrice the monthly average in April–May 1897, but fell below average after August. In Lohardaga, the importation of rice came up to 41,000 md. in 1896–97, as against 16,000 md. in 1895–96, according to the police figures in the annual reports. However, these figures are dismissed by the Deputy Commissioner as the "wildest surmise", being purely speculative in nature. In March 1897, two Ranchi merchants, Babus Hardat Rai Marwari and Tara Prasanna Rai Chowdhry,

17 LRP, Aug. 1898, pt. 1, p. 311. FRFRO, Bhagalpur, ch. 3, paras. 13–14.

began to import small quantities of rice into Ranchi from Singhbhum and elsewhere, through Purulia. In July, prices rose higher due to difficulties of cartage from Purulia. In August, some cartloads of rice came into the district from Chakradharpur via the Chaibassa-Ranchi Road, but it is hard to assess the quantity received, as the carts shed their load in degrees during stopovers at the weekly hats of Bangaon, Murhu and Khunti. Very little rice came in from Manbhum on the east, and none at all from Hazaribagh and Palamau in the north, or from the native states of Sirguja, Gangpur and Jashpur on the west and south of the district. The only import statistics available are for Ranchi, the total amount being 28,083 md. between October 1896 and September 1897, of which Hardat Rai Marwari and Tara Prasanna Rai Chowdhry imported 12,665 and 9,146 md., respectively. Thus, importation in Lohardaga did not begin until March 1897, and failed to pick up even as late as in June. Though some effort was made during 8 August to 8 September 1897 to avail of the government bounty of Re. 1 per maund of rice imported into the district, only 11,050 md. could be brought in due to the difficulties of transport. The total inflow of Burma rice amounted to no more than 2,000 md.[18] In Manbhum, the import trade in grain was larger than usual, rice being brought in from Burdwan, Birbhum and Bankura, as well as from Burma via Calcutta. But an unspecified amount was re-exported to Lohardaga, no particular measures being taken to stimulate the importation of grain. In Palamau Rs. 25,000 was sanctioned by the government after much hesitation for payment of "bounty", and Rs. 75,000 for advances to traders for foodgrain imports. However, only Rs. 9,895-10a-10p on the former count and Rs. 52,500 on the latter were expended, the total quantity of rice imported being no more than 23,692 md. The difficulties of importation into Palamau will be discussed in greater detail later on, while analysing the problems of supply failure in remote and inaccessible tracts during the course of this famine.

In Bengal, exports from the affected district of Bankura in Burdwan Division were "abnormally large" this year, while very

18 LRP, Aug. 1898, pt. 2, p. 742, Report on famine by H. C. Streatfeild, Dept. Comm., Lohardaga, to the Comm., Chotanagpur Div., no. 409 F., Ranchi, 12 Nov. 1897, ch. 3, paras. 12–15.

little rice came by rail or road from Midnapur. No Burma rice was imported either. Exports were heaviest in the lean months from March to May, exhausting stocks in the affected tracts and pushing prices up to unprecedented heights, especially in Saltora. In Nadia in the Presidency Division the local traders, being unaccustomed to imports, were not enterprising enough to undertake such ventures in a crisis. Besides the cartloads of rice brought into the Kalantar from the Rarh in Burdwan and Murshidabad, only about 6,000 md. of Burma rice were imported into the district. Rice imports from Faridpur, Khulna and Bakarganj into Jessore continued in larger quantities than usual until May 1897, when supplies from that quarter fell off. Prices rose to 7 sr. per rupee, and the importation of Burma rice commenced. Approximately 63,000 md. were brought into the district between mid-May and August in 1897. Although Khulna had a deficit, importation was easier as it lay on the direct water route to Calcutta. The amount of foodgrain imported into Murshidabad came up to a mere 17 per cent of the exports from that district. Although in 1874 the imports amounted to only 12 per cent of the exports, altogether 13,388 tons of grain were either sold for cash, distributed as charitable relief, or advanced on loans. In 1897, however, there was no contribution by the government under any of these heads, only 12 and 140 tons being sold and distributed, respectively, by the District Charitable Relief Committee.[19] The available trade returns for the Presidency Division in 1896–97, as given below, show an excess of exports over imports in all districts except Jessore.

TABLE 61

Trade Returns for Presidency Division, 1896–97

Districts	*Imports, md.*	*Exports, md.*	*Excess, E or I*
Nadia	721,099	807,964	86,865 E
Murshidabad	66,203	315,484	249,281 E
Jessore	269,496	74,235	195,261 I
Khulna	14,494	29,769	15,275 E

Source: LRP, Aug. 1898, pt. 2, p. 379.

[19] FRFRO, Murshidabad, p. 3, a comparative statement on the famines of 1874 and 1897.

From Puri district in Orissa, exports of rice continued as usual to Cuttack, Ganjam, Colombo and Mauritius. The imports hardly amounted to anything in ordinary years, and the quantity brought in during the crisis was negligible. The raiyats, under pressure from the prevailing high prices and the inactivity of the local trade, imported small quantities for their own consumption. No statistics are available for this petty trade in foodgrains, as it was on too small a scale to merit notice.

Thus, during the year under review a heavy and incessant stream of exports flowed from the famine-hit districts, in marked contrast to the slow and feeble response of the import trade in foodgrains. The trade followed its own logic. An increased flow of grain towards affected areas in the midst of a crisis, would depend on certain prerequisites such as: an organised and systematic trade mechanism for imports; big traders operating at least at the inter-district level; good communication; and effective demand. These conditions hardly ever prevailed in the famine-hit tracts.

Selective case studies relating to the problem

The problem is brought into focus in four case studies of remote and inaccessible tracts, specifically: (i) Kalantar in Nadia; (ii) Ramnagar-Araraj-Madhuban in Champaran; (iii) the thanas of Garhwa, Daltonganj, Balumath and Latehar in central Palamau; and (iv) the Chilka region in Puri.

Kalantar in Nadia

In the Presidency Division, the affected areas lay mainly in the Nadia Kalantar, and Satkhira in Khulna. The affected areas in Nadia were inadequately served by private traders. The petty banias of the region were "not solvent enough to carry on any extensive import or export trade". Besides, their proportion to the total population of this tract was not even one in a thousand, in sharp contrast to other parts of the district, where the ratio of the commercial to the total population was more than twenty-seven to a thousand.

Trade might have prospered to some extent if communications were better. As it stood, however, people hesitated to open any large business in the interior of this tract, because it was cut off entirely from the outside centres of trade throughout the monsoon.[20] In the Gangni and Nowpara thanas, the means of communication were particularly unsatisfactory. There was no proper trade centre anywhere in the interior of Gangni, none of the nearest markets having proper road connections. The road to Meherpur was un-bridged throughout. The only route across the Bonaj from Chapra to Latuda was an incomplete famine road impassable during the rains. In Nowpara, too, there was no brisk trade and the cart tracks were useless except in the dry season. Trade in the region declined further with the silting up of the Bhagirathi, Bhairab, Mathabanga, Jalangi and Padma. Some of the main commercial centres, such as Gotpara, Debogram, Kaliganj, Tehatta, Meherpur, Hat-Boalia and Taragonia, were located along these rivers.

Traders also complained that the level of purchasing power was not high enough to cover the risk and cost of transporting rice into the Kalantar, which had suffered from successive floods and crop failures in the last five years.

As early as February 1897, the Circle Officers in Nadia found it impossible to locally purchase rice sufficient for distribution, without the aid of contractors. The grain contractors in Karimpur had to be paid 8 an. per md. over market rates. Even by March, no substantial trader had commenced throwing rice into the affected tracts, and cultivators continued to bring in small amounts of paddy by cart from Rarh. On 16 April, the Collector, J. H. E. Garrett, was informed that supplies from Katwa and Rarh had ceased suddenly. Stocks were very poor in Katwa, as mahajans were getting no supplies from the interior. Even relief officials could procure only 200 md. with great difficulty for the Kalantar region. The Katwa dealers refused to sell rice to anyone but their regular customers. The price rose to Rs. 5-8 an. per md., and the contractors failed to supply rice in the affected tracts.

The Collector then entered into contract with a wealthy grain merchant, Babu Pratap Chandra Saha, who was to import 2,000 md. per week from Calcutta, at the market rate, to Debogram in the Kalantar. Two others were also to import rice

[20] FRFRO, Nadia, ch. 1, para. 25.

from Khulna and Calcutta. The price now fell to Rs. 5 or Rs. 5-4 an. per md. in Nadia. Though contractors were appointed to import grain from Calcutta to the Kalantar, and petty importations from the Rarh had recommenced to a slight degree, the northwest part of the district still lay in jeopardy. The Collector publicised the fact that rice may be purchased in Calcutta at less than Rs. 4 per md., hoping in vain to stimulate importation. The only large stores in the district, especially in the northwest, lay with Gregson, an agent of Watson and Company at Shikarpur, who imported from Calcutta and sold freely in Karimpur and Daulatpur.

Disappointed by this poor response of the local traders, the Collector of Nadia arranged to give bounties in aid of grain importation into the district—but to no effect. As supplies failed and exports continued, the Collector proposed to advance Rs. 50,000 to Gregson at 6.25 per cent interest, in order to enable him to enlarge his sphere of activity. The government, however, refused to sanction the loan, on the ground that though Gregson looked for no profit and proposed to sell at cost price, he would undersell all private traders and create a monopoly, thus dislocating trade. Instead, it was proposed to advance money to other traders who would import and sell at any price they found profitable. The Collector maintained that there were no such traders in the tract concerned, and the problem remained unresolved.

Ramnagar-Araraj-Madhuban in Champaran

In the Ramnagar-Araraj-Madhuban tract in Champaran, the local officials, fearing inaction of the traders, persuaded the Commissioner and the Lieutenant Governor to ask for government loans at reasonable rates of interest (about 6 per cent) to responsible local men. They would undertake to import grain from overseas, solely to increase local supplies without any profiteering. Supplies would not be drawn from scarcity districts, and *challan*s (bills) for grain imports into inaccessible tracts would be inspected occasionally. The government, however, thought that this stipulation could be abused in several ways, that the scheme was too generalised, and that it amounted, in effect, to a direct interference with trade, which was likely to paralyse mercantile activity in the region.

In response, the Collector and Governor explained clearly that the proposals were not for financing any general scheme of importation, but for foodgrain imports into precisely defined, specific localities. Besides, contracts with dealers for the supply of grain at relief works would not suffice. Supplies were also running out in the local markets, though purchasing power was still there. This would compel people to flock to relief centres for food, thus overstraining government resources. The administration accepted the logic of these arguments. It agreed to treat Champaran as a special case, while reiterating the principle of laissez-faire as the basis of its general trade policy.

On 17 December 1896, the Collector, emphasising the slackness of trade in Champaran, expressed "grave doubts . . . as to the ability of private enterprise to meet the wants of the people at the proper time". The fear was not unjustified. As Charles Still, the Relief Superintendent of Hardih, observed, Champaran was normally an exporting district, and there were no professional grain dealers in Ramnagar thana who had any stocks of rice or could import at such short notice. The mahajans, who controlled a large portion of the stocks due to excessive prior hypothecation, had also sold out to export agents this year at prices beyond the reach of the local people.

There was still purchasing power in the market, but as the Ramnagar tract was backward and the people poor, great uncertainty prevailed as to how long they could afford to pay famine rates. Even in mid-January 1897, rice was selling at 8.5 sr. and Indian corn at 10 sr. a rupee.

The high cost of carriage partly accounted for the rise in prices. As the Collector wrote on 10 November 1896, with the exception of a few ill-kept tracks, "the tract is without regular communications, the country to the north-east of Ramnagar being particularly defective in this respect". The Tirhut State Railway running through Champaran ended at Bettiah. Shikarpur and Ramnagar in the centre of the famine tract in Champaran lay twenty-four and twenty-eight miles, respectively, from the railway. The severely distressed region extended ten to twelve miles further north. One of the worst tracts to the north of Bagaha was situated fifty miles away from the railway. No subsidiary roads existed to connect the different points in the famine-hit region. The rude tracks along which carts managed to ply were interrupted by numerous watercourses flowing down the hills, involving the risk of a total disruption in communications. "Unfortunately this was the very part of the district in which the need for imported supplies was greatest during the famine".[21]

The danger of a supply failure was so acute in the affected tracts of Champaran as to justify Resolution no. 298F of 20 January 1897 by the Government of India. The Resolution authorised intervention in case of any emergency. The aim would be to stimulate and supplement, though never to supplant, private trade in the region. In effect, however, nothing was done beyond circulating information about the current market situation for the benefit of traders. A bania starting an import business was assured of government purchases for gratuitous relief at rates which, though varying with the Bettiah prices, would leave him with a sufficient profit margin.

However, the breakdown in railway arrangements at Mokama Ghat in mid-May 1897 led to a supply crisis of grave dimensions, Ramnagar being largely dependent on imports of Burma rice. The Bettiah merchants could not afford to order fresh supplies from Calcutta until they realised the value of their earlier consignments, which were taking three to four weeks to arrive instead of the usual ten days. The problems of despatch and pilfering in transit upset all their calculations, causing an almost total suspension of trade in the region. Meanwhile, attempts to start a steamer line from Patna up the Gandak were frustrated by the unprecedentedly low level of the river. The problem intensified with the advent of the rains, as the merchants hesitated to bring in grain lest good bhadoi prospects should draw out the old reserves. Imports failed to pick up throughout the season, as this feeling of uncertainty persisted. They dwindled and ceased altogether in August–September, when the bulk of the bhadoi crops came into the market. The Ramnagar tract, however,

[21] FRFRO, Champaran, 1896–97, by D. J. Macpherson, Magistrate and Collector, ch. 1, para. 17.

remained unrelieved, for there the bhadoi was of little consequence, and always came two to three weeks later than in the rest of the district.

Palamau

The problem assumed greater intensity in the affected regions of Palamau. Even in the best of years Palamau was not self-sufficient in foodgrains, the annual deficit being about 8,484 md. Stocks were further depleted due to successive crop failures in 1895–96 and 1896–97. With the closure of the normal sources of supply, the crisis deepened into famine. Lohardaga sent about 43,000 md. of rice to Palamau by mid-January 1897, and another 10,877 md. by June. Supplies ceased after that, 4,500 pack bullocks being sent back empty from Lohardaga. The Tributary States of Sirguja, Udaypur, Gangpur and Jashpur prohibited grain exports during the crisis. The only hope for Palamau now lay in importing grain into its north-eastern corner from Shahabad and Gaya. But these areas were also suffering from the effects of scarcity and hence could not spare any large consignments.

However, the primary problem in Palamau was the difficulty in transport and communication. It persisted throughout the year under review and upset all calculations regarding the supply of foodgrains in the district. R. H. Renny, the Deputy Commissioner of Palamau, noted: "We may be likened unto a ship at sea with provisions running short—so serious is our situation and so helpless".[22] Palamau was bounded on the west by Mirzapur, the NWP and Sirguja; on the south by Lohardaga; on the north by the Sone in Shahabad; and on the east by Hazaribagh and Gaya. It was at a distinct disadvantage when compared to the districts of Bihar, in having no connection with the railway system of Bengal. The distance from Daltonganj in Palamau to the nearest railway station of Gaya was 101 miles by the Maharajganj Road, and 73 miles to Barun, at the end of the Sone Canal. In internal communications, too, Palamau was worse off. This entire stretch of 101 miles, and 59 of the 73 miles, were *kutcha* (earthen) roads, while the 42 miles from

22 *Selection of Papers*, vol. 4: p. 325.

Maharajganj to Daltonganj lay through hilly and difficult country. By bullock cart it took eight days from Gaya, and six from Barun to carry grain to Palamau in dry weather, and from twelve to twenty days during the rains.

It was very difficult and expensive to procure carts and pack bullocks, which alone could traverse these roads. They were normally scarce, and during the monsoon the rate of cart hire rose to 12 an. per day. There was an unusual demand after the lean season this year for drought cattle of every description for agricultural purposes, especially after the first rains fell.[23] In the early months, combinations of the thakurs or cart owners in the trade marts further held up imports. Even Lohardaga, an isolated district, was better situated than Palamau. It had a metalled road to Purulia, from where supplies could be drawn. Once the prohibitive freight rates were met by the government bounty of Re. 1 per md., carts were forthcoming from Manbhum and the Burdwan Division.

During the rains, the roads became impassable in Palamau. River traffic was now the only recourse, but due to deficient rains the Sone and Koel ran dry. Small boats, which alone could carry grain across the rivers this season, could not be had in sufficient numbers unless they were impressed on the Ganges and brought to Barun.[24] At the height of the crisis, private traders who had taken advances for importing rice could not get carts or boats in time to avail of the bounty, since practically all of them had been impressed for the transport of government rice.[25] Another great obstacle in importing grain from outside, especially from Calcutta, was the absence of telegraphic communication between Daltonganj and the city. As a consequence, local dealers could not get current quotations from the Calcutta market.

There were no big grain-merchants in Palamau who could face such a challenge in the midst of a crisis. The bazaar banias were accustomed only to dealing in bullock loads with the surrounding villages. The bullock drivers were practically the real traders, picking up and carrying supplies from one bania to

23 Ibid., vol. 12: p. 344.
24 Ibid., vol. 10: p. 485.
25 LRP, Aug. 1898, pt. 2, p. 771–72, paras. 30–32.

another, until they could dispose of the stock at a small profit. The dealers at Maharajganj were equally humble, buying paddy by the bullock-load from the beparis and retailing their purchases in the form of rice. In normal years they carried on a petty barter trade in foodgrains in exchange for non-edible products with adjacent areas in the Lohardaga plateau, the Tributary States and, occasionally, with Gaya and Shahabad. These, however, were purely local ventures, involving little capital or knowledge of commercial business, and having no connection with Calcutta or any other important trade centre.

As A. Forbes, the Commissioner of Chotanagpur, reported early in February 1897, Palamau was particularly unfortunate as regards commercial activity and enterprise, so that it would have to "import the contractors as well as the rice".[26] Hazaribagh presented a marked contrast to Palamau in this respect. Both districts were on par as to the stock position and soaring prices, Hazaribagh being perhaps the worse off. Yet Hazaribagh had the great advantage of having several firms of wealthy Marwaris trading directly with Calcutta. They were fully alive to the situation, and traded briskly despite transport problems. Although the railway station at Giridih was over seventy miles from the Sadar by road, these men imported about .25 million md. of rice from Calcutta and other places, between October 1896 and January 1897. To tide over the crisis in Palamau, the Commissioner suggested making import contracts with reliable agencies like Messrs. Jardine, Skinner and Company (who had large lac dealings in the district), and strongly deprecated "a first experiment being tried with a body of inexperienced petty dealers in a matter of such vital importance".[27]

The level of purchasing power in Palamau, however, was not such as to induce outsiders to invest in expensive and risky ventures. The lack of local resources became more evident as the months passed. Enquiries in distress areas such as the Tori pargana and the villages to the north of Daltonganj showed a very uneven distribution of foodstocks. The bulk of the population in these parts were the labouring classes, such as the Ahirs, Dusadhs, Chamars, Kherwars, Bhuiyas, Kahars, Gareris

26 *Selection of Papers*, vol. 4: p. 336.
27 Ibid., p. 328, no. 412T-MR, 27 Jan. 1897.

and others of the kamia class. In normal years they depended on help given by zamindars and other landowners during the slack season. Demand for foodgrains was real and acute. While Section 2 of the Famine Code required officials to be on the alert when prices rose over the normal by 20 per cent, the rise in Palamau by January 1897 varied from 40 to 67 per cent. In January, prices had gone up to 8/8.5 sr. per rupee, yet every ounce was eagerly snapped up even at these high rates. But, already at the end of the month the NWP traders carried off rice from the Garhwa market, outbidding the locals, who returned empty-handed. By the end of February, Palamau was obviously running short of cash, having gone through a long period of scarcity and inflation. Hence, despite acute shortage and an abnormal escalation of rates, importers could not be sure of an effective demand once prices went beyond a certain level. For example, while entire stocks of rice were bought up at 9 sr. or more a rupee, large quantities were left unsold when offered at less than 9 sr.[28] The Commissioner's suggestion on 21 January 1897, that the government should import 0.1 million md. of rice, and the Deputy Commissioner's plea later (on 20 May 1897) for the direct importation of 0.05 million md. were ignored for fear of dislocating the local trade in foodgrains. It was felt that private trade would feel the pulse of the market better. Hence, the task of supplying foodgrains for the local market and relief works were left to private traders, mainly from Gaya.

The Commissioner then proposed indirect measures to stimulate private trade. Traders were repeatedly informed of the market situation. When they failed to respond, government tried to induce the larger Gaya dealers to bring in Burma rice to Daltonganj by offering a bounty of 8 an. per md. The aim of the bounty was to cover the cost of carriage from Gaya to Daltonganj until the end of March. The trade still flagged, mainly due to the difficulty in procuring carts. The Commissioner now suggested extending the bounty to "all rice" instead of Burma rice alone, for country rice outside Palamau might in the near future become cheaper than the latter, in which case the trade in Burma rice would become unprofitable. Moreover, this measure

[28] Ibid., vol. 6: p. 278.

would also place the import trade within the reach of the petty dealers, and bring into play the local system of carts and pack bullocks which would carry across small supplies from Nasirganj, Daudnagar, the irrigated tracts along the Sone Canal, and elsewhere. The suggestion was complied with, and the bounty was extended to a limit of Rs. 25,000 on all rice imported into Palamau until the end of April. A Gaya trader, Ghanshyam Das, was the first to avail of this opportunity. Yet the problems and cost of carriage proved a major constraint, and prices remained high due to lack of competition.

In April, loans up to Rs. 25,000 at 6.25 per cent interest were sanctioned by the government to enable traders—mainly mahajans of Daltonganj, Chainpur and Garhwa—to import rice into Palamau. The bounty was extended as long as the roads were open to traffic, and lasted in effect till early September. The amount sanctioned for advances was increased to Rs. 75,000.

Further, two new routes—one via Manatu to Daltonganj, the other via Dungwar to Garhwa—were thrown open to importers claiming the bounty. Yet imports were not sufficient, and the price rose to the unrealistic level of 6 sr. and less per rupee.

By 21 May, only 7,516 md. of rice had been imported into Palamau over the last three months, while Hazaribagh and Manbhum had imported 125,000 and 91,000 md., respectively, by rail during the same period. Of the Rs. 75,000 sanctioned for advances, only Rs. 52,500 could be expended, while only Rs. 9,895-10 an.-10 p. could be spent from the Rs. 25,000 authorised for payment of the bounty.[29] Importers in Palamau found themselves crippled by the non-availability of carts from Gaya and Barun to Daltonganj. To see to this problem, a Special Officer was sent to Barun. As the rains set in, however, the roads became impassable and imports were blocked still further. On the whole, by September only 13,687 md. of Burma rice and 5,367 md. of country rice had been imported into Palamau since the introduction of the bounty system in February 1897.

[29] LRP, Aug. 1898, pt. 2, no. 322F., Daltonganj, 5 Nov. 1897, from R. H. Renny, Dept. Comm., Palamau, to Comm., Chotanagpur Div., ch. 3, para. 28.

Thus, private trade could not operate effectively in Palamau in 1896–97 despite government bounties and advances. This failure was mainly due to transport difficulties, the absence of big grain merchants, and the wide disparity between prices and purchasing power. Finally, the government decided to directly import 15,440 md. of rice for the relief works, but as the rivers had now become unnavigable, half of the government grain arrived too late. By then the bhadoi and winter crops were practically assured, and it was difficult to dispose of the grain in the local market. The Commissioner of Chotanagpur was sharply critical of the government for carrying its policy of non-interference too far. The entire problem, according to him, could have been solved had it complied with his earlier suggestion to directly import 100,000 md. of foodgrain into Palamau in January 1897.

Chilka Region in Puri

Orissa compared most unfavourably with other parts of the Province, in having "absolutely no machinery for imports".[30] In Cuttack, for instance, there was little or no internal trade, the villagers normally bartering paddy for other necessities. The traders were unaccustomed to importing from outside the district, or even carrying supplies from one part of it to another. Hence, due to the extensive crop failure this year there was very little rice available for sale in the local markets, the stocks being neither large nor easily mobilised. The affected regions of the Chilka tract in Puri were even worse off, as regards trade and communications. The few sarbarahakars, *jagirdar*s (landholders) and zamindars of the region cornered large stocks and refused to sell locally. The people in normal years were self-sufficient in grain, and unused to trade transactions. The Collector noted: "There are no traders here, and trade will not bring the rice".[31] Stocks of grain in a few *math*s (religious institutions) of Chaubiskud and Serai had already been sold to the Ganjam and Bombay traders at high prices.[32]

30 *Selection of Papers,* vol. 4: p. 419.
31 Ibid., p. 421.
32 FRFRO, Puri, 1896–97 and 1897–98; no. 2652, Puri, 2 Dec.

The parganas of Malud, Parikud and Bajrakote on the southern or sea-facing side of the lake consisted of a number of islands intersected by inlets and creeks. During the summer and the rains they were cut off for days at a stretch, as the lake was either too dry or too rough for boats to cross over. These, together with Manikpatna and Satpara, were the "salt parganas", liable to saline floods. Chaubiskud and Serai on the east and north were subjected to the floods of the Daya river, and the brackish waters of the Chilka when the southerly high winds blew. There were no roads, making communication difficult throughout the year. During the rains each village became an island, unapproachable except occasionally by canoes.

Being thus difficult to access and liable to floods and famine, the single-crop region of the Chilka did not naturally have the resources necessary to attract trade. As Mr W. H. Lee, the Collector of Puri, notes in March 1897, "The people being generally poor, and their purchasing power limited, trade does but little in the way of supplying grains to them even in ordinary times".[33] Due to the low level of local resources and abundance of the rice crop in normal years, prices were habitually low in Orissa.

However, though prices were not competitive enough to draw in supplies from without, they were sufficiently high to create pressure within. Yet there was less of an exchange crisis, the real problem being a decline in foodgrain availability in absolute terms, as in the famine year of 1866. Remarking on the relief works in progress in the Nayapara region in Satpara, Mr Lee wrote: "The men already employed there want paddy for pay, and say that money at present is of no value to them". Tanks and wells were being dug and cleaned in Manikpatna, Gopalpur, Deulpara, Sepia, etc., and a road was sanctioned in Parikud. "But all this will not save life, unless paddy is brought here. . . . the people here can buy any quantity of paddy. It is only a few of the very poorest who are out of money.[34]

1897, from W. H. Lee, Offg. Collector, Puri, to the Comm., Orissa Div., ch. 1, para. 4; ch. 3, para. 3.

33 *Selection of Papers,* vol. 4: p. 389, no. 592, Puri, 15 March 1897, from W. H. Lee, Offg. Collector, Puri, to the Comm., Orissa Div.

34 Ibid., p. 419–21, no. 66, Puri, 9/11 Jan. 1897, from W. H. Lee,

As the crisis deepened, the Collector felt the urgency of importing and storing rice in the Chilka region: "I am decidedly of opinion that, in order that terrible scenes may be avoided, it is necessary that rice must be brought here in large quantities, as private trade fails to supply local wants".[35] He therefore advanced small sums of money to respectable persons willing to import paddy into the famine zone. The grain was to be stored in godowns in parts of the distressed tracts at the importers' own risk and expense, without government intervention. The receivers of loans were to pay interest at 6.25 per cent per annum, and furnish adequate security for repayment of the loans before 1 January 1898. Some of the contractors were purchasing grain in Khurda and Rambha, where circumstances were better than in the Sadar. The Collector also ordered ten cartloads of paddy to be purchased at the town and sent to Satpara every week for sale in small quantities at cost price to the needy. This arrangement was to be in place until the godowns set up by persons receiving loans began to function in full swing.

As scarcity had by now extended to the whole of India, a strict adherence to the provisions of the Government Resolution would necessitate the importation of grain from outside India. But as it was impossible in this region to secure local contractors who had the enterprise or resources necessary to undertake importation of grain from outside the country, exemption was sought "in consideration of the special local circumstances". There was hardly any stock of grain or active import trader in Malud, Parikud, Bajrakote or Chaubiskud. Yet these measures of the Collector helped to keep prices down at 10 sr. a rupee at the highest. The Lieutenant Governor, however, disapproved of the Collector's "precipitate" action in importing and selling grain, and maintained that it should in no case have been undertaken before receiving government sanction.[36]

Offg. Collector, Puri, to the Comm., Orissa Div., paras. 6–8.

35 Ibid., p. 389, no. 592. Puri, 15 March 1897, para. 3.

36 *Selection of Papers*, vol. 6: p. 390.

[2.3] Manipulation of the market by speculative traders

The related problems of excessive grain exports from the distressed tracts and a lack of corresponding imports have been discussed above at some length. A third and major constraint on the smooth flow of trade in the famine zone was the manipulation of the market by the local traders, in several different ways. Though the Famine Commission Report of 1898 insisted that there were no combinations by traders worthy of mention during 1896–97, complaints of this were common, especially in Bihar in the early months of the famine. Perhaps there was no large-scale or organised attempt as the millers' combines in Burma in 1882 or 1893, but local manoeuvres were nonetheless effective.

[a] Hoarding and exportation of foodgrains

From the beginning of October 1896, reports poured in of hoardings by grain dealers and their refusal to sell retail in distressed areas. In most districts, especially in bhaoli regions, local zamindars and rich peasants withheld large stocks. A section of the grain dealers in their capacity as mahajans often received their interest in kind. They also secured the crops on the ground by advance payments, the peasant invariably losing out in the bargain. The Mogulbandi dealers in Angul provide an instance in point. In Satkhira in Khulna, too, the raiyats had borrowed money on the security of their aus and jute crops in 1896–97. The rabi foodgrains brought little relief to Champaran this year; they went almost entirely into the hands of the dealers due to extensive prior hypothecation. The pressure of rent and interest payments in Banela, Hitampur, Pabia and Gidhour in the Santhal Parganas likewise forced grain out of the peasant's home and into the mahajan's gola, whence it flowed out of the district altogether.

Tension mounted against such cornering and exportation of grain from famine zones. Yet the government refused to act, on the ground of its much-publicised policy of laissez-faire. For instance, in November 1896, "demonstrations" in Hazaribagh, calling upon the district authorities to stop exports and reduce the price of food, drew no response and quickly fell through. Local merchants bought up all available stocks at prices slightly higher than the market rate, thus cornering supplies and simultaneously raising their own rates.[37] Once prices began to fall in Hazaribagh in August 1897, the mahajans bitterly complained of a loss on the sale of their reserves, confirming once again the existence of hoarded stocks.[38] The Patna Division provides typical examples of hoarding by grain dealers. The *goladars* (stock holders) in many places refused to sell below a rupee's worth of rice at a time. At Naubatpur a number of people had to starve for a day for this reason. Goladars were refusing to sell retail in Phulwari. Similar complaints against several Marwaris came from Khagole on 4 October 1896, and a riot was apprehended. Reports were also received from Barh, Maner and Bihar in Patna district. In Dinapore, four or five golas were looted for this reason on 3 October. Goladars in Saran were said to be changing rates two or three times a day, and unduly inflating prices—they did not actually sell at the rates quoted. The incidents in Patna Division grew more scarce and isolated in November–December, but the problem persisted throughout on a smaller scale. Instances of hoarding were also common in September–October 1896 in Cuttack and Puri, and continued well into 1897. In Angul, there was great difficulty in procuring rice in the market in November. Finally, on receiving complaints from the police and the postal departments, the Deputy Commissioner persuaded the sarbarahakars to sell small quantities to meet pressing demands. Hoarding by local banias also led to grain riots in Rampur-Boalia in Rajshahi in June–July, and in Lohardaga in April 1897.

[b] Rigging of the market

Rigging of the market was a common feature during this famine. In Palamau, for instance, rice was selling in Manatu at 7 sr. or less per rupee in February 1897, while at Hariharganj, only about thirty miles away, it sold at 9.5 sr. The difference was attributed to manipulation of the market by local traders. H. C. Streatfeild,

[37] J. L. Herald, Dept. Comm., Hazaribagh, to the Comm., Chotanagpur Div., no. 1474 R., Hazaribagh, 24/27 Nov. 1897, para. 16.

[38] *Selection of Papers*, vol. 10: p. 442; vol. 11: pp. 428–29.

Deputy Commissioner of Lohardaga, noted certain "suggestive facts" in this context: when the price of rice in Lohardaga rose as high as 5 sr. to the rupee, a zamindar opened his granaries and started selling at lower rates. The local merchants promptly contacted him and dissuaded him from doing so, thus proving that they had stocks to dispose of. The effectiveness of their control over the market was further seen in August 1897 when some Ranchi merchants, fearing a loss on rice imported before the grant of the government bounty, sent part of it out to Lohardaga: prices in Lohardaga fell by 2 sr. to the rupee even before the consignments arrived.[39]

[c] Carters' combines

Not content with rigging the market, the merchants exploited the problems of transport and communication by organising carters' combines to further push up prices. Mr W. H. Lee, the Collector of Puri, wrote in January 1897, "The export merchants have established such a boycott among the carters, that no carter will fetch paddy from Khurda, where rice is 23 sr. (to the rupee), to relieve the town people who cannot get more than 13. If allowed, I will break through this".[40] In July 1897, the difficulties of cartage from Purulia to Ranchi raised the freight charge to Rs. 1-6 an. per md., as against the normal monsoon rate of 13 an. Grain prices rose sharply in consequence, the Ranchi merchants being able to re-import at a profit from Hazaribagh. In Palamau, independent combinations of the thakurs in the trade marts held up imports. The *chaudharies* (cart owners), taking advantage of the great demand for drought cattle on the fields this year after the first showers fell, insisted on a dasturi of 1 to 2 an. a cart from each trader, before arranging to provide for them.[41]

39 H. C. Streatfeild, Dept. Comm., Lohardaga, to the Comm., Chotanagpur Div., no. 409F., Ranchi, 12 Nov. 1897, para. 18.

40 *Selection of Papers*, vol. 4: p. 421, W. H. Lee to the Comm., Orissa Div. No. 116, Puri, 20 Jan. 1897, para. 5.

41 Ibid., vol. 8: p. 416, R. H. Renny, Esq., Dept. Comm. Palamau, to the Comm., Chotanagpur Div., no. 509 R., Daltonganj, 31 May/1 June 1897, para. 10.

[d] Exploitation by middlemen and retailers

The middlemen and retailers exploited both the seller-producer and the consumer by the arbitrary fixing of rates and fraudulent weight measures. In Nadia the zamindars acted as landlord, indigo planter and mahajan, leaving little freedom to the raiyats. The novel manner in which rice was sold in parts of Nadia, such as Tehatta and Gotpara, was anything but a free bargain. At each hat there was a *mahaldar* (middleman) appointed by the zamindar. He paid rent to the zamindar for the privilege of collecting a small tax on each bargain. Every ounce of rice sold was measured by him, the price being calculated at rates he alone had the power to fix, and both the seller and buyer had to act through him. Privileged measurers (*kayali*s) were also met with elsewhere in Bengal; but it was unique for them to fix the rates as well. This local custom might have arisen from the fact that the sellers here were all illiterate women who had to depend on others to do the calculations, and were likewise apt to be cheated. The two mahaldars in Tehatta vied with each other by increasing the rates, to attract the women sellers to their respective parts of the bazaar. Despite rigid government adherence to the policy of non-interference, the police had ultimately to intervene and set the price. In February 1897 Babu Rajendra Narain Mojumdar, overseer in Midnapur, reported that the local grain dealers kept two sets of weight measures (*pai* and *kona)*. They purchased with the correct ones and sold with the others, thus cheating the poor people both ways. In every pai of rice (1.5 sr.) they were cheated of 3 ch. The dealers also sold wet grain, which would swell and weigh more.[42] Referring to the activities of the shopkeepers and dealers in the crisis year of 1896–97, the Famine Report of Shahabad states, "The *baniya* alone thrives at such a time".[43] They profiteered without scruple even on government relief contracts. In Saran, for instance, "they were constantly using short weights, issuing short doles, or doles of grain mixed with earth".[44]

42 Ibid., vol. 4: p. 403, no. 257, 12 Feb. 1897.

43 FRFRO, Shahabad, ch. 4, para. 13.

44 Ibid., Saran, ch. 5, para. 83, Note on Difficulties in the Administration of Gratuitous Relief, point 6.

On the whole, the agrarian crisis of 1896 in Bengal forced a distinct change in the direction and flow of the grain trade, creating new problems and new opportunities. However, the market largely failed to grasp this opportunity and to respond to the price-stimulus in the way expected, due to the several imperfections recounted above.

[3] *The Role of Theory in Policy Failures*

The official approach to famines was not based on a proper understanding of the problems, either of foodgrain availability or entitlement. [i] Exaggerated notions of a surplus often underlay bureaucratic thoughts and action on the subject. [ii] However, it was believed that a shortfall in aggregate production in lean years would directly result in shortage and starvation. Foodgrain prices would naturally shoot up in affected areas. In such a situation, it was thought that the only solution lay in giving free rein to private enterprise, which, undeterred by government interference and regulated by the price-stimulus, would move grain from surplus to scarcity and famine tracts. Hence, the principle of laissez-faire or non-intervention in grain trade remained the basis of government policy during famines. [iii] This policy assumed that the speculator played a positive role in society, for, by raising grain prices in times of scarcity, he helped to control demand and so adjust it to the reduced level of supply.

(i) Official belief in self-sufficiency in food was, however, based on exaggerated estimates of the surplus. A surplus of 3,306,000 tons was estimated for Bengal in 1898, for instance, though the average annual export from this Province in years preceding the famine of 1896–97 amounted to only 305,000 tons. Again, by identifying exports with the surplus, officials like the Collector of Patna in this year of famine ignored the vital role of purchasing power in determining the flow of trade.

(ii) The laissez-faire theory, too, suffered from over-emphasis on the physical aspect of food supply, and did not consider the shift in entitlement patterns. It believed that high prices in the famine zone would naturally attract a free flow of foodgrains. When the volume of this import trade fell far short of expectations, the explanation was sought in the physical problems of transport and communication, rather than in the more fundamental one of market-based entitlements and purchasing power. Adam Smith's political economy was thus concerned with the operation of market forces in meeting a growing demand for food, but ignored a situation when this demand could not be made effective.

(iii) The beneficial effects of speculation in reducing the intensity of the crisis are also open to question. In fact, this view, based on the arguments of Malthus and J. S. Mill, tends to oversimplify the working of market forces. In a famine or scarcity aggravated by speculative hoarding, prices are not depressed even by the release of withheld stocks, for panic creates an abnormal demand. As the Deputy Commissioner of Chotanagpur commented at the end of August 1897, "It is evident much greater pressure is required to lower prices than to raise them".[45] A price rise may be of two types, to each of which the market reacts differently. When a long period of scarcity is anticipated, the universal tendency is to hoard. This further diminishes supply, and the psychosis of greed and fear, thus reinforced, may push up prices to unprecedented heights, as happened in Bengal in 1943. On the other hand, when the shortfall is expected to have only a temporary effect, producers and dealers try to sell their stocks while prices remain high. According to the Lyall Commission, this attitude prevailed in Bengal in 1896–97, there being hardly any large-scale speculation or combination of grain dealers to keep up prices. Yet, complaints against local *banias* were not uncommon this year. There were numerous instances of hoarding and rigging of the market by traders in Patna, Palamau, Lohardaga and other places, as noted earlier in this chapter. This led to widespread grain riots and intensified local distress, as seen in Patna in October 1896, and in Lohardaga and Rajshahi in 1897.

Due to these misconceptions in official policy, the market did not respond to the price stimulus in the way expected. Grain flowed out of acutely affected areas, though famine prices prevailed. Deviations from the official policy in such special cases make

[45] *Selection of Papers,* vol. 11: p. 428., no. 1072R., Chotanagpur, 1 Sept. 1897, memo by J. L. Herald, Dept. Comm., to the Comm., Chotanagpur Div.

interesting reading. For instance Egerton, Collector of Shahabad, forbade grain exports from the district by an order under Section 144, Criminal Procedure Code. Bourdillon, the Commissioner, rebuked him and immediately cancelled his order by wire on the ground that "no direct interference with trade can possibly be allowed". In Champaran, government loans for grain import were allowed after initial reluctance and much haggling with the local officials. In February 1897, Macpherson, Collector of Champaran, noted that the N.W. Railways charged a special reduced rate of 6 an. per md. for downward traffic to, but not for upward traffic from, Howrah. As he observed, "It seems an anomaly under present circumstances to give a bounty like this on exports from Bihar".[46]

In Palamau, suggestions by the Commissioner and Deputy Commissioner for direct importation of 100,000 md. and 50,000 md. of rice, respectively, were brusquely brushed aside—with dire consequences. Local dealers were expected to meet the needs of the district, though A. Forbes, the Commissioner, mentioned in clear terms their inability to do so: "I can assure Government that it is perfectly useless to look for any material help in the present circumstances from the Palamau dealers".[47] His suggestion for an import contract with a reliable Calcutta-based firm like Messrs. Jardine, Skinner and Company was not considered either. He was finally allowed to negotiate imports with the Gaya dealers, only one of whom responded initially and was quite unable to meet the demands of the district. R. H. Renny, the Deputy Commissioner, warned in March 1897, "It appears to me that Government should come to our assistance before it is too late".[48] Even the grain dealers of Hazaribagh could not function effectively in a crisis year like this without government assistance. The Deputy Commissioner noted: "I consider this is one of the districts to which the limitation of the principles laid down by the Famine Commission would expressly apply, that is, a district which cannot be safely left to private enterprise for its food-supplies in time of scarcity".[49]

46 Ibid., vol. 4: p. 174, no. 246 F., 4 Feb. 1897.
47 Ibid., p. 335, 8 Feb. 1897.
48 Ibid., p. 344, no. 2037 R., 12 March 1897.
49 Ibid., p. 347, no. 1399 R., 15–20 Jan. 1897, from J. L. Herald, Dept. Comm., Hazaribagh, to Comm., Chotanagpur Div.

Similarly, as supplies failed in the Kalantar tract in Nadia, the Collector, J. H. E. Garrett, proposed to grant Rs. 50,000 as an advance to Gregson, an agent of Watson and Company, who alone could import grain in large quantities into the region. This, however, was refused, lest Gregson should undersell other grain dealers and dislocate private trade. Garrett wrote in exasperation to F. V. Westmacott, Commissioner of the Presidency Division, on 23 April 1897, "As regards the purchasing public generally, I am afraid nothing can be done beyond endeavouring to stimulate banias into importing from Calcutta by showing them the profit they can make out of it".[50] The Collector was, however, persistent in his attempts to convince the government of the need to finance Gregson, as there were no other local traders big or resourceful enough to undertake imports on this scale. On 8 June, he again wrote to Westmacott:

> As already reported, the whole of the northern portions of the Karimpur and Daulatpur thanas are now entirely dependent on Mr. Gregson, and should the capital which has been placed at his disposal by his firm prove inadequate to meet the drain upon it,—and there is every reason to suppose that it will,—the inevitable result will be that large numbers of persons will be forced to the Government relief works through sheer inability to obtain rice in any other way, and further it is not improbable that deaths from starvation will ensue. Consequently, I beg to request that you will be good enough to move Government to reconsider their decision and accept my proposal . . . or else absolve me from all further responsibility in the matter.[51]

Mr Finucane, Revenue Secretary to the Government of Bengal, wrote back on 17 June, "I am directed to say that the Lieutenant Governor . . . is not convinced that the risk of a failure of supplies is so great as it is believed by you to be. . . . His Honour cannot therefore sanction your proposal to grant a loan to Mr. Gregson".[52]

Garrett's stand was vindicated within a month by the intensity of distress in the Kalantar, and the amount of relief required.

50 Ibid., vol. 8: p. 370, Krishnagar, 23 April 1897.
51 Ibid., p. 372, no. 491 F., Krishnagar, 8 June 1897.
52 Ibid., no. 624 TR./Fam., Darjeeling, 17 June 1897.

Stocks were "non-existent", approximately 109,222 people, i.e. nearly 20 per cent out of a total population of 558,000 in the affected tracts, subsisting on government relief.[53]

In Orissa, the Collector of Puri was pulled up for giving out loans to grain contractors in order to import rice into the Chilka tract. The Collector of Cuttack noted with regret, "Exports must go on and the government forbids interference! At the same time, there is absolutely no machinery for imports".

Too rigid an application of the principle of laissez-faire, irrespective of such special circumstances, led to controversies even at the highest level. In paragraph 13 of the Bengal Government Resolution No. 5133 of 10 December 1896, the Lieutenant Governor, Sir Alexander Mackenzie, applied to the Government of India for sanction of advances to reliable persons at a reasonable rate of interest (about 6 per cent). These advances would be used for the purchase in Calcutta of grain from overseas. The grain was to be sold in remote and inaccessible tracts at the borrowers' own risk and discretion, subject to the occasional inspection of invoices by government officials. This, according to him, was a "question . . . more . . . of finance than of interference with trade". The Governor-General in Council, however, negatived the proposal as being "rather in the nature of a blank cheque presented for his signature". He insisted on a more "localised" scheme of grain advances for remote or inaccessible tracts, where local trade was inactive or unable to cope with the problems of transportation.

Sir Alexander objected to this description of his proposal, and criticised paragraph 8 of the Government of India's letter providing for contracts with grain dealers in "exceptional cases" for the supply of provisions on relief works. As he pointed out, action of this kind was painfully inadequate to meet an emergency of such dimensions, for it did not allow for cases where supplies failed in the local markets as well. There was no difference in principle between advancing money to a contractor, whether for selling grain at relief works or in areas where private trade had failed to cater to local demands. The lengthy correspondence on the subject was finally brought to a close by

53 Ibid., vol. 9: pp. 353, 384.

the sanction of advances only in the most exceptional cases, with a firm rejoinder that "the Government of India still adhere emphatically to the general policy of non-interference with private trade".[54]

As during the Potato Famine in Ireland, the principle of laissez-faire was thus carried too far by the British Government, without reference to the local context. In the process, it ignored even such exceptional cases as had been noted and provided for in the Famine Commission Report of 1880, which was said to form the very basis of this policy. As noted, some local officials like J. H. E. Garrett of Nadia, W. H. Lee of Puri, Macpherson of Champaran and H. C. Streatfeild of Lohardaga questioned the rigidity of the laissez-faire policy; yet even their dissent was not based on an accurate assessment of the situation. Thus, when importations into the famine zone fell far short of expectations, the answer was sought in the physical problems of transport and communication, rather than in those of purchasing power and entitlements. For instance, it was a "mystery" to Garrett that grain flowed out of Nadia, instead of being drawn in by the famine prices ruling in the Kalantar; he did not enquire whether the local people could afford these prices. Similarly, when rice lay unsold in the most distressed tracts of Govindpur in Lohardaga, Streatfeild attributed it to popular superstition rather than the lack of effective demand.[55] The Collector of Patna made the same mistake by identifying exports with the surplus.

Thus, while the "pull failure" reflected the entitlement problems in 1896–97, a massive "response failure" occurred due to the inability of the market or the government to react positively to this abnormal situation by increasing the availability of foodgrains.

54 Ibid., vol. 3: p. 304, no. 298/45-22 F., Calcutta, 20 Jan. 1897; from T. W. Holderness, Dept. Secy. to the Govt. of India, Rev. Dept., to the Secy. to the Govt. of Bengal, Rev. Dept., para. 5.

55 FRFRO, Lohardaga, ch. 3, para. 19, H. C. Streatfeild, Dept. Comm., Lohardaga, to the Comm., Chotanagpur Div., no. 409 F., Ranchi, 12 Nov. 1897.

Epilogue

The analysis so far shows how, during the winter of 1896, the agrarian distress in Bengal deepened into famine, unprecedented in dimension and fierce in extent and intensity. It brings into focus the agony of a peasant society thrown out of gear in an abnormal situation, and the crisis of identities that ensued.

In the process, an attempt has been made to review this famine in terms of Amartya Sen's theory of the Failure of Exchange Entitlements (FEE), as distinct from that of Food Availability Decline or FAD, as he calls it.

The traditional analysis of famines emphasises any reduction in the total output, current supply and per capita availability of foodgrains as the focal points of the crisis. According to this view, a crop failure and decline in aggregate production would directly result in shortage and starvation. This point is repeatedly stressed in the Famine Commission's Reports and policy discussions of the British Indian government throughout the nineteenth century. Contemporary official policies, relying on the political economy of Adam Smith and J. S. Mill, advocated the simple formula that foodgrain prices inflated by crop failure would inevitably attract supplies from surplus to scarcity, and scarcity to famine, tracts. Hence, a free private trade in foodgrains, regulated by this price differential, was looked upon as the only effective remedy in a famine situation, and a policy of laissez-faire or non-intervention in grain trade was strictly emphasised.

This view of Food Availability Decline or FAD is called into question by Amartya Sen's theory of the Failure of Exchange Entitlements. In his monograph *Poverty and Famines*, Sen criticises the FAD approach as being too gross and simplistic, which fails to take note of the finer distinctions of income distribution and changing entitlement values in a market economy. He visualises two types of situations in which the existing pattern of exchange relations might fail, thus leading to abject poverty, starvation and famine. First, even when there is no crop failure or food shortage worthy of mention, a deepening crisis in exchange relations caused by exogenous factors—such as wage depression, unemployment or underemployment of labour, a rise in cost price and fall in profits in the production of certain commodities, or the enrichment of certain sections of society at the expense of others—could lead to a famine situation. Second, famine conditions could develop if a crop failure and general decline in food supply inflated foodgrain prices and correspondingly reduced the food entitlement of different groups in the community; thus, even here the famine is caused not directly by food shortage, but only through its reactions on the existing pattern of exchange relations. Throughout his monograph, Sen emphasises the importance of the first type of situation, that is, a failure of exchange entitlement leading to famine for reasons other than a general decline in food supply. Food shortage is no more than one possible factor in a cluster of variables, some of which might interact to cause strains and shifts within the framework of entitlement relations, and precipitate severe famine conditions "even without receiving any impulse from food production".[1]

[1] *Crop Failure and FAD*

In order to consider the Bengal famine of 1896 in the light of this theory, it is essential to determine the extent of shortfall in the production, current supply and availability of foodgrains that year. Food crops covered 85.61 per cent of the total normal cropped area in the Province, of which 47.74 per cent was taken up by the aman or winter rice, and 19.34 per cent and 18.53 per cent by the bhadoi and rabi crops, respectively. In 1896–97, the estimated outturn of winter rice was 7.5 an. or 46.87 per cent, that of bhadoi 10.5 an. or 65.62 per cent, and of rabi 10.33 an. or 64.56 per cent of an average crop. The crop

[1] Sen, *Poverty and Famine,* p. 158.

failure amounted to much more than 50 per cent in the affected areas of Puri, Bankura, the Presidency Division, Chotanagpur, and the whole of the Patna Division except the Patna and Gaya districts. Crop statistics show that the highest yield of winter rice in the affected districts was only 9 an. or 56 per cent of the average in Puri, while it came down to 1.25, 2.5, 3 and 3.5 an.—7.8, 15.6, 18.75 and 21.8 per cent—in Saran, Nadia, Muzaffarpur and Champaran, respectively.

The current supply and per capita availability of foodgrains in the famine zone went down considerably, due not only to this remarkable shortfall in food production, but also to the low yield and "carry over" stock of the previous year and the excessive exports from famine-hit districts throughout 1896–97. For example, the three affected districts of Chotanagpur showed a deficiency of 30 per cent in 1895–96. In the Patna Division, too, the deficiency of the previous year in Shahabad, Darbhanga and Muzaffarpur was over 30 per cent, while in Champaran a large part of the crop, which was slightly better, was drained off by a brisk export trade in grain.[2] An estimate of the current food supply has been made by the Collectors of the famine-hit districts, by deducting from the total out-turn the amount required for seedgrain, and adding or subtracting the net balance of imports or exports, as the case may be. The per capita availability of food was next ascertained by considering the current supply in relation to the total population of the district, at three-quarters of a seer of foodgrain per head, which, according to A. P. Macdonnell's estimate, would be reduced to approximately half a seer in crisis years. The figures arrived at by this method invariably showed a vast deficit. To take only one example, the five affected districts in the Patna Division showed a total deficit of 6,993,384 md. from September 1896 to September 1897, and by April 1897 none of the north Bihar districts had more than two months' supply of food in hand.[3]

These statistics are no doubt subject to many reservations and cannot give a very clear index of the production or supply position

[2] *Final Resolution*, pp. 11, 16–18.

[3] LRP, Aug. 1898, pt. 2, pp. 933–35; FRFRO, Patna Div., paras. 106–8.

of foodgrains in 1896–97. In recording crop out-turns, for instance, the 16-anna concept created great confusion, for the Government's interpretation of it as a good average crop was never followed by subordinate officers or the peasantry, to whom 16 an. always meant a bumper or ideal crop. Similarly, calculations for the current supply and per capita availability of foodgrains were not always based on a uniform principle, and often took no account of the "carry over" from previous years, or of the inter-district trade by road and river. As the Commissioner of Patna noted, the figures for food stocks provided by the Collectors of Gaya, Muzaffarpur, Saran and other districts were extremely confusing, direct enquiries from the SDOs, the police, the Opium Department and the indigo planters disagreeing hopelessly.[4] In spite of these qualifications, however, the data for 1896–97 are sufficient to indicate an overall food shortage, both real and determinate, in the famine-hit regions of Bengal.

The phenomenal rise in foodgrain prices was a direct indication of the pressure on the food supply. In typical scarcity districts like Champaran, Santhal Parganas and Nadia, the price of common rice per rupee rose abruptly from about 15, 23 and 16 sr. in December–January 1895–96 to 8, 10 and 9 sr. (i.e. by 46.6, 56.5 and 43.75 per cent) respectively, in December–January 1896–97. By the lean period, i.e. May 1897, they moved up to 7.75, 7.75 and 8.25 sr. (i.e. an increase of 54.4, 40.38 and 48.43 per cent) respectively, as against 17, 13 and 16 sr. in May 1896. Thus prices had more than doubled in the scarcity districts, while even in regions beyond the famine zone the increase was more than one-third as compared to normal years.

Case studies of the fifteen affected districts in the Province of Bengal bring out in some detail the starkness of the situation in 1896–97. The crop statistics, whether expressed in fractions of the rupee or in percentages, become meaningful only when considered against the relative contribution of each harvest to the total foodgrain production in the district; the extent of shortfall in the affected areas, as distinct from the district average; the level of reserves as indicated by the yield and carry-over stocks

4 LRP, Aug. 1898, pt. 2, p. 933.

from the previous year; and the trade balance in foodgrains, of the areas concerned. These parameters have been applied as far as possible in chapter 4, to assess the food situation in the famine-hit districts.

[2] *Pull-failure or FEE*

Yet crop failure and famine are not synonymous. An extensive crop failure merely reacted on the peasant economy, aggravating its basic conflicts and entitlement problems until the crisis deepened into famine. Some of these anomalies had persisted throughout the last decade of the nineteenth century, slowly but surely sapping the strength and vitality of a large section of the rural community. It was against this background that the short-term or immediate effects of a widespread crop failure caused an exchange crisis of unprecedented dimensions in 1896, heightened in a few cases by certain coincidental factors.

[2.1] Long-term entitlement failures during the 1890s

As noted, certain long-term developments other than food shortage were persistently undermining the production-, labour- and trade-based entitlements of various sections of the peasant society throughout the 1890s.

Production-based entitlement to foodgrains tended to decline when a crop failure or a fall in agricultural prices directly cut down the consumption of a subsistence farmer.

The Datta Committee, in reviewing the origin and nature of the rising prices between 1895 and 1912, analysed the relative movement of per capita agricultural income and the prices of the commodities generally purchased by the common peasants in Bengal and Bihar, and attempted a comparison of their respective index numbers. The results showed that while the index of agricultural income registered an increase of a mere 2 per cent in the decade 1894–1904, that of commodity prices went up by 10.5 per cent. Though conscious of the imperfections of the available data, Datta concluded, on the basis of the broad trend as indicated by them, that in Bengal and Bihar during this period "the rise in the cost of living has been all along more than the rise in the agricultural income, showing that the cultivators in these parts have been adversely affected by high prices". This applied particularly to foodgrain production, which covered more than 85 per cent of the total cropped area, rather than to cash-crop cultivation, where the peasant traded his product for food. Thus, even during this period of low agricultural income in Bengal and Bihar, some of the cash-crop sectors, as in northern and eastern Bengal, showed that "the cultivators have obtained very large profits on jute and are substantially better off than before".[5] Conversely, aman cultivation, which was extremely susceptible to drought and admitted of no second crop except for a few inferior pulses of the rabi harvest, had a much lower rate of profitability. Hence, mono-crop regions growing aman rice as in the districts of Bihar, Santhal Parganas, Birbhum, Bankura, the Kalantar in Nadia-Murshidabad and the Chilka tract in Puri, invariably showed a low index of prosperity and a high incidence of famine.

The real problem for the peasant or small tenant, however, lay not in the working of market forces, but in the basic contradictions within the rural society. Rising prices were seen to have "adversely affected" the peasants not only because the cost of living was high in relation to food prices, as suggested by the Datta Committee, but also because the peasant economy was conditioned more by the rural power-structure than by secular market forces. In fact, though the agricultural income moved up by only 2 per cent in 1894–1904, its rise during 1895–99 was as high as 7 per cent in relation to a mere 2.5 per cent increase in the cost of living.[6] Yet the rise in agricultural prices did not appreciably improve the peasant's position, for in most cases his surplus was not drawn to the market by a wholesome price stimulus; it was, rather, extracted from him in the form of compulsory payments of rent and interest to the zamindar and mahajan, who ultimately sold it and benefited from the price rise.

While high rent and interest payments and the lack of free market conditions thus reduced the entitlement of the small peasant, they gave the richer classes full scope to perfect their

[5] Datta, *Enquiry into the Rise in Prices,* vol. 1: paras. 435–36.
[6] Ibid., p. 183, para. 436.

mechanism of control over the surplus in their three-fold capacity as zamindar, mahajan and bania. For example, the zamindars, as in the Bihar districts, tried to get a greater share of the rise in agricultural prices since the 1880s by converting cash rents into produce rents wherever possible, particularly in view of the common belief that the rent rates in kind were not subject to the constraints imposed by the tenancy laws on cash rentals.[7] Similarly, the mahajans profited not only from the exorbitant rates of compound interest, but also by monopolising the local markets in their capacity as grain dealers.[8] The loan and interest were often calculated in money while all transactions were in grain at prices fixed arbitrarily by the mahajan, who thus got the profit on the sale and purchase of the grain.

These facts indicate, as Datta noted, "that agricultural indebtedness has increased in the case of cultivators with small holdings, while another section—the larger tenants—has improved and instead of borrowing money they often lend it to their fellows".[9] This was reflected in the growing volume of land sales in this period. Between 1886–87 and 1895–96 sale transactions were "nearly doubled in the case of raiyati holdings at fixed rates, and nearly trebled in the case of raiyati holdings with a right of occupancy".[10] Between 1885 and 1904, land sales increased by about 300 per cent, a large number of them passing into the hands of the affluent peasants functioning as mahajans. According to Amartya Sen, "In empirical studies of actual famines, the question of precision is compromised by data problems . . . and the focus here will be not on characterising entitlements with pretended exactitude, but on studying shifts in some of the main ingredients of entitlements. Big shifts in such ingredients can be decisive in causing entitlement failures, even when there is some 'fuzziness' in the entitlement relations".[11] Hence, the increasing shifts in the ownership of land, which was the basic ingredient in the production of foodgrains, caused

7 Chaudhuri, "Movement of Rent", secs. 3A–3B and 4.

8 Chaudhuri, "The Process of Depeasantization", Sec. 5.

9 Datta, *Enquiry into the Rise in Prices*, para. 389.

10 *Triennial Report,* Registration Dept., Bengal, for the years ending 1898–99, para. 12 of Govt. Resolution.

11 Sen, *Poverty and Famine,* p. 49.

a major change in production-based exchange-relations in the years preceding the famine of 1896, and sharply reduced the food entitlement of the debtor peasants.

This process of depeasantisation and the falling income of the average raiyat increased the labour surplus in agriculture, and forced corresponding cuts in the exchange value of labour. Industrial development was too slow to create any substantial scope for alternative employment, which was further reduced by depression in various agricultural industries like indigo production in south Bihar, date-sugar manufacture in Jessore, or the silk industry in Murshidabad. This, along with the seasonal nature of agricultural labour, reduced the total volume of employment and depressed wage rates in the closing years of the nineteenth century.

The Datta Committee notes: "the rise of prices has been fully met by a rise in wages",[12] and that "the rise has been greatest in rural areas".[13] The indices quoted by Datta move up from 104 in 1895 to 123 in 1900 in nominal wages, and from 102 to 115 between 1895 to 1904 in real wages.[14] These wage data, however, are confined to money wage-rates—that is, to the more developed sector affecting only a fringe of the rural economy—to the exclusion of grain wages as well as the various forms of payment to bonded labourers.

The payment in kind generally tended "to keep down the wage in spite of higher prices".[15] The system was widely prevalent in Bihar and Orissa. In Bihar the wages were particularly low and had remained static for the last 20 years, despite the rise in food prices. Regarding Orissa, too, O'Malley reported in 1907: "Measured by the quantity of grain given, there does not appear to have been any increase in wages paid to agricultural labourers during the last thirty years".[16]

A distinct case was that of the bonded labourers, who always received less than the market rate. The kamiauti system of debt bondage was particularly notorious in the Chotanagpur districts

12 Datta, *Enquiry into the Rise in Prices*, para. 430.
13 Ibid., para. 407.
14 Ibid., para. 419, table 1.
15 *Gazetteer of Bengal*, 1, 1909, p. 72.
16 *DG: Balasore*, 1907, p. 121.

of Palamau, Hazaribagh and Manbhum at the end of the nineteenth century. It has recently been characterised as an attempt of early capitalism to raise the "absolute surplus" in agriculture without any new investment or real increase in labour productivity. The low density of population and a net exodus of over 135,000 labourers per annum from the Lohardaga-Palamau region by 1891 greatly reduced the size of the available labour force. Without a social system of controls like debt bondage, i.e. the dependence and control of labour through indebtedness, the wage rate would have risen sharply.[17] By this system, the labourer was remunerated with two or three kaccha seers of whatever foodgrain his master found convenient to give. At harvest time he received about fifteen kaccha seers in two days. It was clear that at this rate the kamia could never save enough to pay off his debt, and served the mahajan through generations.

Debt-labour on a daily, seasonal or annual basis prevailed also in other districts like Birbhum, Nadia, Malda and Bhagalpur. The daily wage in Bhagalpur left the labourer underfed for about three months in a year. In years of drought his condition worsened, for instead of a fixed quantity of grain his wage dwindled to a small share of the crop reaped. The Collector of Bhagalpur noted: "These grain payments, though they suit the rural economy of the country, are of course the real danger to

17 Mundle, *Backwardness and Bondage,* pp. 4, 91–94. As described more recently by Gyan Prakash, the "plains Hindus . . . used the nineteenth century instruments of land control and Kamiauti advances to make their intrusion more extensive and pervasive than ever before" (Prakash, *Bonded Histories*, pp. 166, 169). The debt contract was reinforced by casteism and money-power. It was juridicial in form, economic in content, yet expressed in terms of reciprocity. As Prakash comments, "The two dimensions (caste and the kamia-malik relationship) were linked because the malik was both an upper-caste person and a landlord." [Gyan Prakash, "Reproducing Inequality: Spirit Cults and Labour Relations in Colonial Eastern India", in *The World of the Rural Labour in Colonial India*, ed. Gyan Prakash (Oxford: Oxford University Press, 1992), p. 295.] For a critical review of Gyan Prakash's study on bonded labour, see *Dalit Movements and the Meanings of Labour in India,* ed. Peter Robb (Oxford: Oxford University Press, 1993), pp. 26–32.

the population". As a result of the meagre surplus, the seasonal or annual employment of debt-labourers developed into a perpetual 'attachment' to their employers. The size of such attached labour was 42 per cent, 50 per cent and 60 per cent, respectively, in the Supaul, Banka and Madhipura sub-divisions in Bhagalpur.[18] In Bankura-Birbhum they had to surrender 25 per cent of their share as interest on the grain advances received by them for their total annual requirements.[19]

Thus, at the close of the nineteenth century there were various types of constraints on the rate of wages, whether paid in cash, kind or by debt-contract. As a result, the exchange value of labour could not keep pace with the rise in agricultural prices. According to a later estimate, real wages rose by only 6 per cent between 1891 and 1901, as against Datta's figure of a 15 per cent rise by 1904, if the index for 1891 be taken as 100.[20]

There was also a definite decline in several areas of the trade-based entitlement to food. Such entitlement groups in the rural economy consisted mainly of local craftsmen, weavers, artisans, fishermen, goalas and cash-crop producers.

Many of the rural crafts, like weaving, ivory carving, pottery making and sericulture, were suffering from great depression. In 1898 the District Officer of Nadia reported: "In almost all villages in this district there are a few families of Tantis and Jolahas. They turn out coarse cloth for the use of cultivators, but their number is gradually decreasing, and the profession is deteriorating on account of English-manufactured cloth, which is cheaper. In several villages which had a reputation for doing business in weaving, this industry is altogether abolished, such as Chakdaha, Tehata, Damurhuda and Dagalbi".[21] The silk industry in Murshidabad suffered not only from foreign competition, but also from frequent silkworm epidemics. In fact, during 1886–96, the noted expert, Nitya Gopal Mukharji, was engaged in

18 *Dufferin Report,* Collector of Bhagalpur to the Comm., 7 April 1888, paras. 8, 13, 15.

19 Ibid., Collector of Birbhum to Comm., Burdwan Div., 30 May 1888.

20 Ghosh, *Agricultural Labourers*, p. 173, table 6: 25; Datta, *Enquiry into the Rise in Prices*, para. 418.

21 *DG: Nadia*, p. 92.

active research on this problem. The profits of sericulture had fallen so low due to these reasons and the reclamation of the asan forests where the cocoons were reared in Angul, that they could hardly finance the high mulberry rentals. Ivory carving also declined so that by 1901 there was not a single *bhaskar* (sculptor) in Mathra, and not more than twenty-five carvers in the entire district.

As to the agricultural industries or cash-crop production, the primary producers were always at a distinct disadvantage irrespective of market conditions. Like the subsistence farmers, they depended totally on unscrupulous middlemen and retailers, and had no direct access to the market. The cultivation of sabai grass by the Paharias in the Rajmahal Hills is a typical case in point. The mahajans arbitrarily fixed the price of the sabai, usually at Rs. 8 to Rs. 10 per 100 loads. The full price was never paid, the greater part of the purchase money being set against 'old debts', i.e. the initial cost borne by the mahajan in clearing the sabai fields. Besides, the produce of the fields was grossly under-estimated, outside labour being employed to cut the grass. The Paharia neither had access to his field to enable him to check the number and size of the bundles, nor the freedom to sell his produce to any other mahajan but his own. In 1898 the Government imposed a royalty of one anna per maund of sabai, which was intended to be raised from the mahajans, who were making immense profits from the sabai trade. In effect, however, the Paharias had to bear the cost, for the mahajans immediately reduced the price of sabai by one-fifth. Thus, while the sabai exports more than doubled between 1901 and 1908 and the mahajans and contractors fast extended their godowns and presses in Sahebganj, the Paharias' entitlement was sharply reduced.[22] A. W. Stark, Deputy Collector on special duty, noted a distinct deterioration in the condition of the Paharia villages in parganas Teliagarhi and Madhuban between 1881 and 1909: "There was scarcely a family that had sufficient grain in store to last them more than a month or two. . . . These people who lived in rude plenty in former days are now living from hand-

[22] Bengal Revenue Proceedings, Sept. 1909, nos. 1–2, p. 136, Patterson, SDO Rajmahal, to Dept. Comm. Santhal Parganas, 14 April 1908, para. 3.

to-mouth and depending on what they can manage to beg from their mahajans".[23]

These broad trends caused much regular starvation among certain sections of the rural society during the last decade of the nineteenth century, and made them peculiarly liable to famines. In this situation, the linkage effects of the extensive crop failure in 1896–97 totally eroded the existing entitlement patterns, creating conditions of acute starvation or famine.

[2.2] Immediate or short-term exchange failures in 1896–97

These were primarily [a] crop-related failures, aggravated occasionally by [b] exogenous or coincidental factors.

[a] Crop-related failures

Production-based entitlements were the first to suffer. Indeed, the peasant proprietor, cash-tenant and bargadar were deeply affected by the direct-entitlement failure. While rent collections went on as usual and the creditor refused to operate, the raiyat's surplus dwindled with the decline in crop size. The sown area contracted for the lack of seedgrain. Very little of the land in Khulna, and only 40 per cent of the total cultivable area in Jessore could be sown in 1897.[24] As the crisis deepened into famine, the sale and mortgage of capital assets by the peasants increased remarkably. Ornaments, utensils and even agricultural implements were being sold at half to two-thirds of their real value. In Athaisi and Banchas in Orissa people were said to have "already parted with their all" by February–March 1897. In Khulna, Jessore, Chotanagpur and western Athaisi, even well-to-do raiyats sold their cattle to beparis, mostly from Calcutta.[25] In fact, it was apprehended that the lack of plough

[23] Ibid., Sept. 1909, nos. 1–2, p. 167. "Report on the Petition of the Hill Manjhis of Pargana Teliagarhi and Tappa Madhuban regarding the dealings of the Mahajans in the Sabai Trade" by A. W. Stark, 12 March 1909, para. 34.

[24] *Selection of Papers,* vol. 8: pp. 290–91.

[25] Ibid., vol. 3: p. 233; vol. 6: p. 404.

cattle would adversely affect cultivation the next season. Credit was raised on the security of the crops on the ground, as on the rabi foodgrains in the famine tract of Shahabad, and the aus and jute crops in Khulna.

This extreme pressure on the cultivators was reflected in their increasing numbers on Government relief works. In Nadia, men of the cultivating classes were seen on earth works, which was considered a most degrading form of labour in these parts.[26] Again, many of the labourers working on a tank near Assasuni in Khulna were cultivators of the better class, some of them owning thirteen to twenty bighas of land which lay fallow for want of seed and plough cattle this year.[27] Many raiyats absconded under this pressure; for example, numerous deserted abads in Shyamnagore and Paikgacha in Satkhira testified to the mass exodus towards the Namal desh or new settlements in the Sunderbans.[28] It was not until July–August in 1897 that the mahajans and zamindars recommenced their lending operations, and that, too, on stringent terms. This often ended in distress sales of peasant holdings. In fact, the vast increase in the registration of land sales by peasants in 1896–97 indicated the extent of their entitlement failure.

The total number of registrations affecting immovable property went up by 15.28 per cent in 1896–97. The number of sales and mortgages rose by 15.4 and 18.63 per cent, respectively.[29] Mortgage was often preferred to sale, as it held a prospect—though remote—of redemption in the future. In the case of deeds of optional registration, instruments of mortgage valued at less than Rs. 100 showed a large increase, as expected, on account of the famine. The number of transactions dealing with the sale of raiyati holdings increased by 19 per cent. Though the entire Province suffered from the prevailing high prices, the signs of stress were most visible in the statistics of sales and mortgages in the famine-hit districts, as analysed in some detail in chapter 5.

Simultaneously, contraction of the sown area and reduction of agricultural operations abruptly reduced employment

26 Ibid., vol. 4: p. 257.
27 Ibid., vol. 7: p. 266.
28 Ibid., vol. 4: p. 239.
29 *Report, Registration Dept., 1896–97*: Minor Statement No. 1.

opportunities for the agricultural labourer. It also affected the numerous small peasants who supplemented their income from land by working as hired farmhands. Due to the poor yield in 1896, the latter pressed down with increasing force on the rural labour market. Faced with this labour surplus and a fall in demand, wages went down visibly by 33 to 50 per cent in most of the famine-hit districts. In south Khulna, for instance, paddy-cutting rates were reduced to one-third of the normal. At Bardal in Satkhira it fell to half of the usual wages. Instead of 3 an. and a meal a day, men worked for 2 an. and no meal.[30] Although emigration increased, wages were sometimes forced down by the closure of alternative fields of employment this year, as in the case of lac, coal and mica production in Chotanagpur, and the silk industry in Murshidabad.

Labourers paid in grain were expected to be in a better position. But, in effect, their share in crisis years dwindled with the decline in production. The kamias were supposed to be relatively well protected during a famine as they were maintained by their masters.[31] Yet they were often ill-treated in such emergencies, as the employer shirked his responsibility to feed and clothe them. Moreover, a famine like that of 1896–97 naturally gave the mahajan increased opportunities to expropriate labour by issuing loans in the later stages of the crisis, when raiyats had to borrow in order to survive and to sow the fields for the next season.

Trade-based entitlements sank low as well, since the weather conditions affecting food-crop production in 1896 had an equally disastrous effect on large areas of the cash-crop sector. The mulberry cultivation in Murshidabad, the tea and lac industry in Manbhum, and the production of sugar-cane, tobacco, jute and oilseeds in all the districts of Chotanagpur suffered a severe setback, adversely affecting the foodgrain entitlement of all those who dealt in them. Hailstorms totally blighted the prospects of the mango crop in Bongaon in Jessore,

30 *Selection of Papers*, vol. 3: p. 204.

31 As Gyan Prakash notes: "The landholders' need for an assured labor supply during the peak periods of agricultural activity and the laborers' need for support during lean months were combined in the Kamia labor system". (Prakash, *Bonded Histories*, p. 170).

as well as in Nadia and Murshidabad.[32] In Jessore-Khulna date trees were plentiful, and the manufacture of jaggery was the chief agricultural industry. But the tapping season, which normally continued until mid-March, ended early this year for the weather was already warm by February. Bongaon in Jessore formed the westernmost part of the important date-palm tract of central Bengal. From November 1896 to February 1897, many of the raiyats subsisted on the income from these date trees. They paid part of their rents out of it, and were able to avoid borrowing from the mahajans at least for three months. But due to the dry nature of the soil in 1896–97, the yield of juice and jaggery ruled about 8 to 12 an. lower per maund than usual.[33]

Moreover, a crop failure naturally reduced the level of purchasing power in an agrarian society, causing an overall depression in rural trades and services. The trade situation in Khulna-Jessore in 1896 was typical of this slump. Thus, at Naubanki, a large hat in Satkhira, all shopkeepers and traders were complaining in 1896 that business was extremely dull. The vegetable growers, fishermen, itinerant dealers in piece goods, the goalas selling *dahi* (curd), the *moira* or confectioner, and the trinket dealers (*manihari*) found their business all but gone.[34] At Jadabpur bazaar in Bongaon, likewise, the books of cloth dealers showed a falling-off in the business to the extent of nearly 40 per cent.[35] In Lakshmipara, Jaipur and Lohagara in Magura, too, the purchasing power of the people had been reduced and general trade suffered quite severely. The books of the cloth dealer and confectioner in the local bazaar showed a 25 per cent and 40 per cent decline in their respective trades this season. Rural services such as those of the barber, washerman, boatman, blacksmith, priest and chaukidar suffered as well, as the average consumer had to cut down on other necessities to be able to buy food at famine prices.

In fact, a fear psychosis which affected the entire peasant economy in a season of scarcity or famine struck at the very basis of the existing value-system determining the patterns of

[32] *Selection of Papers,* vol. 6: p. 239.
[33] Ibid., vol. 5: p. 226.
[34] Ibid., vol. 3: p. 200.
[35] Ibid., vol. 5: p. 230.

exchange entitlement. The price of cereals, touching an all-time high in the winter of 1896, had an erosive effect on society. In the ensuing crisis of identities, the landowner virtually disowned his farmhand, the mahajan his khatak, the bania his client, and the breadwinner his dependants. The existing patterns of loyalty, socio-economic functions and obligations were thus transformed and suspended until the return of normalcy in August–September 1897, when the bhadoi prospects were assured.

Thus, the exchange failure in 1896–97 was primarily due to the linkage effects of a shortfall in agricultural production. The decline in the availability of foodgrains due to crop failure inflated food prices. The average peasant did not benefit from this rise, as he hardly had any marketable surplus, while his direct entitlement to food fell with the reduction in crop size. The rise in grain prices correspondingly reduced the food entitlement of various other groups in the community. Meanwhile, the exchange value of their respective commodities, including labour, not only remained static but fell substantially below its normal level. The process was not unreasoned, as the effect of crop failure in an agrarian society generally depressed the market for field labour and the entire range of consumer goods and services.

[b] Exogenous factors aggravating the exchange crisis in specific areas

There have been instances when food shortage was no more than one possible factor in a complex of variables, some of which might interact to create tensions and shifts within the framework of entitlement relations, and precipitate severe famine conditions "even without receiving any impulse from food production".[36] The exchange crisis in 1896–97, as seen already, was not an instance of this type of situation.

A deficient harvest and a consequent decline in the availability of food staples was the basis of famine in all the districts affected in 1896. Yet one cannot totally ignore the role of certain coincidental factors which, though not drastic in their effects, did intensify the exchange problem arising from food shortage

[36] Sen, *Poverty and Famine,* p. 158.

in this year of famine. However, they were purely localised phenomena, affecting only the areas concerned, and were by no means typical of the non-monetised, or at best partially monetised, exchange-economy of rural Bengal in the late nineteenth century.

The indigo industry in Muzaffarpur, for instance, suffered a sharp decline which first set in during this year of famine, though it took nearly a decade for the full results to show. Indigo cultivation was labour-intensive, drawing four and a half times the labour required by other crops. The industry suffered terribly from the competition of artificial dyes after 1900–1901, the first signs of which were evident in 1896. The number of persons in indigo factories increased during 1891 to 1896. Since then it began to fall, along with a 25 per cent cut in the wages of agricultural labourers precisely in that year. As the supply of labour already exceeded the demand by 68 per cent in Muzaffarpur, the fortunes of the indigo industry had a close bearing on the local problems of labour and exchange-failure.[37]

The year was equally unfavourable to the lac business in Manbhum, due as much to the local failure in produce as to the dullness of trade in the Calcutta market. It led to the closure of 25 per cent of the lac factories in Manbhum, which supported a large proportion of the Kol and Bhuiyan population.[38] This general slackness in transactions and the plague in Bombay hit hard at the coal industry in Chotanagpur. The high additional freight over the Jharia line of the East Indian Railway also placed the Jharia coalfields at a serious disadvantage in comparison with the collieries at Ranigunge, Barakar and other adjacent places. During the year forty collieries stopped work, while others

[37] *D.G.: Muzaffarpur*, p. 84.

[38] Manufacture of lac dye was in fact declining throughout the last two decades of the nineteenth century, due to the competition from cochineal in Europe and aniline dyes in the local markets. Growth of the shellac trade could not absorb the displaced lac-dye workers, as it required a degree of specialisation and, being essentially export-oriented, fluctuated sharply with changes in foreign demand. For further details on the decline of the lac trade, see Ruma Chatterjee, "A Survey of Lac Manufacturers in South Bihar and Bengal: 1872–1921", *Bengal Past and Present* 107, parts 1–2, Jan–Dec 1988.

had their business much reduced. Mica production, too, fell by approximately 12.5 per cent, while no copper and tin mines were worked this year. Tea production declined by 47.17 per cent, while the tussar industry in Raghunathpur and Singhbazaar in Manbhum went down in competition with machine manufactures.[39]

In eastern Bengal, fish were getting scarce as the rivers became saline and particularly rough this year on account of scanty rainfall and high winds. Due to the northwesters, navigation was more perilous; hence the services of the manjhis suffered just as the effects of famine were first being felt in March–April 1897. Fuel sold cheap, and the woodcutters in the Sunderbans had no capital to pay the forest dues.[40] The filatures in Murshidabad, languishing already due to silkworm epidemics and foreign competition, shut down after the failure of the March bund in 1897. They did not re-open until mid-July, thus laying off a very large number of labourers at the height of the famine.[41]

In the tracts along the Chilka and the Devi rivers in Puri, the effects of the prohibition of salt manufacture were being deeply felt precisely at this time by the local molunghee population. The Collector of Cuttack wrote in 1896: "Since the transfer of the salt manufacture of the district from the administration of the Collector, the manufacture has practically ceased and large numbers of persons have been deprived of the means of living which they obtained from it".[42]

[3] *Response Failure of the Market*

"Pull" or exchange failure alone does not explain the entitlement problem in 1896–97. It is equally relevant to assess the strength or ability of the market to respond to any "pull" provided by the regeneration of purchasing power.

In 1896–97, the market did not respond to the price stimulus in the way expected. In fact, there was a "response failure" of

39 *DCAR, Chotanagpur Div.*, 1896–97, secs. 7 and 8, pp. 15–17.

40 *Selection of Papers*, vol. 3: pp. 200, 203; vol. 5: pp. 204–5; vol. 6: p. 220.

41 Ibid., vol. 6: p. 230.

42 *DCAR, Orissa Div.*, 1896–97, p. 12, para. 79.

grave dimensions. Grain flowed out of acutely affected areas, though famine prices prevailed. Again, prices in surplus districts often rose higher than in famine tracts, as seen in the case of Tipperah, Bogra and Gaya. Private trade failed to cater to the needs of remote tracts like Ramnagar in Champaran, Palamau in Chotanagpur, the Chilka region in Puri and the Kalantar in Nadia. An enormous export trade went on in the Patna Division despite acute local scarcity in Bhabua in Shahabad, Siwan-Gopalganj in Saran, Ramnagar-Madhuban-Araraj in Champaran, Muzaffarpur-Sitamarhi in Muzaffarpur, and Madhubani in Darbhanga. Grain flowed out of Bhagalpur Division but did not enter local distress areas like Supaul-Madhipura in Bhagalpur district and Jamtara-Godda in the Santhal Parganas. Nadia and Khulna exported grain as usual, though there were no stocks in the Kalantar tract and Satkhira. Orissa sent grain to Bombay, Madras, Mauritius and Colombo, while parts of Cuttack and the Chilka region in Puri received no supplies, despite acute distress and soaring prices.

This enigma may be explained not only by the lack of "pull" or purchasing capacity, but also by availability problems as in trade and communication, the effects of which were heightened by the imperfections of the market and the misconceptions in government policy. The famine of 1896–97 was of unprecedented dimensions, which created an almost insatiable demand for food. As trade normally moved along established channels, it was no easy task to divert the flow of grain in new directions in order to meet the exigencies of the situation. Certain preconditions were essential for the purpose, viz. (a) an organised trade-base, whether of exports or imports, as the need be; (b) traders rich and resourceful enough to expand on this basis; (c) easy access; and (d) effective demand. It will be seen that few of the tracts affected in 1896 possessed even one of these many advantages.

[3.1] Lack of an organised trade-base

As noted, the trade position was abnormal this year in more ways than one. The widespread apprehension of famine often led to a closure of the normal sources of supply. As a consequence, grain did not flow as in ordinary years from Nepal and the NWP to north Bihar, from Lohardaga, Sirguja, Gangpur and Jashpur to Palamau, or from Dacca-Mymensingh to Rajshahi and Nadia. Due to a growing fear psychosis, the normal surplus districts not only withheld stocks, but also succeeded in drawing out grain from the affected tracts, by virtue of their superior purchasing capacity. Attracted by the high prices offered, there was a voluminous outflow of grain along the existing trade-lines from normally exporting districts in the Patna, Bhagalpur and Orissa Divisions, to the increasing agony of the famine-hit tracts within.

Not only inter-district, but intra-district trade was affected: grain flowed out of Nadia but did not enter the Kalantar, while rice selling at 23 sr. to the rupee in Khurda did not reach Puri town, where it sold at the rate of 13 sr.—a difference of more than 43 per cent. It was difficult for the affected tracts to seek new sources of supply, for the latter usually had prior commitments, and would in any case be reluctant to divert grain to areas lacking in effective demand.

For regions which normally did not import, it was almost impossible to tap fresh sources and start on new ventures in the midst of such a crisis. In this respect districts like Saran, which always imported the greater part of their food requirements enjoyed a distinct advantage, for their traders were familiar with every detail of the local import trade in foodgrains. It is no wonder that supplies flowed liberally into Saran as early as January–February 1897, while surrounding regions suffered from acute scarcity.[43] As noted in Bourdillon's Administrative Report for the year 1891–92, "The district even at the best of times never feeds itself, and in consequence its merchants are thoroughly acquainted with the grain trade; when crops fail and prices rise, the bania merely buys thousands of maunds where he bought hundreds before".[44] Conversely, the importation of grain was a "new experience" for the merchants of Champaran.[45] Likewise, only two Ranchi merchants tried to bring grain into Lohardaga, and importation was "not their normal line of

43 *Selection of Papers*, vol. 4: p. 129, no. 283 F-G, 6 Feb. 1897.
44 FRFRO, Saran, ch. 3, para. 21.
45 FRFRO, Patna Division, ch. 1, para. 30.

business".[46] The traders in Orissa, too, were unused to importing from outside, or even from one part of a district to another. As the Collector of Cuttack noted: "We have a highly organised export trade and no import trade in grain at all".[47] The same applied to Bhagalpur. The Santhal Parganas, too, was normally an exporting district with hardly any fixed source of supply. The administration, however, did not show much interest in this aspect of the problem. As W. B. Oldham, Commissioner of Bhagalpur Division and the Santhal Parganas, remarked: "The question of where supplies are to come from is not to be our concern at all".[48]

[3.2] Absence of rich and resourceful traders

A quick trade response to a crisis of such dimensions as in 1896–97 presumes the existence of an enterprising mercantile community used to operating effectively at least at the inter-district level. However, grain merchants of this calibre could hardly be found anywhere in the famine zone. In Nadia, for instance, people in the Kalantar were dependent for their food on their own reserves or on supplies brought in from the Rarh by cart-men and petty banias as "there is not a single merchant of any wealth or business capacity in the whole tract".[49] The nature of the local trade, if it could be so called, was peculiar, for its fortunes fluctuated with the success or failure of the crops. Foodgrains were sold locally by the village moodies or grocers, who kept modest reserves of oil, tobacco, *chura, moorkee,* rice and pulses. Obviously, in a year of crisis these small-time shopkeepers would be in no position either to replenish their stocks, or to engage in import activities of any consequence.[50] Unlike Nadia, Khulna had direct access to Calcutta; yet, the affected tracts in Satkhira suffered due to the absence of proper traders and mahajans, while the zamindars were uncooperative.

46 FRFRO, Lohardaga, ch. 3, para. 12.
47 *Selection of Papers,* vol. 4: p. 419.
48 Ibid., p. 398, no. 243F, 16–18 Feb. 1897.
49 FRFRO, Nadia, p. 2.
50 FRFRO, Nadia, ch. 1, para. 25.

In the districts of north Bihar, too, one rarely came across local traders of any standing. According to Charles Still, Relief Superintendent of Hardih, there were no stocks for sale in the Ramnagar tract in Champaran, as "there are no big banias or stock-holders at any time". Even the Bettiah traders, on whom the fate of the entire northern half of Bettiah subdivision depended, stopped functioning due to the congestion at Mokama Railway ghat in mid-May 1897; they could not afford to order fresh supplies before realising the value of the earlier consignments stranded at Mokama.[51]

Trade was particularly backward in the Chotanagpur Division. In Lohardaga, the amount of grain trickling in depended almost solely on the efforts of two Ranchi merchants, Babus Hardat Rai Marwari and Tara Prasanna Rai Chowdhry. The grain dealers of Palamau carried on a petty barter trade, having little capital and lesser knowledge of commercial transactions. It is significant that one Ghan Shyam Das, an outsider from Gaya, was the first to avail of the government "bounty" of 8 annas on every maund of Burma rice imported into Palamau from outside. In the affected areas of Orissa, bordering on the Chilka, there was no local trade worth noting. Some wealthy raiyats and maths of Chaubiskud had laid by small reserves for their own use, most of which were sold to the Bombay and Ganjam merchants at high prices this year.

[3.3] Lack of easy access

Non-resident merchants did not show any interest, either, in importing rice into the famine zones, as the risk and expenses of transportation were normally too great to make it worth their while. In Nadia, for instance, they were naturally reluctant to operate on a large scale anywhere in the famine tract, as communications with the outside world were difficult throughout the year, and impossible during the rains. In the dry season carts trudged along numerous tortuous tracts which were wholly or partially submerged during the monsoon, there being practically no proper road in the Kalantar, Bonaj and the bil

51 FRFRO, Champaran, ch. 3, para. 51.

tracts in Gangni. When the floods were too low, as during their commencement or recession, and particularly in the year under review, the khals and bils were neither navigable nor fordable. Moreover, the silting up of the local rivers, which were no longer open even to small country boats in the dry season, was a further 'powerful factor' leading to the decline of trade in this region, as all the sixteen trade-centres of the tract lay along the water routes. In Jessore, grain trade was similarly affected in the last three years by the clogging up of the Muchikhali near its mouth on the Gorai side. It cut off the vital trade-link between Magura and the great rice-producing districts of Faridpur, Khulna and Bakarganj via Kushtia on the Eastern Bengal State Railway, the alternative route across the Gorai being too circuitous for use. Khulna fared better, due largely to its easy accessibility to and from the grain marts of Calcutta.

In the Santhal Parganas, there was only one fully bridged road, and no metalled roads except one or two serving the district headquarters. But, as the Deputy Commissioner of the Santhal Parganas noted, "Famine does not confine itself to district or subdivisional headquarters. If we leave the supply of food to trade, we must help it with good and well-bridged roads".[52]

Due to the broken and uneven surface of the land in Chotanagpur, communications were "necessarily bad". In Lohardaga, for instance, there were hardly any fully bridged or metalled roads for cart traffic. The entire district relied for its imports on the nearest railway station of Purulia, lying seventy-five miles from Ranchi. The long, uphill journey took seven days in fair weather and from ten to fourteen days in the rains, the freight charge running from 9 an. a maund in the dry season to 13 an. during the monsoon. In July 1897 the want of carts pushed it up as high as 1 rupee and 6 an. per maund. The paltry imports (11,050 md.) despite a government bounty of 1 rupee per maund from 8 August to 8 September 1897, indicate the impossibility of provisioning the district via Purulia in a year of crisis. The maximum working power of that traffic was

[52] LRP, Aug. 1898, pt. 1, p. 354, no. 1328F, Dumka, 29 Oct. 1897. From R. Carstairs, Esq., Dept. Comm., Santhal Parganas, to the Comm., Bhagalpur Div. and Santhal Parganas. Note on Precautions against Famine, para. 3.

1 maund per 100 of the district population per month. The difficulties of distribution from Ranchi to the interior were ten times greater. There was only one unmetalled road leading from Ranchi to Palkote in the affected tract, which could not be negotiated by cartmen in the rains. The worst tract was thus inaccessible, lying forty to fifty miles from Ranchi to the west of this road at a distance of two to twelve miles, and being cut off from it by the Karo river, which was often unfordable for days together. In this area of about one hundred sq. miles there was no large hat or grain mart of any kind, the nearest bazaars being Govindpur on the east bank of the Karo, and Dumha and Duria lying beyond this tract to the west.[53]

The situation was worse in Palamau, which was "probably the most isolated district in the whole province of Bengal—a district which in a time of scarcity . . . may not inaptly be compared, in the words of the late Sir George Campbell, to 'a ship at sea running short of provisions'". It had neither railways, nor metalled roads or reliable water communication. Daltonganj lay over one hundred miles from the nearest railway station of Gaya, the journey by bullock cart taking eight to ten days in dry weather and twelve to twenty days during the rains, the usual rate of cart-hire being 12 an. per day.

Transport by road was equally difficult in the summer months due to want of fodder and water for the pack bullocks, while they were virtually impassable during the rains.[54]

In the Patna Division, the rugged hill country covering the southern portion of Bhabhua and Sasaram in Shahabad received their food supplies from the plains through difficult passes which, always unapproachable by wheeled traffic, were closed even to pack animals once the rains set in. Such of the grain marts as existed in Bhabhua subdivision were erratically supplied from Sasaram and Zamania, lying about twenty-eight miles from Bhabhua. Communication was equally difficult, if not more so,

53 H. C. Streatfeild, Dept. Comm., Lohardaga, to the Comm., Chotanagpur Div., no. 409F. chi, 12 Nov. 1897. Report on Famine, ch. 1, paras. 4(b), 5; ch. 3, para. 14.

54 LRP, Aug. 1898, pt. 2, no. 322F., Daltonganj, 5 Nov. 1897. From R. H. Renny, Dept. Comm., Palamau, to the Comm., Chotanagpur Div.; FRFRO, Palamau, ch. 3, para. 24.

in the affected areas of Champaran, the Tirhut State Railway ending at Bettiah. The relatively good means of communication in Saran stand out in sharp contrast, as a major factor stimulating its import trade in foodgrains. It was surrounded on two sides by the great waterways of the Gogra, Ganges and Gandak. The Bengal and North-Western Railway ran across it diagonally for eighty-four miles, while the network of roads was more complete than in any other district of Bihar.

Conversely, the lack of roads made it impossible to supply any foodgrains in the Chilka tract of Puri, either from the interior of the district or from outside, except by boats. Although the East Coast Railway ran close to the northern shore of the lake, it was not feasible to carry supplies across the high floods of the Chilka during the rains.[55]

[3.4] Lack of effective demand

The lack of effective demand was a greater deterrent to trade than the physical difficulties of transport and communication. In fact, traders were often willing to import grain into remote tracts, if the prices paid were high enough to cover the cost of carriage and allow for a substantial profit-margin. The case of Champaran is typical. Despite acute local distress, grain flowed continuously throughout October and the first half of November 1896 from Champaran to the NWP, where higher prices prevailed. In mid-November, however, prices in Champaran rose at a bound by over 16 per cent, checking the outflow and reversing the current into a stream of importations. The process was repeated in mid-March 1897, when prices rose suddenly due to a depletion of stocks, making it remunerative to import Burma rice from Calcutta.[56]

Again, in July–August 1897 difficulties of cartage from Purulia pushed up prices in Lohardaga to a level which enabled a Ranchi trader, Hardat Rai Marwari, to re-import rice at a profit from Hazaribagh, where higher rates had ruled until then. Imports

[55] FRFRO, Puri, 1896–97, ch. 1, para. 5, no. 2652, Puri, 2 Dec. 1897. From W. H. Lee, Offg. Collector, Puri, to the Comm., Orissa Div.

[56] FRFRO, Champaran, ch. 3, para. 49.

were also made during this period from Chakradharpur via the Chaibassa-Ranchi Road.[57]

Famine rates, however, were more often nominal than real, as local people in the scarcity districts could seldom afford to buy grain at competitive prices. The lack of effective demand thus disproved the government theory that the price stimulant would automatically draw supplies from surplus to scarcity regions, and created confusion in bureaucratic circles. J. H. E. Garrett, Collector of Nadia, was baffled by the 'mystery' of grain flowing out constantly from the district instead of being diverted to the Kalantar, where famine prices ruled. Again, the apparent enigma of rice being "taken unsold from the market in the most distressed tracts" of Govindpur in Lohardaga was attributed by the Deputy Commissioner, H. C. Streatfeild, to the superstitious and inconsistent behaviour of the local people.[58] In Palamau, too, rice lay unsold at less than 9 sr. per rupee, and flowed out to the NWP from the Garhwa market.[59] There was a similar outflow from the export centres of Khusropur and Fatwa in Patna. In fact, Bourdillon, Commissioner of Patna Division, had grave doubts as to whether the people there could buy grain at famine prices, had private trade been able to supply the deficiency. As he noted, " lack of adequate purchasing power might account largely for this outflow of grain despite acute local scarcity which was already evident in Bhabhua, Siwan-Gopalganj, the Ramnagar-Araraj-Madhuban tract, Sitamarhi and Madhubani".

The level of purchasing power was habitually low in some districts like Bankura, Balasore and Puri. Shut out from the railways by the Damodar and enjoying a prolific yield of rice in normal years, Bankura had a very restricted trade in foodgrains. Prices and wages were kept down in consequence. The sale of rice at 10 sr. or less per rupee indicated great distress in Bankura, while elsewhere in the famine zones it sold for prices as high as 6 or even 5 sr. to the rupee. The usual abundance of rice in Orissa and its inaccessibility during the rains had a similar effect

[57] H. C. Streatfeild, Dept. Comm., Lohardaga, to the Comm., Chotanagpur Div., no. 409F., Ranchi, 12 Nov. 1897. Report on Famine in Lohardaga, ch. 3, para. 12.

[58] Ibid., para. 19.

[59] *Selection of Papers,* vol. 4: p. 360; vol. 6: p. 278.

on the price and wage levels, enabling others to draw heavily on its food and labour reserves. The price-rise in such districts, while putting great pressure on the local population, was not high enough either to stop exports or to attract imports of any consequence. As the Collector of Cuttack observed: "As long as our prices (relatively high to the normal though they be) are lower than elsewhere, exports must go on".[60]

In certain other areas such as Nadia, Murshidabad, parts of Chotanagpur and north Bihar, crop failure and its linkage effects on related industries in 1896–97 caused an exchange crisis by severely depressing the local wage rates. The closure of the filatures in Murshidabad due to the failure of the Maghi bund this year cut down further on the already dwindling profits of the silk industry, which could no longer finance the high mulberry rentals. Successive crop failures in the Kalantar in Nadia and Satkhira in Khulna for the past few years had greatly reduced their economic staying power. The slackness of the coal and lac trades cut down on the employment opportunities in Chotanagpur. In Muzaffarpur, the decline in indigo cultivation further reduced the local level of entitlement. The prohibition of salt manufacture likewise had a most prejudicial effect in the scarcity tracts of Malud and Parikud in Puri. The Santhal Parganas experienced a fall in the usual demand for labour in the mines and stone quarries, and for reaping crops in the adjacent districts, which had also been hit by famine. While the grain price was alarming by local standards, purchasing power fell as labour, plentiful even in ordinary seasons, had to face further competition this year from small peasants willing to accept lower wages in order to supplement their meagre income from land. Even expenditure on public works was reduced in scarcity areas not officially included in the famine zone. Thus, "The employment on which they had learnt to reckon has been reduced instead of being increased. Their need is great, their demand is loud, but they cannot make it effective".[61]

60 Ibid., vol. 4: p. 419.

61 No. 1328F., Dumka 29 Oct. 1897. R. Carstairs, Dept. Comm., Santhal Parganas, to the Comm., Bhagalpur Div. and Santhal Parganas. Note on Precautions against Famine, paras. 6–7.

Conversely, districts with adequate purchasing power, like Saran, drew a sizeable amount of foodgrain imports. As noted earlier, Saran already had an organised import trade in foodgrains. In crisis years the bania merely expanded on this basis, "knowing well that he cannot fail to sell his stock since the purchasing power of the District is very great indeed owing to the vast sums brought into it by opium, indigo and by the remittances of emigrants".[62] Indeed, Saran received a quarter of the total opium payments to cultivators of poppy in the Patna Division during the five years preceding 1896–97. Again, of the total sum of Rs. 6,574,400 paid in cash for indigo cultivation in the northern districts of the Patna Division during 1896–97, it received Rs. 1,428,000 or 21.7 per cent. Though not impressive in itself, Saran fared better than its neighbours if the opium and indigo payments were considered together. The most potent source of the district resources, however, lay in the cash remittances sent home by its migrant labourers. A rough calculation based on the census statistics of 1891 indicates that 17 per cent of the adult male population in Saran were emigrants who remitted Rs. 2,602,670 to the district in 1896–97, amounting to 23.4 per cent of the total remittances by money orders paid in the Division.[63]

Conclusion

Thus, it follows from the above analysis that:

(i) The decline in food availability due to *crop failure* was both real and determinate during the Bengal famine of 1896–97. Though Sen in his monograph *Poverty and Famine* focuses on FEE almost as an antithesis to FAD, in his later essays he concedes and touches upon the essential links between the two. As he notes, the dissonance arises from the fact that the links do not establish a ratio in aggregates between availability and entitlement, allowing for disparities in income distribution. In fact, in 1896 the possibility of an absolute shortage of food loomed large in several areas of the famine zone, especially in

[62] FRFRO, Saran, ch. 3, para. 21.
[63] LRP, Aug. 1898, pt. 2, p. 923–25. Report on Famine Relief Operations in Patna Div., ch. 2, paras. 77–78.

problem tracts like Palamau, the Nadia Kalantar and the Chilka region of Puri. Even Jean Dre'ze, to whom "the argument that most nineteenth century famines had little to do with a problem of physical availability of food seems convincing enough", makes an exception in favour of the two last great famines of the nineteenth century, those of 1896–97 and 1899–1900. "In these two cases", as he notes, "famines occurred against an exceptional background of massive crop failures virtually throughout the country at times when stocks were already diminished, and much greater caution is required in assessing the aggregate food availability situation. . . . the case against the existence of a food availability problem is much less convincing in this context".[64]

(ii) The availability crisis was due not only to crop deficiency, but also to a widespread *supply failure* in the grain market. The inability of the market to respond and cater to the needs of the moment is explained as much, if not more, by trade, distribution and policy problems, as by the lack of adequate 'pull' or purchasing capacity. As noted, effective demand, though a most potent factor in determining the behaviour of the market, was only one of the many essential prerequisites to ensure a smooth flow of grain into famine-hit tracts. In a paper presented at the WIDER Conference in Helsinki, Sen further qualified the previously conceived role of FEE as the all-pervasive factor in causing and prolonging famines: "The rationale of cash relief rests on the assumption that 'pull failure' is the main problem to deal with, and that the problem of 'response failure' will not provide a barrier to curing the entitlement problem through regenerating purchasing power. This need not always work, and the possibility of using this type of relief must depend to a great extent on the nature of the markets as well as the limits of bureaucratic management".[65] In Bengal in 1896–97 the market was too imperfect and the traders too apathetic to respond to any 'pull' provided by the Government, while the bureaucrats vied with each other in underlining the policy of laissez-faire

64 Jean Dre'ze, "Famine Prevention in India" in *The Political Economy of Hunger,* vol. 2: p. 19.

65 Sen, *Hunger and Entitlements*, p. 35.

and would have nothing to do directly with the import or distribution of food.

(iii) Finally, one should review the most potent question of *exchange failure* in connection with the famine of 1896–97 in Bengal. It has been seen that certain inherent problems in the rural economy were persistently reducing the food entitlement of various sections of the peasant society throughout the 1890s. But, though they increased the vulnerability of these classes to scarcity and famine in general, they did not involve any drastic changes relating specifically to the year under review.

As far as short-term or immediate exchange failures are concerned, the crisis of 1896–97 was primarily the effect of crop-related failures. An exchange crisis resulting exclusively from coincidental shifts in market-based entitlements, independent of food-crop production, was by no means typical of the nineteenth-century peasant economy in Bengal.[66] Manifestations of this type of crisis, as seen in case of the coal and lac industries in Chotanagpur, sericulture in Murshidabad and indigo production in Muzaffarpur, were exceptional phenomena, with a purely localised effect. As agriculture held the basic potential for creating employment opportunities in a rural society (whether in production, labour or trade), the exchange problem in 1896–97 is seen mostly as a sequel to FAD. It manifested itself in various forms of crop-related failures, such as: the reduction in crop size and sown area which cut in directly on the entitlement of the small peasant and agricultural labourer; the effect of adverse weather conditions on the cash-crop sector; the overall depression in rural trades and services; and the trauma

[66] For a comparable study see A. K. Ghosh, "Food Supply and Starvation: A Study of Famines with Reference to the Indian Subcontinent". *Oxford Economic Papers* 34, no. 2, July 1982. As Ghosh notes: "The Bengal Famine of 1943 was somewhat exceptional, both because it was not preceded by any natural disaster and because Bengal's economy at that point of time was far from traditional. Consequently, the framework of analysis developed by Sen is somewhat limited. . . . is it possible for a famine to occur without there being a crop failure ? In the case of a pure peasant economy, it is clearly unlikely. . . . even in a non-monetised exchange economy, a famine is unlikely in the absence of a crop failure."

connected with famine, which temporarily eroded the value-system determining the normal pattern of entitlements and obligations in the rural society.

In conclusion, therefore, it may be said that in 1896–97 food availability decline did indeed occur in Bengal. The crisis deepened into famine, as the scarcity of foodgrains forced a distinct change in entitlement relations. Government relief statistics indicate the extent of distress among different sections of the population. While relief works had to be opened in all the three districts of Khulna, Nadia and Jessore, their extent and duration was the greatest in northwest Nadia, where there was a larger population (about 1/5 to 1/3) of landless day labourers or petty cultivators depending mainly on wage labour. Likewise, in the acutely afffected districts of North Bihar, particularly in Saran, almost the entire population consisted of labourers. In Palamau-Manbhum, too, the pressure on relief works came mostly from landless labourers, especially from the floating population of the kamias. The classes worst hit by the exchange failure were the agricultural labourers and marginal farmers, particularly their women, children, and old and ailing dependents, whose food entitlement, already reduced by various social and institutional problems during the 1890s, collapsed entirely with the crop failure of 1896.

Thus food shortage did not directly lead to famine; it merely intensified the existing tensions, inequalities and entitlement problems within the peasant economy. It affected the supply position, while the change in exchange entitlements reduced the purchasing power or effective demand of a large section of the community. In analysing the famine situation of 1896 in Bengal, therefore, the decline in food availability and the failure in exchange relations appear not as contradictory but rather as complementary factors leading to the crisis.[67] The effects of food shortage were felt through an elaborate network of exchange

[67] Sen negates as too "simplistic" the idea of a "synthesis" being worked out between food availability and entitlement problems, "as 'two sides' of the food story". (Dre'ze and Sen, *Hunger and Public Action*, p. 25.) This, however, hardly applies to the famine under review, for it was marked by crop-related rather than market-based failures in the entitlement structure.

relations: some of them were long-term developments independent of the decline in food supply, which caused much regular starvation, reduced the economic staying power of certain sections of the community, and made them particularly vulnerable to famine; others were short-term fluctuations directly connected with crop failure, which caused a total collapse of the existing entitlement patterns, threw the entire economy out of gear, and led to a sudden outbreak of acute starvation or famine.

Appendix A

Volume of Rural Indebtedness

Though it is not possible to determine and quantify with precision the volume of rural indebtedness in different regions, some statistics may be gleaned from the various official enquiries on the subject. For instance, in the *Report on the Condition of the Lower Orders of the Population* called for by Lord Dufferin in 1888, it was found that in two selected villages in the 24 Parganas, 116 out of 158 families of cultivators (73.4 per cent) were stated to be indebted, their debts amounting on the average to Rs. 72 per family, or "nearly the selling value of one year's crop". Of the 145 labouring families in the two villages, 95 (65.5 per cent) were in debt to the extent of Rs. 42 per family, contracted on a yearly basis. Of the 37 families of artisans, 20 families (more than 50 per cent) were indebted to the extent of Rs. 93 each.[1] According to the Collector, many of the remaining families were free of debt not by choice, but due to lack of sufficient credit; a large number of them probably entered into debt-labour contracts with the mahajan. In "a village of considerable prosperity in Nadia, containing 44 families of cultivators and 58 families of labourers, all the cultivators . . . are said to be more or less indebted. . . . Both cultivators and labourers are more or less the slaves of mahajans and the so-called bhodrolok".[2] Raiyats holding 25/20/15 bighas or less

1 *Dufferin Report*. No. 1MA, Cal., dated 17 May, 1888. From the Collector, 24 Parganas, as forwarded by A. Smith, Comm., Presidency Division, to the Secy. to the Govt. of Bengal, Rev. Dept., paras. 13, 17, 21.

2 Ibid., From Collector, Nadia, as forwarded by the Presidency Comm. to the Secy. to the Govt. of Bengal, Rev. Dept., paras. 29, 33.

usually took loans from the mahajan.[3] Even cultivators who were relatively well-off were not free of debt for, "having been compelled to borrow in a bad year, or on account of a social ceremony or marriage, they find it difficult to extricate themselves from the debt of the *mahajan* with its heavy rate of interest".

Conditions were no better in Bihar. In all but one of six representative villages in Bhagalpur, the number of indebted peasants ranged between 76 and 86 per cent.[4] In Gaya district the Collector, Grierson, estimated the percentage of indebted peasants at 55 and 19 for Aurangabad and the Sadar subdivision, respectively.[5] The kamias constituted 56 per cent of the agricultural labourers, as estimated by C. J. Stevenson-Moore. In Chotanagpur, a study of nine villages in Manbhum showed 75.61 and 55 per cent of the cultivators, artisans and labourers in debt to the extent of Rs. 54, 13 and 10 per family, respectively.[6] The degree of indebtedness thus appeared to be determined by the amount of security offered. In Dhalbhum, Singhbhum district, the manager of the estate wrote that despite the general belief that "about one-half of the agriculturists are in a chronic state of indebtedness to their mahajans . . . My own enquiries . . . tend to show that this proportion is rather below the mark, and that about ten-sixteenth of their class are hopelessly indebted. It is a common saying in the pergunnah that the chashis (agriculturists) cultivate their lands for their mahajans".[7] In Lohardaga, five villages surveyed in Chotanagpur proper by Slack had 129 cultivators, and 76 labourers and artisans, of whom 50 and 25 i.e. 38.75 and 32.89 per cent, respectively, were in debt.[8] In two villages surveyed in Palamau, 74 and 66 per cent of the families were indebted, the latter consisting entirely of

3 Ibid., paras. 54–56.

4 Ibid., Collector, Bhagalpur, to Comm., Bhagalpur, 7 April 1888, para. 12.

5 Grierson, *Notes on the District of Gaya*, Cal. 1893.

6 *Dufferin Report*. C. C. Stevens, Comm., Chotanagpur Division, to the Secy. to the Govt. of Bengal, Rev. Dept., No. 351 R, Ranchi, 31 May 1888, para. 11.

7 Ibid., para. 18.

8 Ibid., para. 33.

cultivators.[9] On the basis of these data, the Commissioner of Chotanagpur concluded that "probably at least half the cultivators are in debt", though "in this division it is peculiarly difficult to arrive at an accurate general conclusion from the consideration of a limited area".[10]

In Orissa, too, the problem of rural indebtedness was remarkably extensive. In Sambalpur village, Balasore, for instance, 7 out of 16 raiyats were in debt to the extent of Rs. 10 to Rs. 50. If one includes the paddy loans, nearly a third of the raiyats were indebted.[11]

[9] Ibid., para. 43.

[10] Ibid., paras. 53–54.

[11] Ibid., from C. F. Worsley, Offg. Comm., Orissa Division, to the Secy. to the Govt. of Bengal, Rev. Dept., No. 20 PT, Camp Pooree, 3 June 1888, para. 8 from Report of Deputy Collector, Balasore.

Appendix B

Lease between a Jotedar and Chukanidar in the Terai Region

[1] *No.138 for 1893*

Meherunnisa, wife of Mehar Ali, of Birnakuri of Rajganj in Jalpaiguri had the following contract with her chukanidar:

"I, Soharu, son of Galu Oraon of Champasori, cultivator, Siliguri, Darjeeling, give this Kabulyat for my chukani land in Mauza Champasori, Pargana Patharghata in Terai for jote No. 517 Kollabari for which Government charges Rs. 40-8 jama. In that jote being necessary to take one hal of land as chukani, I being present agree to pay Rs. 16 for the said land and you have given me a patta for the chukani land for Rs. 16. I voluntarily give the Kabulyat for the land of which boundaries are given below. The term being from 1300 B.S. to 1302 B.S. for three years, during which I will hold it. I will pay the rent to you and take receipt. In the absence of receipt I will get no credit for payment.

If any rent remain in arrear, you have full power to realise the rent by sale of my crops. If I make any objection, it will not be granted. I will pay asmani farmasi or cesses which may be demanded in addition to my rent. I will keep the boundaries of my chukani land correct. I will immediately obey all orders which may come from you or the Government, and will do nothing irregular. All the plantains and bamboos on the land remain as belonging to you and if within the term of this lease, Government makes any settlement I will pay what may be demanded. I will have no title to the chukani on expiration of the term of this lease and I therefore execute this Kabuliyat for the chukani holding".[1]

[1] LRP, 1894, p. 1215. Annexure to the letter of D. Sunder, Settlement Officer, Western Duars.

Map

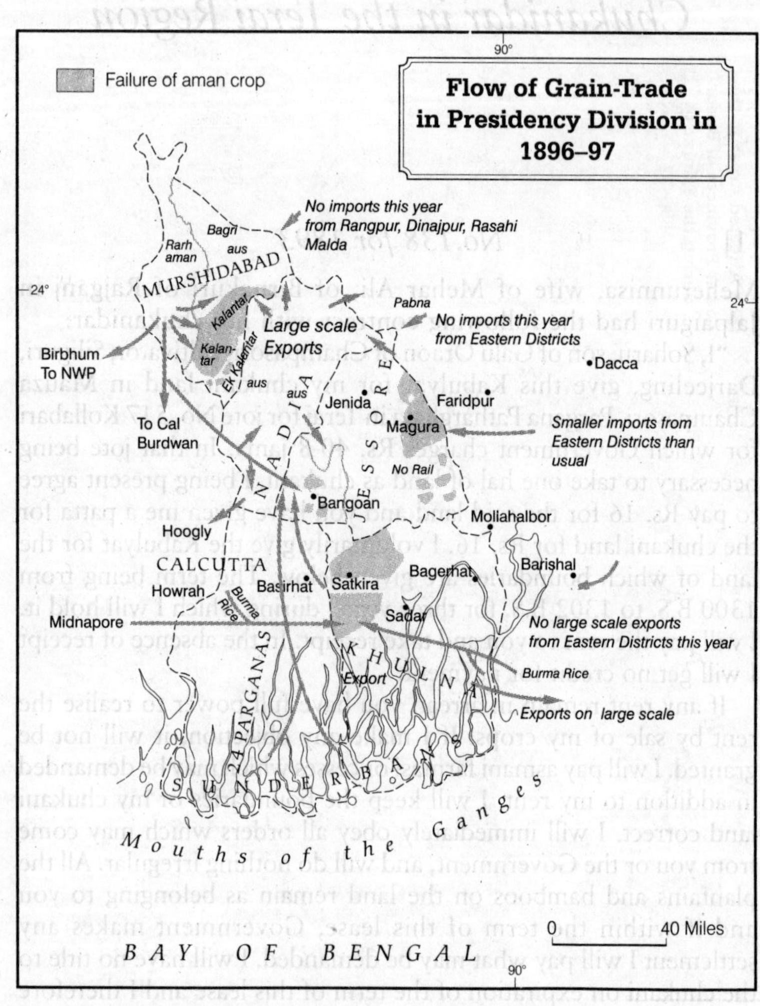

Flow of Grain-Trade in Presidency Division in 1896–97
Failure of aman crop
90°
24°
24°
No imports this year from Rangpur, Dinajpur, Rasahi Malda
Bagri
Rarh aman
aus
MURSHIDABAD
Kalantar
Kalan-tar
Ek Kalantar
aus
aus
Large scale Exports
Pabna
No imports this year from Eastern Districts
Birbhum To NWP
To Cal Burdwan
Dacca
Jenida
Faridpur
Magura
Smaller imports from Eastern Districts than usual
NADIA
JESSORE
No Rail
Bangoan
Moliahalbor
Hoogly
CALCUTTA
Howrah
Burma Rice
Basirhat
Satkira
Bagerhat
Barishal
Sadar
Midnapore
No large scale exports from Eastern Districts this year
24 PARGANAS
KHULNA
Export
Burma Rice
Exports on large scale
SUNDERBAN
Mouths of the Ganges
0 40 Miles
BAY OF BENGAL
90°

Map

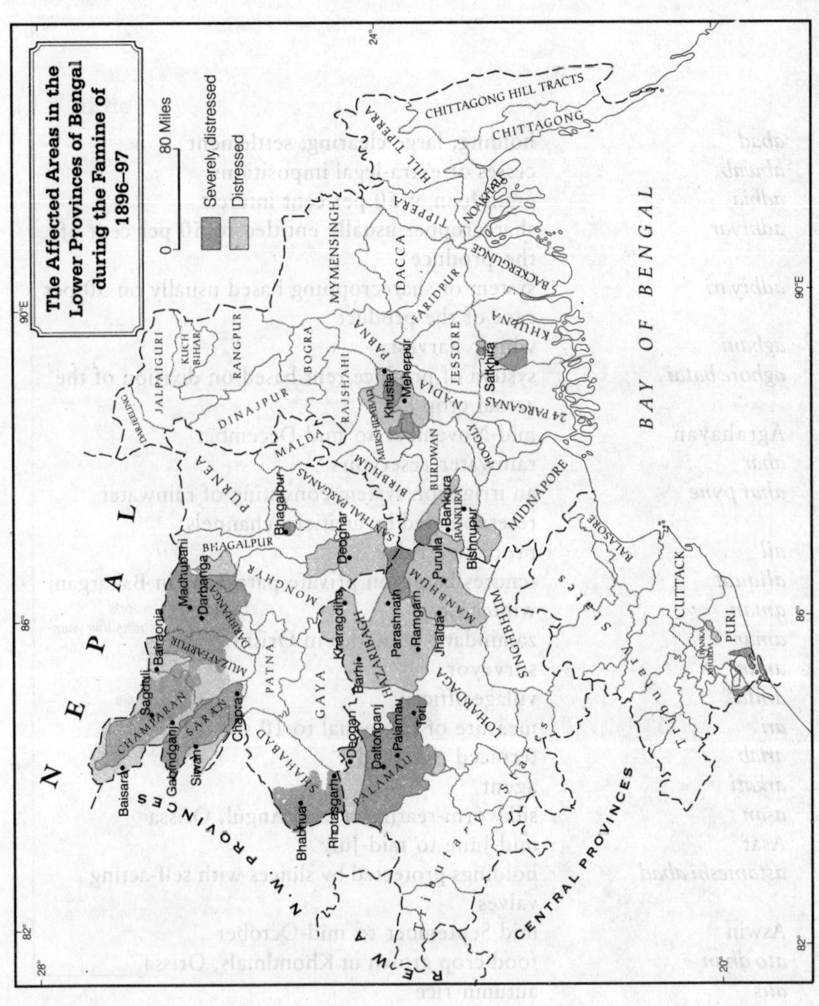

The Affected Areas in the Lower Provinces of Bengal during the Famine of 1896–97
0
80 Miles
Severely distressed
Distressed
90°E
86°
82°
28°
24°
20°
NEPAL
N. W. PROVINCES
CENTRAL PROVINCES
BAY OF BENGAL
DARJEELING
JALPAIGURI
KUCH BIHAR
RANGPUR
DINAJPUR
BOGRA
MYMENSINGH
HILL TIPPERA
CHITTAGONG HILL TRACTS
CHITTAGONG
NOAKHALI
TIPPERA
DACCA
FARIDPUR
BACKERGUNGE
PABNA
RAJSHAHI
MALDA
PURNEA
BHAGALPUR
MONGHYR
SANTHAL PARGANAS
BIRBHUM
MURSHIDABAD
NADIA
JESSORE
KHULNA
24 PARGANAS
HOOGLY
BURDWAN
BANKURA
MIDNAPORE
MANBHUM
HAZARIBAGH
PALAMAU
LOHARDAGA
SINGHBHUM
GAYA
PATNA
SHAHABAD
SARAN
CHAMPARAN
MUZAFFARPUR
DARBHANGA
BALASORE
CUTTACK
PURI
Baisara
Gobindganj
Siwan
Sagauli
Bairagnia
Madhubani
Darbanga
Chapra
Bhabhua
Rhotasgarh
Deogan
Daltonganj
Palamau
Tori
Barhi
Kharagdiha
Parashnath
Ramgarh
Jhalda
Purulia
Deoghar
Bhagalpur
Bankura
Bishnupur
Khustia
Meherpur
Satkhira

Glossary

abad	holding; large clearing, settlement
abwabs	cesses or extra-legal impositions
adhia	grain loan at 50 per cent interest
adhiyar	sharecropper usually entitled to 50 per cent of the produce
adhiyari	system of sharecropping based usually on 50 per cent of the produce
aghani	winter harvest
aghore batai	system of produce rent based on division of the actual crop
Agrahayan	mid-November to mid-December
ahar	rainwater reservoirs
ahar pyne	an irrigation system consisting of rainwater reservoirs fed by artificial channels
ail	protective ridge
aliquat	tenures based on private partitions in Bakarganj
aman	winter rice
amar	zamindars' granaries in Orissa
amin	surveyor
amla	village official
ari	measure of rice equal to 10 sr.
ariab	terraced rice fields
arkati	agent
asan	silkworm-rearing tree in Angul, Orissa
Asar	mid-June to mid-July
astameshi abad	holdings protected by sluices with self-acting valves
Aswin	mid-September to mid-October
ato dhan	food crop grown in Khondmals, Orissa
aus	autumn rice
awal	rice-producing land
aymadar	landholder
babat	on account of
badlan	arrangement among peasants for mutual help and exchange of labour

baicha	aquatic weed injurious to rice crop
baigai	service tenure held by the village priest
Baisakh	mid-April to mid-May
baze-fasal	term for miscellaneous crops in Orissa
bajra	type of millet (*Pennisetum typhoides*)
bakasht	demesne in north Bihar
bandh	high embankment
bangar	hard clay
bania	trader; caste of traders
banokhar	a working arrangement for operating the ahar-pyne system
bara	main winter rice reaped in December-January in Orissa
baramashiya	bonded labour
barga	*batai* system, as known in Bengal
bargadar	sharecropper/tenant on produce rent
barsali	type of interest rate on cash loans
barsha poka	insects causing much damage with nightly attacks on near-ripe corns of rice
batai	system of produce-rent based on actual division of the crop
bawardar	guard
bazaar	market
beejan	seed
begar	forced labour
bel	wild fruit (*Aegle marmelos*)
bemiadi	lease for indefinite period
benami	anonymous, usually describing property held surreptitiously under a different name
bepari	itinerant trader
ber	wild plum (*Zizyphus jujuba*)
beth-begar	free labour
betherkshati	cash commutation of free labour
bhadoi	autumn harvest
Bhadra	mid-August to mid-September
bhadralok	gentlemen, bourgeoisie
bhag	*batai* system, as known in Bengal
bhagchash, bhagjote	sharecropping
bhaiya saheb	landlord
bhandar	granary
bhandari kharach	toll on markets
bhao	outlet from tank
bhaoli	produce rent; produce-rent land
bhaoli nausat	*amla*'s dues
bhaskar	sculptor

bhatua	wild vegetable (*Chenopodium album linn*)
bhelwa	jungle fruit in Chotanagpur
bhet	gifts in kind
bhoora	food crops grown widely in parts of Nadia district
bhukta bandha	form of usufructuary mortgage
bhushan	system of produce rent in Colgong thana, Bhagalpur, varying yearly on the basis of the area or type of crops sown
biali	bhadoi crop in Orissa
bigha	measure of land
bijan	seedgrain
bij-khad	grain loan for seed and food
bil, bilan	lowlands
birahwari	system of produce rent in southeast Purnea, varying yearly on the basis of the area or type of crops sown
birhi	a form of lentil (*Phaseolus radiatus*)
boro	spring rice
brahmajal	insect feeding on rice leaves
brahmottar	rent-free land granted to Brahmins
bund	embankment; out-turn
Chait/Chaitra	mid-March to mid-April
chakband	original Santhal tenures at concessional rates of rent in parts of south Bhagalpur
chakbanddar	tribal headman in the chakband area
chakran	service tenures
challan	bill
chanda	subscription
char	riverside lands/silt formations
chara	petty cash loan repaid in rice
chasha	cultivator
chaudhary	cart owner
chaukidar	guard
chaunra/chaur	higher rice-lands
chhatak, chittak	weight-measure (approx. 58.12 gm.)
chheni	scoop of matting with attached slings
chota	types of interest rates on cash loans
chukanidar	tenure-holder with implicit occupancy rights, most common in northern Bengal
chukti bond	contracts supposedly entered into by mutual consent
chura	parched, flat rice
cutcherry	zamindar's collection office

dadan	advance by merchants against a specified share of the produce
dadni	a contract whereby a specified portion of the produce (of the peasant, weaver or artisan) is hypothecated against the advance of a loan.
dahi	curd
dak kharach	postal levies
dakhila kharach	levies for rent receipts
dakhila	rent receipt
dal	lentil
dalua	summer rice in Orissa
danabandi	produce rent based on estimated crop out-turn
danr	channel
dar-ijaradar	sub-lessee of *ijradar*
dar-thikadar	sub-lessee of *thikadar*
dasturi	allowance
deara	high, riverside lands
dera	grain loan at 50 per cent interest
dhan	paddy
dhani land	rice-producing land
dhankarari	oppressive form of produce rent based on fixed grain payments in Faridpur and Bakarganj
dhoti	loin cloth worn by Indian males
dhulibhag	*batai* system in Orissa
dhurta	type of interest rate on cash loans
diku	foreigners or alien elements in Santhal settlements
doanna sag	wild, edible weed
do-fasal	double-cropped lands
dohar, don	lowlands
dub	bed of reservoir
dubra	grain loan at 100 per cent interest
duni	bent trough
Falgun	mid-February to mid-March
gaicha pharing	insects destroying rice crop in eastern Bengal
gamcha	thinly woven cotton piece used as a towel
ganta	arrangement among peasants for mutual help and exchange of labour
gantidar	tenure-holder in southern Jessore
garha	low-lying rice-lands
gharami	house-building work
ghatwali	service tenures for protection of ghats or hill passes
ghurgril	a type of insect which attacks the gram crop
gilandazi	rent agreement

gohan	wheat
gola	granary
goladar	stock holder
golpatta	leaves used for thatching
gomasta	agent
gondli/gundli	wild fruit; little millet (*Pancium miliare*)
gora	unembanked upland; rice grown on uplands *(Oryza sativa)*
gouni	a unit of measure
gowala	milkman
gur	jaggery
hakim	doctor using traditional remedies for curing diseases
hal	plough; plough-measure
halhansali	distinctive produce-rent system in parts of Bhagalpur, varying yearly on the basis of the area or type of crops sown
haola	tenures featuring prominently in Bakarganj and Khulna
haoladar	tenure-holder in Bakarganj and Khulna regions
harda	rust, a disease of wheat generally caused by continuous cloudy or wet weather
hat	village marts
hath	hand-measure
hathiya	crucial phase for maturing of the rice crop (26 Sept. to 10 Oct.)
hir	small embankment
hisabi debt	running account debt
humrul	arrangement among peasants for mutual help and exchange of labour
ijara	lease
ijaradar	lessee
ikrarnama	rent contract
itmamdar	tenure-holder found mostly in new settlements
jaedadi	system of produce rent distinctive of the Kishanganj-Supaul *thanas* in Bhagalpur, varying yearly on the basis of the area or type of crops sown
jagirdar	landholder
jamabandi	rent roll
jan	bonded labour
janera/janira	millets akin to *bajra*
jau	barley (*Hordeum hexastichum*)
Jeth	mid-May to mid-June
jhulunga	food crop grown in Khondmals, Orissa

jhum	wasteful method of 'slash and burn' agriculture in tribal areas
jol	rice-producing lands
jote	holding
jotedar	landholder
jowar	great millet (*Sorghum vulgare*)
kabuliyat	contract with tenant
kuccha	temporary; raw
kachu	arum (*Colocasia esculenta*)
kaghazi zamin	fictitious land
kalai	type of lentil (*Phaseolus mungo*)
kalimukhi	pests injuring crops in Orissa
kamat	demesne in Bhagalpur Division
kamdar	low rent rates
kamia	bonded labour
kamiauti	bonded-labour contract
kandar	rivulet
kanika	tuber grass
kaon	millets
kapa, kapas	type of cotton
karja	petty cash loan
Karma Puja	a Kol agricultural festival
karup	a type of worm that attacked the wheat crop
kat	measure of rice (*kat* = *poila* ratio)
katkina ijara	lease of land on usufructuary mortgage
katoi	cricket
kayali	licensed measurer
ken	1/73,728,000,000,000th part of an estate
kerker	terraced rice fields
khal	rivulet
khal bandi	levies for roads and embankments
khamar	demesne in north Bihar
khanwa	59-millionth part of an estate
kharar	soil suited for winter rice
kharcha	dues; expense
kharif	winter harvest in northern and western India
khas	demesne lands
khasa	sesamum, an oilseed
khasra	record of lands
khata	account book; record
khatak	debtor
khesari	*Lathyrus sativus*, inferior pulse of the rabi variety
khiyan	foodgrain
khundwat	terraced rice-fields

kist	instalment
kistibandi	agreement to pay rent arrears in instalments
kist-khelapi	interest on arrears of *kist* payments
kodo	a millet (*Paspalum scorbiculatum*)
kolka	food crop grown in Khondmals, Orissa
kona	weight-measure
konga	food crop grown in Khondmals, Orissa
Koomtees	grain traders in Madras
korali	type of interest rate on cash loans
krishan	agricultural servant
kulthi, kurthi	type of black beans (*Dilichos biflorus*)
kunkur	pebbles
kurao	food crop lands of Paharias
kurna	tenant holding within each tikri
kurwa	wasteful method of cultivation in tribal areas
kutcha	earthern (of roads)
laggi	local land measure in Bhagalpur
laggit	record of lands
laghu	early variety of winter rice maturing in September-October in Orissa
laissez-faire	policy of non-intervention
lakh	one hundred thousand (100,000)
lakhiraj	rent-free lands
lakhirajdar	holder of rent-free lands
leda poka	insects damaging paddy
Magh	mid-January to mid-February
mahajan	creditor
mahaldar	middlemen in village hats
mahal	estate
mahua	*Madhuka latifolia*, flower producing country liquor widely consumed in tribal tracts of Chotanagpur and Bhagalpur Divisions
majhi	headman
majhila	winter rice maturing in November-December in Orissa
majoor	labourer
makaddam	tenure-holder in Orissa
makai	maize (*Zea mays*)
malik	master
mamuli	*abwab* for payment of zamindar's officials
manhunda	oppressive form of produce rent based on fixed-grain payments in Bhagalpur
manjhi	headman; boatman
manjhihas	khas lands or demesne

mankhap	produce rent in the form of the market value of a fixed amount of grain/produce at the time of harvest
manki	headman in Chotanagpur tribal areas
manohari	trinket-dealer
maricha pharing	insects destroying rice crop in eastern Bengal
marua	small-grained cereals, *ragi* or African millet (*Eleusine coracana*)
masari than	cloth for mosquito nets
math	monastery, religious institution
maund (md.)	standard weight-measure of the time, approx. 37.20 kg.
mewa	rice hispa
mitha desh	sweet water country
Mogulbandi	grain trader operating all the year round
moira	confectioner
mokarrari	a form of lease by which land was permanently leased out for an advance
molunghees	salt manufacturers in Orissa
moody	retail trader, grocer
moong	green gram (*Vigna radiata*)
moorkee	puffed rice coated with treacle
mridha	village headman/zamindar's peon
muharrir	mate or headman supervising a labour gang
mul raiyat	village headman
munda	headman in Chotanagpur tribal areas
musahar	bonded labour
mustagiri	lease system at enhanced rates
nagdi	cash-paying lands
naib	zamindar's estate manager
Nakodas	grain merchants from Bombay
nakti	wild vegetable eaten in Bihar
namal desh	new settlements in the Sunderbans
napit	barber
nazar	fine, tribute
nazarana	annual charges
nigar	draining of fields
nijchash, nijjote	demesne lands in Bengal and Orissa
pagri	turban
pahi	temporary, non-resident raiyat in Orissa (known as *paikasht* in Bengal)
pai	weight-measure (8 pais = 1 kuri; 16 kuris = 1 ara)
paik	zamindar's guard/agent

pamari	insects damaging winter rice crop after dark in harvesting season
par	ridge
parabandi	rules regulating water rights
parda, purdah	seclusion
pardanashin	women in *parda*, i.e. those who did not venture out in public
pargana	subdivision
pargana laggi	standard unit of land measurement
pargana nirik	prevailing rent rates
pariadari system	rent exemption for uplands
parkhai	temporary rent receipt
paseri	list
patni	popular form of tenure at perpetually fixed rate
patnidar	a category of talukdar holding his taluk by virtue of a direct patta from the zamindar
patwan	system of produce rent in Colgong thana, Bhagalpur, varying yearly on the basis of the area or type of crops sown
patwari	village official
peada	zamindar's guard/agent
piar	wild fruit in tribal tracts
piri	uplands
poila	measure of rice (16 poilas = 1 kuri; 16 kuris = 1 ara)
pol kharach	levies for bridges
Pous	mid-December to mid-January
pradhan	headman
pucca	permanent
pundit	priest, scholar
punya	annual charges
purdar	full rent rates
pyadgan	annual levies for the payment of the landlord's collecting staff
pyne	artificial channel
rabi	spring harvest
rahar	type of pulse (*Cajanus indicas*)
raiyat	peasant
rajdhuti	type of *abwab*
rajhas	khas lands or demesne
rakumat	forced labour
rangi	pests injuring crops in Orissa
rashami	levy for paying the landlord's collecting staff
ropa	transplanted aman rice

sabai	type of grass cultivated by the Paharias
sadiana	levies for marriages
Sahus	trader caste
sal	sal tree (*Shorea robusta*)
salami	fee or purchase money, sometimes in effect a bribe
samaj-band	social ostracism
sanja	oppressive system of produce rent in Midnapur and Orissa
sanki	earthen plate
saradh	winter rice in Orissa
sarai	wild plum (*Barleria cristata linn*)
sarbarahakar	petty trader in Orissa; also tenure-holder
sardar	foreman
sari	a length of cotton or silk draped around the body—the most common garment worn by Indian women
sarkar	government
seer (srs.)	weight measure (930 gm. approx.)
seni	insects damaging winter rice crop after dark in harvesting season
seri	petty cash loan repaid in paddy
shama	grass seed
sharahnama	rent contract
singha	distributary
sikki	money loans with 25 per cent rate of interest
sir	demesne in north Bihar
sonar	goldsmith
Sravan	mid-July to mid-August
tahsilan, tahuri	levies for paying the zamindar's collecting staff
tahsildar	village accountant/revenue official
tàlukdar	tenure holder under zamindar
tanka	system of produce-rent prevalent among the Garos of Susang
tanki	rent-free lands in Orissa
tanr	uplands
tanti	weaver/weaver caste
tappa	measure of land area reclaimed by Santhals within a pargana
taqavi	interest-free agricultural loans given by the zamindar
tean	wild fruit
Telinghee	grain merchants from the South
terai	fertile belt between the Himalayan foothills and the plains

thakur	cart owner
thali	metal plate
thana	area smaller than and within each subdivision or pargana
thani	resident raiyat in Orissa (known as *khudkasht* in Bengal)
thika	lease
thikadar	leaseholder
tikri	*tukra* or piece of land denoting Paharia village or settlement
tikri manjhi	headman of Paharia settlement
tikridar	headman of Paharia settlement
til	*Sesamum indicum*
tisi	linseed (*Linum usitatissimum*)
toila	wasteful practice of *jhum* cultivation in tribal tracts. See *jhum*.
tussar	coarse silk
uchring	cricket
unnochutter	relief kitchen
utbandi	system of produce rent in Nadia varying yearly on the basis of the area or type of crops sown
uttakar system	system of rent assessment for all types of land
zamindar	landlord
zaripeshgi	form of usufructuary mortgage
zimha	system by which zamindars in Bakarganj usurped occupational rights of holdings under neighbouring landlords
zirat	demesne in north Bihar

Bibliography

PRIMARY SOURCES

Archival Records

India Office Records

Bengal Land Revenue Department Proceedings. 1894–1900; 1907–09; 1914–17.

Bengal Irrigation Proceedings. 1872–74, 1877, 1891.

Famine Proceedings (relevant years).

Final Reports on the Famine and Relief Operations in the districts of Bengal in 1896–97 (as incorporated in the Bengal Land Revenue Proceedings, August 1898, parts I and II).

Official Published Sources

Materials Relating to Famine

Administrative experience recorded in former famines. Compiled by J. C. Geddes. Calcutta: Bengal Secretariat (BS) Press, 1874.

Appendices to the Final Resolution of the Government of Bengal on the Famine of 1896–97. 3 vols. Cal: BS Press, 1898.

Bengal: The crops of 1865–66 for comparison with those of 1873–74, compiled from extracts from official papers. Compiled by J. C. Geddes. Cal: BS Press, 1874.

Correspondence relating to the Famine in Bengal and Bihar from Oct. 1873 to May 31st 1874. Cal: Supdt., Govt. Printing, 1874.

Famine Commission Report, 1866. Cal: Superintendent, Government Printing, 1867.

Famine Commission Report, 1880. 3 pts. House of Commons, London: Parliamentary Papers (PP), 1880.

Famine Commission Report, 1898. Simla, Cal: Supdt. , Govt. Printing, 1898.

Famine Inquiry Commission Report on Bengal, 1944. Delhi: Mngr. of Publications, 1945.

Final Resolution of the Government of Bengal on the Famine of 1896–97. Cal: BS Press, 1898.

Further Papers regarding the Famine and Relief Operations in India during 1896–97. London: PP, 1897.

Further Report on the Famine in Bengal and Orissa in 1866, with Appendices by G. Campbell. Nagpur: 1867.

Report of the Commissioners appointed to enquire into the Famine in Bengal and Orissa in1866, along with *Minutes on the Famine in Bengal and Orissa, 1866–67*, by Sir Cecil Beadon. Cal: Supdt., Govt. Printing, 1867.

Report on Foodgrain Supply and Statistical Review of the Operations in the Districts of Bihar and Bengal during the Famine of 1873–74. By A. P. Macdonnell. Cal: BS Press,1876.

Report of the Famine Commission, 1901. London: PP, 1902, LXX.

Selection of Papers Relating to the Famine of 1896–97 in Bengal. 12 vols. Cal: BS Press,1897–98.

Special Narrative of Drought in Bengal and Bihar, 1873–74, together with *Minutes* by the Hon. Sir Richard Temple. Cal: BS Press,1874.

Administrative Reports

Annual Reports of the Dept. of Agriculture, Bengal. Cal: 1894–1900.

Bengal Census Report, 1872, 1881, 1891, 1901, 1911. Cal: B.S. Press

Divisional Commissioners' Annual Reports. Cal: 1894–1900.

Note on Land Transfers and Agricultural Indebtedness in India.. Calcutta, 1895.

Report on the Administration of Bengal, 1894–95, 1895–96, 1896–97, 1897–98. Cal: BS Press.

Report on the Condition of the Lower Orders of the Population in Bengal. Cal: BS Press,1888.

Report of the Drainage Committee, Bengal, 1907. Cal: BS Press, 1907.

Report of the Embankment Committee, 1839–40. Cal: BS Press, 1901.

Report on the Enquiry into the Rise of Prices in India, 1891–1911, by K. L. Datta. Calcutta: Supdt. Govt. Ptg., 1914–15.

Reports on the External and Internal Commerce of Bengal, 1894–98. Cal: BS Press.

Report of the Government of Bengal on the Bengal Tenancy Bill, 1884, vol. 2. Cal: BS Press,1884.

Report of the Indian Irrigation Commission, 1901–3. PP, London: 1903.

Reports of the Irrigation Department, 1879–80; 1881–82; 1885–86. Cal: Bengal Secretariat Book Depot (BSBD).

Report of the Labour Enquiry Commission, 1896. Cal: BS Press,1896.

Reports of the Land Revenue Administration, Lower Provinces, 1894–1900. Cal: Supdt., Govt. Ptg.

Report on Land Transfers from Agricultural to the Non-Agricultural Classes, 1898. Cal: BS Press, 1898.

Reports and Notes on the Administration of the Registration Dept., Bengal. Cal: 1894–1900.

Reports of the Sanitary Commission, 1868, 1882.

Report on the Working of the Tenancy Act. Cal: BS Office, Aug. 1894.

Season and Crop Reports, Bengal. Cal: 1894–1900.

Seed Time and Harvest Time of Crops Grown in Bengal. Cal: BS Press, 1908.

Selection of Papers on Indebtedness and Land Transfer. Cal, 1895.

Bengal District Gazetteers of:

Balasore, compiled by L. S. S. O' Malley. Cal: Bengal Secretariat Book Depot (BSBD), 1907.

Bhagalpur, compiled by J. Byrne. Cal: BSBD, 1911.

Champaran compiled by L. S. S. O'Malley. Cal: BSBD, 1907.

Chittagong compiled by L. S. S. O'Malley. Cal: BSBD, 1908.

Cuttack compiled by L. S. S. O'Malley. Cal: BSBD, 1906.

Darbhanga compiled by L. S. S. O'Malley. Cal: BSBD, 1907.

Gaya compiled by L. S. S. O'Malley. Patna: Supdt., Govt. Printing, Bihar and Orissa, 1906.

Jessore compiled by L. S. S. O'Malley. Cal: BSBD, Cal: BSBD, 1912.

Khulna compiled by L. S. S. O'Malley. Cal: BSBD, 1908.

Manbhum compiled by H. Coupland. Cal: BSBD, Cal: BSBD, 1911.

Midnapur compiled by L. S. S. O'Malley. Cal: BSBD, 1911.

Monghyr compiled by L. S. S. O'Malley. Cal: BSBD, 1909.

Murshidabad compiled by L. S. S. O'Malley. Cal: BSBD, 1914.

Muzaffarpur compiled by L. S. S. O'Malley. Cal: BSBD, 1907.

Nadia compiled by J. H. E. Garrett. Cal: BSBD, 1910.

Palamau compiled by L. S. S. O'Malley. Cal: BSBD, 1907.

Patna compiled by L. S.S. O'Malley. Cal: BSBD, 1907.

Puri compiled by L. S. S. O'Malley. Cal: BSBD, 1908.

Purnea compiled by L. S. S. O'Malley. Cal: BSBD, 1911.

Santhal Parganas compiled by L. S. S. O'Malley. Cal: BSBD, 1910.

Saran compiled by L. S. S. O'Malley. Cal: BSBD, 1908.

Shahabad compiled by L. S. S. O'Malley. Cal: BSBD, 1906.

Singhbhum compiled by L. S. S. O'Malley. Cal: BSBD, 1910.

Final Reports on Survey and Settlement Operations in:

Bakarganj (1900–08), with *Calendar of Estates.* J. C. Jack. Cal: BSBD, 1915.

Bakarganj: Dakhin Shahbazpur Estates (1889–95). P. M. Basu. Cal: BS Press, 1896.

Bakarganj: Tushkhali (1894–98). P. M. Basu. Cal: BS Press, 1898.

Bhagalpur (1902–10). P. W. Murphy. Cal: BSBD,1912.

Birbhum: The Sonthali villages of Rampurhat and several other villages in the Rampurhat and Suri subdivisions (1909–14). P. M. Robertson. Cal: BSBD, 1915.

Burdwan: Burdwan Raj and certain other estates in Burdwan, Hooghly and Bankura (1891–96). S. Haldar. Cal: BS Press, 1897.

Champaran (1892–99). C. J. Stevenson Moore. Cal: BS Press, 1900.

Chittagong (1888–98). C. G. H. Allen. Cal: BS Press, 1900.

Cuttack: Kanika Ward's Estate (1889–94). S. S. Hossein. Cal: BS Press, 1895.

Cuttack: Killa Aul (1892–1901). D. N. Bose. Cal: BS Press, 1904.

Cuttack: Killa Darpan (1901). H. K. Mahanti. Cal: BS Press, 1902.

Dacca (1910–17). F. D. Ascoli. Cal: BSBD, 1917.

Darbhanga (1896–1903). J. H. Kerr. Cal: BS Press, 1904.

Darjeeling:Terai (1898). S. B. Dutt. Cal: BS Press, 1898.

Darjeeling: Kalimpong Govt. Estate (1891–92). J. G. Ritchie. Cal: BS Press, 1892.

Faridpur (1904–14). J. Ç. Jack. Cal: BSBD, 1916.

Faridpur, Calendar of Estates. B. C. Prance. Cal: BSBD, 1917.

Gaya: Deo Estate (1901–4). H. Coupland. Cal: BSBD, 1906.

Gaya: The Tikari Ward's Estates, the Govt. Estates and the Belkhara Mahals (1893–98). C. J. Stevenson Moore. Cal: BS Press, 1899.

Hazaribagh: Koderma Govt. Estate (1902–4). H. Coupland. Cal: BSBD, 1906.

Jalpaiguri (1906–16). J. A. Milligan. Cal: BSBD, 1919.

Jalpaiguri: The Western Duars (1889–95) D. H. E. Sunder. Cal: BS Press, 1895.

Jessore (1920–24). M. A. Momen. Cal: BSBD, 1925.

Khulna: Tantibunia Estate (1894–98). S. C. Sengupta. Cal: BS Press, 1898.

Midnapur: eighteen temporarily settled estates of Pataspur (1893–98). G. C. Dutta. Cal: BS Press, 1898.

Midnapur: minor settlements (1907–13). B, Sanyal. Cal: BSBD, 1916.

Monghyr: Narhan Ward's Estate (1893–98). C. J. Stevenson Moore. Cal: BS Press, 1898.

Monghyr, North (1899–1904). H. Coupland. Cal: BSBD, 1908.

Murshidabad: Fatehsing, Beldanga and Mahisar (1902–9). M. Choinuddin. Cal: BSBD, 1912.

Muzaffarpur (1892–99). C. J. Stevenson Moore. Cal: BS Press, 1901.

Palamau: Palamau Govt. Estate, Chotanagpur (1894–5 to 1896–7). D. H. E. Sunder. Cal: BS Press, 1898.

Patna: Govt and temporarily settled estates and certain pvt estates (1901–4). H. Coupland. Cal: BSBD, 1907.

Puri: Jagirmahals (1906–9). S. Das. Cal: BSBD, 1910.

Puri: Khurda (1897–98). J. H. Taylor (vol. 1) and S. L. Maddox (vol. 2). Cal: BS Press, 1899.

Purnea (1901–8). J. Byrne. Cal: BSBD, 1908.

Saran (1893–1901). J. H. Kerr. Cal: BS Press, 1903.

Singhbhum: The Kolhan Govt. Estate (1897). J. A. Craven. Cal: BS Press, 1898.

Sonthal Parganas (1898–1907). H. Mcpherson. Cal: BSBD, 1909.

Srinagar-Banaili Estates (1887–94). Settlement of 600 villages in the districts of Bhagalpur, Darbhanga, Malda, Monghyr and Purnea. E. W. Collin (1891) and B. Narain (1892). Cal: B. C. M. and others, 1895.

Notes & Monographs

Banerjee, N. N. *Report on the Agriculture of the District of Cuttack*. Cal: BS Press,1893.

Basu, B. C. *Report on the Agriculture of the District of Lohardaga*. 2 parts. Calcutta: BS Press, 1891.

Bentley, C. A. *Malaria and Agriculture in Bengal: how to reduce malaria in Bengal by irrigation*. Cal: BSBD, 1925.

Chandra, R. N. L. *Note on the Cotton Industries of Bengal*. Cal: BS Office, 1898.

Dutt, G. C. *Monograph on Ivory Carving in Bengal*. Cal: 1901.

Geddes, J. C. *Administrative experience recorded in former famines*. Calcutta, 1874.

Grierson, Dr. G. A. *Notes on Gaya District*. Calcutta: 1893.

Hunter, W. W. *Orissa*. Calcutta: Thacker, Spink and Co., 1872.

Jack, J. C. *The Economic Life of a Bengal District*. Oxford: Clarendon Press, 1916.

McAlpin, M. *Report on the condition of the Santhals in the districts of Birbhum, Bankura, Midnapore and North Balasore*. Calcutta: BS Press, 1909.

Prain, Sir D. *Note on the races of wheat cultivated in Bengal*. Cal: BS Press, 1896.

Stevenson-Moore, C. J. *Report on the material condition of small agriculturists and labourers in Gaya*. Cal: 1898.

Warde-Jones, A. W. *Note on Cotton Fabrics*. Cal: BS Office, 1898.

SECONDARY SOURCES

Books and Articles

Alamgir, M. *Famine in South Asia: Political Economy of Mass Starvation.* Cambridge, Mass.: Oelgeschlager, Gunn and Hain, 1980.

Allen, G. "Famines: the Bowbrick-Sen Dispute and some Related Issues". Letters to the Editor, *Food Policy* 11, no. 3, 1986, pp. 259–263.

Ambirajan, S. "Laissez-Faire in Madras". *Indian Economic and Social History Review* 2, no. 3, July 1965, pp. 238–244.

———"Malthusian Population and Theory and Indian Famine Policy in the Nineteenth Century". *Population Studies* 30, no. 1, 1976, pp. 5–14.

Anonymous "The Operation of the Laissez-Faire Principle in Times of Scarcity". *Calcutta Review* 56, Jan. 1867, pp. 102–117.

Arnold, David. "Famine in Peasant Consciousness and Peasant Action: Madras 1876–8". In *Subaltern Studies,* ed. R. Guha, 3: 62–115. Delhi: Oxford University Press, 1984. "Touching the Body: Perspectives on the Indian Plague, 1896–1900". In *Subaltern Studies*, ed. R. Guha, 5: pp. 55–90. Delhi: Oxford University Press, 1987. *Famine.* Oxford: Basil Blackwell, 1988. "Cholera Mortality in British India, 1817–1947". In *India's Historical Demography: Studies in Famine, Disease and Society,* ed. Tim Dyson, pp. 261–83. London: Curzon Press, 1989. *Colonizing the Body: State Medicine and Epidemic Disease in 19th century India.* Berkeley: University of California Press, 1993.

Bailey, F. G. *Caste and the Economic Frontier: Study of a village in highland Orissa.* Manchester: Manchester University Press, 1957.

Banerjee, P. *Calcutta and Its Hinterland: A Study in Economic History of India, 1833–1900.* Calcutta: Progressive Publishers, 1975.

Basu, D. R. "Sen's Analysis of Famine: A Critique". *Journal of Development Studies* 22, 1986, pp. 593–603.

Baulch, B. "Entitlements and the Wollo Famine of 1982–1985". *Disasters* 11, 1987, pp. 195–204.

Becker, J. *Hungry Ghosts: Mao's Secret Famine.* New York: Free Press, 1996.

Bhaduri, A. "The Evolution of Land Relations in Eastern India under British Rule," *Indian Economic and Social History Review* 13, no. 1, January–March 1976, pp. 45–58.

Bhatia, B. M. *Famines in India (1860–1965).* Bombay: Asia Publishing House, 1967.

Bhattacharya, S. *The East India Company and the Economy of Bengal, 1704–1740.* Calcutta: Firma K. L. Mukhopadhyay, 1969.

Bhattacharya, Sabyasachi. "Laissez faire in India". *Indian Economic and Social History Review* 2, no. 1, January 1965, pp. 1–22.

Blair, C. *Indian Famines: Their Historical, Financial and Other Aspects.* Edinburgh and London: W. Blackwell and Sons, 1874.

Blyn, G. *Agricultural Trends in India, 1891–1947.* Philadelphia: University of Pennsylvania Press, 1966.

Borkar, V. V., and Nadkarni, M. V. *Impact of Drought on Rural Life.* Bombay: Popular Prakashan, 1975.

Bose, Sugata. "Starvation amidst Plenty: The Making of Famine in Bengal, Honan and Tonkin, 1942–45". Modern Asian Studies 24, pp. 699–727.

______*Peasant Labour and Colonial Capital: Rural Bengal since 1770.* The New Cambridge History of India, ed. G. Johnson, part 3, vol. 2. Cambridge: Cambridge University Press, 1993.

Boserup, E. *The Conditions of Agricultural Growth.* London: Allen and Unwin, 1965.

______*Population and Technology.* Oxford: Basil Blackwell, 1981.

Bowbrick, P. "The Causes of Famine: A Refutation of Professor Sen's Theory". *Food Policy* 11, no. 2, 1986, pp. 105–124.

______"Rejoinder: An Untenable Hypothesis on the Causes of Famine". *Food Policy* 12, no. 1, 1987, pp. 5–9.

______"Market Margin Investigations and Price Control of Fruits and Vegetables". *Irish Journal of Agricultural Economics and Rural Sociology* 6, 1976, pp. 9–20.

Boyce, J. K. *Agrarian Impasse in Bengal: Institutional Constraints to Technological Change.* Oxford: Oxford University Press, 1987.

Brass, P. "Political Uses of Famine". *Journal of Asian Studies* 45, no. 2, Feb. 1986, pp. 245–67.

Bray, F. *The Rice Economies: Technology and Development in Asian Societies.* Oxford: Basil Blackwell, 1986.

Burns, E., ed. *A Handbook of Marxism.* New York: International Publishers, 1935.

Cahill, K. *Famine.* New York: Orbis Book, 1982.

Cameron, J., H. Ramharak and K. Cole, eds. *Poverty and Power: The Role of Institutions and the Market in Development.* Delhi: Oxford University Press, 1995.

Campbell, Sir George *Memoirs of My Indian Career.* London: Macmillan, 1893.

______*The Irish Land.* London: Trubner, 1869.

______*Systems of Land Tenure in Various Countries,* ed. J. W. Probyn. London: Cobden Club, 1881.

Carlyle, R. W. "Famine in a Bengal District in 1896–97". *Economic Journal* 10, 1900.

Carstairs, R. *The Little World of an Indian District Officer.* London: Macmillan, 1912.

Chakrabarti, M. "The Famine of 1896–97 in the Bengal Presidency: Food Availability Decline or 'Exchange' Crisis?" *The Calcutta Historical Journal* 16, no. 1, Jan.–June 1994, pp. 1–37.

______"Crisis in a Peasant Economy: A Study of the Famine of 1896–97 in Bengal". PhD thesis, University of Calcutta, 1995.

______"Alienation of Raiyati Holdings in Late Nineteenth Century Bengal". In *Retrieving Bengal's Past: Society and Culture in the Nineteenth and Twentieth Centuries,* ed. Ranjit Roy, pp. 96–124. Calcutta: Rabindra Bharati University, 1995.

______"The Lethal Connection: Winter Rice, Poverty and Famine in Late Nineteenth Century Bengal". *The Calcutta Historical Journal* 18, no. 1, Jan.–June 1996, pp. 65–95.

Chandra, B. "Reinterpretation of Nineteenth Century Indian Economic History". *Indian Economic and Social History Review* 5, no. 1, March 1968, pp. 35–75.

Chatterjee, R. "A Survey of Lac Manufactures in South Bihar and Bengal: 1872–1921". *Bengal Past and Present* 107, parts 1 and 2, Jan.–Dec. 1988.

Chaudhuri, B. B. "Agrarian Economy and Agrarian Relations in Bengal, 1859–1885". PhD thesis, University of Oxford, 1968.

______"Agricultural Production in Bengal, 1850–1900: Co-existence of Decline and Growth". *Bengal Past and Present* 88, 1969, pp. 157–170.

______"Rural Credit Relations in Bengal, 1859–85." *Indian Economic and Social History Review* 6, no. 3, September 1969,pp. 203–57.

______"The Process of Depeasantization in Bengal and Bihar, 1885–1947". *Indian Historical Review* 2, no. 1, July 1975, pp. 105–165.

______"Movement of Rent in Eastern India, 1793–1930". *Indian Historical Review* 3, no. 2, January 1977, pp. 320–390.

Cipolla, Carlo. M., ed. *The Emergence of Industrial Societies* 1. 2 vols. The Fontana Economic History of Europe. U.K.: Fontana/Collins, 1973.

Cobb, R. C. *The Police and the People: French Popular Protest, 1789–1820.* London: Oxford University Press, 1970.

Cook, S. B. *Imperial Affinities: Nineteenth Century Analogies and Exchanges between India and Ireland.* New Delhi: Sage Publications, 1993.

Currey, B. and G. Hugo, ed. *Famine as a Geographical Phenomenon.* Riedel: Dordrecht, 1984.

Cutler, P. "Famine Forecasting: Prices and Peasant Behavior in Northern Ethiopia". *Disasters* 8, no. 1, 1984, pp. 48–56.

Darling, M. L. *Punjab Peasant in Prosperity and Debt*. New Delhi: Manohar, 1977.

Dasgupta, P. and D. Ray. "Inequality as a Determinant of Malnutrition and Unemployment: Theory". *Economic Journal* 96, no. 384, Dec. 1986, pp. 1011–34.

Desai, A. R. *Social Background of Indian Nationalism*. Bombay: Popular Prakashan, 1966.

Devereux, S. "Entitlements, Availability and Famine: A Revisionist View of Wollo, 1972–74". *Food Policy* 13, no. 3, 1988, pp. 270–82.

de Waal, A. "A Re-assessment of Entitlement Theory in the Light of Recent Famines in Africa". *Development and Change* 21, no. 3, 1990, pp. 469–490.

Digby, William. *Famine Campaign in Southern India.* 2 vols. London: Longmans Green and Co., 1878.

______*"Prosperous" British India*. London: T. Fisher Unwin, 1901.

Dobb, Maurice. *Studies in the Development of Capitalism.* London: Routledge and Kegan Paul, 1963.

______ *Theories of Value and Distribution since Adam Smith: Ideology and Economic Theory.* Cambridge: Cambridge University Press, 1973.

Dr'eze, J. and A. Sen. *Hunger and Public Action.* Oxford: Clarendon Press, 1989.

______*India: Economic Development and Social Opportunity*. Delhi: Oxford University Press, 1995.

______, ed. *The Political Economy of Hunger*, 3 vols. Oxford: Clarendon Press, 1990.

______ *Indian Development: Selected Regional Perspectives.* Oxford and Delhi: Oxford University Press, 1996.

Dutt, R. C. *Open Letters to Lord Curzon on Famines and Land Assessments in India*. London: Kegan Paul, Trench Trubner and Co., 1900.

______ *The Economic History of India*. London: Kegan Paul, Trench Trubner and Co., 1904.

Dyson, T ed. *India's Historical Demography: Studies in Famine, Disease and Society*. London: Curzon Press, 1989.

Dyson, T. and A, Maharatna. "Bihar Famine, 1966–67 and Maharashtra Drought, 1970–73: The Demographic Consequences". *Economic and Political Weekly* 27, no. 26, 27 June 1992, pp. 1325–1332.

Edwards, R. D. and T. D. Williams. *The Great Famine: Studies in Irish History, 1845–52*. Dublin: 1956. Lilliput Press, 1994.

Engels, F. *Socialism: Utopian and Scientific.* Scientific Socialism Series. Moscow: Progress Publishers, 1970.

Epstein, S. "Productive Efficiency and Customary Systems of Rewards in Rural South India". In *Themes in Economic Anthropology*, ed. R. W Firth, pp. 229–52. London: Tavistock, 1967.

Field, J. O., ed. *The Challenge of Famine: Recent Experience, Lessons Learned.* Kumarian Press, 1993.

Firminger, W. K. *Historical Introduction to the Bengal Portion of the Fifth Report*. Indian Studies Past and Present. Calcutta: R. Cambray, 1962.

Forrest, G. W. *The Famine in India.* London: Horace Cox, 1897.

Franke, R. W. and B. H. Chasin. *Seeds of Famine: Ecological Destruction and the Development Dilemma in the West African Sahel.* U.S.A.: Landmark Studies, 1980.

Freedman, R., ed. *Marx on Economics.* U.S.A.: Harcourt Brace, 1961.

Frere, Sir Bartle. *The Bengal Famine: How It Will be Met and How to Prevent Future Famines in India.* London: John Murray, 1874.

Furnivall, J. S. *Colonial Policy and Practice: A Comparative Study of Burma and Netherlands India.* New York: New York University Press, 1956.

Gadgil, D. R. *The Industrial Evolution of India in Recent Times (1860–1939).* Delhi: Oxford University Press, 1971.

Ganguli, B. N. *Trends of Agriculture and Population in the Ganges Valley.* London: Methuen, 1938.

Ghose, A. K. "Food Supply and Starvation: A Study of Famines with Reference to the Indian Subcontinent". *Oxford Economic Papers* 34, no. 2, July 1982, pp. 368–389.

Ghose, K. C. *Famines in Bengal, 1770–1943.* Calcutta: Indian Associated Publishing Co., 1944.

Ghosh, K. K. *Agricultural Labourers in India: A Study in the History of their Growth and Economic Condition.* Indian Publications Monograph Series, no. 7. Calcutta: 1969.

Glantz, M. ed. *Drought and Hunger in Africa.* Cambridge: Cambridge University Press, 1987.

Gray, P. *Famine, Land and Politics: British Government and Irish Society, 1843–50.* Dublin: Irish Academic Press, 1999.

Greenough, Paul R. "Indian Famines and Peasant Victims: The case of Bengal in 1943–44". *Modern Asian Studies* 14, no. 2, April 1980, pp. 205–35.

______ *Prosperity and Misery in Modern Bengal: The Famine of 1943–44.* Oxford: Oxford University Press, 1982.

Guz, D. "Population Dynamics of Famine in Nineteenth Century Punjab, 1896–97 and 1899–1900". In *India's Historical Demography: Studies in Famine, Disease and Society*, ed. Tim Dyson, pp. 198–221. London: Curzon Press, 1989.

Hardiman, D. "The Bhils and Sahukars of Eastern Gujarat". In *Subaltern Studies,* ed. R. Guha, 5: 1–54 Delhi: Oxford University Press, 1987.

Harrison, G. A. ed. *Famines.* Oxford: Oxford University Press, 1988.

Harriss, B. *Child Nutrition and Poverty in South India.* New Delhi: Concept, 1989.

______"The Intrafamily Distribution of Hunger in South Asia". In *The Political Economy of Hunger,* ed. Jean Dreze and Amartya Sen, vol. I, pp. 351–424. Oxford: Clarendon Press, 1990.

Hill, C. *Reformation to Industrial Revolution.* The Pelican Economic History of Britain, vol. 2. U.K.: Pelican Books, 1969.

Hobsbawm, E. J. *Industry and Empire.* The Pelican Economic History of Britain, vol. 3. U.K.: Pelican Books, 1969.

Hunter, Sir W. W. *Famine Aspects of Bengal Districts.* Simla: 1873.

______*The Annals of Rural Bengal.* Indian Studies Past and Present. Calcutta: 1965.

_____. *Orissa*. Cal: Thacker, Spink and Co., 1872.

Iliffe, J. *The African Poor: A History*. Cambridge: Cambridge University Press, 1987.

Kanbur, R. ed. Q-Squared: Combining Qualitative and Quantitative Methods in Poverty Appraisal. New Delhi: Permanent Black, 2003.

Kanta, R. *The Political Economy of Poverty*. Hyderabad: Orient Longman, 1990.

Kula, E. "The Inadequacy of the Entitlement Approach to Explain and Remedy Famines". *Journal of Development Studies*, 25, 1988, pp. 112–117.

Kumar, D. *Land and Caste in South India: Agricultural Labour in the Madras Presidency during the Nineteenth Century*. Cambridge: Cambridge University Press, 1965.

_____, ed. *Cambridge Economic History of India*. Vol. 2. Cambridge: Cambridge University Press, 1982.

Kynch, Jocelyn. "Some State Responses to Male and Female Need in British India". In *Women, State and Ideology: Studies from Africa and Asia,* ed. H. Afshar, pp. 130–151. London: Macmillan, 1987.

_____"Scarcities, Distress and Crime in British India". Paper presented at the 7th World Congress of Rural Sociology, Bologna, July 1988.

_____"Tightening the Constraints: Famine Relief and Gender Relations". *Gender, Technology and Development* 1, no. 1, Jan.–Apr. 1997, pp. 48–74.

Ladurie, Emmanuel le Roy. *Times of Feast, Times of Famine: A History of Climate since the Year 1000*. Translated by B. Bray. London: George Allen and Unwin 1972.

Lardinois, R. "Famines, Epidemics and Mortality in South India: A Reappraisal of the Demographic Crisis of 1876–78". *Economic and Political Weekly* 20, no. 11, 16 March 1985, p. 454.

Latouche, R. *The Birth of Western Economy*. London: Methuen, 1961.

Loveday, A. *The History and Economics of Indian Famines*. London: A. G. Bell, 1914.

Maharatna, A. "Regional Variation in Demographic Consequences of Famines in Late 19th and Early 20th Century India". *Economic and Political Weekly* 29, no. 23, 4 June, 1994, pp. 1399–1410.

_____ *The Demography of Indian Famines: A Historical Perspective*. New Delhi: Oxford University Press, 1996.

Malthus, T. R. *An Essay on the Principle of Population and a Summary View of the Principle of Population*. Edited by A. Flew. Pelican Classics Series. U.K.: Penguin Books, 1970.

Mann, Harold. H. *Rainfall and Famine*. Bombay: Indian Society of Agricultural Economics, 1955.

_____ *The Social Framework of Agriculture*. Bombay: Vora and Co., 1967.

Marx, Karl. *Articles on India*. Bombay: People's Publishing House, 1945.

Matsui, T. "On the Nineteenth-Century Indian Economic History: A Review of 'Reinterpretation'". *Indian Economic and Social History Review* 5, no. 1, March 1968, pp. 17–33.

McAlpin, Michelle B. "Railroads, Prices and Peasant Rationality, India 1860–1900". *Journal of Economic History* 34, no. 3, Sept. 1974, pp. 662–684.

______"Dearth, Famine and Risk: The Changing Impact of Crop Failures in Western India, 1870–1920". *Journal of Economic History* 39, no. 1, March 1979, pp. 143–157.

______"Impact of Trade on Agricultural Development, Bombay Presidency," *Explorations in Economic History* 17, 1980.—*Subject to Famine: Food Crises and Economic Change in Western India, 1860–1920.* Princeton: Princeton University Press, 1983.

______"Famines, Epidemics and Population Growth: The Case of India". *Journal of Interdisciplinary History* 14, no. 2, 1983.

McCann, J. C. "The Social Impact of Drought in Ethiopia: Oxen, Households and some Implications for Rehabilitation". In *Drought and Hunger in Africa*, ed. M. Glantz, pp. 245–267. Cambridge: Cambridge University Press, 1987.

McMinn, C. W. *Famines: Truths, Half-truths, Untruths*. Calcutta: Thacker, Spink and Co., 1902.

Mellor, J. W. *The Economics of Agricultural Development*. Ithaca, NY: Cornell University Press, 1967.

______*The New Economics of Growth: A Strategy for India and the Developing World*. Ithaca, NY: Cornell University Press, 1976.

Merewether, F. H. S. *A Tour through the Famine Districts of India*. London: A. D. Innes,1898.

Mill, J. S. *Principles of Political Economy, with some of their Applications to Social Philosophy*. Edited by D. Winch. Books 4 and 5. Pelican Classics Series. U.K.: Penguin Books, 1970.

Mitra, Satish Chandra. *Jashohar Khulnar Itihash*. Edited by S. S. Mitra. 2 vols. Calcutta: S. S. Mitra, 1963 (1st edition 1914) and 1965 (1st edition 1922).

Mohanty, B. "Orissa Famine of 1866: Demographic and Economic Consequences". *Economic and Political Weekly* 28, nos. 1–2, 29 Jan. 1993, pp. 55–66.

Morris, M. D. "Economic Change and Agriculture in Nineteenth Century India". *Indian Economic and Social History Review*, 3, no. 2, June 1966, pp. 185–209.

______"Towards a Re-interpretation of Nineteenth Century Indian Economic History". *Indian Economic and Social History Review*, 5, no. 1, March 1968, pp. 1–15.

______"What is a Famine?" *Economic and Political Weekly* 9, no. 44, 2 November 1974, pp. 1855–1864.

Mukherjee, K. M. "Rents and Forms of Tenancy in Birbhum since the Permanent Settlement". *Indian Economic and Social History Review* 14, no. 3, July–September 1977, pp. 363–376.

Mukherjee, R. *The Dynamics of a Rural Society: A Study of the Economic Structure in a Bengal Village*. Berlin: Akademie-Verlag, 1957.

Mundle, Sudipto. *Backwardness and Bondage: Agrarian Relations in a South Bihar District*. New Delhi: Orient Paperbacks (Vision Books), 1979.

Myrdal, G. *Asian Drama: An Inquiry into the Poverty of Nations*. Vol. 2. U.K.: Penguin Press, 1968.

Nag-Chowdhury-Zilly, A. *The Vagrant Peasant: Agrarian Distress and Desertion in Bengal, 1770–1830*. Wiesbaden: Steiner, 1982.

Narain, D. *Impact of Price Movements on Areas under Selected Crops in India, 1900–39*. Cambridge: Cambridge University Press, 1965.

Nash, V. *The Great Famine and Its Causes*. London: Longmans, 1900.

O'Grada, C. *Black '47 and Beyond: The Great Irish Famine in History, Economy and Memory*. Princeton: Princeton University Press, 1999.

Osmani, S. R. *Economic Inequality and Group Welfare: A Theory of Comparison with Application to Bangladesh*. Oxford: Oxford University Press, 1982.

——"The Entitlement Approach to Famine: An Assessment". In *Choice, Welfare and Development: A Festschrift in Honour of Amartya Sen*, ed. K. Basu, P. Pattanaik and K. Suzumora, pp. 253–94. New Delhi: Oxford University Press, 2000.

——"Comments on Alex de Waal's 'Re-assessment of Entitlement Theory in the Light of Recent Famines in Africa,'" *Development and Change* 22, 1991, pp. 587–596.

—, ed. Nutrition and Povert. Oxford:Clarendon Press, 1992.

Palit, C. *Tensions in Bengal Rural Society: Landlords, Planters and Colonial Rule, 1830–60*. Calcutta: Progressive Publishers, 1975.

Palloni, A. "On the Role of Crises in Historical Perspective: An Exchange". *Population and Development Review* 14, 1988, pp. 145–58.

Pati, B., ed. *Issues in Modern Indian History*. Mumbai: Popular Prakashan, 2000.

Pati, B, and Mark Harrison, eds. *Health, Medicine and Empire: Perspectives on Colonial India*. New Delhi: Orient Longman, 2001.

Patnaik, U. "Food Availability Decline and Famine: A Longer View". *Journal of Peasant Studies* 19, no. 1, 1991, pp. 1–25.

Prakash, G. *Bonded Histories: Genealogies of Labor Servitude in Colonial India*. Cambridge: Cambridge University Press, 1990.

Rangasami, A. "Failure of Exchange Entitlement Theory of Famine". *Economic and Political Weekly* 20, no. 41, 12 Oct. 1985, pp. 1747–1752.

Rashid, S. "The Policy of Laissez-faire during Scarcities". *Economic Journal*,

90, no. 359, Sept. 1980, pp. 493–503.

Ravallion, M. "Trade and Stabilisation: Another Look at British India's Controversial Foodgrain Exports". *Explorations in Economic History* 24, 1987.

______ *Markets and Famines.* Oxford: Oxford University Press, 1987.

Ray, P. C. *Indian Famines.* Calcutta: S. Ghosh, 1944.

Ray, R. "The Crisis of Bengal Agriculture, 1870–1927: The Dynamics of Immobility". *Indian Economic and Social History Review* 10, no. 3, Sept. 1973, pp. 244–79.

Ray, S. C. *Economic Causes of Indian Famine.* Calcutta: Baptist Mission Press, 1909.

Raychaudhuri, T. "A Reinterpretation of Nineteenth Century Indian Economic History?" *Indian Economic and Social History Review* 5, no. 1, March 1968, pp. 77–100.

Ricardo, D. *The Works and Correspondence of David Ricardo.* Edited by. P. Sraffa. Vol. 1. Cambridge: Cambridge University Press, 1951.

Rotberg, R. I. and T.K. Rabb eds. *Hunger and History.* Cambridge: Cambridge University Press, 1985.

Rothermund, D. *Government, Landlord and Peasant in India: Agrarian Relations under British Rule, 1865–1935.* Wiesbaden: Steiner, 1978.

Sanyal, S. "Tracing Food-Riots in a Changing Economy: The Riots in the Seine-et-Oise, 1789–1795". *Calcutta Historical Journal* 18, no. 1, Jan–June 1996, pp. 147–202.

Satya, L. D. *Cotton and Famine in Berar, 1850–1900.* New Delhi: Manohar, 1997.

Saxena, D. P. *Rururban Migration in India.* Bombay: Popular Prakashan, 1977.

Schultz, T. W. *Transforming Traditional Agriculture.* New Haven: Yale University Press, 1964.

Scott, James C. *The Moral Economy of the Peasant: Rebellion and Subsistence in Southeast Asia.* New Haven: Yale University Press, 1976.

______ *Weapons of the Weak: Everyday Forms of Peasant Resistance.* Delhi: Oxford University Press, 1990.

Seabrook, J. *Landscapes of Poverty.* Oxford: Basil Blackwell, 1985.

Seavoy, R. E. *Famine in Peasant Societies.* New York: Greenwood Press, 1986.

Sen, Amartya. "Famines as Failures of Exchange Entitlements." *Economic and Political Weekly* 11, nos. 31–33, Special Number 1976, pp. 1273–80.

______"Starvation and Exchange Entitlements: A General Approach and its Application to the Great Bengal Famine". *Cambridge Journal of Economics*, no. 1, 1977, pp. 33–59.

______"Famines". *World Development* 8, no. 9, 1980, pp. 613–21.

______ *Poverty and Famine: An Essay on Entitlement and Deprivation.*

Oxford: Clarendon Press, 1981.

______"Ingredients of Famine Analysis: Availability and Entitlements". *Quarterly Journal of Economics* 95, August 1981, pp. 433–64.

______ *Resources, Values and Development*. Oxford: Blackwell, 1984.

______"Hunger and Entitlements: Research for Action". From monograph based on the WIDER (World Institute for Development Economics Research) study and Conference Paper presented at Helsinki in August, 1986.

______"The Causes of Famine: A Reply". *Food Policy* 11, no. 2, 1986, pp. 125–132.

______"Reply: Famines and Mr Bowbrick". *Food Policy* 12, no. 1, 1987, pp. 10–14.

______. *Development as Freedom*. Oxford University Press, 1999.

Sen, Ashok. "Agrarian Structure and Tenancy Laws in Bengal, 1850–1900." In *Perspectives in Social Sciences*, vol. 2: 1–101. Calcutta: Oxford University Press, Centre for Studies in Social Sciences 1982.

Sharma, S. "The 1837–38 Famine in U.P.: Some Dimensions of Popular Action". *Indian Economic and Social History Review* 30, no. 3, July–Sept. 1993, pp. 337–372.

______ *Famine, Philanthropy and the Colonial State: North India in the Early Nineteenth Century*. New Delhi: Oxford University Press, 2001.

Sheel, A. "South Bihar Geography and the Agricultural Cycle: Gaya and Shahabad in the Nineteenth and Early Twentieth Centuries". *Indian Economic and Social History Review* 30, no. 1, Jan.–Mar. 1993, pp. 85–113.

Singh, K. S. *The Indian Famine 1967: A Study in Crisis and Change*. New Delhi: People's Publishing House, 1975.

Smith, Adam. *The Wealth of Nations*. Edited by A. Skinner. Books 1–3. Pelican Classics Series. U.K.: Penguin Books, 1970.

Srivastava, H. S. *The History of Indian Famines and Development of Famine Policy, 1858–1918*. Agra: Sri Ram Mehra 1968.

Stewart, P. J. "The Ecology of Famine". In *Famines*, ed. G. A. Harrison, pp. 139–61. Oxford University Press, 1988.

Subramanian, V. *Parched Earth: The Maharashtra Drought, 1970–73*. New Delhi: Orient Longman, 1975.

Teklu, T., J. von Braun and E. Zaki. *Drought and Famine Relationships in Sudan: Policy Implications*. Washington, D.C.: E. Int. Food Policy Research Institute (IFPRI), Report 88, 1991.

Temple, Sir Richard. *Men and Events of My Time in India*. London: John Murray, 1882.

Thorner, D. "Long Term Trends in Output in India". In *Economic Growth: Brazil, India, Japan*, ed. S. S. Kuznets, W. E. Moore and J. J. Spengler, pp. 103–128. Durham, N. C.: Duke University Press, 1964.

Thorner, D., and A. Thorner. *Land and Labour in India*. Bombay: Asia

Publishing House, 1962.

Vaughan, M. *The Story of an African Famine: Hunger, Gender and Politics in Malawi*. Cambridge: Cambridge University Press, 1987.

Viner, J. *The Intellectual History of Laissez-Faire*. Chicago: University Law School, 1961.

von Braun, J., T. Teklu and P. Webb. *Famines in Africa: Causes, Responses and Prevention*. Washington D.C.: Int. Food Policy Research Institute, 1999.

Webb, P., J. von Braun and Y. Yohannes. *Famine in Ethiopia: Policy Implications of Coping Failure at National and Household Levels*. Washington, D.C.: International Food Policy Research Institute Report 92, 1992.

Whitcombe, E. *Agrarian Conditions in Northern India*. Vol. 1. *The United Provinces under British Rule, 1860–1900*. New Delhi: Thomson Press (India) 1971.

______"Famine Mortality". *Economic and Political Weekly* 28, no. 23, 5 June 1993, pp. 1169–1179.

Whitehead, A. "A Conceptual Framework for the Analysis of the Effects of Technological Change on Rural Women". *WEP* Working Paper no. 79 (Geneva: ILO), 1981.

Woodham-Smith, C. *The Great Hunger: Ireland, 1845–49*. London: Hamish Hamilton, 1962.

Zurbrigg, S. "Hunger and Epidemic Malaria in Punjab, 1868–1940". *Economic and Political Weekly* 27, no. 4, 25 Jan 1992, PE 2– PE 26.

______. "Aid Starvation Protect from Malaria? Distinguishing between Severity and Lethality of Infectious Disease in Colonial India". Paper presented at the International Commission on Historical Demography Conference, Montreal, 1995.

Newspapers

Calcutta Review.
Hindoo Patriot.
The Englishman.
The Friend of India (later The Statesman. Cal.).
The London Times.

Index